CHALK HILL WINERY

Sommelier Guide

to Restaurants in America

FEATURING 1500 OF THE COUNTRY'S BEST RESTAURANTS
AND ULTIMATE FOOD AND WINE PAIRINGS

YVES SAUBOUA · RONN WIEGAND, M.W., M.S.

2004 EDITION

ACKNOWLEDGEMENTS

Chalk Hill Winery Sommelier Guide to Restaurants in America,
2004 Edition

Published by Chalk Hill Press, Healdsburg, California
Produced and printed by Diablo Custom Publishing,
Walnut Creek, California
ISBN: 0-925437-01-8
All rights reserved.

Copyright © 2004 Chalk Hill Estate Winery, LLC
No part of this book may be reproduced or transmitted in any form or
by any means, electronically or mechanically, without approval from
the publisher and copyright holders.

Special thanks to authors and contributors Richard Betts, M.S.; Brian
Duncan; David Glancy; Andrea Immer, M.S.; Lisa Minucci; Virginia
Philip, M.S.; Madeline Triffon, M.S.; Yves Sauboua, Chalk Hill Estate
Sommelier; Ronn Wiegand, M.W., M.S.; Jean L. Arnold-Sessions and
Michael Merriman of Jean Arnold Group; Annemarie Jones, Marie
Clary and Joanne Peterson of Chalk Hill Estate Winery, LLC.

Cover, inside front cover and chapter cover photography: Lenny Siegel
Inside back cover and chapter covers: Sylvia Steininger,
Sylvia's Photography
Chapter cover photography: Linda McLaughlin, Chalk Hill
Estate Winery, LLC
Photo of Chris Goodheart: Jim Kearns

Although the publisher, authors and editors have done exhaustive
research to ensure the accuracy of the information presented here, we
assume no responsibility for any errors and omissions. We will make
every effort to update the sommelier and restaurant information in
future editions. Updated and new information may be sent to:

Chalk Hill Press
10300 Chalk Hill Road
Healdsburg, CA 95448
jpeterson@chalkhill.com

2004 Edition

C H A L K   H I L L   W I N E R Y

Sommelier Guide

to Restaurants in America

FEATURING 1500 OF THE COUNTRY'S BEST RESTAURANTS
AND ULTIMATE FOOD AND WINE PAIRINGS

Contents

We, as sponsors of the third edition of this Sommelier Guide, are honored and proud to be associated with this project, one that gathers many of the wine industry's most enthusiastic ambassadors into one compendium.

Each page profiles a sommelier and the theater in which he or she plies his or her trade—their restaurant. We have tried to give you a taste of the varied venues where you find sommeliers, those passionate professionals that shepherd us through the occasionally daunting pages of a voluminous wine list.

We all strongly believe in supporting the position of the sommelier. They are our linchpin between the wine producers and the consuming public. They share our passion and communicate our message of commitment to wine's rightful place at table. They breathe life into the wine list and spur the excitement that blossoms when wine is added to the dining experience.

When we ask what it is that gives these sommeliers the most pleasure from their craft they invariably say, "Seeing smiles of satisfaction beam across the faces of my guests."

Use this as your guide to wine friendly establishments across the nation. Ask to talk with the sommeliers, let them guide you and you will be thrilled with the discovery of new vintages, new wine regions and most importantly, new friends.

Frederick & Peggy Furth
Chalk Hill Estate Vineyards &
Winery

Jean Arnold-Sessions
Hanzell Vineyards

Leslie Rudd
Rudd

Jess Jackson & Barbara Banke
Cambria, La Crema, Matanzas
Creek, Stonestreet & Vérité

Tom & Sandra Jordan
Jordan Vineyard and Winery

Raymond Duncan
Silver Oak Cellars

This, our third edition, has thrilled us all with its resounding acceptance by the American sommelier community. A cadre of our comrades, all exuding enthusiasm and dedication to their profession, has submitted their profiles to update and build this guide to its current impressive size. We now have an additional 132 profiles and cover nearly every state. When first embarking on the project of producing this guide we never thought that it would be this successful—this fast!

If there is one tie that binds together all the sommeliers gathered in this guide then it is passion. They all share a common love for the wine industry and the wine consuming public. They must possess an encyclopedic technical knowledge of wines and yet present it with an engaging, enthusiastic demeanor of hospitality and charm—making them a rare breed, indeed.

Our thanks again go to Chalk Hill, and the other sponsoring wineries, for underwriting this educational and career-validating guide. Please use it, as we do, to locate these wine-friendly establishments, each with a sommelier that has crafted a wine program as an extension of their passion and personality.

Cheers!, À votre santé!

Ronn Wiegand, M.W., M.S.
Editor, *Restaurant Wine*
www.restaurantwine.com

Yves Sauboua
Estate Sommelier
Chalk Hill Estate Vineyards & Winery

Chapter One

What is a Sommelier?

BY ANDREA IMMER, MASTER SOMMELIER

What is a Sommelier?

Your dream job? I get an average of three email or phone inquiries per week from sommelier hopefuls. It's easy to see the appeal: you get paid to eat and drink all day, right? Kidding aside, I know exactly where they're coming from in seeking to turn their passion for wine into a profession. I, too, once looked up from my Wall Street spreadsheets and saw that the color of my parachute was not black and white, but red, straw-yellow and rosé.

I. The Sommelier

A sommelier is the person who looks after wine purchases, sales, service and training in a restaurant setting. Although the first two functions seem to capture the imagination of would-be sommeliers—who doesn't love the idea of tasting, traveling, choosing and putting their "stamp" on a wine list?—in my opinion the latter two are where the best sommeliers put their energy. As Madeline Triffon, M.S. (wine director, Unique Restaurant Corporation), puts it, "When I can smell 'cocky' on you, I know you've forgotten that it's not about you and your list, but about the guest, and what makes them happy." Or, as Bobby Stuckey (former sommelier, The French Laundry) says, "You have to bear-hug the room. A lot of people have gotten so caught up in their big lists, they've forgotten it's about taking care of people." And, I'll add, it's about training your teammates so they can handle the wine list and wine service with confidence.

This is a great way to think about it, regardless of how your company's organization chart lays out. Why? Job security—if everyone on the team is selling wine, then they're happy, the guests are happy, and your salary is paid. Some examples:

II. Wine Steward

Wine steward: This was the nature of my first sommelier job, as Cellarmaster at Windows on the World following a stint as a cellar rat. This position usually manages the list and works the dining room floor.

III. Floor Manager/Wine Steward

The person in this role handles both wine list/sommelier duties as well as dining room supervision. You might be managing service, running the door, devising work schedules and more. When I worked as Maître d' and Wine Director at The Dining Room, a five-diamond restaurant in New Jersey, we were very successful with this structure. I gave in-depth wine training to my Captains so they could truly orchestrate the entire evening for their tables, and the guests loved it. I kept the list up to date, ran the room, and could pitch in when the service pace reached a sprint.

IV. Wine Director

Finally, many of the most service-savvy, wine-focused restaurants in America run with the combination of a Wine Director along with Captains with serious wine expertise. For example, Wine Director Karen King of New York City's Gramercy Tavern (and formerly Union Square Café) devotes much of her time to managing the wine list and inventory (a major dollar investment for the company) and to training the floor service team. When you dine there, your Captain is likely to handle every detail of your wine experience, from suggesting to serving. Like most Wine Directors, Karen works the floor periodically to keep tabs on her guests' wine pulse, and because it's a blast to be with colleagues and customers.

V. The Work

What does a sommelier do? Here's a "day in the life" when I was at Windows on the World. Keep in mind it was a very, very large operation, but this encompasses a pretty full array of what sommeliers do when they go to work every day:

On arrival (morning)—Check received invoices to ensure anything you ordered came in. Check vintages – if there's been a change, you'll need to update and reprint the wine lists. Check the banquet wine requisitions for that day's functions to make sure they've got all the product they need. Check the storerooms – temperature OK? Are we running out of anything? Take a look at the previous day's sales reports – how are we doing? How did the new wines by the glass perform?

Midday—Check in with the chef about specials and any menu changes coming up. Collaborate on the next big promotional menu (Mother's Day, Thanksgiving, etc.). Meet with suppliers to taste new products or choose new by-the-glass offerings. Place any next-day wine orders before the cutoff time. Meet with accounting to troubleshoot any inventory or cost problems.

Pre-service—Staff training class, or at least a short pre-shift training or tasting (these should be conducted every day). Announce any wine list changes, and get the reprinted lists into circulation, swapping out the old ones.

Showtime! Work the floor, make wine recommendations, serve and decant wines, and support the service team.

And don't forget to bear-hug the room!

 *Andrea Immer, Master Sommelier, is Dean of Wine Studies of the French Culinary Institute in New York City; author of* Great Wine Made Simple, Andrea Immer's Wine Buying Guide For Everyone, *and* Great Tastes Made Simple; *and president of Great Wine Made Simple, Ltd., a wine consulting company.*

French Culinary Institute of New York City
160 Rockrimmon Road
Stamford, Connecticut 06903
phone 646-254-7516
email andrea@greatwinemadesimple.com

Chapter Two

Maximizing Your Wine Adventure in Restaurants

BY MADELINE TRIFFON, MASTER SOMMELIER

Maximizing Your Wine Adventure in Restaurants

We, the restaurant's front-of-the-house staff, have been waiting to welcome you. We know you're intrigued by wine, having experienced some delicious examples thanks to generous and savvy friends. But you lack practice in negotiating the plethora of oeno-options in a dining situation solo. And you may be fuzzy-minded about what you imagine to be "wine etiquette," meaning how to order what, when to order what, how much to order, whom to tell!

Here are some of the ways that any restaurant with an ambitious wine program is making it easy for you.

I. The Players, and How to Best Access Their Services

The Bartender: As you're sitting at the bar waiting for a table, don't overlook the person making margaritas and cosmos. They're often in charge of some aspect of wine management and are the ones retrieving the wines from the cellar for the waitstaff. These are the folks to ask for tastes of the house wines and chat a bit about the style of the house's wine program.

The Manager: Oftentimes, in this modern age of cross-training, the G.M. or the dining room manager is holding the reins of the wine program as well as running the restaurant. Pipe up with your wine questions when they stop by to do a table check.

The Sommelier: The "official" wine professional, but not often present in casual fine-dining venues. "Does this restaurant have a sommelier or someone else who can make recommendations?" is the question to pose. Hugely important caveat: this is not the person to be scared of, the one who is going to expose all that you don't know; this is the person who is going to take the heat off your wine choices!

The Waitstaff: They can be as helpful as a sommelier. Many servers really enjoy wine themselves. They may not "know" as much as the sommelier, but give them the benefit of the doubt: they taste wine at line-ups with regularity, have a real sense of value, and are the ones taking the pulse of guest preferences. Just as with the food, they know what sells and why, what is interesting, what is a safe bet and what is a steal.

II. Portions and Containers

By the glass: Many restaurants put as much if not more effort into these selections as anything else they do. Good wine-by-the-glass programs are excellent "little wine lists," offering upwards of a dozen to two dozen open bottles. You can design a three-glass wine exploration for yourself and not exceed $35. F.Y.I., a glass of wine measures somewhere between 4 and 6 ounces of liquid. Don't feel cheated if the wine doesn't fill the glass: the restaurant is giving you a nice big vessel in which the wine can release its aroma with abandon.

Tasting portions and half glasses: Don't be shy about asking for a taste. We're happy to make sure you like the flavor before we pour a whole glass. Some places offer a half-glass portion, either as a bigger "taste" or to accompany several courses with different wines. "May I order half glasses?" is a perfectly appropriate question.

Flights: These are lineups of three to five half-glasses/smaller pours grouped by theme, such as "Chardonnays from Around the World" or "Italian Reds." This is an excellent option, pioneered by wine bars, to let the wine educate you.

Half-bottles: The half-bottle list in white-tablecloth venues is a treasure trove of quality and diversity. Don't look for too many moderate values here; the by-the-glass list serves that need. The little-bottle list will fulfill your yen for two and a half glasses of really lovely wine.

Full bottles: Will serve one glass each to five people, give or take. For a champagne toast, one bottle can make it around to eight guests. If you're dining alone and see something irresistible in a whole bottle, go ahead and order it if you don't mind the price tag. You can ask to have what remains saved for you for a return visit the next day (particularly if you're staying in a hotel) or leave the balance for the waitstaff to taste. Send a glass back to the chef!

Larger bottles: They look great and are not an overindulgence for larger parties. Here's the math: if in a party of 12 guests, each person has two glasses of wine, this equals 24 glasses, which equals almost five bottles. A magnum (double bottle) would make complete sense here. Many big wine lists have some of their most interesting selections in larger-format bottles.

III. How Restaurants Announce/Telegraph/ Market Their Wine

The food menu: Many forward-thinking restaurants are now making specific recommendations right on the food menu. Such a simple idea and very effective.

The blackboard: More casual venues will list beverage specials this way, to avoid the hassle of wine list re-prints.

The wine list: These babies come in all shapes and sizes. Take a minute to see how it's organized. Even if they're big, they all have a method, including tables of contents. Some sections may be arranged by taste (drier to sweeter), and some lists offer "50 under $50" lists. It's worth your while to have a quick browse, even if you're having wine by the glass. Seeds for future wine ordering!

The specials card or table tent: Casual venues will use cards clipped to the menus or point-of-sale materials on the table to telegraph wine specials along with food. You'll cheat yourself if you ignore them.

The reserve wine list: An addendum to the "regular" list, usually offering more expensive wines that are in limited stock (one or two bottles on hand).

In the waitstaff's head: Verbal specials are not just food items.

IV. Parting Shots to Wine-and-Dine Happiness

Speak: The more you tell us, the happier you'll be! Be utterly straightforward about how much money you'd like to spend. Give the server or sommelier a "price window" that honestly represents your budget, and we'll breathe a sigh of relief. No self-respecting restaurant pro wants you to spend more than you feel comfortable spending. We want you to be comfortable and happy.

Speak some more: Tell us what wine(s) you've had that really did the trick for you. It's the most efficient way we have of reading your taste.

Write: Make a note of wines you really liked and wines you didn't enjoy at all in a pocket notebook. This exercise results in a handy resource for future forays.

Surf: Check out the restaurant's website. The wine list is often posted and you can get a taste for its style and any wine values ahead of time.

Take the menus: Ask for copies on your way out the door. Digesting them over a cup of morning coffee can give you ideas for your next dining adventure.

Be honest: About what you don't know. "Please pick out wines for each course, I don't feel like reading the wine list." "I love big reds but don't know the first thing about Spain."

Ask: "Is it appropriate for me to tip you?" "Do you have wine tastings here?" "Can you serve us something off-beat in a half-bottle?"

Taste: Don't let that offered sip before accepting the bottle make you tense. Just like food, if it smells good, it probably is!

Trust: Trust your own instincts and common sense. You order food with abandon whether or not you can cook, don't you?

Relax and play: Beeline to the more obscure-sounding wine or category, particularly if they're modestly priced. These are the hiding spots for the wine buyer's true loves that are rarely ordered. You might end up with a great wine discovery.

Madeline Triffon, Master Sommelier, is wine director of Unique Restaurant Corporation, where she oversees the wine programs in the company's five full-service restaurants. Triffon was the first American woman to pass the Master Sommelier exam.

Unique Restaurant Corp.
30100 Telegraph Road, Suite #251
Bingham Farms, Michigan 48025
phone 248-646-0370, x220
email Mtriffon01@UniqueRestaurants.com

Chapter Three

Food & Wine:
Together Forever

BY BRIAN DUNCAN, OWNER/WINE DIRECTOR, BIN 36

Food & Wine: Together Forever

After working with food and wine over the
years, I have found a couple of things to be
absolutely true. One is that food and wine
inherently belong together. Secondly, that
experimentation breeds incredible opportunities for discovery.

As a child, I have vivid memories of my parents going to
great lengths in preparing meals for our family and visiting
guests. Certain types of meats had to come from a specific
butcher; seafood was only selected from a particular market and so
on. This attention to detail has had a profound and lasting impression on me. It perhaps has ruined me for being suited for anything
else but running a restaurant and creating menus with the sole pur-
pose of optimizing and harmonizing flavors. I also realized that
through thoughtful selection, it is possible to create unforgettable
combinations with food and wine. Here, I am going to share some
of the most amazing pairings with you to provide a resource for
creating your own food and wine magic.

In December 1999, I opened a restaurant/wine bar/market called
BIN 36. We created it to provide a non-intimidating environment
for our guests to taste, experiment and ultimately make discoveries
about food and wine without the pretense normally associated
with wine. To make things simple and fun, I pair each dish on the
menu with at least one or two wine recommendations so that our
guests don't have to struggle making selections for dishes they have
never tasted.

Soon after opening I began teaching wine classes that always
included sampling food components, and spices and herbs to illus-
trate and magnify flavor cohesion and contrasts. The lessons are
powerful tools in clarifying and understanding food and wine synergy.

Each class begins with tasting a broad array of wine styles from
sparkling to dessert wines. We compare and contrast each wine
observing aromas, flavors, weight, intensity and the finish. One of
the clearest rules for pairing involves choosing wines that match the
intensity of each dish and the intensity of the cooking method.
Once this is understood, it becomes apparent that the main protein

(meat, fish, poultry, vegetables, etc…) of each dish may become secondary in considering the wine choice.

Quite often the sauce, herbs, spices and cooking method require more attention and can dictate the wine choice. Example: Grilling is more intense than sautéeing. If I grill a fresh piece of halibut, it creates a meatier impression of the fish and may require a more robust white wine or even a hearty red wine. It all comes down to balance. At BIN 36, we break the old "white wine with fish" rule because we understand the versatility of the components in both the food and wine. We treat meatier fish like tuna and swordfish like meat. Our peppercorn-crusted swordfish sings when paired with a hearty Australian Shiraz. This robust red wine shows off the intense flavors infused from our wood grill and accents the peppery flavors in the wine.

Generally, people think of Riesling and Gewürztraminer as sweet wines, and therefore not necessarily ideal food wines. In these sessions, I always have the class begin by smelling the aromas, then encourage them to taste by holding the wine in their mouths for six to eight seconds. This is longer than most of them have ever done this. What happens is that the wine has an opportunity to reveal a greater array of flavors and provides clues for possible nuances to highlight in food. I then pass around a bowl of wasabi-flavored dried peas and have them sample the peas with the Riesling. It never fails that at the end of the session virtually everyone purchases the Riesling to take home with them. It is fun to watch because they are discovering that they like something they've been told they are not supposed to enjoy. The combination of intense eye-watering spice and the relief of fruit-juicy acidity finally makes sense. This combo leads to animated discussions. It also provides the chance for me to recommend trying these wines with spicy and exotic cuisines such as Chinese, Thai, Indian and Mexican, as well as sushi.

It is really very simple. There are basically two ways to approach food and wine pairing. You can elect to enhance or echo flavors in a dish, or you might choose to contrast the flavors. I call the latter the question-and-answer session in your mouth. For instance, if you eat something hot and spicy you most likely want to drink something to decrease or put the fire out. That is where fruity, high-acid versions of wines like Pinot Gris, Riesling and Gewürztraminer come in handy.

I also enjoy seeing the reaction when I offer simple ripe tomatoes with crisp Gewürztraminer. It's as if they are eating tomatoes for the first time. Remember that tomatoes are a highly acidic fruit and Gewürztraminer is a richly flavored wine. Recognize any themes here? Acid is the key. The acid in the tomato creates that sensation on the sides of your tongue that makes you salivate and desire something more; either more food or more wine. It serves to cut right through the fat in food, creating a pleasurable sensation akin to butter melting in your mouth. The acid also performs the function of cleansing your mouth so that each taste of food or wine is fresh and new.

Since we have been discussing spice, I want to add another discovery. One of my favorite wines to take to sushi bars is a ripe, young red Zinfandel. Before you recommend that I seek counseling, try this test. Pour soy sauce in the little dish they provide, add as much wasabi as you like, stir it up, dip your sushi, then taste the red Zinfandel. You will taste flavors in the fish that sake and beer just can't unleash. Why? Zinfandel is a grape that possess a higher sugar content; it achieves a higher level of ripeness. This allows it to tame sour, salty and spicy flavors such as soy, mustard, wasabi and BBQ sauce.

Let's focus on one of my favorite subjects : cheese! It is a popular myth that red wine is the best choice for cheese. What is usually neglected is attention to which type of cheese with which type of wine. Let's start with goat cheese. My preference for these tangy wonders are usually Chenin Blanc (Savennières, Vouvray), Sauvignon Blanc or white Bordeaux, and Pinot Noir.

What is common to both the cheese and the wines is a high acid content. Creamy buttery cheeses like Camembert, double- and triple-cream cheeses work beautifully with sparkling wines and buttery Chardonnays by mimicking the smooth texture and echoing the flavors in the cheese. Firm cow's milk cheeses do better with heartier red wines like Cabernet Sauvignon, Merlot, Rioja, and a variety of Italian reds. The delicious stinky blue-veined cheeses work beautifully with robust reds like Amarone (an almost port-like Italian red), red Zinfandel and a variety of fortified wines such as dessert-style Sherries, Australian Muscat, Madeira and Port. Late-harvest Riesling, Hungarian Tokaji and Sauternes are just a few of the choices built for the salty pungency of blue cheese.

There is one hard-and-fast rule that cannot be broken when choosing wine for dessert. The wine you select must be at least as sweet or sweeter than the dessert you choose.

How many times have you found yourself at the end of a meal with just enough dry red wine to go around and then dessert arrives. You begin eating the dessert and need a little wine to wash it down. So you reach for the red wine and it tastes sour, even foul. Here's my point: the dessert is sweeter than your dry red wine. Chocolate might work, but it had better be of the bittersweet or dark chocolate varieties or you will have that awful bitter aftertaste at the end of a potentially delightful meal.

While I covered a small variety of options, I hope these examples are useful in providing a foundation for discovery in planning meals and menus, or creating your own food and wine magic. As always, my motto is "The best way to learn about it is to drink it."

Brian Duncan is owner and wine director of Chicago's highly regarded wine bar, restaurant, and wine shop BIN 36. A second BIN 36 was recently opened in Lincolnshire.

BIN 36
339 North Dearborn
Chicago, Illinois 60610
phone 312-560-4660
email brian@bin36.com

BIN 36 Lincolnshire
275 Parkway Drive
Lincolnshire, Illinois 60069
phone 847-808-9463
website www.bin36.com

Chapter Four

Tasting Wine: Making the Restaurant Ritual Useful

by Richard Betts, Master Sommelier

Tasting Wine: Making the Restaurant Ritual Useful

You are at dinner, the sommelier arrives with your wine, it's opened, a taste is poured, you give it a sniff, a sip, and you're not sure; is it off or just not that good? Do you send it back or simply hope for better luck next time? All of a sudden dinner is not much fun.

I t should never be this way when you're dining out; wine is an integral and essential part of the meal and not one that should cause angst. The reality of the experience, however, requires the diner to take some initiative to ensure vinous success. Here's how to do it with confidence and ease.

First of all, realize that the sommelier is your advocate and your friend. This is someone who is there only to help you get exactly what you want without pretense or intimidation. The best sommeliers are keenly aware that putting the guests' desires first is the only road to success.

It is also important to be a thoughtful taster. As a sommelier, I taste many wines and do my best to evaluate them all consistently. The same principles that I use to taste can be used to your advantage when tasting in a restaurant, in spite of distractions.

Before you actually taste, you are usually presented the cork. While nothing is gleaned from smelling, tasting or throwing the cork, do look at it. As silly as it may sound, you should be sure that whatever is printed on the cork does not contradict what is written on the label. Also, look to see if wine has seeped out, which never indicates by itself that the wine is bad but occasionally gives storage clues.

When you are poured a taste, make sure it is a good one; you need something to work with, after all, so it is absolutely in order to have a healthy splash. Then there are actually three parts to consider for any wine: appearance, smell and taste. Begin by looking at the wine and ask yourself if it makes sense. Red wines will be, obviously, shades of red, while white wines are shades of yellow and green but all wines take on brown as they age.

We expect a young Napa Cabernet to be deep red/purple and a traditional Chianti to be garnet/orange in color. However, if our young Cab is garnet/orange, there may be a problem. Also, look for bubbles and sediment. Unless you're drinking Champagne, you can do without the fizz, and, while sediment is harmless to you, most old wines do "throw" sediment and require special handling and possibly decanting.

Before giving the wine a sniff, get it moving in the glass. Swirling it around does make it easier to smell. Does the wine smell correct or flawed? If you have no idea of what the wine is supposed to be like, then ask whoever sold it to you! It's not an exact science, but our Cabernet should smell something like Cab after all. Do remember to give it time, since few wines give you everything they have immediately. The wine has been slumbering in that bottle and probably needs some time to get the sleep out of its eyes before it can get up and dance. When more time is required, it is reasonable to say, "I'd like to give it a minute to open up." This way you can buy yourself an extra moment to decide.

In the rare instance of a flaw such as oxidation or "cork" taint (that wet-dog, moldy, cardboard smell), you may have some sense of it right away, but it generally gets stronger as the wine sits in your glass so you can confirm any suspicions with time.

Then when sipping, take in the flavors and the texture. Consider how the wine feels and how it finishes (longer usually means better quality). All of the elements such as fruit, oak, acidity and tannin should be in balance; this harmony is a mark of quality. Our well-made young Cabernet is going to have lots of tannin but it is also brimming with lush fruit, identifying it as a "big" wine.

You might also consider how the wine is going to pair with food. For example, many Americans find Chianti to be acidic or "sour" on its own, but when paired with a lusty pasta dish that acidity brings verve and life to the food creating a great marriage. Lastly, be sure the temperature is it to your liking. Wines too warm or too cool can be iced or left on the table respectively. No ice bucket is necessary (I frequently find whites served too cool, so I let them warm on the table). Hot wines are mostly unacceptable.

Now we are ready to make our judgment. Is it an objective (is it a good-quality wine) or subjective (do I like this wine) decision? It is both, really. If the wine is flawed (e.g.: corked, oxidized or otherwise), it is going back. If you're uncertain, feel free to ask for another opinion either from a companion or your advocate and friend the sommelier. If the sommelier says that the wine is sound, consider it useful information, but still make your decision independently.

If you do not like the wine, even if it is sound, and you were sold the wine by your enthusiastic sommelier, then the dialogue is open to return it because it is not what you were led to expect. If you chose the wine on your own and are unsure of the restaurant's policy, you might say, "I believe the wine is sound, but I am not certain I like it."

Return policies vary wildly but your friendly sommelier will be eager to please and is likely to take this cue and either offer to replace it with another selection or share with you the restaurant's policy on returned bottles. Better restaurants will take back wine on the basis of your taste alone. However, I would not advocate using this approach to find the "perfect" bottle each time. In addition to keeping the friendly sommelier smiling, breadth of experience in wine drinking is very important. Only through experience can we truly develop our own palates and build our knowledge base. In any event, by remaining composed and thoughtful throughout the process the old adage will hold true for you: "The guest is (almost) always right."

Richard Betts is wine director and sommelier at The Little Nell, in Aspen, Colorado. He recently passed the Master Sommelier exam (on his first try), to become the ninth Master Sommelier Krug Cup Winner. He lives in Aspen with his wife, Mona, his daughter, Claudia, and two golden retrievers.

Montagna at The Little Nell
675 East Durant Avenue
Aspen, Colorado 81611
phone 970-920-6339
email rbetts@thelittlenell.com

Chapter Five

Wine Service in Restaurants

BY LISA MINUCCI, SOMMELIER, MARTINI HOUSE

Wine Service in Restaurants

"Welcome to Martini House. If I can answer
any questions on the wine list or pair any of
your courses with wine this evening, please
don't hesitate to ask me," is my usual greet-
ing to guests who have been seated in our
Napa Valley restaurant.

Our guests come from all over the world to visit Napa Valley
and to learn about wine, and they possess varied levels
of expertise with the grape. Though the list contains
700 entries from around the world, my mission is to make our
guests feel comfortable and excited about our wine program.
With pages devoted to "Women Winemakers We Love" and
"Restaurateurs Who Are Winemakers," to "The Voodoo That You
Do: Biodynamic Wines" and "Elevations: Wines With Altitude,"
I strive to make it as entertaining as it is educational.

As soon as you are seated, we offer a glass of either sparkling wine
or Champagne to enjoy while you peruse Chef Humphries' seasonal menu. If bubbles are not your preference, perhaps a glass of
wine, Sherry or a cocktail to begin your evening? The forty wines
offered by the glass are listed in sections such as crisp, medium-
bodied and lush, providing tastes for every palate. All wines offered
by the glass are served in Spiegelau stemware with the exception of
our "Dream Wines" (older or exceptional Napa Valley wines),
which are poured in Riedel "Extreme Series" crystal glasses.

Once a guest has made a selection from the wine list, I retrieve the
bottle from one of our five temperature-controlled storage units.
The server sets the table with proper stemware, a coaster and a
decanter. The bottle is presented to the diner who selected the
wine, while verbalizing the name of the wine and its vintage.
Sometimes a guest will touch the bottle to feel the temperature
of the bottle. We keep different wines at different temperatures.
Sauvignon Blanc and Rieslings are kept cooler than Chardonnay
and Viognier, while red wines are stored at cellar temperature.
This is a luxury many restaurants do not possess, as storage is
always an issue in any restaurant. While most diners are pleased
with Chardonnay served at 53-54 degrees, some will ask for the wine
to be kept on ice. Any way you enjoy your wine is the correct way.

I extract the cork with a waiter's corkscrew, which I feel is the most reliable tool. Unlike service personnel at most restaurants, I do not present the cork to the guest unless it is an older bottling or the guest requests it. A cork from a younger bottle of wine has little information to reveal, and guests are sometimes confused as to what to do with it. Since I have added a page of "Cork Free Wines," sometimes a twist of the wrist is all that is necessary!

Unlike most restaurants, we decant all wines, both red and white, with the exception of Champagne and older Burgundy. The majority of wines consumed at Martini House are between three and seven years old and have not thrown any sediment. These wines are poured quickly into the decanter in order to aerate them. If the wine has more than seven years' bottle age, I bring a pillar candle to the table and carefully decant the wine at the table, checking for sediment. I then give the decanter a little swish and sniff from it. If the wine is corked or smells faulty, I quickly replace it. Sometimes a guest will ask to smell a corked wine in order to become familiar with that flaw. Education is the best armament in the battle against drinking faulty wines!

Many of our diners comment that they have never witnessed young wines being decanted, particularly white wines. I explain that decanting introduces oxygen into the wine, which helps it to open up more quickly, revealing its wonderful aromas and flavors. (I am often asked where one can purchase a good decanter!) A healthy splash is offered to the person who selected the wine. If he or she appears pleased, I pour the wines for the other guests, always ladies first, finishing with the host. If a second bottle is requested, a clean tasting glass is presented. If it is an older wine, all guests will get a clean stem.

While Martini House is a white-tablecloth restaurant and wine service is, hopefully, conducted properly, I never want it to feel pretentious, contrived or stuffy. I am familiar with all of the wines on the list and will ask what the guest is enjoying for dinner and then make appropriate suggestions in different price categories, often using conversational, food-based terminology to describe the wines.

I have been a sommelier at fairly formal restaurants and more casual dining rooms, and proper wine service should not differ from one to the next. Yes, I am fortunate to work in a restaurant that believes its wine program is important enough to employ a sommelier and that invests serious money in wine inventory, good glassware and decanters.

Whatever the style of restaurant or the cuisine, however, it is often the attitude and approach of the person offering the wine guidance—choosing and creating the list, training the staff and pairing the menu—that makes a guest feel comfortable, relaxed and excited about the wine that is headed to their table.

I remind myself of this with a quote on the opening page of the wine list from wine writer Hubrecht Duijker that reads: "Never apologize for, or be ashamed of, your own taste in wine. Preferences for wine vary just as much as those for art or music."

Lisa Minucci is sommelier at The Martini House, in St. Helena, California. The wine list at the restaurant is known for its intelligence and sense of fun, both in terms of its selections and its organization.

The Martini House
1245 Spring Street
St. Helena, California 94574
phone 707-963-2233
email amgadw@excite.com

Chapter Six
Wine Prices in Restaurants
BY DAVID GLANCY

Wine Prices in Restaurants

Many people question the prices that restaurants charge for wine. It is sometimes difficult to swallow finding your favorite $20
retail bottle of wine on the restaurant's list
for $40. Is this typical of restaurant wine
markups, and if so, why?

I. Typical Markups

There is a wide variety of pricing schedules for restaurants, but
most use a sliding scale where inexpensive wines are marked up
more than expensive wines. Typical markups range from 1.5 to
3.0 times the wholesale cost for wines offered by the bottle. Wines
by the glass are generally marked up more, ranging from 3.0 to
5.0 times the wholesale cost for the bottle, divided by four to five
glasses served per bottle. According to the Golden Gate Restaurant
Association's Economic Study 2001, the national average wine cost
for restaurants ranges from 36 percent to 40 percent. This is the
equivalent of average markups of 2.5 to 2.8 times. The markup
schedule the sommelier uses is the tool for them to achieve the
budgeted wine product cost dictated to them by the restaurant
owner, manager or corporation.

II. Costs Involved in Wine Programs

So, what expenses compel restaurateurs to mark up that $20 bottle
to $40 on their wine list? The costs that directly impact wine pric-
ing include the salary of the wine director or sommelier(s), the cost
of maintaining wine inventory, construction cost of a proper wine
cellar, utility bills for air-conditioning and refrigeration, menu
printing, stemware breakage, staff training, product spoilage and
insurance costs associated with liquor liability. Construction costs
for a basic wine cellar range from about $10,000 to $25,000 and
can be substantially higher if upgraded materials such as mahogany
are used. Fine stemware can cost anywhere from $5 to $50 each
and are broken constantly. A large white-tablecloth restaurant can
easily spend $5,000 to $10,000 a year on replacement glasses.
Staff training is another large expense of the wine program. Staff
members are paid their hourly rate to attend training sessions,
the sommelier spends time planning these sessions, and there is

product cost involved in opening wines for the staff to taste. This is an ongoing process because wine lists regularly change, and staff turnover averages around 50 percent a year, often running 200 percent and higher for new restaurant openings.

Wines by the glass have additional costs compared to bottle sales. These costs include spoilage, spillage and over-pouring. If fewer than four glasses of a by-the-glass selection are sold in a day, the unsold portion of the bottle may spoil. This is often a problem when a dozen or more selections are available. Money may also be spent on various wine preservation systems. There is also an opportunity for a spill on every glass served. The price of the glass may be based on getting five glasses out of each bottle, and the generous bartender may only be getting four out of each, as well as offering a glass or two to their regular guests "on the house."

There are other expenses that impact the entire restaurant. Food, wine, beer, liquor and nonalcoholic beverage profits all go toward paying for initial construction costs, ongoing maintenance, insurance, taxes, loan costs and repaying investors. Average new construction is around $250 per square foot and can run that high for an extensive renovation of an existing property. At the end of the day, restaurants eke out an average of 5 percent income before taxes. Compare that to the pharmaceutical industry at over 18 percent, banks at more than 10 percent and consumer products at over 9 percent. These slim profit margins are why 90 percent of all restaurants fail within five years.

III. Corkage Fees

Corkage is the fee a restaurant charges for handling and serving a bottle of wine that a customer brings into the restaurant. Most restaurants charge from $5 to $30 per bottle corkage fee. Restaurants that have a sommelier on staff, offer a large selection of wines, provide fine stemware, and have proper wine storage tend to be at the top of this range. The fee is often doubled for magnums, and some restaurants charge a stem fee for each glass used instead of a corkage fee. Many restaurants will waive one corkage charge for every bottle ordered from the wine list. Of note is that it is illegal to bring wine into a restaurant in several states, while some restaurants do not allow it even where it is legal to do so.

IV. Finding Value Wines

Although sommeliers have formulas they use for pricing wines, these are not set in stone. Some wines are marked up less than others. Lesser-known wines and regions, or wines that have not sold well, may be offered at lower markups. One well-known wine director uses a lower markup on the first page of the wine list in order to make a good first impression on guests. Most sommeliers will gladly point out value wines on the list at whatever price point the guest is comfortable with. Straying beyond Chardonnay and Cabernet can also be helpful in finding the best values on any wine list.

David Glancy is the proprietor of SFsommelier Consulting (www.sfsommelier.com), a firm that provides beverage and operations consulting to the hospitality and retail industries, and to consumers.

Sfsommelier Consulting
66 Crestline Drive, #7
San Francisco, California 94131
phone 415-505-9382
email sfglancy@earthlink.net

Chapter Seven
Featured Wineries

Cambria

Cambria

5475 Chardonnay Lane
Santa Maria, California 93454
(888) 339-9463
cambriawines.com
(tasting room open Sat. and
Sun. 10 a.m.–5 p.m. and
weekdays by appointment)

Cambria creates the ultimate expression of estate bottled Santa Barbara County Pinot Noir, Chardonnay and Syrah from our family-owned estate vineyard in the heart of the Santa Maria Bench. The Santa Maria Bench, home to Cambria, is a study in contrasts. There is the understated beauty of the landscape—the wide-angle vistas of undulating vineyards and gently rolling hills; the cool Pacific breezes that cloak the vineyards in morning coastal fog. And then there are the wines—head turning, opulent, larger-than-life affairs that impress with their power and seduce with their texture. At Cambria we celebrate these contrasts, from the restrained beauty of our land to the bold intensity of our wines.

First Vintage
The inaugural vintage for Cambria was 1988 with the introduction of Sur Lees Chardonnay and Julia's Vineyard Pinot Noir.

Winemaker
Denise Shurtleff

Vineyard Manager
Patrick Huguenard

Wines
Chardonnay, Pinot Noir and Syrah

Vineyard Sources
Cambria Estate Vineyards
Santa Maria Valley

Chalk Hill

Sonoma County
10300 Chalk Hill Road
Healdsburg, California 95448
(707) 838-4306
www.chalkhill.com
(visit by appointment only)

Chalk Hill Estate Vineyards & Winery is family-owned and operated in the Chalk Hill sub-appellation of Russian River Valley in Sonoma County, California. Since 1972 Founders and Proprietors Frederick and Peggy Furth have lived on the 1200-acre estate, 350 acres planted in vineyard. Each one of more than 80 vineyard parcels has been created up and down the hillsides and on the valley floors to grow naturally balanced vines. Winemaking consistently conveys the individuality of each site by using natural, traditional methods. The hallmark of all Chalk Hill wines is the land that sustains the vines and the winemaking that authenticates this incomparable terroir.

First Vintage
The inaugural vintage for Chalk Hill was 1980 with the introduction of Estate Bottled Chardonnay, Cabernet Sauvignon and Sauvignon Blanc.

Winemaker
Steven Leveque

Vineyard Manager
Mark Lingenfelder

Proprietors
Frederick & Peggy Furth

Wines
Chardonnay, Sauvignon Blanc, Merlot, Cabernet Sauvignon, Pinot Gris, Botrytised Semillon

Vineyard Source
Chalk Hill Estate, Chalk Hill Valley, Russian River Valley

VINEYARDS

Hanzell Vineyards
18596 Lomita Avenue
Sonoma, California 95476
(707) 996-3860
fax: (707) 996-3862
hanzell.com

Hanzell Vineyards, located in the hills above Sonoma Valley, is a private estate winery and vineyard founded in 1957 by Ambassador J. D. Zellerbach. Zellerbach's passion for the great wines of Burgundy prompted his planting of Chardonnay and Pinot Noir vines and the building of an architectural jewel of a winery inspired by Clos de Vougeot. Hanzell Vineyards is renowned for its innovative introduction (in the 1960s) of stainless steel for fermenting its wines and French oak for barrel aging.

As it has been for the past thirty years, Hanzell Vineyards today, now under President, Jean L. Arnold and Winemaker Daniel Docher's stewardship, is still under Bob Session's watchful eye. His new team continues to live the "Hanzell Way"—absolute commitment to quality, the singular expression of terroir from this land, and honoring the tremendous heritage of this unique estate. Hanzell Vineyards is owned by the de Brye Family and has been since 1975.

First Vintage
In 1953, Ambassador Zellerbach and his wife Hanna planted Chardonnay and Pinot Noir on the Hanzell Estate. The winery's first offering was the 1957 Hanzell Vineyards Chardonnay.

Winemaker
Daniel Docher became the Hanzell Vineyards winemaker in January 2002, after apprenticing for seven years under longtime Hanzell winemaker Bob Sessions.

Vineyard Manager
Jose de Jesus Ramos began working at Hanzell in 1977 and has been Hanzell vineyard manager since 1985.

Wines
Estate grown and produced Chardonnay and Pinot Noir

Vineyard Sources
Since 1962, the Hanzell Estate has been the sole vineyard source.

Jordan

Jordan

1474 Alexander Valley Road
Healdsburg, California 95448
(707) 431-5250
fax: (707) 431-5259
www.jordanwinery.com

Founded in 1972, Jordan Vineyard & Winery has specialized in the production of ultra-premium Sonoma County Cabernet Sauvignon and Russian River Valley Chardonnay. Located in Sonoma County's renowned Alexander Valley, the winery stands on an oak-covered knoll overlooking 375 acres of carefully tended hillside and valley floor vineyards. Situated less than twenty miles from the Pacific Ocean, the topography, soil and climate impart a distinctive character to Jordan wines. For over twenty-five years Jordan has consistently produced elegant, balanced wines with the philosophy that winemaking is simply a logical completion of nature's work.

First Vintage

The inaugural vintage for Jordan Cabernet Sauvignon was 1976; the inaugural vintage of Jordan Chardonnay was 1979.

Winemaker

Rob Davis joined Jordan Winery as enologist and assistant to Andre Tchelistcheff in 1976 and was made winemaker in 1977.

Vineyard Manager

Mark Bailey

Wines

Cabernet Sauvignon and Chardonnay

Vineyard Sources

Jordan Estate, Alexander Valley, Russian River Valley and Mendocino County

La Crema

3690 Laughlin Road
Windsor, CA 95492
707-571-1504
www.lacrema.com
(visit by appointment only)

La Crema Winery is a family owned estate and is situated in the heart of Sonoma County's Russian River Valley. Founded in 1979, La Crema is considered one of the pioneers in producing intensely flavored Chardonnay and Pinot Noir from the Russian River Valley. Creating great Chardonnay and Pinot Noir wines is restricted by the ability to grow the finest, cold coastal grapes. La Crema searches for grapes grown in well drained soils where the coastal fog allows long hang time and slow ripening. The result is small intense berries which provide the elegance and balance that mark the signature of La Crema handcrafted wines.

First Vintage
The inaugural vintage for La Crema was 1979 with Chardonnay and Pinot Noir.

Winemaker
Jeff Stewart

Vineyard Manager
Hector Bedolla

Proprietors
La Crema is owned by sisters Laura Jackson-Giron and Jennifer Jackson.

Wines
Chardonnay and Pinot Noir. Limited production of Viognier, Syrah and Zinfandel.

Vineyard Sources
La Crema Estate, Russian River Valley, Sonoma Coast, Carneros and Anderson Valley

mATANZAS CREEK WINERY

Matanzas Creek
6097 Bennett Valley Road
Santa Rosa, CA 95404
(707) 528-6464

Located in the cool climate Bennett Valley area of Sonoma County, Matanzas Creek Winery was founded on a simple precept—quality first, always. This philosophy quickly earned the winery a reputation as one of California's top producers of Chardonnay, Sauvignon Blanc and Merlot. Winemaker Gary Patzwald and Consulting Winemaker Pierre Seillan continue to strive for balance, elegance and consistency in all of their wines. Proprietors Barbara Banke and Jess Jackson are dedicated to continuing the winery's tradition of excellence by improving the quality of the estate vineyards while making exciting new vineyard sources available.

First Vintage
The inaugural vintage for Matanzas Creek 1978 Sonoma Valley Chardonnay released in 1979.

Winemaker
Gary Patzwald

Vineyard Manager
Brandon Axell

Wines
Chardonnay, Sauvignon Blanc, Merlot and Syrah

Vineyard Sources
Matanzas Creek Estate (Bennett Valley), Nicholas (Bennett Valley), Jackson Park (Bennett Valley), Nolan (Bennett Valley), Durell (Carneros), Sangiacomo-Catarina (Carneros), Sangiacomo-Kiser (Carneros), Hopkins (Russian River Valley), Bock (Redwood Valley)

RUDD

Rudd
500 Oakville Crossroad
Oakville, California 94562
(707) 944-8577
www.ruddwines.com
(visit by appointment only)

Rudd winery was established in 1996, when Leslie Rudd purchased the 54-acre estate in Oakville. Since the purchase, Mr. Rudd has made extensive renovations to the property that include a complete replanting of the vineyards to close-spaced, red Bordeaux varietals and the expansion and renovation of the winery, adding custom-designed tanks and a gentle, gravity-flow system. In addition, 22,000 square feet of caves have been dug below the winery to provide ideal aging conditions. In April 2002, Charles Thomas joined the Rudd team as Director of Vineyards & Winemaking. Charles brings to Rudd over 25 years of winemaking and vineyard experience. Rudd uses a blend of tradition and innovation, adhering to a philosophy of continuous improvement, to provide discriminating consumers with an exceptional wine-drinking experience.

First Vintage
The first wines under the Rudd label were released in October 2000.

Winemaker
Charles Thomas

Vineyard Manager
Terry Mathison

Wines
Cabernet Sauvignon, Proprietary Red Blend, Chardonnay and Sauvignon Blanc

Vineyard Sources
Oakville and Russian River Valley

SILVER OAK CELLARS
CABERNET SAUVIGNON

Silver Oak Cellars
(800) 273-8809
www.silveroak.com

Napa Valley
915 Oakville Crossroad
Oakville, California 94562

Alexander Valley
24625 Chianti Road
Geyserville, California 95441

In the early 1970s Silver Oak Cellars emerged as a dream tied to an intrepid idea: to create a Cabernet Sauvignon of fully developed flavors and velvety soft textures on the day it was released for sale.

Silver Oak is consistently the most requested Cabernet Sauvignon in America's finest restaurants. The elegance and finesse of our wines have attracted as zealous a circle of customers as any winery, and we are truly grateful for their allegiance, although we will never relax in our pursuit of perfection. We believe that we have yet to make our best bottle of wine, and we will never stop trying.

First Vintage
The inaugural vintage for Silver Oak was 1972 North Coast Cabernet Sauvignon.

Winemaker
Daniel Baron

Vineyard Manager
Dane Petersen

Wine
Cabernet Sauvignon

Vineyard Sources
Alexander Valley and Napa Valley vineyards

STONESTREET

Stonestreet
7111 Highway 128
Healdsburg, California 95448
(707) 433-9463
stonestreetwines.com

Located on the outskirts of Healdsburg at the base of the Mayacamas Mountains lies Stonestreet's new winery. Ideally located, the winery lies minutes from our vineyards at Alexander Mountain Estate, a 5,000-acre parcel that rises on the crest of the Alexander Valley appellation of eastern Sonoma County. Its unique mountain terroir is ideal for producing world-class estate and single-vineyard Cabernet Sauvignon, Merlot, Sauvignon Blanc and Chardonnay.

First Vintage
The inaugural vintage for Stonestreet was 1989 with the introduction of Cabernet Sauvignon and Merlot. In the autumn of 1989, Jess Jackson established and named Stonestreet in honor of his late father, Jess Stonestreet Jackson. Mike Westrick, winemaker since 1996, continues to build upon the legacy of producing distinctive wines to savor, collect and age.

Winemaker
Mike Westrick

Vineyard Manager
Tony Viramontes

Wines
Cabernet Sauvignon, Merlot, Sauvignon Blanc, Chardonnay and Legacy "Meritage"

Vineyard Sources
Alexander Mountain Estate

VÉRITÉ

Vérité

4611 Thomas Road,
Healdsburg, California 95448
(707) 433-9000
www.veritewines.com
(visit by appointment only)

Simply put, but profound in its intent, Vérité is dedicated to producing red wines of style and substance along a traditional model. The winery selects the finest Merlot, Cabernet Sauvignon, Cabernet Franc and Malbec from a handful of outstanding mountain and hillside sites or micro-crus along the Mayacamas Mountain range. Each micro-crus or "vineyard within a vineyard" is based on diverse criteria of soil, climate and other aspects specifically selected for their potential to express a strong sense of terroir. Our winemaker's approach is to envision a model of the wine he would like to create, then to obtain precisely the fruit needed to express that vision.

First Vintage
The inaugural vintage for Vérité was 1998 with two wines, Vérité, Merlot based, and La Joie, Cabernet Sauvignon based.

Vigneron (Winemaker)
Pierre Seillan

Assistant Vignerons
Olivier Rousset

Wines
La Muse (Merlot, Cabernet Sauvignon), La Joie (Cabernet Sauvignon, Merlot), Le Désir (Merlot, Cabernet Franc, Cabernet Sauvignon)

Vineyard Sources
John Alexander Mountain Estate, Alexander Valley, Mt. Taylor, Bennett Valley, Kellogg, Knights Valley, Diamondback, Chalk Hill

Chapter Eight
The Restaurants

Crow's Nest in the Hotel Captain Cook

Fifth and K Streets
Anchorage, Alaska 99501
phone 907-276-6000 fax 907-343-2298
website www.captaincook.com

Randal S. Lindsey
SOMMELIER

LIST ANY FORMAL AND INFORMAL WINE TRAINING, DEGREES, CERTIFI-
CATES AND AWARDS.
Master Sommelier program first level; our list receives the Wine Spectator and
Tier awards annually.

WHAT INSPIRED YOU TO PURSUE A CAREER THAT INVOLVES WINE?
I was inspired attending a Wines of the World class twenty years ago.

NAME RECENT WINE DISCOVERIES THAT HAVE EXCITED YOU.
Wines of Austria.

WHAT BITS OF INFORMATION WOULD YOU LIKE YOUR CUSTOMERS TO
KNOW ABOUT YOU?
I have traveled the world and bring perspectives from the areas I've traveled to
(that are not always known to the wine world) to the table.

IF YOU WERE NOT IN THIS PROFESSION, WHAT WOULD YOU BE DOING?
I'd pursue cultural studies. I love to study relationships between people.

DESCRIBE YOUR WINE SELECTIONS, BOTH BY THE GLASS AND ON YOUR
LIST.
We have 10,000 bottles with more than 1,400 different selections and more
than thirty wines by the glass available in thirteen different varietals. We are
known for our large selection of French and California wines.

WHAT ARE THE MOST UNIQUE FEATURES IN YOUR WINE PROGRAM?
We have wine flights in the Whale Tail restaurant and hold special wine dinners
with winemakers. Each month the Crow's Nest has a five-course tasting menu
paired with wine.

IN THE PAST YEAR, WHAT WINES IN YOUR WINE PROGRAM HAVE CUS-
TOMERS BECOME MORE WILLING TO ORDER?
Oregon Pinot Noir.

Atlas Bistro
2515 North Scottsdale Road
Scottsdale, Arizona 85257
phone 480-990-2433 fax 480-990-2435
website www.atlasbistro.com

David M. Johnson
SOMMELIER

WHAT INSPIRED YOU TO PURSUE A CAREER THAT INVOLVES WINE?
The Johnstons of Scotland, my ancestral clan, have historically been significant negotiants in Bordeaux. It's a heritage I'm proud to follow.

WHAT BITS OF INFORMATION WOULD YOU LIKE YOUR CUSTOMERS TO KNOW ABOUT YOU?
I am a vintage wine and cask whisky broker in addition to my duties as sommelier. I also represent fine Italian wine crystal from Bottega del Vino in Verona.

IF YOU WERE NOT IN THIS PROFESSION, WHAT WOULD YOU BE DOING?
I'd be an artisanal food producer or merchant such as a cheesemonger, an heirloom chili farmer or a purebred cattle breeder.

NAME A COUPLE OF YOUR RESTAURANT'S SIGNATURE DISHES. WHAT TYPES OF WINE DO YOU PREFER TO RECOMMEND WITH EACH?
Ginger-cured duck with wild mushroom risotto and wilted spinach accompanied by Sonoma Pinot Noir; lamb tamale with salsa and crème fraîche with Australian Shiraz.

IN THE PAST YEAR, WHAT WINES IN YOUR WINE PROGRAM HAVE CUSTOMERS BECOME MORE WILLING TO ORDER?
California Viognier, Rhône wine, Spanish Crianza, Italian and Cal-Italian Arneis, Australian Port, Okanagan Pinot Noir and Arizona red blends.

WHAT ARE SOME OTHER ULTIMATE WINE AND FOOD PAIRINGS?
French Sauvignon Blanc with smoked eels; Amarone with pastissada de caval (horsemeat stew); Beaujolais with New Mexico chiles rellenos; Châteauneuf-du-Pape and roast turkey; Alsatian Pinot Blanc and eggs Benedict; Zinfandel and buffalo wings.

Christopher's Fermier Brasserie and Paola's Wine Bar

2584 East Camelback Road
Phoenix, Arizona 85016
phone 602-522-2344 fax 602-468-0314
website www.fermier.com

Paola M. Embry-Gross
OWNER AND SOMMELIER

WHAT INSPIRED YOU TO PURSUE A CAREER THAT INVOLVES WINE?
Chef Christopher Gross, my former husband and current business partner, planted the seed. I love wine and was inspired to build a career in it because wine brings people together.

NAME ONE OR TWO OF YOUR FAVORITE WINE DISTRICTS OR WINE REGIONS FROM AROUND THE WORLD.
Last year it was southern Italy with its exotic grape varieties like Negroamaro, Primitivo and Nero d'Avola. This year it is Spain.

NAME RECENT WINE DISCOVERIES THAT HAVE EXCITED YOU.
2001 Mulderbosch Sauvignon Blanc from South Africa, 2001 Clos Mimi Petite Rousse Syrah from Paso Robles, California.

WHAT BITS OF INFORMATION WOULD YOU LIKE YOUR CUSTOMERS TO KNOW ABOUT YOU?
I love all kinds of music, especially music from Buddha Bar, Barrio Latino and Nirvana Lounge.

WHAT ARE THE MOST UNIQUE FEATURES IN YOUR WINE PROGRAM?
Our menu indicates my wine suggestions with all appetizers and main courses. We also offer a complimentary 1-ounce taste of any of our 100 wines by the glass.

WHAT CATEGORY OF WINE IS THE BEST VALUE IN YOUR RESTAURANT?
ABC (Anything But Chardonnay and Cabernet) and whites and reds from Spain, New Zealand, the south of Italy and Portugal.

IN THE PAST YEAR, WHAT WINES IN YOUR WINE PROGRAM HAVE CUSTOMERS BECOME MORE WILLING TO ORDER?
Oregon Pinot Noir, Petite Sirah from California and Sauvignon Blanc from New Zealand.

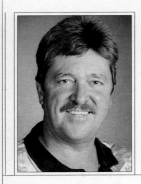

Different Pointe of View at the Pointe-Hilton Tapatio Cliffs Resort

11111 North Seventh Street
Phoenix, Arizona 85020
phone 602-863-0912 fax 602-866-6358
website www.differentpointeofview.com

Eric Spragett
CELLAR MASTER

LIST ANY FORMAL AND INFORMAL WINE TRAINING, DEGREES, CERTIFICATES AND AWARDS.
Certified Wine Educator; Certificate Course, Court of Master Sommeliers.

WHAT INSPIRED YOU TO PURSUE A CAREER THAT INVOLVES WINE?
It beats working for a living!

NAME ONE OR TWO OF YOUR FAVORITE WINE REGIONS.
I love the Anderson Valley in Mendocino because it is pleasantly unspoiled. Also, Saint-Émilion is the epitome of a wine town

NAME RECENT WINE DISCOVERIES THAT HAVE EXCITED YOU.
Old Pedro Ximinez Sherry.

WHAT WOULD YOU LIKE YOUR CUSTOMERS TO KNOW ABOUT YOU?
I neither pretend to understand nor use "winespeak."

IF YOU WERE NOT IN THIS PROFESSION, WHAT WOULD YOU BE DOING?
Brewing.

DESCRIBE YOUR WINE SELECTIONS, BOTH BY THE GLASS AND ON YOUR LIST.
We have a global selection with an emphasis on Bordeaux and California reds.

WHAT ARE THE MOST UNIQUE FEATURES IN YOUR WINE PROGRAM?
Our "birthday" list offers twenty wines at deep discounts.

WHAT CATEGORY OF WINE IS THE BEST VALUE IN YOUR RESTAURANT?
South African reds and Spanish Tempranillo.

WHAT WINES DO YOU RECOMMEND WITH YOUR SIGNATURE DISHES?
Lobster bisque with Cienega or San Benito Viognier; rack of lamb with Willamette Pinot Noir.

WHAT WINES ARE CUSTOMERS NOW MORE WILLING TO ORDER?
Oregon Pinot Gris.

Elements

5700 East McDonald Drive
Paradise Valley, Arizona 85253
phone 480-607-2305
website www.elementsrestaurant.com

Patricia M. Jasmin
RESTAURANT MANAGER
AND BEVERAGE DIRECTOR

NAME TWO OF YOUR FAVORITE WINES FROM AROUND THE WORLD.
Pinot Noir from Oregon and white wines from Friuli, especially Sauvignon
Blanc.

IF YOU WERE NOT IN THIS PROFESSION, WHAT WOULD YOU BE DOING?
Working in the movies, not as an actor, but behind the scenes. I'm a huge
movie fan, especially of old classics and smaller production films.

DESCRIBE YOUR WINE SELECTIONS, BOTH BY THE GLASS AND ON YOUR
LIST.
Our list has many offerings including a large bubbly section and wines from
California, Washington and Oregon, with some fun imports like Grüner
Veltliner, New Zealand Pinot Noir and Italian Sauvignon Blanc.

WHAT ARE THE MOST UNIQUE FEATURES IN YOUR WINE PROGRAM?
We have more than twenty-five wines by the glass, many half-bottle selections
in each category, and we make frequent changes to the list.

WHAT CATEGORY OF WINE IS THE BEST VALUE IN YOUR RESTAURANT?
The "alternative" reds like Zinfandel, Grenache and Syrah.

NAME A COUPLE OF YOUR RESTAURANT'S SIGNATURE DISHES. WHAT
TYPES OF WINE DO YOU PREFER TO RECOMMEND WITH EACH?
Our menu changes monthly, but maintains an emphasis on seafood with Asian
accents. We love to pair our food with Gewürztraminer, Grüner Veltliner and
Sauvignon Blanc from the Loire Valley.

IN THE PAST YEAR, WHAT WINES IN YOUR WINE PROGRAM HAVE CUS-
TOMERS BECOME MORE WILLING TO ORDER?
California Zinfandel, Syrah, Petite Sirah and Oregon Pinot Noir.

Mary Elaine's at the Phoenician Resort

6000 East Camelback Road
Scottsdale, Arizona 85251
phone 480-941-8200 fax 480-947-4311
website www.thephoenician.com

Greg A. Tresner
MASTER SOMMELIER

LIST ANY WINE TRAINING, DEGREES, CERTIFICATES AND AWARDS.
Master Sommelier Diploma in 2000, Court of Master Sommeliers; Wine Spectator Grand Award since 2000.

WHAT INSPIRED YOU TO PURSUE A CAREER THAT INVOLVES WINE?
I love all the evocative musings, poetic waxing, romantic evenings, prosaic inspirations and creative storytelling that my sensory adventures with wine deliver.

NAME RECENT WINE DISCOVERIES THAT HAVE EXCITED YOU.
I like the second labels of top Spanish red wine producers, like Artadi and Palacios, for value and quality.

WHAT BIT OF INFORMATION WOULD YOU LIKE YOUR CUSTOMERS TO KNOW ABOUT YOU?
I like flamenco music.

DESCRIBE YOUR WINE SELECTIONS, BOTH BY THE GLASS AND ON YOUR LIST.
We have a global, comprehensive list designed to please our hotel guests, satisfy our local clientele and educate our staff.

WHAT ARE THE MOST UNIQUE FEATURES IN YOUR WINE PROGRAM?
We have a large half-bottle selection and verticals of California red varietals. We also enjoy choosing wines for Chef de Cuisine Brad Thompson's "Chef's Table" and his daily tasting menus.

WHAT CATEGORY OF WINE IS THE BEST VALUE IN YOUR RESTAURANT?
Red Bordeaux and Australian Shiraz are well-priced.

NAME ONE OF YOUR RESTAURANT'S SIGNATURE DISHES. WHAT WINE DO YOU PREFER TO RECOMMEND WITH IT?
Dover sole meunière, baby beets and sauce Bercy with top Oregon Pinot Noir.

IN THE PAST YEAR, WHAT WINES IN YOUR WINE PROGRAM HAVE CUSTOMERS BECOME MORE WILLING TO ORDER?
Oregon Pinot Noir, Riesling and Grüner Veltliner from Austria's Wachau.

Mary Elaine's at the Phoenician Resort

6000 East Camelback Road
Scottsdale, Arizona 85251
phone 480-941-8200 fax 480-947-4311
website www.thephoenician.com

Paul T. Botamer
LEAD SOMMELIER

LIST ANY FORMAL AND INFORMAL WINE TRAINING, DEGREES, CERTIFICATES AND AWARDS.
Certificate Course, Court of Master Sommeliers, 1997.

WHAT INSPIRED YOU TO PURSUE A CAREER THAT INVOLVES WINE?
I have always loved history, and every great wine has an interesting story behind it.

NAME ONE OF YOUR FAVORITE WINE DISTRICTS OR WINE REGIONS FROM AROUND THE WORLD.
Alsace. The wines pair well with food and can be so diverse.

DESCRIBE YOUR WINE SELECTIONS, BOTH BY THE GLASS AND ON YOUR LIST.
Our list is designed to be user-friendly, starting with an excellent by-the-glass section. We also strive to have the best half-bottle selection possible.

WHAT ARE THE MOST UNIQUE FEATURES IN YOUR WINE PROGRAM?
Having five sommeliers on staff enables us to ensure that every guest receives personalized service.

WHAT CATEGORIES OF WINE ARE THE BEST VALUES IN YOUR RESTAURANT?
Wines from Spain and South Africa.

NAME A COUPLE OF YOUR RESTAURANT'S SIGNATURE DISHES. WHAT TYPES OF WINE DO YOU PREFER TO RECOMMEND WITH EACH?
Buffalo tenderloin paired with Australian Shiraz; salmon with Oregon Pinot Noir.

IN THE PAST YEAR, WHAT WINES IN YOUR WINE PROGRAM HAVE CUSTOMERS BECOME MORE WILLING TO ORDER?
Australian Shiraz.

Mary Elaine's at the Phoenician Resort

6000 East Camelback Road
Scottsdale, Arizona 85251
phone 480-941-8200 fax 480-947-4311
website www.thephoenician.com

Thomas A. Ratcliff
CELLAR MASTER AND SOMMELIER

LIST ANY FORMAL AND INFORMAL WINE TRAINING, DEGREES, CERTIFI-
CATES AND AWARDS.
Advanced Certificate Course, Court of Master Sommeliers, 2000; Certificate
Course, Court of Master Sommeliers, 1994; Wine Captain's certificate,
American Sommelier Society, 1991.

WHAT PART OF YOUR JOB DO YOU ENJOY THE MOST?
I enjoy having someone say that my wine suggestion was the highlight of his or
her evening.

NAME ONE OF YOUR FAVORITE WINE DISTRICTS OR WINE REGIONS
FROM AROUND THE WORLD.
New Zealand for Riesling, Pinot Noir and Sauvignon Blanc.

NAME RECENT WINE DISCOVERIES THAT HAVE EXCITED YOU.
The Piedmont region of Italy is a rediscovery for me, with its Barbera and
Dolcetto. I also like the Veneto region for white wine.

WHAT ARE THE MOST UNIQUE FEATURES IN YOUR WINE PROGRAM?
We have a 200-plus half-bottle selection and an extensive by-the-glass selection
of Madeira.

WHAT CATEGORY OF WINE IS THE BEST VALUE IN YOUR RESTAURANT?
Second wines from the great Châteaux of Bordeaux. For example, we have three
vintages of Petite Cheval from Cheval-Blanc.

NAME A COUPLE OF YOUR RESTAURANT'S SIGNATURE DISHES. WHAT
TYPES OF WINE DO YOU PREFER TO RECOMMEND WITH EACH?
Cream of lobster soup paired with Amontillado Sherry; lamb with northern
Rhône Syrah, especially Cornas.

IN THE PAST YEAR, WHAT WINES IN YOUR WINE PROGRAM HAVE CUS-
TOMERS BECOME MORE WILLING TO ORDER?
Italian and Washington State wines.

Mary Elaine's at the Phoenician Resort

6000 East Camelback Road
Scottsdale, Arizona 85251
phone 480-941-8200 fax 480-947-4311
website www.thephoenician.com

Troy J. Smith
SOMMELIER

WHAT INSPIRED YOU TO PURSUE A CAREER THAT INVOLVES WINE?
Tasting for the first time a German Riesling Trockenbeerenauslese.

NAME ONE OF YOUR FAVORITE WINE DISTRICTS OR WINE REGIONS
FROM AROUND THE WORLD.
Alsace for the crisp acidity of its wines and the wines' ability to pair so well
with a wide variety of foods

WHAT BITS OF INFORMATION WOULD YOU LIKE YOUR CUSTOMERS TO
KNOW ABOUT YOU?
Yes, I really am old enough to drink.

IF YOU WERE NOT IN THIS PROFESSION, WHAT WOULD YOU BE DOING?
Cooking professionally.

DESCRIBE YOUR WINE SELECTIONS, BOTH BY THE GLASS AND ON YOUR LIST.
Our selection is an exceptional representation of wines from around the world,
with a particular focus on France and California.

WHAT CATEGORY OF WINE IS THE BEST VALUE IN YOUR RESTAURANT?
Wines from South Africa.

NAME A COUPLE OF YOUR RESTAURANT'S SIGNATURE DISHES. WHAT
TYPES OF WINE DO YOU PREFER TO RECOMMEND WITH EACH?
A savory preparation of foie gras with grand cru red Burgundy; rack of lamb
with reds from the Rhône.

IN THE PAST YEAR, WHAT WINES IN YOUR WINE PROGRAM HAVE CUS-
TOMERS BECOME MORE WILLING TO ORDER?
Red and white Burgundy.

WHAT ARE SOME OTHER ULTIMATE WINE AND FOOD PAIRINGS?
Old Australian Muscat with Reese's Sticks. It's amazing what you can learn at
4 a.m. with an empty refrigerator.

Mary Elaine's at the Phoenician Resort

6000 East Camelback Road
Scottsdale, Arizona 85251
phone 480-941-8200 fax 480-947-4311
website www.thephoenician.com

Jake Underhill
CAPTAIN AND SOMMELIER

NAME RECENT WINE DISCOVERIES THAT HAVE EXCITED YOU.
Wines from Provence and the Midi, an often-overlooked corner of France.

WHAT BITS OF INFORMATION WOULD YOU LIKE YOUR CUSTOMERS TO KNOW ABOUT YOU?
I'll take fishing over sleep any day.

DESCRIBE YOUR WINE SELECTIONS, BOTH BY THE GLASS AND ON YOUR LIST.
Our list is broad. If I pour a glass of wine for someone and they respond with "Wow!" then I've done my job.

WHAT CATEGORY OF WINE IS THE BEST VALUE IN YOUR RESTAURANT?
We have some great prices on older Bordeaux and feature quite a few large-format bottles at good prices.

NAME ONE OF YOUR RESTAURANT'S SIGNATURE DISHES. WHAT WINE DO YOU PREFER TO RECOMMEND WITH IT?
Our lobster soup goes great with a medium-bodied Sherry. I can usually "win over" guests who think they don't, or won't, like Sherry.

WHAT ARE SOME OTHER ULTIMATE WINE AND FOOD PAIRINGS?
Hot buttered popcorn with an oaky California Chardonnay. It sounds weird, but it can't be beat.

Tarbell's

3213 East Camelback Road
Phoenix, Arizona 85018
phone 602-955-8100 fax 602-955-8181
website www.tarbells.com

Jim Gallen
OPERATIONS MANAGER
AND WINE GUY

WHAT INSPIRED YOU TO PURSUE A CAREER THAT INVOLVES WINE?
I sold my first bottle and saw how it changed the guests' experience. I knew then that I always wanted to do that.

NAME RECENT WINE DISCOVERIES THAT HAVE EXCITED YOU.
The reds coming from Argentina are simply delicious. They offer structure and big, bold flavors for everyone's palate.

WHAT BITS OF INFORMATION WOULD YOU LIKE YOUR CUSTOMERS TO KNOW ABOUT YOU?
I like piña coladas and getting caught in the rain ... Oh, never mind!

DESCRIBE YOUR WINE SELECTIONS, BOTH BY THE GLASS AND ON YOUR LIST.
We choose our wines, both by the glass and by the bottle, for their individuality, value, and the guest's opportunity to experience something new.

WHAT ARE THE MOST UNIQUE FEATURES IN YOUR WINE PROGRAM?
We change our lists, both by the glass and by the bottle, every week to present new wines to our guests.

WHAT CATEGORIES OF WINE ARE THE BEST VALUES IN YOUR RESTAURANT?
Australian and Argentine reds.

NAME A COUPLE OF YOUR RESTAURANT'S SIGNATURE DISHES. WHAT TYPES OF WINE DO YOU PREFER TO RECOMMEND WITH EACH?
Spice-crusted New England scallops with cipollini and shiitake couscous and wild scallion vinaigrette served with German Riesling; jumbo pasta shells stuffed with braised veal and tomato basil broth with Chianti Classico.

IN THE PAST YEAR, WHAT WINES IN YOUR WINE PROGRAM HAVE CUSTOMERS BECOME MORE WILLING TO ORDER?
Australian Shiraz and Italian reds.

Wright's at the Arizona Biltmore

2400 East Missouri Avenue
Phoenix, Arizona 85016
phone 602-955-6600 fax 602-381-7600
website www.azbiltmore.com

Philman Chan
SOMMELIER

WHAT PART OF YOUR JOB DO YOU ENJOY THE MOST?
Making conversation with the guests and suggesting nontraditional wine pairings, because I like to see their surprise when they have something together that they may not have experienced before.

NAME ONE OF YOUR FAVORITE WINE DISTRICTS OR WINE REGIONS FROM AROUND THE WORLD.
French Burgundy. I enjoy the diversity of wines from this region.

DESCRIBE YOUR WINE SELECTIONS, BOTH BY THE GLASS AND ON YOUR LIST.
Our wine list focuses on Californian and French selections, particularly the first growth of Bordeaux. The wines by the glass are eclectic. They include varietals from around the world, from regions like California, Chile, Australia, Germany, France and Italy.

WHAT ARE THE MOST UNIQUE FEATURES IN YOUR WINE PROGRAM?
For the past ten years, we have hosted extravagant wine dinners that showcase producers from around the world. We present a five-course dinner with wines from the featured vineyards.

WHAT CATEGORIES OF WINE ARE THE BEST VALUES IN YOUR RESTAURANT?
Wines from Chile and the Loire Valley.

NAME A COUPLE OF YOUR RESTAURANT'S SIGNATURE DISHES. WHAT TYPES OF WINE DO YOU PREFER TO RECOMMEND WITH EACH?
Grilled veal porterhouse paired with a top California Zinfandel-Cabernet blend; duck hash appetizer with excellent Russian River Pinot Noir.

IN THE PAST YEAR, WHAT WINES IN YOUR WINE PROGRAM HAVE CUSTOMERS BECOME MORE WILLING TO ORDER?
Reds from the Rhône Valley, and Pinot Gris and Sauvignon Blanc from New Zealand.

Wrigley Mansion Club

2501 East Telawa Trail
Phoenix, Arizona 85016
phone 602-955-4079 fax 602-956-8439
website www.wrigleymansionclub.com

David C. Torkko
RESTAURANT MANAGER
AND SOMMELIER

WHAT INSPIRED YOU TO PURSUE A CAREER THAT INVOLVES WINE?
A magical evening meal in Hawaii. The food and wines were perfect and perfectly presented, and this experience motivates me to this day.

NAME ONE OF YOUR FAVORITE WINE DISTRICTS OR WINE REGIONS FROM AROUND THE WORLD.
Burgundy. When they catch lightning in a bottle, there is nothing better.

NAME RECENT WINE DISCOVERIES THAT HAVE EXCITED YOU.
I have found that wines from some high-altitude vineyards, like Malbecs from Argentina, are incredibly concentrated, extracted and enjoyable.

DESCRIBE YOUR WINE SELECTIONS, BOTH BY THE GLASS AND ON YOUR LIST.
We offer many of California's greatest wines, as well as representations from the major wine regions of the world. Classic wines for classic dining.

WHAT ARE THE MOST UNIQUE FEATURES IN YOUR WINE PROGRAM?
We have beautiful monthly wine dinners featuring principals from prominent wineries, and have a great by-the-glass selection.

NAME A COUPLE OF YOUR RESTAURANT'S SIGNATURE DISHES. WHAT TYPES OF WINE DO YOU PREFER TO RECOMMEND WITH EACH?
Red king prawns on butternut squash risotto with Marlborough, New Zealand Sauvignon Blanc; braised lamb shank cannelloni with Dolcetto d'Alba.

IN THE PAST YEAR, WHAT WINES IN YOUR WINE PROGRAM HAVE CUSTOMERS BECOME MORE WILLING TO ORDER?
Oregon Pinot Gris and Australian red blends.

Barcelona Restaurant
ROBERT HOLDER, WINE BUYER
900 North 54th Street, Chandler
480-785-9004

Barmouche
JIM GALLEN, SOMMELIER
3131 East Camelback Road, Phoenix
602-956-6900

Cowboy Ciao
PETER KASPERSKI, SOMMELIER
7133 East Stetson Drive, Scottsdale
480-946-3111

Durant's
JACK McELROY, SOMMELIER
2611 North Central Avenue, Phoenix
602-264-5967

Eddie Matney's
BETTINA STERN, WINE BUYER
2398 East Camelback Road, Phoenix
602-957-3214

Fleming's Prime Steakhouse and Wine Bar
MARIANE OP DE HAAR, SOMMELIER
905 North 54th Street, Chandler
480-940-1900

Gregory's World Bistro
KIM CASALE, SOMMELIER
8120 North Hayden Road, Scottsdale
480-946-8700

The Grill at Fairmont Scottsdale Princess Resort
MAT REINHART, FOOD AND BEVERAGE DIRECTOR
7575 East Princess Drive, Scottsdale
480-585-4848

Harris'
ELI RICHARDSON, SOMMELIER
3101 East Camelback Road, Phoenix
602-508-8888

Kazimierz World Wine Bar
PETER KASPERSKI, SOMMELIER
7137 East Stetson Drive, Scottsdale
480-946-3004

Kincaid's Fish, Chop & Steak House
JEAN DALZELL, GENERAL MANAGER
2 South Third Street, Phoenix
602-340-0000

Latilla at the Boulders Resort
MARK POPE, WINE STEWARD
34631 North Tom Darlington Drive, Carefree
480-488-7316

Mancuso's at the Borgata
CHRIS BLAZER, SOMMELIER
6166 North Scottsdale Road, Scottsdale
480-948-9988

Marco Polo Supper Club
MIKE LOMBARDO, SOMMELIER
2621 East Camelback Street, Phoenix
602-468-0100

Marquesa at the Fairmont Scottsdale Princess Resort
REED GROBAN, FOOD AND BEVERAGE DIRECTOR
7575 East Princess Drive, Scottsdale
480-585-4848

The Melting Pot

LARRY SMITH, WINE BUYER

8320 North Hayden Road, Scottsdale
480-607-1799

Meritage Steakhouse at JW Marriott Desert Ridge Resort

DAVID NEALON, WINE BUYER

5350 East Marriott Drive, Phoenix
480-293-5000

Michael's at the Citadel

HARLAN BERMAN, SOMMELIER

8700 East Pinnacle Peak Road, Scottsdale
480-515-2575

Mosaic

MATHEW RINN, SOMMELIER

10600 East Jomax Road, Scottsdale
480-563-9600

Rancho Pinot Grill

TOM KAUFMAN, OWNER AND SOMMELIER

6208 North Scottsdale Road, Scottsdale
480-367-8030

Ruth's Chris Steak House

BARRY GARRISON, GENERAL MANAGER AND WINE BUYER

2201 East Camelback Road, Phoenix
602-957-9600

Ruth's Chris Steak House

MICHAEL LEICHTSUSS, GENERAL MANAGER AND WINE BUYER

7001 North Scottsdale Road, Scottsdale
480-991-5988

Sea Saw

PETER KASPERSKI, SOMMELIER

7133 East Stetson Drive, Scottsdale
480-481-9463

T. Cook's at the Royal Palms Hotel

ROBERT REEVES, SOMMELIER

5200 East Camelback Road, Phoenix
602-808-0766

Top of the Rock Restaurant at Wyndham Buttes Resort

STEPHEN JOHNSON, RESORT SOMMELIER

200 Westcourt Way, Tempe
602-431-2370

Village Tavern

MATT HAMILTON, SOMMELIER

8787 North Scottsdale Road, Scottsdale
480-951-6445

Vincent Guerithault on Camelback

VINCENT GUERITHAULT, OWNER, CHEF AND WINE BUYER

3930 East Camelback Road, Phoenix
602-224-0225

The Asylum Restaurant at the Jerome Grand Hotel

200 Hill Street
Jerome, Arizona 86331
phone 928-639-3197 fax 928-639-0299
website www.theasylum.biz

Paula T. Woolsey
OWNER AND CELLAR MASTER

LIST ANY FORMAL AND INFORMAL WINE TRAINING, DEGREES, CERTIFICATES AND AWARDS.
Certified Wine Specialist, Society of Wine Educators; Wine Spectator Award of Excellence, 1995, 1998 and 2002.

WHAT INSPIRED YOU TO PURSUE A CAREER THAT INVOLVES WINE?
My father was an importer of fine wines in the 1970s and early 1980s, so growing up I was exposed to fine wine.

NAME RECENT WINE DISCOVERIES THAT HAVE EXCITED YOU.
Wine from Casa de La Ermita in Jumilla, Spain, is a super value. Marquis Philips S2 Shiraz #9 is a New World wine that's very juicy.

WHAT BITS OF INFORMATION WOULD YOU LIKE YOUR CUSTOMERS TO KNOW ABOUT YOU?
I'm known as the "wine witch" of Sedona. My specialty is tarot cards and numerology.

DESCRIBE YOUR WINE SELECTIONS, BOTH BY THE GLASS AND ON YOUR LIST.
We have 100 wines on our list, with twenty by the glass. It's a living, beautiful, changing list.

WHAT CATEGORIES OF WINE ARE THE BEST VALUES IN YOUR RESTAURANT?
Spain, Australia, Italian red wines and German Rieslings.

NAME A COUPLE OF YOUR RESTAURANT'S SIGNATURE DISHES. WHAT TYPES OF WINE DO YOU PREFER TO RECOMMEND WITH EACH?
Santa Lucia Pinot Noir served with salmon Florentine with bacon; Riesling from Germany with fried calamari and atomic cocktail sauce.

IN THE PAST YEAR, WHAT WINES IN YOUR WINE PROGRAM HAVE CUSTOMERS BECOME MORE WILLING TO ORDER?
Ports and dessert wines, German Riesling, Austrian Grüner Veltliner, New Zealand Pinot Noir and Spanish Garnacha.

L'Auberge de Sedona

301 L'Auberge Lane
Sedona, Arizona 86339
phone 928-282-1661 fax 928-282-2885
website www.lauberge.com

Mark J. Buzan
CELLAR MASTER

LIST ANY FORMAL AND INFORMAL WINE TRAINING, DEGREES, CERTIFI-
CATES AND AWARDS.
Certificate Course, Court of Master Sommeliers; Wine Spectator Award of
Excellence, 1992 to present; DiRona Award of Excellence, 1992 to present; and
many more awards.

WHAT INSPIRED YOU TO PURSUE A CAREER THAT INVOLVES WINE?
I'm inspired by the culture that surrounds wine.

NAME TWO OF YOUR FAVORITE WINE DISTRICTS OR WINE REGIONS
FROM AROUND THE WORLD.
Burgundy, Côte de Beaune for the great values one can find, and Argentina for
its red wine.

NAME RECENT WINE DISCOVERIES THAT HAVE EXCITED YOU.
The dry whites of the Loire, other than Sancerre.

WHAT BITS OF INFORMATION WOULD YOU LIKE YOUR CUSTOMERS TO
KNOW ABOUT YOU?
After a hard day's work, for the most part, the most satisfying thing for me is a beer.

DESCRIBE YOUR WINE SELECTIONS, BOTH BY THE GLASS AND ON YOUR
LIST.
The list is global, as is the by-the-glass list, offering wines from Rhône reds to
Alsatian Gewürztraminer.

NAME A COUPLE OF YOUR RESTAURANT'S SIGNATURE DISHES. WHAT
TYPES OF WINE DO YOU PREFER TO RECOMMEND WITH EACH?
Our chef loves to use game such as venison and elk. With these, full-bodied
Australian Cabernet Sauvignons or Shirazs work well.

IN THE PAST YEAR, WHAT WINES IN YOUR WINE PROGRAM HAVE CUS-
TOMERS BECOME MORE WILLING TO ORDER?
German Riesling.

L'Auberge de Sedona

301 L'Auberge Lane
Sedona, Arizona 86339
phone 928-282-1661 fax 928-282-2885
website www.lauberge.com

Paul M. Fried
SOMMELIER

LIST ANY FORMAL AND INFORMAL WINE TRAINING, DEGREES, CERTIFICATES AND AWARDS.

Certificate Course, Court of Master Sommeliers; Wine Spectator Award of Excellence, 1992 to present; DiRona Award of Excellence, 1992 to present; and many more.

WHAT INSPIRED YOU TO PURSUE A CAREER THAT INVOLVES WINE?

A passion for pairing wines with food that came from my training as both a chef and a tea taster and tea blender for Celestial Seasonings.

NAME ONE OR TWO OF YOUR FAVORITE WINE DISTRICTS OR WINE REGIONS FROM AROUND THE WORLD.

Côte de Beaune for elegance and finesse; Barossa Valley, Australia, for powerful Cabernet Sauvignon, Shiraz and exceptional dessert wines.

NAME RECENT WINE DISCOVERIES THAT HAVE EXCITED YOU.

August Kessler's Rheingau Rieslings are incredibly deep and well-crafted, and Heinrich Blaufränkisch of Burgenland, Austria, is a style all its own.

WHAT BITS OF INFORMATION WOULD YOU LIKE YOUR CUSTOMERS TO KNOW ABOUT YOU?

The more you know, the more you know you don't know!

WHAT ARE THE MOST UNIQUE FEATURES IN YOUR WINE PROGRAM?

Our large half-bottle selection, a pairing menu that changes weekly and a worldwide list in a French country restaurant setting.

WHAT CATEGORIES OF WINE ARE THE BEST VALUES IN YOUR RESTAURANT?

Côtes du Lubéron and Côtes du Ventoux.

IN THE PAST YEAR, WHAT WINES IN YOUR WINE PROGRAM HAVE CUSTOMERS BECOME MORE WILLING TO ORDER?

South American reds and Australian Shiraz.

Bistro Zin

1865 East River Road
Tucson, Arizona 85718
phone 520-299-7799 fax 520-615-4534
website www.tasteofbistrozin.com

Regan D. Jasper
CORPORATE SOMMELIER

WHAT ARE SOME OF YOUR ULTIMATE FOOD AND WINE PAIRINGS?
Pan-seared scallops over saffron Israeli couscous and lobster demi-glaze with Viognier or Alsatian Pinot Gris; Mapleleaf duck with a drunken cherry sauce with Russian River Valley Pinot Noir; foie gras with Sauternes; beef carpaccio with Valpolicella.

DESCRIBE YOUR WINE SELECTIONS.
We offer seventy wines, all by the glass and all incorporated into flights. The flights showcase wines from important growing regions for each varietal.

WHAT CATEGORY OF WINE IS THE BEST VALUE IN YOUR RESTAURANT?
Pinot Gris in white, and Syrah and Shiraz in red.

NAME RECENT WINE DISCOVERIES THAT HAVE EXCITED YOU.
Soave from Italy. New Zealand Sauvignon Blanc, with its bright tropical fruit. The wines of Alvaro Palacios from Spain are amazing.

WHAT IS YOUR FAVORITE WINE REGION IN THE WORLD TODAY?
Russian River, because of its Pinot Noir, which is my favorite varietal.

WHAT LED YOU TO PURSUE A CAREER THAT INVOLVES WINE?
I was a captain in a fine dining restaurant, where the sommelier was my mentor. Wine became my favorite aspect of the dining experience.

WHAT IS THE BEST ASPECT OF YOUR JOB?
The thrill of the find. Discovering the next quality wine, varietal or region that few yet recognize is both rewarding and thrilling.

IF YOU WERE NOT IN THE WINE PROFESSION, WHAT WOULD YOU BE DOING?
Buying and selling real estate.

The Grill at Hacienda Del Sol

5601 North Hacienda Del Sol Road
Tucson, Arizona 85718
phone 520-529-3500 fax 520-299-5554
website www.haciendadelsol.com

Daniel A. McCoog
DIRECTOR OF WINE
AND SOMMELIER

WHAT INSPIRED YOU TO PURSUE A CAREER THAT INVOLVES WINE?
Wine was a hobby that turned into an obsession that turned into a career.

WHAT PART OF YOUR JOB DO YOU ENJOY THE MOST?
Making the perfect match between the guest, food and wine.

NAME ONE OF YOUR FAVORITE WINE DISTRICTS OR REGIONS FROM
AROUND THE WORLD.
Dry Creek in Sonoma County. I have lived and made wine there for seven
years. I love the Dry Creek Zinfandel fruit.

NAME RECENT WINE DISCOVERIES THAT HAVE EXCITED YOU.
Uruguayan Tannat and Merlot blends because they're rich, mouth-filling wines
of a new character.

WHAT BITS OF INFORMATION WOULD YOU LIKE YOUR CUSTOMERS TO
KNOW ABOUT YOU?
I'm an award-winning amateur winemaker and ale maker.

WHAT ARE THE MOST UNIQUE FEATURES IN YOUR WINE PROGRAM?
Our "Taste the Greats" dinners: The Iron Chef and Iron Sommelier dinners
where the guests judge and vote on the winners for food, wine and food-and-
wine pairing categories for three courses.

WHAT CATEGORY OF WINE IS THE BEST VALUE IN YOUR RESTAURANT?
Argentine Malbec.

NAME A COUPLE OF YOUR RESTAURANT'S SIGNATURE DISHES. WHAT
TYPES OF WINE DO YOU PREFER TO RECOMMEND WITH EACH?
Southwestern cioppino with Pinot Noir from the Russian River Valley; pecan
wood-grilled rib-eye steak and Tempranillo from Ribera del Duero.

Janos

3770 East Sunrise Drive
Tucson, Arizona 85718
phone 520-615-6100 fax 520-615-3334
website www.janos.com

Ryan J. Schwartz
DIRECTOR OF WINE
AND SOMMELIER

WHAT ARE SOME OF YOUR ULTIMATE FOOD AND WINE PAIRINGS?
Seared sea scallops, carrot nage, with lobster and potato galette paired with an Albariño from Rias Baixas, Spain. Mediterranean roast rack of lamb, pomegranate sauce and fingerling potatoes paired with a mature, traditional Barolo or Barbaresco.

DESCRIBE YOUR WINE SELECTIONS.
We have more than 800 selections, specializing in rare, artisan wines whose makers are dedicated to being the best while remaining unique.

WHAT CATEGORY OF WINE IS THE BEST VALUE IN YOUR RESTAURANT?
Red Rhône.

NAME RECENT WINE DISCOVERIES THAT HAVE EXCITED YOU.
Schwarz wines from Austria. The winery is producing a wonderful Chardonnay, Zweigelt and Rosé of Zweigelt.

WHAT IS YOUR FAVORITE WINE REGION IN THE WORLD TODAY?
Rhône Valley. I can't think of any other region that consistently gives higher quality wine for the money.

WHAT LED YOU TO PURSUE A CAREER THAT INVOLVES WINE?
A passion and interest in the marriage of wine and food.

WHAT IS THE BEST ASPECT OF YOUR JOB?
Searching out small, artisan wines to give our guests unique experiences.

IF YOU WERE NOT IN THE WINE PROFESSION, WHAT WOULD YOU BE DOING?
Playing professional golf, which is what I did for a few years before I became a sommelier.

Ventana Room at Loews Ventana Canyon Resort

7000 North Resort Drive
Tucson, Arizona 85750
phone 520-299-2020 fax 520-299-6832
website www.ventanaroom.com

Kevin P. Brady
MAÎTRE D'HÔTEL

LIST ANY FORMAL AND INFORMAL WINE TRAINING, DEGREES, CERTIFI-
CATES AND AWARDS.
Certificate Course and Advanced Certificate Course (audited), Court of Master
Sommeliers.

HOW MANY DAYS A WEEK ARE YOU A SOMMELIER ON THE FLOOR IN
YOUR RESTAURANT?
When I am needed, I work as a sommelier in some capacity every day.

WHAT INSPIRED YOU TO PURSUE A CAREER THAT INVOLVES WINE?
Working with René Chazottes.

NAME RECENT WINE DISCOVERIES THAT HAVE EXCITED YOU.
I am studying the Champagne region again. I recently tasted Salon 1982
Le Mesnil. It was stellar!

WHAT BITS OF INFORMATION WOULD YOU LIKE YOUR CUSTOMERS TO
KNOW ABOUT YOU?
I love making people feel like "gold" in this restaurant and that they matter
most.

DESCRIBE YOUR WINE SELECTIONS, BOTH BY THE GLASS AND ON YOUR LIST.
We want to have the best wine by-the-glass program, because we believe that
patrons should be able to taste anything, from a Latour to a d'Yquem.

NAME A COUPLE OF YOUR RESTAURANT'S SIGNATURE DISHES. WHAT
TYPES OF WINE DO YOU PREFER TO RECOMMEND WITH EACH?
Chef Trosch creates well-balanced, fresh dishes every day. We owe it to him to
choose the best pairings for whatever he prepares.

IN THE PAST YEAR, WHAT WINES IN YOUR WINE PROGRAM HAVE CUS-
TOMERS BECOME MORE WILLING TO ORDER?
Northwest reds because our sommelier, Mr. Sullivan, has taken the time to help
educate our guests.

Anthony's in the Catalinas

JOE MASCARI, PROPRIETOR AND
WINE BUYER
6440 North Campbell Avenue, Tucson
520-299-1771

Café Terra Cotta

DON LURIA, SOMMELIER
3500 East Sunrise Drive, Tucson
520-577-8100

Elle

TODD BURNHART, SOMMELIER
3048 East Broadway Boulevard,
Tucson
520-327-0500

Fuego Restaurant Bar & Grill

JOE POSEY, WINE DIRECTOR
6958 East Tanque Verde Road,
Tucson
520-886-1745

J Bar at the Westin La Paloma Hotel

KATIE POWERS, SOMMELIER
3770 East Sunrise Drive, Tucson
520-615-6100

Kingfisher Bar & Grill

TIM IVANKOVICH, SOMMELIER
2564 East Grant Street, Tuscon
520-323-7739

McMahon's Prime Steakhouse

JOE ECKRIDGE, SOMMELIER
2959 North Swan Road, Tucson
520-327-7463

Michaelangelo Ristorante

JOE ALI, WINE BUYER
420 West Magee Road, Tucson
520-297-5772

Ovens Bistro and Wine Bar at Saint Philips Plaza

CANDENCE GROGAN, SOMMELIER
4280 North Campbell Street, Tucson
520-577-9001

Red Sky Café

STEVEN SCHULTZ, SOMMELIER
1661 North Swan Road, Tucson
520-326-5454

Sullivan's Steakhouse

CHRIS ROCKWOOD, SOMMELIER
1785 East River Road, Tucson
520-299-4275

The Tack Room

RICHARD TYLER, WINE BUYER
7300 East Vactor Ranch Trail, Tucson
520-722-2800

Wildflower

REGAN JASPER,
CORPORATE SOMMELIER
7037 North Oracle Road, Tucson
520-219-4230

A.P. Stumps
163 West Santa Clara Street
San Jose, California 95113
phone 408-292-9928 fax 408-292-9927
website www.apstumps.com

Randall W. Bertao
GENERAL MANAGER

WHAT INSPIRED YOU TO PURSUE A CAREER THAT INVOLVES WINE?
My first taste of a 1961 Château Lafite-Rothschild.

NAME ONE OR TWO OF YOUR FAVORITE WINE DISTRICTS OR WINE
REGIONS FROM AROUND THE WORLD.
Mosel Riesling and Côte de Nuits reds are the most food-friendly wines
produced.

WHAT BITS OF INFORMATION WOULD YOU LIKE YOUR CUSTOMERS TO
KNOW ABOUT YOU?
I was raised on a small farm in California and lived in London, Ontario, for
ten years.

DESCRIBE YOUR WINE SELECTIONS, BOTH BY THE GLASS AND ON YOUR
LIST.
We have numerous wine flights. Both the flights and our list represent wine
from world-class wine regions along with new, up-and-coming areas.

WHAT CATEGORIES OF WINE ARE THE BEST VALUES IN YOUR RESTAURANT?
New World Pinot Noir and German Riesling.

NAME A COUPLE OF YOUR RESTAURANT'S SIGNATURE DISHES. WHAT
TYPES OF WINE DO YOU PREFER TO RECOMMEND WITH EACH?
Thai tuna with red Burgundy; cold-smoked salmon and hot-smoked sturgeon
with German Riesling.

IN THE PAST YEAR, WHAT WINES IN YOUR WINE PROGRAM HAVE CUS-
TOMERS BECOME MORE WILLING TO ORDER?
Pinot Noir.

Alioto's Restaurant
No. 8 Fisherman's Wharf
San Francisco, California 94133
phone 415-673-0183

Nunzio S. Alioto
PRESIDENT, GENERAL MANAGER AND MASTER
SOMMELIER

WHAT INSPIRED YOU TO PURSUE A CAREER THAT INVOLVES WINE?
I was born and raised in the business.

WHAT PART OF YOUR JOB DO YOU ENJOY THE MOST?
Making recommendations and tastings.

NAME SOME FAVORITE WINE REGIONS FROM AROUND THE WORLD.
Germany, Italy, America and France.

NAME RECENT WINE DISCOVERIES THAT HAVE EXCITED YOU.
Northern Italy and Alsace.

IF YOU WERE NOT IN THIS PROFESSION, WHAT WOULD YOU BE DOING?
Fly fisherman, winemaker or professional golfer.

DESCRIBE YOUR WINE SELECTIONS, BOTH BY THE GLASS AND ON YOUR
LIST.
We offer light, fruity, uncomplicated white wines, since this is a seafood
restaurant.

WHAT CATEGORIES OF WINE ARE THE BEST VALUES IN YOUR RESTAURANT?
Italian and domestic white wines.

NAME A COUPLE OF YOUR RESTAURANT'S SIGNATURE DISHES. WHAT
TYPES OF WINE DO YOU PREFER TO RECOMMEND WITH EACH?
Seafood sausage with Italian white wine or California white varietals with no
oak; cioppino and Bandol Rosé.

IN THE PAST YEAR, WHAT WINES IN YOUR WINE PROGRAM HAVE CUS-
TOMERS BECOME MORE WILLING TO ORDER?
German Riesling, white Italian and Alsatian wines.

Ana Mandara

891 Beach Street
San Francisco, California 94109-1102
phone 415-771-6800 fax 415-771-5275
website www.anamandara.com

Joanna R. Breslin
SOMMELIER

WHAT ARE SOME OF YOUR ULTIMATE FOOD AND WINE PAIRINGS?
Turbinado sugar and chili–glazed freshwater prawns with a rich Pinot Gris
from Alsace or Austria; seared Mekong basa with lemon-chili sauce and off-dry
Riesling; lobster with Cognac and lobster roe sauce paired with Châteauneuf-
du-Pape blanc; oysters and Chablis; chocolate and young, fruity Banyuls.

DESCRIBE YOUR WINE SELECTIONS.
Our Vietnamese cuisine calls for wines with fruit and firm acidity, so we focus
on Riesling, Pinot Gris and white Rhônes, as well as Pinot Noir and
Mediterranean red varietals and blends.

WHAT CATEGORIES OF WINE ARE THE BEST VALUES ON YOUR WINE LIST?
German whites and southern French reds offer particularly stellar quality for
the price.

NAME RECENT WINE DISCOVERIES THAT HAVE EXCITED YOU.
A modern-style Cahors that is 100-percent Malbec; Austrian Grauburgunder;
Pinot Noir from New Zealand; Sauvignon Blanc from South Africa.

WHAT LED YOU TO PURSUE A CAREER THAT INVOLVES WINE?
I started part-time at Ana Mandara to learn floor service, and loved it.

WHAT ARE THE BEST ASPECTS OF YOUR JOB?
The opportunity to taste the great range of wines available; the improvisational
element of working on the floor; the diversity of our clientele and co-workers;
being able to help people find wines they love that they would not have chosen
on their own.

IF YOU WERE NOT IN THIS PROFESSION, WHAT WOULD YOU BE DOING?
Coffee, or chocolate or psychotherapy.

Aqua

252 California Street
San Francisco, California 94111
phone 415-956-9662 fax 415-956-5229
website www.aqua-sf.com

Mauro Cirilli
SOMMELIER

NAME ONE OF YOUR FAVORITE WINE DISTRICTS FROM AROUND THE WORLD.

Valpolicella. This region produces three very unique wines, each very different from the other, with a long tradition using the same grapes.

NAME RECENT WINE DISCOVERIES THAT HAVE EXCITED YOU.

Rieslings from Austria, for their quality and style.

WHAT BITS OF INFORMATION WOULD YOU LIKE YOUR CUSTOMERS TO KNOW ABOUT YOU?

I started to make and drink wine when I was seven years old on my grandfather's property. Wine has been an important part of the family meal my entire life.

IF YOU WERE NOT IN THIS PROFESSION, WHAT WOULD YOU BE?

A Maître d'.

WHAT ARE THE MOST UNIQUE FEATURES IN YOUR WINE PROGRAM?

We have carefully selected a large number of wines from all over the world with many hard-to-find wines from small producers.

NAME A COUPLE OF YOUR RESTAURANT'S SIGNATURE DISHES. WHAT TYPES OF WINE DO YOU PREFER TO RECOMMEND WITH EACH?

Thai snapper with white Chassagne-Montrachet; surf and turf with a rich Sangiovese from Tuscany.

IN THE PAST YEAR, WHAT WINES IN YOUR WINE PROGRAM HAVE CUSTOMERS BECOME MORE WILLING TO ORDER?

Italian wines.

Asia SF

201 Ninth Street
San Francisco, California 94103
phone 415-255-2742 fax 415-255-8887
website www.asiasf.com

Matthew J. Metcalf

EXECUTIVE CHEF AND WINE DIRECTOR

WHAT INSPIRED YOU TO PURSUE A CAREER THAT INVOLVES WINE?
The realization that food was only one component of a restaurant. I wanted to excel in all areas, not only the kitchen.

NAME TWO OF YOUR FAVORITE WINES FROM AROUND THE WORLD.
Amador Zinfandel. They are rich, balanced wines. And Alsatian Gewürztraminer, the world's best white wine!

NAME RECENT WINE DISCOVERIES THAT HAVE EXCITED YOU.
Inexpensive table wines from France and Italy, which are affordable and unpretentious.

WHAT WOULD YOU LIKE YOUR CUSTOMERS TO KNOW ABOUT YOU?
I love comfort foods (pasta with butter) and prefer to eat simple things rather than fancier restaurant foods.

IF YOU WERE NOT IN THIS PROFESSION, WHAT WOULD YOU BE DOING?
Nonprofit work, because I enjoy working to make others happy.

DESCRIBE YOUR WINE SELECTIONS, BOTH BY THE GLASS AND ON YOUR LIST.
We have a careful selection of wines. I enjoy it when a customer says, "I think it's so cool that you have Albariño and Marsanne. They go so well with your menu."

WHAT ARE THE MOST UNIQUE FEATURES IN YOUR WINE PROGRAM?
Because of our unique entertainment, customers don't expect a well-thought-out, 100-bottle list or three-star cuisine. That we have both makes us unique.

NAME A COUPLE OF YOUR RESTAURANT'S SIGNATURE DISHES. WHAT TYPES OF WINE DO YOU PREFER TO RECOMMEND WITH EACH?
Orange lamb with a big, juicy Shiraz from Australia; ahi burger with a crisp, aromatic Riesling or Gewürztraminer.

WHAT WINES ARE CUSTOMERS NOW MORE WILLING TO ORDER?
Italian Pinot Grigio, Oregon Pinot Gris and Australian Shiraz.

Bacar

448 Brannan Street
San Francisco, California 94107
phone 415-904-4100 fax 415-904-4113
website www.bacarsf.com

Debbie F. Zachareas
PARTNER AND WINE DIRECTOR

WHAT INSPIRED YOU TO PURSUE A CAREER THAT INVOLVES WINE?

I fell in love with wine and decided to pursue a career in it rather than a career that would afford me the income to spend all of my extra time and money on my true love.

NAME RECENT WINE DISCOVERIES THAT HAVE EXCITED YOU.

Austria has been most exciting over the last few years, especially the fact that it is the only place in the world for Grüner Veltliner. It fits all price ranges, too.

WHAT BITS OF INFORMATION WOULD YOU LIKE YOUR CUSTOMERS TO KNOW ABOUT YOU?

My background is in education. The greatest joy, outside of sharing wine with friends, is bringing it into the center of other people's lives through education and experimentation.

DESCRIBE YOUR WINE SELECTIONS, BOTH BY THE GLASS AND ON YOUR LIST.

Bacar has a well-rounded, international list with an emphasis on boutique wines from all over the world. We have food-friendly whites from the Loire Valley, Austria, Germany and Champagne and a large by-the-glass list with sixty-four selections.

NAME A COUPLE OF YOUR RESTAURANT'S SIGNATURE DISHES. WHAT TYPES OF WINE DO YOU PREFER TO RECOMMEND WITH EACH?

Oysters with Txakolina (from the Basque Country in Spain); wok-roasted mussels with Austrian Grüner Veltliner; house-made sausages with a selection of Riesling.

IN THE PAST YEAR, WHAT WINES IN YOUR WINE PROGRAM HAVE CUSTOMERS BECOME MORE WILLING TO ORDER?

German Riesling, Austrian Grüner Veltliner, American Pinot Noir and Washington Syrah.

Big Four Restaurant at the Huntington Hotel

1075 California Street
San Francisco, California 94108
phone 415-771-1140 fax 415-474-6227
website www.big4restaurant.com

Eric Janssen
DIRECTOR OF FOOD AND BEVERAGE

NAME ONE OR TWO OF YOUR FAVORITE WINE DISTRICTS OR WINE REGIONS FROM AROUND THE WORLD.

Rhône, as well as most Rhône varietals from around the world. They are such great food wines.

NAME RECENT WINE DISCOVERIES THAT HAVE EXCITED YOU.

I rediscovered German Rieslings. I had always enjoyed those wines, but somehow I'd moved away from them. Their quality is at its peak now.

DESCRIBE YOUR WINE SELECTIONS, BOTH BY THE GLASS AND ON YOUR LIST.

We mostly focus on California wines with great depth in Cabernet. We have a balanced list that offers wines from around the world, with multiple styles of the most familiar varieties.

WHAT ARE THE MOST UNIQUE FEATURES IN YOUR WINE PROGRAM?

We pride ourselves on our growing half-bottle collection.

WHAT CATEGORY OF WINE IS THE BEST VALUE IN YOUR RESTAURANT?

Our high-end wines, which have a lower markup than our other wines.

NAME A FEW OF YOUR RESTAURANT'S SIGNATURE DISHES. WHAT TYPES OF WINE DO YOU PREFER TO RECOMMEND WITH EACH?

The chef specializes in game. Most of these dishes pair well with Rhône wines.

IN THE PAST YEAR, WHAT WINES IN YOUR WINE PROGRAM HAVE CUSTOMERS BECOME MORE WILLING TO ORDER?

German Riesling and Rhône wines, based on our recommendations, are well received.

Boulevard Restaurant

1 Mission Street
San Francisco, California 94105
phone 415-543-6084 fax 415-495-2936

John M. Lancaster
WINE DIRECTOR AND SOMMELIER

WHAT IS ONE OF YOUR ULTIMATE FOOD AND WINE PAIRINGS?
Papardella pasta, pressed with truffles, with shaved truffles on top paired with a
Paolo Scavino Barolo.

DESCRIBE YOUR WINE SELECTIONS.
California wines are the anchor of our list, but like the menu, we take a global
view of food and wine.

WHAT IS YOUR FAVORITE WINE REGION IN THE WORLD TODAY?
Probably the south of France. I love the wines, and every trip I've taken has
been magical.

WHAT LED YOU TO PURSUE A CAREER THAT INVOLVES WINE?
I was working in a restaurant and it became obvious I cared more than anyone
about wine, so they made me the buyer. I've been doing it ever since.

WHAT ARE THE MOST CHALLENGING ASPECTS OF YOUR JOB?
Managing my time between meetings with purveyors, educating our staff,
doing service and having a family life.

IF YOU WERE NOT IN THE WINE PROFESSION, WHAT WOULD YOU BE?
A sportswriter.

Café Marcella

368 Village Lane
Los Gatos, California 95030
phone 408-354-8006 fax 408-354-9086

Robert (Larry) Stepek
GENERAL MANAGER

NAME TWO OF YOUR FAVORITE WINE DISTRICTS FROM AROUND THE WORLD.
Buzet, south of Bordeaux, is where wines with great nobility and grand Bordeaux character cost half the price. The wines from Vosne-Romanée are like no others.

NAME RECENT WINE DISCOVERIES THAT HAVE EXCITED YOU.
The wines from Torres in Penedès, Spain. They are now using rediscovered vines from pre-phylloxera vineyards.

WHAT BITS OF INFORMATION WOULD YOU LIKE YOUR CUSTOMERS TO KNOW ABOUT YOU?
I have a home in Gers, France, in the heart of Armagnac country near the Pyrénées. Here, the great country wines are abundant and are a great value.

TO WHAT WINE ORGANIZATIONS OR SOCIETIES DO YOU BELONG?
Society of Wine Educators.

DESCRIBE YOUR WINE SELECTIONS, BOTH BY THE GLASS AND ON YOUR LIST.
Our by-the-glass and list offerings work together. Our specialty is French "Vin de Pays" and Burgundy.

WHAT ARE THE MOST UNIQUE FEATURES IN YOUR WINE PROGRAM?
Our wine program is consistent. Guests know that we make recommendations based on personal experience and that we offer great value, always.

WHAT CATEGORY OF WINE IS THE BEST VALUE IN YOUR RESTAURANT?
Burgundy. We seek out small producers who offer good value.

NAME A COUPLE OF YOUR RESTAURANT'S SIGNATURE DISHES. WHAT TYPES OF WINE DO YOU PREFER TO RECOMMEND WITH EACH?
Foie Gras au Torchon with Monbazillac because it's subtler than Sauternes; Colorado rack of lamb with Pommard.

IN THE PAST YEAR, WHAT WINES IN YOUR WINE PROGRAM HAVE CUS-TOMERS BECOME MORE WILLING TO ORDER?
Zinfandel.

Campton Place Hotel and Restaurant

340 Stockton Street
San Francisco, California 94108
phone 415-781-5555 fax 415-955-5536
website www.camptonplace.com

Sean S. Crowley
WINE DIRECTOR AND SOMMELIER

CALIFORNIA, SAN FRANCISCO BAY AREA

WHAT INSPIRED YOU TO PURSUE A CAREER THAT INVOLVES WINE?
My brother-in-law taught me how to open Champagne as a teenager, and I've been fascinated ever since.

NAME SEVERAL OF YOUR FAVORITE WINES FROM AROUND THE WORLD.
Champagne is the most versatile wine with food because of the high acidity. I also love German, Alsatian and Austrian whites.

NAME RECENT WINE DISCOVERIES THAT HAVE EXCITED YOU.
It is not so much of a recent discovery, but Txakoli from the Basque region of Spain is always a treat.

WHAT BITS OF INFORMATION WOULD YOU LIKE YOUR CUSTOMERS TO KNOW ABOUT YOU?
I grew up as a competitive ice skater.

WHAT ARE THE MOST UNIQUE FEATURES IN YOUR WINE PROGRAM?
I change the wines on our six-course tasting menu nightly to accommodate different palates and the needs of guests.

WHAT CATEGORY OF WINE IS THE BEST VALUE IN YOUR RESTAURANT?
Loire Valley whites.

NAME ONE OF YOUR RESTAURANT'S SIGNATURE DISHES. WHAT TYPE OF WINE DO YOU PREFER TO RECOMMEND WITH IT?
Foie Gras Parfait (soft polenta, fig and foie gras foam served in a martini glass) with Champagne Rosé.

WHAT ARE SOME OTHER ULTIMATE WINE AND FOOD PAIRINGS?
Triple-crème cheese and Champagne; foie gras and Jurançon; oysters and Txakoli (from Spain's Basque region).

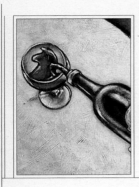

Cetrella Bistro and Café

845 Main Street
Half Moon Bay, California 94019
phone 650-726-4090 fax 650-726-4291
website www.cetrella.com

Saeed Amini
BEVERAGE DIRECTOR AND SOMMELIER

WHAT ARE SOME OF YOUR ULTIMATE FOOD AND WINE PAIRINGS?
Goat cheese, bacon, caramelized onion and thyme pizza with Pinot Gris; lamb kabob with Bordeaux; baked escargot with tarragon butter and Chablis; zarzuela and Rosé; short ribs and Châteauneuf-du-Pape; grilled calamari and Chianti.

DESCRIBE YOUR WINE SELECTIONS.
Mediterranean; simple and affordable, with many unknown wines. I try to educate the customers without intimidation.

WHAT CATEGORY OF WINE IS THE BEST VALUE IN YOUR RESTAURANT?
Italian whites.

NAME RECENT WINE DISCOVERIES THAT HAVE EXCITED YOU.
Refosco offers good value and diversity. Lagrein—it's elegant and complex.

WHAT IS YOUR FAVORITE REGION IN THE WORLD TODAY?
Tuscany. The wines are simple enough to drink every day, but age well and are food-friendly.

WHAT LED YOU TO PURSUE A CAREER THAT INVOLVES WINE?
Besides my love of wine, I feel that it brings people together in peace and harmony!

WHAT ARE THE BEST ASPECTS OF YOUR JOB?
Getting customers to experience new wines and watching them enjoy them.

IF YOU WERE NOT IN THE WINE PROFESSION, WHAT WOULD YOU BE DOING?
The Peace Corps. I love people and always want to help anyone in need.

Le Colonial

20 Cosmo Place
San Francisco, California 94109
phone 415-931-3600 fax 415-931-2933
website www.lecolonialsf.com

Steven Oliver

WINE DIRECTOR AND PURCHASING
MANAGER

WHAT PART OF YOUR JOB DO YOU ENJOY THE MOST?

Discovering smaller, lesser-known wineries early on is an enjoyable part of what I do. I incorporate these wines into our list. It allows customers to broaden their tastes and helps develop a following for these smaller vintners.

NAME RECENT WINE DISCOVERIES THAT HAVE EXCITED YOU.

Domestic, Rhône-style wines or blends like Niebaum-Coppola's Blancaneaux or Chalk Hill Pinot Gris.

WHAT BITS OF INFORMATION WOULD YOU LIKE YOUR CUSTOMERS TO KNOW ABOUT YOU?

I enjoy traveling and cooking as a combination. Utilizing the ingredients of the areas I'm visiting allows me to broaden my experience and create a different type of memory.

DESCRIBE YOUR WINE SELECTIONS, BOTH BY THE GLASS AND ON YOUR LIST.

We feature fifteen wines by the glass, forty-five half-bottles and 250 full bottles, both domestic and foreign. We have limited our wines by the glass in an attempt to promote sales in the other categories. We feel strongly that this offers the customer a well-rounded experience and exposure to more complex offerings that is only available through the server's wine presentation.

NAME ONE OF YOUR RESTAURANT'S SIGNATURE DISHES. WHAT WINE DO YOU PREFER TO RECOMMEND WITH IT?

Cha Ca pan-seared Alaskan halibut with turmeric and dill sauce, Bermuda onions, jalapeño peppers, scallion rice noodles, peanuts and an English cucumber salad with rice wine vinaigrette with top Alsace white (specifically a blend of Riesling and Pinot Gris).

Le Colonial

20 Cosmo Place
San Francisco, California 94109
phone 415-931-3600 fax 415-931-2933
website www.lecolonialsf.com

William Boumier

SOMMELIER

NAME SOME OF YOUR FAVORITE WINE REGIONS FROM AROUND THE WORLD.

There are few other regions like Alsace in the world in terms of complexity, terroir, white varietals, food-pairing ability and talented winemakers. Alsace has it all. Of course, one cannot omit the Rhône Valley and Germany.

NAME A RECENT WINE DISCOVERY THAT EXCITED YOU.

Torrontès from Argentina is a little-known grape in the United States. It's like a cross between Muscat and Gewürztraminer, but with higher acid.

WHAT BITS OF INFORMATION WOULD YOU LIKE YOUR CUSTOMERS TO KNOW ABOUT YOU?

I enjoy life and, at the end of the day or week, there is nothing more special to me than celebrating by dining out. It makes me appreciate life even more. Forget therapy and eat out!

WHAT ARE THE MOST UNIQUE FEATURES IN YOUR WINE PROGRAM?

Our half-bottle program and the presence of many allocated wines.

WHAT CATEGORIES OF WINE ARE THE BEST VALUES IN YOUR RESTAURANT?

Our Rhône selections, lesser-known "Other Whites" and Rosé.

NAME ONE OF YOUR RESTAURANT'S SIGNATURE DISHES. WHAT WINE DO YOU PREFER TO RECOMMEND WITH IT?

Bo Luc Lac, wok-seared beef tenderloin with crispy julienne Yukon gold potatoes, Bermuda onions and baby tomatoes with a Willamette Valley Pinot Noir.

Crustacean

1475 Polk Street
San Francisco, California 94109
phone 415-776-2722 fax 415-776-1069
website www.secretkitchen.com

David Glancy
SOMMELIER AND WINE CONSULTANT

WHAT INSPIRED YOU TO PURSUE A CAREER THAT INVOLVES WINE?
Peter Granoff, Evan Goldstein and Kevin Zraly inspired me early in my restaurant management career.

WHAT PART OF YOUR JOB DO YOU ENJOY THE MOST?
Turning a guest on to a new favorite wine.

NAME ONE OR TWO OF YOUR FAVORITE WINE DISTRICTS OR WINE REGIONS FROM AROUND THE WORLD.
Champagne for the world's best sparkling wine. It's versatile with food and great for everyday occasions, as well as those special celebrations. Also, the many regions of Germany for all styles of Riesling, from bone dry to incredibly sweet. They are wonderful in their youth, but age exceptionally well.

NAME RECENT WINE DISCOVERIES THAT HAVE EXCITED YOU.
Dry Furmint wines from Hungary. They have great richness, bracing acidity and are truly unique.

WHAT ARE THE MOST UNIQUE FEATURES IN YOUR WINE PROGRAM?
We have an excellent variety of aromatic white wines at all price points that go very well with our Euro-Asian cuisine.

WHAT CATEGORY OF WINE IS THE BEST VALUE IN YOUR RESTAURANT?
Our "Crisp, Dry Whites" and "Eclectic Reds" sections are the best values.

NAME A FEW OF YOUR RESTAURANT'S SIGNATURE DISHES. WHAT TYPES OF WINE DO YOU PREFER TO RECOMMEND WITH EACH?
Garlic-roasted crab with German Spätlese Riesling; mussels with Asian pesto and Marlborough Sauvignon Blanc; baked Alaska with Australian fortified Muscat.

IN THE PAST YEAR, WHAT WINES IN YOUR WINE PROGRAM HAVE CUSTOMERS BECOME MORE WILLING TO ORDER?
German Rieslings. Their sales have increased considerably.

Il Davide

901 A Street
San Rafael, California 94901
phone 415-454-8080 fax 415-453-9590
website www.ildavide.com

Bill Woodbridge
BAR MANAGER AND WINE BUYER

NAME ONE OF YOUR FAVORITE WINE REGIONS FROM AROUND THE WORLD.
Russian River Valley for its earthy Pinot Noirs.

NAME RECENT WINE DISCOVERIES THAT HAVE EXCITED YOU.
The Sierra Foothills have been surprising in the last few years with some very rich, deep reds.

IF YOU WERE NOT IN THIS PROFESSION, WHAT WOULD YOU BE DOING?
Traveling.

DESCRIBE YOUR WINE SELECTIONS, BOTH BY THE GLASS AND ON YOUR LIST.
We have more than 300 wines on our list. We usually run about twenty wines by the glass. We offer a large selection of current and aged Cabernet Sauvignon, as well as a very exciting selection of Zinfandel.

WHAT ARE THE MOST UNIQUE FEATURES IN YOUR WINE PROGRAM?
Our wine-by-the-glass program offers two flights a day and a constantly changing list. We feature high-end wines and older vintages to introduce customers to wines they may not have the opportunity to taste.

WHAT CATEGORY OF WINE IS THE BEST VALUE IN YOUR RESTAURANT?
Many of our early to mid-'90s Cabernet Sauvignon, and some lesser-known Chianti.

NAME A COUPLE OF YOUR RESTAURANT'S SIGNATURE DISHES. WHAT TYPES OF WINE DO YOU PREFER TO RECOMMEND WITH EACH?
Our smoked chicken ravioli with a Carneros Chardonnay; braised lamb shanks with a Russian River Pinot Noir.

IN THE PAST YEAR, WHAT WINES IN YOUR WINE PROGRAM HAVE CUSTOMERS BECOME MORE WILLING TO ORDER?
Central Coast wines, especially Syrah.

The Dining Room
at the Ritz-Carlton

600 Stockton at California Street
San Francisco, California 94108
phone 415-296-7465 fax 415-951-8730

Stephane Lacroix
WINE DIRECTOR AND SOMMELIER

WHAT ARE SOME OF YOUR ULTIMATE FOOD AND WINE PAIRINGS?
Lobster salad paired with Sauvignon Blanc from New Zealand; squab breast paired with a Rhône such as Côte Rôtie; large asparagus, chicken with parmesan and olive oil paired with Chablis Premier Cru or Pouilly-Fumé from Dageneau; frog legs and snails meunière with white Rhônes.

DESCRIBE YOUR WINE SELECTIONS.
Our list offers 1,200 selections, mainly from California and France, with depth in old vintages and a good representation of top vineyards from around the world.

WHAT CATEGORY OF WINE IS THE BEST VALUE IN YOUR RESTAURANT?
Red Rhône, especially selections from the smaller appellations of Crozes-Hermitage, Cairanne, Gigondas and St. Joseph.

NAME A RECENT WINE DISCOVERY THAT EXCITED YOU.
The Rioja blanco from Remelluri is an incredible white from Spain with personality, complexity and balance.

WHAT IS YOUR FAVORITE WINE REGION IN THE WORLD TODAY?
Alsace. I love the tradition and the typicity of the wines. They are great, food-friendly wines.

WHAT LED YOU TO PURSUE A CAREER THAT INVOLVES WINE?
Passion for the restaurant business, good grades in wine class in catering school, interaction with the guests and the staff's passion for wine.

WHAT ARE THE BEST ASPECTS OF YOUR JOB?
Discovering new people and new regions. Enjoying a passion as my job!

IF YOU WERE NOT IN THE WINE PROFESSION, WHAT WOULD YOU BE DOING?
I love the outdoors and exercise, so maybe I'd be a trainer.

Emile's

545 South Second Street
San Jose, California 95112
phone 408-289-1960 fax 408-998-1245
website www.emiles.com

Emile Mooser
CHEF AND OWNER

NAME TWO OF YOUR FAVORITE WINE DISTRICTS FROM AROUND THE WORLD.

Napa Valley and the Santa Cruz Mountains.

NAME RECENT WINE DISCOVERIES THAT HAVE EXCITED YOU.

New blends like Viognier and Sauvignon Blanc, red and white Meritage and the newer Rhône blends.

WHAT BITS OF INFORMATION WOULD YOU LIKE YOUR CUSTOMERS TO KNOW ABOUT YOU?

I love travel, skiing all over the world and mountaineering. I work with the Sherpas developing new recipes for Everest Expectations.

DESCRIBE YOUR WINE SELECTIONS, BOTH BY THE GLASS AND ON YOUR LIST.

We feature a tasting menu every day, and I customize menus for individuals or groups with complementary wines. We also feature twelve wines by the glass.

WHAT ARE THE MOST UNIQUE FEATURES IN YOUR WINE PROGRAM?

A good selection of half-bottles, fair pricing and a selection of Swiss wines.

WHAT CATEGORY OF WINE IS THE BEST VALUE IN YOUR RESTAURANT?

California wines.

NAME A COUPLE OF YOUR RESTAURANT'S SIGNATURE DISHES. WHAT TYPES OF WINE DO YOU PREFER TO RECOMMEND WITH EACH?

Fresh apricot tart (when in season) with late-harvest California white; Foie Gras au Torchon with Sauternes; lamb shanks with Zinfandel.

IN THE PAST YEAR, WHAT WINES IN YOUR WINE PROGRAM HAVE CUSTOMERS BECOME MORE WILLING TO ORDER?

Meritage wines, New Zealand Sauvignon Blanc and new blends.

Farallon

450 Post Street
San Francisco, California 94102
phone 415-956-6969 fax 415-834-1234
website www.farallonrestaurant.com

Peter J. Palmer

WINE DIRECTOR AND SOMMELIER

WHAT IS ONE OF YOUR ULTIMATE FOOD AND WINE PAIRINGS?
Prosciutto and summer melon with mint chiffonade paired with off-dry
Gewürztraminer.

DESCRIBE YOUR WINE SELECTIONS.
I want our wine program to be fun, exciting and accessible. The list offers 475
international selections, with the majority from California and France. Our
menu is mainly seafood, so lots of Burgundy and New World Pinot Noir is
available for red wine drinkers.

WHAT CATEGORY OF WINE IS THE BEST VALUE IN YOUR RESTAURANT?
Italian whites. They are inexpensive and better than ever.

NAME RECENT WINE DISCOVERIES THAT HAVE EXCITED YOU.
Bonaccorsi Pinot Noir; the white wines from Francois Villard, Yves Gangloff
and Yves Cuilleron in the northern Rhône; and the wines of Quintarelli in the
Veneto—utterly unique and always memorable.

WHAT IS YOUR FAVORITE WINE REGION IN THE WORLD TODAY?
Burgundy, followed very closely by the northern Rhône Valley.

WHAT LED YOU TO PURSUE A CAREER THAT INVOLVES WINE?
I moved to San Francisco as a bartender and this, coupled with the proximity
of the wine country and a couple of great bottles of Burgundy, got me hooked.

WHAT ARE THE BEST ASPECTS OF YOUR JOB?
The most rewarding by far is getting to know the people and personalities
behind the wines.

IF YOU WERE NOT IN THIS PROFESSION, WHAT WOULD YOU BE DOING?
Something outdoors like nature and travel writing and photography.

Fifth Floor Restaurant at the Palomar Hotel

12 Fourth Street
San Francisco, California 94103
phone 415-348-1555 fax 415-348-1551
website www.fifthfloor.citysearch.com

Belinda Chang
WINE DIRECTOR

HOW MANY DAYS A WEEK ARE YOU A SOMMELIER ON THE FLOOR IN YOUR RESTAURANT?
Every day!

WHAT INSPIRED YOU TO PURSUE A CAREER THAT INVOLVES WINE?
Watching Joseph Spellman work his magic on the floor at Charlie Trotter's inspired me.

DESCRIBE YOUR WINE SELECTIONS, BOTH BY THE GLASS AND ON YOUR LIST.
To make it more fun for our guests, we feature a rotating selection of approximately thirty wines by the glass that are intended for pairing with the ever-changing dishes on the menu. Classic pairings like Sauternes with seared foie gras are respected, while neoclassic pairings like California Viognier with Lobster Cappuccino are also explored.

NAME A COUPLE OF YOUR RESTAURANT'S SIGNATURE DISHES. WHAT TYPES OF WINE DO YOU PREFER TO RECOMMEND WITH EACH?
Squab breast roasted with almonds and cumin paired with grand cru red Burgundy; skate wing with artichokes and bordelaise sauce paired with Collioure Rouge.

La Folie Restaurant

2316 Polk Street
San Francisco, California 94109
phone 415-776-5577 fax 415-776-3431

George Passot

SOMMELIER, WINE BUYER AND MANAGER

WHAT IS ONE OF YOUR ULTIMATE FOOD AND WINE PAIRINGS?
Sautéed foie gras with wild huckleberries and a glass of Château d'Yquem 1989.

DESCRIBE YOUR WINE SELECTIONS.
A good balance between California and French wines. Not too large.
Customers are not intimidated by the wine list.

WHAT IS YOUR FAVORITE WINE REGION IN THE WORLD TODAY?
For the scenery I would say Beaujolais. For white wines, Bourgogne and New
Zealand. For red wines, the Rhône Valley and Bordeaux.

WHAT LED YOU TO PURSUE A CAREER THAT INVOLVES WINE?
The passion for wine and food pairing.

WHAT IS THE BEST ASPECT OF YOUR JOB?
Finding the right wine for my customer, whatever his budget.

IF YOU WERE NOT IN THE WINE PROFESSION, WHAT WOULD YOU BE?
A clown!

Gary Danko

800 North Point Street
San Francisco, California 94109
phone 415-749-2060 fax 415-775-1805
website www.garydanko.com

Christie R. Dufault
SOMMELIER

NAME ONE OF YOUR FAVORITE WINES FROM AROUND THE WORLD.
Champagne. I prefer the lean, crisp and mineral styles. Visually, a glass of
Champagne is exquisite.

NAME RECENT WINE DISCOVERIES THAT HAVE EXCITED YOU.
Several Syrahs from California that had incredible concentration and depth of flavor.

WHAT BITS OF INFORMATION WOULD YOU LIKE YOUR CUSTOMERS TO
KNOW ABOUT YOU?
I like to go on cycling trips in wine regions around the world. I enjoy French
films and I love to cook.

IF YOU WERE NOT IN THIS PROFESSION, WHAT WOULD YOU BE DOING?
If not a professional wine taster, I would be a professional spa tester.

DESCRIBE YOUR WINE SELECTIONS, BOTH BY THE GLASS AND ON YOUR LIST.
We have a Grand Award wine list specializing in the classics. We also have more
than 200 half-bottle selections.

WHAT ARE THE MOST UNIQUE FEATURES IN YOUR WINE PROGRAM?
We have nine Sub-Zero wine storage units in addition to the cellar, ensuring
that all of the different white wines are served at the proper temperatures.

WHAT CATEGORIES OF WINE ARE THE BEST VALUES IN YOUR RESTAURANT?
German and Austrian whites and Spanish reds.

NAME ONE OF YOUR RESTAURANT'S SIGNATURE DISHES. WHAT WINE DO
YOU PREFER TO RECOMMEND WITH IT?
Pancetta-wrapped frog legs with sunchoke-garlic purée and lentils served with
premier cru Côte de Beaune white Burgundy.

IN THE PAST YEAR, WHAT WINES IN YOUR WINE PROGRAM HAVE CUS-
TOMERS BECOME MORE WILLING TO ORDER?
Grüner Veltliners from Austria and white Rhône Valley wines.

Greens Restaurant

Fort Mason, Building A
San Francisco, California 94123
phone 415-771-6222 fax 415-771-3470
website www.greensrestaurant.com

Chaylee A. Priete

WINE DIRECTOR AND
DINING ROOM MANAGER

WHAT PART OF YOUR JOB DO YOU ENJOY THE MOST?
Tasting with the winemakers and hearing the stories behind their wine and
career choices.

NAME ONE OR TWO OF YOUR FAVORITE WINE DISTRICTS OR WINE
REGIONS FROM AROUND THE WORLD.
The Rhône. The wines are ultimately food-friendly and express gorgeous ter-
roir; Spain, particularly Priorat, for all the exciting changes happening there.

DESCRIBE YOUR WINE SELECTIONS, BOTH BY THE GLASS AND ON YOUR LIST.
There are 325 wines on our list. I rotate wine from our cellars quite frequently.
The list is global and eclectic with a concentration on boutique California
wines and quite a bit of Burgundy. The sixteen by-the-glass choices reflect the
same.

WHAT ARE THE MOST UNIQUE FEATURES IN YOUR WINE PROGRAM?
I do a selection of wines paired by the glass every Saturday night with our four-
course prix fixe menu. There are usually ten hard-to-find or allocated wines
offered.

WHAT CATEGORIES OF WINE ARE THE BEST VALUES IN YOUR RESTAURANT?
Great, affordable Burgundies and reds from small producers in the south of
France.

NAME A COUPLE OF YOUR RESTAURANT'S SIGNATURE DISHES. WHAT
TYPES OF WINE DO YOU PREFER TO RECOMMEND WITH EACH?
Marinated tofu brochettes with a charmoula glaze paired with Alsace Pinot
Blanc; winter gratin with manchego cheese paired with Napa Valley Cabernet
Sauvignon.

IN THE PAST YEAR, WHAT WINES IN YOUR WINE PROGRAM HAVE CUS-
TOMERS BECOME MORE WILLING TO ORDER?
Alsatian Rieslings and both red and white wines from Spain.

Incanto

1550 Church Street
San Francisco, California 94131
phone 415-641-4500 fax 415-641-4546
website www.incanto.biz

Claudio Villani
WINE MANAGER AND SOMMELIER

NAME ONE OF YOUR FAVORITE WINE REGIONS FROM AROUND THE WORLD.

Southern Italy, with its rediscoveries of varieties like Fiano, Vermentino, Greco, Aglianico, Nero d'Avola and Primitivo.

NAME RECENT WINE DISCOVERIES THAT HAVE EXCITED YOU.

We were recently visited by the winemaker Aleç Kristancic of the Movia estate in Slovenia. Aleç is a true inspiration.

IF YOU WERE NOT IN THIS PROFESSION, WHAT WOULD YOU BE DOING?

I briefly played semi-professional baseball in Italy and would love to have pursued a life in sports.

WHAT ARE THE MOST UNIQUE FEATURES IN YOUR WINE PROGRAM?

The most unique feature of Incanto's wine program is the small paper disc that we place around the stem of each wine that we serve by the glass, indicating the denomination, vintage and producer of the wine.

WHAT CATEGORY OF WINE IS THE BEST VALUE IN YOUR RESTAURANT?

Southern Italian reds.

NAME A COUPLE OF YOUR RESTAURANT'S SIGNATURE DISHES. WHAT TYPES OF WINE DO YOU PREFER TO RECOMMEND WITH EACH?

Fiore Sardo cheese served with a Barbera d'Alba; flourless chocolate torte with Aleatico di Maremma, an ancient red dessert wine that nearly became extinct in the 1960s and 1970s.

IN THE PAST YEAR, WHAT WINES IN YOUR WINE PROGRAM HAVE CUSTOMERS BECOME MORE WILLING TO ORDER?

Delicate, elegant, perfumed wines from the Alps like Lagrein, Teroldego, Pinot Nero and aromatic white wines such as Sylvaner, Mueller-Thurgau and Sauvignon Blanc with little or no oak influence.

Indigo Restaurant

687 McAllister Street
San Francisco, California 94102
phone 415-673-9353 fax 415-673-9369
website www.indigorestaurant.com

Greg Quinn

GENERAL MANAGER AND
WINE DIRECTOR

LIST AWARDS YOU HAVE RECEIVED.
We have received six consecutive Awards of Excellence from Wine Spectator.

WHAT INSPIRED YOU TO PURSUE A CAREER THAT INVOLVES WINE?
Serendipity. I never intended this as a career, but I came to love the lifestyle.

NAME ONE OF YOUR FAVORITE WINE REGIONS FROM AROUND THE WORLD.
I love Dry Creek; it's the best region for Zinfandel. Its Zins typically are not overblown and are food-friendly.

NAME RECENT WINE DISCOVERIES THAT HAVE EXCITED YOU.
I think the wines made on the Sonoma Coast, particularly at Peay Vineyards, are some of the most distinctive wines made in California. Also, Oregon's Pinot Gris is great.

DESCRIBE YOUR WINE SELECTIONS, BOTH BY THE GLASS AND ON YOUR LIST.
We focus primarily on California wines, offering California's best producers at great prices.

WHAT CATEGORIES OF WINE ARE THE BEST VALUES IN YOUR RESTAURANT?
Offbeat white wines like Oregon Pinot Gris, Rhône whites, Riesling and varietals like Albariño, Pinot Blanc and Chenin Blanc.

NAME A FEW OF YOUR RESTAURANT'S SIGNATURE DISHES. WHAT TYPES OF WINE DO YOU PREFER TO RECOMMEND WITH EACH?
Off-dry Riesling with our spicy ahi tuna poke; Oregon Pinot Gris with our grilled mahi mahi with mango coulis; Dry Creek Zinfandel with our spicy pork loin dish.

IN THE PAST YEAR, WHAT WINES IN YOUR WINE PROGRAM HAVE CUSTOMERS BECOME MORE WILLING TO ORDER?
Red and white Rhône-style blends, Burgundian varietals from Sonoma Coast and anything in a half-bottle. Our customers have come to trust us over time and are more adventurous than before.

Jardinière

300 Grove Street
San Francisco, California 94102
phone 415-861-5555 fax 415-861-5580
website www.jardiniere.com

Eugenio V. Jardim
WINE DIRECTOR

WHAT PART OF YOUR JOB DO YOU ENJOY THE MOST?
I enjoy everything about my job: Tasting, buying, selling and, above all, discovering new wines.

NAME TWO OF YOUR FAVORITE WINE DISTRICTS OR WINE REGIONS FROM AROUND THE WORLD.
The Rhône, because of the incredible diversity of its wines, and Austria's Wachau because of the superb purity and freshness of its wines.

NAME RECENT WINE DISCOVERIES THAT HAVE EXCITED YOU.
The wines of South Africa and lesser-known appellations there, as well as producers from the Loire Valley, all for their very high quality and value.

WHAT ARE THE MOST UNIQUE FEATURES IN YOUR WINE PROGRAM?
Our half-bottle selection that caters to the opera and symphony patrons and our very exciting after-dinner wine flights.

WHAT CATEGORY OF WINE IS THE BEST VALUE IN YOUR RESTAURANT?
Southern Hemisphere whites and reds.

NAME A COUPLE OF YOUR RESTAURANT'S SIGNATURE DISHES. WHAT TYPES OF WINE DO YOU PREFER TO RECOMMEND WITH EACH?
Maine diver scallops with pommes purée and truffle nage with Chambolle-Musigny; red wine braised short ribs with herb salad and Sonoma County Zinfandel.

IN THE PAST YEAR, WHAT WINES IN YOUR WINE PROGRAM HAVE CUSTOMERS BECOME MORE WILLING TO ORDER?
Loire Valley Chenin Blanc from Montlouis, Rhône Valley Syrah from Collines Rhodaniennes and Riesling and Grüner Veltliner from Austria.

WHAT ARE SOME OTHER ULTIMATE WINE AND FOOD PAIRINGS?
Slow-braised pork cheeks with creamy morels and potato gnocchi with Rioja Crianza.

Marché Aux Fleurs

23 Ross Common
Ross, California 94957
phone 415-925-9200
website www.marcheauxfleursrestaurant.com

Holly S. Baker
PROPRIETOR AND SOMMELIER

WHAT PART OF YOUR JOB DO YOU ENJOY THE MOST?
I enjoy making recommendations to customers and introducing European wines to the local Northern California consumers.

NAME ONE OF YOUR FAVORITE WINES OR WINE REGIONS FROM AROUND THE WORLD.
Champagne, because it makes any day a special occasion. The wines are versatile and taste great with or without food.

NAME RECENT WINE DISCOVERIES THAT HAVE EXCITED YOU.
Germany has great variety in styles, and its wines are undervalued and can pair with challenging dishes.

IF YOU WERE NOT IN THIS PROFESSION, WHAT WOULD YOU BE DOING?
Law was the original plan, but I've turned a passion and hobby into my profession. Now I can't imagine another job that would be as gratifying.

WHAT ARE THE MOST UNIQUE FEATURES IN YOUR WINE PROGRAM?
We do wine classes through the local recreation department. We also have wine dinners that feature the wines and foods of various regions.

WHAT CATEGORY OF WINE IS THE BEST VALUE IN YOUR RESTAURANT?
In all categories we have wines beginning in the $20 range. We have more than fifty wines that are under $40.

NAME A COUPLE OF YOUR RESTAURANT'S SIGNATURE DISHES. WHAT TYPES OF WINE DO YOU PREFER TO RECOMMEND WITH EACH?
Salade de chêvre chaud with Sancerre; duck confit with Côtes du Rhône.

IN THE PAST YEAR, WHAT WINES IN YOUR WINE PROGRAM HAVE CUSTOMERS BECOME MORE WILLING TO ORDER?
White and red Burgundy, Sancerre, Malbec and Cabernet Franc.

The Matterhorn Swiss Restaurant

2323 Van Ness Avenue
San Francisco, California 94109
phone 415-885-6116 fax 415-885 6116
website www.matterhorn.citysearch.com

Brigitte Thorpe
OWNER

WHAT INSPIRED YOU TO PURSUE A CAREER THAT INVOLVES WINE?
I got involved at a very early age while drinking wine in Switzerland at the age of four years old. My father loved French Burgundies and Bordeaux. His wine cellar was so interesting that I often spent time in there. Being in the top 100 restaurants in San Francisco for the last six years has been inspiring and gives me the tools to provide a nice wine list.

NAME ONE OF YOUR FAVORITE WINE REGIONS FROM AROUND THE WORLD.
I love the wine region around Lake Geneva. As a native Swiss, I adore Swiss white wines.

NAME RECENT WINE DISCOVERIES THAT HAVE EXCITED YOU.
Riesling, in any style. Rieslings are very interesting and so diverse.

IF YOU WERE NOT IN THIS PROFESSION, WHAT WOULD YOU BE DOING?
I am a good profiler. I'd probably be in law enforcement.

WHAT ARE THE MOST UNIQUE FEATURES IN YOUR WINE PROGRAM?
I have more than thirty half-bottles of wine available. People love to try different wines, and half-bottles give them that chance.

WHAT CATEGORY OF WINE IS THE BEST VALUE IN YOUR RESTAURANT?
Swiss wines are the best value. They are generally expensive to buy, but my markup is low.

NAME A COUPLE OF YOUR RESTAURANT'S SIGNATURE DISHES. WHAT TYPES OF WINE DO YOU PREFER TO RECOMMEND WITH EACH?
Cheese fondue Valaisanne with a fine Dezaley L'Arbalete; beef fondue Bourguignonne with rich Zinfandel.

McCormick and Kuleto's Seafood

900 North Point Street
San Francisco, California 94109
phone 415-929-1730 fax 415-567-2919

Steve E. Deniz
FOOD AND BEVERAGE MANAGER

NAME TWO OF YOUR FAVORITE WINE DISTRICTS OR WINE REGIONS FROM AROUND THE WORLD.
Burgundy, France, for the purest form of Pinot Noir; California's Central Coast for the variety and type of its undiscovered treasures.

NAME RECENT WINE DISCOVERIES THAT HAVE EXCITED YOU.
Washington State Cabernet, a region that yearly improves in quality.

WHAT BITS OF INFORMATION WOULD YOU LIKE YOUR CUSTOMERS TO KNOW ABOUT YOU?
I started my hospitality career painting hotel rooms and, one day, they needed help in the dining room. The rest is history.

IF YOU WERE NOT IN THIS PROFESSION, WHAT WOULD YOU BE DOING?
Working for an auto racing team.

DESCRIBE YOUR WINE SELECTIONS, BOTH BY THE GLASS AND ON YOUR LIST.
A focus on premium California wine, while highlighting French, German and Italian imports.

WHAT CATEGORY OF WINE IS THE BEST VALUE IN YOUR RESTAURANT?
California Sauvignon Blanc and Pinot Noir.

NAME A COUPLE OF YOUR RESTAURANT'S SIGNATURE DISHES. WHAT TYPES OF WINE DO YOU PREFER TO RECOMMEND WITH EACH?
Dungeness crab cakes with Placer County Viognier; smoked alder salmon with Carneros Pinot Noir.

IN THE PAST YEAR, WHAT WINES IN YOUR WINE PROGRAM HAVE CUSTOMERS BECOME MORE WILLING TO ORDER?
California Zinfandel and New Zealand Sauvignon Blanc.

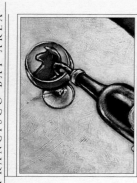

Merenda

1809 Union Street
San Francisco, CA 94123
phone 415-346-7373

Keith Fergel

SOMMELIER

WHAT INSPIRED YOU TO PURSUE A CAREER THAT INVOLVES WINE?
The allure of figuring out what makes different wines unique and the challenge of pairing food and wine drew me to this career.

WHAT PART OF YOUR JOB DO YOU ENJOY THE MOST?
The sommelier inherently must be a shrewd and analytical wine buyer by day and also a compassionate and caring servant by night. I like the dichotomy; it makes us well-rounded.

NAME ONE OR TWO OF YOUR FAVORITE WINE DISTRICTS OR WINE REGIONS FROM AROUND THE WORLD.
I love wines from cooler regions and cool spots in warmer regions: Burgundy, the Mosel, Austria and the northern Rhône.

DESCRIBE YOUR WINE SELECTIONS, BOTH BY THE GLASS AND ON YOUR LIST.
We offer a custom-tailored wine and food experience for our guests. We don't have a "flight of wines" to accompany our tasting menu, opting rather to have enough sommeliers on the floor in order to find out what our guests love to drink and make them feel comfortable.

WHAT CATEGORY OF WINE IS THE BEST VALUE IN YOUR RESTAURANT?
There are values throughout our selections.

NAME ONE OF YOUR RESTAURANT'S SIGNATURE DISHES. WHAT WINE DO YOU PREFER TO RECOMMEND WITH IT?
Our sweet pea ravioli with fresh tomatoes, mint and green almonds with crisp, northern Italian white wine, such as a Sauvignon Blanc from Alto Adige.

IN THE PAST YEAR, WHAT WINES IN YOUR WINE PROGRAM HAVE CUS-TOMERS BECOME MORE WILLING TO ORDER?
Off-dry reds like Amarone or wines from Collio.

Mistral

370-6 Bridge Parkway
Redwood Shores, California 94065
phone 650-802-9222 fax 650-802-9221
website www.mistraldining.com

Morgan L. Plant

GENERAL MANAGER AND
WINE DIRECTOR

WHAT INSPIRED YOU TO PURSUE A CAREER THAT INVOLVES WINE?
My parents really inspired me to learn more. They taught me to pursue with a passion those things that interested me.

WHAT PART OF YOUR JOB DO YOU ENJOY THE MOST?
Making that one-on-one connection with the guests and seeing a recommendation turn out to be a highlight of their evening.

NAME ONE OR TWO OF YOUR FAVORITE WINE DISTRICTS OR WINE REGIONS FROM AROUND THE WORLD.
I am really a big fan of the Northwest, the Willamette Valley especially. The Pinots are so complex and fun.

NAME RECENT WINE DISCOVERIES THAT HAVE EXCITED YOU.
Wines from Chile and Argentina.

IF YOU WERE NOT IN THIS PROFESSION, WHAT WOULD YOU BE?
An accountant or professional college student!

WHAT ARE THE MOST UNIQUE FEATURES IN YOUR WINE PROGRAM?
We sell almost fifty wines by the glass that change regularly. We try to highlight a winery a month and add a page in our wine list for them. We usually try to pair this with a wine dinner.

WHAT CATEGORY OF WINE IS THE BEST VALUE IN YOUR RESTAURANT?
California Cabernet Sauvignon. We don't mark it up as much as other restaurants do.

NAME A COUPLE OF YOUR RESTAURANT'S SIGNATURE DISHES. WHAT TYPES OF WINE DO YOU PREFER TO RECOMMEND WITH EACH?
Marinated grilled skirt steak with Amador County Zinfandel; Thai crab and shrimp spring rolls with Alsatian whites.

Navio at the Ritz-Carlton Half Moon Bay

One Miramontes Point Road
Half Moon Bay, California 94019
phone 650-712-7055 fax 650-712-7070
website www.ritzcarlton.com

Michael H. Rasmussen
DIRECTOR OF WINE AND SOMMELIER

WHAT INSPIRED YOU TO PURSUE A CAREER THAT INVOLVES WINE?
Ten years ago I had the best food and wine pairing that I'd ever had, and it was that year that I changed my career as a chef to that of a sommelier.

NAME ONE OF YOUR FAVORITE WINE DISTRICTS OR WINE REGIONS FROM AROUND THE WORLD.
Ribera del Duero, Spain, has earthy, spicy, food-friendly wines that are great values.

NAME RECENT WINE DISCOVERIES THAT HAVE EXCITED YOU.
Washington Syrahs! Big, bold, super-ripe, jammy. I cannot help but like these wines.

WHAT BITS OF INFORMATION WOULD YOU LIKE YOUR CUSTOMERS TO KNOW ABOUT YOU?
I drink Miller beer at home.

IF YOU WERE NOT IN THIS PROFESSION, WHAT WOULD YOU BE DOING?
Teaching high school history.

DESCRIBE YOUR WINE SELECTIONS, BOTH BY THE GLASS AND ON YOUR LIST.
We offer the most highly sought-after selections, mainly from California, but with representation of much of the rest of the wine world.

WHAT CATEGORY OF WINE IS THE BEST VALUE IN YOUR RESTAURANT?
California Syrah.

NAME ONE OF YOUR RESTAURANT'S SIGNATURE DISHES. WHAT WINE DO YOU PREFER TO RECOMMEND WITH IT?
Lobster in red wine sauce with Russian River Pinot Noir.

Niebaum-Coppola Café

473 University Avenue
Palo Alto, California 94301
phone 650-752-0350 fax 650-752-0359
website www.cafecoppola.com

John E. Aylward

DIRECTOR OF CAFÉ OPERATIONS AND
SOMMELIER

WHAT INSPIRED YOU TO PURSUE A CAREER THAT INVOLVES WINE?
I became hooked when I moved to California and was surrounded by the magic of the Wine Country.

NAME ONE OF YOUR FAVORITE WINE REGIONS FROM AROUND THE WORLD.
Washington State. Its reds show such wonderful ripeness with an almost sweet acidity to them.

NAME RECENT WINE DISCOVERIES THAT HAVE EXCITED YOU.
Spain for its crisp whites, full-bodied reds and elegant dessert wines at affordable prices.

WHAT BITS OF INFORMATION WOULD YOU LIKE YOUR CUSTOMERS TO KNOW ABOUT YOU?
I was born in Walla Walla before it was an appellation. It is fun to have that connection.

IF YOU WERE NOT IN THIS PROFESSION, WHAT WOULD YOU BE DOING?
Woodworking.

DESCRIBE YOUR WINE SELECTIONS, BOTH BY THE GLASS AND ON YOUR LIST.
Our wine list is comprised of wines from around the globe, more than thirty by-the-glass selections and nearly 200 available by the bottle, priced from $15 to $295. We also have an extensive variety of Francis Ford Coppola wines because we are an extension of his winery.

NAME ONE OF YOUR RESTAURANT'S SIGNATURE DISHES. WHAT WINE DO YOU PREFER TO RECOMMEND WITH IT?
Branzino al Sale, a whole Mediterranean-style sea bass with a California white blend, like Coppola's Blancaneaux.

IN THE PAST YEAR, WHAT WINES IN YOUR WINE PROGRAM HAVE CUSTOMERS BECOME MORE WILLING TO ORDER?
Italian wines, from the simple rustic styles to the flashier international ones.

Pacific's Edge Restaurant at Highlands Inn

120 Highlands Drive
Carmel, California 93923
phone 831-622-5445 fax 831-626-1574
website www.highlands-inn.com

Bernabe De Luna
WINE DIRECTOR

WHAT INSPIRED YOU TO PURSUE A CAREER THAT INVOLVES WINE?
The inspiration came from my first taste of serious wines: Champagne Salon and Château d'Yquem.

NAME TWO OF YOUR FAVORITE WINES.
Champagne and Burgundy.

NAME RECENT WINE DISCOVERIES THAT HAVE EXCITED YOU.
Numanthia-Thermes 2000 Termanthia, from Spain's Toro district (a Grenache produced from vines that date back to the nineteenth century).

IF YOU WERE NOT IN THIS PROFESSION, WHAT WOULD YOU BE DOING?
I would be in the kitchen!

WHAT ARE THE MOST UNIQUE FEATURES IN YOUR WINE PROGRAM?
Our most unique feature is the Master's of Food and Wine event that is held at the hotel annually. But we also offer a selection of more than 1,700 wines.

WHAT CATEGORY OF WINE IS THE BEST VALUE IN YOUR RESTAURANT?
We have good values in every category. But the best are found in the "Sommelier's Wine Pairing" category, where different wines are offered for a fraction of the price of one bottle.

NAME ONE OF YOUR RESTAURANT'S SIGNATURE DISHES. WHAT WINE DO YOU PREFER TO RECOMMEND WITH IT?
Marinated tuna and hamachi yuzu, mustard oil and opal basil with dry Furmint, from Hungary.

IN THE PAST YEAR, WHAT WINES IN YOUR WINE PROGRAM HAVE CUS-TOMERS BECOME MORE WILLING TO ORDER?
Wines from Austria, Spain and Germany.

Pacific's Edge Restaurant at Highlands Inn

120 Highlands Drive
Carmel, California 93923
phone 831-622-5445 fax 831-626-1574
website www.highlands-inn.com

Arvind P. Dutt

CELLAR MASTER

NAME TWO OF YOUR FAVORITE WINES FROM AROUND THE WORLD.
Champagne, because I just love to drink it and it matches almost all foods; red Burgundy because of its aroma.

NAME RECENT WINE DISCOVERIES THAT HAVE EXCITED YOU.
Nicolas Catena Zapata 1999, Mendoza, Argentina, for great value compared to California. Termanthia 2000 from Numanthia-Thermes, Spain.

DESCRIBE YOUR WINE SELECTIONS, BOTH BY THE GLASS AND ON YOUR LIST.
We have about thirty different wines by the glass (three Champagnes, ten whites and fifteen reds), and the wine list offers a huge selection of California wines, French whites and reds, as well as many Italian, Chilean, Argentinean, Australian, German (Riesling) and Oregon wines.

WHAT ARE THE MOST UNIQUE FEATURES IN YOUR WINE PROGRAM?
We have a huge selection of half-bottles of Champagne, California and French reds and whites, and Italian and Chilean reds. We also pair wines for three-, four- or five-course meals.

WHAT CATEGORY OF WINE IS THE BEST VALUE IN YOUR RESTAURANT?
California Cabernet and French white and red Burgundy.

NAME A FEW OF YOUR RESTAURANT'S SIGNATURE DISHES. WHAT TYPES OF WINE DO YOU PREFER TO RECOMMEND WITH EACH?
Marinated tuna with Austrian Grüner Veltliner; seared foie gras with German Riesling Auslese; Duck, Duck, Goose with red Burgundy.

IN THE PAST YEAR, WHAT WINES IN YOUR WINE PROGRAM HAVE CUS-TOMERS BECOME MORE WILLING TO ORDER?
German Riesling and Austrian Grüner Veltliner.

Pajaro Street Grill

435 Pajaro Street
Salinas, California 93901
phone 831-754-3738 fax 831-754-2779
website www.psgrill.net

Deamer Dunn
PRESIDENT AND WINE BUYER

WHAT INSPIRED YOU TO PURSUE A CAREER THAT INVOLVES WINE?
During academic travel to Châteauneuf-du-Pape in 1978, I fell in love with the romance of wine.

NAME ONE OR TWO OF YOUR FAVORITE WINE DISTRICTS OR WINE REGIONS FROM AROUND THE WORLD.
My personal passion has always been Italy, and professionally my interest has been in the growth of Monterey County wines.

NAME RECENT WINE DISCOVERIES THAT HAVE EXCITED YOU.
Argentinean Malbecs. They pair well with grilled foods and are such great values.

IF YOU WERE NOT IN THIS PROFESSION, WHAT WOULD YOU BE DOING?
Art. I began painting in 1999 and have fallen in love with portraying emotions through the use of color and shape.

DESCRIBE YOUR WINE SELECTIONS, BOTH BY THE GLASS AND ON YOUR LIST.
To match our "Central Coast Cuisine," we specialize in the wines of Monterey County; they make up about thirty-five percent of our list. We also have wines from most of the important wine regions of the world, including some rare wines on our reserve list.

IN THE PAST YEAR, WHAT WINES IN YOUR WINE PROGRAM HAVE CUS-TOMERS BECOME MORE WILLING TO ORDER?
Syrah and imported wines.

WHAT ARE SOME OF YOUR FAVORITE WINE AND FOOD PAIRINGS?
Hearty Cabernet Sauvignon with a juicy, grilled rib-eye; Syrah with venison; and either Pinot Noir or Chardonnay with duck or salmon, depending on the dish's sauce.

Parcel 104 at the Marriott Hotel Santa Clara

2700 Mission College Boulevard
Santa Clara, California 95054
phone 408-970-6104 fax 408-970-6190
website www.parcel104.com

Robert Sharpe
GENERAL MANAGER AND WINE DIRECTOR

NAME ONE OF YOUR FAVORITE WINE REGIONS FROM AROUND THE WORLD.

Germany is a favorite wine region because of the quality and diversity of Riesling. Germany provides some diverse expressions, from the dry wines of the Rheingau (especially Charta) to the yin-yang sweetness and balanced acidity of the Mosel.

NAME RECENT WINE DISCOVERIES THAT HAVE EXCITED YOU.

Pinot Gris from Marlborough, New Zealand, has excited me both in terms of quality as well as value. Huia Vineyards especially comes to mind.

WHAT BITS OF INFORMATION WOULD YOU LIKE YOUR CUSTOMERS TO KNOW ABOUT YOU?

I have a delightful eight-year-old daughter named Melissa.

DESCRIBE YOUR WINE SELECTIONS, BOTH BY THE GLASS AND ON YOUR LIST.

We have more than 500 selections, with an emphasis on California and international classics. We offer twenty-five selections by the glass.

WHAT ARE THE MOST UNIQUE FEATURES IN YOUR WINE PROGRAM?

We feature six flights that consist of three 2-ounce portions to compare and contrast wine styles and appellations. We have an extensive half-bottle program and unique offerings by the glass.

WHAT CATEGORY OF WINE IS THE BEST VALUE IN YOUR RESTAURANT?

Red Bordeaux.

NAME A COUPLE OF YOUR RESTAURANT'S SIGNATURE DISHES. WHAT TYPES OF WINE DO YOU PREFER TO RECOMMEND WITH EACH?

Pancetta-wrapped Sierra quail with California Sangiovese; rhubarb barbecue Berkshire pork chops and Coca-Cola-braised bacon with German Riesling.

Passionfish Restaurant

701 Lighthouse Avenue
Pacific Grove, California 93950
phone 831-655-3311 fax 831-655-3454
website www.passionfish.net

Ted Walter
OWNER, CHEF,
AND WINE BUYER

WHAT PART OF YOUR JOB DO YOU ENJOY THE MOST?
Recommending an obscure wine to diners and witnessing their excitement at a
new discovery.

NAME YOUR FAVORITE WINE DISTRICTS.
Martinborough, New Zealand, offers great Pinot Noir with lots of aging potential. Rioja is a great value for delicious wines.

NAME RECENT WINE DISCOVERIES THAT HAVE EXCITED YOU.
The 2001 Rieslings from Australia, with their great structure and balance.

WHAT WOULD YOU LIKE YOUR CUSTOMERS TO KNOW ABOUT YOU?
My daughter, Megan, has acquired my passion for wine and is studying winemaking at Adelaide University in Australia.

IF YOU WERE NOT IN THIS PROFESSION, WHAT WOULD YOU BE DOING?
I love design. I have a professional interest in houseware design such as table-
ware, plates, chairs, kitchens and restaurants.

DESCRIBE YOUR WINE SELECTIONS, BOTH BY THE GLASS AND ON YOUR LIST.
Our wine list is priced at retail. We have many rare and desirable wines for serious aficionados, and many delightfully obscure wines available for occasions
when customers feel adventurous.

NAME A COUPLE OF YOUR RESTAURANT'S SIGNATURE DISHES. WHAT
TYPES OF WINE DO YOU PREFER TO RECOMMEND WITH EACH?
Fresh Monterey Bay squid with a spicy orange-cilantro dipping sauce with
German Riesling Kabinett; Monterey sea bass with artichokes in a red
wine–basil fish fumet with Martinborough Pinot Noir.

IN THE PAST YEAR, WHAT WINES IN YOUR WINE PROGRAM HAVE CUS-
TOMERS BECOME MORE WILLING TO ORDER?
New Zealand Sauvignon Blanc, German Riesling, Oregon Pinot Noir, Spanish
reds, Australian Grenache.

The Plumed Horse

14555 Big Basin Way
Saratoga, California 95070
phone 408-867-4711 fax 408-867-6919
website www.plumedhorse.com

Paul S. Mekis
CELLAR MASTER

WHAT INSPIRED YOU TO PURSUE A CAREER THAT INVOLVES WINE?
Blind tastings in the early 1980s hosted by my friends and me, where we tasted wines from a specific varietal, discussed them, and compared notes. At the end of the evening was the grand unveiling.

NAME TWO OF YOUR FAVORITE WINE DISTRICTS FROM AROUND THE WORLD.
Santa Lucia Highlands in Monterey County, for its dark plum and full-flavored Pinot Noirs. And Priorat in Spain; its wines are inky, and have massive structure and ripe blackberry, chocolate and licorice flavors.

WHAT BITS OF INFORMATION WOULD YOU LIKE YOUR CUSTOMERS TO KNOW ABOUT YOU?
Don't challenge Paul to ping-pong, a pool game or anything else competitive.

WHAT ARE THE MOST UNIQUE FEATURES IN YOUR WINE PROGRAM?
We offer a tasting flight of top-rated wines by a 2-ounce or 5-ounce pour. On each placemat there is a description of the grape varietal and the winery's history.

WHAT CATEGORIES OF WINE ARE THE BEST VALUES IN YOUR RESTAURANT?
Older red Burgundies, South African wine, older German Riesling, Syrah and Paso Robles wines.

NAME A COUPLE OF YOUR RESTAURANT'S SIGNATURE DISHES. WHAT TYPES OF WINE DO YOU PREFER TO RECOMMEND WITH EACH?
Rack of lamb in our secret marinade with roasted garlic demi-glaze paired with a new style Côte-Rôtie or Syrah; pine-crusted ahi tuna seared rare with Pinot Noir.

IN THE PAST YEAR, WHAT WINES IN YOUR WINE PROGRAM HAVE CUSTOMERS BECOME MORE WILLING TO ORDER?
Oregon Pinot Noir; Washington Merlot and Cabernet; and Australian, New Zealand and South African wines in general.

Prima

1522 North Main Street
Walnut Creek, California 94596
phone 925-935-7780 fax 925-935-7780

J. D. (John) Massler

SOMMELIER
TEAM: MARCUS GARCIA,
ASSISTANT SOMMELIER

WHAT IS ONE OF YOUR ULTIMATE FOOD AND WINE PAIRINGS?
2000 Domaine Tempier Rosé with a bowl of steamed mussels—a little spicy.

DESCRIBE YOUR WINE SELECTIONS.
We have three wine lists: A 1,600-item, complete list from around the world; a
100-bottle "Selected List" (including a comparative tasting of five wines), with
twenty to twenty-five wines by the glass; and a dessert wine list.

WHAT IS YOUR FAVORITE WINE REGION?
I love everything about Provence. The wines are improving, especially Bandol,
and drink wonderfully with the Mediterranean cuisine of Provence.

WHAT LED YOU TO PURSUE A CAREER THAT INVOLVES WINE?
I've collected and loved wine for thirty years and have worked in all parts of the
restaurant business.

WHAT ARE THE BEST ASPECTS OF YOUR JOB?
I love all aspects of my job. My major challenge is keeping the waiters pumped
up about wine.

IF YOU WERE NOT A SOMMELIER, WHAT WOULD YOU BE DOING?
Another restaurant job: Owner, chef, waiter.

Rubicon

San Francisco, California 94111
phone 415-434-4100 fax 415-421-7648
website www.sfrubicon.com

Larry N. Stone
MASTER SOMMELIER
AND PARTNER

WHAT INSPIRED YOU TO PURSUE A CAREER THAT INVOLVES WINE?
A chance encounter with a bottle of 1967 Châteauneuf-du-Pape at an uncle's home.

NAME SOME OF YOUR FAVORITE WINE REGIONS FROM AROUND THE WORLD.
Napa Valley because of the elegance it has attained in its wines in such a short
time; Burgundy for the joyousness of its wines and the joie de vivre of its
vignerons; Tuscany for the renaissance of Sangiovese.

WHAT BITS OF INFORMATION WOULD YOU LIKE YOUR CUSTOMERS TO
KNOW ABOUT YOU?
I love classical and modern music and serve on the board of Kronos Quartet, as
well as on the Chicago Lyric Opera and the San Francisco Opera fundraising
committees.

IF YOU WERE NOT IN THIS PROFESSION, WHAT WOULD YOU BE DOING?
Making wine under the name of my daughter, Sirifa.

DESCRIBE YOUR WINE SELECTIONS, BOTH BY THE GLASS AND ON
YOUR LIST.
We have a comprehensive list selected for the current menu and value by the
glass. We are known for our selection of Napa Cabernet and Meritage,
Burgundy and Rhône wines and the values that we offer.

WHAT ARE THE MOST UNIQUE FEATURES IN YOUR WINE PROGRAM?
Many vertical selections of wines of consequence.

WHAT CATEGORIES OF WINE ARE THE BEST VALUES IN YOUR RESTAURANT?
German Riesling and Austrian Grüner Veltliner.

NAME A COUPLE OF YOUR RESTAURANT'S SIGNATURE DISHES. WHAT
TYPES OF WINE DO YOU PREFER TO RECOMMEND WITH EACH?
Pheasant with Pinot Noir from the Russian River; tuna tartare and New
Zealand Sauvignon Blanc; pork with Shiraz from McLaren Vale or Côte-Rôtie.

Sardine Factory

701 Wave Street
Monterey, California 93940
phone 831-373-3775 fax 831-373-4241
website www.sardinefactory.com

Marc S. Cutino
CELLAR MASTER

WHAT INSPIRED YOU TO PURSUE A CAREER THAT INVOLVES WINE?
Wine motivated me to be part of this restaurant, which is a family-run business.

WHAT PART OF YOUR JOB DO YOU ENJOY THE MOST?
Watching customers try wines new to them and being blown away.

NAME ONE OF YOUR FAVORITE WINE REGIONS.
Anything Italian. They are such great food wines and have recently had a string
of great vintages.

WHAT WOULD YOU LIKE YOUR CUSTOMERS TO KNOW ABOUT YOU?
I love to hike the Big Sur coastline.

IF YOU WERE NOT CELLAR MASTER HERE, WHAT WOULD YOU BE?
A chef.

DESCRIBE YOUR WINE SELECTIONS.
We have a very extensive list that covers all the important wine regions of the
world, with a special emphasis on local Monterey County wineries.

WHAT ARE THE MOST UNIQUE FEATURES IN YOUR WINE PROGRAM?
The depth of selection and pricing of our older Burgundies and Bordeaux, and
the private dining room in our famous wine cellar.

WHAT CATEGORIES OF WINE ARE THE BEST VALUES IN YOUR RESTAURANT?
German Riesling and older red Burgundies.

**NAME ONE OF YOUR RESTAURANT'S SIGNATURE DISHES. WHAT WINE DO
YOU PREFER TO RECOMMEND WITH IT?**
Seared coriander-crusted ahi tuna or a 16-ounce prime New York steak paired
with Santa Lucia Highlands Pinot Noir.

WHAT WINES ARE CUSTOMERS NOW MORE WILLING TO ORDER?
Rhône varietals, both red and white, from California and France.

Wente Vineyards Restaurant

5050 Arroyo Road
Livermore, California 94550
phone 925-456-2450 fax 925-456-2401
website www.wentevineyards.com

Jorge A. Tinoco
SOMMELIER

WHAT INSPIRED YOU TO PURSUE A CAREER THAT INVOLVES WINE?
One birthday, we enjoyed rib-eye steaks with a bottle of 1967 Mouton-Rothschild. That was the first time I felt a wine connection.

NAME ONE OF YOUR FAVORITE WINE REGIONS FROM AROUND THE WORLD.
Livermore Valley, with its long history and its very intense Cabernet Sauvignon, Merlot, Zinfandel and Sangiovese.

NAME RECENT WINE DISCOVERIES THAT HAVE EXCITED YOU.
New World Sangiovese generally; also, the Phoenix Vineyards wines by Steven Kent. These are exciting wines of good quality and value.

DESCRIBE YOUR WINE SELECTIONS, BOTH BY THE GLASS AND ON YOUR LIST.
Our by-the-glass selections represent the whole Livermore Valley, especially up-and-coming wineries. Our selection of dessert wines is something we're very proud of. It includes a fine selection of tawnies, vintage and colheita Portos as well as sweet wines from Inniskillen and Avignonesi. Our wine list, at about 500 wine selections, contains mostly California wine.

WHAT ARE THE MOST UNIQUE FEATURES IN YOUR WINE PROGRAM?
We have winemaker dinners and a series of concerts hosted right in the back of the restaurant. Past performers like Bill Cosby, Chris Isaak and Jewel keep coming back for a beautiful night at the vineyard.

WHAT CATEGORY OF WINE IS THE BEST VALUE IN YOUR RESTAURANT?
Zinfandel, because of its high quality and generally low price.

NAME A COUPLE OF YOUR RESTAURANT'S SIGNATURE DISHES. WHAT TYPES OF WINE DO YOU PREFER TO RECOMMEND WITH EACH?
Applewood-smoked pork chop and Monterey Pinot Noir or Zinfandel; fresh salmon and Livermore Valley Chardonnay.

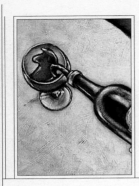

XYZ Restaurant at the W Hotel

181 Third Street
San Francisco, California 94103
phone 415-817-7836 fax 415-817-7873
website www.xyz-sf.com

Jerad J. Ruhl
FLOOR MANAGER
AND SOMMELIER

LIST ANY OF YOUR FORMAL WINE TRAINING, CERTIFICATES OR AWARDS.
Certificate Course, Court of Master Sommeliers.

WHAT INSPIRED YOU TO PURSUE A CAREER THAT INVOLVES WINE?
The fact that learning about wine is a never-ending process and that you can never know everything about it.

WHAT PART OF YOUR JOB DO YOU ENJOY THE MOST?
Making recommendations and watching the customer's response to something new.

NAME ONE OR TWO OF YOUR FAVORITE WINE DISTRICTS OR WINE REGIONS FROM AROUND THE WORLD.
Ribera del Duero from Spain for reds, and Kamptal in Austria for whites. Both are producing exciting wines at a lower price than most.

NAME RECENT WINE DISCOVERIES THAT HAVE EXCITED YOU.
Rosé Sancerre. I recently had the chance to taste it for the first time. The liveliness of this wine shocked me.

IF YOU WERE NOT IN THIS PROFESSION, WHAT WOULD YOU BE DOING?
Writing.

TO WHAT WINE ORGANIZATIONS OR SOCIETIES TO YOU BELONG?
Guild of Master Sommeliers.

DESCRIBE YOUR WINE SELECTIONS, BOTH BY THE GLASS AND ON YOUR LIST.
We specialize in a compact yet eclectic selection of wines with heavy influences from California and France.

WHAT CATEGORY OF WINE IS THE BEST VALUE IN YOUR RESTAURANT?
There are gems to be found in all categories.

Yabbies Coastal Kitchen

2237 Polk Street
San Francisco, California 94109
phone 415-474-4088 fax 415-474-4962
website www.yabbiesrestaurant.com

Windee B. Smith
OWNER AND WINE DIRECTOR

WHAT INSPIRED YOU TO PURSUE A CAREER THAT INVOLVES WINE?
Spending a summer with friends who had a 20,000-bottle cellar, I was able to try wines from all over the world.

WHAT PART OF YOUR JOB DO YOU ENJOY THE MOST?
Selling a bottle of wine to customers that they have never tried and seeing the smile of delight after the first sip.

NAME YOUR FAVORITE WINE DISTRICTS.
Carneros and Russian River Valley. I find that Pinot Noir goes well with our food, and these are my two favorite California Pinot regions.

NAME RECENT WINE DISCOVERIES THAT HAVE EXCITED YOU.
Pinot Noirs from Robledo, Sonoma Valley, and Castalia, Russian River Valley.

WHAT WOULD YOU LIKE YOUR CUSTOMERS TO KNOW ABOUT YOU?
Wine was my hobby in my twenties. I had never worked in a restaurant prior to opening Yabbies. I did it for the wine.

DESCRIBE YOUR WINE SELECTIONS, BOTH BY THE GLASS AND ON YOUR LIST.
Our selection features small California producers. Our wine program is all about making their wines available.

WHAT CATEGORIES OF WINE ARE THE BEST VALUES IN YOUR RESTAURANT?
California Pinot Noir and Sauvignon Blanc.

NAME A COUPLE OF YOUR RESTAURANT'S SIGNATURE DISHES. WHAT TYPES OF WINE DO YOU PREFER TO RECOMMEND WITH EACH?
Oysters with crisp Sauvignon Blanc; Thai snapper (spicy) with dry Gewürztraminer or German Riesling.

IN THE PAST YEAR, WHAT WINES IN YOUR WINE PROGRAM HAVE CUS-TOMERS BECOME MORE WILLING TO ORDER?
Pinot Noir and Sauvignon Blanc.

231 Ellsworth
RICHARD MILKOVICH, WINE
DIRECTOR
231 South Elllsworth Avenue, San Mateo
650-347-7231

A. Sabella's Restaurant
ANTONE SABELLA, SOMMELIER
2766 Taylor Street, San Francisco
415-771-6775

Absinthe Brasserie & Bar
NEAL MECHANIC, WINE BUYER
398 Hayes Street, San Francisco
415-551-1590

Asia de Cuba at the Clift Hotel
NICOLE BURKE, ASSISTANT MANAGER
AND WINE BUYER
495 Geary Street, San Francisco
415-775-4700

Azie
JOE MERLINO, BEVERAGE DIRECTOR
826 Folsom Street, San Francisco
415-538-0918

Bay Wolf Restaurant
MICHAEL WILD, OWNER
AND WINE BUYER
3853 Piedmont Avenue, Oakland
510-655-6004

Blackhawk Grille
KATE SCHUMACHER, SOMMELIER
3540 Black Hawk Plaza Circle, Danville
510-736-4295

Bob's Steak and Chop House
ERIK SANDSTEDT, MANAGER
AND WINE BUYER
500 California Street, San Francisco
415-273-3085

The Caprice
PAUL ROBERTS, WINE BUYER
2000 Paradise Drive, Tiburon
415-435-3400

Carnelian Room
MIKE AL-JABARI, SOMMELIER
555 California Street, San Francisco
415-433-7500

Le Central Bistro
PAUL TANPHANICH, WINE BUYER
453 Bush Street, San Francisco
415-391-2233

Charles Nob Hill
JANE RATE, SOMMELIER
1250 Jones Street, San Francisco
415-771-5400

Chez Panisse
JONATHAN WATERS, WINE BUYER
1517 Shattuck Avenue, Berkeley
510-548-5525

Cielo at Ventana Inn and Spa
MATTHEW HISCOCK, WINE BUYER
Big Sur Highway 1, Big Sur
831-667-2331

Club XIX at The Lodge at Pebble Beach
JOHN WINFIELD, BEVERAGE MANAGER
Seventeen Mile Drive, Pebble Beach
831-625-8519

The Cosmopolitan Café
ROY AUSTIN, SOMMELIER
121 Spear Street, San Francisco
415-543-4001

The Covey at Quail Lodge

KEN PERRY, MANAGER
AND WINE BUYER
8205 Valley Greens Drive, Carmel
831-624-2888

Cozmo's Corner Grill

ROY AUSTIN, WINE DIRECTOR
2001 Chestnut Street, San Francisco
415-351-0175

Dal Baffo

VINCENZO LOGRASMO, CHEF,
OWNER AND WINE BUYER
878 Santa Cruz Avenue, Menlo Park
650-325-1588

Domenico's on the Wharf

JUHRIE SIVLOVE, WINE BUYER
50 Fisherman's Wharf, Monterey
831-372-3655

Eastside West Restaurant and Bar

JOHN MARRS, SOMMELIER
3154 Fillmore Street, San Francisco
415-885-4000

Elizabeth Daniel Restaurant

BRITT GUILDERSLEEVE, SOMMELIER
550 Washington Street, San Francisco
415-397-6129

EOS Restaurant

DARIN SNOW, WINE DIRECTOR
901 Cole Street, San Francisco
415-566-3063

Fandango

PIERRE BAIN, WINE BUYER
223 17th Avenue, Pacific Grove
831-372-3456

Fior d'Italia

GIANNI ANDIERI, CHEF
AND WINE BUYER
601 Union Street, San Francisco
415-986-1886

First Crush Restaurant

JESSE SCHWARTZ, SOMMELIER
101 Cyril Magnin Street, San Francisco
415-982-7874

Fleur de Lys

MICKEY CLEVINGER, WINE BUYER
777 Sutter Street, San Francisco
415-673-7779

Il Fornaio

SUE PEY, CORPORATE WINE BUYER
223 Town Center, Corte Madera
415-927-4400

Fournou's Ovens at the Stanford Court Hotel

ROLF BUEHLMANN,
RESTAURANT MANAGER
905 California Street, San Francisco
415-989-1910

Frascati

RICH WOOD, WINE BUYER
1901 Hyde Street, San Francisco
415-928-1406

Fresh Cream Restaurant

STEVE CHESNY, WINE BUYER
99 Pacific Street, Monterey
831-375-9798

Globe

MARY KLINGBEIL, CO-OWNER
AND WINE BUYER
290 Pacific Avenue, San Francisco
415-391-4132

Grasing's

KURT GRUSSING, WINE BUYER
Sixth and Mission Streets, Carmel
831-624-6562

The Grill on the Alley

PHILIPPE AZOULAY, WINE DIRECTOR
AND GENERAL MANAGER
172 South Market Street, San Jose
408-294-2244

Hap's

MIKE CONNORS, WINE BUYER
122 West Neal Street, Pleasanton
925-600-9200

Harris' Restaurant

JONATHAN TENNENBAUM,
WINE BUYER
2100 Van Ness Avenue, San Francisco
415-673-1888

Hawthorne Lane

NABILE ABI'GHANEM, SOMMELIER
22 Hawthorne Street, San Francisco
415-777-9779

Hayes Street Grill

RICHARD SANDERS, SOMMELIER
320 Hayes Street, San Francisco
415-863-5545

Jordan's at the Claremont Resort & Spa

DOUGLAS SMITH, WINE BUYER
41 Tunnel Road, Berkeley
510-843-3000

Julius' Castle Restaurant

JEFFREY POLLACK, OWNER
AND WINE BUYER
1541 Montgomery Street, San Francisco
415-362-3042

Kingfish

ROBERT KIRKBRIDE, WINE BUYER
201 South B Street, San Mateo
650-343-1226

Kuleto's Trattoria

LEANNE KAUFMAN, WINE BUYER
1095 Rollins Road, Burlingame
650-342-4922

Lafayette Park Hotel

JAY LIFSON, FOOD AND
BEVERAGE DIRECTOR
3287 Mount Diablo Boulevard, Lafayette
925-283-3700

Lark Creek Inn

JORDAN MUSICANT, BAR MANAGER
234 Magnolia Avenue, Larkspur
415-924-7766

Left Bank

LANCE BELLAMY, WINE BUYER
60 Crescent Drive, Pleasant Hill
925-288-1222

London Wine Bar

GARY LOCKE, WINE BUYER
415 Sansome Street, San Francisco
415-788-4811

Los Gatos Brewing Co.

RANDY BERTO, SOMMELIER
130-G North Santa Cruz Avenue, Los Gatos
408-395-9929

Lulu
JOE MERLINO, WINE BUYER
816 Folsom Street, San Francisco
415-495-5775

Manka's Inverness Lodge
MARGRITT GRAADE, WINE BUYER
30 Callendar Way, Inverness
415-669-1034

Marinus Restaurant at Bernardus Lodge
MARK JENSEN, WINE DIRECTOR
415 Carmel Valley Road, Carmel Valley
831-658-3500

Masa's
ALAN MURRAY, SOMMELIER
648 Bush Street, San Francisco
415-989-7154

MC2
BRIAN HOWARD, GENERAL MANAGER
AND WINE BUYER
470 Pacific Avenue, San Francisco
415-956-0666

Mecca
GENE TARTAGLIA, OWNER
AND WINE BUYER
2029 Market Street, San Francisco
415-621-7000

Montrio
DANA MEIKIRK, WINE DIRECTOR
414 Calle Principal, Monterey
831-648-8880

Moose's
BURTON BRADLEY, WINE DIRECTOR
1652 Stockton Street, San Francisco
415-989-7800

Morton's of Chicago
VEDRAN KOMAZEC, SOMMELIER
400 Post Street, San Francisco
415-986-5830

Nepenthe Restaurant
LONE PETERSON, SOMMELIER
Highway 1, Big Sur
831-667-2345

North Beach Restaurant
LORENZO PETRONI, WINE BUYER
1512 Stockton, San Francisco
415-392-1587

Old Bath House Restaurant
GARY VAN DENDRIES, SOMMELIER
620 Ocean View, Pacific Grove
831-375-5195

Oliveto
JOHN BATES, WINE STEWARD
5655 College Avenue, Oakland
510-547-5356

One Market Restaurant
STEVE IZZO, SOMMELIER
AND WINE BUYER
One Market Street, San Francisco
415-777-5577

Palio d'Asti
GIANNI FASSIO, WINE BUYER
640 Sacramento Street, San Francisco
415-395-9800

Paolo's Restaurant
JALIL SAMAVAVARCHIAN, SOMMELIER
333 West San Carlos Street #150, San Jose
408-294-2558

Le Papillon Restaurant

CAMERON MASHAYEKH, WINE BUYER

410 Saratoga Avenue, San Jose

408-296-3730

Park Grill
at the Park Hyatt Hotel

PETER DONNELLY, FOOD AND

BEVERAGE DIRECTOR

333 Battery Street, Embarcadero Center,

San Francisco

415-392-1234

El Paseo

GUNTHER KELLNER, WINE BUYER

7 El Paseo Lane, Mill Valley

415-388-0741

Patrick David's

BOB CASCERDO, WINE BUYER

416 Sycamore Valley Road West, Danville

925-838-7611

Pearl Alley Bistro

MARK CURTIS, SOMMELIER

110 Pearl Alley, Santa Cruz

831-429-8070

Peppoli
at the Inn at Spanish Bay

JOHN WINTHROP, BEVERAGE DIRECTOR

2700 17 Mile Drive, Pebble Beach

831-647-7433

Piacere

TONY GUNDOGDU, SOMMELIER

727 Laurel Street, San Carlos

650-592-3536

Plumpjack Café

ROSIE GIBSON, SOMMELIER

3127 Fillmore Street, San Francisco

415-563-4755

Postrio

BJORN KOCK, WINE BUYER

545 Post Street, San Francisco

415-776-7825

Rio Grill

BRENT PUCHRIK, WINE BUYER

101 Crossroads Boulevard, Carmel

831-625-5437

Rose Pistola

JAMES ATWOOD, WINE DIRECTOR

532 Columbus Avenue, San Francisco

415-399-0499

Roy's of San Francisco

J. DIETRECH, WINE BUYER

101 Second Street, San Francisco

415-777-0277

Ruth's Chris
Steak House

BILL PARDY, SOMMELIER

1601 Van Ness Avenue, San Francisco

415-673-0557

Scala's Bistro
at the Sir Francis Drake

RAND NIELSEN, SOMMELIER

432 Powell Street, San Francisco

415-392-7755

Shadowbrook Restaurant

TED BURKE, OWNER AND WINE BUYER

1750 Wharf Road, Capitola

831-475-1511

Shanghai 1930

GEORGE CHEN, WINE BUYER

133 Steuart Street, San Francisco

415-896-5600

Sierra Mar
at the Post Ranch Inn
DOMINIQUE DA CRUZ, WINE BUYER
Highway 1, Big Sur
831-667-2800

Silks
at the Mandarin Oriental
CRAIG TUPPER, SOMMELIER
222 Sansome Street, San Francisco
415-986-2020

Slanted Door
MARK ELLENBOGEN, SOMMELIER
100 Brannan Street, San Francisco
415-861-8032

Solano Grill and Bar
PHILIP CHEN, SOMMELIER
1133 Solano Avenue, Albany
510-525-8686

Spago Palo Alto
ALEX RESNIC, WINE BUYER
265 Lytton Avenue, Palo Alto
650-833-1000

Spivac's Restaurant
RACHEL SPIVAC, CHEF
AND WINE BUYER
5635 Silver Creek Valley Road, San Jose
408-528-1203

Sundance
The Steakhouse
ARON FLETCHER, WINE BUYER
1921 El Camino Real, Palo Alto
650-321-6798

Tommy Toy's Restaurant
STEVE LEE, WINE BUYER
655 Montgomery Street, San Francisco
415-397-4888

Valhalla Restaurant
NUNZIO ALIOTO, PRESIDENT,
GENERAL MANAGER AND
MASTER SOMMELIER
201 Bridgeway, Sausalito, San Fransisco
415-332-2777

The Village Pub
MARK SULLIVAN, CHEF
AND WINE BUYER
2967 Woodside Road, Woodside
650-851-9888

Viognier
KEN KNOX, WINE BUYER
222 East Fourth Street, San Mateo
650-685-3727

Waterfront Restaurant
AL FALCHI, WINE BUYER
Pier 7 at Embarcardero, San Francisco
415-391-2696

Zibibbo
JOE MERLINO, WINE BUYER
430 Kipling Street, Palo Alto
650-328-6722

Zuni Café
STEVEN KOPP, SOMMELIER
1658 Market Street, San Francisco
415-552-2522

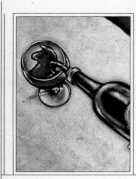

All Seasons Bistro and Wine Shop

1400 Lincoln Avenue
Calistoga, California 94515
phone 707-942-9111 fax 707-942-9420
website www.allseasonsnapavalley.com

Sean Q. Meyer
SOMMELIER

WHAT INSPIRED YOU TO PURSUE A CAREER THAT INVOLVES WINE?
I have a great passion for food and wine.

NAME ONE OF YOUR FAVORITE WINE REGIONS FROM AROUND THE WORLD.
The northern Rhône. There is just so much variety and expression, even with the same varietal.

NAME RECENT WINE DISCOVERIES THAT HAVE EXCITED YOU.
The wines of South Africa are amazing, and its Shiraz is rapidly becoming one of my favorites.

WHAT BITS OF INFORMATION WOULD YOU LIKE YOUR CUSTOMERS TO KNOW ABOUT YOU?
My undergraduate degree is in opera performance. I also love water sports such as kayaking, scuba, snorkeling, sailing and water skiing.

IF YOU WERE NOT IN THIS PROFESSION, WHAT WOULD YOU BE?
A race car driver.

WHAT ARE THE MOST UNIQUE FEATURES IN YOUR WINE PROGRAM?
There is an on-premise wine shop, so the restaurant sells all of our offerings at retail plus a small corkage fee.

NAME A COUPLE OF YOUR RESTAURANT'S SIGNATURE DISHES. WHAT TYPES OF WINE DO YOU PREFER TO RECOMMEND WITH EACH?
Perigord truffle chip ice cream with an Austrian Scheurebe dessert wine; salmon tartare with crispy taro root, wakame seaweed salad and wasabi emulsion paired with an Alsace Riesling.

IN THE PAST YEAR, WHAT WINES IN YOUR WINE PROGRAM HAVE CUSTOMERS BECOME MORE WILLING TO ORDER?
Spanish wines. I am very excited about this, as the wines are particularly wonderful with food.

Applewood Inn and Restaurant

13555 Highway 116
Guerneville, California 95446
phone 707-869-9093 fax 707-869-9170
website www.applewoodinn.com

Chad Gardner

RESTAURANT MANAGER

WHAT PART OF YOUR JOB DO YOU ENJOY THE MOST?
Introducing guests to new and unique wines, then watching the surprised and delighted expressions on their faces.

NAME ONE OF YOUR FAVORITE WINE REGIONS FROM AROUND THE WORLD.
Sonoma County's Russian River Valley because I grew up here and I feel a deeply rooted connection to the earth, climate and wines that are produced.

WHAT BITS OF INFORMATION WOULD YOU LIKE YOUR CUSTOMERS TO KNOW ABOUT YOU?
I enjoy boating, skiing, classic movies, entertaining friends at home and traveling.

IF YOU WERE NOT IN THIS PROFESSION, WHAT WOULD YOU BE DOING?
I can't imagine myself doing anything other than what I'm doing right now.

WHAT ARE THE MOST UNIQUE FEATURES IN YOUR WINE PROGRAM?
Reasonably priced, hard-to-find Sonoma County wines.

NAME A COUPLE OF YOUR RESTAURANT'S SIGNATURE DISHES. WHAT TYPES OF WINE DO YOU PREFER TO RECOMMEND WITH EACH?
Our menu changes constantly. Now we are offering a lightly curried cauliflower soup with pear salad that I would pair with a crisp, clean Sauvignon Blanc; and seared Maine dayboat scallops with vanilla orange and warm spring vegetable salad paired with a complex and full-bodied Chardonnay.

IN THE PAST YEAR, WHAT WINES IN YOUR WINE PROGRAM HAVE CUS-TOMERS BECOME MORE WILLING TO ORDER?
The relatively rare wines we feature in our by-the-glass program (such as Williams Selyem Sonoma County Pinot Noir 2000).

Carneros Restaurant at the Lodge at Sonoma

1325 Broadway Street
Sonoma, California 95476
phone 707-931-2042 fax 707-931-2047
website www.carnerosrestaurant.com

Kimberly Z. Fallon
WINE STEWARD

WHAT PART OF YOUR JOB DO YOU ENJOY THE MOST?

Discovering new and historic producers, vineyards and life stories, and then sharing that information with servers and guests; also, facilitating the highest food and wine pairing experiences for our guests.

NAME ONE OF YOUR FAVORITE WINE REGIONS FROM AROUND THE WORLD.

My native state, California, because the viticulture is evolving constantly.

NAME RECENT WINE DISCOVERIES THAT HAVE EXCITED YOU.

Chalk Hill Pinot Gris is rich and layered, unlike most other California examples. Peter Michael Le Moulin Rouge Pinot Noir is a deep, extracted and velvety expression of this varietal.

WHAT BITS OF INFORMATION WOULD YOU LIKE YOUR CUSTOMERS TO KNOW ABOUT YOU?

My husband and I moved to Sonoma County to raise our family in this agricultural and wine-producing community. We strive to be productive, contributing members of the community.

WHAT CATEGORIES OF WINE ARE THE BEST VALUES IN YOUR RESTAURANT?

Dry Creek Zinfandel and Russian River and Carneros Pinot Noir and Chardonnay.

NAME A COUPLE OF YOUR RESTAURANT'S SIGNATURE DISHES. WHAT TYPES OF WINE DO YOU PREFER TO RECOMMEND WITH EACH?

Wood oven-smoked rotisserie rib-eye with Knights Valley Meritage red; in-season halibut with crab-smashed potatoes, morel mushrooms and cherry tomatoes with corn nage paired with Carneros Chardonnay.

IN THE PAST YEAR, WHAT WINES IN YOUR WINE PROGRAM HAVE CUSTOMERS BECOME MORE WILLING TO ORDER?

Sonoma County Pinot Blanc and Pinot Gris, Syrah, wines from mountain fruit sources and vineyard-designated wines.

Cole's Chop House

1122 Main Street
Napa, California 94559
phone 707-224-6328 fax 707-254-9692

Greg R. Gevurtz
WINE DIRECTOR

WHAT INSPIRED YOU TO PURSUE A CAREER THAT INVOLVES WINE?
I enjoy trying menus and learning about wine. I am a chef also, so it is natural for me to incorporate wine knowledge with my culinary experience.

WHAT PART OF YOUR JOB DO YOU ENJOY THE MOST?
Learning about wine, how the grapes are grown and then made into wine.

NAME TWO OF YOUR FAVORITE WINE REGIONS FROM AROUND THE WORLD.
Napa Valley, because I live here and enjoy being part of a community that makes great wines; Burgundy, France, because I really like its Pinot Noir and Chardonnay.

WHAT BITS OF INFORMATION WOULD YOU LIKE YOUR CUSTOMERS TO KNOW ABOUT YOU?
I am also a chef, and I really enjoy the restaurant business, especially meeting people and entertaining guests.

DESCRIBE YOUR WINE SELECTIONS, BOTH BY THE GLASS AND ON YOUR LIST.
We serve wonderful steaks and chops and our wine list reflects this. We specialize in high-end red wines and wines from local and boutique wineries.

WHAT ARE THE MOST UNIQUE FEATURES IN YOUR WINE PROGRAM?
We have a good variety of wines from lesser-known producers and a large selection of Cabernet Sauvignons and proprietary blends.

NAME ONE OF YOUR RESTAURANT'S SIGNATURE DISHES. WHAT WINE DO YOU PREFER TO RECOMMEND WITH IT?
Our dry-aged New York steak with Napa or Carneros Syrahs or Napa Valley Cabernet Sauvignons.

IN THE PAST YEAR, WHAT WINES IN YOUR WINE PROGRAM HAVE CUSTOMERS BECOME MORE WILLING TO ORDER?
California Rhône varietals, dessert wines and Portos.

Equus Restaurant at the Fountain Grove Inn

101 Fountain Grove Parkway
Santa Rosa, California 95403
phone 707-578-6101 fax 707-544-3126
website www.fountaingroveinn.com

Larry Van Aalst
SOMMELIER

WHAT INSPIRED YOU TO PURSUE A CAREER THAT INVOLVES WINE?
A search for truth, because "In wine there's truth."

WHAT PART OF YOUR JOB DO YOU ENJOY THE MOST?
The hospitality that this Wine Country affords.

NAME ONE OF YOUR FAVORITE WINE DISTRICTS FROM AROUND THE WORLD.
California's Russian River produces my favorite Pinot Noir, Chardonnay and Sauvignon Blanc. The great fruit makes for bold wines.

NAME RECENT WINE DISCOVERIES THAT HAVE EXCITED YOU.
Spanish Grenache for value and unique style.

WHAT BITS OF INFORMATION WOULD YOU LIKE YOUR CUSTOMERS TO KNOW ABOUT YOU?
Roller-coaster riding and snorkeling in the southern hemisphere.

DESCRIBE YOUR WINE SELECTIONS, BOTH BY THE GLASS AND ON YOUR LIST.
Our selection is Sonoma County with a great quality-to-price ratio. We also have the best selections from other areas.

WHAT ARE THE MOST UNIQUE FEATURES IN YOUR WINE PROGRAM?
Our flights and our specials on "Winemaker Friday" every week.

WHAT CATEGORY OF WINE IS THE BEST VALUE IN YOUR RESTAURANT?
Great Sonoma County Zinfandels.

NAME A COUPLE OF YOUR RESTAURANT'S SIGNATURE DISHES. WHAT TYPES OF WINE DO YOU PREFER TO RECOMMEND WITH EACH?
Hardwood-grilled beef with Dry Creek Zinfandel; local rabbit with Russian River Sauvignon Blanc.

IN THE PAST YEAR, WHAT WINES IN YOUR WINE PROGRAM HAVE CUSTOMERS BECOME MORE WILLING TO ORDER?
Local Pinot Gris.

The French Laundry

6640 Washington Street
Yountville, California 94599
phone 707-944-2380 fax 707-944-1974
website www.frenchlaundry.com

Paul N. Roberts

WINE DIRECTOR AND MASTER SOMMELIER
TEAM: NATE READY, SOMMELIER

WHAT INSPIRED YOU TO PURSUE A CAREER THAT INVOLVES WINE?
The first great glass of wine that I experienced in a wine-tasting class—a 1970 Latour.

WHAT PART OF YOUR JOB DO YOU ENJOY THE MOST?
The constant balance between the business aspect and the emotional aspect of the business, which can truly raise the overall experience.

NAME ONE OF YOUR FAVORITE WINE REGIONS FROM AROUND THE WORLD.
Mosel-Saar-Ruwer. The delicate nature of Mosel Riesling makes for the most dynamic food match in the world.

NAME RECENT WINE DISCOVERIES THAT HAVE EXCITED YOU.
Jumilla in Spain. Its wines are remarkable values that display fruit and structure that will appeal to any person who usually drinks New World wine.

WHAT BITS OF INFORMATION WOULD YOU LIKE YOUR CUSTOMERS TO KNOW ABOUT YOU?
I love gifts of wine from their personal cellars.

IF YOU WERE NOT IN THIS PROFESSION, WHAT WOULD YOU BE DOING?
Living off my wife.

DESCRIBE YOUR WINE SELECTIONS, BOTH BY THE GLASS AND ON YOUR LIST.
Subtle selections based upon balance and finesse.

WHAT WINES ARE THE BEST VALUES IN YOUR RESTAURANT?
Collioure and Marsannay.

NAME ONE OF YOUR RESTAURANT'S SIGNATURE DISHES. WHAT WINE DO YOU PREFER TO RECOMMEND WITH IT?
Pig's head and bacon and eggs. Chef Keller rolls out the skin and stuffs it with sweetbreads, pig's ear and cheek meat, which is sautéed and served with a poached quail egg. It's great with Châteauneuf-du-Pape.

Glen Ellen Inn Restaurant

13670 Arnold Drive
Glen Ellen, California 95442
phone 707-996-6409 fax 707-996-1634
website www.glenelleninn.com

Karen J. Bertrand
CO-OWNER AND "WINE ANGEL"

WHAT INSPIRED YOU TO PURSUE A CAREER THAT INVOLVES WINE?
My husband is a chef, and we love food and wine.

NAME TWO OF YOUR FAVORITE WINE REGIONS FROM AROUND THE WORLD.
Sonoma Valley and Napa Valley. This is the "New Wild West," where wine is bold. I am happy to live in the most exciting wine area in the world.

NAME RECENT WINE DISCOVERIES THAT HAVE EXCITED YOU.
I really love the new style of Chardonnay. It has style with very light to no oak, with full malolactic fermentation.

WHAT BITS OF INFORMATION WOULD YOU LIKE YOUR CUSTOMERS TO KNOW ABOUT YOU?
I have a beautiful four-year-old who keeps me running all day long.

IF YOU WERE NOT IN THIS PROFESSION, WHAT WOULD YOU BE DOING?
I can't imagine anything else. The restaurant is my life!

WHAT ARE THE MOST UNIQUE FEATURES IN YOUR WINE PROGRAM?
We are the smallest restaurant with the biggest wine list (twenty-four tables, 600 wines).

WHAT CATEGORY OF WINE IS THE BEST VALUE IN YOUR RESTAURANT?
Value is determined by being satisfied with your wine selection. All of our pricing on wine is very fair.

NAME ONE OF YOUR RESTAURANT'S SIGNATURE DISHES. WHAT WINE DO YOU PREFER TO RECOMMEND WITH IT?
We have a lovely Dungeness crab pot sticker with leek cream and soy oil that pairs delightfully with Sonoma Sauvignon Blanc.

IN THE PAST YEAR, WHAT WINES IN YOUR WINE PROGRAM HAVE CUSTOMERS BECOME MORE WILLING TO ORDER?
Syrah.

Langleys on the Green

610 McClelland
Windsor, California 95492
phone 707-837-7984
website www.langleysonthegreen.com

Walter R. Inman
WINE AND BEVERAGE DIRECTOR
AND SOMMELIER

WHAT INSPIRED YOU TO PURSUE A CAREER THAT INVOLVES WINE?
My mother told me I needed a summer job, so I started in production and
quickly fell in love with wine.

WHAT PART OF YOUR JOB DO YOU ENJOY THE MOST?
Tasting some of the best wines in the world and getting paid for it.

NAME TWO OF YOUR FAVORITE WINE REGIONS FROM AROUND THE WORLD.
The Rhône Valley and Alsace. The Rhône offers such a wide array of wines,
from powerful and meaty to soft and delicate. Alsace offers great refreshing
wines that are perfect with food.

NAME RECENT WINE DISCOVERIES THAT HAVE EXCITED YOU.
German Riesling for its quality, value and many strong vintages; Spanish wines
for their great quality and prices.

IF YOU WERE NOT IN THIS PROFESSION, WHAT WOULD YOU BE?
A scuba instructor or treasure hunting.

WHAT ARE THE MOST UNIQUE FEATURES IN YOUR WINE PROGRAM?
Our wine list rotates with the menu, is ever-changing and focuses on food and
wine pairing. Each course has multiple wine pairing recommendations and the
wines are organized by weight.

WHAT CATEGORY OF WINE IS THE BEST VALUE IN YOUR RESTAURANT?
We think that the whole wine program offers value.

NAME A COUPLE OF YOUR RESTAURANT'S SIGNATURE DISHES. WHAT
TYPES OF WINE DO YOU PREFER TO RECOMMEND WITH EACH?
Pot stickers with German Riesling; seared ahi with Pinot Noir.

IN THE PAST YEAR, WHAT WINES IN YOUR WINE PROGRAM HAVE CUS-
TOMERS BECOME MORE WILLING TO ORDER?
Spanish Tempranillo and Italian Pinot Grigio.

Martini House

1245 Spring Street
St. Helena, California 94574
phone 707-963-2233 fax 707-967-9237
website www.kuleto.com/Martini.htm

Lisa E. Minucci
SOMMELIER

WHAT INSPIRED YOU TO PURSUE A CAREER THAT INVOLVES WINE?
I worked in retail in New York City and learned a great deal, especially about French and German wines, so I decided to study wine seriously.

WHAT PART OF YOUR JOB DO YOU ENJOY THE MOST?
Working with the chef to create sublime matches, introducing guests to new wines and regions and pairing wines to specific dishes.

NAME ONE OF YOUR FAVORITE WINE REGIONS FROM AROUND THE WORLD.
Napa Valley. Its best wines are produced by creative, fastidious winemakers interested in achieving the absolute best.

NAME A RECENT WINE DISCOVERY THAT EXCITED YOU.
Aglianico from Italy for its quality-to-price ratio.

IF YOU WERE NOT IN THIS PROFESSION, WHAT WOULD YOU BE?
An art restorer, an antique dealer or a diplomat.

DESCRIBE YOUR WINE SELECTIONS, BOTH BY THE GLASS AND ON YOUR LIST.
We feature more than forty-five wines by the glass and an international selection of 700 wines on our wine list. Most wines are from smaller producers.

NAME A FEW OF YOUR RESTAURANT'S SIGNATURE DISHES. WHAT TYPES OF WINE DO YOU PREFER TO RECOMMEND WITH EACH?
Venison and game sauce with Napa Valley Cabernet Sauvignon; foie gras with Tokaji Aszù; lobster with white Burgundy; veal cheeks with Willamette Valley Pinot Noir; cheese with Northern Italy white wines; chocolate desserts with tawny Portos.

IN THE PAST YEAR, WHAT WINES IN YOUR WINE PROGRAM HAVE CUS-TOMERS BECOME MORE WILLING TO ORDER?
Australian Riesling and Grüner Veltliner, German and Alsatian Riesling and Oregon Pinot Noir.

Pinot Blanc

641 Main Street
St. Helena, California 94574
phone 707-963-6191 fax 707-963-6192

Ronald D. Wolf
MANAGER AND WINE BUYER

WHAT INSPIRED YOU TO PURSUE A CAREER THAT INVOLVES WINE?
I was a brewer for Anchor Steam Beer in 1976–77. Upon returning home to Portland, Oregon, my wife gave me a twelve-week Wines of the World course from Harris Wine Cellars as my Christmas gift.

NAME ONE OR TWO OF YOUR FAVORITE WINE DISTRICTS OR WINE REGIONS FROM AROUND THE WORLD.
Alsace and Burgundy. These regions produce some of the most exciting, food-friendly wines in the world. Inspirational!

WHAT BITS OF INFORMATION WOULD YOU LIKE YOUR CUSTOMERS TO KNOW ABOUT YOU?
I brew, barbecue, hike, fish, camp under the stars and head to the beach to shuck oysters.

WHAT ARE THE MOST UNIQUE FEATURES IN YOUR WINE PROGRAM?
We have more than twenty by-the-glass wines and fifty-five half-bottles. As our season starts, we'll expand and offer flights and daily specials.

WHAT CATEGORIES OF WINE ARE THE BEST VALUES IN YOUR RESTAURANT?
Riesling, Viognier, Pinot Noir, Zinfandel and Syrah offer the best values.

NAME A COUPLE OF YOUR RESTAURANT'S SIGNATURE DISHES. WHAT TYPES OF WINE DO YOU PREFER TO RECOMMEND WITH EACH?
Foie gras with Tokaji Aszù 5 Puttonyos; ricotta gnocchi with braised veal cheeks paired with Pinot Noir or Zinfandel from Napa, Sonoma or the Central Coast.

IN THE PAST YEAR, WHAT WINES IN YOUR WINE PROGRAM HAVE CUSTOMERS BECOME MORE WILLING TO ORDER?
German Riesling, Oregon Pinot Noir, Santa Lucia Highlands Pinot Noir and old-vine Zinfandel from anywhere.

Rendezvous Inn and Restaurant

647 North Main Street
Fort Bragg, California 95437
phone 707-964-8142
website www.rendezvousinn.com

Kim Badenhop
OWNER, CHEF AND WINE BUYER

WHAT INSPIRED YOU TO PURSUE A CAREER THAT INVOLVES WINE?
One night I was dining and staying at Georges Blanc. I decided that if I were ever to start enjoying wine this would probably be the place. I had a half-bottle of Bâtard-Montrachet with my dinner.

NAME ONE OF YOUR FAVORITE WINE REGIONS FROM AROUND THE WORLD.
Alsace for the various styles of wine produced, and also the price-to-quality ratio offered.

NAME A RECENT WINE DISCOVERY THAT EXCITED YOU.
Limerick Lane's Late Harvest Furmint, made in the style of a Tokaji.

WHAT WOULD YOU LIKE YOUR CUSTOMERS TO KNOW ABOUT YOU?
While pursuing a career on Wall Street, I attended restaurant school, moonlighting as a chef.

IF YOU WERE NOT IN THIS PROFESSION, WHAT WOULD YOU BE DOING?
It's hard to imagine doing anything else.

NAME A FEW OF YOUR RESTAURANT'S SIGNATURE DISHES. WHAT TYPES OF WINE DO YOU PREFER TO RECOMMEND WITH EACH?
Rack of spring lamb with ratatouille and a red wine reduction sauce with chicken livers and anchovies paired with a California red Rhône-style blend; roasted loin of venison with an Anderson Valley Zinfandel; pan-seared Muscovy duck breast with a huckleberry-lavender sauce paired with a Russian River Valley Pinot Noir.

IN THE PAST YEAR, WHAT WINES IN YOUR WINE PROGRAM HAVE CUSTOMERS BECOME MORE WILLING TO ORDER?
Sauvignon Blanc and Pinot Noir.

WHAT ARE SOME OTHER ULTIMATE WINE AND FOOD PAIRINGS?
Corn on the cob with a slightly off-dry Riesling with good acidity. Each summer, my wife and I have our annual corn and Riesling dinner.

Restaurant 301
at the Hotel Carter

301 L Street
Eureka, California 95501
phone 707-444-8062 fax 707-444-8067
website www.carterhouse.com

Mark J. Carter
WINE DIRECTOR

WHAT INSPIRED YOU TO PURSUE A CAREER THAT INVOLVES WINE?
Opening the restaurant, inn and hotel began my career in wine buying sixteen years ago. I also have Italian roots, and wine was always a part of dinner with my grandparents.

WHAT PART OF YOUR JOB DO YOU ENJOY THE MOST?
Getting to personally know the winemakers and vintners from my favorite wineries and developing personal and business relationships with them.

NAME TWO OF YOUR FAVORITE WINES FROM AROUND THE WORLD.
Napa Valley Cabernet Sauvignon is my favorite (surprise!). I also enjoy Oregon Pinot Noir. Eureka is approximately halfway between Napa and Oregon, and I've always had a strong tendency toward "local flavor."

NAME RECENT WINE DISCOVERIES THAT HAVE EXCITED YOU.
The beginning of a new wine region right here in Humboldt County, California.

WHAT ARE THE MOST UNIQUE FEATURES IN YOUR WINE PROGRAM?
The enormous (approximately 3,800-bottle) wine list is constantly evolving and is my pride and joy. I like to offer a 2.5-ounce pour to a full-glass pour. The food and wine pairings of Restaurant 301's "Discovery Menu" are unforgettable.

WHAT CATEGORIES OF WINE ARE THE BEST VALUES IN YOUR RESTAURANT?
From Italy, Chianti; from France, Sancerre. Chilean wines as well.

NAME A COUPLE OF YOUR RESTAURANT'S SIGNATURE DISHES. WHAT TYPES OF WINE DO YOU PREFER TO RECOMMEND WITH EACH?
Fresh Dungeness crab and homemade mayonnaise with a crisp Viognier, Sancerre or Riesling; salmon in beurre blanc with Oregon Pinot Gris; grilled steak and lightly salted French fries with Napa Valley Cabernet Sauvignon.

River's End Restaurant and Inn

11048 Highway One
Jenner, California 95450
phone 707-865-2484 fax 707-865-9621
website www.rivers-end.com

Bert Rangel
OWNER AND WINE BUYER

WHAT INSPIRED YOU TO PURSUE A CAREER THAT INVOLVES WINE?
During a salmon tasting, a server brought me a glass of Paul Hobbs Chardonnay. The salmon was elevated to another level. It was a revelation in my culinary career.

WHAT PART OF YOUR JOB DO YOU ENJOY THE MOST?
If I can make a wine recommendation that makes a memorable dining experience, I've done my job.

NAME TWO OF YOUR FAVORITE WINE DISTRICTS FROM AROUND THE WORLD.
Russian River Valley and Sonoma Coast. I enjoy drinking Chardonnay and Pinot Noir. These regions are rich in complexity and variety.

NAME RECENT WINE DISCOVERIES THAT HAVE EXCITED YOU.
Pinot Noir made by different wineries from the same vineyard, Pisoni Vineyards, in the Santa Lucia Highlands. All versions were beautiful.

IF YOU WERE NOT IN THIS PROFESSION, WHAT WOULD YOU BE DOING?
I appreciate modern architecture. I would have made a great architect.

WHAT CATEGORY OF WINE IS THE BEST VALUE IN YOUR RESTAURANT?
Sauvignon Blanc has not increased in price over the years and pairs very well with our Asian-style dishes.

NAME A COUPLE OF YOUR RESTAURANT'S SIGNATURE DISHES. WHAT TYPES OF WINE DO YOU PREFER TO RECOMMEND WITH EACH?
King salmon with Russian River Sauvignon Blanc; Dungeness crab bisque paired with Sonoma Coast Chardonnay.

IN THE PAST YEAR, WHAT WINES IN YOUR WINE PROGRAM HAVE CUSTOMERS BECOME MORE WILLING TO ORDER?
Pinot Gris, which I introduced to our by-the-glass list.

Santé at the Fairmont Sonoma Mission Inn

100 Boyes Boulevard
Boyes Hot Springs, California 95416
phone 707-938-9000 fax 707-938-4250
website www.fairmont.com

John B. Burdick
SOMMELIER

WHAT INSPIRED YOU TO PURSUE A CAREER THAT INVOLVES WINE?
I was pruning in a vineyard on a cold January in the Russian River region when I saw the light!

NAME ONE OF YOUR FAVORITE WINE REGIONS FROM AROUND THE WORLD.
The Carneros district for supreme Pinot Noir and Chardonnay.

NAME RECENT WINE DISCOVERIES THAT HAVE EXCITED YOU.
I am looking for the backyard winemakers these days. I may order 500 cases a year from Berthoud Vineyards, Favero Vineyards and others.

WHAT BITS OF INFORMATION WOULD YOU LIKE YOUR CUSTOMERS TO KNOW ABOUT YOU?
I have been a musician for thirty years. I have a vineyard touring business and I play guitar on my tours.

DESCRIBE YOUR WINE SELECTIONS, BOTH BY THE GLASS AND ON YOUR LIST.
Our wine by-the-glass list shines! We are known for our local selection of micro-wineries with production under 200–300 cases. People love to taste wines that were vinified only a few miles away.

WHAT CATEGORIES OF WINE ARE THE BEST VALUES IN YOUR RESTAURANT?
Spanish whites, wines from New Zealand and Australia and California Zinfandels.

NAME A COUPLE OF YOUR RESTAURANT'S SIGNATURE DISHES. WHAT TYPES OF WINE DO YOU PREFER TO RECOMMEND WITH EACH?
Pan-seared sea scallops, caramelized cauliflower purée with toasted almond butter and a five- to seven-year-old Carneros Chardonnay; mustard and thyme-marinated rack of lamb, sweet corn fritters, rosemary jus with Russian River Pinot Noir.

IN THE PAST YEAR, WHAT WINES IN YOUR WINE PROGRAM HAVE CUSTOMERS BECOME MORE WILLING TO ORDER?
Pinot Noir.

CALIFORNIA, NORTHERN

La Toque
at the Rancho Caymus Inn

1140 Rutherford Road
Rutherford, California 94573
phone 707-963-9770 fax 707-963-9072
website www.latoque.com

Scott Tracy
SOMMELIER

WHAT ARE SOME OF YOUR ULTIMATE FOOD AND WINE PAIRINGS?
Foie gras with Sauternes; Banyuls with chocolate; sashimi with Tocai Friulano; ginger desserts with Malvasia delle Lipari; and properly chilled French Champagne with the reading of a fine dining menu.

DESCRIBE YOUR WINE SELECTIONS.
We have an extensive wine list, but most guests order wines that I have paired with the eleven dishes on our menu, which changes weekly.

WHAT CATEGORY OF WINE IS THE BEST VALUE IN YOUR RESTAURANT?
The concept of "value" for our guests is in the value of the experience. Most of our diners are not concerned with the best buys of the wine world because they are on vacation, often with their spouses. The pleasure of sharing ten dishes and ten wines with the one you love is a very valuable memory.

NAME RECENT WINE DISCOVERIES THAT HAVE EXCITED YOU.
Loire Valley Chenin Blanc. Dry versions with cheese and sweet versions with strawberries.

WHAT IS YOUR FAVORITE WINE REGION IN THE WORLD TODAY?
Napa Valley.

WHAT LED YOU TO PURSUE A CAREER THAT INVOLVES WINE?
I found that wine returned the passion that I had for it exponentially.

WHAT IS THE BEST ASPECT OF YOUR JOB?
The ever-changing, nightly wine pairing allows for a wonderful opportunity to learn and teach and share the love of wine.

IF YOU WERE NOT IN THE WINE PROFESSION, WHAT WOULD YOU BE DOING?
Teaching.

Albion River Inn

MARK BOWERY, SOMMELIER

3790 North Highway One, Albion

707-937-1919

Auberge du Soleil Restaurant

KRIS MARGERUM, SOMMELIER

180 Rutherford Hill Road, Rutherford

707-963-1211

Brix Restaurant

CURT JONES, SOMMELIER

7377 St. Helena Highway, Napa

707-944-2749

Catahoula Restaurant & Saloon

JAN BIRNBAUM, WINE BUYER

1457 Lincoln Avenue, Calistoga

707-942-2275

Celadon

GREG GEVURTZ, WINE BUYER

1040 Main Street, Napa

707-254-9690

Cucina Rustica at the Depot Hotel

MIKE GHILARDUCCI, WINE BUYER

241 First Street West, Sonoma

707-938-2980

Domaine Chandon

JOHN GRETZ, WINE BUYER

One California Drive, Yountville

707-944-2892

Dry Creek Kitchen

LEO HANSEN, SOMMELIER

317 Healdsburg Avenue, Healdsburg

707-431-0330

Fusilli Ristorant

DAN GIACALONI, OWNER AND WINE BUYER

620 Jackson Street, Fairmont

707-428-4211

The Girl and the Gaucho

SONDRA BERNSTEIN, PROPRIETOR AND WINE BUYER

13690 Arnold Drive, Glen Ellen

707-938-2130

Greystone at the Culinary Institute of America

MICHAEL PRYOR, FOOD AND BEVERAGE DIRECTOR

2555 Main Street, St. Helena

707-967-1010

The Harbor House Inn

CRAIG ROBY, CHEF AND WINE BUYER

5600 South Highway One, Elk

707-877-3203

J.M. Rosen's Waterfront Grill

JAN ROSEN, WINE BUYER

54 East Washington Street, Petaluma

707-773-3200

Madrona Manor

KEN STIRITZ, SOMMELIER

1001 Westside Road, Healdsburg

707-433-4231

Manzanita Restaurant

GREG DOLGUSHLEIN, WINE BUYER

336 Healdsburg Avenue, Healdsburg

707-433-8111

Mixx Restaurant
DAN BERMAN, WINE BUYER
135 Fourth Street, Santa Rosa
707-573-1344

Mustard's Grill
NATALIE SCHLEIP, WINE BUYER
7399 St. Helena Highway, Yountville
707-944-2424

Napa Valley Grille
STEVE DUSTIMYER, SOMMELIER
6795 Washington Street, Yountville
707-944-8686

Pangaea
ROB HUNTER, WINE BUYER
250 Main Street, Point Arena
707-882-3001

The Restaurant at Meadowood
JOHN THOREEN, DIRECTOR OF WINE
900 Meadowood Lane, St. Helena
707-963-3646

Syrah Restaurant
KEN GOLDFINE, WINE BUYER
205 Fifth Street, Santa Rosa
707-568-4002

The Victorian Restaurant at the Mendocino Hotel
JOHN LODIN, SOMMELIER
45080 Main Street, Mendocino
707-937-0511

Wappo Bar Bistro
ARON BAUMAN, WINE BUYER
1226-B Washington Street, Calistoga
707-942-4712

Zin Restaurant & Wine Bar
JEANETTE FRANK, WINE BUYER
344 Center Street, Healdsburg
707-473-0946

Zinsvalley Restaurant
TERESA JOHNSON, WINE BUYER
3253 Browns Valley Road, Napa
707-224-0695

Miro at
Bacara Resort and Spa

8301 Hollister Avenue
Santa Barbara, California 93103
phone 805-968-0100 fax 805-571-3271
website www.bacararesort.com

Gillian M. Ballance
WINE DIRECTOR

WHAT INSPIRED YOU TO PURSUE A CAREER THAT INVOLVES WINE?
A grand cru Burgundy tasting with Patrick Seré from Dreyfus-Ashby.

NAME TWO OF YOUR FAVORITE WINE REGIONS FROM AROUND THE
WORLD.
Champagne; bubbles always make me feel great! And I'm crazy about Northern
Italian whites from Friuli because they are so food-friendly.

NAME RECENT WINE DISCOVERIES THAT HAVE EXCITED YOU.
Portuguese red wines have delicious native grapes with good value and a distinctive brambly flavor.

IF YOU WERE NOT IN THIS PROFESSION, WHAT WOULD YOU BE DOING?
Teaching dance classes.

DESCRIBE YOUR WINE SELECTIONS, BOTH BY THE GLASS AND ON YOUR LIST.
We definitely specialize in local wines since the Wine Country is only fifty
miles from the resort. People at Bacara definitely want to be educated about
Santa Barbara wines.

WHAT CATEGORY OF WINE IS THE BEST VALUE IN YOUR RESTAURANT?
Rhône Valley reds and red and white Burgundy.

NAME ONE OF YOUR RESTAURANT'S SIGNATURE DISHES. WHAT WINE DO
YOU PREFER TO RECOMMEND WITH IT?
Sautéed sweetbreads with hazelnuts and crêpes confit with great white
Burgundy.

IN THE PAST YEAR, WHAT WINES IN YOUR WINE PROGRAM HAVE CUS-
TOMERS BECOME MORE WILLING TO ORDER?
Pinot Noir. It is now our hottest-selling red.

The Patio at the Four Seasons Biltmore Hotel

1260 Channel Drive
Santa Barbara, California 93101
phone 805-969-2261 fax 805-565-8232
website www.fourseasons.com

David A. Asam

MANAGER AND SOMMELIER

WHAT INSPIRED YOU TO PURSUE A CAREER THAT INVOLVES WINE?
Attending the wine class at Cornell University. It began as a source for free drinks and developed into a passion.

NAME SOME OF YOUR FAVORITE WINES FROM AROUND THE WORLD.
Loire Valley Sauvignon Blanc and Santa Barbara Syrah and Viognier. The fresh, clean, minerally Sauvignon Blancs are perfect for any day, and Santa Barbara is producing unique, rich and affordable Rhône varietals.

NAME RECENT WINE DISCOVERIES THAT HAVE EXCITED YOU.
Melville Winery in Santa Barbara. They produce solid, well-made Pinot Noir, Chardonnay and Syrah at great prices.

WHAT BITS OF INFORMATION WOULD YOU LIKE YOUR CUSTOMERS TO KNOW ABOUT YOU?
I grew up in a small town called Shepherdstown, West Virginia, and will never turn down a glass of bubbly.

DESCRIBE YOUR WINE SELECTIONS, BOTH BY THE GLASS AND ON YOUR LIST.
The list has a base in Santa Barbara County wines while maintaining a solid representation of wines from the world's other great wine regions.

WHAT CATEGORY OF WINE IS THE BEST VALUE IN YOUR RESTAURANT?
Santa Barbara Rhône varietals.

NAME A COUPLE OF YOUR RESTAURANT'S SIGNATURE DISHES. WHAT TYPES OF WINE DO YOU PREFER TO RECOMMEND WITH EACH?
Crabmeat gazpacho with Santa Barbara Viognier; marinated duck breast with red Burgundy, preferably Chambolle-Musigny.

IN THE PAST YEAR, WHAT WINES IN YOUR WINE PROGRAM HAVE CUS-TOMERS BECOME MORE WILLING TO ORDER?
Rhône varietals such as Viognier and Syrah, especially from Santa Barbara County. Also, Pinot Gris and Pinot Blanc.

Ranch House
Restaurant
MICHAEL DENNEY, WINE BUYER
500 South Lomita Avenue, Ojai
805-646-2360

San Ysidro Ranch
SCOTT ABATE, WINE BUYER
900 San Ysidro Lane, Montecito
805-969-5046

Wine Cask Restaurant
WENDY VAN HORN, WINE BUYER
813 Anacapa Street, Santa Barbara
805-966-9463

Barney Greengrass Restaurant at Barneys New York

9570 Wilshire Boulevard, Fifth Floor
Beverly Hills, California 90212
phone 310-777-5877 fax 310-777-5760

Sharyn L. Kervyn de Volkaersbeke
GENERAL MANAGER

WHAT INSPIRED YOU TO PURSUE A CAREER THAT INVOLVES WINE?
In my college years I was a bartender and wine buyer for restaurants. Later my interest in wine was developed with the help of my French-speaking husband and his family.

NAME TWO OF YOUR FAVORITE WINE REGIONS FROM AROUND THE WORLD.
California regions are exciting. They are dynamic and are becoming more focused on producing quality wines. However, there will always be the timeless beauty of Bourgogne.

WHAT BITS OF INFORMATION WOULD YOU LIKE YOUR CUSTOMERS TO KNOW ABOUT YOU?
I paint mixed-media collage and used to have an art business. I grew up in a family in the restaurant business and started helping them at age nine.

DESCRIBE YOUR WINE SELECTIONS, BOTH BY THE GLASS AND ON YOUR LIST.
We specialize in California wines, as well as French Champagne. Our list is small, yet it offers a wide selection of styles within each varietal.

WHAT ARE THE MOST UNIQUE FEATURES IN YOUR WINE PROGRAM?
We carry half-bottles and a wide selection of wines by the glass. We recently developed an afternoon "Twilight on the Terrace" food and wine pairing menu for the summer season.

NAME A COUPLE OF YOUR RESTAURANT'S SIGNATURE DISHES. WHAT TYPES OF WINE DO YOU PREFER TO RECOMMEND WITH EACH?
Eastern smoked fish and caviar with Champagne or domestic white wine; peppered ahi with Pinot Noir.

IN THE PAST YEAR, WHAT WINES IN YOUR WINE PROGRAM HAVE CUSTOMERS BECOME MORE WILLING TO ORDER?
Rhône wines and blends.

Billy's at the Beach

2751 West Pacific Coast Highway
Newport Beach, California 92663
phone 949-722-1100 fax 949-722-1374
website www.billysatthebeach.com

Rick Craig
GENERAL MANAGER
AND WINE DIRECTOR

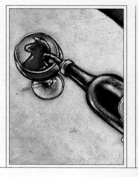

CALIFORNIA, LOS ANGELES AREA

WHAT INSPIRED YOU TO PURSUE A CAREER THAT INVOLVES WINE?
When I was seventeen, my father opened a bottle of 1945 Margaux for his fortieth birthday. It was my first exposure to great wine.

NAME SOME OF YOUR FAVORITE WINE REGIONS FROM AROUND THE WORLD.
Alsace and Rhône Valley in France, Napa Valley in California and Marlborough in New Zealand.

WHAT BITS OF INFORMATION WOULD YOU LIKE YOUR CUSTOMERS TO KNOW ABOUT YOU?
I am an avid rock climber and father of two.

IF YOU WERE NOT IN THIS PROFESSION, WHAT WOULD YOU BE DOING?
I can't imagine not being in this business, but being a winemaker would be okay.

DESCRIBE YOUR WINE SELECTIONS, BOTH BY THE GLASS AND ON YOUR LIST.
Our list features 260 selections, mainly from California and France, but also from Australia, New Zealand, Germany, Chile and South Africa. We feature several verticals from top producers.

WHAT ARE THE MOST UNIQUE FEATURES IN YOUR WINE PROGRAM?
We feature about 20 wines by the glass and do several winemaker dinners each year.

NAME A FEW OF YOUR RESTAURANT'S SIGNATURE DISHES. WHAT TYPES OF WINE DO YOU PREFER TO RECOMMEND WITH EACH?
Pan-seared opakapaka and shiitake mushrooms with Oregon Pinot Noir; grilled mahi-mahi with tropical salsa paired with New Zealand Sauvignon Blanc; rack of lamb with red Rhône.

IN THE PAST YEAR, WHAT WINES IN YOUR WINE PROGRAM HAVE CUSTOMERS BECOME MORE WILLING TO ORDER?
New Zealand Sauvignon Blanc, California Syrah, California Zinfandel and Alsace.

The Cellar

305 North Harbor Boulevard
Fullerton, California 92832
phone 714-525-5682 fax 714-525-3853
website www.imenu.com/thecellar

Ernest Zingg
OWNER AND MANAGER

WHAT ARE SOME OF YOUR ULTIMATE FOOD AND WINE PAIRINGS?
Roasted breast of Muscovy duck and sour cherries with a fruity Australian or Central Coast Syrah; Châteaubriand bouquetière with a Côte de Beaune (Burgundy).

DESCRIBE YOUR WINE SELECTIONS.
We are next to a major convention center and our wine selection caters to international customers. We carry wines from more than fifteen countries.

WHAT CATEGORY OF WINE IS THE BEST VALUE IN YOUR RESTAURANT?
The older wines, especially red Burgundies and California Cabernets, where a ten-year-old to twenty-year-old bottle is priced only a little less than the latest release from the same producer.

NAME A RECENT WINE DISCOVERY THAT EXCITED YOU.
A Marsanne from Chateau Tahbilk in Victoria, Australia.

WHAT IS YOUR FAVORITE WINE REGION IN THE WORLD TODAY?
Burgundy is my favorite region and Pinot Noir my favorite wine.

WHAT LED YOU TO PURSUE A CAREER THAT INVOLVES WINE?
Wine service has always been close to my heart and when I became a proprietor, I continued to serve and recommend wine.

WHAT IS THE BEST ASPECT OF YOUR JOB?
Tasting all the new wines. I have personally tasted 98 percent of the wine I buy.

IF YOU WERE NOT IN THE WINE PROFESSION, WHAT WOULD YOU DO?
Return to the hotel business.

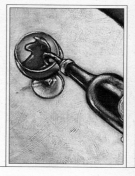

Chez Melange

1716 South Pacific Coast Highway
Redondo Beach, California 90277
phone 310-540-1222 fax 310-316-9283
website www.chezmelange.com

Michael I. Franks
Co-Owner

WHAT ARE SOME OF YOUR ULTIMATE FOOD AND WINE PAIRINGS?
Sausage and Zinfandel; Cajun meatloaf and southern Rhône; oysters and
California Pinot Gris; lamb ossobuco and Pinot Noir; chicken curry and
California Gewürztraminer.

DESCRIBE YOUR WINE SELECTIONS.
We specialize in California wines, new releases, hard-to-find wines and
great values.

WHAT CATEGORY OF WINE IS THE BEST VALUE IN YOUR RESTAURANT?
Interesting reds.

NAME RECENT WINE DISCOVERIES THAT HAVE EXCITED YOU.
Joe Gott Cabernet Sauvignon 2000—a great value; Waterbrook Melange
1999—a Cabernet Merlot-Sangiovese blend. It is a great value and has a
great name.

WHAT IS YOUR FAVORITE WINE REGION IN THE WORLD TODAY?
Napa Valley, for its quality, people and innovation.

WHAT LED YOU TO YOUR CURRENT POSITION?
Passion for wine.

WHAT ARE THE BEST ASPECTS OF YOUR JOB?
The constant motivation to get things right.

IF YOU WERE NOT IN THE WINE PROFESSION, WHAT WOULD YOU BE?
I would be in marketing.

Cuistot

72505 El Paseo Street
Palm Desert, California 92260
phone 760-340-1000 fax 760-340-1254

Fred M. Gerber
SOMMELIER

WHAT INSPIRED YOU TO PURSUE A CAREER THAT INVOLVES WINE?
My first wine class during my server apprenticeship.

WHAT PART OF YOUR JOB DO YOU ENJOY THE MOST?
Meeting with winemakers and others in the industry and helping our guests discover "new" wines to enjoy.

NAME TWO OF YOUR FAVORITE WINE REGIONS FROM AROUND THE WORLD.
Russian River, for its many styles of Pinot Noir, and Carneros for its crisp, citrus-flavored Chardonnay.

NAME RECENT WINE DISCOVERIES THAT HAVE EXCITED YOU.
Kalin Cellars Chardonnay and Sauvignon Blanc, which show that California whites can age well.

WHAT WOULD YOU LIKE YOUR CUSTOMERS TO KNOW ABOUT YOU?
I was raised in Switzerland, and enjoy hiking, camping and scuba diving.

IF YOU WERE NOT IN THIS PROFESSION, WHAT WOULD YOU BE DOING?
Private tours around the world or running a Wine Country inn.

DESCRIBE YOUR WINE SELECTIONS, BOTH BY THE GLASS AND ON YOUR LIST.
Our list concentrates on California and France. We feature small producers whose wines reflect great quality-to-price ratios.

WHAT ARE THE MOST UNIQUE FEATURES IN YOUR WINE PROGRAM?
We hold winemaker dinners and have a fabulous tasting menu with wine pairings.

NAME A COUPLE OF YOUR RESTAURANT'S SIGNATURE DISHES. WHAT TYPES OF WINE DO YOU PREFER TO RECOMMEND WITH EACH?
Lightly seared foie gras with Sauternes; quail and sweetbreads with Central Coast Syrah.

WHAT WINES ARE CUSTOMERS NOW MORE WILLING TO ORDER?
Red Burgundy and California Sauvignon Blanc and Zinfandel.

Diplomate Café

2112 Brea Mall Drive
Brea, California 92821
phone 714-256-0303 fax 714-256-1563
website www.lediplomatecafe.com

Michael P. Magoski
MANAGER

NAME TWO OF YOUR FAVORITE WINE REGIONS FROM AROUND THE WORLD.
Russian River Valley and Mendocino. A lot of it has to do with their long growing seasons and the presence of coastal fog.

IF YOU WERE NOT IN THIS PROFESSION, WHAT WOULD YOU BE?
A travel photographer, a director, a teacher or a DJ mixing the hot sounds of modern Brazilian electronic bossa nova with deeply spiritual Indian ragas.

DESCRIBE YOUR WINE SELECTIONS, BOTH BY THE GLASS AND ON YOUR LIST.
We specialize in esoteric, small-production wines. We look for wines that either define their varietal or are unique in portraying the variations within a varietal. We look for "the fifth taste."

WHAT ARE THE MOST UNIQUE FEATURES IN YOUR WINE PROGRAM?
We have a large and very esoteric wine by-the-glass program. Tuesday through Thursday all wines by the glass are twenty-five percent off between 3 and 7:30 p.m.

NAME A FEW OF YOUR RESTAURANT'S SIGNATURE DISHES. WHAT TYPES OF WINE DO YOU PREFER TO RECOMMEND WITH EACH?
Baked Brie with almonds and apples with mature California Chardonnay; fruit and cheese with Mendocino Zinfandel; charbroiled salmon salad with avocado, tomato and papaya with Russian River Pinot Noir; feta, garlic and tomato (pannini-style) with Sangiovese or New Zealand Sauvignon Blanc; portobello mushroom sandwich with Santa Barbara Syrah.

IN THE PAST YEAR, WHAT WINES IN YOUR WINE PROGRAM HAVE CUSTOMERS BECOME MORE WILLING TO ORDER?
Pinot Noir, Zinfandel, Malbec, Syrah, Pinot Gris, Sauvignon Blanc and Gewürztraminer.

Drago

2628 Wilshire Boulevard
Santa Monica, California 90403
phone 310-828-1585 fax 310-582-2294
website www.celestinodrago.com

Jeff Morgenthal
WINE DIRECTOR AND SOMMELIER

WHAT INSPIRED YOU TO PURSUE A CAREER THAT INVOLVES WINE?
The door was opened through bicycle racing where, historically, the most important countries for racing also paralleled wine regions like France, Italy and Spain.

NAME RECENT WINE DISCOVERIES THAT HAVE EXCITED YOU.
Red Burgundies from Domaine Arlaud, a young producer making wines with real texture at very fair prices; Enrico Fossi from Tuscany, especially the Malbec and Riesling.

WHAT BITS OF INFORMATION WOULD YOU LIKE YOUR CUSTOMERS TO KNOW ABOUT YOU?
That cycling is the greatest parallel for wine. In cycling, one can only achieve success through suffering. The same is true of wine growing.

IF YOU WERE NOT IN THIS PROFESSION, WHAT WOULD YOU BE DOING?
I'd be a jazz drummer, writing novels or designing shoes.

WHAT ARE THE MOST UNIQUE FEATURES IN YOUR WINE PROGRAM?
We have forty wines from Bruno Giacosa, thirty-five wines from Gaja in all sizes and lots of Brunello. We have an all-Italian wine by-the-glass program.

WHAT CATEGORY OF WINE IS THE BEST VALUE IN YOUR RESTAURANT?
Reds from Southern Italy: Aglianico-based reds from Campania; Nero d'Avola–based reds from Sicily; Cannonau from Sardinia.

NAME A COUPLE OF YOUR RESTAURANT'S SIGNATURE DISHES. WHAT TYPES OF WINE DO YOU PREFER TO RECOMMEND WITH EACH?
Carpaccio di salmone with Alto Adige Sylvaner; coniglio al forno con olive e pepperoni with Tuscan Syrah.

IN THE PAST YEAR, WHAT WINES IN YOUR WINE PROGRAM HAVE CUS-TOMERS BECOME MORE WILLING TO ORDER?
Barolo and Barbaresco.

Eldorado Country Club

46000 Fairway Drive
Indian Wells, California 92210
phone 760-346-8081 fax 760-340-1325

Joshua S. Blackman
SOMMELIER

WHAT INSPIRED YOU TO PURSUE A CAREER THAT INVOLVES WINE?
A visit to my uncle's vineyard in Northern California. He told me that I was going to help with the harvest and crush some of the Zinfandel grapes. Since that day, I fell in love with "the juice."

NAME ONE OF YOUR FAVORITE WINE REGIONS FROM AROUND THE WORLD.
California. It is producing great wine, even without the help of previous, generational experience.

IF YOU WERE NOT IN THIS PROFESSION, WHAT WOULD YOU BE DOING?
Playing golf.

WHAT ARE THE MOST UNIQUE FEATURES IN YOUR WINE PROGRAM?
Our wine pricing. We mark up wines about forty percent. For example, our cost on the 1997 Bryant Family Cabernet Sauvignon is $200 and we sell it for $260.

WHAT CATEGORY OF WINE IS THE BEST VALUE IN YOUR RESTAURANT?
California wines, especially Merlot.

NAME A COUPLE OF YOUR RESTAURANT'S SIGNATURE DISHES. WHAT TYPES OF WINE DO YOU PREFER TO RECOMMEND WITH EACH?
Blackened salmon with Alsatian Riesling or Pinot Blanc; rack of lamb with Russian River Pinot Noir or Syrah.

IN THE PAST YEAR, WHAT WINES IN YOUR WINE PROGRAM HAVE CUSTOMERS BECOME MORE WILLING TO ORDER?
Oddly enough, my guests are still living in the Merlot and Chardonnay era. However, I've been actively recommending Pinot Noir, Syrah, Petite Sirah, Pinot Blanc, Pinot Gris and Riesling to allow them to expand their horizons.

WHAT ARE SOME OTHER ULTIMATE WINE AND FOOD PAIRINGS?
Curry with Gewürztraminer; shellfish with Champagne, Pinot Gris or Pinot Blanc; wild game with Petite Sirah.

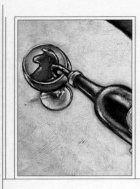

Gardens Restaurant at the Four Seasons Hotel

300 South Doheny Drive
Los Angeles, California 90048
phone 310-273-2222 fax 310-385-4927

Ekrem Tercanoglu
FOOD AND BEVERAGE DIRECTOR

NAME ONE OF YOUR FAVORITE WINE REGIONS FROM AROUND THE WORLD.
Burgundy, because of my passion for great food and wine.

NAME RECENT WINE DISCOVERIES THAT HAVE EXCITED YOU.
L'Aventure Optimus Paso Robles for the winemakers' philosophy of quality.

WHAT BITS OF INFORMATION WOULD YOU LIKE YOUR CUSTOMERS TO KNOW ABOUT YOU?
I enjoy fishing, hunting and cooking.

IF YOU WERE NOT IN THIS PROFESSION, WHAT WOULD YOU BE DOING?
I don't know if I can do anything else.

DESCRIBE YOUR WINE SELECTIONS, BOTH BY THE GLASS AND ON YOUR LIST.
Our 700-selection wine list is diverse with a strong influence in California. It has complete showings of Bordeaux, Burgundy, Rhône and Italian wines, which complement the California-Mediterranean cuisine. We offer fourteen to twenty white and red wines by-the-glass.

WHAT ARE THE MOST UNIQUE FEATURES IN YOUR WINE PROGRAM?
We have a good half-bottle selection and great Porto and sweet wines by-the-glass.

WHAT CATEGORY OF WINE IS THE BEST VALUE IN YOUR RESTAURANT?
California Syrah, Spain, Chile, Alsatian wines.

NAME ONE OF YOUR RESTAURANT'S SIGNATURE DISHES. WHAT WINE DO YOU PREFER TO RECOMMEND WITH IT?
Maine lobster poached in beurre blanc sauce with steamed vegetables paired with a top Meursault.

The Hobbit Restaurant

2932 East Chapman Avenue
Orange, California 92869
phone 714-997-1972 fax 714-997-3181
website hobbitrestaurant.com

Brian W. Harley
MANAGER AND SOMMELIER

WHAT INSPIRED YOU TO PURSUE A CAREER THAT INVOLVES WINE?
I didn't choose this career; it chose me. Boy, am I glad.

WHAT PART OF YOUR JOB DO YOU ENJOY THE MOST?
Gee, let me think ... drinking great wine.

NAME ONE OR TWO OF YOUR FAVORITE WINE REGIONS.
I enjoy many Pinot Noirs and Chardonnays from Carneros, but it really is all
about Burgundy.

WHAT ELSE WOULD YOU LIKE YOUR CUSTOMERS TO KNOW ABOUT YOU?
Nothing. They know too much already!

IF YOU WERE NOT IN THIS PROFESSION, WHAT WOULD YOU BE DOING?
I'd be unemployed. There's no better occupation than this.

DESCRIBE YOUR WINE SELECTIONS, BOTH BY THE GLASS AND ON YOUR LIST.
We have more than 1,200 selections in the cellar from both the Old and New
World. We also have two different wine-tasting flights that coincide with our
seven-course menu.

WHAT ARE THE MOST UNIQUE FEATURES IN YOUR WINE PROGRAM?
We have some rare large-format bottles. The restaurant also hosts four or five
winemaker dinners every year.

WHAT CATEGORIES OF WINE ARE THE BEST VALUES IN YOUR RESTAURANT?
Loire Valley whites and Zinfandel.

NAME ONE OF YOUR RESTAURANT'S SIGNATURE DISHES. WHAT WINES
DO YOU PREFER TO RECOMMEND WITH IT?
Prime New York steak paired with a Spring Mountain District Cabernet
Sauvignon or a Bordeaux first-growth.

WHAT WINES ARE CUSTOMERS NOW MORE WILLING TO ORDER?
Syrah from California and Australia.

James' Beach Café

60 North Venice Boulevard
Venice, California 90291
phone 310-823-5396 fax 310-827-8560

Daniel C. Samakow
PROPRIETOR

WHAT ARE SOME OF YOUR ULTIMATE FOOD AND WINE PAIRINGS?
Steak and Cabernet Sauvignon; foie gras and Château d'Yquem 1989; salmon and Pouilly-Fumé.

DESCRIBE YOUR WINE SELECTIONS.
We specialize in comfort food. Our list is a comfort list of great names and exciting newcomers, all sold at excellent prices.

WHAT CATEGORY OF WINE IS THE BEST VALUE IN YOUR RESTAURANT?
California wines.

NAME RECENT WINE DISCOVERIES THAT HAVE EXCITED YOU.
1999 Justin Isosceles, for its great complexity and value; 1997 Peter Michael "Bellecote" Chardonnay and 1999 Kistler Chardonnay for their wonderful balance.

WHAT ARE YOUR FAVORITE WINE REGIONS IN THE WORLD TODAY?
Rhône for its quality and versatility with food; Bordeaux for complexity.

WHAT LED YOU TO YOUR CURRENT POSITION?
I create perfume for my cosmetic company and for other companies. There are many similarities regarding notes and understanding complexity that made me appreciate wine when I started my restaurants.

WHAT ARE THE BEST ASPECTS OF YOUR JOB?
Buying wine at auction, explaining rare vintages to customers and trying new, exciting producers.

IF YOU WERE NOT IN THE WINE PROFESSION, WHAT WOULD YOU BE DOING?
Making art. I am a painter.

Jer-ne Restaurant at the Ritz-Carlton Marina Del Rey

4375 Admiralty Way
Marina Del Rey, California 90292
phone 310-823-1700 fax 310-823-2403

Alison Junker
WINE DIRECTOR AND SOMMELIER

WHAT INSPIRED YOU TO PURSUE A CAREER THAT INVOLVES WINE?
Andrea Immer. I took the sommelier course in New York that she was teaching.

NAME ONE OF YOUR FAVORITE WINE REGIONS.
Loire Valley. It has both white and red wines that are like no other. And the prices can't be beat.

NAME RECENT WINE DISCOVERIES THAT HAVE EXCITED YOU.
New Zealand reds. I was amazed at how far they have come, especially the Cabernets and Merlots.

IF YOU WERE NOT IN THIS PROFESSION, WHAT WOULD YOU BE DOING?
Cartography.

DESCRIBE YOUR WINE SELECTIONS, BOTH BY THE GLASS AND ON YOUR LIST.
We have a good by-the-glass selection of about thirty-five wines that is constantly changing. Our list represents all the major regions with a strong California representation.

WHAT ARE THE MOST UNIQUE FEATURES IN YOUR WINE PROGRAM?
We have great wine dinners with winemakers, a large by-the-glass selection and a tasting menu with wine.

WHAT CATEGORY OF WINE IS THE BEST VALUE IN YOUR RESTAURANT?
Italian reds.

NAME A COUPLE OF YOUR RESTAURANT'S SIGNATURE DISHES. WHAT TYPES OF WINE DO YOU PREFER TO RECOMMEND WITH EACH?
Grilled lamb chops, Maui onions and blue cheese fondue paired with California Zinfandel; diver scallops rumaki on fava bean ragout with a Santa Barbara Chardonnay.

WHAT WINES ARE CUSTOMERS NOW MORE WILLING TO ORDER?
More aromatic whites, like Vouvray and Gewürztraminer.

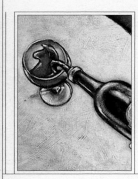

Linq Restaurant & Lounge

8338 West Third Street
Los Angeles, California 90048
phone 323-655-4555 fax 323-655-1144
website www.linqlounge.com

Matthew P. Kay
BEVERAGE DIRECTOR

LIST YOUR FORMAL AND INFORMAL WINE TRAINING.
Multiple wine-training seminars at UCLA.

WHAT INSPIRED YOU TO PURSUE A CAREER THAT INVOLVES WINE?
It began as a hobby.

WHAT PART OF YOUR JOB DO YOU ENJOY THE MOST?
Making unusual suggestions to customers and seeing them enjoy wines they
wouldn't normally choose.

NAME ONE OF YOUR FAVORITE WINE REGIONS FROM AROUND THE WORLD.
Rhône Valley for its many different varietals and different styles.

NAME RECENT WINE DISCOVERIES THAT HAVE EXCITED YOU.
Red Car for its dedication to its vineyards and wines; Clos Mimi for exceptional
quality.

DESCRIBE YOUR WINE SELECTIONS, BOTH BY THE GLASS AND ON YOUR LIST.
We offer wines from both hemispheres. We have a large selection of Bordeaux
wines as well as wines from throughout the New World.

WHAT ARE THE MOST UNIQUE FEATURES IN YOUR WINE PROGRAM?
We have a large by-the-glass selection, wines are available by the half-glass or
taste, and we have special wine pricing.

WHAT CATEGORIES OF WINE ARE THE BEST VALUES IN YOUR RESTAURANT?
California Syrah and dessert wines, especially Banyuls.

NAME A COUPLE OF YOUR RESTAURANT'S SIGNATURE DISHES. WHAT
TYPES OF WINE DO YOU PREFER TO RECOMMEND WITH EACH?
Whole sizzling catfish with crisp California Sauvignon Blanc; Chilean sea bass
with Sancerre.

WHAT WINES ARE CUSTOMERS NOW MORE WILLING TO ORDER?
Wines from South Africa, especially Pinotage.

Lucques

8474 Melrose Avenue
Los Angeles, California 90069
phone 323-655-6277 fax 323-655-3925
website www.lucques.com

Caroline P. Styne
OWNER AND SOMMELIER

WHAT INSPIRED YOU TO PURSUE A CAREER THAT INVOLVES WINE?
I began helping with the wine list at my previous job and became totally obsessed!

WHAT PART OF YOUR JOB DO YOU ENJOY THE MOST?
I find making recommendations the most exciting and rewarding part of the job, particularly when I can surprise someone with an unusual selection.

NAME TWO OF YOUR FAVORITE WINE REGIONS.
Northern Rhône because of Syrah's incredible diversity and Umbria for its hearty, herbal red wines.

NAME RECENT WINE DISCOVERIES THAT HAVE EXCITED YOU.
I've been falling in love with St. Chinian. What flavors, what values, what rich wines!

WHAT WOULD YOU LIKE YOUR CUSTOMERS TO KNOW ABOUT YOU?
I'm a crossword puzzle fanatic.

DESCRIBE YOUR WINE PROGRAM AND WINE SELECTIONS.
We specialize in small-production wineries. Our list is known for showcasing wines that are off the beaten path.

WHAT CATEGORY OF WINE IS THE BEST VALUE IN YOUR RESTAURANT?
The wines of Provence and southern France, an area of great, rich wines at reasonable prices.

NAME A COUPLE OF YOUR RESTAURANT'S SIGNATURE DISHES. WHAT TYPES OF WINE DO YOU PREFER TO RECOMMEND WITH EACH?
Arroz negro (Spanish black rice) with Rioja; braised beef short ribs with hearty Châteauneuf-du-Pape.

WHAT WINES ARE CUSTOMERS NOW MORE WILLING TO ORDER?
German Rieslings. We're having a hard time keeping them in stock.

Max Restaurant

13355 Ventura Boulevard
Sherman Oaks, California 91423
phone 818-784-2915 fax 818-784-2918
website www.maxrestaurant.com

Michael J. Lamb
CO-OWNER AND WINE DIRECTOR

WHAT INSPIRED YOU TO PURSUE A CAREER THAT INVOLVES WINE?
While attending Pepperdine, I started dating a girl from Sonoma. It was all wine and roses from then on.

NAME ONE OF YOUR FAVORITE WINE DISTRICTS.
Santa Rita Hills, just north of Santa Barbara, offers a unique microclimate that produces intense wines, especially Pinot Noir.

NAME RECENT WINE DISCOVERIES THAT HAVE EXCITED YOU.
The quality and value of Australian wines, and up-and-coming Mexican wines with great potential.

WHAT WOULD YOU LIKE YOUR CUSTOMERS TO KNOW ABOUT YOU?
I run marathons in my spare time.

DESCRIBE YOUR WINE SELECTIONS, BOTH BY THE GLASS AND ON YOUR LIST.
Our wines are from both well-known producers and boutique wineries, with a strong California presence (for our clientele) with additional wines from Oregon, France, Italy, Australia and New Zealand.

WHAT ARE THE MOST UNIQUE FEATURES IN YOUR WINE PROGRAM?
We pour a dozen wines by-the-glass selected to go with the menu, including Shiraz. All wines are selected with the menu in mind.

WHAT CATEGORY OF WINE IS THE BEST VALUE IN YOUR RESTAURANT?
Australian wines and red table wines from California.

NAME A COUPLE OF YOUR RESTAURANT'S SIGNATURE DISHES. WHAT TYPES OF WINE DO YOU PREFER TO RECOMMEND WITH EACH?
Indian-crusted Marsala cod with Sancerre; wok-sautéed filet mignon with Shiraz.

IN THE PAST YEAR, WHAT WINES IN YOUR WINE PROGRAM HAVE CUSTOMERS BECOME MORE WILLING TO ORDER?
Shiraz from Australia and wines from smaller, lesser-known producers.

Melisse

1104 Wilshire Boulevard
Santa Monica, California 90401
phone 310-395-0881 fax 310-395-3810
website www.melisse.com

Brian K. Kalliel
BEVERAGE DIRECTOR
AND WINE BUYER

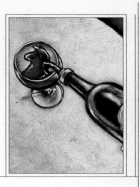

NAME ONE OR TWO OF YOUR FAVORITE WINE DISTRICTS OR WINE
REGIONS FROM AROUND THE WORLD.
Loire Valley and Rhône Valley, for their amazing food wines.

NAME RECENT WINE DISCOVERIES THAT HAVE EXCITED YOU.
Arbois Rouge is very light, vibrant and inexpensive and goes well with fish and
chicken.

WHAT WOULD YOU LIKE YOUR CUSTOMERS TO KNOW ABOUT YOU?
I'm an avid golfer. Need a fourth?

IF YOU WERE NOT IN THIS PROFESSION, WHAT WOULD YOU BE DOING?
Running from the law.

DESCRIBE YOUR WINE SELECTIONS, BOTH BY THE GLASS AND ON YOUR LIST.
Our list is predominantly French. The wines by the glass are chosen as part of
our wine-pairing program. We're trying to expose great wines from southern
France.

WHAT ARE THE MOST UNIQUE FEATURES IN YOUR WINE PROGRAM?
Wine pairings. We go out of our way to have what we consider to be the best
pairing program in town.

WHAT CATEGORY OF WINE IS THE BEST VALUE IN YOUR RESTAURANT?
A good list has value in all categories.

NAME A COUPLE OF YOUR RESTAURANT'S SIGNATURE DISHES. WHAT
TYPES OF WINE DO YOU PREFER TO RECOMMEND WITH EACH?
Lobster Thermador served with aged Savennières; rib-eye with a beautiful
Barbera d'Alba.

IN THE PAST YEAR, WHAT WINES IN YOUR WINE PROGRAM HAVE CUS-
TOMERS BECOME MORE WILLING TO ORDER?
Loire Valley and Austria.

Michael's Restaurant

1147 Third Street
Santa Monica, California 90403
phone 310-451-0843 fax 310-394-1830

Jennifer L. Benzie
SOMMELIER

NAME A COUPLE OF YOUR RESTAURANT'S SIGNATURE DISHES. WHAT
TYPES OF WINE DO YOU PREFER TO RECOMMEND WITH EACH?
A juicy Barbera d'Alba with 28-day dry-aged New York steak.

DESCRIBE YOUR WINE SELECTIONS, BOTH BY THE GLASS AND ON THE LIST.
We have about 500 selections from different regions, grape varieties and price
points. We also offer about twenty wines by the glass. We have a large selection
of half-bottles that pair wonderfully with the chef's tasting menu.

WHAT CATEGORY OF WINE IS THE BEST VALUE IN YOUR RESTAURANT?
Red Rhônes.

NAME ONE OF YOUR FAVORITE WINE REGIONS FROM AROUND THE
WORLD.
Italy, a country that is examining its Old World concepts and now evolving
with New World ideas.

NAME RECENT WINE DISCOVERIES THAT HAVE EXCITED YOU.
The wines from Lewis Cellars. There's not a bad one in the bunch!

WHAT INSPIRED YOU TO PURSUE A CAREER THAT INVOLVES WINE?
I thought I would be serving cocktails on the beach when I moved to the
Virgin Islands, but I knew enough about wine to land a job as a wine steward.

WHAT PART OF YOUR JOB DO YOU ENJOY THE MOST?
When pieces of the "wine puzzle" fall into place, and when I get a wine right in
a blind tasting.

IF YOU WERE NOT IN THE WINE PROFESSION, WHAT WOULD YOU BE DOING?
A pastry chef, except that I don't do early mornings!

IN THE PAST YEAR, WHAT WINES IN YOUR WINE PROGRAM HAVE CUS-
TOMERS BECOME MORE WILLING TO ORDER?
Oregon Pinot Noir.

Mr. Stox

1105 East Katella Avenue
Anaheim, California 92651
phone 714-634-2994 fax 714-634-0561
website www.mrstox.com

Ronald W. Marshall
CO-OWNER

NAME TWO OF YOUR FAVORITE WINE REGIONS FROM AROUND THE WORLD.
The Russian River in Sonoma for its great Pinot Noir; Burgundy for wines that are truly distinctive and reflect their terroir.

NAME RECENT WINE DISCOVERIES THAT HAVE EXCITED YOU.
Shiraz Paringa is a great value from Australia. I've also rediscovered Sauvignon Blanc, which is great with food.

WHAT BITS OF INFORMATION WOULD YOU LIKE YOUR CUSTOMERS TO KNOW ABOUT YOU?
I love to read, travel and exercise.

IF YOU WERE NOT IN THIS PROFESSION, WHAT WOULD YOU BE?
A professor.

DESCRIBE YOUR WINE SELECTIONS, BOTH BY THE GLASS AND ON YOUR LIST.
We offer wine at good values with more than twenty-five half-bottles available.

WHAT ARE THE MOST UNIQUE FEATURES IN YOUR WINE PROGRAM?
We have a large listing of old Bordeaux and half-bottle selections.

WHAT CATEGORY OF WINE IS THE BEST VALUE IN YOUR RESTAURANT?
Almost all our categories do, and should, have good values.

NAME ONE OF YOUR RESTAURANT'S SIGNATURE DISHES. WHAT WINE DO YOU PREFER TO RECOMMEND WITH IT?
Maryland crab cakes with Russian River Sauvignon Blanc.

IN THE PAST YEAR, WHAT WINES IN YOUR WINE PROGRAM HAVE CUSTOMERS BECOME MORE WILLING TO ORDER?
California Syrah, Chianti, Brunello and Barolo.

Napa Rose at the Disneyland Grand Californian Resort

1600 South Disneyland Drive
Anaheim, California 92802
phone 714-300-7170 fax 714-300-7122

Michael A. Jordan
SOMMELIER, GENERAL MANAGER
AND WINE EDUCATOR

WHAT ARE SOME OF YOUR ULTIMATE FOOD AND WINE PAIRINGS?
Seared scallops with coastal-style Chardonnay; pork rack with Zinfandel; Scharffen Berger chocolate velvet pâté with Pinot Noir Port; Sauternes with seared foie gras; venison with California Zinfandel; oysters and Sancerre; braised rabbit ragoût with Chianti Classico Riserva.

DESCRIBE YOUR WINE SELECTIONS.
There are 330 wines on the list and fifty by the glass. Ninety percent are California wines, from cult wines to affordable "discovery" wines.

WHAT CATEGORIES OF WINE ARE THE BEST VALUES ON YOUR WINE LIST?
Rhône varietals, Cal-Italian varietals, Pinot Noir and Zinfandel.

NAME RECENT WINE DISCOVERIES THAT HAVE EXCITED YOU.
Fanucchi Trousseau Gris is a crisp, fruity, limited-production wine at a great price; Tantara Pinot Noir is a fine version of the varietal.

WHAT IS YOUR FAVORITE WINE REGION IN THE WORLD TODAY?
California. With seventy-one AVAs and so many varieties being grown well, there is both diversity and great quality among them.

WHAT LED YOU TO PURSUE A CAREER THAT INVOLVES WINE?
I am passionate about the experience of great dining and of enhancing meals with selected wines. And I enjoy sharing that.

WHAT ARE THE BEST ASPECTS OF YOUR JOB?
Teaching wine classes that have resulted in the certification of thirty sommeliers on staff at the resort and managing the wine program at the restaurant.

IF YOU WERE NOT IN THE WINE PROFESSION, WHAT WOULD YOU BE DOING?
Helping children with special needs.

The Pacific Club

4110 MacArthur Boulevard
Newport Beach, California 92660
phone 949-955-1123 fax 949-252-7680

René E. Chazottes

DIRECTOR OF WINE AND
MAÎTRE SOMMELIER
TEAM: ERICK STRONG,
ASSISTANT SOMMELIER

WHAT ARE SOME OF YOUR ULTIMATE FOOD AND WINE PAIRINGS?
Roasted partridge with fresh raisin with Château Gazin 1995 Pomerol; yellowtail with oyster mushrooms, fresh ginger and roasted peppers with King Estate 1998 Pinot Gris from Oregon.

DESCRIBE YOUR WINE SELECTIONS.
Open-minded, balanced and affordable.

WHAT IS YOUR FAVORITE WINE REGION IN THE WORLD TODAY?
Burgundy. Great people, fantastic food, amazing wines.

WHAT LED YOU TO PURSUE A CAREER THAT INVOLVES WINE?
Passion.

WHAT IS THE BEST ASPECT OF YOUR JOB?
Objectivity.

IF YOU WERE NOT IN THE WINE PROFESSION, WHAT WOULD YOU BE?
A clown.

Patina Restaurant

5955 Melrose Avenue
Los Angeles, California 90038
phone 323-467-1108 fax 323-467-0215
website www.patinagroup.com

Christopher A. Meeske
SOMMELIER

WHAT INSPIRED YOU TO PURSUE A CAREER THAT INVOLVES WINE?
It's just such a unique field, very diverse and ever-changing. It is so interesting from geography to history. It has it all. No other agricultural product is as complex.

NAME TWO OF YOUR FAVORITE WINE REGIONS FROM AROUND THE WORLD.
Burgundy for its individuality and the Mosel for its delicacy and finesse.

NAME A RECENT WINE DISCOVERY THAT EXCITED YOU.
Garys' Vineyard Syrah from the Santa Lucia Highlands, from the Miura winery. It has incredible aromatic complexity and intensity.

WHAT BITS OF INFORMATION WOULD YOU LIKE YOUR CUSTOMERS TO KNOW ABOUT YOU?
I raced bicycles professionally for a short period of time. I still love to ride.

IF YOU WERE NOT IN THIS PROFESSION, WHAT WOULD YOU BE?
A PGA tour professional.

WHAT ARE THE MOST UNIQUE FEATURES IN YOUR WINE PROGRAM?
The breadth and depth of our wine program. We have different wines from all over the world. We have been a Wine Spectator Grand Award winner since 1994.

WHAT CATEGORY OF WINE IS THE BEST VALUE IN YOUR RESTAURANT?
Riesling from Germany.

NAME A COUPLE OF YOUR RESTAURANT'S SIGNATURE DISHES. WHAT TYPES OF WINE DO YOU PREFER TO RECOMMEND WITH EACH?
Seasonal vegetables, raw and braised, with Sancerre; duck breast with turnips and cabbage with red Burgundy.

IN THE PAST YEAR, WHAT WINES IN YOUR WINE PROGRAM HAVE CUSTOMERS BECOME MORE WILLING TO ORDER?
Loire Valley whites and Austrian Grüner Veltliner.

Pinot Provence

686 Anton Boulevard
Costa Mesa, California 92626
phone 714-444-5900 fax 714-444-5906

Scott S. Teruya
GENERAL MANAGER
AND SOMMELIER

WHAT ARE SOME OF YOUR ULTIMATE FOOD AND WINE PAIRINGS?
Braised rabbit with grilled portobella mushroom, foie gras raviolis and braised red chard with red Burgundy or Gigondas; our Belgian endive and wild cress salad with candied pecans Roquefort and walnut vinaigrette pairs well with an Alsatian Gewürztraminer with some residual sugar.

DESCRIBE YOUR WINE SELECTIONS.
A 500-selection list of older and current vintages from all major wine regions and in all price categories, including many great finds at reasonable prices. We also feature fifty to seventy-five half-bottles.

WHAT CATEGORY OF WINE IS THE BEST VALUE IN YOUR RESTAURANT?
The "Old World Interesting Alternatives" section of our list, featuring the wines of Spain and Portugal.

NAME RECENT WINE DISCOVERIES THAT HAVE EXCITED YOU.
Spanish red and white wines. Many are extremely good values, high quality and consistent from vintage to vintage.

WHAT IS YOUR FAVORITE WINE REGION IN THE WORLD TODAY?
Burgundy. It is amazing that a wine produced from Pinot Noir can develop flavors, concentration, complexity and be defined by terroir.

WHAT IS THE BEST ASPECT OF YOUR JOB?
Wine education is the most rewarding.

IF YOU WERE NOT IN THE WINE PROFESSION, WHAT WOULD YOU BE DOING?
Something in the medical field. I was ready to run off to medical school before I decided to attend the Culinary Institute of America.

Rattlesnake

46200 Harrison Place
Coachella, California 92236
phone 760-775-2880 fax 760-863-4651
website www.trump29.com

David F. Manzella
SOMMELIER

WHAT INSPIRED YOU TO PURSUE A CAREER THAT INVOLVES WINE?
Tasting a bottle of Stag's Leap SLV as a busboy. This chance encounter with
leftover wine planted the seed for my fascination with wine.

NAME TWO OF YOUR FAVORITE WINES OR WINE REGIONS FROM AROUND
THE WORLD.
Chardonnay from Burgundy, with its sleek style and mineral qualities; and
Niagara Peninsula, with its great ice wines. I'm from Buffalo, New York, so I
guess this is my hometown team!

NAME RECENT WINE DISCOVERIES THAT HAVE EXCITED YOU.
Wines from Santa Barbara County. Foxen's Chenin Blanc is the perfect example
of mind-blowing quality and great pricing of Santa Barbara wines.

WHAT ARE THE MOST UNIQUE FEATURES IN YOUR WINE PROGRAM?
We feature biweekly wine dinners, limited to forty guests. These dinners range
in theme from Paul Hobbs to Veuve Clicquot five-course pairings.

WHAT CATEGORY OF WINE IS THE BEST VALUE IN YOUR RESTAURANT?
Syrah.

NAME A COUPLE OF YOUR RESTAURANT'S SIGNATURE DISHES. WHAT
TYPES OF WINE DO YOU PREFER TO RECOMMEND WITH EACH?
Hawaiian yellowfin tuna steak, cooked to temperature, served over quinoa and
spoon spinach with a mango-chili sesame salsa, with Riesling; veal porterhouse
steak, served with Pinot Noir essence, gingered squash and Maui onion rings
with Santa Barabara Syrah.

Rembrandt's Beautiful Food

909 East Yorba Linda Boulevard
Placentia, California 92870
phone 714-528-6222 fax 714-528-6202

Bernie Gordon
PARTNER AND SOMMELIER

NAME ONE OR TWO OF YOUR FAVORITE WINE DISTRICTS OR WINE REGIONS FROM AROUND THE WORLD.
Number one is Burgundy for both white and red, especially red. I also much admire and enjoy the Rhône varietals from Paso Robles and its environs. I love the flavors.

NAME RECENT WINE DISCOVERIES THAT HAVE EXCITED YOU.
Chalk Hill Sauvignon Blanc for its perfume and texture, and many of Winebow's Italian selections, which are great values!

WHAT BITS OF INFORMATION WOULD YOU LIKE YOUR CUSTOMERS TO KNOW ABOUT YOU?
I have interests in numismatics and astronomy, and I'm an old movie buff.

IF YOU WERE NOT IN THIS PROFESSION, WHAT WOULD YOU BE DOING?
Outside of restaurant and wine activities, I love to read, mostly history. I would like to write.

DESCRIBE YOUR WINE SELECTIONS, BOTH BY THE GLASS AND ON YOUR LIST.
We have a versatile and varied (rather than specialized) list, but promote Pinot Noir. We are attempting to broaden our guests' enjoyment of different kinds of wines; for instance, sometimes recommending a dry Gewürztraminer instead of a Chardonnay.

WHAT CATEGORY OF WINE IS THE BEST VALUE IN YOUR RESTAURANT?
Australian wines in many varietals. They have an excellent price-to-quality ratio.

NAME A COUPLE OF YOUR RESTAURANT'S SIGNATURE DISHES. WHAT TYPES OF WINE DO YOU PREFER TO RECOMMEND WITH EACH?
Salmon with Oregon Pinot Noir; culotte steak with Paso Robles Syrah.

IN THE PAST YEAR, WHAT WINES IN YOUR WINE PROGRAM HAVE CUSTOMERS BECOME MORE WILLING TO ORDER?
American Riesling and Pinot Noir from any appellation.

Renato Ristorante at Portofino Beach Hotel

2304 West Ocean Front Boulevard
Newport Beach, California 92663
phone 949-673-8058 fax 949-723-4370
website www.renatoristorante.com

Kenneth J. Ricamore
OWNER AND WINE BUYER

WHAT INSPIRED YOU TO PURSUE A CAREER THAT INVOLVES WINE?
When I first came to own this restaurant, the manager was buying the wine. When he left, I was forced to educate myself.

WHAT PART OF YOUR JOB DO YOU ENJOY THE MOST?
I enjoy making recommendations and really surprising the guest with a selection.

NAME ONE OF YOUR FAVORITE WINE DISTRICTS FROM AROUND THE WORLD.
Montalcino, Tuscany. We are Italian and I find that this region provides wines that enhance our food wonderfully.

DESCRIBE YOUR WINE SELECTIONS.
We offer sixteen selections in our by-the-glass program ranging from $9.95 to $13.50.

WHAT ARE THE MOST UNIQUE FEATURES IN YOUR WINE PROGRAM?
Our semi-monthly wine dinners.

WHAT CATEGORY OF WINE IS THE BEST VALUE IN YOUR RESTAURANT?
Our by-the-glass wines.

NAME ONE OF YOUR RESTAURANT'S SIGNATURE DISHES. WHAT WINE DO YOU PREFER TO RECOMMEND WITH IT?
Homemade pasta rotelle with Rosso di Montalcino.

IN THE PAST YEAR, WHAT WINES IN YOUR WINE PROGRAM HAVE CUS-TOMERS BECOME MORE WILLING TO ORDER?
Washington and Oregon wines.

La Rive Gauche

320 Tejon Place
Palos Verdes Estate, California 90274
phone 310-378-0267 fax 310-373-5837
website www.chowbaby.com/larivegauche

Jacques M. Grenier
OWNER AND WINE BUYER

NAME ONE OR TWO OF YOUR FAVORITE WINE DISTRICTS OR WINE REGIONS FROM AROUND THE WORLD.
France for its good selection of earthy wines; Canada for its ice wines.

NAME RECENT WINE DISCOVERIES THAT HAVE EXCITED YOU.
Château Cordet, from Margaux, is a great value.

WHAT BITS OF INFORMATION WOULD YOU LIKE YOUR CUSTOMERS TO KNOW ABOUT YOU?
I'm a discoverer of unusual backgrounds and would like to be known as a young son of a farmer. I learned a lot from my father.

IF YOU WERE NOT IN THIS PROFESSION, WHAT WOULD YOU BE DOING?
I would be a winemaker, for starters. I'd get fresh air all day, like my father.

TO WHAT WINE ORGANIZATIONS OR SOCIETIES TO YOU BELONG?
A private group, "Fifteen Friends From Around the World." We meet once a year for special wine meetings.

DESCRIBE YOUR WINE SELECTIONS, BOTH BY THE GLASS AND ON YOUR LIST.
My wine list is recognized as being very reasonably priced compared to others, especially in the French and American selections.

WHAT CATEGORY OF WINE IS THE BEST VALUE IN YOUR RESTAURANT?
Petites Châteaux from Bordeaux, especially Margaux.

NAME A FEW OF YOUR RESTAURANT'S SIGNATURE DISHES. WHAT TYPES OF WINE DO YOU PREFER TO RECOMMEND WITH EACH?
Veal Oscar, crabmeat sauce, béarnaise foie gras with a rich, German wine; ostrich with Pinot Noir; coquilles St. Jacques with Carneros Chardonnay.

WHAT ARE SOME OTHER ULTIMATE WINE AND FOOD PAIRINGS?
Bordeaux Saint-Estèphe and a nice veal chop with wild mushroom sauce.

Röckenwagner Restaurant

2435 Main Street
Santa Monica, California 90405
phone 310-399-6504 fax 310-399-7984
website www.rockenwagner.com

David Osenbach
SOMMELIER

WHAT INSPIRED YOU TO PURSUE A CAREER THAT INVOLVES WINE?
I've always been tremendously interested in wine and food.

WHAT PART OF YOUR JOB DO YOU ENJOY THE MOST?
I enjoy having our customers fall in love with a wine that they've never heard of before.

NAME RECENT WINE DISCOVERIES THAT HAVE EXCITED YOU.
Pinot Noir from some of the newer AVAs in California, like Santa Rita Hills.

IF YOU WERE NOT IN THIS PROFESSION, WHAT WOULD YOU BE DOING?
I'd be an orchestra conductor.

DESCRIBE YOUR WINE SELECTIONS, BOTH BY THE GLASS AND ON YOUR LIST.
We have one of the largest selections of German and Austrian wines in the area, although we're not a German restaurant (despite the name). These wines are great values and pair wonderfully with our food. Also, very few of our customers know about them, so it makes my job more of an educational experience for everyone involved.

WHAT CATEGORY OF WINE IS THE BEST VALUE IN YOUR RESTAURANT?
Austrian whites and reds from the Rhône.

NAME ONE OF YOUR RESTAURANT'S SIGNATURE DISHES. WHAT WINE DO YOU PREFER TO RECOMMEND WITH IT?
Simple steamed white asparagus with Austrian Grüner Veltliner.

IN THE PAST YEAR, WHAT WINES IN YOUR WINE PROGRAM HAVE CUSTOMERS BECOME MORE WILLING TO ORDER?
German and Austrian wines, especially Grüner Veltliner.

Rosa's Italian Restaurant

425 North Vineyard Avenue
Ontario, California 91764
phone 909-937-1220 fax 909-937-7022
website www.rosasitalian.com

Melissa Herzog
WINE BUYER

WHAT INSPIRED YOU TO PURSUE A CAREER THAT INVOLVES WINE?
I grew up in a family where wine was always a part of the dining experience.

WHAT PART OF YOUR JOB DO YOU ENJOY THE MOST?
Pairing wines with foods, recommending wines with certain foods and giving the guests a pleasurable experience.

NAME A COUPLE OF YOUR FAVORITE WINES FROM AROUND THE WORLD.
I love Napa Cabernet Sauvignon as well as Russian River Valley Chardonnay and Pinot Noir.

NAME RECENT WINE DISCOVERIES THAT HAVE EXCITED YOU.
California Zinfandels.

WHAT BITS OF INFORMATION WOULD YOU LIKE YOUR CUSTOMERS TO KNOW ABOUT YOU?
We like our customers to feel that they are part of our family here.

DESCRIBE YOUR WINE SELECTIONS, BOTH BY THE GLASS AND ON YOUR LIST.
We provide a wide range of selections by the glass in order to give our customers an opportunity to try new wines.

WHAT CATEGORY OF WINE IS THE BEST VALUE IN YOUR RESTAURANT?
California Cabernet and Italian varietals.

NAME ONE OF YOUR RESTAURANT'S SIGNATURE DISHES. WHAT WINE DO YOU PREFER TO RECOMMEND WITH IT?
Osso buco paired with Brunello di Montalcino.

IN THE PAST YEAR, WHAT WINES IN YOUR WINE PROGRAM HAVE CUSTOMERS BECOME MORE WILLING TO ORDER?
California Merlot.

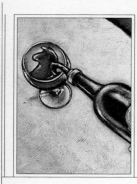

Le St. Germain
74-985 Highway 111
Indian Wells, California 92210
phone 760-773-6511 fax 760-773-6510
website www.lestgermain.com

David Yaquinto
SOMMELIER

NAME ONE OR TWO OF YOUR FAVORITE WINE DISTRICTS OR WINE
REGIONS FROM AROUND THE WORLD.
Bordeaux is a favorite because of the complexity of its wines, and Australia
because its winemakers truly know how to make good Shiraz.

NAME RECENT WINE DISCOVERIES THAT HAVE EXCITED YOU.
Australian Shiraz is now some of the best in the world; Mexico, because it now
produces world-class red and white wines.

IF YOU WERE NOT IN THIS PROFESSION, WHAT WOULD YOU BE DOING?
Golfing. I love the game.

DESCRIBE YOUR WINE SELECTIONS, BOTH BY THE GLASS AND ON YOUR LIST.
Our wine selections are geared toward optimal buying for seasonal business.

WHAT ARE THE MOST UNIQUE FEATURES IN YOUR WINE PROGRAM?
We have a large red Bordeaux selection.

WHAT CATEGORY OF WINE IS THE BEST VALUE IN YOUR RESTAURANT?
Red Bordeaux.

NAME A COUPLE OF YOUR RESTAURANT'S SIGNATURE DISHES. WHAT
TYPES OF WINE DO YOU PREFER TO RECOMMEND WITH EACH?
Seared foie gras with Sauternes; rack of lamb with mature red Bordeaux, from
Pauillac.

IN THE PAST YEAR, WHAT WINES IN YOUR WINE PROGRAM HAVE CUS-
TOMERS BECOME MORE WILLING TO ORDER?
Red Bordeaux, Oregon Pinot Noirs and Australian reds.

Villa Nova Restaurant

3131 West Pacific Coast Highway
Newport Beach, California 92663
phone 949-642-7880 fax 949-642-1865
website www.villanovarestaurant.com

John W. Caneer
WINE BUYER

WHAT INSPIRED YOU TO PURSUE A CAREER THAT INVOLVES WINE?
I was a bartender for about ten years, and when the opportunity to get involved with wine came along, I couldn't pass it up.

WHAT PART OF YOUR JOB DO YOU ENJOY THE MOST?
Finding the right wine for customers, especially when they appreciate our efforts.

NAME ONE OR TWO OF YOUR FAVORITE WINE DISTRICTS OR WINE REGIONS FROM AROUND THE WORLD.
Oregon Pinot Noirs, because they represent the true nature of great Pinot Noir. Also super-Tuscans, because they pair so well with our menu.

IF YOU WERE NOT IN THIS PROFESSION, WHAT WOULD YOU BE DOING?
Fishing in Mexico.

DESCRIBE YOUR WINE SELECTIONS, BOTH BY THE GLASS AND ON YOUR LIST.
Our wine list has mostly wine from California and Italy, which suit our customers' palates and our menu. I try to get the staff excited by adding new wines from South Africa and Australia when I can.

WHAT ARE THE MOST UNIQUE FEATURES IN YOUR WINE PROGRAM?
Our California verticals of Cabernet Sauvignon and Sauvignon Blanc are quite spectacular.

WHAT CATEGORY OF WINE IS THE BEST VALUE IN YOUR RESTAURANT?
Most of our wines are good values.

IN THE PAST YEAR, WHAT WINES IN YOUR WINE PROGRAM HAVE CUS-TOMERS BECOME MORE WILLING TO ORDER?
Syrah.

230 Forest Avenue
RICHARD ROTHBARD, SOMMELIER
230 Forest Avenue, Laguna Beach
949-494-2545

Alto Palato Trattoria
DANILLO TERRIBILI, OWNER
AND WINE BUYER
755 North La Cienega Boulevard,
Los Angeles
310-657-9271

Angelini Osteria
GINO ANGELINI, OWNER
AND WINE BUYER
7313 Beverly Boulevard, Los Angeles
323-297-0070

Antonello Ristorante
STEVE NEBOL, SOMMELIER
1611 Sunflower Avenue, Santa Ana
714-751-7153

Aubergine
TIM GOODELL, OWNER, CHEF
AND WINE BUYER
508 29th Street, Newport Beach
714-723-4150

Café Del Rey
PHILIP GRANT, MANAGER
AND WINE STEWARD
4451 Admiralty Way, Marina Del Rey
310-823-6395

Café La Boheme
RAY CACCIOLI, WINE BUYER
8400 Santa Monica Boulevard,
West Hollywood
323-848-2360

Campanile Restaurant
GEORGE COSSETTE, WINE BUYER
624 South La Brea Avenue, Los Angeles
323-938-1447

Capo Restaurant
BRUCE MARDER, OWNER
AND WINE BUYER
1810 Ocean Avenue, Santa Monica
310-394-5550

Chanteclair
BULENT YAGIZ, MANAGER
AND WINE BUYER
18921 MacArthur Boulevard, Irvine
949-752-8001

Crustacean Restaurant and Lounge
DAVID JONES, SOMMELIER
9646 Little Santa Monica Boulevard,
Beverly Hills
310-205-8990

The Dining Room at the Ritz-Carlton Laguna Niguel
HANNA DABROWSKI, BEVERAGE
MANAGER AND SOMMELIER
One Ritz Carlton Drive, Dana Point
949-240-2000

Le Dome
EDDY KERKHOFS, WINE BUYER
8720 Sunset Boulevard, Los Angeles
310-659-6919

Doug Arango's
ROBERT EVANS, WINE BUYER
73520 El Paseo, Palm Desert
760-341-4120

Duane's Prime Steaks at the Mission Inn
TOM SZALLAY, WINE BUYER
3649 Mission Inn Avenue, Riverside
909-784-0300

Five Crowns Restaurant

CHRIS SZCHENYI, WINE BUYER
3801 East Coast Highway,
Corona Del Mar
949-760-0331

Granita

PHOITOS KYRIAKOUZIS, WINE BUYER
23725 West Malibu Road, Malibu
310-456-0488

Jensen's

CHRIS LONGO, WINE BUYER
73601 Highway 111, Palm Desert
760-346-9393

JiRaffe

STEPHEN PARRA, WINE BUYER
502 Santa Monica Boulevard,
Santa Monica
310-917-6671

L'Opera

CHRISTOPHER LAVINE, GENERAL
MANAGER AND SOMMELIER
101 Pine Avenue, Long Beach
562-491-0066

Los Angeles Country Club

BRUCE PRUITT, GENERAL MANAGER
10101 Wilshire Boulevard, Los Angeles
323-272-2134

Morton's of Chicago

WILLIAM LEWIS, WINE BUYER
1641 West Sunflower, Santa Ana
714-444-4834

Napa Valley Grille

RAFAEL DUMAS, SOMMELIER
Westwood Center, 1100 Glendon
Avenue, Los Angeles
310-824-3322

New York Grill

RICHARD JOOS, MANAGER
AND WINE BUYER
950 Ontario Mills Drive, Ontario
909-987-1928

Opaline

DAVID ROSOFF, MANAGING PARTNER
AND WINE DIRECTOR
7450 Beverly Boulevard, Los Angeles
323-857-6725

L'Orangerie

STEPHANE CLASQUIN, MAÎTRE D'
903 North La Cienega Boulevard,
Los Angeles
310-652-9770

The Polo Lounge at the Beverly Hills Hotel

CLAUDE BOUDOUX, FOOD AND
BEVERAGE DIRECTOR
9641 Sunset Boulevard, Beverly Hills
310-276-2251

The Regency Club

MATHIAS ORELLANA, FOOD AND
BEVERAGE DIRECTOR
10900 Wilshire Boulevard, Los Angeles
310-208-1443

Saddle Peak Lodge

GERHARD TRATTER, GENERAL
MANAGER AND WINE BUYER
419 Cold Canyon Road, Calabasas
818-222-3888

Spago Beverly Hills

DAVID ORGANIZAK, MANAGER
AND SOMMELIER
KEVIN O'CONNOR, SOMMELIER
176 North Canon Drive, Beverly Hills
310-385-0880

Studio at Montage Resort and Spa

CHRIS COON, DIRECTOR OF WINE
30801 South Coast Highway,
Laguna Beach
949-715-6420

Troquet

SYLVIE CAHUZAC, SOMMELIER
333 Bristol Street, Costa Mesa
714-708-6865

Valentino

PIERO SELVAGGIO, OWNER
AND WINE BUYER
3115 Pico Boulevard, Santa Monica
310-829-4313

La Vie en Rose

LOUIS LAULHERE, OWNER
AND WINE BUYER
240 South State College Boulevard, Brea
714-529-8333

Vincenti Ristorante

GARY FREEDMAN, WINE BUYER
11930 San Vincente Boulevard,
Los Angeles
310-207-0127

The Wine Country

TIM HARTWIG, WINE BUYER
2301 Redondo Avenue, Signal Hill
562-597-8303

Alfiere Mediterranean Bistro

1590 Harbor Island Drive
San Diego, California 92101
phone 619-692-2778 fax 619-692-2737
website alfiereonline.com

Antonio C. Friscia
EXECUTIVE CHEF AND WINE BUYER

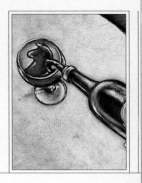

WHAT INSPIRED YOU TO PURSUE A CAREER THAT INVOLVES WINE?
A lifelong passion for food and wine.

WHAT PART OF YOUR JOB DO YOU ENJOY THE MOST?
Recommending different varietals that pair with my food, and making people happy.

NAME SEVERAL OF YOUR FAVORITE WINE DISTRICTS FROM AROUND THE WORLD.
Alsace for its complex and elegant varietals; Burgundy for its complex, earthy wines; Piedmont for its rich, complex and earthy varietals.

IF YOU WERE NOT IN THIS PROFESSION, WHAT WOULD YOU BE DOING?
Making wine or working in a vineyard.

DESCRIBE YOUR WINE SELECTIONS, BOTH BY THE GLASS AND ON YOUR LIST.
We have an international selection that focuses on Italy and Old World–style wines. We offer more than fifty wines by the glass. We are committed to turning people on to new varietals that will complement their dining experience.

WHAT CATEGORY OF WINE IS THE BEST VALUE IN YOUR RESTAURANT?
All categories are values, since we don't overprice anything.

NAME A COUPLE OF YOUR RESTAURANT'S SIGNATURE DISHES. WHAT TYPES OF WINE DO YOU PREFER TO RECOMMEND WITH EACH?
Seared Hudson Valley foie gras and caramelized pears with ice wine; chocolate soufflé with Brachetto d'Acqui.

IN THE PAST YEAR, WHAT WINES IN YOUR PROGRAM HAVE CUSTOMERS BECOME MORE WILLING TO ORDER?
Wines from Alsace, New Zealand and Italy.

Azzura Point Restaurant at Loews Coronado Bay Resort

4000 Coronado Bay Road
Coronado, California 92118
phone 619-424-4000 fax 619-628-5468
website www.loews.com

Kurt A. Kirschenman
SOMMELIER

WHAT ARE SOME OF YOUR ULTIMATE FOOD AND WINE PAIRINGS?
Lobster risotto paired with Italian white (Gavi, Greco di Tufo); seared ahi tuna with dry Riesling from Alsace or Austria; roasted venison loin wrapped in bacon with massive Australian Shiraz blend.

DESCRIBE YOUR WINE SELECTIONS.
We are strong on California white and red wines, but also feature wines from many regions around the world.

WHAT CATEGORIES OF WINE ARE THE BEST VALUES ON YOUR WINE LIST?
California Sauvignon Blancs, Bordeaux and Australian wines.

NAME RECENT WINE DISCOVERIES THAT HAVE EXCITED YOU.
Australia whites are outstanding; its reds great value.

WHAT IS YOUR FAVORITE WINES REGION IN THE WORLD TODAY?
Whites and reds from the Rhône Valley. They are tremendous. Also, Australian wines are outstanding and are usually great values.

WHAT LED YOU TO PURSUE A CAREER THAT INVOLVES WINE?
I became highly motivated to learn about wine both during my time as a bartender here at the restaurant and during my travels to the major wine regions in Europe.

WHAT ARE THE BEST ASPECTS OF YOUR JOB?
It is very rewarding to have guests say "Wow!" when they try a wine I've recommended for the first time.

IF YOU WERE NOT IN THIS PROFESSION, WHAT WOULD YOU BE DOING?
Making wine, growing grapes or being a travel guide.

El Bizcocho at the Rancho Bernardo Inn

17550 Bernardo Oaks Drive
San Diego, California 92128
phone 858-675-8500 fax 858-675-8501
website www.jcresorts.com

Michael D. Dalton
HEAD SOMMELIER

WHAT ARE SOME OF YOUR ULTIMATE FOOD AND WINE PAIRINGS?
Spanish red pepper–lacquered scallops with orange and corn ravioli, white asparagus and vanilla bean butter with rich Australian Sauvignon Blanc; our roasted duck with caramelized root vegetables and Pinot Noir; sautéed sea bass with braised short ribs and Port wine reduction with jammy Australian Shiraz; grilled veal chop with morel mushroom sauce and red Bordeaux.

DESCRIBE YOUR WINE SELECTIONS.
Our list features 1,600 selections with breadth and depth in many areas. We encourage our guests to allow us to guide and assist them with their selections, and this is indicated on our cover page.

WHAT CATEGORIES OF WINE ARE THE BEST VALUES ON YOUR WINE LIST?
California Zinfandel and wines from the southern Rhône.

NAME RECENT WINE DISCOVERIES THAT HAVE EXCITED YOU.
New Zealand Sauvignon Blancs—tremendous character and great value; Australian Shirazs and blends, which offer a lot of character and early accessibility.

WHAT IS YOUR FAVORITE WINE REGION IN THE WORLD TODAY?
The Rhône. I love the terroir of the wines and their compatibility with our chef's cuisine.

WHAT LED YOU TO PURSUE A CAREER THAT INVOLVES WINE?
A love of wine and an exposure to a great wine program.

WHAT IS THE BEST ASPECT OF YOUR JOB?
The opportunity to sell, serve and taste the best wines in the world nightly.

IF YOU WERE NOT IN THE WINE PROFESSION, WHAT WOULD YOU BE DOING?
Professional golf.

Donovan's Steak and Chop House

4340 La Jolla Village Drive
San Diego, California 92122
phone 858-450-6666 fax 858-450-6664
website www.donovanssteakhouse.com

Carl J. Essert
GENERAL MANAGER AND SOMMELIER

NAME TWO OF YOUR FAVORITE WINES FROM AROUND THE WORLD.
Oregon Pinot Noirs are especially interesting. Oregon has had several good vintages in a row and is establishing itself as a serious region. Washington State Meritages and varietals are some of the most flavorful, diverse and accessible value wines in the marketplace today.

NAME RECENT WINE DISCOVERIES THAT HAVE EXCITED YOU.
South African Stellenbosch Delheim Grand Reserve Cabernet Sauvignon. I was impressed by its balance, terroir and profile. It's complex, yet not over the top. A diamond in the rough.

DESCRIBE YOUR WINE SELECTIONS, BOTH BY THE GLASS AND ON YOUR LIST.
Wines of the world, offered both by the glass and our wine list. We are attempting to broaden the consumers' horizons and give them a chance to experience either New World or Old World wines categorized by their region.

WHAT ARE THE MOST UNIQUE FEATURES IN YOUR WINE PROGRAM?
Wine categorized by regions and price point, and our large vertical of wines from Domaine de la Romanée-Conti.

WHAT CATEGORY OF WINE IS THE BEST VALUE IN YOUR RESTAURANT?
All white wines except California Chardonnay and Champagne.

NAME A COUPLE OF YOUR RESTAURANT'S SIGNATURE DISHES. WHAT TYPES OF WINE DO YOU PREFER TO RECOMMEND WITH EACH?
Argentinean Malbec, paired with any of our steaks; Canadian ice wines with crème brûlée.

Fleming's Prime Steakhouse and Wine Bar

8970 University Center Lane
La Jolla, California 92122
phone 858-535-0078 fax 858-535-0096

David P. Trainer
WINE MANAGER

WHAT INSPIRED YOU TO PURSUE A CAREER THAT INVOLVES WINE?
My family has always enjoyed wine as an art.

WHAT PART OF YOUR JOB DO YOU ENJOY THE MOST?
Getting the servers and bartenders excited about new and interesting wines.

NAME ONE OF YOUR FAVORITE WINE REGIONS FROM AROUND THE WORLD.
Oregon, for its cutting-edge farming methods and superior wine.

WHAT BITS OF INFORMATION WOULD YOU LIKE YOUR CUSTOMERS TO KNOW ABOUT YOU?
I wrote a travel guide about Alaska and British Columbia in 1999.

IF YOU WERE NOT IN THIS PROFESSION, WHAT WOULD YOU BE?
A professional golfer.

DESCRIBE YOUR WINE SELECTIONS, BOTH BY THE GLASS AND ON YOUR LIST.
By offering more than 100 wines by the glass and 100 by the bottle, we are trying to give guests the chance to order great wines by the glass.

WHAT CATEGORY OF WINE IS THE BEST VALUE IN YOUR RESTAURANT?
Expensive Cabernet Sauvignons, which have low markups in our restaurant.

NAME ONE OF YOUR RESTAURANT'S SIGNATURE DISHES. WHAT WINE DO YOU PREFER TO RECOMMEND WITH IT?
Bone-in filet mignon with Napa Valley Cabernet Sauvignon.

IN THE PAST YEAR, WHAT WINES IN YOUR PROGRAM HAVE CUSTOMERS BECOME MORE WILLING TO ORDER?
California Syrah and Petite Sirah.

George's at The Cove

1250 Prospect Place
La Jolla, California 92037
phone 858-454-4244 fax 858-454-5458
website www.georgesatthecove.com

Steve J. Josefski

RESTAURANT MANAGER
AND WINE BUYER

WHAT ARE SOME OF YOUR ULTIMATE FOOD AND WINE PAIRINGS?
A carrot–coconut milk soup with lemongrass and ginger with lobster cannelloni and mint paired with Mendocino Gewürztraminer; roasted grouper with a ragoût of corn, cranberry beans, zucchini blossom, calamari and Spanish chorizo with lightly oaked Tempranillo.

DESCRIBE YOUR WINE SELECTIONS.
We have 500 selections on the list and hundreds more in the cellar. Our focus is on California, but we incorporate all styles from most wine-growing regions in the world at reasonable prices.

WHAT CATEGORY OF WINE IS THE BEST VALUE IN YOUR RESTAURANT?
Rhône-style wines, which offer great value. We feature selections from many regions of the world, such as France, Australia and California.

NAME RECENT WINE DISCOVERIES THAT HAVE EXCITED YOU.
Spanish wines. Better viticulture, marketing and shipping have brought these wines to a higher level in the United States.

WHAT IS YOUR FAVORITE WINE REGION IN THE WORLD TODAY?
I love them all. After thirty years in the business, I couldn't pick just one.

WHAT LED YOU TO YOUR CURRENT POSITION?
The support of George Hauer (owner of the restaurant), who recognized my passion for wine and provided the means for pursuing it.

WHAT IS THE MOST CHALLENGING PART OF YOUR JOB?
The minute-to-minute challenge of providing a high level of service and satisfaction (and succeeding most of the time).

IF YOU WERE NOT IN THE WINE PROFESSION, WHAT WOULD YOU BE DOING?
Gardening.

Mille Fleurs

6009 Paseo Delisias
Rancho Santa Fe, California 92067
phone 858-756-3085 fax 858-756-9945
website www.millefleurs.com

Bertrand R. Hug
OWNER AND WINE BUYER

DESCRIBE YOUR WINE SELECTIONS.

Our selections reflect my personal taste, although I do try to please more people by having an eclectic selection. Our wine cellar offers more than 700 choices, a selection of wines spanning the globe which includes all price ranges.

WHAT IS YOUR FAVORITE WINE REGION IN THE WORLD TODAY?

I love all the regions.

WHAT LED YOU TO PURSUE A CAREER THAT INVOLVES WINE?

I am the owner, but I handle all the wine purchases and training for both restaurants.

WHAT IS THE MOST CHALLENGING ASPECT OF YOUR JOB?

Wine list management is a constant, evolving job. I taste twenty to fifty wines every day, Monday through Thursday, and write a wine column for the Rancho Santa Fe Review.

IF YOU WERE NOT IN THE WINE PROFESSION, WHAT WOULD YOU BE?

An actor.

Baron's

MOE SHEMIRANI, WINE BUYER
11828 Rancho Berrnardo, Suite 108-09,
San Diego
858-485-8686

Bertrand at Mister A's

BERTRAND HUG, OWNER
AND WINE BUYER
2550 Fifth Avenue, San Diego
619-239-1377

Brigantine

JOHN AZEVEDO, GENERAL MANAGER
AND WINE BUYER
3263 Camino del Mar, Del Mar
858-481-1166

Candelas

ALBERTO MESTRE, PROPRIETOR
AND WINE BUYER
416 Third Avenue, San Diego
619-702-4455

Croce's

CHRIS MILLER, RESTAURANT MANAGER
AND BEVERAGE DIRECTOR
802 Fifth Avenue, San Diego
619-233-4355

Delicias

KEVIN MABBUTT, OWNER
AND WINE BUYER
6106 Paseo Delicias B, Rancho Santa Fe
858-756-8000

Harbor House Restaurant

DEBI MCLAUGHLIN,
CO-WINE DIRECTOR
831 West Harbor Drive, San Diego
619-232-1141

Hornblower Yacht

HILARY ROSSI, FOOD AND
BEVERAGE MANAGER
2825 Fifth Avenue, San Diego
619-686-8700

Jake's Del Mar

CHRIS HOWE, WINE SPECIALIST
1660 Coast Boulevard, Del Mar
858-755-2002

Pacifica Del Mar

ROBERT CARTER, WINE BUYER
1555 Camino Del Mar, Suite 321,
Del Mar
858-792-0476

Pamplemousse Grille

PAM SCHWARTZ, MANAGER
AND WINE BUYER
514 Via De La Valle, Solana Beach
858-792-9090

Rainwater's

LAUREL RAINWATER, OWNER
AND WINE BUYER
1202 Kettner Boulevard, San Diego
619-233-5757

Rancho Valencia Restaurant at the Rancho Valencia Resort

DON BRIGHT, BAR MANAGER
5921 Valencia Circle, Rancho Santa Fe
858-756-1123

Santé Ristorante

TONY BUONSANT, WINE BUYER
7811 Herschel Avenue, La Jolla
858-454-1315

Star of the Sea

Brian Johnston, Executive Chef
and Wine Buyer
1360 North Harbor Drive, San Diego
619-232-7408

Thee Bungalow

Edmund Moore, Owner
and Wine Buyer
4996 West Point Loma Boulevard,
San Diego
619-224-2884

Top of the Cove

Josef Helphinstine, Sommelier
1216 Prospect Street, La Jolla
858-454-7779

Wine Bistro

Bryan Ferres, Wine Buyer
363 Fifth Avenue, San Diego
619-234-7487

The Winesellar &
Brasserie

David Derby, Wine Buyer
Terry Hudson, Wine Buyer
9550 Waples Street, San Diego
858-450-9557

Enotria Café and Wine Bar

1431 Del Paso Boulevard
Sacramento, California 95815
phone 916-922-6792 fax 916-922-6794
website www.enotria.com

Michael B. Chandler
WINE DIRECTOR

NAME TWO OF YOUR FAVORITE WINE REGIONS FROM AROUND THE
WORLD.
Napa Valley and Burgundy. Napa Valley because I love the ripeness of its
Cabernet Sauvignon, Syrah and Zinfandel; and Burgundy because the variety of
styles and character in its wines amaze me.

NAME RECENT WINE DISCOVERIES THAT HAVE EXCITED YOU.
Lodi Viognier produced by Vino Con Brio Winery. It's a delicious wine, and
although the quality is amazing, the value is even more so.

IF YOU WERE NOT IN THIS PROFESSION, WHAT WOULD YOU BE DOING?
Architecture. Before getting into the wine industry, I was going to school to
become an architect.

DESCRIBE YOUR WINE SELECTIONS, BOTH BY THE GLASS AND ON YOUR
LIST.
We offer seven flights of three wines daily that include sparkling wine and
Champagne, white wine and an array of regional red wines. We also have a 395-
bottle wine list that focuses on all the major wine-growing regions of the world.

WHAT ARE THE MOST UNIQUE FEATURES IN YOUR WINE PROGRAM?
We feature a thirty percent discount on all wine purchases every Tuesday
evening.

WHAT CATEGORY OF WINE IS THE BEST VALUE IN YOUR RESTAURANT?
California Cabernet Sauvignon.

NAME A COUPLE OF YOUR RESTAURANT'S SIGNATURE DISHES. WHAT
TYPES OF WINE DO YOU PREFER TO RECOMMEND WITH EACH?
Our paella with Zinfandel or Syrah; our pepper-crusted pork tenderloin with
Russian River Valley Pinot Noir.

Nepheles

1169 Ski Run Boulevard
South Lake Tahoe, California 96150
phone 530-544-8130 fax 530-544-8131
website www.nepheles.com

Timothy R. Halloran

PRESIDENT AND CELLAR MASTER

WHAT ARE SOME OF YOUR ULTIMATE FOOD AND WINE PAIRINGS?
Rack of New Zealand lamb roasted with a grain mustard crust, then finished
with a tequila, garlic, feta cheese demi-glaze with a Shiraz or Zinfandel;
Château d'Yquem with foie gras.

DESCRIBE YOUR WINE SELECTIONS.
Current and aged California wines at reasonable prices with more than 100
items on the list and 3,500 bottles in the cellar.

WHAT CATEGORY OF WINE IS THE BEST VALUE IN YOUR RESTAURANT?
California Cabs that are ten years old or more.

NAME A RECENT WINE DISCOVERY THAT EXCITED YOU.
A 1985 Mondavi Reserve Napa Valley Cabernet Sauvignon.

WHAT IS YOUR FAVORITE WINE REGION IN THE WORLD TODAY?
California, with its cutting-edge technology.

WHAT LED YOU TO YOUR CURRENT POSITION?
My love of food and wine and a B.S. in hotel and restaurant administration
from Oklahoma State University, 1974.

WHAT IS THE BEST ASPECT OF YOUR JOB?
Having a well-trained, experienced staff to work with.

IF YOU WERE NOT IN THE WINE PROFESSION, WHAT WOULD YOU BE
DOING?
I'd be retired.

Le Petit Pier

7238 North Lake Boulevard
Tahoe Vista, California 96148
phone 530-546-4464 fax 530-546-7508

Patricia Dufau-McCarthy
OWNER AND WINE DIRECTOR

NAME ONE OR TWO OF YOUR FAVORITE WINE REGIONS FROM AROUND THE WORLD.
I love wine from all districts around the world. There are too many to name a favorite.

WHAT BITS OF INFORMATION WOULD YOU LIKE YOUR CUSTOMERS TO KNOW ABOUT YOU?
I love exercise, yoga and Pilates. I am a grandmother.

IF YOU WERE NOT IN THIS PROFESSION, WHAT WOULD YOU BE DOING?
I would love to be involved in helping the elderly or very young children.

DESCRIBE YOUR WINE SELECTIONS, BOTH BY THE GLASS AND ON YOUR LIST.
We have an extensive wine list specializing in wines from California and France. Our by-the-glass list usually has about fifteen wines from many varietals.

WHAT ARE THE MOST UNIQUE FEATURES IN YOUR WINE PROGRAM?
We have extravagant wine dinners. We try to bring wines into all dinner parties. It's just as important as the food.

WHAT CATEGORY OF WINE IS THE BEST VALUE IN YOUR RESTAURANT?
Other red varietals, such as those from the Rhône; Zinfandel; Sangiovese.

NAME A COUPLE OF YOUR RESTAURANT'S SIGNATURE DISHES. WHAT TYPES OF WINE DO YOU PREFER TO RECOMMEND WITH EACH?
Maine lobster with white Burgundy; medallions of venison with Cabernet Sauvignon, either from France or Napa Valley.

IN THE PAST YEAR, WHAT WINES IN YOUR WINE PROGRAM HAVE CUSTOMERS BECOME MORE WILLING TO ORDER?
Napa Sangiovese and blends.

The Vintage Press Restaurante

216 North Willis Street
Visalia, California 93291
phone 559-733-3033 fax 559-738-5262
website www.thevintagepress.com

Gregory A. Vartanian
WINE DIRECTOR

NAME SOME OF YOUR FAVORITE WINES FROM AROUND THE WORLD.
Bandol, Austrian white wines and red wines from Paso Robles.

NAME RECENT WINE DISCOVERIES THAT HAVE EXCITED YOU.
Any dry Rosé is a delicious wine, but a challenge to sell.

WHAT BITS OF INFORMATION WOULD YOU LIKE YOUR CUSTOMERS TO KNOW ABOUT YOU?
I am a third-generation restaurateur, and have ten brothers and sisters.

DESCRIBE YOUR WINE SELECTIONS, BOTH BY THE GLASS AND ON YOUR LIST.
We are building a global list that will cover the major areas and also the small producers.

WHAT ARE THE MOST UNIQUE FEATURES IN YOUR WINE PROGRAM?
We have a complete twenty-one-year vertical of Opus One, and verticals in other areas as well. Large bottles are well-represented. Our wines by the glass change weekly.

WHAT CATEGORIES OF WINE ARE THE BEST VALUES IN YOUR RESTAURANT?
Wines from Australia, New Zealand, South Africa and California.

NAME A COUPLE OF YOUR RESTAURANT'S SIGNATURE DISHES. WHAT TYPES OF WINE DO YOU PREFER TO RECOMMEND WITH EACH?
Wild mushrooms sautéed with Cognac in puff pastry paired with a Russian River Pinot Noir; chicken sautéed with roasted garlic and candied lemon peel with a Paso Robles Syrah.

IN THE PAST YEAR, WHAT WINES IN YOUR WINE PROGRAM HAVE CUSTOMERS BECOME MORE WILLING TO ORDER?
Australian reds, New Zealand whites and South African reds.

Biba

SCOTT SMITH, SOMMELIER
2801 Capital Avenue, Sacramento
916-455-2422

Café Fiore

NICK ASHMORE, WINE BUYER
1169 Ski Run Boulevard,
South Lake Tahoe
916-541-2908

Camps at Greenhorn Creek Resort

ROBERT ANDERSON, EXECUTIVE CHEF
AND WINE BUYER
711 McCauley Ranch Road, Angels Camp
209-736-8181

Christophe's French Restaurant

ESAAN MACKANI, WINE BUYER
2304 East Bidwell Street, Folsom
916-983-4883

Christy Hill

DEBBIE MACRORIE, SOMMELIER
115 Grove Street, Tahoe City
530-583-8551

Citronée Bistro & Wine Bar

ROBERT PEREZ, WINE BUYER
320 Broad Street, Nevada City
530-265-5697

City Hotel

TOM BENDER, WINE BUYER
Main Street, Columbia
209-532-1479

City Treasure Restaurant

MICHAEL STUMBOS, OWNER
AND WINE BUYER
1730 L Street, Sacramento
916-447-7380

Elbow Room

MICHAEL SHIRNIAN, OWNER
AND WINE BUYER
731 West San Jose, Fresno
559-227-1234

Erna's Elderberry House

CHRIS SHACKELFORD, WINE BUYER
48688 Victoria Lane, Oakhurst
209-683-6800

The Firehouse

MARIO ORTIZ, WINE BUYER
1112 Second Street, Sacramento
916-442-4772

Il Fornaio

CLIFFORD BURK, WINE BUYER
400 Capital Mall Drive, Sacramento
916-446-4100

Glissandi in the Resort at Squaw Valley

DOUG CARLSON, WINE BUYER
400 Squaw Creek Road, Olympic Valley
530-583-6300

The Kitchen

DOUG NITCHMAN, WINE BUYER
2225 Hurley Way, Sacramento
916-568-7171

Lahontan Country Club Lake Tahoe

RUSSEL KOBAYASHI, MANAGER
AND WINE BUYER
12700 Lodge Trail Drive, Truckee
530-550-2400

Lewmarnels Restaurant at Best Western Station Inn

LEW MARNEL, WINE BUYER

901 Park Avenue, South Lake Tahoe

530-542-1101

Redwood Forest Restaurant

LES HORD, OWNER AND WINE BUYER

121 West Third Street, Chico

530-343-4315

Sicilian Café

JAMES TAYLOR, OWNER, CHEF
AND WINE BUYER

1020 Main Street, Chico

530-345-2233

Victorian Room at the Groveland Hotel

PEGGY MOSLEY, WINE BUYER

18767 Main Street, Groveland

209-962-4000

Wolfdale's

JAN BINNEWEG, WINE BUYER

640 North Lake Boulevard, Tahoe City

530-583-5700

1515 Restaurant
1515 Market Street
Denver, Colorado 80202
phone 303-571-0011 fax 303-431-0940
website www.1515restaurant.com

Gene Tang
OWNER AND SOMMELIER
TEAM: OLAV PETERSON,
EXECUTIVE CHEF AND SOMMELIER

WHAT PART OF YOUR JOB DO YOU ENJOY THE MOST?
Pairing wine with our innovative cuisine and, of course, the joy of trying at least fifty wines weekly.

NAME ONE OR TWO OF YOUR FAVORITE WINE DISTRICTS OR WINE REGIONS FROM AROUND THE WORLD.
Sonoma and Napa for their very different styles of Chardonnay and Cabernet Sauvignon.

NAME RECENT WINE DISCOVERIES THAT HAVE EXCITED YOU.
South African wines for their style and price; New Zealand wines for their freshness, quality and new screwcap stoppers; Italian wine for its variety.

WHAT BITS OF INFORMATION WOULD YOU LIKE YOUR CUSTOMERS TO KNOW ABOUT YOU?
I enjoy fly-fishing and collecting wine.

IF YOU WERE NOT IN THIS PROFESSION, WHAT WOULD YOU BE DOING?
Traveling. I love tasting local wines, foods and culture.

DESCRIBE YOUR WINE SELECTIONS, BOTH BY THE GLASS AND ON YOUR LIST.
We carry more than 200 wines on our list, primarily from California.

WHAT ARE THE MOST UNIQUE FEATURES IN YOUR WINE PROGRAM?
Great wine dinners that are great values, and our wines available by the glass.

NAME A COUPLE OF YOUR RESTAURANT'S SIGNATURE DISHES. WHAT TYPES OF WINE DO YOU PREFER TO RECOMMEND WITH EACH?
Kobe steak, celery root, parsnip gratin and tart cherry reduction served with a California Cabernet blend or Meritage; strawberry balsamic Chilean sea bass with Sonoma County Chardonnay.

IN THE PAST YEAR, WHAT WINES IN YOUR WINE PROGRAM HAVE CUSTOMERS BECOME MORE WILLING TO ORDER?
New Zealand Sauvignon Blanc and Pinot Noir and Oregon Pinot Noir.

Antares Restaurant

57-1/2 Eighth Street
Steamboat Springs, Colorado 80477
phone 970-879-9939 fax 970-879-0718

Douglas W. Enochs

OWNER AND SOMMELIER

WHAT ARE SOME OF YOUR ULTIMATE FOOD AND WINE PAIRINGS?
Pistachio-crusted rack of lamb with Napa Valley Cabernet Sauvignon; Thai curry prawns over jasmine rice with New Zealand Riesling.

DESCRIBE YOUR WINE SELECTIONS.
We offer twenty wines by the glass and have an international list of 175 selections, with an emphasis on American wines.

WHAT CATEGORY OF WINE IS THE BEST VALUE IN YOUR RESTAURANT?
California Chardonnay.

NAME RECENT WINE DISCOVERIES THAT HAVE EXCITED YOU.
Rancho Zabaco Dancing Bull Zinfandel. Well priced with big flavors.

WHAT IS YOUR FAVORITE WINE REGION IN THE WORLD TODAY?
Piedmont. Barolos are my current favorites. I visited the region last year and fell in love.

WHAT LED YOU TO PURSUE A CAREER THAT INVOLVES WINE?
Love of wine and the restaurant business.

WHAT ARE THE BEST ASPECTS OF YOUR JOB?
Drinking wine and socializing with the guests.

IF YOU WERE NOT IN THE WINE PROFESSION, WHAT WOULD YOU BE DOING?
Catering.

Barolo Grill
3030 East Sixth Avenue
Denver, Colorado 80206
phone 303-393-1040 fax 303-333-9240

Mark S. Sandusky
SOMMELIER

WHAT ARE SOME OF YOUR ULTIMATE FOOD AND WINE PAIRINGS?
Our signature dish of duckling braised in red wine paired with aged Barolo (sublime!); Stilton with vintage Port; New Mexican cuisine with Châteauneuf-du-Pape.

DESCRIBE YOUR WINE SELECTIONS.
We specialize in the wines of Italy with a strong selection of wines from Barolo and Barbaresco, Tuscany and the Veneto.

WHAT CATEGORY OF WINE IS THE BEST VALUE IN YOUR RESTAURANT?
Barbera.

NAME RECENT WINE DISCOVERIES THAT HAVE EXCITED YOU.
The wines of Sicily. They are good values and have an entirely different flavor profile from wines from other Italian regions.

WHAT IS YOUR FAVORITE WINE REGION IN THE WORLD TODAY?
The Piedmont region of northern Italy for its Barolo and Barbaresco wines. They're powerful, yet polished and elegant.

WHAT LED YOU TO PURSUE A CAREER THAT INVOLVES WINE?
Fourteen years in the restaurant business, a love of wine and the excitement in introducing people to the joys of great food and wine.

WHAT ARE THE BEST ASPECTS OF YOUR JOB?
When a customer leaves happy and satisfied, satiated by food and wine, that's rewarding.

IF YOU WERE NOT IN THE WINE PROFESSION, WHAT WOULD YOU BE DOING?
Playing trombone in a jazz combo.

Bravo! Ristorante
at the Adams Mark Hotel

1550 Court Place
Denver, Colorado 80202
phone 303-893-3333 fax 303-626-2542
website www.adamsmark.com

Maxence Ariza
SOMMELIER

WHAT INSPIRED YOU TO PURSUE A CAREER THAT INVOLVES WINE?
I grew up in France. At home and on a regular basis, my mother served Alsace Riesling, Pommard, Saint-Émilion and Châteauneuf-du-Pape, to name a few.

NAME ONE OF YOUR FAVORITE WINE REGIONS FROM AROUND THE WORLD.
The wines of the south of France, from Séguret (next to Châteauneuf) to Bellet (next to Nice).

NAME RECENT WINE DISCOVERIES THAT HAVE EXCITED YOU.
Tokaji wines (Hungary) that can be paired with foie gras as well as pork and chocolate.

WHAT BITS OF INFORMATION WOULD YOU LIKE YOUR CUSTOMERS TO KNOW ABOUT YOU?
I teach beverage classes at Johnson and Wales University in Denver. Judo is the only thing that I feel more comfortable doing than tasting wine.

IF YOU WERE NOT IN THIS PROFESSION, WHAT WOULD YOU BE?
A chef or a stuntman.

WHAT ARE THE MOST UNIQUE FEATURES IN YOUR WINE PROGRAM?
We serve a free sample of wine with our complimentary appetizer from our Bravo Vineyard selection. The response has been great, and customers have been able to taste wine a little more outside the box.

NAME A COUPLE OF YOUR RESTAURANT'S SIGNATURE DISHES. WHAT TYPES OF WINE DO YOU PREFER TO RECOMMEND WITH EACH?
Cider-glazed pork chop and sun-dried tomatoes with Valpolicella Ripasso or Breganze Merlot; grilled lamb chops with mustard and goat cheese vinaigrette paired with a super-Tuscan or Barbaresco.

IN THE PAST YEAR, WHAT WINES IN YOUR WINE PROGRAM HAVE CUS-TOMERS BECOME MORE WILLING TO ORDER?
Pinot Grigio.

Brook's Steak House and Cellar

6538 South Yosemite Circle
Greenwich Village, Colorado 80111
phone 303-770-1177 fax 303-770-0193
website www.brookssteakhouse.com

Jeremy J. Reimann
SOMMELIER

WHAT INSPIRED YOU TO PURSUE A CAREER THAT INVOLVES WINE?
When I began fine dining service as a waiter, my biggest weakness was wine knowledge. I wanted to learn, and developed a passion for it.

WHAT PART OF YOUR JOB DO YOU ENJOY THE MOST?
Making recommendations to our guests and building relationships through the love of wine.

NAME ONE OF YOUR FAVORITE WINE DISTRICTS OR WINE REGIONS FROM AROUND THE WORLD.
Burgundy for its incredible depth and character and its interesting history (Napoleon, inheritance laws and World War II).

WHAT WOULD YOU LIKE YOUR CUSTOMERS TO KNOW ABOUT YOU?
I'm a native of Denver, Colorado.

IF YOU WERE NOT IN THIS PROFESSION, WHAT WOULD YOU BE?
A high school history teacher.

DESCRIBE YOUR WINE SELECTIONS, BOTH BY THE GLASS AND ON YOUR LIST.
We try to create a well-balanced list with an emphasis on international and domestic red wines. We have a large variety of wine by the glass, in half-bottles and large-format bottles.

WHAT ARE THE MOST UNIQUE FEATURES IN YOUR WINE PROGRAM?
We have an extensive by-the-glass and half-bottle selection, in addition to a selection of 1,200 standard bottles.

WHAT CATEGORY OF WINE IS THE BEST VALUE IN YOUR RESTAURANT?
Bordeaux, Italian wine and domestic Cabernet Sauvignon.

IN THE PAST YEAR, WHAT WINES IN YOUR WINE PROGRAM HAVE CUSTOMERS BECOME MORE WILLING TO ORDER?
German Silvaner, Italian Soave and domestic Syrah.

California Café

8505 Park Meadows Center Drive
Littleton, Colorado 80124
phone 303-649-1111 fax 303-649-1731
website www.constellationconcepts.com

Justin I. Brown
MANAGER AND WINE BUYER

NAME TWO OF YOUR FAVORITE WINE REGIONS FROM AROUND THE
WORLD.
Chablis for its style and its aging in stainless steel (allowing the true flavor of
the grape to come through); Santa Maria Valley for its outstanding Pinot Noir.

NAME A RECENT WINE DISCOVERY THAT EXCITED YOU.
Carignane is a great food wine and pairs well with game meats. It has power
and the ability to stand up to rich sauces.

WHAT BITS OF INFORMATION WOULD YOU LIKE YOUR CUSTOMERS TO
KNOW ABOUT YOU?
I'm an avid golfer and fly fisherman. I'm also an amateur carpenter and plan to
build my own 200-bottle redwood wine cellar.

IF YOU WERE NOT IN THIS PROFESSION, WHAT WOULD YOU BE?
A civil engineer.

DESCRIBE YOUR WINE SELECTIONS, BOTH BY THE GLASS AND ON YOUR LIST.
We are known for our large selection of wines (265 selections). I always look
for values to pass on to the customer.

WHAT ARE THE MOST UNIQUE FEATURES IN YOUR WINE PROGRAM?
We hold six to ten wine dinners a year; have thirty wines by the glass (all available for free tastes); have thirty-one half-bottles; and several wine flights.

NAME A COUPLE OF YOUR RESTAURANT'S SIGNATURE DISHES. WHAT
TYPES OF WINE DO YOU PREFER TO RECOMMEND WITH EACH?
Grilled salmon with garlic mashed potatoes, sautéed spinach and grapefruit
sauce with Carneros Pinot Noir; grilled ostrich with truffle mashed potatoes,
spaghetti squash and Port wine sauce with Napa Cabernet Sauvignon.

IN THE PAST YEAR, WHAT WINES IN YOUR WINE PROGRAM HAVE CUS-
TOMERS BECOME MORE WILLING TO ORDER?
California Viognier, Syrah, Petite Sirah, Pinot Noir and Sangiovese.

The Cliff House
at Pikes Peak

306 Cañon Avenue
Manitou Springs, Colorado 80829
phone 719-685-3000 fax 719-685-3913
website www.thecliffhouse.com

Paul A. York
GENERAL MANAGER
AND SOMMELIER

WHAT INSPIRED YOU TO PURSUE A CAREER THAT INVOLVES WINE?
My father worked for Heublein, Gallo and United Vintners in the 1970s.
Consequently, I was inspired by Spañada, Annie Green Springs and Thunderbird.

NAME TWO OF YOUR FAVORITE WINE REGIONS FROM AROUND THE WORLD.
Sonoma County for its opulent yet spicy Zinfandel and Napa for its world-class
Cabernet Sauvignon.

NAME RECENT WINE DISCOVERIES THAT HAVE EXCITED YOU.
Pezzi King "SLR" Zinfandel's quality for the price is exceptional; PlumpJack
Chardonnay is so perfect a wine that it cuts through sauces.

WHAT BITS OF INFORMATION WOULD YOU LIKE YOUR CUSTOMERS TO
KNOW ABOUT YOU?
I was a rock musician from L.A. in the 1970s. I own a 24-track digital record-
ing studio in my home.

IF YOU WERE NOT IN THIS PROFESSION, WHAT WOULD YOU BE DOING?
Rock star—definitely!

DESCRIBE YOUR WINE SELECTIONS, BOTH BY THE GLASS AND ON YOUR LIST.
We focus on New World wines from the United States, Australia and New
Zealand. We are known for our California Syrah, Zinfandel and Pinot Noir.

IN THE PAST YEAR, WHAT WINES IN YOUR WINE PROGRAM HAVE CUS-
TOMERS BECOME MORE WILLING TO ORDER?
California Zinfandel and Syrah, primarily because of our enthusiasm about
these wines.

WHAT ARE SOME ULTIMATE WINE AND FOOD PAIRINGS?
Chocolate with Champagne or sparkling wine (like Blanc de Blanc); foie gras
with Zinfandel or Syrah; pepper steak with a heavy Cabernet Sauvignon;
chanterelles with Pinot Noir; peach tarts with Auslese; blue cheese with
vintage Porto.

The Cliff House
at Pikes Peak

306 Cañon Avenue
Manitou Springs, Colorado 80829
phone 719-685-3000 fax 719-685-3913
website www.thecliffhouse.com

Julius R. Watson
DIRECTOR OF FOOD AND BEVERAGE

WHAT PART OF YOUR JOB DO YOU ENJOY THE MOST?
Helping guests make selections and offering wine education to staff and guests.

NAME TWO OF YOUR FAVORITE WINE REGIONS FROM AROUND THE WORLD.
Rhône Valley—I love Syrah and the big, full-bodied, smoky styles produced there; Sonoma County for its Chardonnay and Pinot Noir.

NAME RECENT WINE DISCOVERIES THAT HAVE EXCITED YOU.
Côtes du Rhône from 1998 is full-flavored and great value; New Zealand Sauvignon Blanc is fresh, fruity and floral, with good balance.

IF YOU WERE NOT IN THIS PROFESSION, WHAT WOULD YOU BE DOING?
I'd be in computers.

WHAT ARE THE MOST UNIQUE FEATURES IN YOUR WINE PROGRAM?
We have a good half-bottle selection and an extensive range of dessert wines, all served in Riedel crystal glassware.

WHAT CATEGORY OF WINE IS THE BEST VALUE IN YOUR RESTAURANT?
Approximately forty top-quality California Zinfandels priced from $25 to $150, and several Turley single vineyard bottlings.

NAME A COUPLE OF YOUR RESTAURANT'S SIGNATURE DISHES. WHAT TYPES OF WINE DO YOU PREFER TO RECOMMEND WITH EACH?
Rabbit en crépinette with Oregon Willamette Valley Pinot Noir; tamarind-lacquered half duckling, d'Anjou pear, persimmon coulis with a Côtes du Rhône or Australian Shiraz.

IN THE PAST YEAR, WHAT WINES IN YOUR WINE PROGRAM HAVE CUS-TOMERS BECOME MORE WILLING TO ORDER?
Pinot Noir from California and Oregon and red Zinfandel.

Larkspur Restaurant
458 Vail Valley Drive
Vail, Colorado 81657
phone 970-479-8050 fax 970-479-8052
website www.larkspurvail.com

Kevin M. Furtado
BEVERAGE DIRECTOR
AND SOMMELIER

DESCRIBE YOUR WINE SELECTIONS.
Very diverse, with an emphasis on wines that are food-friendly and good values.

WHAT CATEGORY OF WINE IS THE BEST VALUE IN YOUR RESTAURANT?
Italian wines. With the run of great vintages, there have been many great,
affordable wines available.

WHAT IS YOUR FAVORITE REGION OR AREA IN THE WORLD TODAY?
Alsace. This exceptional region produces wine of elegance and intensity. It is
also a thrill to see the look of enjoyment and amazement when a person tastes
an Alsatian Pinot Gris for the first time.

WHAT LED YOU TO PURSUE A CAREER THAT INVOLVES WINE?
My passion for food led me to restaurants, which led me to wine.

WHAT ARE THE BEST AND MOST CHALLENGING ASPECTS OF YOUR JOB?
Educating myself, my staff and our guests.

IF YOU WERE NOT IN THE WINE PROFESSION, WHAT WOULD YOU BE
DOING?
I could not imagine not being in the restaurant business.

The Lodge at Vail

174 East Gore Creek Drive
Vail, Colorado 81657
phone 970-476-5011 fax 970-476-7425
website www.lodgeatvail.rockresorts.com

Willem A. Johnson
CELLAR MASTER AND SOMMELIER

NAME TWO OF YOUR FAVORITE WINE REGIONS FROM AROUND THE WORLD.

Alsace and Italy. Alsace because I think it's a magical place for pairing food and wine. Italy because I believe, for all tastes, more good wine comes out of Italy than all other wine-producing regions combined.

NAME RECENT WINE DISCOVERIES THAT HAVE EXCITED YOU.

Several great Austrian Rieslings that go beyond styles from Alsace or Germany; not bone-dry or laden with residual sugar, these wines are approachable for more palates than their predecessors.

WHAT BITS OF INFORMATION WOULD YOU LIKE YOUR CUSTOMERS TO KNOW ABOUT YOU?

Take everything I say with a grain of salt and a sense of humor. After all, I drink for a living.

IF YOU WERE NOT IN THIS PROFESSION, WHAT WOULD YOU BE DOING?

Making wine or flying helicopters. Either way, my head would still be in the clouds.

NAME A COUPLE OF YOUR RESTAURANT'S SIGNATURE DISHES. WHAT TYPES OF WINE DO YOU PREFER TO RECOMMEND WITH EACH?

Bison atop Nueske grits with Côte-Rôtie or Carneros Syrah; arborio-crusted sea scallops atop potato-parsnip purée with old-style Soave Classico Superiore.

IN THE PAST YEAR, WHAT WINES IN YOUR WINE PROGRAM HAVE CUS-TOMERS BECOME MORE WILLING TO ORDER?

Dedicated red drinkers have been trying different whites and even blush wines more often. I have also seen a resurgence in Champagne's popularity as a wine to enjoy with dinner, not just at celebrations.

Ludwig's Restaurant

20 Vail Road
Vail, Colorado 81657
phone 970-476-5656 fax 970-476-1639
website www.sonnenalp.com

Andreas Wickhoff
SOMMELIER

NAME TWO OF YOUR FAVORITE WINE REGIONS FROM AROUND THE WORLD.

The Loire Valley is so distinctive, so diverse and offers the best Sauvignon Blanc in the world. Tuscany has consistently great vintages and has both indigenous grape-style wines and international-style wines.

NAME RECENT WINE DISCOVERIES THAT HAVE EXCITED YOU.

Priorat, Spain, has great reds with a very distinctive style derived from the grapes and climate. Also, California Cabernets from the 1980s are great.

WHAT BITS OF INFORMATION WOULD YOU LIKE YOUR CUSTOMERS TO KNOW ABOUT YOU?

I'm a winter sports enthusiast (especially snowboarding) and a "world explorer," as I've worked in Australia, France, Austria, and both the East Coast and now Colorado in the United States.

IF YOU WERE NOT IN THIS PROFESSION, WHAT WOULD YOU BE?

A professional soccer player.

DESCRIBE YOUR WINE SELECTIONS, BOTH BY THE GLASS AND ON YOUR LIST.

We have a balance between Old and New World wines, with a great selection of Bordeaux and Napa reds.

NAME A COUPLE OF YOUR RESTAURANT'S SIGNATURE DISHES. WHAT TYPES OF WINE DO YOU PREFER TO RECOMMEND WITH EACH?

Colorado rack of lamb with Bordeaux Médoc or California Cabernet Sauvignon; Dover sole with Sancerre or New Zealand Sauvignon Blanc.

IN THE PAST YEAR, WHAT WINES IN YOUR WINE PROGRAM HAVE CUSTOMERS BECOME MORE WILLING TO ORDER?

Austrian reds and Italian whites from Friuli and Veneto.

Montagna
at the Little Nell

675 East Durant Avenue
Aspen, Colorado 81611
phone 970-920-4600 fax 970-920-6328
website www.thelittlenell.com

Richard Betts
MASTER SOMMELIER
AND WINE DIRECTOR

WHAT INSPIRED YOU TO PURSUE A CAREER THAT INVOLVES WINE?
Living in Italy and enjoying great local wine every day!

NAME ONE OR TWO OF YOUR FAVORITE WINE DISTRICTS OR WINE
REGIONS FROM AROUND THE WORLD.
Burgundy and the northern Rhône. Both offer wines of great specificity,
elegance and finesse with an incredibly sensual appeal.

NAME RECENT WINE DISCOVERIES THAT HAVE EXCITED YOU.
Old-vine Grenache from Spain. Its quality is amazing, and it's such a good value.

WHAT BITS OF INFORMATION WOULD YOU LIKE YOUR CUSTOMERS TO
KNOW ABOUT YOU?
I view wine as a grocery and not a luxury. I drink it with meals every day and
believe it is essential to good health.

DESCRIBE YOUR WINE SELECTIONS, BOTH BY THE GLASS AND ON YOUR LIST.
The scope of the list is very broad. I want to have something for everyone. We
are known for artisan wine from all vintages at amazing prices. The program is
designed to help people have fun.

WHAT CATEGORY OF WINE IS THE BEST VALUE IN YOUR RESTAURANT?
Burgundy, Germany and Champagne.

NAME A COUPLE OF YOUR RESTAURANT'S SIGNATURE DISHES. WHAT
TYPES OF WINE DO YOU PREFER TO RECOMMEND WITH EACH?
Crab cakes with German Riesling; duck with red Burgundy.

IN THE PAST YEAR, WHAT WINES IN YOUR WINE PROGRAM HAVE CUS-
TOMERS BECOME MORE WILLING TO ORDER?
Red and white Burgundy are by far the best sellers—and growing.

WHAT ARE SOME OTHER ULTIMATE WINE AND FOOD PAIRINGS?
Whatever you like with whatever you like—this is supposed to be fun!

Range Restaurant
304 East Hopkins
Aspen, Colorado 81611
phone 970-925-2402 fax 970-925-6634
website www.renaissancerestaurant.com

Robert A. Ittner
OWNER, GENERAL MANAGER
AND SOMMELIER

WHAT INSPIRED YOU TO PURSUE A CAREER THAT INVOLVES WINE?
Love for wine. No other beverage touches our hearts more than wine.

NAME TWO OF YOUR FAVORITE WINE REGIONS FROM AROUND THE WORLD.
I love Sonoma Valley for the complexity of the wines. Also, Rhône Valley,
whose wines go great with food.

NAME RECENT WINE DISCOVERIES THAT HAVE EXCITED YOU.
New Zealand and Australia offer great values and are really exciting wines.

**WHAT BITS OF INFORMATION WOULD YOU LIKE YOUR CUSTOMERS TO
KNOW ABOUT YOU?**
I love the outdoors and life in Aspen.

IF YOU WERE NOT IN THIS PROFESSION, WHAT WOULD YOU BE DOING?
Teaching and consulting.

DESCRIBE YOUR WINE SELECTIONS, BOTH BY THE GLASS AND ON YOUR LIST.
It's mostly American and French, with all areas represented.

WHAT ARE THE MOST UNIQUE FEATURES IN YOUR WINE PROGRAM?
We have tasting menus nightly, with matched wines.

WHAT CATEGORY OF WINE IS THE BEST VALUE IN YOUR RESTAURANT?
We have a "Best Value" section on our list with many great wines.

**NAME A COUPLE OF YOUR RESTAURANT'S SIGNATURE DISHES. WHAT
TYPES OF WINE DO YOU PREFER TO RECOMMEND WITH EACH?**
Hot date rack of lamb with California Zinfandel; prosciutto-wrapped monkfish
with white Burgundy.

**IN THE PAST YEAR, WHAT WINES IN YOUR WINE PROGRAM HAVE CUS-
TOMERS BECOME MORE WILLING TO ORDER?**
New Zealand, South American and Spanish wines.

Ruth's Chris Steak House

1445 Market Street
Denver, Colorado 80202
phone 303-446-2233 fax 303-446-2244
website www.ruthschrisdenver.com

Marc A. Taylor

GENERAL MANAGER AND
WINE DIRECTOR

WHAT INSPIRED YOU TO PURSUE A CAREER THAT INVOLVES WINE?
I really just took an interest as a busser at our Las Vegas location.

NAME TWO OF YOUR FAVORITE WINE REGIONS FROM AROUND THE WORLD.
Australia for its big, rich, extracted and complex wines at great prices; Spain for wines that are great with our steaks.

NAME RECENT WINE DISCOVERIES THAT HAVE EXCITED YOU.
Chalk Hill Sauvignon Blanc for its Old World style, mineral characteristics and value.

WHAT BITS OF INFORMATION WOULD YOU LIKE YOUR CUSTOMERS TO KNOW ABOUT YOU?
I was born and raised in Las Vegas and moved to Colorado at the age of twenty-one. I love to fly-fish, hunt and golf, all of which go great with wine.

IF YOU WERE NOT IN THIS PROFESSION, WHAT WOULD YOU BE DOING?
I really can't imagine anything else.

DESCRIBE YOUR WINE SELECTIONS, BOTH BY THE GLASS AND ON YOUR LIST.
We have more than 750 selections, with a large selection of California Cabernet Sauvignon and wines from Spain to South Africa.

WHAT ARE THE MOST UNIQUE FEATURES IN YOUR WINE PROGRAM?
We offer more than thirty wines by the glass, several wine flights and a large selection of half-bottles.

WHAT CATEGORIES OF WINE ARE THE BEST VALUES IN YOUR RESTAURANT?
Australian Shiraz and wines from Toro, Spain.

NAME A COUPLE OF YOUR RESTAURANT'S SIGNATURE DISHES. WHAT TYPES OF WINE DO YOU PREFER TO RECOMMEND WITH EACH?
New York strip with a big Tinto de Toro or Priorat; filet mignon with Russian River Pinot Noir.

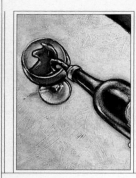

Ship Tavern
at the Brown Palace Hotel

321 17th Street
Denver, Colorado 80202
phone 303-297-3111 fax 303-297-5900
website www.brownpalace.com

William Davis
RESTAURANT MANAGER
AND SOMMELIER

NAME ONE OF YOUR FAVORITE WINE REGIONS FROM AROUND THE
WORLD.
Oregon, especially the Willamette Valley. It makes both delicate and muscular
wines that appeal to a great many palates.

NAME RECENT WINE DISCOVERIES THAT HAVE EXCITED YOU.
Chilean Syrahs, with their wonderful fruit extraction and expression at a great
price.

IF YOU WERE NOT IN THIS PROFESSION, WHAT WOULD YOU BE?
A milkman, if they are still around.

DESCRIBE YOUR WINE SELECTIONS, BOTH BY THE GLASS AND ON YOUR
LIST.
We attempt to offer a broad selection, while always striving to find artisanal
wines. We have the oldest and most extensive cellar in Denver, with more than
1,000 selections.

WHAT ARE THE MOST UNIQUE FEATURES IN YOUR WINE PROGRAM?
Our Cruvinet system allows us to offer by-the-glass library selections from various producers.

WHAT CATEGORY OF WINE IS THE BEST VALUE IN YOUR RESTAURANT?
Strangely enough, due to our futures programs, our lesser growths in 2000
Bordeaux and southern Rhônes are our best values.

NAME ONE OF YOUR RESTAURANT'S SIGNATURE DISHES. WHAT WINE DO
YOU RECOMMEND WITH IT?
The prime rib has been on our menu for fifty years, and I like to serve it with
Willamette Valley Pinot Noir, or something similar.

IN THE PAST YEAR, WHAT WINES IN YOUR WINE PROGRAM HAVE CUS-
TOMERS BECOME MORE WILLING TO ORDER?
Syrah from all areas of the world, Pinot Gris and dessert wines.

Sweet Basil

193 Gore Creek Drive
Vail, Colorado 81657-4549
phone 970-476-0125 fax 970-476-0137
website www.sweetbasil-vail.com

Patrick T. Welch

BEVERAGE DIRECTOR

WHAT ARE SOME OF YOUR ULTIMATE FOOD AND WINE PAIRINGS?
Beef tenderloin and béarnaise sauce with a big California Cabernet Sauvignon;
Colorado rack of lamb with a red Hermitage or Châteauneuf-du-Pape.

DESCRIBE YOUR WINE SELECTIONS.
Our list consists of 425 selections and we offer twenty wines by the glass. We
focus on California and France, but we also have a broad selection of wines
from all over the world.

WHAT CATEGORY OF WINE IS THE BEST VALUE IN YOUR RESTAURANT?
Rhône varietals.

NAME RECENT WINE DISCOVERIES THAT HAVE EXCITED YOU.
The wines from Priorat, Ribera del Duero and other lesser-known wines of
Spain and Portugal have excited me recently.

WHAT IS YOUR FAVORITE WINE REGION IN THE WORLD TODAY?
Burgundy. I love its rich history and the extensive microclimates that create
such diverse wines in this small region.

WHAT LED YOU TO YOUR CURRENT POSITION?
I became involved in fine dining after high school and fell in love with how
wine is made, its history and, of course, the taste.

WHAT ARE THE BEST ASPECTS OF YOUR JOB?
Training the staff and inspiring younger servers to learn about wine.

IF YOU WERE NOT IN THE WINE PROFESSION, WHAT WOULD YOU BE
DOING?
Something related to art or art history.

Tante Louise
4900 East Colfax Avenue
Denver, Colorado 80220-1208
phone 303-355-4488 fax 303-321-6312
website www.tantelouise.com

Emma M. Healion
SOMMELIER

WHAT ARE SOME OF YOUR ULTIMATE FOOD AND WINE PAIRINGS?
Ribera del Duero reds with deer rack; white Châteauneuf-du-Pape with scallops; pan-seared foie gras with Monbazillac; lamb and truffles with Échezeaux; wild mushroom charlotte with Rioja.

DESCRIBE YOUR WINE SELECTIONS.
Our 500-item wine list is predominantly French, with an emphasis on Burgundy.

WHAT CATEGORY OF WINE IS THE BEST VALUE IN YOUR RESTAURANT?
Spanish whites.

NAME A RECENT WINE DISCOVERY THAT EXCITED YOU.
Carmelo Rodero Ribera del Duero Riserva 1996 is a beautiful wine with unique character.

WHAT IS YOUR FAVORITE WINE REGION IN THE WORLD TODAY?
The Rhône Valley. It has a huge variety of wines, many great values and some dynamic new winemakers. There also have been some phenomenal vintages here in the late 1990s.

WHAT LED YOU TO PURSUE A CAREER THAT INVOLVES WINE?
I have a passion for food and wine pairing and was approached to take this position.

WHAT ARE THE BEST ASPECTS OF YOUR JOB?
Seeing customers try something different and get really excited about it. It is extremely rewarding to see customers return again and again to the restaurant, asking for recommendations and totally trusting my judgment.

IF YOU WERE NOT IN THE WINE PROFESSION, WHAT WOULD YOU BE DOING?
Sculpting, or something in the perfume business or art world.

Trios Enoteca

1730 Wynkoop Street
Denver, Colorado 80202
phone 303-293-2887 fax 303-293-8475
website www.triosenoteca.com

Gabriele (Gibbie) Whelehan

GENERAL MANAGER
AND SOMMELIER

NAME TWO OF YOUR FAVORITE WINE REGIONS FROM AROUND THE
WORLD.
Sardinia and Priorat. Sardinia because no one ever thinks of this beautiful place
off the coast of Italy; Priorat because I was absolutely stunned when I saw this
Spanish landscape.

NAME A RECENT WINE DISCOVERY THAT EXCITED YOU.
Poderi di Luigi Einaudi Dolcetto di Dogliani 2000. Its silky earth tones combined with rich cherry fruit make this wine my recent favorite.

WHAT ARE THE MOST UNIQUE FEATURES IN YOUR WINE PROGRAM?
We have an extensive by-the-glass program that allows us to showcase unfamiliar wines as well as old favorites. These wines change every three months. We
also have several themed wine flights.

WHAT CATEGORY OF WINE IS THE BEST VALUE IN YOUR RESTAURANT?
Our French reds category, which excludes Burgundy, Bordeaux and the Rhône
Valley. There are many finds here for less than $30.

NAME A COUPLE OF YOUR RESTAURANT'S SIGNATURE DISHES. WHAT
TYPES OF WINE DO YOU PREFER TO RECOMMEND WITH EACH?
Fresh mozzarella and tomato bruschetta with New Zealand Sauvignon Blanc;
chocolate fondue with Spanish Grenache.

DO YOUR CUSTOMERS FREQUENTLY ORDER WINE BEFORE MENU ITEMS?
Yes. Trios Enoteca is a wine bar, first and foremost, with an excellent small plate
and dessert menu. The immediate reaction for guests is to try one of our wines
by the glass, then to order food. Our servers have great knowledge of the food
menu as well as the wine list, so we practice plenty of "reverse pairing."

Adega Restaurant and Wine Bar

CHRIS FARNUM, SOMMELIER
1700 Wynkoop Street, Denver
303-534-2222

Allred's

PETE CHEROSKE, SOMMELIER
2 Coonskin Ridge, Telluride
970-728-7474

L'Apogee

JAMI JANNY, OWNER AND WINE BUYER
911 Lincoln Avenue, Steamboat Springs
970-879-1919

Beano's Cabin

ROBERT BATTLE, WINE BUYER
Beaver Creek Service Center, Avon
970-949-9090

Bloom

MICHAEL WILCOX, GENERAL MANAGER
AND SOMMELIER
One West Flatiron Circle, Broomfield
720-887-2800

Le Bosquet

CANDACE SHEPHERD, WINE STEWARD
Majestic Plaza, Sixth and Belleview
Streets, Crested Butte
970-349-5808

Bristol at Arrowhead

WENDALL MURRAY, OWNER
AND WINE BUYER
676 Sawatch Drive, Edwards
970-926-2111

The Broker Restaurant

JERRY FRITZLER, WINE BUYER
821 17th Street, Denver
303-292-5065

Café Alpine

KEITH MAHONEY, CHEF, OWNER
AND WINE BUYER
106 East Adams Street, Breckenridge
970-453-8218

The Caribou Club

OLIVER JADERKO, WINE BUYER
411 East Hopkins, Aspen
970-925-2929

Charles Court at the Broadmoor

TIM WEUSTNECK, SOMMELIER
1 Lake Avenue, Colorado Springs
719-634-7711

Chefs'

DAVE DAME, OWNER AND WINE BUYER
936 North Avenue, Grand Junction
970-243-9673

Cool River Café

SPENCER BURTON, SOMMELIER
8000 East Belleview Avenue,
Greenwood Village
303-771-4117

Cucina Colore

KYLE MCGRATH, GENERAL MANAGER
AND WINE STEWARD
3041 East Third Avenue, Denver
303-393-6917

La Cueva Restaurant

ALFONSO NUNEZ, WINE BUYER
9742 East Colfax Avenue, Aurora
303-367-1422

Del Frisco's Double Eagle

JUSTIN WHARRY, SOMMELIER
8100 East Orchard Road,
Greenwood Village
303-796-0100

Diamond Caberet

MARK THOMAS, WINE STEWARD
1222 Glenarm Place, Denver
303-571-4242

Flagstaff House Restaurant

SCOTT MONETTE, MANAGING
PARTNER AND WINE BUYER
1138 Flagstaff Road, Boulder
303-442-4640

Gabriel's

MARCEL KOOYENGA, SOMMELIER
5450 West Highway 67, Sedalia
303-688-2323

Giovanni's Ristorante and Trattoria

DAVE SYPERT, OWNER
AND WINE BUYER
127 11th Street, Steamboat Springs
970-879-4141

The Greenbriar Inn

PHILLIP GODDARD, OWNER
AND SOMMELIER
8735 North Foothills Highway, Boulder
303-440-7979

Krabloonik

DAN MacEACHEN, OWNER
AND WINE BUYER
4250 Divide Road, Snowmass Village
970-923-3953

Laudisio

MARK KRETZ, GENERAL MANAGER
AND WINE STEWARD
2785 Iris Avenue, Boulder
303-442-1300

Mirabelle Restaurant at Beaver Creek

DANIEL JOLY, OWNER AND CHEF
55 Village Road, Avon
970-949-7728

Nico's Catacombs

NICO ZENTFELD, OWNER
AND WINE BUYER
115 South College Avenue, Fort Collins
970-484-6029

Olives at the St. Regis Aspen

IMRE KAUSZ, WINE DIRECTOR
315 East Dean Street, Aspen
970-920-3300

Palace Arms at the Brown Palace Hotel

GARY KELLER, MAÎTRE D'
321 17th Street, Denver
303-297-3111

Pinons

JEFF WALKER, WINE BUYER
105 South Mill Street, Aspen
970-920-2021

Potager

LYNN McGINNIS, WINE MANAGER
1109 Ogden Street, Denver
303-832-5788

Primitivo

ANASTASIA LAMMEY, SOMMELIER

28 South Tejon Street, Colorado Springs

719-473-4900

Rustique

ROBERT ITTNER, OWNER,

GENERAL MANAGER AND SOMMELIER

216 South Monarch Street, Aspen

970-920-2555

Splendido
at the Chateau

JIM LAY, WINE DIRECTOR

17 Chateau Lane, Avon

970-845-8808

Sullivan's Steakhouse

JIM SHUMATE, GENERAL MANAGER

AND WINE BUYER

1745 Wazee Street, Denver

303-295-2664

Syzygy Restaurant

WALT HARRIS, SOMMELIER

520 East Hyman Avenue,

Second Floor, Aspen

970-925-3700

Terra Bistro
at the Vail Mountain
Lodge and Spa

TOMMY LECLARE, WINE STEWARD

352 East Meadow Drive, Vail

970-476-6836

La Tour Restaurant

PAUL FERZACCA, OWNER, CHEF

AND WINE BUYER

122 East Meadow Drive, Vail

970-476-4403

Trios Grille & Wine Bar

NANDO RODRIGUEZ, BAR MANAGER

1155 Canyon Boulevard, Boulder

303-442-8400

The Tyrolean Inn

SIG LANGEGGER, OWNER

AND WINE BUYER

400 East Meadow Drive, Vail

970-476-2204

Rebecca's

265 Glenville Road
Greenwich, Connecticut 06831
phone 203-532-9270 fax 203-532-9271

Rebecca Kirhoffer

Co-Owner

Name your favorite wine regions from around the world.
Burgundy, Burgundy, Burgundy—so incredibly complex and yet so simple.

Name recent wine discoveries that have excited you.
Charles Heidsieck Cuvée de Millenaire 1990; Marquis d'Angerville Volnay; Robert Arnoux Vosne-Romanée, Les Suchots; King Estate Reserve Pinot Noir 1999; Quilceda Creek Cabernet Sauvignon 1999.

What bits of information would you like your customers to know about you?
My husband is Reza Khorshidi, the chef at Rebecca's. Surprisingly, even after being in business for five years, not all of our customers and guests know this!

If you were not in this profession, what would you be?
A designer for homes, clothing or jewelry.

Describe your wine selections, both by the glass and on your list.
The list consists mostly of American and French wines. I have chosen wines that I think are well-suited to our cuisine, which is marked with classical French technique and simplicity.

Name a few of your restaurant's signature dishes. What types of wine do you prefer to recommend with each?
Foie gras dumplings in a truffle broth with red Burgundy; grilled Alaskan ivory king salmon with white asparagus and red Burgundy sauce with Oregon Pinot Noir; roasted guinea hen with glazed carrot rounds, Swiss noodles, lemon and fresh thyme with red Burgundy, from Nuits-SaintGeorges.

In the past year, what wines in your wine program have customers become more willing to order?
Pinot Noir ... hallelujah!

CONNECTICUT

Cavey's Restaurant
STEVEN CAVAGNARO, WINE BUYER
NANCY HAMMARSTROM, SOMMELIER
45 East Center Street, Manchester
860-649-0344

Elms Restaurant
and Tavern
VERN GAUDET, GENERAL MANAGER
AND WINE BUYER
500 Main Street, Ridgefield
203-438-9206

Telluride Restaurant
MARY SCHAFFER, OWNER
AND WINE BUYER
245 Bedford Street, Stamford
203-357-7679

Columbus Inn

2216 Pennsylvania Avenue
Wilmington, Delaware 19806
phone 302-571-1492 fax 302-571-1111
website www.columbusinn.com

Claire D. Mauk
WINE CELLAR MANAGER

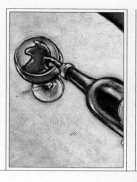

WHAT INSPIRED YOU TO PURSUE A CAREER THAT INVOLVES WINE?
My wine mentor, Ezio Reynaud.

WHAT PART OF YOUR JOB DO YOU ENJOY THE MOST?
Introducing a guest to a totally new wine, especially New World varietals.

NAME YOUR FAVORITE WINE REGION FROM AROUND THE WORLD.
Oregon's Willamette Valley has gorgeous scenery, friendly winemakers and excellent Pinot Noir.

NAME RECENT WINE DISCOVERIES THAT HAVE EXCITED YOU.
The value of wines from Chile and Argentina and the bold tastes and values of Washington State wines.

IF YOU WERE NOT IN THIS PROFESSION, WHAT WOULD YOU BE?
A baseball umpire.

DESCRIBE YOUR WINE SELECTIONS, BOTH BY THE GLASS AND ON YOUR LIST.
We are moving to an all–New World wine list.

WHAT ARE THE MOST UNIQUE FEATURES IN YOUR WINE PROGRAM?
We have monthly wine classes for our guests, women-and-wine nights, and half-price bottles after 9 p.m. on weekends.

WHAT CATEGORY OF WINE IS THE BEST VALUE IN YOUR RESTAURANT?
California Sangiovese.

NAME A COUPLE OF YOUR RESTAURANT'S SIGNATURE DISHES. WHAT TYPES OF WINE DO YOU PREFER TO RECOMMEND WITH EACH?
Crispy soft-shell crabs with Rhône-style white; pan-seared Dover sole with crab, capers and lemon, paired with Sonoma County Chardonnay.

IN THE PAST YEAR, WHAT WINES IN YOUR WINE PROGRAM HAVE CUS-TOMERS BECOME MORE WILLING TO ORDER?
Oregon Pinot Noir.

Café Zeus
MARK BOGIA, MANAGER
AND WINE BUYER
37 Wilmington Avenue, Rehoboth Beach
302-226-0400

Chez La Mer
THOMAS WAYSON, WINE BUYER
210 Second Street, Rehoboth Beach
302-227-6494

Cloud 9
JOHN BERDINI, WINE BUYER
234 Rehoboth Avenue, Rehoboth Beach
302-226-1999

Fusion
JONATHAN SPIVAK, WINE BUYER
50 Wilmington Avenue, Rehoboth Beach
302-226-1940

The Inn at Canal Square
TED BECKER, INN KEEPER
AND WINE BUYER
122 Market Street, Lewes
302-644-3377

La La Land
JEFF BRADY, WINE BUYER
22 Wilmington Avenue, Rehoboth Beach
302-227-3887

Bistro Bis

15 East Street Northwest
Washington, District of Columbia 20001
phone 202-661-2700 fax 202-661-2747
website www.bistrobis.com

Ted P. Wynot
SOMMELIER

WHAT INSPIRED YOU TO PURSUE A CAREER THAT INVOLVES WINE?
I grew up around wine and it was always part of our meals at home. After college, I attended culinary school.

NAME TWO OF YOUR FAVORITE WINE REGIONS FROM AROUND THE WORLD.
The Rhône Valley because the wines offer great complexity and depth; Champagne because it has the greatest sparkling wine in the world and it, Champagne, is the best way to begin a meal.

WHAT BITS OF INFORMATION WOULD YOU LIKE YOUR CUSTOMERS TO KNOW ABOUT YOU?
I am a LSU football nut and I am fascinated with airplanes. I have an undergraduate degree in political science with a concentration in legal studies.

IF YOU WERE NOT IN THIS PROFESSION, WHAT WOULD YOU BE?
A chef or pilot.

DESCRIBE YOUR WINE SELECTIONS, BOTH BY THE GLASS AND ON YOUR LIST.
On our list and by the glass we present wines from lesser-known regions and varieties that are excellent value as well. I'm a firm believer that a guest should not have to spend over $50 a bottle to get a truly remarkable wine.

WHAT CATEGORY OF WINE IS THE BEST VALUE IN YOUR RESTAURANT?
Spanish reds.

NAME A COUPLE OF YOUR RESTAURANT'S SIGNATURE DISHES. WHAT TYPES OF WINE DO YOU PREFER TO RECOMMEND WITH EACH?
Sea scallops Provençale with white Rhône; braised lamb shank with tarbais beans with Cornas, Côte-Rôtie or Madiran.

WHAT IS ANOTHER ULTIMATE WINE AND FOOD PAIRING?
Dark chocolate and Banyuls. There is no better combination.

Café Milano

3251 Prospect Street Northwest
Washington, District of Columbia 20007
phone 202-965-8990 fax 202-965-7119
website www.cafemilano.net

Franco Nuschese
PRESIDENT
TEAM: LAURENT MENOUD, SOMMELIER

WHAT ARE SOME OF YOUR ULTIMATE FOOD AND WINE PAIRINGS?
Pastas go very well with California wines; Italian wines with salads and cheeses.

DESCRIBE YOUR WINE SELECTIONS.
We have a great Italian and American wine list.

WHAT CATEGORY OF WINE IS THE BEST VALUE IN YOUR RESTAURANT?
Super-Tuscans.

NAME A RECENT WINE DISCOVERY THAT EXCITED YOU.
Almaviva from Chile.

WHAT IS YOUR FAVORITE WINE REGION IN THE WORLD TODAY?
Number one is Tuscany, Italy. And I also like Napa Valley.

WHAT LED YOU TO YOUR CURRENT POSITION?
My background in Italy.

WHAT ARE THE BEST ASPECTS OF YOUR JOB?
Meeting new people every day and the ability to share the knowledge of wine with customers.

IF YOU WERE NOT IN THIS PROFESSION, WHAT WOULD YOU BE DOING?
Show business.

The Historic Georgetown Club

1530 Wisconsin Avenue Northwest
Washington, District of Columbia 20007
phone 202-333-9330 fax 202-333-3183

Gino Ballarin
DINING ROOM MANAGER
AND WINE DIRECTOR

WHAT PART OF YOUR JOB DO YOU ENJOY THE MOST?
Pairing proper wines with any given dish for the club's patrons.

NAME TWO OF YOUR FAVORITE WINES.
California and Oregon Pinot Noirs for their fullness, versatility and value.

NAME A RECENT WINE DISCOVERY THAT EXCITED YOU.
Viognier from the United States and Europe. It has been quickly accepted by many who had not experienced this great wine before.

WHAT WOULD YOU LIKE YOUR CUSTOMERS TO KNOW ABOUT YOU?
After a round of golf and a good swim (I was a swimmer for Italy), I enjoy a nice meal and a good bottle of wine.

IF YOU WERE NOT IN THIS PROFESSION, WHAT WOULD YOU BE?
It's hard to imagine anything else, but if I had to, the captain of a ship would be fine.

DESCRIBE YOUR WINE SELECTIONS, BOTH BY THE GLASS AND ON YOUR LIST.
Our wines by the glass and wine list reflect quality and good values, keeping in mind that our members are also our diners.

WHAT CATEGORIES OF WINE ARE THE BEST VALUES IN YOUR RESTAURANT?
California Chardonnay and red Burgundy.

NAME A FEW OF YOUR RESTAURANT'S SIGNATURE DISHES. WHAT TYPES OF WINE DO YOU PREFER TO RECOMMEND WITH EACH?
Seared foie gras with Sauternes; potato-crusted Chilean sea bass with Sauvignon Blanc; venison with Amarone.

IN THE PAST YEAR, WHAT WINES IN YOUR WINE PROGRAM HAVE CUS-TOMERS BECOME MORE WILLING TO ORDER?
California Sauvignon Blanc, Italian Pinot Grigio (by the glass) and high-end California Cabernet Sauvignon.

Kinkeads, An American Brasserie

2000 Pennsylvania Avenue Northwest
Washington, District of Columbia 20006
phone 202-296-7700 fax 202-296-7688
website www.kinkead.com

Michael D. Flynn
WINE DIRECTOR AND SOMMELIER

WHAT INSPIRED YOU TO PURSUE A CAREER THAT INVOLVES WINE?
My academic background in French, my love of cooking and a chance
encounter with the late chef and sommelier Jean-Louis Palladin.

NAME YOUR FAVORITE WINE REGION FROM AROUND THE WORLD.
Burgundy because it's so elusive and unpredictable, and so sublime when it all
comes together.

NAME RECENT WINE DISCOVERIES THAT HAVE EXCITED YOU.
Biblia Chora white, a Sauvignon Blanc and Assyrtico blend, for its value and
lovely pistachio flavor; and Coma d'en Pou, from Spain's Terra Alta—it's
sinful and a great value!

WHAT WOULD YOU LIKE YOUR CUSTOMERS TO KNOW ABOUT YOU?
Sailing, photography, French films and my slavish devotion to current events.

IF YOU WERE NOT IN THIS PROFESSION, WHAT WOULD YOU BE DOING?
Diplomacy or academia.

WHAT ARE THE MOST UNIQUE FEATURES IN YOUR WINE PROGRAM?
The color-coded "thermometers" that run along the margin of each page, showing the approximate body, richness and flavor characteristics of the wines.

WHAT CATEGORY OF WINE IS THE BEST VALUE IN YOUR RESTAURANT?
Red blends from the south of France.

**NAME A COUPLE OF YOUR RESTAURANT'S SIGNATURE DISHES. WHAT
TYPES OF WINE DO YOU PREFER TO RECOMMEND WITH EACH?**
Tuna with flageolet, grilled portobello mushrooms paired with red Burgundy;
pepita-crusted salmon with crab, shrimp, corn and chile ragout paired with
Austrian Riesling.

WHAT WINES ARE CUSTOMERS NOW MORE WILLING TO ORDER?
Austrian Grüner Veltliner, Oregon Pinot Noir, South African Cabernet
Sauvignon and red blends.

The Occidental

1475 Pennsylvania Avenue Northwest
Washington, District of Columbia 20004
phone 202-783-1475 fax 202-783-1478
website www.occidentaldc.com

Kathryn Morgan
WINE DIRECTOR AND SOMMELIER

WHAT INSPIRED YOU TO PURSUE A CAREER THAT INVOLVES WINE?
As the only child of a wine collector and amateur chef, I was hooked early on!

NAME TWO OF YOUR FAVORITE WINE REGIONS FROM AROUND THE WORLD.
Germany for whites and Burgundy for reds; you can taste the soul in these wines.

NAME RECENT WINE DISCOVERIES THAT HAVE EXCITED YOU.
The excellent price-to-value ratio in "grower Champagnes."

DESCRIBE YOUR WINE SELECTIONS, BOTH BY THE GLASS AND ON YOUR LIST.
It is an international selection, with enticing choices in every price range, and with an emphasis on food and wine pairing.

WHAT ARE THE MOST UNIQUE FEATURES IN YOUR WINE PROGRAM?
The list is very user-friendly. Wines are listed by varietal, with colorful maps and catchy headings like "Tasty Tongue Twisters" and "Pinot Envy."

WHAT CATEGORIES OF WINE ARE THE BEST VALUES IN YOUR RESTAURANT?
Our "Cutting Edge Whites" category that includes Riesling, Grüner Veltliner and Chenin Blanc and "Italian Reds" category.

WHAT WINES ARE CUSTOMERS NOW MORE WILLING TO ORDER?
German Riesling, South African Bordeaux varietals and Loire Valley Cabernet Franc.

NAME A FEW OF YOUR RESTAURANT'S SIGNATURE DISHES. WHAT TYPES OF WINE DO YOU PREFER TO RECOMMEND WITH EACH?
Roasted lobster with chestnut spaetzle and chanterelle mushrooms with Meursault premier cru; Port-marinated venison chop and blackberry sauce with Australian Shiraz; oven-roasted vegetable crêpe with celery root sauce and red pepper oil with Vouvray sec; seared bluefin tuna with roasted garlic potato cakes, shiitake relish and lobster soy sauce with Châteauneuf-du-Pape blanc; Granny Smith apple tart, walnut streusel, caramel and cinnamon ice cream with Hungarian Tokaji.

Olives
1600 K Street Northwest
Washington, District of Columbia 20006
phone 202-452-1866 fax 202-452-8580
website www.toddenglish.com

Benjamin J. Sevilla
RESTAURANT MANAGER
AND WINE DIRECTOR

NAME TWO OF YOUR FAVORITE WINE REGIONS FROM AROUND THE
WORLD.
Rioja and Napa Valley. Rioja is an excellent wine and an exceptional value.
Napa Valley wines are very alluring, with a wide selection of varietals and many
great wines.

NAME A RECENT WINE DISCOVERY THAT EXCITED YOU.
Caro by Catena and Baron Eric Rothschild is a great blended wine with fasci-
nating characteristics.

WHAT BITS OF INFORMATION WOULD YOU LIKE YOUR CUSTOMERS TO
KNOW ABOUT YOU?
I really love to travel, play basketball and listen to music.

IF YOU WERE NOT IN THIS PROFESSION, WHAT WOULD YOU BE DOING?
I would own a do-it-yourself dog wash.

DESCRIBE YOUR WINE SELECTIONS, BOTH BY THE GLASS AND ON YOUR
LIST.
Our wine list represents a wide range of regions with wines at nearly all price
points. We also showcase wines of high quality that are great values from "new"
regions such as Spain and Argentina.

NAME ONE OF YOUR RESTAURANT'S SIGNATURE DISHES. WHAT WINE DO
YOU PREFER TO RECOMMEND WITH IT?
Spicy tuna tartare with Alsatian Riesling.

IN THE PAST YEAR, WHAT WINES IN YOUR WINE PROGRAM HAVE CUS-
TOMERS BECOME MORE WILLING TO ORDER?
Spanish and Argentinean wines.

Vidalia

1990 M Street Northwest
Washington, District of Columbia 20036
phone 202-659-1990 fax 202-223-8572
website www.vidaliadc.com

Michael A. Nevarez
GENERAL MANAGER AND SOMMELIER

WHAT INSPIRED YOU TO PURSUE A CAREER THAT INVOLVES WINE?
I worked in a fine dining restaurant, where the sommelier, the chef and the other managers introduced me to the exciting world of fine food and good wine.

NAME ONE OF YOUR FAVORITE WINE REGIONS FROM AROUND THE WORLD.
The Rhône Valley, for several reasons: its wines are very diverse in style, from north to south, they pair well with food and they are very expressive of terroir.

WHAT BITS OF INFORMATION WOULD YOU LIKE YOUR CUSTOMERS TO KNOW ABOUT YOU?
I enjoy hunting, fishing and cooking gourmet dinners for my friends and family.

WHAT CATEGORIES OF WINE ARE THE BEST VALUES IN YOUR RESTAURANT?
California cult wines and Alsatian wines.

NAME A COUPLE OF YOUR RESTAURANT'S SIGNATURE DISHES. WHAT TYPES OF WINE DO YOU PREFER TO RECOMMEND WITH EACH?
Shrimp and grits (sautéed shrimp with caramelized onions, spinach, yellow corn grits with shrimp cream and fresh thyme), with Sonoma County Chardonnay and Australian or Californian Viognier; and crab cakes (lump crabmeat with creamy, sweet onion slaw and stone-ground mustard sauce) with dry Chenin Blanc from the Loire Valley or fresh, light-bodied Sauvignon Blanc from New Zealand or California.

IN THE PAST YEAR, WHAT WINES IN YOUR WINE PROGRAM HAVE CUS-TOMERS BECOME MORE WILLING TO ORDER?
Alsatian Riesling and Pinot Gris and Australian Shiraz and Viognier.

WHAT ARE SOME OTHER ULTIMATE WINE AND FOOD PAIRINGS?
Goat cheese cheesecake with strawberry compote and balsamic vinegar reduction served with a 5 Puttonyos Tokaji Aszu.

1789 Restaurant
WILLIAM WATTS, WINE BUYER
1226 36th Street Northwest, Washington
202-965-1789

Andale
CHRIS CUNNINGHAM, MANAGER
AND WINE BUYER
401 Seventh Street Northwest,
Washington
202-783-3133

Beduci
JEAN GARRAT, OWNER
AND WINE BUYER
2100 P Street Northwest, Washington
202-223-3824

Café Atlantico
FRANCISCO ASTUDILLO, RESTAURANT
MANAGER AND SOMMELIER
405 Eighth Street Northwest, Washington
202-393-0812

The Capital Grille
JIM KINNEY, WINE BUYER
601 Pennsylvania Avenue, Washington
202-737-6200

The Caucus Room
ED D'ALESSANDRO, MANAGER
AND WINE BUYER
401 Ninth Street Northwest, Washington
202-393-1300

Citronelle at the Latham Hotel
MARK SLATER, SOMMELIER
3000 M Street Northwest, Washington
202-625-2150

Equinox
TRAVIS GRAY, WINE DIRECTOR
818 Connecticut Avenue Northwest,
Washington
202-331-8118

Galileo Restaurant
MICHAEL NAYERI, GENERAL MANAGER
AND WINE BUYER
1110 21st Street Northwest, Washington
202-293-7191

Jaleo at the Lansburgh
SANDY LEWIS, WINE BUYER
ANTONI YELAMO, SOMMELIER
480 Seventh Street Northwest,
Washington
202-628-7949

Jeffrey's at the Watergate Hotel
JEAN-BAPTIST LAGLACE, RESTAURANT
MANAGER AND WINE BUYER
2650 Virginia Avenue Northwest,
Washington
202-298-4455

McCormick and Schmick's
JAVIER BAQUERO, BEVERAGE MANAGER
1652 K Street Northwest, Washington
202-861-2233

Mendocino Grill
TROY BOCK, MANAGER AND WINE BUYER
2917 M Street Northwest, Washington
202-333-2912

Morrison-Clark Restaurant
MANDY SILVER, RESTAURANT
MANAGER AND WINE BUYER
Massachusetts Avenue and 11th Street
Northwest, Washington
800-332-7898

Morton's of Chicago

LARRY THOMAS, JR.,
ASSISTANT GENERAL MANAGER
AND WINE BUYER
1050 Connecticut Avenue, Washington
202-955-5997

Old Ebbitt Grill

KYLE GAFFNEY, ASSISTANT GENERAL
MANAGER AND WINE BUYER
675 15th Street Northwest, Washington
202-347-4801

The Prime Rib

JIM ROSS, WINE BUYER
2020 K Street Northwest, Washington
202-466-8811

Red Sage

RALPH ROSENBURG, MANAGER
AND WINE BUYER
605 14th Street Northwest, Washington
202-638-4444

Seasons at the Four Seasons Hotel

DAVID BERNAND, SOMMELIER
2800 Pennsylvania Avenue, Washington
202-944-2000

Smith & Wollensky

RICHARD FITZGERALD, SOMMELIER
1112 19th Street Northwest,
Washington
202-466-1100

Taberna del Alabardero

DAVID BUENO, ASSISTANT MANAGER
AND SOMMELIER
JAVIER REGATTO, WINE BUYER
1776 Eye Street Northwest, Washington
202-429-2200

Tenpenh

SCOTT CLIME, DIRECTOR
OF BEVERAGES
1001 Pennsylvania Avenue Northwest,
Washington
202-393-4500

Willard International Continental

JITKA WIELAND, FOOD AND
BEVERAGE DIRECTOR
1401 Pennsylvania Avenue Northwest,
Washington
202-637-7440

Beech Street Grill

801 Beech Street
Fernandina Beach, Florida 32034
phone 904-277-3662 fax 904-277-5611
website www.beechstreetgrill.com

Elizabeth Smiddy
OWNER AND SOMMELIER

NAME ONE OF YOUR FAVORITE WINE REGIONS FROM AROUND THE WORLD.
Southern Rhône Valley, wines with style and complexity at great prices.

NAME RECENT WINE DISCOVERIES THAT HAVE EXCITED YOU.
Italian wines are interesting and always challenge the palate.

WHAT WOULD YOU LIKE YOUR CUSTOMERS TO KNOW ABOUT YOU?
The only job I had before the restaurant business was a paper route.

IF YOU WERE NOT IN THIS PROFESSION, WHAT WOULD YOU BE DOING?
I'd have to go back to the paper route.

DESCRIBE YOUR WINE SELECTIONS, BOTH BY THE GLASS AND ON YOUR LIST.
Currently we are trying to balance the list, moving somewhat away from pricey
boutique wines and California Cabernets to a more global, well-rounded list.

WHAT ARE THE MOST UNIQUE FEATURES IN YOUR WINE PROGRAM?
We print our lists in-house, and change our by-the-glass list every ten days.
Our whole program is always changing, always moving forward.

WHAT CATEGORY OF WINE IS THE BEST VALUE IN YOUR RESTAURANT?
Alternative whites like Sauvignon Blanc, Pinot Gris, Pinot Blanc and Chenin
Blanc.

**NAME A COUPLE OF YOUR RESTAURANT'S SIGNATURE DISHES. WHAT
TYPES OF WINE DO YOU PREFER TO RECOMMEND WITH EACH?**
Our restaurant focuses on fresh, regional seafood, so the "Alternative White"
and "Lighter Red" categories are both active.

WHAT WINES ARE CUSTOMERS NOW MORE WILLING TO ORDER?
Offbeat reds like Syrah, Primitivo, Rhône blends and offbeat whites like
Grüner Veltliner and Pinot Blanc.

Bern's Steak House

1208 South Howard Avenue
Tampa, Florida 33606
phone 813-251-2421 fax 813-251-5001
website www.bernssteakhouse.com

Eric A. Renaud
SOMMELIER
TEAM: KEN COLLURA,
HEAD SOMMELIER

WHAT ARE SOME OF YOUR ULTIMATE FOOD AND WINE PAIRINGS?
Steak and Rhône wines; foie gras and Sauternes; shellfish with Austrian white wines; barbecue with Zinfandel or Ribera del Duero.

DESCRIBE YOUR WINE SELECTIONS.
We have 6,500 table wines, 1,000 dessert wines and about 185 wines by the glass from vintages dating back to 1971. We want to offer all styles of wine.

WHAT CATEGORY OF WINE IS THE BEST VALUE IN YOUR RESTAURANT?
Older red wines from virtually any region. Our pricing is inexpensive because Bern Laxer, the founder, began buying wines in quantity in the 1960s.

NAME RECENT WINE DISCOVERIES THAT HAVE EXCITED YOU.
The crisp, refreshing white wines of Austria and South African wines, which are rapidly improving in quality and are very reasonably priced.

WHAT IS YOUR FAVORITE WINE REGION IN THE WORLD TODAY?
Burgundy, for white and red wines. For everyday reds, Spain.

WHAT LED YOU TO PURSUE A CAREER THAT INVOLVES WINE?
It happened by accident. I began working part-time at the restaurant as a wine steward. I began studying and asking questions.

WHAT IS THE MOST REWARDING ASPECT OF YOUR JOB?
Finding the wine my guests say they love, a wine they might not have ever thought of asking for, from a region they may not ever have known existed.

IF YOU WERE NOT IN THE WINE PROFESSION, WHAT WOULD YOU BE?
A jet mechanic.

Charley's Aged Steak and Market Fresh Fish

4444 West Cypress Street
Tampa, Florida 33607
phone 813-353-9706 fax 813-353-9510
website www.charleyssteakhouse.com

Lee M. Fuettere
SOMMELIER

NAME TWO OF YOUR FAVORITE WINE REGIONS FROM AROUND THE WORLD.
Oakville and Burgundy; Oakville for the roundness and depth of fruit of its wines and Burgundy for its finesse and diversity.

NAME RECENT WINE DISCOVERIES THAT HAVE EXCITED YOU.
Reds from Argentina, especially those of Susana Balbo and Ben Marco.

WHAT BITS OF INFORMATION WOULD YOU LIKE YOUR CUSTOMERS TO KNOW ABOUT YOU?
After attending college, I spent seven years in professional theater and then moved to New York to "make it." Like so many actors, I became a full-time waiter.

DESCRIBE YOUR WINE SELECTIONS, BOTH BY THE GLASS AND ON YOUR LIST.
We offer more than 750 selections on our wine list and more than thirty selections by the glass. We feature wines from around the world, but our selection is primarily from California. To satisfy a variety of wine tastes, we offer rare and allocated wines and great wines that are well-known.

NAME A COUPLE OF YOUR RESTAURANT'S SIGNATURE DISHES. WHAT TYPES OF WINE DO YOU PREFER TO RECOMMEND WITH EACH?
Grilled lamb chop topped with pesto butter with Australian Shiraz; blue cheese–stuffed filet mignon and peppercorn sauce with Russian River Valley Pinot Noir.

IN THE PAST YEAR, WHAT WINES IN YOUR WINE PROGRAM HAVE CUSTOMERS BECOME MORE WILLING TO ORDER?
Syrah and Shiraz.

WHAT ARE SOME OTHER ULTIMATE WINE AND FOOD PAIRINGS?
Steak au poivre with Amarone; lobster with grand cru white Burgundy; red snapper with Monterey Pinot Noir.

Charley's Steakhouse

8255 International Drive
Orlando, Florida 32819-9350
phone 407-363-0228 fax 407-354-4617

Edward A. Marsh
WINE STEWARD AND SOMMELIER

NAME TWO OF YOUR FAVORITE WINE REGIONS FROM AROUND THE WORLD.
Piedmont and Napa Valley. I never tire of deep, rich reds from Napa, particularly Cabernets and Meritage blends. The earthy, rich, tannic Barolos and Barbarescos from Piedmont are fabulous.

NAME RECENT WINE DISCOVERIES THAT HAVE EXCITED YOU.
Australian Shiraz and blends. They are so fruit-forward, deep in color and concentrated; also, the price is right.

WHAT ARE THE MOST UNIQUE FEATURES IN YOUR WINE PROGRAM?
We have nearly 200 selections and a selection of magnums and larger-format bottles. We also feature older Bordeaux and many half-bottles.

WHAT CATEGORIES OF WINE ARE THE BEST VALUES IN YOUR RESTAURANT?
California Chardonnay and Washington Riesling.

NAME A COUPLE OF YOUR RESTAURANT'S SIGNATURE DISHES. WHAT TYPES OF WINE DO YOU PREFER TO RECOMMEND WITH EACH?
Our 20-ounce filet mignon, paired with a spicy California Zinfandel or an Australian Shiraz; our 2-pound lobster with California Chardonnay.

IN THE PAST YEAR, WHAT WINES IN YOUR WINE PROGRAM HAVE CUSTOMERS BECOME MORE WILLING TO ORDER?
Australian Shiraz and Napa Valley red Meritage; Zinfandel is a close third.

Del Frisco's Steak House

729 Lee Road
Orlando, Florida 32810
phone 407-645-4443 fax 407-645-0483
website www.delfriscosorlando.com

Dan Colgan
SOMMELIER

NAME TWO OF YOUR FAVORITE WINE REGIONS FROM AROUND THE
WORLD.
Australia and Germany. I like Australia for its ripeness, richness and oakiness;
Germany for its Riesling. They both make profound wine.

NAME RECENT WINE DISCOVERIES THAT HAVE EXCITED YOU.
The new way of "thinking" is Spain. The newer styles are fun and affordable,
and can even be earthmoving.

WHAT BITS OF INFORMATION WOULD YOU LIKE YOUR CUSTOMERS TO
KNOW ABOUT YOU?
I blind-taste almost every day. Plus, I spend most of my disposable income on
wine.

IF YOU WERE NOT IN THIS PROFESSION, WHAT WOULD YOU BE DOING?
I'd be a contractor doing finish carpentry. I build wine cellars and racking systems during the day.

DESCRIBE YOUR WINE SELECTIONS, BOTH BY THE GLASS AND ON YOUR
LIST.
We specialize in American reds like Cabernets, Merlots and blends, with a good
by-the-glass selection. We have 375 wines.

WHAT CATEGORY OF WINE IS THE BEST VALUE IN YOUR RESTAURANT?
Australian red.

NAME A COUPLE OF YOUR RESTAURANT'S SIGNATURE DISHES. WHAT
TYPES OF WINE DO YOU PREFER TO RECOMMEND WITH EACH?
Aged, hand-cut steaks with Zinfandel or Australian Shiraz; Australian cold-
water lobster tail with Pinot Noir.

IN THE PAST YEAR, WHAT WINES IN YOUR WINE PROGRAM HAVE CUS-
TOMERS BECOME MORE WILLING TO ORDER?
Australian Shiraz.

Elephant Walk Restaurant at Sandestin Golf and Beach Resort

9300 Emerald Coast Parkway West
Sandestin, Florida 32550-7268
phone 850-267-4800 fax 850-267-6121
website www.sandestin.com

Stewart M. Smith
GENERAL MANAGER AND SOMMELIER

NAME TWO OF YOUR FAVORITE WINE REGIONS FROM AROUND THE WORLD.
Red wines from the Napa Valley and Alexander Valley because of the typically bold and often complex nature of these wines.

NAME RECENT WINE DISCOVERIES THAT HAVE EXCITED YOU.
Bordeaux from the 2000 vintage. Wines of classic styling.

WHAT BITS OF INFORMATION WOULD YOU LIKE YOUR CUSTOMERS TO KNOW ABOUT YOU?
I have a surprisingly small wine collection at home because I think that great wine is made to drink. I have no patience for waiting.

IF YOU WERE NOT IN THIS PROFESSION, WHAT WOULD YOU BE DOING?
I would be a food and wine critic. It would be nice to have a critic who actually knew about wine and food. There are far too few.

DESCRIBE YOUR WINE SELECTIONS, BOTH BY THE GLASS AND ON YOUR LIST.
We have a large selection of excellent wines and wines that sell.

WHAT ARE THE MOST UNIQUE FEATURES IN YOUR WINE PROGRAM?
Monthly wine dinners with various producers. And our incentive wine sales program for servers.

NAME A COUPLE OF YOUR RESTAURANT'S SIGNATURE DISHES. WHAT TYPES OF WINE DO YOU PREFER TO RECOMMEND WITH EACH?
Pan-seared filet of grouper with jumbo lump crabmeat, spinach and saffron cream with Napa Valley Chardonnay; USDA prime filet of beef or New York strip steak with Sonoma County or Napa Valley Cabernet Sauvignon.

Fetishes Fine Dining

6690 Gulf Boulevard
Saint Pete Beach, Florida 33706
phone 727-363-3700 fax 727-360-1642
website www.beachdirectory.com/fetishes

Bruce Caplan
OWNER AND WINE BUYER

NAME TWO OF YOUR FAVORITE WINE REGIONS FROM AROUND THE WORLD.

The Rhône region in France and Paso Robles in central California. I love the wines from these regions because they are smooth and full-bodied.

NAME RECENT WINE DISCOVERIES THAT HAVE EXCITED YOU.

Ridge Coast Range. I'm anxious to see what the blend will be each year. Also, Artesa Merlot from Sonoma County; what a bargain!

IF YOU WERE NOT IN THIS PROFESSION, WHAT WOULD YOU BE?

A photographer.

DESCRIBE YOUR WINE SELECTIONS, BOTH BY THE GLASS AND ON YOUR LIST.

Heavy in California and known for having highly allocated wines.

WHAT ARE THE MOST UNIQUE FEATURES IN YOUR WINE PROGRAM?

Extended verticals of California Cabernets and Bordeaux such as a Hess Collection, Ridge Montebello and Lafon-Rochet.

WHAT CATEGORY OF WINE IS THE BEST VALUE IN YOUR RESTAURANT?

Syrah and Shiraz.

NAME A COUPLE OF YOUR RESTAURANT'S SIGNATURE DISHES. WHAT TYPES OF WINE DO YOU PREFER TO RECOMMEND WITH EACH?

Duck with Chambord sauce with full-bodied Pinot Noir; Maryland-style crab cakes with Sauvignon Blanc.

IN THE PAST YEAR, WHAT WINES IN YOUR WINE PROGRAM HAVE CUSTOMERS BECOME MORE WILLING TO ORDER?

Australian and Chilean wines.

Fish Bones Restaurant

6707 Sand Lake Road
Orlando, Florida 32819
phone 407-352-0135 fax 407-352-3480

David A. Shoemaker
WINE DIRECTOR AND SOMMELIER

WHAT INSPIRED YOU TO PURSUE A CAREER THAT INVOLVES WINE?
In all honesty, it goes back to when I was twelve or thirteen and was watching James Bond. I was so intrigued by his knowledge that I asked my mom to buy me a book about wine.

WHAT BITS OF INFORMATION WOULD YOU LIKE YOUR CUSTOMERS TO KNOW ABOUT YOU?
I live, eat and breathe my profession. This is what I love. Every day I discover something new, both professionally and personally. My goal is to help the people around me do the same.

IF YOU WERE NOT IN THIS PROFESSION, WHAT WOULD YOU BE DOING?
I have twenty-one years of metal fabrication experience. I am an artist blacksmith in my spare time. I also have been a competitive water-skier for the last twelve years.

WHAT CATEGORY OF WINE IS THE BEST VALUE IN YOUR RESTAURANT?
Australian wines. They seem to have value in every price range.

NAME A COUPLE OF YOUR RESTAURANT'S SIGNATURE DISHES. WHAT TYPES OF WINE DO YOU PREFER TO RECOMMEND WITH EACH?
Peppercorn and sesame seed–crusted yellowfin tuna, paired with German Riesling; T-bone lamb with Australian Shiraz.

IN THE PAST YEAR, WHAT WINES IN YOUR WINE PROGRAM HAVE CUSTOMERS BECOME MORE WILLING TO ORDER?
Pinot Noir, definitely.

Flying Fish Café
at Walt Disney World's Boardwalk Resort
2101 North Epcot Resort Boulevard
Lake Buena Vista, Florida 32830
phone 407-939-3463 fax 407-939-5158

Gary P. Lee
RESTAURANT MANAGER AND SOMMELIER

NAME ONE OF YOUR FAVORITE VARIETALS. WHAT DISTRICTS DO YOU PREFER?.
Rieslings from Margaret River and from Alsace because of their ripeness and crisp acidity.

NAME RECENT WINE DISCOVERIES THAT HAVE EXCITED YOU.
Wines from Spain; extremely good in quality, with great combinations of fruit and structure, and at super prices.

WHAT BITS OF INFORMATION WOULD YOU LIKE YOUR CUSTOMERS TO KNOW ABOUT YOU?
I enjoy long-distance bicycling and am working on an MBA through Stetson University.

DESCRIBE YOUR WINE SELECTIONS, BOTH BY THE GLASS AND ON YOUR LIST.
The offerings on the current list include wines from New Zealand, France, Germany, Spain, Italy, Australia and, of course, the United States. But the selections have to match well with the chef's cuisine.

WHAT CATEGORIES OF WINE ARE THE BEST VALUES IN YOUR RESTAURANT?
Currently the best values are California Zinfandel, Australian Shiraz and Chardonnay, and Washington State sparkling wine.

NAME A COUPLE OF YOUR RESTAURANT'S SIGNATURE DISHES. WHAT TYPES OF WINE DO YOU PREFER TO RECOMMEND WITH EACH?
Potato-wrapped snapper with Paso Robles Cabernet Sauvignon; mahi-mahi with Sancerre; salmon with Sonoma County Chardonnay.

WHAT ARE SOME OF YOUR OTHER ULTIMATE WINE AND FOOD PAIRINGS?
Char-crusted steak with Priorat; sea bass with Rheinhessen Riesling Spätlese Trocken.

The Grill Room
at the Ritz-Carlton
4750 Amelia Island Parkway
Fernandina Beach, Florida 32034
phone 904-277-1100 fax 904-277-1144
website www.ritzcarlton.com

John L. Pugliese
WINE STEWARD

WHAT IS ONE OF YOUR ULTIMATE FOOD AND WINE PAIRINGS?
Foie gras with Austrian dessert wines such as Eiswein and Beerenauslese.

DESCRIBE YOUR WINE SELECTIONS.
Our wine list is diverse and complex.

WHAT CATEGORY OF WINE IS THE BEST VALUE IN YOUR RESTAURANT?
California Zinfandel.

NAME RECENT WINE DISCOVERIES THAT HAVE EXCITED YOU.
Austrian wines. They are good values and taste wonderful!

WHAT IS YOUR FAVORITE WINE REGION IN THE WORLD TODAY?
Alsace. The wines are so food-friendly.

WHAT LED YOU TO PURSUE A CAREER THAT INVOLVES WINE?
A passion for food and wine.

WHAT ARE THE BEST ASPECTS OF YOUR JOB?
Meeting guests who love to try new wines. The rewards are the smiles I receive
for choosing a great wine.

IF YOU WERE NOT IN THE WINE PROFESSION, WHAT WOULD YOU BE?
A chef, because I love to cook.

Jiko, The Cooking Place at Disney World Animal Kingdom

2901 Osceola Parkway
Lake Buena Vista, Florida 32830
phone 407- 939-3463 fax 407-938-7102

Keith Landry
AREA MANAGER

NAME RECENT WINE DISCOVERIES THAT HAVE EXCITED YOU.
Austrian wines from the Wachau. I love Rieslings and they are the best wines. They age well, make wonderful food pairings and are crisp and clean.

WHAT BITS OF INFORMATION WOULD YOU LIKE YOUR CUSTOMERS TO KNOW ABOUT YOU?
I am a food-TV junkie. I tape all kinds of cooking shows. And I love to travel.

IF YOU WERE NOT IN THIS PROFESSION, WHAT WOULD YOU BE?
A scuba-diving instructor in the Caribbean.

DESCRIBE YOUR WINE SELECTIONS, BOTH BY THE GLASS AND ON YOUR LIST.
Jiko is an African cuisine restaurant. We only sell South African wines, and we have the largest all–South African wine list in North America. We have more than eighty bottles of South African wine on the list and offer a majority of them by the glass.

NAME A FEW OF YOUR RESTAURANT'S SIGNATURE DISHES. WHAT TYPES OF WINE DO YOU PREFER TO RECOMMEND WITH EACH?
Pan-roasted monkfish with "vegetables of the moment," crispy parsnips and tomato butter sauce with South African Shiraz; berbere-braised lamb shank with toasted couscous, baby spinach and berbere sauce with South African Shiraz; cucumber, tomato and red onion salad with swirled cottage cheese and watermelon vinaigrette with South African Sauvignon Blanc.

IN THE PAST YEAR, WHAT WINES IN YOUR WINE PROGRAM HAVE CUSTOMERS BECOME MORE WILLING TO ORDER?
Chenin Blanc and Pinotage.

WHAT ARE SOME OTHER ULTIMATE WINE AND FOOD PAIRINGS?
Champagne with salty popcorn and mussels with Muscadet.

Maison & Jardin Restaurant

430 South Wymore Road
Altamonte Springs, Florida 32714
phone 407-862-4410 fax 407-862-5507

William R. Beuret

OWNER AND SOMMELIER

WHAT IS ONE OF YOUR ULTIMATE FOOD AND WINE PAIRINGS?
1970 Vega Sicilia Unico with fresh-roasted, whole suckling lamb.

DESCRIBE YOUR WINE SELECTIONS.
We have 1,300 selections from all the major wine areas of the world, with special emphasis on California, Bordeaux, Burgundy, Germany and Italy. Food and wine pairings are on the wine list.

WHAT ARE YOUR FAVORITE WINE REGIONS IN THE WORLD TODAY?
The Mosel, for the beauty; Burgundy, for the wine; and Italy, for food and wine compatibility.

WHAT LED YOU TO YOUR CURRENT POSITION?
Love of wine and dining, and it's a part of the job owning a fine restaurant.

WHAT IS THE MOST CHALLENGING ASPECT OF YOUR JOB?
Never-ending staff training. Finding motivated and enthusiastic staff in a tight labor market.

IF YOU WERE NOT IN THE WINE PROFESSION, WHAT WOULD YOU BE DOING?
Teaching.

Maison and Jardin Restaurant

430 South Wymore Road
Altamonte Springs, Florida 32714
phone 407-862-4410 fax 407-862-5507
website www.maison-jardin.com

Daniel M. Albert
WINE SOMMELIER

NAME SOME OF YOUR FAVORITE WINES FROM AROUND THE WORLD.
Champagne, which I associate with happy celebrations; Saint-Émilion for the early drinkability and richness of its wines; Burgundy for its wide range of styles and flavors.

NAME RECENT WINE DISCOVERIES THAT HAVE EXCITED YOU.
White wines from the northern Rhône, with their exotic fruit.

WHAT WOULD YOU LIKE YOUR CUSTOMERS TO KNOW ABOUT YOU?
I am currently working toward my BSBA in finance at the University of Central Florida.

IF YOU WERE NOT IN THIS PROFESSION, WHAT WOULD YOU BE?
A chef.

DESCRIBE YOUR WINE SELECTIONS, BOTH BY THE GLASS AND ON YOUR LIST.
We offer 1,600 selections from around the world to satisfy the needs of all of our guests. All of the wines have a lower markup than many other restaurants.

WHAT ARE THE MOST UNIQUE FEATURES IN YOUR WINE PROGRAM?
We offer forty wines by the glass and 150 half-bottle selections. Wine pairing dinners are offered five nights a week.

WHAT CATEGORY OF WINE IS THE BEST VALUE IN YOUR RESTAURANT?
Red Bordeaux.

NAME A FEW OF YOUR RESTAURANT'S SIGNATURE DISHES. WHAT TYPES OF WINE DO YOU PREFER TO RECOMMEND WITH EACH?
Beef Wellington with black truffle bordelaise with Pauillac (red Bordeaux); rack of lamb with tarragon lamb jus paired with Australian Shiraz; shrimp and scallops with Alsatian Riesling; ostrich and quail with Saint-Émilion (red Bordeaux).

WHAT WINES ARE CUSTOMERS MORE MORE WILLING TO ORDER?
German Riesling and Australian reds, especially Shiraz and Cabernet-Shiraz.

Michael's on East Restaurant

1212 East Avenue South
Sarasota, Florida 34239
phone 941-366-0007 fax 941-955-1945

Michael Klauber

PROPRIETOR, SOMMELIER
AND WINE BUYER

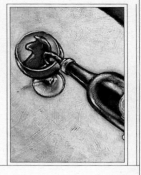

WHAT IS ONE OF YOUR ULTIMATE FOOD AND WINE PAIRINGS?
Roasted quail with rich, red Burgundy.

DESCRIBE YOUR WINE SELECTIONS.
We focus primarily on estate and domain-bottled wines, with 200 to 250 wines and twelve to fifteen wine flights.

WHAT IS YOUR FAVORITE WINE REGION IN THE WORLD TODAY?
Burgundy! I love the wines. It is a place where the style of food is so beautifully complemented by the amazing wines.

WHAT LED YOU TO PURSUE A CAREER THAT INVOLVES WINE?
Actually, I was thrown into it while working at Arnaud's Restaurant in New Orleans.

WHAT ARE THE MOST CHALLENGING ASPECTS OF YOUR JOB?
To constantly create opportunities for our guests to experience new wines. To continue to find emerging wineries and wine regions.

IF YOU WERE NOT IN THIS PROFESSION, WHAT WOULD YOU BE DOING?
Living in the wine country, growing grapes and making wine.

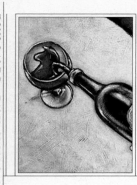

Narcoossee's at Disney's Grand Floridian Beach Resort

4401 Grand Floridian Way
Lake Buena Vista, Florida 32832
phone 407-939-3463

Robert T. Dunham
AREA MANAGER AND SOMMELIER

WHAT INSPIRED YOU TO PURSUE A CAREER THAT INVOLVES WINE?
A very fun and educational wine trip through Burgundy, Champagne and the south of France.

WHAT PART OF YOUR JOB DO YOU ENJOY THE MOST?
Making recommendations to customers and educating our staff about wine.

NAME YOUR FAVORITE WINE REGIONS FROM AROUND THE WORLD.
Burgundy is by far my favorite region because of its wine, food and atmosphere.

WHAT BITS OF INFORMATION WOULD YOU LIKE YOUR CUSTOMERS TO KNOW ABOUT YOU?
I love to play hockey.

IF YOU WERE NOT IN THIS PROFESSION, WHAT WOULD YOU BE DOING?
Probably a chef.

DESCRIBE YOUR WINE SELECTIONS, BOTH BY THE GLASS AND ON YOUR LIST.
Just trying to keep it fun, fresh and cutting-edge. I love to try new things and introduce them to our guests.

WHAT ARE THE MOST UNIQUE FEATURES IN YOUR WINE PROGRAM?
We will sell almost any wine by the glass.

WHAT CATEGORY OF WINE IS THE BEST VALUE IN YOUR RESTAURANT?
Our "Alternative" category.

NAME ONE OF YOUR RESTAURANT'S SIGNATURE DISHES. WHAT WINE DO YOU PREFER TO RECOMMEND WITH IT?
Our salmon and potato salad with California Pinot Noir.

Ocean Grill

1050 Sexton Plaza
Vero Beach, Florida 32963
phone 772-231-5409 fax 772-234-8389
website www.ocean-grill.com

C. Thayer Kern

MANAGER, BEVERAGE DIRECTOR
AND SOMMELIER

NAME TWO OF YOUR FAVORITE WINE REGIONS FROM AROUND THE
WORLD.
Sonoma's Russian River Valley because it produces such great fruit flavors in its
wines, and Beaujolais because I think I just like saying "carbonic maceration."

NAME A RECENT WINE DISCOVERY THAT EXCITED YOU.
I became aware of "whole cluster" (carbonic maceration) fermentation when I
first tasted Willamette Valley Vineyards' Whole Cluster Pinot Noir. The flavor,
style and value of this wine is really first rate. As for Beaujolais, I just thought it
was supposed to taste that way.

WHAT BITS OF INFORMATION WOULD YOU LIKE YOUR CUSTOMERS TO
KNOW ABOUT YOU?
Before my kids, I used to play both ice and street hockey.

WHAT ARE THE MOST UNIQUE FEATURES IN YOUR WINE PROGRAM?
We offer signature wines from quality, limited-production wineries and quality
wines from established producers. We feature ten to fourteen by-the-glass
selections and many half-bottles.

WHAT CATEGORY OF WINE IS THE BEST VALUE IN YOUR RESTAURANT?
All wines on the list are values. We use the same pricing formula for all our
wines, and our customers win as a result.

NAME A FEW OF YOUR RESTAURANT'S SIGNATURE DISHES. WHAT TYPES
OF WINE DO YOU PREFER TO RECOMMEND WITH EACH?
Crab au gratin with California Pinot Grigio; broiled pompano with apricot
butter with an aromatic white wine; roast duckling with California late-picked
Zinfandel.

WHAT ARE SOME OTHER ULTIMATE WINE AND FOOD PAIRINGS?
Stone crab claws with Gewürztraminer; Cajun New York strip with late-picked
Zinfandel; rack of lamb with Shiraz.

Ruth's Chris Steak House

610 North Orlando Avenue
Winter Park, Florida 32789
phone 407-622-2444 fax 407-622-4455
website www.ruthchris.com

Kevin J. Boyer
SOMMELIER
AND BEVERAGE MANAGER

WHAT INSPIRED YOU TO PURSUE A CAREER THAT INVOLVES WINE?

My family. My mother owned and operated a demonstrating company that specialized in wine and spirits. My mother's passion for teaching really shaped what I came to know and love about the wine industry. (Not to mention having all that wine around the house at an early age!)

NAME YOUR FAVORITE WINE REGION FROM AROUND THE WORLD.

I have always been a tried-and-true Pacific Northwest wine lover.

NAME RECENT WINE DISCOVERIES THAT HAVE EXCITED YOU.

Wines from southeastern Europe, including those from Romania, Bulgaria and Hungary. I've tasted excellent Mavrud and Melnik wines from Bulgaria and wonderful Tokaji Aszu from small producers in Hungary.

IF YOU WERE NOT IN THIS PROFESSION, WHAT WOULD YOU BE DOING?

I can't imagine another profession that could make me half as happy, short of crafting my own wine.

NAME ONE OF YOUR RESTAURANT'S SIGNATURE DISHES. WHAT WINE DO YOU PREFER TO RECOMMEND WITH IT?

Veal chop with sweet and hot peppers paired with old vine Zinfandel.

WHAT ARE SOME OTHER ULTIMATE WINE AND FOOD PAIRINGS?

Bluefin or ahi tuna, lightly grilled rare with a touch of spice, paired with German Riesling Kabinett or a New World dry Riesling.

Sawgrass Marriott Resort and Beach Club

1000 PGA Tour Boulevard
Ponte Verde Beach, Florida 32082
phone 904-285-7777 fax 904-285-7003

Vincenzo E. D'Agostino
FOOD AND BEVERAGE MANAGER
AND SOMMELIER

WHAT INSPIRED YOU TO PURSUE A CAREER THAT INVOLVES WINE?
Wine is a part of my Italian culture and my career in the restaurant industry.

WHAT PART OF YOUR JOB DO YOU ENJOY THE MOST?
I enjoy talking to people about wine and tasting wine. I have met so many great people in this profession.

NAME ONE OF YOUR FAVORITE WINE REGIONS FROM AROUND THE WORLD.
Italy in general and Tuscany in particular, because it's a beautiful region filled with history, great food and excellent wines.

NAME RECENT WINE DISCOVERIES THAT HAVE EXCITED YOU.
Rioja, Spain, for the grapes like Tempranillo and Garnacha. Spanish wines are underrated and great values, too.

WHAT WOULD YOU LIKE YOUR CUSTOMERS TO KNOW ABOUT YOU?
I love to travel and I have a passion for food and wine.

IF YOU WERE NOT IN THIS PROFESSION, WHAT WOULD YOU BE DOING?
I'd represent a winery or teach wine seminars.

DESCRIBE YOUR WINE SELECTIONS.
Our wine list aims to please our guests, whether they want a $23 bottle of wine or a $1,000 bottle.

NAME A FEW OF YOUR RESTAURANT'S SIGNATURE DISHES. WHAT TYPES OF WINE DO YOU PREFER TO RECOMMEND WITH EACH?
Hawaiian bigeye tuna with Szechwan sauce and soba noodles with Australian Shiraz; mascarpone cheese with extra-dry Champagne; smoked mozzarella with Sonoma County Chardonnay.

WHAT WINES ARE CUSTOMERS NOW MORE WILLING TO ORDER?
Pinotage from South Africa and Sangiovese from Italy; and Portuguese and Chilean wines. Half-bottles, also.

Victoria and Albert's at Disney's Grand Floridian Beach Resort

4401 Floridian Way
Lake Buena Vista, Florida 32830
phone 407-824-3000 fax 407-824-0093

Brian J. Koziol
AREA MANAGER AND WINE BUYER

WHAT INSPIRED YOU TO PURSUE A CAREER THAT INVOLVES WINE?
As a student at the University of Wisconsin-Stout, I had the opportunity to attend a wine education class as part of the curriculum

WHAT PART OF YOUR JOB DO YOU ENJOY THE MOST?
Our wine-pairing program. Discussing and tasting wines with Chef Scott Hunnel is a key focus of mine.

NAME TWO OF YOUR FAVORITE WINES FROM AROUND THE WORLD.
Champagne and Germany. Bubbles are perfect for celebrating, and the balance of acidity and sweetness in German Riesling offer many options for food pairings.

NAME RECENT WINE DISCOVERIES THAT HAVE EXCITED YOU.
Wines from Capçanes winery in Spain, which are high quality and excellent value for money; Bertani 1976 Amarone della Valpolicella, still delicious after all these years!

IF YOU WERE NOT IN THIS PROFESSION, WHAT WOULD YOU BE DOING?
I wish my athletic ability had allowed me to be a baseball player.

DESCRIBE YOUR WINE SELECTIONS, BOTH BY THE GLASS AND ON YOUR LIST.
Our wine list has 700 selections and is focused on Champagne, Bordeaux, Burgundy and California.

WHAT ARE THE MOST UNIQUE FEATURES IN YOUR WINE PROGRAM?
Our wine-pairing program. We match six wines from around the world with a menu selection.

WHAT ARE SOME OTHER ULTIMATE WINE AND FOOD PAIRINGS?
Our Kona chocolate soufflé with Brachetto d'Acqui; Iranian Karabarun osetra caviar with Blanc de Blancs Champagne.

Antonio's at Sandlake

FRANCESCO D'ANGELO,
WINE BUYER
7559 West Sandlake Road, Orlando
407-363-9191

Antonio's La Fiamma

JOEL CABAN, WINE BUYER
611 South Orlando Avenue, Maitland
407-645-1043

Armani's at the Grand Hyatt

CHERYL WHITE, WINE BUYER
6200 West Courtney Campbell
Causeway, Tampa
813-281-9165

Arthur's 27 at the Wyndham Palace Resort

JAY FINKELSTEIN, MANAGER
AND WINE BUYER
1900 Lake Buena Vista Drive,
Lake Buena Vista
407-827-2727

Ashley Street Grille at the Radisson River Walk Hotel

RICK DORMAN, FOOD AND
BEVERAGE DIRECTOR
200 North Ashley Street, Tampa
813-226-4400

Bacco Italian Restaurant

LILIANA BADAMO, SOMMELIER
10065 University Boulevard, Orlando
407-678-8833

Bay Hill Country Club

FRED HANSEN, FOOD AND
BEVERAGE DIRECTOR
6200 Bay Hill Boulevard, Orlando
407-876-2429

Beach Bistro

BOB VALENTINO, WINE DIRECTOR
6600 Gold Drive, Holmes Beach
941-778-6444

Big City Tavern

KIRA ASTLE, GENERAL MANAGER
1600 East Seventh Avenue, Tampa
813-247-3000

Bob Heilman's Beachcomber Restaurant

BOB HEILMAN, OWNER
AND WINE BUYER
447 Mandalay Avenue,
Clearwater Beach
727-442-4144

Café de France

DOMINIQUE GUTIERREZ,
PRESIDENT, OWNER
AND WINE PURCHASER
526 Park Avenue South, Winter Park
407-647-1869

Café in the Court at the Ramada Resort Parkway

DANIEL MEYS, FOOD AND
BEVERAGE DIRECTOR
2900 Parkway Boulevard, Kissimmee
407-396-7000

Charlie's Lobster House

JEFF EICHER, WINE BUYER
8445 International Drive,
Suite 122, Orlando
407-352-6929

Chatham's Place

MAURICE COLINDRES, MANAGING
PARTNER AND WINE BUYER
7575 Dr. Phillips Boulevard, Orlando
407-345-2992

Christinis Restaurant

CHRIS CHRISTINI, OWNER
AND WINE BUYER
7600 Dr. Phillips Boulevard, Orlando
407-345-8770

Citricos at the Disney Grand Floridian Resort

JOHN BLAZON, CORPORATE
WINE DIRECTOR
4401 Grand Floridian Way, Lake
Buena Vista
407-566-5808

Citrus Club

JED ZIEGLER, FOOD AND
BEVERAGE DIRECTOR
255 South Orange Avenue, Orlando
407-843-1080

Columbia Restaurant

RENE CAUSSEY, WINE BUYER
2117 East Seventh Avenue, Tampa
813-248-4961

Le Coq Au Vin

PETER BURKE, SOMMELIER
4800 South Orange Avenue, Orlando
407-851-6980

La Coquina at the Hyatt Grand Cypress Resort

FRED HOFFMAN, FOOD AND
BEVERAGE DIRECTOR
1 Grand Cypress Boulevard, Orlando
407-239-1234

Criolla's

MICHEL THIBAULT, SOMMELIER
170 East Scenic Highway, 30-A,
Santa Rosa Beach
850-267-1267

Destin Chops

JIM ALTAMURA, OWNER
AND WINE BUYER
320 Highway 98 East, Destin
850-654-4944

Donatello

TED LEWIS, SOMMELIER
232 North Dale Mabry, Tampa
813-875-6660

Dux at the Peabody Orlando

JOHN ASKEW, FOOD AND
BEVERAGE DIRECTOR
9801 International Drive, Orlando
407-345-4540

Ellie's

BOB MOULDER, GENERAL MANAGER
AND WINE BUYER
41 Royal Palm Pointe, Vero Beach
772-778-2600

Emeril's Restaurant

DAVID PENISI, SOMMELIER
6000 Universal Boulevard, Orlando
407-224-2424

Enzo's Restaurant

ENZO PERLINI, CO-OWNER
AND WINE BUYER
JOANNE ROSS, CO-OWNER
AND WINE BUYER
1130 South Highway 17-92,
Longwood
407-834-9872

Epping Forest Yacht Club

CHRIS MILLER,
BEVERAGE MANAGER
1830 Epping Forest Drive,
Jacksonville
904-739-7200

Fleming's Prime Steakhouse

PAUL DeMEZA, WINE BUYER
4322 Boy Scout Road, Tampa
813-874-9463

Fulton's Crab House

MELESEINI PENITANI,
BEVERAGE DIRECTOR
1670 North Buena Vista Drive,
Lake Buena Vista
407-934-2628

Governor's Club

BARRY HERMAN, SOMMELIER
202 South Adams Street, Tallahassee
850-222-4065

Grosvenor Resort

MICHAEL GRAY, FOOD AND
BEVERAGE DIRECTOR
1850 Hotel Plaza Boulevard,
Lake Buena Vista
407-828-4444

Harvey's Bistro

BENJ RAY, GENERAL MANAGER
390 North Orange Avenue, Orlando
407-246-6965

Hemingway's at the Hyatt Regency Grand Cypress Resort

ROBERT FOHR, SOMMELIER
One Grand Cypress Boulevard,
Lake Buena Vista
407-239-3854

Interlachen Country Club

RYAN KLING, WINE BUYER
2245 Interlachen Center, Winter Park
407-657-0850

Island Way Grill

BRAD DIXON, WINE
AND SPIRITS MANAGER
20 Island Way, Clearwater Beach
727-461-6617

Jack's Place at the Rosen Plaza Hotel

STACI RAMPHAL,
RESTAURANT MANAGER
9700 International Drive, Orlando
407-996-9700

Jackson's Bistro

ERIC LITCHFIELD, GENERAL
MANAGER AND WINE BUYER
601 South Harbor Island Boulevard,
Tampa
813-277-0112

Karlings Inn

KARL CAENERS, WINE BUYER
4640 North US Highway 17,
De Leon Springs
386-985-5535

Kelly's For Just About Anything!

VIRGIL KELLY, OWNER, CHEF
AND WINE BUYER
319 Main Street, Dunedin
727-736-5284

Lafite's at the Melbourne Hilton

BILL GRIFFITH, FOOD AND
BEVERAGE DIRECTOR
200 Rialto Place, Melbourne
321-768-0200

Lando Sams at the Radisson Plaza Hotel

RICHARD BITNER, MANAGER
AND WINE BUYER
60 South Ivanhoe Boulevard, Orlando
407-425-4455

Linda's La Cantina Steakhouse

KAREN HART, SOMMELIER
4721 East Colonial Drive, Orlando
407-894-4491

Manuel's on the 28th

DARREL HORMEL, FOOD
AND BEVERAGE DIRECTOR
AND SOMMELIER
RALPH KRAUS, WINE BUYER
390 North Orange Avenue,
Winter Park
407-246-6580

Marina Café

JIM ALTAMURA, WINE BUYER
404 Highway 98 East, Destin
850-837-7960

The Maritana Grill at the Don Cesar Beach Resort

DON GORDON,
BEVERAGE MANAGER
3400 Gulf Boulevard, St. Pete Beach
727-360-1881

Marker 32

BEN GROSHELL, OWNER
AND WINE BUYER
14549 Beach Boulevard, Jacksonville
904-223-1534

Mise en Place

MARYANN FERENCE, OWNER AND
WINE BUYER
442 West Kennedy Boulevard, Tampa
813-254-5373

Monte's

JACK PIEMONTE, OWNER
AND WINE BUYER
1517 South Ocean Drive, Vero Beach
772-231-6612

Moon Fish

TODD BOWLIN, MANAGER
AND WINE BUYER
7525 West Sand Lake Road, Orlando
407-363-7262

Morton's of Chicago

SETH MILLER, GENERAL MANAGER
AND WINE BUYER
7600 Dr. Phillips Boulevard, Orlando
407-248-3485

Orlando Airport Marriott

VINOD BAJAJ, FOOD AND
BEVERAGE DIRECTOR
7499 Augusta National Drive, Orlando
407-851-9000

Oystercatcher's

KENNY HUNSBERGER, CHEF
AND WINE BUYER
6200 Courtney Campbell Causeway,
Tampa
813-207-6815

The Palm

CHERYL HILL, MANAGER AND
WINE BUYER
205 Westshore Plaza Drive, Tampa
813-849-7256

Paul's Surfside Restaurant

PAOLO FORLINI, OWNER
AND WINE BUYER
435 Mandalay Avenue, Clearwater
727-445-1155

Portobello Yacht Club at Pleasure Island

MELISSA REMINGTON,
BEVERAGE DIRECTOR
1650 Buena Vista Drive, Lake Buena
Vista
407-934-8888

Ronnie's Steakhouse

RON ELIAS, OWNER
AND WINE BUYER
7500 International Drive, Orlando
407-313-3000

Roy's

CHRIS AULD, BEVERAGE MANAGER
7760 Sand Lake Road, Orlando
407-352-4844

Roy's

JON VURGINAC, WINE DIRECTOR
4342 West Boy Scout Boulevard,
Tampa
813-873-7697

Ruth's Chris Steak House

MARK MONAHAN, MANAGER
AND WINE BUYER
1700 North Westshore Boulevard,
Tampa
813-282-1118

Seasons 52

GEORGE MILIOTES, GENERAL
MANAGER AND WINE BUYER
7700 Sand Lake Road, Orlando
407-354-5212

Sideburn's

AMY CAIRNS, WINE BUYER
2208 West Morrison Avenue, Tampa
813-258-2233

Silver Lake Golf and Country Club

SARA STEVENS, WINE BUYER
9435 Silver Lake Drive, Leesburg
352-787-4035

St. Tropez al Fresco Bistro

JASON GARDNER, CO-OWNER
AND WINE BUYER
2075 Indian River Boulevard,
Vero Beach
772-778-9565

Tangos

JILL TENCH, CO-OWNER
AND WINE BUYER
3001 Ocean Drive, Suite 107,
Vero Beach
772-231-1550

The Tides

MARY LISA ALFALLA, WINE BUYER
3103 Cardinal Drive, Vero Beach
772-234-3966

Tio Pepe Restaurant
JESUS EXPOSITO, OWNER
AND WINE BUYER
2930 Gulf to Bay Boulevard,
Clearwater
727-799-3082

Vito's Chop House
FRANK BRUNO, MANAGER AND
WINE BUYER
8633 International Drive, Orlando
407-354-2467

Walt Disney World Swan and Dolphin
MENZE HEROIAN, WINE BUYER
1200 Epcot Resort, Lake Buena Vista
407-934-3000

Windermere at the Isleworth Country Club
RANDY LUEDDERS, CHEF
AND WINE BUYER
6100 Deacon Drive, Windermere
407-876-6034

Wyndham Palace Resort
LUC ANDRES, FOOD AND
BEVERAGE DIRECTOR
1900 Lake Buena Vista Drive,
Lake Buena Vista
407-827-2727

The Addison

2 East Camino Real
Boca Raton, Florida 33432
phone 561-395-9335 fax 561-393-6255
website www.theaddison.com

Zachary N. Smith

SOMMELIER

NAME TWO OF YOUR FAVORITE WINES FROM AROUND THE WORLD.
Alsatian white wines for their elegance, fruit expression and complexity.
Proprietary red wines from Napa for the wonderful range of styles, from elegant to powerful.

NAME RECENT WINE DISCOVERIES THAT HAVE EXCITED YOU.
Pinot Noirs from the Santa Lucia Highlands and Santa Maria in California for their beautiful fruit and flexibility with food. Small Shiraz producers in Barossa and McClaren Vale in Australia for the depth and power of their wines.

WHAT WOULD YOU LIKE YOUR CUSTOMERS TO KNOW ABOUT YOU?
I love the outdoors, whether hiking or enjoying the beaches in Florida or the Caribbean.

IF YOU WERE NOT IN THIS PROFESSION, WHAT WOULD YOU BE?
A fishing guide or commercial pilot.

DESCRIBE YOUR WINE SELECTIONS, BOTH BY THE GLASS AND ON YOUR LIST.
We serve eighteen wines by the glass and have about 300 wines by the bottle, with an emphasis on California, Italy, France and Australia.

WHAT CATEGORY OF WINE IS THE BEST VALUE IN YOUR RESTAURANT?
California Zinfandel and Syrah, and wines from the south of France.

NAME A COUPLE OF YOUR RESTAURANT'S SIGNATURE DISHES. WHAT TYPES OF WINE DO YOU PREFER TO RECOMMEND WITH EACH?
Pan-seared lump crab cakes with a Pommery mustard–cayenne butter sauce paired with Alsatian Gewürztraminer or Riesling; herb-crusted ahi tuna with a Port wine sauce and Australian Shiraz.

WHAT WINES ARE CUSTOMERS NOW MORE WILLING TO ORDER?
Washington State Riesling, New Zealand Sauvignon Blanc, California Syrah and Australian Shiraz.

Bacchus & Co.

13499 South Cleveland Avenue
Fort Meyers, Florida 33907
phone 239-415-9463
website www.bacchusandco.com

Robert "Bone" Mulroy

GENERAL MANAGER

NAME TWO OF YOUR FAVORITE WINE REGIONS FROM AROUND THE WORLD.

Carneros produces world-class Pinot Noir and Chardonnay. I also like Piedmont for its big Barolos.

NAME RECENT WINE DISCOVERIES THAT HAVE EXCITED YOU.

South African wines, for their value.

WHAT BITS OF INFORMATION WOULD YOU LIKE YOUR CUSTOMERS TO KNOW ABOUT YOU?

I love to travel.

IF YOU WERE NOT IN THIS PROFESSION, WHAT WOULD YOU BE DOING?

Sports marketing.

DESCRIBE YOUR WINE SELECTIONS, BOTH BY THE GLASS AND ON YOUR LIST.

We offer something for everyone. We have private-label wines by the glass as well as selections from boutique producers from all over the world. Educating the guest is one of our daily goals. If I can teach one person something new each day, I'm satisfied!

WHAT CATEGORY OF WINE IS THE BEST VALUE IN YOUR RESTAURANT?

Our Burgundy and Rhône wines are the best values.

NAME A COUPLE OF YOUR RESTAURANT'S SIGNATURE DISHES. WHAT TYPES OF WINE DO YOU PREFER TO RECOMMEND WITH EACH?

Seafood paella (shrimp, scallops, clams, mussels and chorizo sausage with saffron rice) with white Bordeaux or New Zealand Sauvignon Blanc; our sushi dishes with Alsace Pinot Gris and German Riesling.

IN THE PAST YEAR, WHAT WINES IN YOUR WINE PROGRAM HAVE CUS-TOMERS BECOME MORE WILLING TO ORDER?

Red Zinfandel.

WHAT IS ONE OF YOUR ULTIMATE WINE AND FOOD PAIRINGS?

Lamb and Australian Shiraz. You just can't go wrong.

Bistro Chez Jean-Pierre

132 North County Road
Palm Beach, Florida 33480
phone 561-833-1171 fax 561-835-0482

David Leverrier
MANAGER AND WINE BUYER

NAME ONE OR TWO OF YOUR FAVORITE WINE REGIONS FROM AROUND THE WORLD.
Burgundy reds. Not often does one region offer an array of different styles, from light Volnays to huge Cortons.

NAME RECENT WINE DISCOVERIES THAT HAVE EXCITED YOU.
Alsatian wines. Although a hard sell, they are very food-friendly and a perfect match for our Florida weather.

WHAT WOULD YOU LIKE YOUR CUSTOMERS TO KNOW ABOUT YOU?
I play golf and tennis, but my girlfriend and my job are my life.

IF YOU WERE NOT IN THIS PROFESSION, WHAT WOULD YOU BE DOING?
This is all I know and all I've ever done. I don't know what else I could do.

DESCRIBE YOUR WINE SELECTIONS, BOTH BY THE GLASS AND ON YOUR LIST.
We only have French and American wines. We have twelve selections by the glass, twelve by the half-bottle and 327 wines by the bottle.

WHAT ARE THE MOST UNIQUE FEATURES IN YOUR WINE PROGRAM?
It is a very straightforward wine list with good choices at every price range in every category. Balance is the key.

WHAT CATEGORY OF WINE IS THE BEST VALUE IN YOUR RESTAURANT?
California Sauvignon Blancs and red Rhône wines.

NAME A COUPLE OF YOUR RESTAURANT'S SIGNATURE DISHES. WHAT TYPES OF WINE DO YOU PREFER TO RECOMMEND WITH EACH?
Fresh sautéed foie gras with caramelized pears and Gewürztraminer; braised beef short ribs and Côte-Rôtie.

WHAT WINES ARE CUSTOMERS NOW MORE WILLING TO ORDER?
California Zinfandel and red Burgundy.

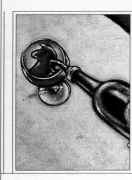

Bistro La Tavernetta

926 Northeast 20th Avenue
Fort Lauderdale, Florida 33304
phone 954-463-2566 fax 954-524-2777
website www.latavernetta.net

Ute E. Stork
MASTER CHEF AND
RESTAURANT MANAGER

WHAT INSPIRED YOU TO PURSUE A CAREER THAT INVOLVES WINE?
I enjoy being in the hospitality industry. A great wine rounds up every great experience.

WHAT PART OF YOUR JOB DO YOU ENJOY THE MOST?
Interaction with the customer. In the hospitality and tourism industry the customers are usually in a good mood. It is great to enhance their experience and to try to create something memorable.

NAME ONE OF YOUR FAVORITE WINES.
Amarone. Great care is taken in producing it, from harvest to the bottle.

NAME RECENT WINE DISCOVERIES THAT HAVE EXCITED YOU.
Italian wines, especially Chiantis, which can be found at very affordable prices.

WHAT BITS OF INFORMATION WOULD YOU LIKE YOUR CUSTOMERS TO KNOW ABOUT YOU?
I have a background as a hands-on chef, as well as a Ph.D. in hospitality and tourism.

WHAT ARE THE MOST UNIQUE FEATURES IN YOUR WINE PROGRAM?
We have a description of the wines on the list to make them more accessible.

WHAT CATEGORIES OF WINE ARE THE BEST VALUES IN YOUR RESTAURANT?
Amarone della Valpolicella and Chianti Classico.

NAME A COUPLE OF YOUR RESTAURANT'S SIGNATURE DISHES. WHAT TYPES OF WINE DO YOU PREFER TO RECOMMEND WITH EACH?
Mero Ischia with scallops, mussels and asparagus with Italian Pinot Grigio; 16-ounce veal chop with grilled portobello mushroom served with Italian Barbera from Piedmont.

City Cellar
Wine Bar and Grill

700 South Rosemary Avenue
West Palm Beach, Florida 33401
phone 561-366-0071 fax 561-366-8541
website www.bigtimerestaurants.com/city_cellar_citycellar.html

Ryan M. Morgan
MANAGER AND SOMMELIER

WHAT INSPIRED YOU TO PURSUE A CAREER THAT INVOLVES WINE?
I was in fine dining throughout college. I eventually realized that people were paying to go out and experience what I was doing for a living.

NAME ONE OF YOUR FAVORITE WINES.
I love Oregon Pinot Noir; New World fruit matched with body and structure.

NAME A RECENT WINE DISCOVERY THAT EXCITED YOU.
I recently had an exceptional dry German Riesling. To search for the fruit, instead of having it smack you in the palate, was refreshing, both literally and figuratively.

IF YOU WERE NOT IN THIS PROFESSION, WHAT WOULD YOU BE DOING?
I have a bachelor's degree in computer science, so I would probably pursue a career in that field.

WHAT ARE THE MOST UNIQUE FEATURES IN YOUR WINE PROGRAM?
We offer a wide selection of wines, including fifty wines by the glass and half-glass, forty half-bottle selections and wine flights that feature special wines not usually served by the glass.

WHAT CATEGORY OF WINE IS THE BEST VALUE IN YOUR RESTAURANT?
Napa Valley Cabernet Sauvignon.

NAME A COUPLE OF YOUR RESTAURANT'S SIGNATURE DISHES. WHAT TYPES OF WINE DO YOU PREFER TO RECOMMEND WITH EACH?
A 16-ounce lamb shank on the bone, braised in red wine with mashed potatoes and fried parsnips paired with California Syrah; Chilean sea bass (broiled with garlic aioli) served with julienne-sliced and sautéed vegetables and white beans flavored with pancetta, with Napa Chardonnay.

L'Escalier
at the Breakers Hotel

One South County Road
Palm Beach, Florida 33480
phone 561-659-8480 fax 561-655-3740
website www.thebreakers.com

Virginia A. Philip
CHEF SOMMELIER AND
MASTER SOMMELIER

LIST SOME OF YOUR WINE DEGREES AND AWARDS.
Master Sommelier diploma, November 2002; Best Sommelier in the United States, November 2002; American Sommelier Association; Restaurant Wine "On-Premise Wine Marketer of the Year," 2002.

WHAT INSPIRED YOU TO PURSUE A CAREER THAT INVOLVES WINE?
I love the challenge of wine and all the other subjects that revolve around it.

NAME TWO OF YOUR FAVORITE WINES OR WINE REGIONS.
German Rieslings because they are excellent food wines; Spain for its quality and value.

WHAT BITS OF INFORMATION WOULD YOU LIKE YOUR CUSTOMERS TO KNOW ABOUT YOU?
My husband and I own a 110-seat restaurant. He runs and operates it. I usually work there on my days off.

IF YOU WERE NOT IN THIS PROFESSION, WHAT WOULD YOU BE DOING?
I'd own my own wine shop and gourmet food store.

DESCRIBE YOUR WINE SELECTIONS, BOTH BY THE GLASS AND ON YOUR LIST.
Our wine list has been a Grand Award winner since 1981. We have 1,250 selections from all over the globe. We have a great food and wine pairing program.

WHAT ARE THE MOST UNIQUE FEATURES IN YOUR WINE PROGRAM?
We have a selection of 110 half-bottles and more than 200 California Cabernet selections alone. All wines by the glass are offered in 3-ounce or 6-ounce pours.

NAME A COUPLE OF YOUR RESTAURANT'S SIGNATURE DISHES. WHAT TYPES OF WINE DO YOU PREFER TO RECOMMEND WITH EACH?
Tournedos Rossini with Washington State Merlot; squab or quail with red Burgundy; Florida pompano with Rioja.

Harry's Continental Kitchens

525 Saint Judes Drive
Longboat Key, Florida 34228
phone 941-383-0777 fax 941-383-2029
website www.harryskitchen.com

Harold R. Christensen
OWNER AND CHEF

NAME TWO OF YOUR FAVORITE WINE REGIONS FROM AROUND THE WORLD.
The Champagne region in France because I like the small towns, the vineyards and the method of production. Also, Sonoma County because the people are casual and unpretentious, and the wines are great.

NAME RECENT WINE DISCOVERIES THAT HAVE EXCITED YOU.
South African Rhône-style wines such as Fairview Goats Rotie and Rust-en-Vrede Shiraz. They are as good as, if not better than, those from France.

WHAT BITS OF INFORMATION WOULD YOU LIKE YOUR CUSTOMERS TO KNOW ABOUT YOU?
I've been a master chef for thirty years and first level–certified sommelier for twelve years. I was one of the first chefs to pass the certification exam.

IF YOU WERE NOT IN THIS PROFESSION, WHAT WOULD YOU BE DOING?
Farming or something in agriculture.

WHAT ARE THE MOST UNIQUE FEATURES IN YOUR WINE PROGRAM?
We have half-bottles in all major varietals. We have prix fixe dinner specials with wine pairings, as well as winemaker dinners every other Wednesday night. The dinners are very casual and intimate, for a maximum of twenty-eight people.

WHAT WINES ARE THE BEST VALUES IN YOUR RESTAURANT?
1995 red Bordeaux and 1995 California Cabernet.

NAME A FEW OF YOUR RESTAURANT'S SIGNATURE DISHES. WHAT TYPES OF WINE DO YOU PREFER TO RECOMMEND WITH EACH?
Roast duck with Napa Valley Rosé; crab cakes with New Zealand Sauvignon Blanc; grouper Française with California Chardonnay; lamb chops with Sonoma County Zinfandel.

WHAT ARE SOME OTHER ULTIMATE WINE AND FOOD PAIRINGS?
Oysters with Sauvignon Blanc; butter, cream and Chardonnay; grilled fish and Pinot Gris.

Harry's Continental Kitchens

525 Saint Judes Drive
Longboat Key, Florida 34228
phone 941-383-0777 fax 941-383-2029
website www.harryskitchen.com

Hal R. Christensen
GENERAL MANAGER

WHO INSPIRED YOU TO PURSUE A CAREER THAT INVOLVES WINE?
My parents. Their love of wine and their involvement and relationships with different people in the wine industry were a real inspiration.

NAME RECENT WINE DISCOVERIES THAT HAVE EXCITED YOU.
Kim Crawford wines for their great quality and price; Lolonis organically grown wines are all top-quality and fairly priced, and the reserve Zinfandel and Petite Syrah are wonderful.

WHAT BITS OF INFORMATION WOULD YOU LIKE YOUR CUSTOMERS TO KNOW ABOUT YOU?
I'm a Florida native and a Florida State alumnus. I love the water, sport fishing, sport diving and free diving. I grew up in the restaurant business.

IF YOU WERE NOT IN THIS PROFESSION, WHAT WOULD YOU BE DOING?
I would have a career in upper-level management or own my own business. My dream is to own my own marina with a sport fishing fleet.

WHAT ARE THE MOST UNIQUE FEATURES IN YOUR WINE PROGRAM?
We have wine pairings with five-course prix fixe dinners and intimate, twenty guest, bi-weekly wine dinners in a private room with a speaker.

WHAT CATEGORY OF WINE IS THE BEST VALUE IN YOUR RESTAURANT?
Older Cabernet Sauvignons.

NAME A COUPLE OF YOUR RESTAURANT'S SIGNATURE DISHES. WHAT TYPES OF WINE DO YOU PREFER TO RECOMMEND WITH EACH?
Grouper pescatore sautéed with angel hair pasta with leek and garlic cream sauce and Sonoma County Chardonnay or Viognier; New Zealand rack of lamb with rosemary-scallion crust and Shiraz sauce with Napa Valley Petite Sirah.

Hi-Life Café

3000 North Federal Highway 12
Fort Lauderdale, Florida 33306
phone 954-563-1395 fax 954-563-1615
website www.hilifecafe.com

Chuck Smith
OWNER AND WINE DIRECTOR

NAME TWO OF YOUR FAVORITE WINES.
Napa Valley Cabernet Sauvignons for their distinctive depth and intense fruit character; New Zealand Sauvignon Blancs for their crisp acidity and compatibility with food.

NAME RECENT WINE DISCOVERIES THAT HAVE EXCITED YOU.
Jade Mountain Viognier for its intensity of flavor; Numanthia from the Toro region of Spain for its unique qualities.

WHAT BITS OF INFORMATION WOULD YOU LIKE YOUR CUSTOMERS TO KNOW ABOUT YOU?
I have a theatrical background.

IF YOU WERE NOT IN THIS PROFESSION, WHAT WOULD YOU BE DOING?
Teaching in the wine field, probably.

DESCRIBE YOUR WINE SELECTIONS, BY THE GLASS AND ON YOUR LIST.
We offer twenty wines by the glass and 90 to 100 wines on our list. We try to offer a diverse range of wines, reflecting great value and quality.

WHAT ARE THE MOST UNIQUE FEATURES IN YOUR WINE PROGRAM?
Besides the above, we print our own list and offer ongoing promotions.

NAME A FEW OF YOUR RESTAURANT'S SIGNATURE DISHES. WHAT TYPES OF WINE DO YOU PREFER TO RECOMMEND WITH EACH?
Salmon in a light Dijon sauce with Sancerre or Sauvignon Blanc; roast duckling with Burgundy or California Merlot; filet mignon in Dutch Dijon cream with Napa Cabernet.

IN THE PAST YEAR, WHAT WINES IN YOUR WINE PROGRAM HAVE CUSTOMERS BECOME MORE WILLING TO ORDER?
Oregon Pinot Noir, Burgundy and New Zealand Sauvignon Blanc.

Jackson's Steakhouse
450 East Las Olas Boulevard
Fort Lauderdale, Florida 33301
phone 954-522-4450 fax 954-522-1911
website www.jacksonssteakhouse.com

Patrick E. Morey
GENERAL MANAGER

NAME TWO OF YOUR FAVORITE WINE REGIONS FROM AROUND THE WORLD.
South Australia for reds of quality, richness and complexity; Santa Lucia
Highlands for its exceptional Pinot Noir.

NAME RECENT WINE DISCOVERIES THAT HAVE EXCITED YOU.
Northstar Merlot—amazing Merlot quality at a reasonable price; and Casa
Lapostolle Clos Apalta, the first world-class South American wine I have tasted.

WHAT BITS OF INFORMATION WOULD YOU LIKE YOUR CUSTOMERS TO
KNOW ABOUT YOU?
My educational background is in business. Many guests don't realize that I am
also the restaurant's general manager. As a hobby I raise large, exotic fish.

IF YOU WERE NOT IN THIS PROFESSION, WHAT WOULD YOU BE DOING?
Restoring old homes.

DESCRIBE YOUR WINE SELECTIONS.
We have a well-rounded, international program with 250 to 340 selections and
20 to 25 wines available by the glass. Our focus is high-quality American reds
like Cabernet, Syrah and Pinot Noir in all price ranges.

NAME A COUPLE OF YOUR RESTAURANT'S SIGNATURE DISHES. WHAT
TYPES OF WINE DO YOU PREFER TO RECOMMEND WITH EACH?
A 22-ounce USDA prime rib chop (bone-on-rib style) with American Syrah;
herb-crusted New Zealand rack of lamb with Santa Lucia Highlands Pinot Noir.

IN THE PAST YEAR, WHAT WINES IN YOUR WINE PROGRAM HAVE CUS-
TOMERS BECOME MORE WILLING TO ORDER?
American Syrah sales have tripled and our offerings have doubled.

WHAT ARE SOME OTHER ULTIMATE WINE AND FOOD PAIRINGS?
Dry-aged beef with a Côtes du Rhône; macadamia-crusted scallops with Santa
Barbara Chardonnay; barbecued New York strip with red Zinfandel.

Joe's Stone Crab Restaurant

11 Washington Avenue
Miami Beach, Florida 33139
phone 305-673-0365 fax 305-673-0295

Paul R. Kozolis
BEVERAGE DIRECTOR

WHAT IS YOUR ULTIMATE FOOD AND WINE PAIRING?
Kim Crawford Sauvignon Blanc with ice-cold Florida stone crab and Joe's mustard sauce, garlic spinach and french-fried sweet potatoes.

DESCRIBE YOUR WINE SELECTIONS.
We have a good selection of wines from around the world.

WHAT IS YOUR FAVORITE WINE REGION IN THE WORLD TODAY?
Burgundy. I am so passionate about Pinot Noir.

WHAT LED YOU TO YOUR CURRENT POSITION?
An insatiable desire for knowledge of wine.

WHAT ARE THE MOST CHALLENGING ASPECTS OF YOUR JOB?
Keeping my list fresh, and training my staff to understand fine wine and how to sell it.

IF YOU WERE NOT IN THIS PROFESSION, WHAT WOULD YOU BE DOING?
Living on a boat in Key West and fishing for a living.

Lucca at the Boca Raton Resort and Club

501 East Camino Real
Boca Raton, Florida 33432
phone 561-447-3000 fax 561-447-5023
website www.bocaresort.com

CJ "Charlie" Arturaola
WINE DIRECTOR AND SOMMELIER

WHO INSPIRED YOU TO PURSUE A CAREER INVOLVING WINE?
My father. As a kid, I helped him decant wine once a week from demijohns to bottles.

WHAT PART OF YOUR JOB DO YOU ENJOY THE MOST?
Teaching guests not to be intimidated by labels, and relating history and facts about the wine regions the wines come from.

NAME ONE OR TWO OF YOUR FAVORITE WINE DISTRICTS OR WINE REGIONS FROM AROUND THE WORLD.
Bordeaux for its history and Chianti because I love to single out the character and structure of wines from its various districts.

NAME RECENT WINE DISCOVERIES THAT HAVE EXCITED YOU.
Sauvignon Blanc from New Zealand and Chile! Awesome wines that are great for everyday sipping in sunny Florida.

IF YOU WERE NOT IN THIS PROFESSION, WHAT WOULD YOU BE?
A shepherd in the Basque country, making my own cheese and producing wine.

WHAT ARE THE MOST UNIQUE FEATURES IN YOUR WINE PROGRAM?
Our winter wine dinners, featuring special wines from various wine regions and boutique wineries, and our great selection of half-bottles.

NAME A COUPLE OF YOUR RESTAURANT'S SIGNATURE DISHES. WHAT TYPES OF WINE DO YOU PREFER TO RECOMMEND WITH EACH?
"27 Ocean Blue," a Colorado lamb rack with a Dijon mustard crust, paired with Gevrey-Chambertin; osso buco alla Milanese with Carmignano Riserva.

IN THE PAST YEAR, WHAT WINES IN YOUR PROGRAM HAVE CUSTOMERS BECOME MORE WILLING TO ORDER?
Oregon Pinot Noir, Shiraz from Coonawarra, Malbec from Argentina, Rioja from Spain, Brunello di Montalcino from Tuscany, Primitivo from Apulia and Nero d'Avola from Sicily.

Norman's

21 Almeria Avenue
Coral Gables, Florida 33134
phone 305-446-6767 fax 305-446-7909
website www.normans.com

Ian Falconi
GENERAL MANAGER

NAME TWO OF YOUR FAVORITE WINE DISTRICTS.
Nuits-Saint-Georges for finesse, elegance and power; Howell Mountain for luxury, richness and exuberance.

NAME RECENT WINE DISCOVERIES THAT HAVE EXCITED YOU.
Muddy Waters Chardonnay from New Zealand, a great value and a fabulous, classical expression; Venus Garnacha blend, from Montsant, Spain, a very good value that is fresh and rich.

WHAT WOULD YOU LIKE YOUR CUSTOMERS TO KNOW ABOUT YOU?
I like history and sociology, looking for the connections between human culture and society.

IF YOU WERE NOT IN THIS PROFESSION, WHAT WOULD YOU BE DOING?
Cinematography, economics or history.

DESCRIBE YOUR WINE SELECTIONS. WHAT ARE THE MOST UNIQUE FEATURES IN YOUR WINE PROGRAM?
We view our program as a collection of rare and unique bottles and therefore offer a range of eclectic and esoteric selections. In what we offer, we seek out values and new and fresh ideas and producers.

WHAT CATEGORY OF WINE IS THE BEST VALUE IN YOUR RESTAURANT?
New World Pinot Noir.

NAME A COUPLE OF YOUR RESTAURANT'S SIGNATURE DISHES. WHAT TYPES OF WINE DO YOU PREFER TO RECOMMEND WITH EACH?
Yucca-stuffed crispy shrimp with sour mojo and habañero tartar salsa with Austrian Grüner Veltliner; "Pan Stew" (Maine lobster, scallop and shrimp) with melted tomatoes paired with Flowers Perennial from California.

WHAT WINES ARE CUSTOMERS NOW MORE WILLING TO ORDER?
Grüner Veltliner; Syrah; and Alsatian Riesling, Pinot Gris and Pinot Blanc.

Pierre's Restaurant at Morada Bay

81600 Overseas Highway
Islamorada, Florida 33036
phone 305-664-3225 fax 305-664-3227

Yoann A. Bagat
SOMMELIER

NAME YOUR FAVORITE WINE REGION.
Bordeaux, which is where I'm from.

NAME RECENT WINE DISCOVERIES THAT HAVE EXCITED YOU.
Shafer 2000 Firebreak is a very nice blend of Sangiovese and Cabernet Sauvignon and great with spicy food, fish and meat.

WHAT BITS OF INFORMATION WOULD YOU LIKE YOUR CUSTOMERS TO KNOW ABOUT YOU?
Trust me, and you will be pleased.

DESCRIBE YOUR WINE SELECTIONS, BOTH BY THE GLASS AND ON YOUR LIST.
Forty-five percent French, fifty percent American and five percent Italian.

WHAT IS THE MOST UNIQUE FEATURE IN YOUR WINE PROGRAM?
Its diversity.

WHAT CATEGORY OF WINE IS THE BEST VALUE IN YOUR RESTAURANT?
Meritage.

NAME A COUPLE OF YOUR RESTAURANT'S SIGNATURE DISHES. WHAT TYPES OF WINE DO YOU PREFER TO RECOMMEND WITH EACH?
Curry broiled yellowtail snapper with Sancerre or Pouilly Fumé; seared Hudson Valley duck breast with mature red Bordeaux (Médoc).

HOW DO YOU RECOMMEND WINES TO CUSTOMERS FROM A FOOD PAIRING POINT OF VIEW?
I usually try to find out what wines our customers drink and then introduce them to something new that they would not normally order or have never had before. The old-fashioned white with fish and red with meat is over. There are new pairings that are so exciting, like tuna with Pinot Noir, fish with red Sancerre, or meat with a white wine.

Ruth's Chris Steak House

6700 South Tamiami Trail
Sarasota, Florida 34231
phone 941-924-9442 fax 941-924-8982
website www.ruthchris.com

Brian P. Lanigan
BEVERAGE MANAGER

WHAT INSPIRED YOU TO PURSUE A CAREER THAT INVOLVES WINE?
I worked with several Master Sommeliers during my restaurant career.

WHAT PART OF YOUR JOB DO YOU ENJOY THE MOST?
I enjoy studying about wine and the wine industry. Sharing this knowledge
with staff and customers is quite fulfilling.

NAME TWO OF YOUR FAVORITE WINES FROM AROUND THE WORLD.
The Champagne region because its sparkling wine is so enjoyable to drink. In
red wine, Burgundy because of the Pinot Noir grape's many interesting qualities.

NAME RECENT WINE DISCOVERIES THAT HAVE EXCITED YOU.
Sparkling wines from the Pacific Northwest. These wines are great values and
great quality.

IF YOU WERE NOT IN THIS PROFESSION, WHAT WOULD YOU BE DOING?
Comedy and travel. I would love to do stand-up.

DESCRIBE YOUR WINE SELECTIONS, BOTH BY THE GLASS AND ON YOUR LIST.
With 140 wines, we strive to present a cross-section of price points, flavor profiles and regions of origin. In our by-the-glass program, every three months we
feature one red wine and one white wine selection (along with twenty others),
which are typically unique and of high quality. Our wine list also has a large
Meritage section.

WHAT ARE THE MOST UNIQUE FEATURES IN YOUR WINE PROGRAM?
Every bottle of red wine ordered at Ruth's Chris is decanted using a wine aera-
tor and served in a hand-blown glass carafe.

Andre's Steakhouse
ANDRE COTTOLONI, OWNER
AND WINE BUYER
2800 North Tamiami Trail, Naples
941-263-5851

Arturo's Restaurant
VINCENT GISMALDE, WINE BUYER
6750 North Federal Highway,
Boca Raton
561-997-7373

Au Paradis
MICHEL CARBONNEAU, SOMMELIER
11412 Tamiami East Trail, Naples
239-775-7676

Baleen at Grove Isle Club and Resort
THOMAS WRIGHT, WINE BUYER
4 Grove Isle Drive, Coconut Grove
305-285-7973

Bijou Café
JEAN-PIERRE KNAGGS, OWNER
AND WINE BUYER
1287 First Street, Sarasota
941-366-8111

Blue Door at the Delano Hotel
TIMOTHY WAGNER, SOMMELIER
1685 Collins Avenue, Miami Beach
305-674-6400

Boheme Bistro
JOSEPH BOUER, MANAGER
AND WINE BUYER
1118 East Atlantic Avenue,
Delray Beach
561-278-4899

Burt and Jack's
STEVE BROWN, SOMMELIER
Berth 23 — Port Everglades,
Fort Lauderdale
954-522-5225

Café Baci
ROBERTO MEI, OWNER
AND WINE BUYER
4001 South Tamiami Trail, Sarasota
941-921-4848

Café Boulud at the Brazilian Court Hotel
KURT TAYLOR, SOMMELIER
301 Australian Avenue, Palm Beach
561-655-7740

Café Chardonnay
BRIAN CHAMIS, SOMMELIER
4533 PGA Boulevard, Palm Beach
561-627-2662

Café L'Europe
RAINER SCHONHERR, SOMMELIER
331 South County Road, Palm Beach
561-655-4020

Café Maxx
RON LABADIE, BEVERAGE MANAGER
2601 East Atlantic Boulevard,
Pompano Beach
954-782-0606

The Capital Grill
RON ADELMAN, MANAGER
AND WINE BUYER
444 Brickell Avenue, Miami
305-374-4500

Casa d'Angelo

ANGELO ELIA, OWNER
AND WINE BUYER
1201 North Federal Highway,
Fort Lauderdale
954-564-1234

Casa Juancho

JOSE RODRIGUEZ, GENERAL
MANAGER AND WINE BUYER
2436 Southwest Eighth Street, Miami
305-642-2452

Chantalle's

DAVID McKINNEY, OWNER,
CHEF AND WINE BUYER
3822 Tamiami Trail, Port Charlotte
941-766-1251

Chardonnay

RENE NICOLAS, WINE DIRECTOR
2331 Tamiami Trail North, Naples
941-261-1744

Chef Allen

ALLEN SUSSER, OWNER,
CHEF AND WINE BUYER
19088 North East 29th Avenue,
Miami
305-935-2900

China Grill

MADALINE HEILWEIL,
BAR MANAGER
404 Washington Avenue,
Miami Beach
305-534-2211

The Club at Edgewater Beach Hotel

AARON STALLINGS, FOOD
AND BEVERAGE DIRECTOR
1905 Golf Shore Boulevard North,
Naples
941-403-2156

The Colony Beach and Tennis Resort

MICHAEL GAREY, FOOD AND
BEVERAGE DIRECTOR
1620 Gulf of Mexico Drive,
Longboat Key
941-383-6464

Crow's Nest Marina

STEVE HARNER, OWNER
AND WINE BUYER
1968 Tarpon Center Drive, Venice
941-484-9551

Darrel and Oliver's Bistro 17 at Renaissance Fort Lauderdale

MAX UBILLA, MANAGER
AND WINE BUYER
WALTER RUANO, WINE BUYER
1617 Southeast 17th Street,
Fort Lauderdale
954-626-1701

The Dining Room at the Ritz-Carlton Naples

BILL HARRIS, HOTEL SOMMELIER
280 Vanderbilt Beach, Naples
941-598-6644

Eden Roc
at the Renaissance
Resort and Spa

MARK BUTCHER, WINE BUYER

4525 Collins Avenue, Miami Beach

305-531-0000

Flagler Grill

VICTORIA PAONESSA, WINE BUYER

47 Southwest Flagler Avenue, Stuart

772-221-9517

The Forge

GINO ST. ANGELO, SOMMELIER

432 41st Street, Miami Beach

305-538-8533

Fred's

GRAHAM THOMPSON, SOMMELIER

1924 South Osprey Avenue, Sarasota

941-364-5811

Gigi's Tavern, Oyster
Bar & Café

RICHIE PANELLA,
GENERAL MANAGER

346 Plaza Real Mizner Park,

Boca Raton

561-368-4488

Green Street Café

IMMANUAL DELLEPINE, MANAGER

AND WINE BUYER

3110 Commodore Plaza,

Coconut Grove

305-444-0244

The Grill
at the Four Seasons
Resort at Palm Beach

DANIEL BRAUN, MANAGER

AND WINE BUYER

2800 South Ocean Boulevard,

Palm Beach

561-582-2800

The Grill
at the Ritz-Carlton
Palm Beach

JOEL LAVERDURE, MANAGER AND

WINE BUYER

100 South Ocean Boulevard,

Manalapan

561-533-6000

Hobo's Fish Joint

JANET LABINER, WINE BUYER

10317 Royal Palm Boulevard,

Coral Springs

954-346-5484

Ian's Tropical Grill

ERIC GRUTKA, CO-OWNER

AND WINE BUYER

927 North US Highway 1, Fort Pierce

772-595-5950

Johannes

PETER IMRE, SOMMELIER

47 East Palmetto Park Road,

Boca Raton

561-394-0007

Lafite
at the Registry Resort

IAN HAWTHORNE, FOOD

AND BEVERAGE DIRECTOR

475 Seagate Drive, Naples

239-597-3232

Legal Sea Foods
JOHN EDWARD, BAR MANAGER
550 South Rosemary Avenue,
West Palm Beach
561-838-9000

Lemont Restaurant
JOHN KOHSIEK, BAR MANAGER
515 North Flagler Drive,
West Palm Beach
561-820-2442

Louie's Backyard
DONNA HASTIE, WINE BUYER
700 Waddell Avenue, Key West
305-294-1061

Mancini's
MARIO BRANDIMARATE,
WINE BUYER
1017 East Las Olas Boulevard,
Fort Lauderdale
954-764-5510

Mangia Mangia
ELIOT BARON, OWNER
AND WINE BUYER
900 Southard Street, Key West
305-294-2469

Mario's Tuscan Grill
SANDE WEINSTEIN, WINE BUYER
1450 North Federal Highway,
Boca Raton
561-362-7407

Mark's South Beach at the Hotel Nash
SCOTT KLEIN, GENERAL MANAGER
AND WINE BUYER
1120 Collins Avenue, Miami Beach
305-604-9050

Mark's Las Olas
THOMAS HILAN, SOMMELIER
1032 East Las Olas Boulevard,
Fort Lauderdale
954-463-1000

Mezzanotte Restaurant
PIERO FILIPI, WINE BUYER
1777 Michigan Avenue, Miami Beach
818-242-4885

Morton's of Chicago
JOHN JANETTE, GENERAL MANAGER
AND WINE BUYER
1200 Brickell Avenue, Miami
305-400-9990

Munroe's Restaurant and Jazz Tavern
RICK MONROE, OWNER
AND WINE BUYER
1296 First Street, Sarasota
941-316-0609

Opus Restaurant
MARK MINOR, GENERAL MANAGER
AND SOMMELIER
5200 Tamiami Trail, Naples
941-261-2555

Ortanique
MICHAEL MCCARTHY, SOMMELIER
278 Miricle Mile, Coral Gables
305-446-7710

The Palm
MAX RUDBERG, ASSISTANT
GENERAL MANAGER
AND WINE BUYER
9650 East Bay Harbor Drive, Bay Harbor
305-868-7256

Pazzo
DANA WILSON, BEVERAGE
MANAGER
853 Fifth Avenue South, Naples
941-434-8494

La Petite Maison
OLIVIER ADAMS, SOMMELIER
366 East Palmetto Park Road,
Boca Raton
561-750-7483

Pises
RALPH SAMPSON, WINE DIRECTOR
1007 Simonton Street, Key West
305-294-7100

Primavera Restaurant
GIACOMO DRESSENO, OWNER
AND WINE BUYER
830 East Oakland Park Boulevard,
Fort Lauderdale
954-564-6363

Renato's
BRAD STAPLETON, WINE BUYER
87 Via Mizner, Palm Beach
561-655-9752

The River House Restaurant
DOUG PENNELL, MANAGER
AND WINE BUYER
2373 PGA Boulevard,
Palm Beach Gardens
561-694-1188

Roessler's
KLAUS ROESSLER, OWNER
AND WINE BUYER
2033 Vamo Way, Sarasota
941-966-5688

Ruth's Chris Steak House
TOMMY BLUME, GENERAL
MANAGER AND WINE BUYER
2320 Salzedo Street, Coral Gables
305-461-8360

Ruth's Chris Steak House
CRAIG CONNLEY, WINE BUYER
661 US Highway 1,
North Palm Beach
561-863-0660

Sands Pointe at the Resort at Longboat Key
JEFF MONDAY, WINE BUYER
301 Gulf of Mexico Drive,
Longboat Key
941-387-1626

Sanibel Steakhouse
SCOTT KAUFMANN,
RESTAURANT MANAGER
24041 South Tamiami Trail,
Bonita Springs
941-390-0400

Shula's Steak House at the Miami Lakes Golf Resort
CHRISTIAN DAMMERT, GENERAL
MANAGER AND WINE BUYER
7601 North West 154th Street,
Miami
305-820-8047

Silver Cricket
BRIAN LaPALM, WINE BUYER
1923 Ringling Boulevard, Sarasota
941-955-9179

Smith & Wollensky at South Point Park

MICHAEL MAYER,
BEVERAGE DIRECTOR
1 Washington Avenue, Miami Beach
305-673-2800

Snapper's Seafood & Pasta

JOHN STILLEY, OWNER
AND WINE BUYER
398 North Congress Avenue,
Boynton Beach
561-375-8600

Stefano's

ALEXANDER MAVRIS, DIRECTOR
OF WINE AND SPIRITS
24 Crandon Boulevard, Key Biscayne
305-361-7007

The Summerhouse

DOUG VALTZ, WINE BUYER
6101 Midnight Pass Road, Sarasota
941-349-1100

Syrah Restaurant

GARY BUELL, OWNER
AND WINE BUYER
457 Bayfront Place, Naples
941-417-9724

The Tasting Room at JD Ford

GRAHAM THOMPSON, SOMMELIER
1925 South Osprey Avenue, Sarasota
941-364-5811

The Temptation Restaurant

DANNY KAHL, BEVERAGE MANAGER
350 Park Avenue, Boca Grande
941-964-2610

Il Tulipano

FILITTO IL GRANDE, OWNER
AND WINE BUYER
11052 Biscayne Boulevard,
North Miami
305-893-4811

Vesuvio Restaurant

TONY RICOTTI, OWNER
AND WINE BUYER
2715 East Atlantic Boulevard,
Pompano Beach
954-941-1594

La Vieille Maison

LEONCE PICOT, WINE BUYER
770 East Palmetto Park, Boca Raton
561-391-6701

Village Café

PAUL MINOUI, OWNER
AND WINE BUYER
14970 Captiva Drive, Captiva Island
941-472-1956

Zemi

ANTHONY HOBBS, MANAGER
AND WINE BUYER
5050 Town Center Circle, Boca Raton
561-391-7177

Anthony's Restaurant
3109 Piedmont Road Northeast
Atlanta, Georgia 30305-2531
phone 404-262-7379 fax 404-261-6009

Asif Edrish
SOMMELIER

WHAT ARE SOME OF YOUR ULTIMATE FOOD AND WINE PAIRINGS?
Sautéed foie gras served with peaches and peach balsamic sauce paired with
Errazuriz Late Harvest Sauvignon Blanc from Chile. For an entrée, classic Surf
and Turf served with Burgundy sauce paired with Penfolds Bin 707 Cabernet
from South Australia.

DESCRIBE YOUR WINE SELECTIONS.
Our wine list is diverse and dynamic with more than 475 selections. My goal is
to provide quality wines from different parts of the world.

WHAT IS YOUR FAVORITE WINE REGION IN THE WORLD TODAY?
South Australia. I like its big, fat, heavy, fruity, often jammy red wines. I also
like the use of American oak to add flavors.

WHAT LED YOU TO PURSUE A CAREER THAT INVOLVES WINE?
I have been involved in the food-service industry since 1991, starting from the
kitchen and then moving to the floor. My passion, interest and, ultimately, the
opportunity pushed me into becoming a sommelier.

IF YOU WERE NOT A SOMMELIER, WHAT WOULD YOU BE DOING?
Definitely in the food service industry, probably as a manager.

Bacchanalia
1198 Howell Mill Road
Atlanta, Georgia 30318
phone 404-365-0410 fax 404-365-8020

Daniel J. Rudiger
SOMMELIER
AND FLOOR MANAGER

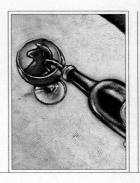

WHAT ARE SOME OF YOUR ULTIMATE FOOD AND WINE PAIRINGS?
Medjool dates with shaved Parmigiano-Reggiano paired with a Sauternes-style wine; blue crab fritter with avocado, citrus and Thai pepper essence with an off-dry, crisp Mosel Riesling.

DESCRIBE YOUR WINE SELECTIONS.
I maintain a core wine list and seek out different and unfamiliar wines that I promote through our food and wine program.

WHAT CATEGORIES OF WINE ARE THE BEST VALUES ON YOUR WINE LIST?
White and red varietals other than Chardonnay, Merlot, Pinot Noir, etc.

NAME A RECENT WINE DISCOVERY THAT EXCITED YOU.
Drinking a 1980 Riesling from the Barossa Valley with a screw cap. It was a classic, developed Riesling with depth and finesse. Who knew!

WHAT IS YOUR FAVORITE WINE REGION IN THE WORLD TODAY?
Alsace.

WHAT LED YOU TO PURSUE A CAREER THAT INVOLVES WINE?
A desire to know about what I was drinking and why it tasted the way it did.

WHAT ARE THE BEST ASPECTS OF YOUR JOB?
Discovering new wines, finding good value/quality wines and having satisfied guests.

Buckhead Diner

3073 Piedmont Road
Atlanta, Georgia 30305
phone 404-262-3336 fax 404-262-3593
website www.buckheadrestaurants.com

Mark C. Cromer
ASSISTANT GENERAL MANAGER

WHAT INSPIRED YOU TO PURSUE A CAREER THAT INVOLVES WINE?
A good friend in the business was pursuing an education in winemaking at
UC, Davis.

NAME TWO OF YOUR FAVORITE WINE REGIONS FROM AROUND THE
WORLD.
Burgundy, because my favorite varietal is Pinot Noir (and Chardonnay from
Burgundy is a close second); Oregon, because its climate is perfect for Pinot Gris.

NAME A RECENT WINE DISCOVERY THAT EXCITED YOU.
Domestic Barbera, which is of relatively high quality.

WHAT BITS OF INFORMATION WOULD YOU LIKE YOUR CUSTOMERS TO
KNOW ABOUT YOU?
I enjoy the interaction with guests from all walks of life and backgrounds.

IF YOU WERE NOT IN THIS PROFESSION, WHAT WOULD YOU BE?
A used car salesman.

DESCRIBE YOUR WINE SELECTIONS, BOTH BY THE GLASS AND ON YOUR
LIST.
Our list provides inexpensive, high-quality wines that pair well with our menu.

WHAT ARE THE MOST UNIQUE FEATURES IN YOUR WINE PROGRAM?
Our "Spotlight" section of the wine list changes monthly, and includes selections of rare grapes, unusual regions and boutique wineries.

WHAT CATEGORY OF WINE IS THE BEST VALUE IN YOUR RESTAURANT?
Other whites, from Viura to Marsanne to Pinot Gris.

NAME A COUPLE OF YOUR RESTAURANT'S SIGNATURE DISHES. WHAT
TYPES OF WINE DO YOU PREFER TO RECOMMEND WITH EACH?
Veal mushroom meatloaf with Spanish Tempranillo; seared sea scallops with
Oregon Pinot Gris.

Chops Steak and Lobster Bar

70 West Paces Ferry Road
Atlanta, Georgia 30305
phone 404-262-2675 fax 404-233-2762
website www.buckheadrestaurants.com

Eddie Valente
DIRECTOR OF OPERATIONS

LIST ANY FORMAL AND INFORMAL WINE TRAINING, DEGREES, CERTIFI-
CATES AND AWARDS.
Advanced Certificate Course, Court of Master Sommeliers.

WHAT INSPIRED YOU TO PURSUE A CAREER THAT INVOLVES WINE?
A 1973 Le Musigny I tasted in 1978 opened my eyes to great wine.

NAME ONE OR TWO OF YOUR FAVORITE WINE DISTRICTS OR WINE
REGIONS FROM AROUND THE WORLD.
Oregon Pinot Noir and Pinot Gris for their fresh flavors and balance; Alsatian
whites for their purity of flavor.

NAME RECENT WINE DISCOVERIES THAT HAVE EXCITED YOU.
Greek wines. When we opened our Greek restaurant, Kyma, we were exposed
to many of these wines.

DESCRIBE YOUR WINE SELECTIONS, BOTH BY THE GLASS AND ON YOUR
LIST.
With thirteen restaurants, our wine program varies from a 450-plus selection at
Chops and Bluepointe to a sixty-five-item list at Buckhead Diner. We have
Italian concepts with excellent Italian selections and a Greek restaurant with
seventy Greek wines.

WHAT ARE THE MOST UNIQUE FEATURES IN YOUR WINE PROGRAM?
Pricci and Veni, Vidi, Vici have quartinos and Kyma serves an 8-ounce personal
carafe. Our restaurants offer flight nights and early specials.

IN THE PAST YEAR, WHAT WINES IN YOUR WINE PROGRAM HAVE CUS-
TOMERS BECOME MORE WILLING TO ORDER?
Greek and Alsatian wines and Viognier.

Chops Steak and Lobster Bar

70 West Paces Ferry Road
Atlanta, Georgia 30305
phone 404-262-2675 fax 404-233-2762
website www.buckheadrestaurants.com

John L. Ford
BEVERAGE DIRECTOR

WHAT PART OF YOUR JOB DO YOU ENJOY THE MOST?
Having the opportunity to taste so many diverse wines from the great to the not-so-great and the ugly.

NAME ONE OF YOUR FAVORITE WINE REGIONS FROM AROUND THE WORLD.
Burgundy. I am a real fan of both red and white Burgundies because they are so diverse.

NAME RECENT WINE DISCOVERIES THAT HAVE EXCITED YOU.
Late-harvest dessert wine (Chenin Blanc) from South Africa, Pinot Noir from New Zealand and Chardonnay from Casablanca Valley, Chile.

IF YOU WERE NOT IN THIS PROFESSION, WHAT WOULD YOU BE?
An advertising or marketing executive.

DESCRIBE YOUR WINE SELECTIONS, BOTH BY THE GLASS AND ON YOUR LIST.
Our focus is big California reds and verticals of first-growth Bordeaux. We seek out boutique wineries while attracting the guests' attention with "heavy hitters."

WHAT CATEGORY OF WINE IS THE BEST VALUE IN YOUR RESTAURANT?
Australian Shiraz is the best value anywhere at the moment. Some Spanish Ribera del Dueros are also great values.

NAME A COUPLE OF YOUR RESTAURANT'S SIGNATURE DISHES. WHAT TYPES OF WINE DO YOU PREFER TO RECOMMEND WITH EACH?
Triple-cut domestic lamb chops with a smoky Syrah; lobster bar "shellfish tower" (gulf shrimp, chilled Maine lobster, Blue Point oysters) with horseradish and red wine mignonette with Sancerre.

IN THE PAST YEAR, WHAT WINES IN YOUR WINE PROGRAM HAVE CUSTOMERS BECOME MORE WILLING TO ORDER?
Australian reds, Willamette Valley Pinot Noir and Columbia Valley Merlot.

The Cloister and Sea Island Company

100 First Street
Sea Island, Georgia 31561
phone 800-732-4752 fax 912-638-3932
website www.seaisland.com

Louis T. Wesslund

SOMMELIER AND WINE BUYER
TEAM: JOHN MCCUNE, SOMMELIER FOR LODGE

NAME ONE OF YOUR FAVORITE WINE DISTRICTS OR WINE REGIONS
FROM AROUND THE WORLD.
The Rhône Valley and surrounding sub-regions.

NAME RECENT WINE DISCOVERIES THAT HAVE EXCITED YOU.
The south of France (Rhône, Languedoc and Roussillon) for their immensely
flavorful and food-friendly wines, some of which are the best values in France.

WHAT BITS OF INFORMATION WOULD YOU LIKE YOUR CUSTOMERS TO
KNOW ABOUT YOU?
I'm a former golf professional and a former soccer professional.

WHAT ARE THE MOST UNIQUE FEATURES IN YOUR WINE PROGRAM?
Our by-the-glass selection is eclectic, offering wines from regions like Yecla,
Spain, to McLaren Vale, Australia, to Kremstal, Austria, and varietals from Petit
Verdot and Grüner Veltliner to Cabernet Franc. We also have extremely fair
bottle prices on our main list.

WHAT CATEGORY OF WINE IS THE BEST VALUE IN YOUR RESTAURANT?
Bordeaux and Burgundy.

NAME A COUPLE OF YOUR RESTAURANT'S SIGNATURE DISHES. WHAT
TYPES OF WINE DO YOU PREFER TO RECOMMEND WITH EACH?
Many variations of lamb, most often herb-crusted, with Spanish Mourvèdre;
many variations of lobster with German off-dry Riesling.

IN THE PAST YEAR, WHAT WINES IN YOUR WINE PROGRAM HAVE CUS-
TOMERS BECOME MORE WILLING TO ORDER?
Alternative whites like Grüner Veltliner, Riesling and Albariño, and Australian
reds, especially Grenache.

WHAT ARE SOME OTHER ULTIMATE WINE AND FOOD PAIRINGS?
Foie gras with Alsatian Pinot Gris; rack of lamb with Spanish Grenache.

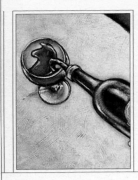

Eno Restaurant and Wine Bar

800 Peachtree Street
Atlanta, Georgia 30308
phone 404-685-3191 fax 404-685-3199
website www.eno-atlanta.com

Doug Strickland
MANAGING PARTNER
AND WINE DIRECTOR

NAME THREE OF YOUR FAVORITE WINE REGIONS FROM AROUND THE
WORLD.
Burgundy, because its Pinot Noir shows such finesse; Piedmont, for its unique
wines and expressive producers; and the Rhône Valley, for the ever-versatile
Syrah.

NAME RECENT WINE DISCOVERIES THAT HAVE EXCITED YOU.
French Rhônes and Rhône-style wines that are excellent value; Spanish reds and
whites from developing regions and rapidly advancing producers, who are innovative mavericks.

IF YOU WERE NOT IN THIS PROFESSION, WHAT WOULD YOU BE DOING?
Cooking, acting and painting.

DESCRIBE YOUR WINE SELECTIONS, BOTH BY THE GLASS AND ON YOUR
LIST.
We have a strong by-the-glass program, we offer European-Mediterranean vari-
etals, and we take an adventurous approach in our wine selections.

WHAT CATEGORY OF WINE IS THE BEST VALUE IN YOUR RESTAURANT?
Red wine from the south of France and northern Spain.

NAME A COUPLE OF YOUR RESTAURANT'S SIGNATURE DISHES. WHAT
TYPES OF WINE DO YOU PREFER TO RECOMMEND WITH EACH?
Provençal seafood stew with Bandol Rosé; North African–style braised lamb
with Côtes du Rhône.

IN THE PAST YEAR, WHAT WINES IN YOUR WINE PROGRAM HAVE CUS-
TOMERS BECOME MORE WILLING TO ORDER?
Rhône Valley and Rhône-style wines; Sangiovese, Chenin Blanc and Viognier.

WHAT ARE SOME OTHER ULTIMATE WINE AND FOOD PAIRINGS?
Zinfandel and quail with chocolate-infused sauce.

Joël Restaurant

The Forum, 3290 Northside Parkway
Atlanta, Georgia 30327
phone 404-233-3500 fax 404-467-4750
website www.joelrestaurant.com

Philippe J. R. Buttin
HEAD SOMMELIER

NAME TWO OF YOUR FAVORITE WINE DISTRICTS FROM AROUND THE WORLD.
Burgundy and Stellenbosch (South Africa) because of the diversity of their microclimates.

NAME RECENT WINE DISCOVERIES THAT HAVE EXCITED YOU.
Morandé late-harvest Sauvignon Blanc, from Chile, for its great freshness and acidity; Gruet Pinot Noir from New Mexico, for its generosity and earthiness.

IF YOU WERE NOT IN THIS PROFESSION, WHAT WOULD YOU BE?
A winemaker.

DESCRIBE YOUR WINE SELECTIONS, BOTH BY THE GLASS AND ON YOUR LIST.
We have a very wide selection of wines by the glass.

WHAT ARE THE MOST UNIQUE FEATURES IN YOUR WINE PROGRAM?
Year-round food and wine pairings and a large selection of half-bottles, covering most of the regions of the world.

WHAT CATEGORIES OF WINE ARE THE BEST VALUES IN YOUR RESTAURANT?
White and red wines from Chile, Argentina and South Africa.

NAME A COUPLE OF YOUR RESTAURANT'S SIGNATURE DISHES. WHAT TYPES OF WINE DO YOU PREFER TO RECOMMEND WITH EACH?
Roast breast of quail with lentils, salsa and daikon radish with Niagara Peninsula dry Riesling; sautéed sweetbread and braised cheeks with seven spices with New Mexico Pinot Noir.

IN THE PAST YEAR, WHAT WINES IN YOUR WINE PROGRAM HAVE CUSTOMERS BECOME MORE WILLING TO ORDER?
Grüner Veltliner from Austria and Pinotage from South Africa.

Joël Restaurant
The Forum, 3290 Northside Parkway
Atlanta, Georgia 30327
phone 404-233-3500 fax 404-841-0906
website www.joelrestaurant.com

Raul M. Yague
ASSISTANT CHEF
AND SOMMELIER

NAME ONE OF YOUR FAVORITE WINES.
Côte-Rôtie, because of the concentration, delicacy, smoothness, smokiness, acidity and complexity that the Shiraz grape variety expresses there.

NAME RECENT WINE DISCOVERIES THAT HAVE EXCITED YOU.
Sparkling wine from New Mexico for its big extraction of fruit, great acidity and finesse.

WHAT BITS OF INFORMATION WOULD YOU LIKE YOUR CUSTOMERS TO KNOW ABOUT YOU?
I have also been working in the kitchen and am passionate about food as well. Cooking is something that I really enjoy. It helps me to harmonize the wines with my customer's food choices.

IF YOU WERE NOT IN THIS PROFESSION, WHAT WOULD YOU BE DOING?
Cooking.

WHAT CATEGORY OF WINE IS THE BEST VALUE IN YOUR RESTAURANT?
South American and South African wines.

NAME ONE OF YOUR RESTAURANT'S SIGNATURE DISHES. WHAT WINE DO YOU PREFER TO RECOMMEND WITH IT?
Fresh oysters served on the shell with a Japanese dressing made of soy sauce, ginger, nori powder, rice wine, sugar and olive oil with a southern France Syrah-blend.

IN THE PAST YEAR, WHAT WINES IN YOUR WINE PROGRAM HAVE CUS-TOMERS BECOME MORE WILLING TO ORDER?
South African Pinotage and New Mexican sparkling wine.

Joël Restaurant

The Forum, 3290 Northside Parkway
Atlanta, Georgia 30327
phone 404-233-3500 fax 404-467-4750
website www.joelrestaurant.com

Chantelle Grilhot
ASSISTANT SOMMELIER

WHAT INSPIRED YOU TO PURSUE A CAREER THAT INVOLVES WINE?
Philippe Buttin, my mentor and chef and sommelier, and Yves Durant have each helped me to take that passion to a professional level.

DESCRIBE YOUR WINE SELECTIONS, BOTH BY THE GLASS AND ON YOUR LIST.
We have 25 wines by the glass and 1,600 selections from around the world. We are strong in major regions, as well as wines in popular styles from regions most people wouldn't typically choose.

WHAT ARE THE MOST UNIQUE FEATURES IN YOUR WINE PROGRAM?
We have a large selection of half-bottles, 6-liters and large formats.

WHAT CATEGORY OF WINE IS THE BEST VALUE IN YOUR RESTAURANT?
Wines from South Africa, to which we devote four pages of our wine list. They are low in price and of stellar quality, and should not missed when dining here!

NAME A FEW OF YOUR RESTAURANT'S SIGNATURE DISHES. WHAT TYPES OF WINE DO YOU PREFER TO RECOMMEND WITH EACH?
Roast breast of quail with lentils flavored with coriander, served with dry Riesling from Canada or Germany; sautéed veal sweetbreads and braised cheek, seven spices Asian sauce, confit apple, with either Faugères or Minervois; Pavlova, a meringue filled with diplomat cream and mango, marinated in passion fruit juice or mango coulis exotic fruit sorbet, paired with Marlborough, New Zealand, late-harvest Sauvignon Blanc.

IN THE PAST YEAR, WHAT WINES IN YOUR WINE PROGRAM HAVE CUSTOMERS BECOME MORE WILLING TO ORDER?
Wines from South Africa, Chile, Argentina and Spain.

Nava

3060 Peachtree Road Northwest
Atlanta, Georgia 30305
phone 404-240-1984 fax 404-240-1831
website www.buckheadrestaurants.com

Sara Trinkwalder
BEVERAGE MANAGER

WHAT INSPIRED YOU TO PURSUE A CAREER THAT INVOLVES WINE?
While waiting tables earlier in my career I developed a love of wine, both tasting and learning about it.

NAME TWO OF YOUR FAVORITE WINE REGIONS FROM AROUND THE WORLD.
Burgundy and the California Central Coast, both for the quality of winemaking and their history.

NAME RECENT WINE DISCOVERIES THAT HAVE EXCITED YOU.
Charlotte Street Shiraz Chardonnay Cabernet Sauvignon from Australia is a great value, a unique blend and has a great taste profile.

WHAT WOULD YOU LIKE YOUR CUSTOMERS TO KNOW ABOUT YOU?
I grew up in Buffalo, New York, and moved to Atlanta in 1995.

IF YOU WERE NOT IN THIS PROFESSION, WHAT WOULD YOU DO?
Own and operate a bed-and-breakfast or a wine shop.

DESCRIBE YOUR WINE SELECTIONS, BOTH BY THE GLASS AND ON YOUR LIST.
Value, value, value! We go for value and a great selection of unique varietals and blends, along with more typical wines.

WHAT ARE THE MOST UNIQUE FEATURES IN YOUR WINE PROGRAM?
Weekly wine flight specials.

WHAT ARE THE BEST WINE VALUES IN YOUR RESTAURANT?
Eighty percent of the wines on the list are under $50.

NAME A COUPLE OF YOUR RESTAURANT'S SIGNATURE DISHES. WHAT TYPES OF WINE DO YOU PREFER TO RECOMMEND WITH EACH?
Suncorn-crusted red snapper with Alsace Riesling; cowboy-cut beef tenderloin with California Zinfandel.

WHAT WINES ARE CUSTOMERS NOW MORE WILLING TO ORDER?
Italian super-Tuscans, Tempranillo, and California Sauvignon Blanc.

Nikolai's Roof
at the Hilton Atlanta
255 Courtland Street Northeast
Atlanta, Georgia 30303
phone 404-221-6362 fax 404-221-6811

Cristophe Orlarei
ASSISTANT MANAGER
AND SOMMELIER

WHAT ARE SOME OF YOUR ULTIMATE FOOD AND WINE PAIRINGS?
Seared scallops and New Zealand Sauvignon Blanc 2000.

DESCRIBE YOUR WINE SELECTIONS.
We have more than 500 wines, emphasizing Californian and French selections, but with some great catches from New Zealand and Australia.

WHAT CATEGORY OF WINE IS THE BEST VALUE IN YOUR RESTAURANT?
Australian.

NAME RECENT WINE DISCOVERIES THAT HAVE EXCITED YOU.
Oregon Pinot Gris and Pinot Noir, which both offer superb value.

WHAT IS YOUR FAVORITE REGION OR AREA IN THE WORLD TODAY?
New Zealand, for the refreshing quality of its Sauvignon Blanc and Pinot Noir.

WHAT LED YOU TO PURSUE A CAREER THAT INVOLVES WINE?
Love of wine and food.

WHAT IS THE MOST CHALLENGING ASPECT OF YOUR JOB?
Promoting and maintaining an extensive selection of wine by the glass.

IF YOU WERE NOT IN THE WINE PROFESSION, WHAT WOULD YOU BE DOING?
Running my own bar.

Pano and Paul's Restaurant

1232 West Paces Ferry Road
Atlanta, Georgia 30327
phone 404-261-3662 fax 404-261-4512
website www.buckheadrestaurants.com

Markus Rutz
ASSISTANT MANAGER

WHAT INSPIRED YOU TO PURSUE A CAREER THAT INVOLVES WINE?
The idea of touching and handling specialty goods.

NAME TWO OF YOUR FAVORITE WINE REGIONS FROM AROUND THE WORLD.
Napa Valley, for all the gems that constantly emerge from it; McClaren Vale,
for its awesome Shiraz.

NAME RECENT WINE DISCOVERIES THAT HAVE EXCITED YOU.
Hartman Lane Pinot Noir, a California Pinot Noir that will rival any
Burgundy; Mason Sauvignon Blanc, an incredible wine at an excellent price.

WHAT WOULD YOU LIKE YOUR CUSTOMERS TO KNOW ABOUT YOU?
I love to do research on news about wines in the market, something outside the
boundaries of employment.

IF YOU WERE NOT IN THIS PROFESSION, WHAT WOULD YOU BE DOING?
Architecture and design.

DESCRIBE YOUR WINE SELECTIONS, BOTH BY THE GLASS AND ON YOUR LIST.
Great price-to-value relationships and unadvertised specialty wines.

WHAT ARE THE MOST UNIQUE FEATURES IN YOUR WINE PROGRAM?
Seasonal prix fixe wine pairings and complimentary corkage.

WHAT CATEGORY OF WINE IS THE BEST VALUE IN YOUR RESTAURANT?
Our rare, old red wines.

NAME A COUPLE OF YOUR RESTAURANT'S SIGNATURE DISHES. WHAT
TYPES OF WINE DO YOU PREFER TO RECOMMEND WITH EACH?
Fried lobster with a buttery Chardonnay; sautéed sole with Sauvignon Blanc.

WHAT WINES ARE CUSTOMERS NOW MORE WILLING TO ORDER?
Oregon, German and Alsatian Pinot Gris and white varietals.

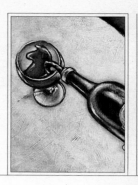

Pricci

500 Pharr Road
Atlanta, Georgia 30305
phone 404-237-2941 fax 404-261-0058
website www.buckheadrestaurants.com

Robert Koch

MANAGER AND SOMMELIER

NAME TWO OF YOUR FAVORITE WINE REGIONS FROM AROUND THE WORLD.
Tuscany, for its Brunello di Montalcino, which is robust and full of character;
Piedmont, for its Arneis and Nebbiolo.

NAME RECENT WINE DISCOVERIES THAT HAVE EXCITED YOU.
There are more than 2,000 grape varieties in Italy and we know only a handful.

WHAT BITS OF INFORMATION WOULD YOU LIKE YOUR CUSTOMERS TO
KNOW ABOUT YOU?
I was born in the Czech Republic. I had thirteen years of restaurant experience.
I'm very competitive and I love all sports.

IF YOU WERE NOT IN THIS PROFESSION, WHAT WOULD YOU BE?
A professional athlete.

DESCRIBE YOUR WINE SELECTIONS, BOTH BY THE GLASS AND ON YOUR LIST.
Our wine selection is entirely Italian. We present major regions and grape varieties, while bringing excellent values to our patrons.

WHAT ARE THE MOST UNIQUE FEATURES IN YOUR WINE PROGRAM?
Pasta night on Thursdays with featured red and white flights and our new quartino decanter for by-the-glass wines.

WHAT CATEGORIES OF WINE ARE THE BEST VALUES IN YOUR RESTAURANT?
Nero d'Avola from Sicily and Verdicchio from the Marches region.

NAME A COUPLE OF YOUR RESTAURANT'S SIGNATURE DISHES. WHAT
TYPES OF WINE DO YOU PREFER TO RECOMMEND WITH EACH?
Osso buco with saffron risotto and Barbaresco or Barolo; whole grilled sea bass
with a Vernaccia di San Gimignano.

IN THE PAST YEAR, WHAT WINES IN YOUR WINE PROGRAM HAVE CUSTOMERS BECOME MORE WILLING TO ORDER?
Tuscan reds and Pinot Grigio from Trentino-Alto Adige.

The River Room Restaurant and Tavern

4403 Northside Parkway, Suite150
Atlanta, Georgia 30327
phone 404-233-5455 fax 404-233-3073
website www.riverroom.com

Eric S. Simpkins
WINE AND BAR MANAGER

WHAT PART OF YOUR JOB DO YOU ENJOY THE MOST?
Good wine shared with good people is a delicious recipe.

NAME ONE OR TWO OF YOUR FAVORITE WINE DISTRICTS OR WINE REGIONS FROM AROUND THE WORLD.
Paso Robles and South Australia. Paso Robles wines have such intense fruit. South Australian wines are excellent blends of innovation and value.

IF YOU WERE NOT IN THIS PROFESSION, WHAT WOULD YOU BE DOING?
Writing or teaching philosophy, photography or literature.

DESCRIBE YOUR WINE SELECTIONS, BOTH BY THE GLASS AND ON YOUR LIST.
Our list is known for being creative, diverse and balanced while offering proven quality wines, including a few American legends.

WHAT ARE THE MOST UNIQUE FEATURES IN YOUR WINE PROGRAM?
We have a very large by-the-glass selection featuring nightly pairings with the specials and desserts. We also have "Wines on Wednesday," our weekly tastings featuring wineries and importers.

WHAT CATEGORY OF WINE IS THE BEST VALUE IN YOUR RESTAURANT?
Red Vin de Pays.

NAME A COUPLE OF YOUR RESTAURANT'S SIGNATURE DISHES. WHAT TYPES OF WINE DO YOU PREFER TO RECOMMEND WITH EACH?
Jumbo lump crab cakes with beurre blanc and vanilla essence with lightly oaked or unoaked white Burgundy; pork tenderloin over Parmesan whipped potatoes and wild mushrooms, with a Rhône varietal Vin de Pays or an Oregon Pinot Noir.

IN THE PAST YEAR, WHAT WINES IN YOUR WINE PROGRAM HAVE CUSTOMERS BECOME MORE WILLING TO ORDER?
Rhône Valley reds, white Burgundies and red and white esoteric blends from California.

Seeger's

111 West Paces Ferry Road Northwest
Atlanta, Georgia 30305
phone 404-846-9779 fax 404-846-9217
website www.seegers.com

Mark E. Mendoza

SOMMELIER

WHAT INSPIRED YOU TO PURSUE A CAREER THAT INVOLVES WINE?
I have always had restaurant jobs and it seemed a natural progression for me.
Wine is a huge subject. I've been drawn to it by geography as well as history.

WHAT PART OF YOUR JOB DO YOU ENJOY THE MOST?
I enjoy interacting with guests, which is a paramount connection. Plus, working the floor is a good workout.

NAME ONE OF YOUR FAVORITE WINE DISTRICTS.
The Mosel wines of Germany are underrated and truly world-class wines.

NAME RECENT WINE DISCOVERIES THAT HAVE EXCITED YOU.
Fürst Pinot Noir "Barrique," Franken 1998. Who knew that the Germans could mirror Burgundy so well?

IF YOU WERE NOT IN THIS PROFESSION, WHAT WOULD YOU BE DOING?
Teaching young people to view the world via a soccer ball.

DESCRIBE YOUR WINE SELECTIONS, BOTH BY THE GLASS AND ON YOUR LIST.
The list emphasizes German whites; however, there is a strong commitment to Burgundy and the Rhône Valley, as well as verticals of top-growth Bordeaux.

WHAT ARE THE MOST UNIQUE FEATURES IN YOUR WINE PROGRAM?
We do quarterly wine dinners with renowned winemakers. The chef and I also collaborate once a month on a small, intimate wine dinner.

NAME A COUPLE OF YOUR RESTAURANT'S SIGNATURE DISHES. WHAT TYPES OF WINE DO YOU PREFER TO RECOMMEND WITH EACH?
Grilled turbot fillet, vegetable á la grecque, tomato confiture with Hermitage blanc; squab in five spices, date chutney and glazed carrots with Chambolle-Musigny.

WHAT WINES ARE CUSTOMERS NOW MORE WILLING TO ORDER?
German Riesling and Alsace whites.

Seeger's

111 West Paces Ferry Road
Atlanta, Georgia 30305
phone 404-846-9779 fax 404-846-9217
website www.seegers.com

Florian Spiegelberger
ASSISTANT SOMMELIER

WHAT INSPIRED YOU TO PURSUE A CAREER THAT INVOLVES WINE?
I started working by accident at a wine merchant (vinothek).

WHAT PART OF YOUR JOB DO YOU ENJOY THE MOST?
Making unusual recommendations to customers.

NAME ONE OF YOUR FAVORITE WINE REGIONS FROM AROUND THE
WORLD.
Austria, especially its undiscovered reds.

WHAT BITS OF INFORMATION WOULD YOU LIKE YOUR CUSTOMERS TO
KNOW ABOUT YOU?
I came from Munich, Germany, to work for one of the best chefs in the United
States, Guenter Seeger.

IF YOU WERE NOT IN THIS PROFESSION, WHAT WOULD YOU BE DOING?
I'd be a professional soccer player.

WHAT ARE THE MOST UNIQUE FEATURES IN YOUR WINE PROGRAM?
Special wine dinners featuring winemakers like Peter Hall, Robert Weil and
Gunderloch.

45 South
CHRISTOPER CAMPBELL,
WINE BUYER
20 East Broad Street, Savannah
912-233-1881

The Abbey
GEORGE GORE, WINE BUYER
163 Ponce De Leon Avenue
Northeast, Atlanta
404-876-8532

Aspen's Signature Steaks
WILLIAM PAGE, GENERAL MANAGER
AND WINE BUYER
2942 Shallowford Road, Marietta
678-236-1400

Atlanta Grill
SILVIO GARCIA, WINE MANAGER
181 Peachtree Street Northeast,
Atlanta
404-659-0400

BluePointe
STEVENSON ROSSLO, WINE BUYER
3455 Peachtree Road, Atlanta
404-237-9070

Bone's
RON PETERSON, WINE BUYER
3130 Piedmont Road, Atlanta
404-237-2663

Canoe
KEVIN GOOD, MANAGER
AND WINE BUYER
4199 Paces Ferry Road Northwest,
Atlanta
770-432-2663

Capital Grille
JOHN ST. JOHN, MANAGER
AND WINE BUYER
255 East Paces Ferry Road, Atlanta
404-262-1162

Chez Philippe's
PHILIPPE HADDAD, OWNER,
CHEF AND WINE BUYER
10 Kings Circle at Peachtree Hills,
Atlanta
404-231-4113

City Grill
BRAD REGISTER, GENERAL
MANAGER AND WINE BUYER
55 Hurt Plaza, Atlanta
404-681-9042

Dailey's Restaurant & Bar
CHRIS LOWRY, ASSISTANT GENERAL
MANAGER AND WINE BUYER
17 International Boulevard, Atlanta
404-681-3303

The Dining Room at the Ritz-Carlton Buckhead
MICHAEL MCNEILL, SOMMELIER
3434 Peachtree Road Northeast,
Atlanta
404-237-2700

Elizabeth's On 37th
GARY BUTCH, WINE BUYER
105 East 37th Street, Savannah
912-236-5547

Fogo De Chao

JEAN BOSCHETTI, MANAGER
AND WINE BUYER
3101 Piedmont Road, Atlanta
404-266-9988

The Food Studio

SUZANNE REINHARD, GENERAL
MANAGER AND WINE BUYER
887 West Marietta Street, Atlanta
404-815-6677

Goldfish

DAVID ABES, DIRECTOR OF
OPERATIONS AND WINE BUYER
4400 Ashford Dunwoody Road,
Atlanta
770-671-0100

La Grotta

ANTONIO ABIZANDA, CHEF,
OWNER AND WINE BUYER
SERGIO SAVALLI, OWNER
AND SOMMELIER
2637 Peachtree Road Northeast,
Atlanta
404-231-1368

Sapphire Grill

DAVID TUMBLIN, GENERAL
MANAGER AND WINE BUYER
110 West Saint Julian Street,
Savannah
912-443-9962

South City Kitchen

JOE FERRIS, ASSISTANT MANAGER
AND WINE BUYER
1144 Crescent Avenue Northeast,
Atlanta
404-873-7358

La Tavola Trattoria

MATTHEW COGGIN, MANAGER
AND WINE BUYER
992 Virginia Avenue Northeast,
Atlanta
404-873-5430

Veni, Vidi, Vici

DAN MILLMAN,
BEVERAGE MANAGER
41 14th Street, Atlanta
404-875-8424

La Mer
at the Halekulani Hotel

2199 Kalia Road
Honolulu, Hawaii 96815
phone 808-923-2311 fax 808-931-5039
website www.halekulani.com

Randolph H. Ching
WINE MANAGER

WHAT ARE SOME OF YOUR ULTIMATE FOOD AND WINE PAIRINGS?
Chef Yves Garnier's bouillabaisse and Rosé from Provence; crustaceans and
Sauvignon Blanc from around the world.

DESCRIBE YOUR WINE SELECTIONS.
We have a wide selection of international wines and a representation of those
countries producing world-class wines.

WHAT CATEGORIES OF WINE ARE THE BEST VALUES ON YOUR WINE LIST?
Italian, Australian and South American wines.

NAME RECENT WINE DISCOVERIES THAT HAVE EXCITED YOU.
Domaine Tempier Bandol rouge. This wine has a sense of place. Wonderful terroir. Older vintages are also wonderful and very balanced.

WHAT IS YOUR FAVORITE WINE REGION IN THE WORLD TODAY?
Wherever you can grow good Pinot Noir.

WHAT LED YOU TO PURSUE A CAREER THAT INVOLVES WINE?
Wine was my hobby. I have always had a big interest in wine.

WHAT IS THE BEST ASPECT OF YOUR JOB?
I love matching food and wine.

IF YOU WERE NOT IN THE WINE PROFESSION, WHAT WOULD YOU BE?
A chef.

Hoku's at the Kahal Mandarin Oriental Hotel

WAYNE WOODS, FOOD
AND BEVERAGE DIRECTOR
5000 Kahala Avenue, Honolulu
808-739-8888

Hy's Steak House

BOB PANTER, GENERAL MANAGER
AND WINE BUYER
2440 Kuhio Avenue, Honolulu
808-922-5555

Lodge at Koele

INGRIDA COUTO, WINE BUYER
1 Keomoku Highway, Lana'i City
808-565-7300

Roy's Kahana Bar and Grill

MICHAEL WEBBER, GENERAL
MANAGER AND WINE BUYER
4405 Hanoapiilani Highway,
Kahana, Maui
808-669-6999

Roy's Restaurant

MIKE ONO, WINE BUYER
6600 Kananianaole Highway,
Honolulu
808-396-7697

Beverly's
at the Coeur d'Alene
SAM LANGE, WINE BUYER

250 Northwest Boulevard,
Coeur d'Alene
208-765-4000

Evergreen Restaurant
BURKE SMITH, WINE DIRECTOR

115 Rivers West, Ketchum
208-726-3888

The Capital Grille
633 North St. Clair Street
Chicago, Illinois 60611
phone 312-337-9400 fax 312-337-1259

Paul R. Calzaretta
SOMMELIER

WHAT ARE SOME OF YOUR ULTIMATE FOOD AND WINE PAIRINGS?
Our dry-aged steak au poivre with a Cognac cream sauce paired with Gigondas;
farm-raised bluepoint oysters with Chablis; live, whole Maine lobsters broiled
and steamed, with Chassagne-Montrachet.

DESCRIBE YOUR WINE SELECTIONS.
Our wine program is primarily Cabernet-based because we are a steakhouse,
but I am expanding our selections to include more varietals like Syrah and
Zinfandel.

WHAT CATEGORY OF WINE IS THE BEST VALUE IN YOUR RESTAURANT?
"Interesting Red," which focuses on less common red varietals and blends.

NAME RECENT WINE DISCOVERIES THAT HAVE EXCITED YOU.
Château Camou, El Gran Vino Tinto from Mexico, a Bordeaux-style red that
offers superior quality for the price.

WHAT IS YOUR FAVORITE WINE REGION IN THE WORLD?
Spring Mountain District, Napa Valley.

WHAT LED YOU TO PURSUE A CAREER THAT INVOLVES WINE?
I have had an avid interest in wine and food since my first restaurant job in
high school.

WHAT IS THE BEST ASPECT OF YOUR JOB?
Being in a profession that is always changing and improving is both challenging
and rewarding. It enables me to remain dedicated.

IF YOU WERE NOT IN THIS PROFESSION, WHAT WOULD YOU BE DOING?
Performing various styles of music. I have been an instrumentalist
(trumpet/cornet) for nearly twenty years.

Carlos' Restaurant

429 Temple Avenue
Highland Park, Illinois 60035
phone 847-432-0770 fax 847-432-2047
website www.carlos-restaurant.com

Marcello Cancelli
SOMMELIER

ILLINOIS

NAME RECENT WINE DISCOVERIES THAT HAVE EXCITED YOU.
California's Central Coast, especially Santa Barbara County, with its deep and characterful Syrahs at great prices. South Africa is a budding superstar.

WHAT BITS OF INFORMATION WOULD YOU LIKE YOUR CUSTOMERS TO KNOW ABOUT YOU?
That despite my Italian ancestry, I am really a hot-blooded Brazilian.

IF YOU WERE NOT IN THIS PROFESSION, WHAT WOULD YOU BE DOING?
Writing, and living within steps of a beautiful beach.

DESCRIBE YOUR WINE SELECTIONS.
Our list features 2,000 selections, focusing on French and California wines, with a significant presence of Italian, German and Australian producers. We offer nineteen wines by the glass.

WHAT ARE THE MOST UNIQUE FEATURES IN YOUR WINE PROGRAM?
We offer a tasting menu matched with popular wines, monthly wine dinners, a large selection of half-bottles and, on Mondays, no corkage fee. We taste some amazing wines on that night.

NAME A COUPLE OF YOUR RESTAURANT'S SIGNATURE DISHES. WHAT TYPES OF WINE DO YOU PREFER TO RECOMMEND WITH EACH?
Sautéed John Dory and Hawaiian shrimp with shrimp and tarragon emulsion paired with premier cru Chablis; pan-roasted Kobe beef tenderloin with wild mushroom ragout and a blood orange, black truffle sauce paired with Washington State Merlot.

WHAT WINES ARE CUSTOMERS NOW MORE WILLING TO ORDER?
Pinot Noir from Oregon and Burgundy and American Syrah.

WHAT ARE SOME OTHER ULTIMATE WINE AND FOOD PAIRINGS?
Oysters and Champagne, duck and red Côte de Beaune, and Bleu d'Auvergne cheese with Oloroso Sherry.

Charlie Trotter's

816 West Armitage Avenue
Chicago, Illinois 60614
phone 773-248-6228 fax 773-248-6088
website www.charlietrotters.com

Serafin Alvarado
SOMMELIER

WHAT INSPIRED YOU TO PURSUE A CAREER THAT INVOLVES WINE?
It was more like being chosen, and for that I feel privileged.

WHAT PART OF YOUR JOB DO YOU ENJOY THE MOST?
Without a doubt, the one-on-one interaction with our guests. Everything else builds up toward that involvement.

NAME TWO OF YOUR FAVORITE WINE REGIONS FROM AROUND THE WORLD.
Burgundy and Alsace. For me, it all comes down to the identity of a wine, and the wines from these regions are expressive of their origins and are versatile at the table with a great variety of food.

NAME RECENT WINE DISCOVERIES THAT HAVE EXCITED YOU.
Spain, all of it. It's exciting to see how this country is rediscovering itself, showing its potential for great food wines; the wines are also great values.

WHAT BITS OF INFORMATION WOULD YOU LIKE YOUR CUSTOMERS TO KNOW ABOUT YOU?
I studied chemistry and played bass for several bands while at college. I'm also a New York Mets fan.

IF YOU WERE NOT IN THIS PROFESSION, WHAT WOULD YOU BE?
A wine journalist.

Charlie Trotter's

816 West Armitage Avenue
Chicago, Illinois 60614
phone 773-248-6228 fax 773-248-6088
website www.charlietrotters.com

Jason L. Smith
SOMMELIER

WHAT INSPIRED YOU TO PURSUE A CAREER THAT INVOLVES WINE?
After attending the wine course at the Culinary Institute of America, I became totally fascinated by wine.

WHAT PART OF YOUR JOB DO YOU ENJOY THE MOST?
There are too many amazing aspects of my job to pick just one.

NAME ONE OF YOUR FAVORITE WINES FROM AROUND THE WORLD.
Burgundy. There's no need to continue!

NAME RECENT WINE DISCOVERIES THAT HAVE EXCITED YOU.
Washington State, Spanish wines and Merus Cabernet, Napa.

WHAT BITS OF INFORMATION WOULD YOU LIKE YOUR CUSTOMERS TO KNOW ABOUT YOU?
I enjoy skiing and beautiful beaches.

IF YOU WERE NOT IN THIS PROFESSION, WHAT WOULD YOU BE DOING?
I'd be a cook in the kitchen at Charlie Trotter's.

DESCRIBE YOUR WINE SELECTIONS, BOTH BY THE GLASS AND ON YOUR LIST.
We highlight small-production wineries and attempt to challenge our guests and each other by offering the unexpected, like sake and wines from lesser-known regions.

WHAT CATEGORIES OF WINE ARE THE BEST VALUES IN YOUR RESTAURANT?
German and Washington State wines.

NAME A COUPLE OF YOUR RESTAURANT'S SIGNATURE DISHES. WHAT TYPES OF WINE DO YOU PREFER TO RECOMMEND WITH EACH?
Our restaurant specializes in spontaneity, and the same goes for the wine program.

WHAT WINES ARE CUSTOMERS NOW MORE WILLING TO ORDER?
Spanish and Austrian wines.

Charlie Trotter's

816 West Armitage Avenue
Chicago, Illinois 60614
phone 773-248-6228 fax 773-248-6088
website www.charlietrotters.com

Linda Violago
SOMMELIER

WHAT INSPIRED YOU TO PURSUE A CAREER THAT INVOLVES WINE?

I have always worked as a waiter. A friend introduced me to a Frank Schoonmaker book. Both my friend and the book inspired me to explore the world of wine.

WHAT PART OF YOUR JOB DO YOU ENJOY THE MOST?

I love one-on-one interaction, whether it's with guests, suppliers, peers or colleagues talking about our passions.

NAME TWO OF YOUR FAVORITE WINE REGIONS FROM AROUND THE WORLD.

Burgundy for the history and the respect for the land, vines and culture; New Zealand for the great inquisitive minds of those who make its world-class wines.

NAME RECENT WINE DISCOVERIES THAT HAVE EXCITED YOU.

New Zealand Pinot Noir for great quality, Spain for both its exciting "new" regions and wines from Ribera del Duero that are profound.

WHAT BITS OF INFORMATION WOULD YOU LIKE YOUR CUSTOMERS TO KNOW ABOUT YOU?

I love traveling and immersing myself in different cultures. I studied ballet for ten years before my knee betrayed me. And I love yoga and the search for the divine.

IF YOU WERE NOT IN THIS PROFESSION, WHAT WOULD YOU BE DOING?

Working in vineyards and wineries around the world that produce Pinot Noir, or a midwife advocate for women's health and alternative health care options.

Cité Restaurant

505 North Lake Shore Drive
Chicago, Illinois 60610
phone 312- 644-4050 fax 312-644-4066
website www.citechicago.com

Fariborz D. Rouchi

GENERAL MANAGER
AND SOMMLIER

WHAT INSPIRED YOU TO PURSUE A CAREER THAT INVOLVES WINE?
My passion for food and cooking led me to fine dining. The culture, history
and people who enjoy wine and food led me to pursue a career in the restaurant business.

NAME TWO OF YOUR FAVORITE WINE REGIONS FROM AROUND THE
WORLD.
Loire Valley for its versatility and broad selections, ranging from sparkling
wines to dessert wines; Burgundy for its reds and my passion for Pinot Noir.

NAME A RECENT WINE DISCOVERY THAT EXCITED YOU.
1997 Quinta do Mouro from Portugal is a red wine with immense complexity
and charm; one of the hidden gems of the wine world.

DESCRIBE YOUR WINE SELECTIONS, BOTH BY THE GLASS AND ON YOUR LIST.
Sixty percent of the wine list is dedicated to red wines. Our half-bottle category
has increased to more than forty offerings.

WHAT ARE THE MOST UNIQUE FEATURES IN YOUR WINE PROGRAM?
We offer a "Flight of the Month" that is chosen by our wine club members. It
debuts on the first Wednesday of every month.

WHAT CATEGORIES OF WINE ARE THE BEST VALUES IN YOUR RESTAURANT?
Austrian whites and Spanish and Portuguese reds.

NAME A COUPLE OF YOUR RESTAURANT'S SIGNATURE DISHES. WHAT
TYPES OF WINE DO YOU PREFER TO RECOMMEND WITH EACH?
Pan-seared veal chop and foie gras with red wine reduction paired with red
Burgundy; Tuscan bean soup with fried sage and garlic oil paired with
California Chardonnay.

WHAT ARE SOME OTHER ULTIMATE WINE AND FOOD PAIRINGS?
Passion fruit caramel custard with a late-harvest Muscat.

The Dining Room at the Ritz-Carlton

160 East Pearson Street
Chicago, Illinois 60611
phone 312-573-5223 fax 312-266-9623
website www.fourseasons.com/chicagorc/index.html

Fernando Beteta
DINING ROOM MANAGER
AND SOMMELIER

NAME YOUR FAVORITE WINE REGION.
Italy, because of the variety of wines produced, which perfectly complement the food and culture.

NAME A RECENT WINE DISCOVERY THAT EXCITED YOU.
Quarts de Chaume, Domaine des Baumard, a beautiful dessert wine from the Loire Valley.

IF YOU WERE NOT IN THIS PROFESSION, WHAT WOULD YOU BE DOING?
Something in the arts.

WHAT ARE THE MOST UNIQUE FEATURES IN YOUR WINE PROGRAM?
We offer an eight-wine flight to pair with each course of our Chef's Menu, and a five-wine flight with the tasting menu. There are more than forty wines and Ports available by the glass, and we boast fourteen vintages of Château Latour, and an average of eight to ten vintages of Bordeaux's other first growths.

WHAT WINES ARE THE BEST VALUES IN YOUR RESTAURANT?
There are many: St. Aubin, Volnay and Santenay in Burgundy; Saint-Joseph in the Rhône; California Pinot Noir and a number of wines from Austria and Germany.

NAME A COUPLE OF YOUR RESTAURANT'S SIGNATURE DISHES. WHAT TYPES OF WINE DO YOU PREFER TO RECOMMEND WITH EACH?
Sautéed duck liver, homemade quince jam, black mission fig compote, medjool date purée, Port reduction and toasted brioche with Hungarian Tokaji Aszù 5 Puttonyos; grilled marinated rack of Colorado lamb, white beans with lamb shank and parsley bread crumbs, candied fennel lamb sausage with Columbia Valley Merlot.

WHAT ARE SOME OTHER ULTIMATE WINE AND FOOD PAIRINGS?
Tokaji Aszù with Roquefort; Banyuls with chocolate soufflé; Brunello di Montalcino with Tuscany salami and Pecorino Sardo.

Erawan Royal Thai Cuisine

729 North Clark Street
Chicago, Illinois 60610
phone 312-642-6888 fax 312-642-6811
website www.erawangroup.com

Anoroth "Noth" Chitdamrong

FOOD AND BEVERAGE DIRECTOR AND
GENERAL MANAGER

NAME TWO OF YOUR FAVORITE WINE DISTRICTS FROM AROUND THE
WORLD.
Wachau, Austria, for its Rieslings and Grüner Veltliners that are pure, focused
and expressive; Loire Valley, France, for the wines' food compatibility and
expression of terroir.

NAME RECENT WINE DISCOVERIES THAT HAVE EXCITED YOU.
Australian Shiraz for its ability to show vibrancy of fruit and still be food-
friendly and elegant; Argentine Malbec for its underappreciated potential and
virtuosity.

WHAT WOULD YOU LIKE YOUR CUSTOMERS TO KNOW ABOUT YOU?
I am a true adventurer and lover of international wines.

DESCRIBE YOUR WINE SELECTIONS, BOTH BY THE GLASS AND ON YOUR LIST.
We specialize in wines that have both a high acidity that lends an affinity with
food and a true expression of varietal and terroir. With our menu, the great
whites of Austria, Germany, Alsace and Loire work extremely well.

WHAT CATEGORY OF WINE IS THE BEST VALUE IN YOUR RESTAURANT?
German Riesling. There is no other area that combines such good affinity,
expressiveness and focus.

NAME A COUPLE OF YOUR RESTAURANT'S SIGNATURE DISHES. WHAT
TYPES OF WINE DO YOU PREFER TO RECOMMEND WITH EACH?
Lamb Mussaman curry with soft, rich Australian Shiraz; garlic truffle prawns
with Austrian Grüner Veltliner.

WHAT WINES ARE CUSTOMERS NOW MORE WILLING TO ORDER?
Australian, Austrian and German wines.

WHAT ARE SOME OTHER ULTIMATE WINE AND FOOD PAIRINGS?
Blanc de Blancs Champagne with fried tempura items (soft-shell crab or crab
pouches) and German Riesling with Thai chilies.

Nomi
at the Park Hyatt Chicago

800 North Michigan Avenue
Chicago, Illinois 60611
phone 312-335-1234 fax 312-239-4000
website www.parkhyattchicago.com

Robert Jovic
SOMMELIER

WHAT ARE SOME OF YOUR ULTIMATE FOOD AND WINE PAIRINGS?
Nomi's chilled cucumber soup with Oregon Pinot or Sancerre. Our sushi is perfect with German Riesling or Sauvignon Blanc.

DESCRIBE YOUR WINE SELECTIONS.
Our wine list represents the entire world, from rare jewels to simple vintages. We are constantly seeking out new wines from small producers that pair well with our cuisine.

WHAT CATEGORIES OF WINE ARE THE BEST VALUES ON YOUR WINE LIST?
Red wines from South Africa and white wines from New Zealand.

NAME RECENT WINE DISCOVERIES THAT HAVE EXCITED YOU.
Darioush Winery Signature Viognier 2001—nice acidity and a wonderful aroma; Vall-Llach from Spain's Priorato region—it's a monster wine, big, bold and intense with a nice finish; Lemelson Pinot Noir Jerome Reserve 1999— just the right combination of spice.

WHAT ARE YOUR FAVORITE WINE REGIONS IN THE WORLD TODAY?
Alsace, Burgundy and Oregon.

WHAT LED YOU TO PURSUE A CAREER THAT INVOLVES WINE?
My grandfather was a winemaker, and as a child I worked in his vineyard and became fascinated with wine.

WHAT ARE THE BEST ASPECTS OF YOUR JOB?
I get to taste amazing wines and meet interesting people from all over the world. I also like getting feedback from my customers after making suggestions.

IF YOU WERE NOT A SOMMELIER, WHAT WOULD YOU BE DOING?
Own my own restaurant or be an opera singer.

Le Titi De Paris

1015 West Dundee Road
Arlington Heights, Illinois 60004
phone 847-506-0222 fax 847-506-0474
website www.letitideparis.com

Marcel G. Flori
SOMMELIER

WHAT INSPIRED YOU TO PURSUE A CAREER THAT INVOLVES WINE?
Both my passion for wine and food and Steven Spurrier at L'Académie du Vin in Paris.

NAME TWO OF YOUR FAVORITE WINE REGIONS FROM AROUND THE WORLD.
Provence and the Loire Valley in France. They are both underrated, yet have very impressive wines.

NAME RECENT WINE DISCOVERIES THAT HAVE EXCITED YOU.
The sweet wines from the Loire Valley offer very good value compared with Sauternes.

WHAT BITS OF INFORMATION WOULD YOU LIKE YOUR CUSTOMERS TO KNOW ABOUT YOU?
I play classical guitar and custom-build furniture.

WHAT IS THE MOST UNIQUE FEATURE IN YOUR WINE PROGRAM?
We have regional wine dinners once a month.

WHAT CATEGORY OF WINE IS THE BEST VALUE IN YOUR RESTAURANT?
All of our wines are good values.

NAME A COUPLE OF YOUR RESTAURANT'S SIGNATURE DISHES. WHAT TYPES OF WINE DO YOU PREFER TO RECOMMEND WITH EACH?
Sautéed salmon in a cider sauce with Gamay from Touraine; New Zealand venison with huckleberry sauce paired with New Zealand Syrah.

IN THE PAST YEAR, WHAT WINES IN YOUR WINE PROGRAM HAVE CUSTOMERS BECOME MORE WILLING TO ORDER?
Red Bordeaux and reds from Provence.

Tuscany

1014 West Taylor Street
Chicago, Illinois 60607
phone 312-829-1990 fax 312-829-8023
website www.stefanirestaurants.com

Peter H. Bovis
GENERAL MANAGER
AND WINE BUYER

WHAT INSPIRED YOU TO PURSUE A CAREER THAT INVOLVES WINE?
Pairing different types of food and wine.

WHAT PART OF YOUR JOB DO YOU ENJOY THE MOST?
Serving new and different people every day.

NAME ONE OF YOUR FAVORITE WINE DISTRICTS OR WINE REGIONS
FROM AROUND THE WORLD.
The Tuscany region in Italy.

NAME RECENT WINE DISCOVERIES THAT HAVE EXCITED YOU.
Wines from Greece.

WHAT BITS OF INFORMATION WOULD YOU LIKE YOUR CUSTOMERS TO
KNOW ABOUT YOU?
I am always looking to help guests with their selections.

IF YOU WERE NOT IN THIS PROFESSION, WHAT WOULD YOU BE DOING?
I would probably be a doctor.

DESCRIBE YOUR WINE SELECTIONS, BOTH BY THE GLASS AND ON YOUR LIST.
We specialize in Tuscan wines.

WHAT ARE THE MOST UNIQUE FEATURES IN YOUR WINE PROGRAM?
We have fantastic wine dinners every other month.

WHAT CATEGORY OF WINE IS THE BEST VALUE IN YOUR RESTAURANT?
Chianti, by the glass and by the bottle.

NAME A COUPLE OF YOUR RESTAURANT'S SIGNATURE DISHES. WHAT
TYPES OF WINE DO YOU PREFER TO RECOMMEND WITH EACH?
Veal osso buco with Barolo; rack of lamb with Chianti.

WHAT WINES ARE CUSTOMERS NOW MORE WILLING TO ORDER?
Chianti.

Tuscany

1014 West Taylor Street
Chicago, Illinois 60607
phone 312-829-1990 fax 312-829-8023
website www.stefanirestaurants.com

Alexander J. Prekurat
MAÎTRE D'
AND SOMMELIER

WHAT INSPIRED YOU TO PURSUE A CAREER THAT INVOLVES WINE?
Working in restaurants and getting to taste different wines on a regular basis.

WHAT PART OF YOUR JOB DO YOU ENJOY MOST?
Tasting and doing seminars.

NAME TWO OF YOUR FAVORITE WINE REGIONS FROM AROUND THE WORLD.
Chianti and Napa Valley.

NAME RECENT WINE DISCOVERIES THAT HAVE EXCITED YOU.
Wines from Australia.

WHAT BITS OF INFORMATION WOULD YOU LIKE YOUR CUSTOMERS TO
KNOW ABOUT YOU?
I like to drink fine wine and play golf.

IF YOU WERE NOT IN THIS PROFESSION, WHAT WOULD YOU BE?
Probably be a car dealer in Vegas.

DESCRIBE YOUR WINE SELECTIONS, BOTH BY THE GLASS AND ON YOUR LIST.
We feature an extensive range of Italian wines.

WHAT ARE THE MOST UNIQUE FEATURES IN YOUR WINE PROGRAM?
Our selection of Italian wines and our wine dinners, held every other month.

WHAT CATEGORY OF WINE IS THE BEST VALUE IN YOUR RESTAURANT?
Italian.

NAME A COUPLE OF YOUR RESTAURANT'S SIGNATURE DISHES. WHAT
TYPES OF WINE DO YOU PREFER TO RECOMMEND WITH EACH?
Rack of lamb with Chianti; penne brivido with Barolo.

IN THE PAST YEAR, WHAT WINES IN YOUR WINE PROGRAM HAVE CUS-
TOMERS BECOME MORE WILLING TO ORDER?
German Riesling and Australian wines.

Ambria

BOB BANSBERG, SOMMELIER

2300 North Lincoln Park West,
Chicago

773-472-5959

Angelo's Ristorante

ANGELO BATTAGLIA,
OWNER AND WINE BUYER

247 North York Road, Elmhurst

630-833-2400

Arun's

SUE PIKULSOM, WINE BUYER
AND SOMMELIER

4156 North Kedzie Avenue, Chicago

773-539-1909

BIN 36

BRIAN DUNCAN, SOMMELIER

339 North Dearborn Street, Chicago

312-755-9463

Blackbird

EDUARD SEITAN, SOMMELIER
RICK DIARMIT, BAR MANAGER

619 West Randolph Street, Chicago

312-715-0708

Cab's Wine Bar & Bistro

ALIXE LISCHETT, WINE BUYER

430 North Main Street, Glen Ellyn

630-942-9463

Cape Cod Room

CYRILLE PAWELKO, WINE BUYER

140 East Walton, Chicago

312-787-2200

Carlton Club and Four Seasons at the Ritz-Carlton

PIERRE LASSERRE, SOMMELIER

160 East Pearson Street, Chicago

312-266-1000

Chicago Prime Steakhouse

STELIO KALKOUNOS, WINE BUYER

1370 Bank Drive, Schaumburg

847-969-9900

Edgewood Valley Country Club

CAROLE WHITE, FOOD AND
BEVERAGE DIRECTOR

7500 South Willow Springs Road,
LaGrange

708-246-2800

Everest

ALPANA SINGH,
MASTER SOMMELIER

440 La Salle, 40th Floor, Chicago

312-663-8920

Froggy's French Café

PASCAL ROCHELEMAGNE,
WINE BUYER

306 Green Bay Road, Highwood

847-433-7080

Harry Caray's Restaurant

MICHELE ANDERSON,
WINE DIRECTOR

33 West Kinzie Street, Chicago

312-828-0966

Italian Village

RAY CAPITINI, OWNER
AND WINE BUYER
Ron Balter, Wine Director
71 West Monroe, Second Floor,
Chicago
312-332-7005

Joe's Seafood, Prime Steak and Stone Crab

KEVIN BRATT, WINE DIRECTOR
60 East Grand Avenue, Chicago
312-379-5637

Maggiano's Little Italy

DAVID PENNACHETTI,
WINE AND BEVERAGE MANAGER
101 West Grand, Suite 400, Chicago
312-644-7766

MK

JOHN ARENTS, WINE BUYER
868 North Franklin, Chicago
312-482-9179

Nine

LARRY FLAM, MANAGER
AND WINE BUYER
440 West Randolph Street, Chicago
312-575-9900

North Pond

BRIAN O'CONNOR, GENERAL
MANAGER AND SOMMELIER
2610 North Cannon Drive, Chicago
773-477-5845

One Sixty Blue

MYRON MARKEWYCZ, SOMMELIER
160 North Loomis Street, Chicago
312-850-0303

Printers Row Restaurant

GINGER MORALES, WINE BUYER
550 South Dearborn Street, Chicago
312-461-0780

Pump Room at the Omni Ambassador East

BILL BORDEN, BEVERAGE MANAGER
1301 North State Parkway, Chicago
312-266-0360

Rushmore

JOE KAHN, WINE BUYER
1023 West Lake Street, Chicago
312-421-8845

Shaw's Crab House & Blue Crab Lounge

STEVE SHERMAN, WINE BUYER
1900 East Higgins Road,
Schaumburg
847-517-2722

Spago

GERRY MULDOON, SOMMELIER
520 North Dearborn, Chicago
312-527-3704

Spiaggia Restaurant

HENRY BISHOP, SOMMELIER
980 North Michigan Avenue,
Chicago
312-280-2750

Tallgrass

TOM ALVES, WINE BUYER
1006 South State Street, Lockport
815-838-5566

Thyme

JOHN BUBALA, CHEF
AND SOMMELIER
464 North Halsted, Chicago
312-226-4300

Tournesol

MICHAEL SMITH, GENERAL
MANAGER AND SOMMELIER
4343 North Lincoln, Chicago
773-477-8820

Tru

R. SCOTT TYREE, WINE DIRECTOR
AND SOMMELIER
AARON ELLIOT,
ASSISTANT SOMMELIER
676 North Saint Clair Street, Chicago
312-202-0001

Va Pensiero

JOHN BOWERS, WINE BUYER
1566 Oak Avenue, Evanston
847-475-7779

Vivere

RON BALTER, WINE BUYER
71 West Monroe Street, Chicago
312-332-4040

Wildfire

BRAD WERMAGER, WINE MANAGER
232 Oakbrook Center, Chicago
312-787-9000

Zealous Restaurant

KEVIN HALMIHIAK, WINE BUYER
419 West Superior Street, Chicago
312-475-0165

The Carriage House Dining Room

24460 Adams Road
South Bend, Indiana 46628
phone 574-272-9220 fax 574-272-6179

Judith L. Coté
OWNER AND SOMMELIER

WHAT INSPIRED YOU TO PURSUE A CAREER THAT INVOLVES WINE?
My mother, who established The Carriage House Dining Room in 1975. The complementary relationship with food and wine was one that she stressed.

NAME ONE OR TWO OF YOUR FAVORITE WINE DISTRICTS OR WINE REGIONS FROM AROUND THE WORLD.
Stags Leap District of Napa County. I've never tasted a wine from there that wasn't luscious and praiseworthy.

NAME RECENT WINE DISCOVERIES THAT HAVE EXCITED YOU.
Eroica Riesling from Chateau Ste. Michelle.

WHAT BITS OF INFORMATION WOULD YOU LIKE YOUR CUSTOMERS TO KNOW ABOUT YOU?
I have an avid interest in fine art. My collection of twentieth-century Indiana Hoosier Salon paintings is on display throughout the Carriage House.

WHAT ARE THE MOST UNIQUE FEATURES IN YOUR WINE PROGRAM?
We have hosted an extravagant holiday wine dinner for more than fifteen years. Each year we have a different theme.

WHAT CATEGORY OF WINE IS THE BEST VALUE IN YOUR RESTAURANT?
Pinot Noir.

NAME A FEW OF YOUR RESTAURANT'S SIGNATURE DISHES. WHAT TYPES OF WINE DO YOU PREFER TO RECOMMEND WITH EACH?
Apple walnut raisin pie with tawny Porto; oysters Rockefeller and vintage Champagne; smoked salmon with a caper mayonnaise and red onions paired with German Riesling; beef Wellington with a Burgundian sauce paired with Pinot Noir.

IN THE PAST YEAR, WHAT WINES IN YOUR WINE PROGRAM HAVE CUSTOMERS BECOME MORE WILLING TO ORDER?
Oregon Pinot Noir and white wines in general, especially Riesling.

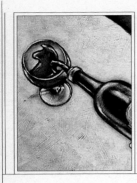

LaSalle Grill

115 West Colfax Avenue
South Bend, Indiana 46601
phone 574-288-1155 fax 219-288-2012
website www.lasallegrille.com

Joseph R. Wilfing
BEVERAGE DIRECTOR
AND SOMMELIER

DESCRIBE YOUR WINE SELECTIONS.
Our wine program is geared toward wines that are drinkable now. We have 350 wines on our list from the finest vineyards around the world. We also have a great selection of wines by the glass and half-bottle.

WHAT CATEGORY OF WINE IS THE BEST VALUE IN YOUR RESTAURANT?
The Rhône Valley.

NAME RECENT WINE DISCOVERIES THAT HAVE EXCITED YOU.
Wines from the Loire Valley and New Zealand.

WHAT ARE YOUR FAVORITE WINE REGIONS IN THE WORLD TODAY?
The Russian River Valley. Most of the Chardonnay is produced to the Burgundy standard, and the scenery is to die for. Secondly, Pomerol. The wine is exquisite and the land is remarkable.

WHAT LED YOU TO PURSUE A CAREER THAT INVOLVES WINE?
It is based on my own enjoyment. I personally enjoy talking to and educating people about wine and its production.

WHAT ARE THE BEST ASPECTS OF YOUR JOB?
The people I serve. Customers seem to enjoy and engage in conversation about wine, not only because it is pertinent to the evening, but also because wine is a wonderful beverage. I am also able to gain a personal knowledge of culture and regions of the world through travel and study, something I would not be doing if I were not in the wine business.

IF YOU WERE NOT IN THE WINE PROFESSION, WHAT WOULD YOU BE DOING?
Public speaking.

40 Sardines

11942 Roe Avenue
Overland Park, Kansas 66209
phone 913-451-1040 fax 913-451-1048
website www.40sardines.com

Ryan W. Sciara
GENERAL MANAGER
AND SOMMELIER

NAME ONE OF YOUR FAVORITE WINE REGIONS FROM AROUND THE WORLD.
Southern Rhône Valley, from the everyday drinking Côtes du Rhône to the elegant and powerful Châteauneuf-du-Pape. They represent some of the best values in the world.

NAME A RECENT WINE DISCOVERY THAT EXCITED YOU.
The Grenache-based wines of Priorat. They offer a lot of bang for the buck.

WHAT BITS OF INFORMATION WOULD YOU LIKE YOUR CUSTOMERS TO KNOW ABOUT YOU?
I was an intern with BATF and once considered a career in law enforcement. I decided that carrying a corkscrew to work was much safer than carrying a gun.

WHAT ARE THE MOST UNIQUE FEATURES IN YOUR WINE PROGRAM?
Our twenty wines at $20 and the arrangement of our list by flavor profile and weight, which makes it very user- and food-friendly.

WHAT CATEGORY OF WINE IS THE BEST VALUE IN YOUR RESTAURANT?
Champagne and sparkling wine specifically, but the more expensive the wine gets, the better the value for our guests.

NAME A FEW OF YOUR RESTAURANT'S SIGNATURE DISHES. WHAT TYPES OF WINE DO YOU PREFER TO RECOMMEND WITH EACH?
Braised shortribs and Rosso di Montalcino; slow-roasted salmon and premier cru Chablis; lemon meringue pie with Moscato d'Asti; grilled Portuguese sardines and Verdicchio.

WHAT WINES ARE CUSTOMERS NOW MORE WILLING TO ORDER?
Light, crisp French Chardonnay and medium- to light-bodied reds like Pinot Noir and Sangiovese-based Italian wines.

WHAT ARE SOME OTHER ULTIMATE WINE AND FOOD PAIRINGS?
Buttered popcorn and Brut Champagne; Cabrales blue cheese with Pedro Ximenez Sherry.

The Oakroom
at the Seelbach Hilton
500 Fourth Avenue
Louisville, Kentucky 40202
phone 502-585-3200 fax 502-585-9240
website www.seelbachhilton.com

Jerry Slater
MAÎTRE D'

WHAT PART OF YOUR JOB DO YOU ENJOY THE MOST?
Turning customers on to wines that they never had before, like a recent guest who loved a La Scolca Gavi di Gavi.

NAME TWO OF YOUR FAVORITE WINE REGIONS FROM AROUND THE WORLD.
Alsace, where the wines have beautiful aromas and crisp acidity; Mount Veeder Cabernets for their big, muscular and ripe flavors.

NAME RECENT WINE DISCOVERIES THAT HAVE EXCITED YOU.
Wines from Spain, beyond Rioja. I really liked Spanish wines from the eastern shores or the French border.

WHAT BITS OF INFORMATION WOULD YOU LIKE YOUR CUSTOMERS TO KNOW ABOUT YOU?
I came to this profession as a necessity. I was a literature student. I wasn't in food and beverage.

IF YOU WERE NOT IN THIS PROFESSION, WHAT WOULD YOU BE DOING?
I'd be a college literature professor, or perhaps a filmmaker.

DESCRIBE YOUR WINE SELECTIONS, BOTH BY THE GLASS AND ON YOUR LIST.
We have about 1,270 selections on the list. We try to offer a broad range of wines, from the most classic to those from the younger regions of the world.

NAME ONE OF YOUR RESTAURANT'S SIGNATURE DISHES. WHAT WINE DO YOU PREFER TO RECOMMEND WITH IT?
White-truffle oil scrambled free-range eggs with foie gras and jump-fried morels with Tokaji Aszù 5 Puttonyos.

WHAT ARE SOME OTHER ULTIMATE WINE AND FOOD PAIRINGS?
Albariño with salads; French or American Syrah with lamb.

The Oakroom
at the Seelbach Hilton

500 Fourth Avenue
Louisville, Kentucky 40202
phone 502-585-3200 fax 502-585-9240
website www.seelbachhilton.com

Robert W. Munson

SOMMELIER

WHAT PART OF YOUR JOB DO YOU ENJOY THE MOST?
I enjoy tasting and making recommendations to customers. I also enjoy watching how trends change from week to week.

NAME ONE OR TWO OF YOUR FAVORITE WINE DISTRICTS OR WINE REGIONS FROM AROUND THE WORLD.
The Rhône Valley because I enjoy big, rustic wines and appreciate what that region does with Syrah and Grenache.

NAME RECENT WINE DISCOVERIES THAT HAVE EXCITED YOU.
Coturri Wines from Sonoma Valley. Tony Coturri makes the most interesting and diverse red Zinfandels while using strictly organic methods.

WHAT BITS OF INFORMATION WOULD YOU LIKE YOUR CUSTOMERS TO KNOW ABOUT YOU?
I was born and raised in Kentucky and, while living and serving an internship at Mary Ann's Restaurant and Bar as senior barman in Castletownshend, Ireland, I met my wife who was working in a work-abroad program from Russia.

IF YOU WERE NOT IN THIS PROFESSION, WHAT WOULD YOU BE DOING?
Seeking a master's degree in business, sooner than later.

WHAT ARE THE MOST UNIQUE FEATURES IN YOUR WINE PROGRAM?
We offer a large half-bottle list to meet the needs of single diners. We also feature a wine-decanting cart stocked with aerating funnels, Reidel decanters and wine cradles.

WHAT CATEGORIES OF WINE ARE THE BEST VALUES IN YOUR RESTAURANT?
Spanish and Australian reds.

IN THE PAST YEAR, WHAT WINES IN YOUR WINE PROGRAM HAVE CUSTOMERS BECOME MORE WILLING TO ORDER?
American Cabernet Sauvignon and Italian and Australian reds.

Le Relais Restaurant
ANTHONY DIKE, OWNER
AND WINE BUYER
Bowman Field, Taylorsville Road,
Louisville
502-451-9020

Vincenzo's
PAULA FISCHER, WINE BUYER
150 South Fifth Street, Louisville
502-580-1350

Andrea's Restaurant

3100 19th Street at Ridgelake
Metairie, Louisiana 70002
phone 504-834-8583 fax 504-834-6698
website www.andreasrestaurant.com

Andrea Apuzzo
PROPRIETOR AND SOMMELIER

WHAT IS ONE OF YOUR ULTIMATE FOOD AND WINE PAIRINGS?
Red snapper with Fontanelle Chardonnay.

DESCRIBE YOUR WINE SELECTIONS.
I select wines from around the world and then try to share my passion for wine with friends, family and guests.

WHAT CATEGORIES OF WINE ARE THE BEST VALUES ON YOUR WINE LIST?
Zinfandel, red Bordeaux.

NAME RECENT WINE DISCOVERIES THAT HAVE EXCITED YOU.
Ca' Montini Pinot Grigio L'Aristocratico and Bastianich Vespa Bianco.

WHAT IS YOUR FAVORITE WINE REGION IN THE WORLD TODAY?
Tuscany.

WHAT LED YOU TO PURSUE A CAREER THAT INVOLVES WINE?
Love of wine. I made wine in my home in Capri.

WHAT ARE THE BEST ASPECTS OF YOUR JOB?
Being able to create a fine wine list from wines around the world; encouraging my guests to have discriminating taste.

IF YOU WERE NOT IN THE WINE PROFESSION, WHAT WOULD YOU BE?
A doctor or musician.

Bayona Restaurant

430 Dauphine Street
New Orleans, Louisiana 70112
phone 504-525-4455 fax 504-522-0589

Dan Brown
WINE STEWARD

NAME ONE OR TWO OF YOUR FAVORITE WINE DISTRICTS OR WINE REGIONS FROM AROUND THE WORLD.
Rhône Valley. I love the northern Rhône. Its wines are great values.

NAME RECENT WINE DISCOVERIES THAT HAVE EXCITED YOU.
Spain, Austria, New Zealand Pinot Noir and the 2001 German wines.

WHAT BITS OF INFORMATION WOULD YOU LIKE YOUR CUSTOMERS TO KNOW ABOUT YOU?
I keep some special wine glasses and dessert spoons from the 1700s on hand for my friends and regular customers.

IF YOU WERE NOT IN THIS PROFESSION, WHAT WOULD YOU BE DOING?
I recently finished a master's degree in preservation at Tulane and am currently working there on my Ph.D.

DESCRIBE YOUR WINE SELECTIONS, BOTH BY THE GLASS AND ON YOUR LIST.
Six hundred wines by the bottle, fifteen by the glass and more than sixty dessert wines by the glass.

WHAT ARE THE MOST UNIQUE FEATURES IN YOUR WINE PROGRAM?
Our red Burgundies and Rhône Valley selections.

NAME A COUPLE OF YOUR RESTAURANT'S SIGNATURE DISHES. WHAT TYPES OF WINE DO YOU PREFER TO RECOMMEND WITH EACH?
Grilled duck breast with Côte-Rôtie; salmon with Austrian whites; foie gras with Sauternes.

IN THE PAST YEAR, WHAT WINES IN YOUR WINE PROGRAM HAVE CUS-TOMERS BECOME MORE WILLING TO ORDER?
Pinot Noir and Sauvignon Blanc. Customers seem more open to suggestions than ever before.

The Bistro at Maison de Ville Hotel

727 Rue Toulouse
New Orleans, Louisiana 70130
phone 504-528-9206 fax 504-528-9939
website www.maisondeville.com/new-bistro.html

Patrick P. Van Hoorebeek
"MASTER OF CEREMONIES"

WHAT INSPIRED YOU TO PURSUE A CAREER THAT INVOLVES WINE?
Auguste Escoffier.

WHAT PART OF YOUR JOB DO YOU ENJOY THE MOST?
Meeting wonderful people every day and trying to make them feel very special.

NAME ONE OR TWO OF YOUR FAVORITE WINE DISTRICTS OR WINE REGIONS FROM AROUND THE WORLD.
Spain for its great value and great potential while still being very underrated.

NAME RECENT WINE DISCOVERIES THAT HAVE EXCITED YOU.
Bajoz Crianza from the Toro region of Spain.

WHAT WOULD YOU LIKE YOUR CUSTOMERS TO KNOW ABOUT YOU?
The Krewe of Cork's "king for life" (Mardi Gras parade) and my collection of signed jeroboams.

IF YOU WERE NOT IN THIS PROFESSION, WHAT WOULD YOU BE?
An Oscar ceremony presenter!

WHAT ARE THE MOST UNIQUE FEATURES IN YOUR WINE PROGRAM?
We offer special selections in our "Vin du Jour," "Best-Kept Secrets" and our half-bottle categories. The Bistro strives to satisfy the diverse palates and "noses" that grace our establishment.

NAME ONE OF YOUR RESTAURANT'S SIGNATURE DISHES. WHAT WINE DO YOU PREFER TO RECOMMEND WITH IT?
Mussels Bruxelloise with french fries and California Sauvignon Blanc.

WHAT WINES ARE CUSTOMERS NOW MORE WILLING TO ORDER?
Cabernet Sauvignon and Oregon Pinot Noir.

WHAT ARE SOME OTHER ULTIMATE WINE AND FOOD PAIRINGS?
Boiled crayfish with California sparkling wine or Champagne; sushi with Chianti.

Café Margaux

765 Bayou Pines Drive East
Lake Charles, Louisiana 70601
phone 337-433-2902 fax 337-494-0606

D. C. Flynt
MASTER OF WINE, OWNER
AND EXECUTIVE CHEF

WHAT ARE SOME OF YOUR ULTIMATE FOOD AND WINE PAIRINGS?
Classical cuisine and wine created from the regional varietals that come from
the same area as the food, but the wine does not have to come from the same
region.

DESCRIBE YOUR WINE SELECTIONS.
Our list features 450 wines, which are arranged by varietal, region and appellation and are listed from fullest to lightest body in each category.

WHAT IS YOUR FAVORITE WINE REGION IN THE WORLD TODAY?
Australia. No other region in the world is as successful in providing the greatest
quality wines at the best price.

WHAT LED YOU TO YOUR CURRENT POSITION?
The love of the world's most natural fermented beverage.

WHAT IS THE MOST CHALLENGING ASPECT OF YOUR JOB?
Training the wait staff to understand that their role is to add value at every level
(wine, food and pleasure) and that wine is not a trophy hunt, but part of a
pleasurable lifestyle.

IF YOU WERE NOT IN THE WINE PROFESSION, WHAT WOULD YOU BE
DOING?
If I was not involved in wine, I would not be involved in life.

Bacco at the W Hotel of New Orleans

RICHARD KRUMM, SOMMELIER
310 Chartres Street, New Orleans
504-522-2426

Bourbon House at the Astor Crown Hotel

NEIL GERNON,
BEVERAGE MANAGER
144 Bourbon Street, New Orleans
504-962-0500

Brennan's Restaurant

HARRY HILL, WINE BUYER
417 Royal Street, New Orleans
504-525-9711

Broussard's Restaurant

MARC PREUSS, WINE BUYER
819 Conti Street, New Orleans
504-581-3866

Café Giovanni's

DUKE LOCICENO, CO-OWNER
AND WINE BUYER
117 Decatur Street, New Orleans
504-529-2154

Commander's Palace

JOHN PADDON, SOMMELIER
1403 Washington Avenue,
New Orleans
504-899-8221

Court of Two Sisters

JOE FEIN, OWNER
AND WINE BUYER
613 Royal Street, New Orleans
504-522-7261

The Dakota

KENNETH LA COUR, OWNER
AND WINE BUYER
629 North Highway 190, Covington
985-892-3712

Delmonico Restaurant & Bar

ALEKSANDAR JOVANOVIC,
SOMMELIER
1300 Saint Charles Avenue,
New Orleans
504-525-4937

Dominique's at Maison Depuy Hotel

WALTER BERTOD, SOMMELIER
1001 Rue Toulouse, New Orleans
504-522-8800

Emeril's

MATT LIRETTE, SOMMELIER
800 Tchoupitoulas Street,
New Orleans
504-528-9393

The French Table

JONATHAN INGLES, GENERAL
MANAGER AND WINE BUYER
3216 West Esplanade Avenue North,
Metairie
504-833-8108

Gabrielle Restaurant

MARY SONNIER, OWNER
AND SOMMELIER
3201 Esplanade Street, New Orleans
504-948-6233

Galatoire's

DAVID GOOCH, WINE MANAGER
209 Bourbon Street, New Orleans
504-525-2021

Gino's Restaurant
GINO MARINO, OWNER
AND WINE BUYER
4542 Bennington Avenue,
Baton Rouge
225-927-7156

The Grill Room at the Windsor Court Hotel
CLIVE O'DONOGHUE, FOOD AND
BEVERAGE DIRECTOR
300 Gravier Street, New Orleans
504-523-6000

Juban's Restaurant
CAROL JUBAN, WINE BUYER
3739 Perkins Road, Baton Rouge
225-346-8422

Lafitte's Landing
PATRICIA TATE,
BEVERAGE MANAGER
10275 Highway 70, New Orleans
225-473-1232

Mansur's
BRANDON MCDONALD,
WINE BUYER
3044 College Drive, Baton Rouge
225-923-3366

Palace Café
BARRY HIMEL, BEVERAGE MANAGER
605 Canal Street, New Orleans
504-523-1661

The Pelican Club Restaurant and Bar
RICHARD HUGHES, PROPRIETOR
AND WINE BUYER
312 Exchange Alley, New Orleans
504-523-1504

La Provence
CHRIS KERAGEORGIOU, SOMMELIER
25020 Highway 190, Lacombe
504-626-7662

Red Fish Grill
STEVE LESSING, GENERAL MANAGER
AND WINE BUYER
115 Bourbon Street, New Orleans
504-598-1200

Restaurant Cuvée
KENNETH LA COUR, OWNER
AND WINE BUYER
JEFF CUNDINGER, WINE DIRECTOR
322 Rue Magazine, New Orleans
504-587-9001

Upperline Restaurant
HEATHER CHEUZRONT, GENERAL
MANAGER AND WINE BUYER
1413 Upperline Street, New Orleans
504-891-9822

The White Barn Inn

CHRISTOPHER BAILEY, SOMMELIER

37 Beech Street, Kennebunkport

207-967-2321

Antrim 1844 Country Inn

30 Trevanion Road
Taneytown, Maryland 21787
phone 410-756-6812 fax 410-756-2744
website www.antrim1844.com

Sia Ayrom
RESTAURANT MANAGER
TEAM: RICHARD MOLLETT, SOMMELIER

NAME ONE OF YOUR FAVORITE WINE REGIONS FROM AROUND THE WORLD.
Bordeaux, for the simplicity of the wineries and the complexity of its wines.

NAME RECENT WINE DISCOVERIES THAT HAVE EXCITED YOU.
McLaren Vale Shiraz, particularly choices imported by the Grateful Palate. They are exceptional wines and great values.

IF YOU WERE NOT IN THIS PROFESSION, WHAT WOULD YOU BE?
A television producer. That's what I studied in school.

DESCRIBE YOUR WINE SELECTIONS, BOTH BY THE GLASS AND ON YOUR LIST.
We try to offer the best possible wines by the glass. We also have a 1,500-bin wine list for our guests to choose from.

WHAT ARE THE MOST UNIQUE FEATURES IN YOUR WINE PROGRAM?
We have an exceptionally large vertical listing of Cabernet Sauvignon, Meritage, Chardonnay and Merlot, and monthly winemaker dinners.

WHAT CATEGORY OF WINE IS THE BEST VALUE IN YOUR RESTAURANT?
Australian and New Zealand reds.

NAME A COUPLE OF YOUR RESTAURANT'S SIGNATURE DISHES. WHAT TYPES OF WINE DO YOU PREFER TO RECOMMEND WITH EACH?
Venison rib with chèvre and apple gratin paired with California Zinfandel; crab porcupine with sweet corn paired with Russian River Valley Viognier.

IN THE PAST YEAR, WHAT WINES IN YOUR WINE PROGRAM HAVE CUSTOMERS BECOME MORE WILLING TO ORDER?
Rieslings, Australian reds and California Petite Sirahs.

L'Auberge Chez Francois

Three Pooks Hill Road
Bethseda, Maryland 20814
phone 301-571-7331
website www.laubergechezfrancois.com

Adriano F. Rossi
SOMMELIER

NAME ONE OF YOUR FAVORITE WINE DISTRICTS FROM AROUND THE WORLD.

Burgundy and, in particular, Pommards that bring together personality, complexity and silkiness.

NAME RECENT WINE DISCOVERIES THAT HAVE EXCITED YOU.

New Zealand wines, for their intensity, fruitiness, unmistakable style and good value; Austrian wines, for their style, structure and balance.

IF YOU WERE NOT IN THIS PROFESSION, WHAT WOULD YOU BE DOING?

Working in a farm winery where I can further utilize my skills and make full use of my experience.

DESCRIBE YOUR WINE SELECTIONS, BOTH BY THE GLASS AND ON YOUR LIST.

We offer a selection of good wines from the United States, France and Italy, including a range of wines by the glass and a short wine list with some recommended wines that are particularly good values. Our regular wine list includes roughly 300 items and several wines offered in half-bottles.

NAME A FEW OF YOUR RESTAURANT'S SIGNATURE DISHES. WHAT TYPES OF WINE DO YOU PREFER TO RECOMMEND WITH EACH?

Sautéed Alaska sablefish, shrimp, mussels, saffron rice and tomato concassé niçoise with a California Viognier; Alsatian feast with sausages, duck, goose, confit, foie gras, pork and sauerkraut cooked with Crémant d'Alsace with Pinot Gris from Alsace; medallions of antelope, boar, deer chop, breast of pheasant, mushrooms, spaetzle, chestnuts and roebuck sauce with a Napa Valley Petite Sirah.

IN THE PAST YEAR, WHAT WINES IN YOUR WINE PROGRAM HAVE CUSTOMERS BECOME MORE WILLING TO ORDER?

Oregon and California Pinot Noir and red Burgundy.

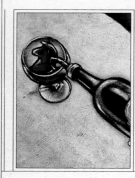

Hamptons Restaurant at the Harbor Court Hotel
550 Light Street
Baltimore, Maryland 21202
phone 410-234-0550

David P. Cawthorne
SOMMELIER

NAME ONE OR TWO OF YOUR FAVORITE WINE DISTRICTS OR WINE REGIONS FROM AROUND THE WORLD.
Loire Valley, for its traditional winemaking, and New Zealand, for its up-and-coming, promising new wines and wineries.

NAME RECENT WINE DISCOVERIES THAT HAVE EXCITED YOU.
Priorat. I love the wines from this region and especially the history behind them.

WHAT BITS OF INFORMATION WOULD YOU LIKE YOUR CUSTOMERS TO KNOW ABOUT YOU?
I'm a classical trumpet player.

IF YOU WERE NOT IN THIS PROFESSION, WHAT WOULD YOU BE?
A male exotic dancer.

DESCRIBE YOUR WINE SELECTIONS, BOTH BY THE GLASS AND ON YOUR LIST.
We offer a global selection of wines, catering to our international clientele and their needs.

WHAT ARE THE MOST UNIQUE FEATURES IN YOUR WINE PROGRAM?
The set menus with wine pairings are terrific.

NAME A COUPLE OF YOUR RESTAURANT'S SIGNATURE DISHES. WHAT TYPES OF WINE DO YOU PREFER TO RECOMMEND WITH EACH?
Our menu changes seasonally, so it allows a great deal of flexibility in tasting and pairing wines and after-dinner liquors.

IN THE PAST YEAR, WHAT WINES IN YOUR WINE PROGRAM HAVE CUSTOMERS BECOME MORE WILLING TO ORDER?
Wines from Alsace and Gewürztraminer.

Tragara Ristorante

4935 Cordell Avenue
Bethesda, Maryland 20814
phone 301-951-4935 fax 301-951-0401
website www.tragara.com

Claude Amsellem
OWNER

NAME SOME OF YOUR FAVORITE WINE DISTRICTS FROM AROUND THE WORLD.
Tuscany (for its Brunellos), the Napa Valley and Châteauneuf-du-Pape.

NAME RECENT WINE DISCOVERIES THAT HAVE EXCITED YOU.
Louis Bernard Côtes du Rhône 2000, for both its quality and value.

WHAT BITS OF INFORMATION WOULD YOU LIKE YOUR CUSTOMERS TO KNOW ABOUT YOU?
I'm a food and wine lover and have lived in several countries.

IF YOU WERE NOT IN THIS PROFESSION, WHAT WOULD YOU BE?
A stockbroker or a wine merchant.

DESCRIBE YOUR WINE SELECTIONS, BOTH BY THE GLASS AND ON YOUR LIST.
We are known for the depth and breadth of our wine selections, which span many countries and prices.

WHAT ARE THE MOST UNIQUE FEATURES IN YOUR WINE PROGRAM?
On request we hold wine and dinner parties and multiple-course dinners with wine tastings.

WHAT CATEGORY OF WINE IS THE BEST VALUE IN YOUR RESTAURANT?
California wines.

NAME A FEW OF YOUR RESTAURANT'S SIGNATURE DISHES. WHAT TYPES OF WINE DO YOU PREFER TO RECOMMEND WITH EACH?
Our osso buco Milanese with a Chianti; our pasta combination dish with Australian Sauvignon Blanc; buffalo steak with Napa Valley Cabernet Sauvignon.

IN THE PAST YEAR, WHAT WINES IN YOUR WINE PROGRAM HAVE CUSTOMERS BECOME MORE WILLING TO ORDER?
Zinfandel from California and Pinot Noir from the Pacific Northwest.

Beechtree Golf Club
JASON BRAITHWAIT, WINE BUYER
811 South Stephany Road, Aberdeen
410-297-9700

Black Olive
DEMITRIS SPILIADIS, SOMMELIER
814 South Bond Street, Baltimore
410-276-7141

Brass Elephant
JACK ELSBY, WINE BUYER
924 North Charles Street, Baltimore
410-547-8480

Bulle Rock Golf Club
DOUG WILSON, SOMMELIER
320 Blenheim Lane, Havre de Grace
410-939-8887

Caesar's Den
GUIDO DE FRANCO, SOMMELIER
223 South High Street, Baltimore
410-547-0820

Chiapparelli's
BRIAN CHIAPPARELLI, OWNER
AND WINE BUYER
237 High Street, Baltimore
410-837-0309

The Crossing at Casey Jones
LISA BALES, WINE BUYER
417 Charles Street, La Plata
301-932-6226

Dalesio's of Little Italy
PAUL OLIVER, SOMMELIER
829 Eastern Avenue, Baltimore
410-539-1965

Due
LESLEY DESAUTELS, SOMMELIER
25 Crossroads Drive, Owings Mills
410-356-3030

Fager's Island at the Lighthouse Club Hotel
RICK PAIRO, SOMMELIER
201 60th Street, Ocean City
410-524-5500

Harryman House
JOHN WORTHINGTON, OWNER
AND WINE BUYER
340 Main Street, Reisterstown
410-833-8850

Henninger's Tavern
KENNY VIETH, OWNER
AND WINE BUYER
1812 Bank Street, Baltimore
410-342-2172

Horizons Restaurant at the Clarion Resort Fontainebleu
RICHARD HUEBECK, SOMMELIER
101st Street and Oceanfront,
Ocean City
410-524-3535

Inn at Perry Cabin
THAD HOY, WINE BUYER
308 Watkins Lane, St. Michaels
410-745-2200

Ixia
TREVOR IFILL, GENERAL MANAGER
AND WINE BUYER
518 North Charles Street, Baltimore
410-727-1800

Kent Manor Inn & Restaurant
DENNIS SHAKAN, WINE BUYER
500 Kent Manor Drive, Stevensville
410-643-5757

King's Contrivance
RICHARD ACKMAN, SOMMELIER
10150 Shaker Drive, Columbia
410-995-0550

Lewnes's Steakhouse
ERIC PETERSON, SOMMELIER
4th and Severn Avenues, Annapolis
410-263-1617

Linwood Café
PAUL WRIGHT, WINE DIRECTOR
25 Crossroads Drive, Owings Mill
410-356-3030

Nicks Airport Inn
PAUL GIANNARIS, WINE BUYER
Route 11 North, Hagerstown
301-733-8560

Northwoods Inn
RUSSELL BROWN, OWNER
AND WINE BUYER
809 Melvin Avenue, Annapolis
410-269-6775

Old Angler's Inn
ANDRE CONDON, SOMMELIER
10801 McArthur Boulevard, Potomac
301-365-2425

The Oregon Grille
BLANE BOERI, GENERAL MANAGER
AND WINE BUYER
1201 Shawan Road, Hunt Valley
410-771-0505

The Prime Rib
DAVID DEREWICZ, WINE BUYER
1101 North Calvert Street, Baltimore
410-539-1804

Purple Orchid Restaurant
RICHARD WONG, OWNER
AND WINE BUYER
419 North Charles Street, Baltimore
410-837-0080

Reflections at the Holiday Inn Oceanfront
JASON STONE, WINE BUYER
67th Street and Coastal Highway,
Ocean City
410-524-5252

Ristorante Della Notte
RITA LYMPEROPOULOS, GENERAL
MANAGER AND WINE BUYER
801 Eastern Avenue, Baltimore
410-837-5500

Roccoco's
SUZI O'BOYLE, BAR MANAGER
AND WINE BUYER
20 West Washington Street,
Hagerstown
301-790-3331

Rudy's 2900
RUDY PAUL, MAÎTRE D'
2900 Baltimore Boulevard, Finksburg
410-833-5777

Sam's Waterfront
MARY RANDALL, WINE BUYER
2020 Chesapeake Harbor Drive,
Annapolis
410-263-3600

Spike & Charlie's
KENNY CARPS, SOMMELIER
1225 Cathedral Street, Baltimore
410-752-8144

Tilghman Island Inn
DAVID McCALLUM, SOMMELIER
21384 Coopertown Road,
Tilghman Island
410-886-2141

Tio Pepe Restaurant
MIGUEL SANC, SOMMELIER
10 East Franklin Street, Baltimore
410-539-4675

Boston College Club

100 Federal Street, 36th Floor
Boston, Massachusetts 02110
phone 617-946-2828 fax 617-345-9172

Shaun P. Hubbard
BEVERAGE MANAGER

WHAT IS ONE OF YOUR ULTIMATE FOOD AND WINE PAIRINGS?
Artichoke terrine with warm foie gras and truffle vinaigrette with Château Mont-Redon Châteuneuf-du-Pape blanc 1998.

DESCRIBE YOUR WINE SELECTIONS.
It is a collaboration of efforts, staff input and exposure to outside influence such as local wine tastings, reading materials and dining experiences.

WHAT ARE SOME OF YOUR FAVORITE WINE REGIONS IN THE WORLD TODAY?
From Italy, the Piedmont region for reds, the Veneto for some floral whites. But I also truly enjoy the Châteauneuf-du-Pape region of France for both red and white wines.

WHAT LED YOU TO YOUR CURRENT POSITION?
The excitement and passion of experiencing and learning about the world of wine and the pleasure of sharing that knowledge with family, friends, co-workers and guests.

WHAT ARE THE BEST ASPECTS OF YOUR JOB?
Expanding the horizons of others, getting people to try something new, which is sometimes a challenge.

IF YOU WERE NOT IN THE WINE PROFESSION, WHAT WOULD YOU BE?
Captain of my own charter fishing boat.

The Federalist
at Fifteen Beacon Hill
Fifteen Beacon Street
Boston, Massachusetts 02108
phone 617-670-2515 fax 617-670-2525

James J. Flynn
SOMMELIER

NAME TWO OF YOUR FAVORITE WINE REGIONS FROM AROUND THE WORLD.
Willamette Valley and Rhône Valley, both of which make good-value wines that are very versatile at the table.

NAME RECENT WINE DISCOVERIES THAT HAVE EXCITED YOU.
1999 Clark-Claudon Cabernet and 1999 Turnbull Syrah; both offer astounding fruit at a great price.

WHAT WOULD YOU LIKE YOUR CUSTOMERS TO KNOW ABOUT YOU?
Only that I love wine.

IF YOU WERE NOT IN THIS PROFESSION, WHAT WOULD YOU BE DOING?
I'd probably write.

DESCRIBE YOUR WINE SELECTIONS, BOTH BY THE GLASS AND ON YOUR LIST.
We offer twenty-eight wines by the glass and specialize in Bordeaux, Burgundy and Rhône wines as well as Napa Cabernet Sauvignon.

WHAT ARE THE MOST UNIQUE FEATURES IN YOUR WINE PROGRAM?
The wine program has great by-the-glass and half-bottle options. There is great depth in first growths, Williams-Selyem and Napa Cabernets like Harlan, Colgin and Grace Family.

WHAT CATEGORY OF WINE IS THE BEST VALUE IN YOUR RESTAURANT?
Rhône Valley reds, Zinfandels, New Zealand and Chilean reds.

NAME A FEW OF YOUR RESTAURANT'S SIGNATURE DISHES. WHAT TYPES OF WINE DO YOU PREFER TO RECOMMEND WITH EACH?
Dover sole with top Meursault; Maine lobster with California Chardonnay; beef Wellington with California Syrah.

IN THE PAST YEAR, WHAT WINES IN YOUR WINE PROGRAM HAVE CUSTOMERS BECOME MORE WILLING TO ORDER?
Oregon Pinot Noir, red Rhône wines and New Zealand Sauvignon Blanc.

Lala Rokh on Beacon Hill

97 Mount Vernon Street
Boston, Massachusetts 02108
phone 617-720-5511 fax 617-720-0489

Babak Bina
GENERAL MANAGER
AND CO-OWNER

WHAT ARE SOME OF YOUR ULTIMATE FOOD AND WINE PAIRINGS?
A German Riesling (von Hövel) with our pâté of olive and walnuts; Chalk Hill Estate Vineyard Selection Pinot Gris 1997 with our spinach, caramelized onion, yogurt and walnuts.

DESCRIBE YOUR WINE SELECTIONS.
Particular, concise and ever-changing.

WHAT IS YOUR FAVORITE WINE REGION IN THE WORLD TODAY?
Sonoma County. Dedication, while being relaxed about it.

WHAT LED YOU TO YOUR CURRENT POSITION?
The love of wine and food.

WHAT IS THE MOST CHALLENGING ASPECT OF YOUR JOB?
Keeping up with the vintages as well as new winemakers from around the world.

IF YOU WERE NOT IN THE WINE PROFESSION, WHAT WOULD YOU BE?
A professional polo player.

Legal Sea Foods Park Square

26 Park Square
Boston, Massachusetts 02116
phone 617-426-4444 fax 617-338-7629
website www.leagalseafoods.com

David J. Alphonse
DIRECTOR OF BEVERAGE OPERATIONS

WHAT INSPIRED YOU TO PURSUE A CAREER THAT INVOLVES WINE?
I grew up in the restaurant business. My family owned and operated two. I worked at an early age and decided to concentrate on the beverage side of the business when I was old enough.

NAME ONE OR TWO OF YOUR FAVORITE WINE DISTRICTS OR WINE REGIONS FROM AROUND THE WORLD.
Alsace and Loire Valley for white wines and their versatility with food; Burgundy and Tuscany for reds.

NAME RECENT WINE DISCOVERIES THAT HAVE EXCITED YOU.
Austrian whites offer complexity and are very approachable; some are great values.

WHAT BITS OF INFORMATION WOULD YOU LIKE YOUR CUSTOMERS TO KNOW ABOUT YOU?
Wine is both a profession and a hobby.

IF YOU WERE NOT IN THIS PROFESSION, WHAT WOULD YOU BE DOING?
I can't imagine not being in this industry.

DESCRIBE YOUR WINE SELECTIONS, BOTH BY THE GLASS AND ON YOUR LIST.
Our wine selection, both list items and by-the-glass selections, is extensive and value-oriented. We specialize in half-bottle selections. We have comprehensive wine lists for twenty-eight restaurants.

WHAT ARE THE MOST UNIQUE FEATURES IN YOUR WINE PROGRAM?
Our extensive wine by-the-glass program, half-bottle offerings and our wine flights.

IN THE PAST YEAR, WHAT WINES IN YOUR WINE PROGRAM HAVE CUS-TOMERS BECOME MORE WILLING TO ORDER?
Wines from Alsace and New Zealand.

Mistral

223 Columbus Avenue
Boston, Massachusetts 02116
phone 617-867-9300 fax 617-351-2601
website www.mistralbistro.com

Dawn M. Lamendola
BEVERAGE MANAGER
AND SOMMELIER

NAME ONE OF YOUR FAVORITE WINE REGIONS FROM AROUND THE WORLD.
Burgundy, for its beautiful wines.

NAME RECENT WINE DISCOVERIES THAT HAVE EXCITED YOU.
New Zealand Pinot Noirs often have a great flavor profile at affordable prices.

IF YOU WERE NOT IN THIS PROFESSION, WHAT WOULD YOU BE DOING?
Organic farming.

DESCRIBE YOUR WINE SELECTIONS, BOTH BY THE GLASS AND ON YOUR LIST.
We have an international list of 500-plus selections to complement our French-Mediterranean cuisine. Our program includes exciting new discoveries as well as the classics at every price point.

WHAT ARE THE MOST UNIQUE FEATURES IN YOUR WINE PROGRAM?
We offer over forty wines by the glass at all price points. We also offer an extensive half-bottle and large format list.

WHAT CATEGORY OF WINE IS THE BEST VALUE IN YOUR RESTAURANT?
Italian reds, as well as California Cabernets and red Bordeaux.

NAME A FEW OF YOUR RESTAURANT'S SIGNATURE DISHES. WHAT TYPES OF WINE DO YOU PREFER TO RECOMMEND WITH EACH?
Truffle-scented gnocchi, wild mushrooms and shaved Parmesan with premier cru or grand cru white Burgundy; pappardelle, braised rabbit and prosciutto with Valpolicella; grilled salmon with citrus and winter greens with Rosé Champagne: roast duckling and root vegetables, date and fig hash and cherry gastrique with northern Rhône red.

IN THE PAST YEAR, WHAT WINES IN YOUR WINE PROGRAM HAVE CUSTOMERS BECOME MORE WILLING TO ORDER?
Spanish reds, by the glass and bottle; great new styles at great prices.

No. 9 Park

9 Park Street
Boston, Massachusetts 02108-4804
phone 617-742-9991 fax 617-742-9993

Catherine Silirie
WINE DIRECTOR

WHAT IS ONE OF YOUR ULTIMATE FOOD AND WINE PAIRINGS?
Wellfleet oysters and Louis Michel, Grossot or Raveneau Chablis.

DESCRIBE YOUR WINE SELECTIONS.
Our wine list is mostly French, Italian and American wines because our menu is based in these traditions. We pride ourselves on staff wine training (ten sommeliers are better than one).

WHAT IS YOUR FAVORITE WINE REGION IN THE WORLD TODAY?
Tuscany, for its natural and man-made beauty and for its straightforward cooking that goes so well with Chianti and Brunello.

WHAT LED YOU TO YOUR CURRENT POSITION?
Bacchus spoke to me in a dream, and I was then determined to find my way in the trade.

WHAT IS THE MOST CHALLENGING ASPECT OF YOUR JOB?
Continued staff training; trying to keep servers constantly involved and enthusiastic.

IF YOU WERE NOT IN THIS PROFESSION, WHAT WOULD YOU BE DOING?
I would still find a way to be involved with wine, as it is my ultimate interest.

Olives

90 Main Street
Charlestown, Massachusetts 02129
phone 617-242-9715 fax 617-242-1333
website www.toddenglish.com

Glenn A. Tanner
WINE DIRECTOR
AND SOMMELIER

WHAT ARE SOME OF YOUR ULTIMATE FOOD AND WINE PAIRINGS?
Todd's tuna tartare with Grüner Veltliner; soft-shell crab with big California Chardonnay; beef with Argentine Malbec.

DESCRIBE YOUR WINE SELECTIONS.
We offer a broad variety of wines, which we try to make user-friendly and accessible.

WHAT CATEGORY OF WINE IS THE BEST VALUE IN YOUR RESTAURANT?
The "Other Red" section of the Olives' wine lists offers funky, delicious stuff that doesn't fit into mainstream varietal categories.

NAME A RECENT WINE DISCOVERY THAT EXCITED YOU.
Frank Potts' 1999 by Bleasdale Vineyards in South Australia. Delicious stuff and a ridiculous bargain.

WHAT IS YOUR FAVORITE WINE REGION IN THE WORLD TODAY?
Austria. I love Austrian wines.

WHAT LED YOU TO PURSUE A CAREER THAT INVOLVES WINE?
Love of food, wine and people. I enjoy turning people on to new tastes and flavors.

WHAT ARE THE BEST ASPECTS OF YOUR JOB?
Training staff, guest interaction and the theater of the floor.

IF YOU WERE NOT IN THIS PROFESSION, WHAT WOULD YOU BE DOING?
Teaching and writing.

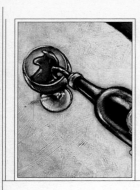

Plaza III,
A Kansas City Steakhouse
101 South Market Boulevard, Faneuil Hall Marketplace
Boston, Massachusetts 02109
phone 617-720-5570 fax 617-720-5071
website www.plazaiii.com

Paul J. McKeever
SOMMELIER

WHAT INSPIRED YOU TO PURSUE A CAREER THAT INVOLVES WINE?
The love of wine. I have a passion for learning how wine achieves its varying
degrees of perfection.

NAME ONE OF YOUR FAVORITE WINE REGIONS FROM AROUND THE
WORLD.
South Africa. I am very impressed with the recent level of wine quality as well
as the value the wines offer.

NAME A RECENT WINE DISCOVERY THAT EXCITED YOU.
Volker Eisele 1999 Estate Cabernet. It is an outstanding example of quality and
value in Napa Valley.

IF YOU WERE NOT IN THIS PROFESSION, WHAT WOULD YOU BE DOING?
I would be ruling the world.

DESCRIBE YOUR WINE SELECTIONS, BOTH BY THE GLASS AND ON YOUR
LIST.
Through our wine by-the-glass program, we are able to expose our guests to
different varietals and new wines. Our wine list is dominated by California red
wines to capitalize on our concept of an American steakhouse.

WHAT ARE THE MOST UNIQUE FEATURES IN YOUR WINE PROGRAM?
We believe that half-bottles are an extension of the by-the-glass program and
therefore offer a broad selection of them.

75 Chestnut

DAVID ARMARAL, GENERAL
MANAGER AND WINE BUYER
75 Chestnut Street, Boston
617-227-2175

Anthony's Pier 4

GEORGE PEPIONOVIC,
WINE STEWARD
140 Northern Avenue, Boston
617-482-6262

Aquitaine

DON BAILEY, GENERAL MANAGER
AND WINE BUYER
569 Tremont Street, Boston
617-424-8577

Aujourd'hui
at the Four
Seasons Hotel

JASON WATERLOW, MANAGER
AND WINE BUYER
200 Boylston Street, Boston
617-451-1392

Azure

MARK PETERSON, GENERAL
MANAGER AND WINE BUYER
65 Exeter Street, Boston
617-266-6222

The Bay Tower

DAVID WHEELER, WINE BUYER
60 State Street, Boston
617-723-1666

Black Rhino

MATT ROSSI, GENERAL MANAGER
AND WINE BUYER
21 Broad Street, Boston
617-263-0101

The Blue Room

DEANNA BRIGGS, WINE BUYER
1 Kendall Square, Cambridge
617-494-9034

Boston Harbor Hotel

ED COSTA, FOOD AND
BEVERAGE DIRECTOR
70 Rowes Wharf, Boston
617-439-7000

Café Louis

BRICK LOOMIS, WINE DIRECTOR
234 Berkeley Street, Boston
617-266-4680

Capital Grille

MICHAEL MCBRIDE, WINE BUYER
359 Newbury Street, Boston
617-262-8900

Clio's
at the Elliot Hotel

BETH IANNICELLI, WINE BUYER
370-A Commonwealth Avenue,
Boston
617-536-7200

Davide Restaurant

FRANK GESUALDI, OWNER
AND WINE BUYER
326 Commercial Street, Boston
617-227-5745

Durgin Park

SUSAN KELLEY, WINE BUYER
5 Faneuil Hall Market Plaza, Boston
617-227-2038

L'Espalier

ERIK JOHNSON, SOMMELIER
30 Gloucester Street, Boston
617-262-3023

Hamersley's Bistro
FIONA HAMERSLEY, WINE BUYER
553 Tremont Street, Boston
617-423-2700

Icarus
MICHAEL MARTIN, WINE STEWARD
3 Appleton Street, Boston
617-426-1790

Julien at the Meridien Boston
MAX COMPAGNON, WINE BUYER
250 Franklin Street, Boston
617-451-1900

Maison Robert
MONDETH PHAN, WINE BUYER
45 School Street, Boston
617-227-3370

Prezza
DAVID PETRILLI, GENERAL
MANAGER AND WINE BUYER
24 Fleet Street, Boston
617-227-1577

Radius
SCOTT FRALEY, SOMMELIER
8 High Street, Boston
617-426-1234

Rialto
PATRICK DUBSKY, GENERAL
MANAGER AND WINE BUYER
1 Bennett Street, Cambridge
617-661-5050

Ritz-Carlton Café at the Ritz-Carlton Hotel
PETER GREERTY,
DIRECTOR OF WINE
15 Arlington Street, Boston
617-536-5700

Salamander Restaurant
MORIYA BODIE, WINE BUYER
1 Huntington Avenue, Boston
617-451-2150

Seaport Hotel Boston
STEVE WOOD, WINE BUYER
1 Seaport Lane, Boston
617-385-4000

Seasons Restaurant at the Millennium Bostonian Hotel
SEAN WILCOX, FOOD AND
BEVERAGE DIRECTOR
6 Faneuil Hall Marketplace, Boston
617-523-3600

Somerset Club
A. DENNIS MICHEL, GENERAL
MANAGER AND WINE BUYER
42 Beacon Street, Boston
617-227-1731

Top of the Hub at the Prudential Center
RAPHAEL OLIVER, GENERAL
MANAGER AND WINE BUYER
800 Boylston Street, Boston
617-536-1775

The Vault Bistro and Wine Bar
KARIN MICHAELS, GENERAL
MANAGER AND WINE BUYER
105 Water Street, Boston
617-292-9966

21 Federal

21 Federal Street
Nantucket, Massachusetts 02554
phone 508-228-2121 fax 508-228-2962
website www.21federal.net

Amber Stevens

FLOOR MANAGER
AND WINE DIRECTOR

WHAT INSPIRED YOU TO PURSUE A CAREER THAT INVOLVES WINE?
The wine program was assigned to me by the founder of the restaurant before he passed away. It is an honor to continue his work.

NAME ONE OR TWO OF YOUR FAVORITE WINE DISTRICTS OR WINE REGIONS FROM AROUND THE WORLD.
Willamette Valley, Oregon; its Pinot Noirs are exquisite and more similar to the wines of Burgundy than those from California.

NAME RECENT WINE DISCOVERIES THAT HAVE EXCITED YOU.
1997 Brunellos from Tuscany. These are very comforting wines to drink on a blustery winter day on Nantucket.

WHAT BITS OF INFORMATION WOULD YOU LIKE YOUR CUSTOMERS TO KNOW ABOUT YOU?
I have a bachelor's degree in dance. An injury prevented me from performing, although performing on the restaurant floor is just as rewarding.

IF YOU WERE NOT IN THIS PROFESSION, WHAT WOULD YOU BE DOING?
There's no business like show business.

DESCRIBE YOUR WINE SELECTIONS, BOTH BY THE GLASS AND ON YOUR LIST.
Our wine list matches our cuisine, which is a blend of new and traditional styles.

WHAT CATEGORY OF WINE IS THE BEST VALUE IN YOUR RESTAURANT?
California Sauvignon Blanc and Spanish reds.

NAME ONE OF YOUR RESTAURANT'S SIGNATURE DISHES. WHAT WINE DO YOU PREFER TO RECOMMEND WITH IT?
Pan-crisped salmon with morels and roasted beet butter with Willamette Valley Pinot Noir.

WHAT WINES ARE CUSTOMERS NOW MORE WILLING TO ORDER?
California Meritages.

American Seasons

80 Centre Street
Nantucket, Massachusetts 02554
phone 508-228-7111 fax 508-325-0779
website www.americanseasons.com

Orla B. Murphy-LaScola
GENERAL MANAGER
AND SOMMELIER

WHAT INSPIRED YOU TO PURSUE A CAREER THAT INVOLVES WINE?
I worked in Cognac as a tour guide while in college.

NAME ONE OR TWO OF YOUR FAVORITE WINE REGIONS FROM AROUND
THE WORLD.
South Africa. I enjoyed Pinotage while visiting wineries there. It is great with
food. Also, Alsace has great dry Rieslings.

NAME RECENT WINE DISCOVERIES THAT HAVE EXCITED YOU.
Lavenier Winery in Africa; American ports, especially Heitz Ink Grade, a Port
finally worthy of inclusion on our wine list.

WHAT BITS OF INFORMATION WOULD YOU LIKE YOUR CUSTOMERS TO
KNOW ABOUT YOU?
I trained as a journalist and freelanced for two years. I have worked at American
Seasons for eight years, and I'm married to executive chef Michael LaScola.

IF YOU WERE NOT IN THIS PROFESSION, WHAT WOULD YOU BE DOING?
Writing. I took a chef's course at Ballymaloe Cookery School in Ireland.

DESCRIBE YOUR WINE SELECTIONS, BOTH BY THE GLASS AND ON YOUR LIST.
Our list is all-American. We look for small producers who excel in specific
grape varietals.

WHAT ARE THE MOST UNIQUE FEATURES IN YOUR WINE PROGRAM?
Our wine dinners in the fall and spring and our reserve wines available by the glass.

NAME A COUPLE OF YOUR RESTAURANT'S SIGNATURE DISHES. WHAT
TYPES OF WINE DO YOU PREFER TO RECOMMEND WITH EACH?
Foie gras crème brûlée with Moscato.

IN THE PAST YEAR, WHAT WINES IN YOUR WINE PROGRAM HAVE CUS-
TOMERS BECOME MORE WILLING TO ORDER?
American white varietals.

Il Capriccio

888 Main Street
Waltham, Massachusetts 02453
phone 781-894-2234 fax 781-891-3227

Jeannie Rogers
OWNER AND WINE BUYER

NAME ONE OF YOUR FAVORITE WINE REGIONS FROM AROUND THE WORLD.
Piedmont. I love the combination of the vineyards with the Alps, the almost painful tannin of young Nebbiolos with the rich cuisine and the region's great, minerally whites.

NAME RECENT WINE DISCOVERIES THAT HAVE EXCITED YOU.
2001 Tocai from Borgo San Daniele in Friuli; 2001 Castel Noarna Bianco di Castelnuovo.

DESCRIBE YOUR WINE SELECTIONS, BOTH BY THE GLASS AND ON YOUR LIST.
Our wine selection changes often. We specialize in mainly Northern Italian wine, but we also have wines from Germany, Austria and other countries.

WHAT ARE THE MOST UNIQUE FEATURES IN YOUR WINE PROGRAM?
We have wine dinners, our wine pricing is very fair, and our wines selections are interesting.

WHAT WINES ARE THE BEST VALUES IN YOUR RESTAURANT?
Italian Barbera and Chianti Classico and German Riesling.

NAME ONE OF YOUR RESTAURANT'S SIGNATURE DISHES. WHAT WINE DO YOU PREFER TO RECOMMEND WITH IT?
Porcini mushroom soufflé with Pinot Bianco or Barbera.

IN THE PAST YEAR, WHAT WINES IN YOUR WINE PROGRAM HAVE CUSTOMERS BECOME MORE WILLING TO ORDER?
Barolo, Barbera and Austrian Grüner Veltliner and Riesling.

WHAT ARE SOME OTHER ULTIMATE WINE AND FOOD PAIRINGS?
Soft-shell crab and Grüner Veltliner; truffles and Barolo.

The Chanticleer Inn
9 New Street
Siasconset, Massachusetts 02564
phone 508-257-6231 fax 508-257-4154
website www.thechanticleerinn.com

Cécile J. Chauveau
SOMMELIER

WHAT INSPIRED YOU TO PURSUE A CAREER THAT INVOLVES WINE?
I was brought up in a wine family in Burgundy. My grandfather made labels for DRC and others, and my uncle is a vineyard owner.

NAME ONE OF YOUR FAVORITE WINE REGIONS FROM AROUND THE WORLD.
I love Burgundy for its Pinot Noir. It's where I had my first tasting and first harvest.

NAME A RECENT WINE DISCOVERY THAT EXCITED YOU.
Dalla Valle Maya 1998; very concentrated and powerful with lots of fruit and complexity.

WHAT WOULD YOU LIKE YOUR CUSTOMERS TO KNOW ABOUT YOU?
I love the history of wine. I also participate in harvest every year.

IF YOU WERE NOT IN THIS PROFESSION, WHAT WOULD YOU BE DOING?
I would be in the kitchen cooking and matching food with wine.

DESCRIBE YOUR WINE SELECTIONS, BOTH BY THE GLASS AND ON YOUR LIST.
I like wines that are unknown to the public. I encourage customers to try new things.

WHAT ARE THE MOST UNIQUE FEATURES IN YOUR WINE PROGRAM?
Wine flights and wine dinners.

WHAT CATEGORY OF WINE IS THE BEST VALUE IN YOUR RESTAURANT?
White Burgundy, Zinfandel and Rhône wines.

NAME A COUPLE OF YOUR RESTAURANT'S SIGNATURE DISHES. WHAT TYPES OF WINE DO YOU PREFER TO RECOMMEND WITH EACH?
Lobster soufflé with white Burgundy; stuffed squab and prune dressing with California Zinfandel.

WHAT WINES ARE CUSTOMERS NOW MORE WILLING TO ORDER?
Alsace, Vendange Tardive Riesling and Rhône wine.

Cioppino's Restaurant

20 Broad Street
Nantucket, Massachusetts 02554
phone 508-228-4622 fax 508-228-2152
website www.cioppinos.com

Tracy W. Root
PROPRIETOR AND SOMMELIER

WHAT INSPIRED YOU TO PURSUE A CAREER THAT INVOLVES WINE?
When I started in the restaurant trade, I was amazed at the lack of wine-knowledgeable staff. I think we should know all aspects of our field.

WHAT PARTS OF YOUR JOB DO YOU ENJOY THE MOST?
Making customers feel at ease when talking about wine and introducing quality wines to them that are good values.

NAME ONE OF YOUR FAVORITE WINE REGIONS FROM AROUND THE WORLD.
Champagne. The people and the wines are so bubbly!

NAME RECENT WINE DISCOVERIES THAT HAVE EXCITED YOU.
Argentine Malbec is a good, hearty, flavorful wine.

IF YOU WERE NOT IN THIS PROFESSION, WHAT WOULD YOU BE DOING?
Running a small Caribbean island.

DESCRIBE YOUR WINE SELECTIONS, BOTH BY THE GLASS AND ON YOUR LIST.
We are strong in California selections.

WHAT ARE THE MOST UNIQUE FEATURES IN YOUR WINE PROGRAM?
We do four wine dinners in the summer season, and we offer red and white premium wine pours that change every two weeks.

WHAT CATEGORY OF WINE IS THE BEST VALUE IN YOUR RESTAURANT?
Cabernet, Chardonnay, Syrah and Zinfandel.

NAME A COUPLE OF YOUR RESTAURANT'S SIGNATURE DISHES. WHAT TYPES OF WINE DO YOU PREFER TO RECOMMEND WITH EACH?
Braised pork shank with California Syrah; fillet of sole with Rully Blanc.

IN THE PAST YEAR, WHAT WINES IN YOUR WINE PROGRAM HAVE CUSTOMERS BECOME MORE WILLING TO ORDER?
Oregon Pinot Noir, California Syrah and Argentine Malbec.

Le Soir Bistro

51 Lincoln Street
Newton, Massachusetts 02458
phone 617-965-3100 fax 617-964-5069
website www.lesoirbistro.com

Paul Westerkamp
SOMMELIER AND WINE BUYER

NAME ONE OR TWO OF YOUR FAVORITE WINE DISTRICTS OR WINE
REGIONS FROM AROUND THE WORLD.

Alsace, France, for its ability to provide wines that work well with Pacific Rim
cuisine (Asian produce with French technique).

NAME RECENT WINE DISCOVERIES THAT HAVE EXCITED YOU.

Banyuls, which can enhance either a chocolate or a blue cheese course.

IF YOU WERE NOT IN THIS PROFESSION, WHAT WOULD YOU BE DOING?

A cheesemaker.

DESCRIBE YOUR WINE SELECTIONS, BOTH BY THE GLASS AND ON YOUR
LIST.

Our wine list features 115 to 150 different wines, and we pour 18 to 23 wine
by-the-glass daily. We specialize in the wines of Burgundy and California, especially Chardonnay and Pinot Noir. The wine list is re-created daily to enhance
the menu for each evening.

NAME A FEW OF YOUR RESTAURANT'S SIGNATURE DISHES. WHAT TYPES
OF WINE DO YOU PREFER TO RECOMMEND WITH EACH?

Lobster and fennel profiterole, whipped dill cream with Sancerre or Menetou-
Salon; pan-roasted whole monkfish with carrots and bacon lardons, pommes
purée with Sonoma Coast Chardonnay, Carneros Pinot Noir or premier cru
Chablis; slow-cooked rabbit pot pie with Russian River Pinot Noir, Sonoma
old-vine Zinfandel or Hermitage.

IN THE PAST YEAR, WHAT WINES IN YOUR WINE PROGRAM HAVE CUS-
TOMERS BECOME MORE WILLING TO ORDER?

Alsace Gewürztraminer, Pinot Blanc, Pinot Gris and Riesling.

WHAT ARE SOME OTHER ULTIMATE WINE AND FOOD PAIRINGS?

Sancerre and goat cheese; Central Coast or Russian River Pinot Noir and white
tuna; Santenay and seared foie gras; Banyuls and chocolate.

Topper's at the Wauwinet

120 Wauwinet Road
Nantucket, Massachusetts 02584
phone 508-228-8768 fax 508-325-0657

Craig R. Hanna
CELLAR MASTER

NAME TWO OF YOUR FAVORITE WINE REGIONS FROM AROUND THE WORLD.
Burgundy and Piedmont for their small, artisanal family producers.

NAME RECENT WINE DISCOVERIES THAT HAVE EXCITED YOU.
Many small producers in France and Italy made such lovely wines in 2002, a
difficult vintage. I've also recently enjoyed Pinot Noirs from Central Otago,
New Zealand.

IF YOU WERE NOT IN THIS PROFESSION, WHAT WOULD YOU BE DOING?
Philosopher, auto restorer, chef or psychic.

DESCRIBE YOUR WINE SELECTIONS, BOTH BY THE GLASS AND ON YOUR LIST.
We have a small by-the-glass program because of our large half-bottle selection.
Our greatest strengths are in wines from Burgundy, the Rhône, Champagne
and Italy.

WHAT CATEGORY OF WINE IS THE BEST VALUE IN YOUR RESTAURANT?
Red Provence, white Loire, Alsatian, Portuguese and Spanish, and red Côte de
Beaune.

NAME A COUPLE OF YOUR RESTAURANT'S SIGNATURE DISHES. WHAT
TYPES OF WINE DO YOU PREFER TO RECOMMEND WITH EACH?
Glidden Point oysters on the half shell with tête de cuvée Champagne; lobster
and scallop Navarin with grand cru white Burgundy.

WHAT ARE SOME OTHER ULTIMATE WINE AND FOOD PAIRINGS?
Seared foie gras with quince–black pepper jam and a sweet late-harvest Chenin
Blanc; roasted pheasant with cipollini and a cider sauce and New World Pinot
Noir; bluefin tuna tartare with cucumber, lime and peppercress and dry
Champagne; seared sea scallops with roasted root vegetables and truffles with
white northern Rhône; beet risotto with sautéed greens, aged goat cheese and
horseradish with older Barbaresco; grilled lamb loin with a parsnip-pear purée,
arugula, pine nuts and rosemary with mature red Hermitage.

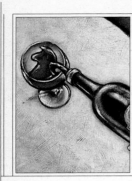

Wheatleigh

11 Hawthorne Road
Lenox, Massachusetts 01240
phone 413-637-0610 fax 413-637-4507
website www.wheatleigh.com

Pascal J.D. Fiancette
SOMMELIER

NAME RECENT WINE DISCOVERIES THAT HAVE EXCITED YOU.

Austrian wines. I visited there, and appreciated both the beauty of the country and the typicity of their varietals.

WHAT BITS OF INFORMATION WOULD YOU LIKE YOUR CUSTOMERS TO KNOW ABOUT YOU?

After my diploma in France, I started my professional career in the U.K. at a two-star Michelin restaurant. I still have not worked in France, despite being a French sommelier.

DESCRIBE YOUR WINE SELECTIONS, BOTH BY THE GLASS AND ON YOUR LIST.

Our wine selection is mainly French and American from some of the best producers. We are striving now for a more global selection.

WHAT ARE THE MOST UNIQUE FEATURES IN YOUR WINE PROGRAM?

We have an extensive half-bottle selection and we hold wine dinners with great producers. We also offer every afternoon a complimentary tasting of wine and cheese to our in-house guests.

NAME A COUPLE OF YOUR RESTAURANT'S SIGNATURE DISHES. WHAT TYPES OF WINE DO YOU PREFER TO RECOMMEND WITH EACH?

Dungeness crab salad, spring pea and roe vinaigrette with New Zealand Sauvignon Blanc; baby spring farm lamb, with wild morels and locally foraged ramps, with Oregon Pinot Noir.

IN THE PAST YEAR, WHAT WINES IN YOUR WINE PROGRAM HAVE CUSTOMERS BECOME MORE WILLING TO ORDER?

White Burgundy, Napa Valley Cabernets and some Italian and Spanish wines.

WHAT IS ANOTHER ULTIMATE WINE AND FOOD PAIRING?

Whole-roasted lobster with cardamom and butter paired with Viognier from the Rhône Valley.

Abbicci

GIORGIO TESSARI, SOMMELIER
43 Main Street, Yarmouthport
508-362-3501

Atlantica

JOE DOOLEY, WINE BUYER
44 Border Street, Cohasset
781-383-0900

Bistro Zinc

THIERY BREARD, WINE BUYER
56 Church Street, Lenox
413-637-8800

Blantyre

CHRISTELLE REGNIER,
WINE BUYER
16 Blantyre Road, Lenox
413-637-3556

Blue Ginger

ROB MULLER, MANAGER
AND WINE BUYER
583 Washington Street, Wellesley
781-283-5790

Brae Burn
Country Club

RICK SHAUGHNESSY, ASSISTANT
GENERAL MANAGER AND
WINE BUYER
326 Fuller Street, Newtonville
617-244-0680

Brant Point Grill
at the White Elephant

DANIEL THOMAS, SOMMELIER
50 Easton Street, Nantucket Island
508-325-1320

Carambola

RICHARD PILE, WINE BUYER
663 Main Street, Waltham
781-899-2244

Chancellors
at the Point Breeze

PAUL GONNELLA, WINE BUYER
71 Eastern Street, Nantucket
508-228-8674

Charles River
Country Club

DANIEL O'CONNELL, WINE BUYER
483 Dedham Street, Newton
617-332-1320

Chester

JOHN GUERRA, WINE BUYER
404 Commercial Street, Provincetown
508-487-8200

Chillingsworth

KATHY ALLEN, WINE BUYER
N/S Route 6A, Brewster
508-896-3640

Church Street Café

LINDA FORMAN, WINE BUYER
65 Church Street, Lenox
413-637-2745

The Daniel
Webster Inn

WALLY BLANCHETTE, SOMMELIER
149 Main Street, Sandwich
508-888-3622

DeMarco Restaurant

BRIAN HAWKINS, WINE BUYER
9 India Street, Nantucket
508-228-1836

Flora

JOE ANTOUN, WINE BUYER

190 Massachusetts Avenue, Arlington

781-641-1664

The Pearl

DAVID LOWER, SOMMELIER

12 Federal Street, Nantucket

508-228-9622

Silks
at Stonehedge Inn

MICHAEL OTAKA, SOMMELIER

160 Pawtucket Boulevard, Tyngsboro

978-649-4400

The Grill
at Hobbs Brook
at the Doubletree
Guest Suites

LYNNE NEWTON, FOOD

AND BEVERAGE DIRECTOR

550 Winter Street, Waltham

617-890-6767

Tosca

JOSEPH ERROL, WINE BUYER

14 North Street, Hingham

781-740-0080

Big Rock Chop House

245 South Eton
Birmingham, Michigan 48009
phone 248-647-7774 fax 248-647-2103
website www.bigrockchophouse.com

Vera D. Rizer

GENERAL MANAGER

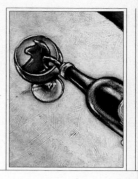

WHAT INSPIRED YOU TO PURSUE A CAREER THAT INVOLVES WINE?

I was asked to write a wine list twenty years ago and one of my salesmen at the time was very helpful. I'll never forget his pairing of Moscato with plain cheese-cake. What a match!

NAME TWO OF YOUR FAVORITE WINE REGIONS FROM AROUND THE WORLD.

The Rhône and Burgundy, for their earthy complexity that matches so perfectly with food.

WHAT BITS OF INFORMATION WOULD YOU LIKE YOUR CUSTOMERS TO KNOW ABOUT YOU?

My husband and I make one to two wine trips per year, in which everything is centered around wine and food. I incorporate our finds on these trips into the wine list and menu specials.

WHAT ARE THE MOST UNIQUE FEATURES IN YOUR WINE PROGRAM?

We have more than 350 selections. Our by-the-glass wines are changed season-ally. We host at least one or two wine-related events per quarter. Our markups are moderate and we turn over our inventories five times a year.

WHAT CATEGORIES OF WINE OFFER THE BEST VALUE IN YOUR RESTAURANT?

California Zinfandel and Syrah.

NAME A FEW OF YOUR RESTAURANT'S SIGNATURE DISHES. WHAT TYPES OF WINE DO YOU PREFER TO RECOMMEND WITH EACH?

A 20-ounce bone-in filet mignon with Cabernet Sauvignon; potato-wrapped salmon with mustard-leek sauce with Chardonnay or Viognier; spiced Maryland crab cakes or crispy calamari with New Zealand Sauvignon Blanc; ostrich tenderloin with Oregon Pinot Noir.

IN THE PAST YEAR, WHAT WINES IN YOUR WINE PROGRAM HAVE CUS-TOMERS BECOME MORE WILLING TO ORDER?

Syrah and Zinfandel.

Café Cortina

30715 West Ten Mile Road
Farmington Hills, Michigan 48025
phone 248-474-3033 fax 248-474-9064
website www.cafecortina.com

Adriano L. Tonon
OWNER, MAÎTRE D'
AND SOMMELIER

WHAT ARE SOME OF YOUR ULTIMATE FOOD AND WINE PAIRINGS?
Gnocchetti con funghi selvatici with Pinot Grigio or Chalk Hill Chardonnay;
Amarone with meats; Barolo with pasta; Chardonnay or Pinot Grigio with fish.

DESCRIBE YOUR WINE SELECTIONS.
We specialize in Italian wines, but offer some wonderful American (California,
Michigan) wines, as well.

WHAT CATEGORIES OF WINE ARE THE BEST VALUES ON YOUR WINE LIST?
Sangiovese and California Cabernet Sauvignon.

NAME A RECENT WINE DISCOVERY THAT EXCITED YOU.
Carpineto Chianti Classico. I am not an avid Chianti connoisseur, but
Carpineto is a delightful discovery.

WHAT IS YOUR FAVORITE WINE REGION IN THE WORLD TODAY?
We are very biased toward Italian wines, but California wines are my personal
favorites.

WHAT LED YOU TO PURSUE A CAREER THAT INVOLVES WINE?
A passion for food, wine and Italian hospitality.

WHAT IS THE BEST ASPECT OF YOUR JOB?
Creating lifelong memories for our cherished clientele.

IF YOU WERE NOT IN THE WINE PROFESSION, WHAT WOULD YOU BE?
An actor or rock star. I enjoy the art of entertainment.

The Lark

6430 Farmington Road
West Bloomfield, Michigan 48322
phone 248-661-4466 fax 248-661-8891
website www.thelark.com

James D. Lark

PROPRIETOR, MAÎTRE D'
AND SOMMELIER

WHAT INSPIRED YOU TO PURSUE A CAREER THAT INVOLVES WINE?
I was served wine at home from the age of three. After several other careers, my love of fine wine and cuisine led me to open my own restaurant in 1981.

NAME ONE OR TWO OF YOUR FAVORITE WINE DISTRICTS OR WINE REGIONS FROM AROUND THE WORLD.
Burgundy for the incomparable pleasure of a great Pinot Noir; Bordeaux for the tremendous variety of fine wines and both regions for the beauty of their countryside, fine restaurants and the hospitality of their vintners.

NAME RECENT WINE DISCOVERIES THAT HAVE EXCITED YOU.
Wines from previously mediocre Italian regions such as Lazio, Umbria and Sicily.

WHAT BITS OF INFORMATION WOULD YOU LIKE YOUR CUSTOMERS TO KNOW ABOUT YOU?
I have wined and dined, hunted and fished around the world and recounted these adventures in my book, *The Ultimate Lark*.

WHAT CATEGORY OF WINE IS THE BEST VALUE IN YOUR RESTAURANT?
Ten top Champagnes priced between $50 and $70.

NAME A FEW OF YOUR RESTAURANT'S SIGNATURE DISHES. WHAT TYPES OF WINE DO YOU PREFER TO RECOMMEND WITH EACH?
Rack of lamb Genghis Khan with red Bordeaux; roasted Maine lobster with California Chardonnay; Chinese oven crisp-roasted duck with Sangiovese.

IN THE PAST YEAR, WHAT WINES IN YOUR WINE PROGRAM HAVE CUSTOMERS BECOME MORE WILLING TO ORDER?
Châteauneuf-du-Pape; New Zealand Sauvignon Blanc; California Syrah; Alsace whites; California Viognier.

WHAT ARE SOME OTHER ULTIMATE WINE AND FOOD PAIRINGS?
Sauternes and foie gras; late-harvest Gewürztraminer and foie gras; red Burgundy and pheasant.

No. VI Chophouse and Lobster Bar at the Hotel Baronette

27790 Novi Road
Novi, Michigan 48377
phone 248-305-5210 fax 248-349-7467
website www.uniquerestaurants.com

Richard G. Rubel
WINE MANAGER AND SOMMELIER

WHO INSPIRED YOU TO PURSUE A CAREER THAT INVOLVES WINE?
Madeline Triffon.

NAME TWO OF YOUR FAVORITE WINE REGIONS FROM AROUND THE WORLD.
Germany, for its pure and layered white wines, and southern Rhône, for its concentrated and stylish red wines.

NAME RECENT WINE DISCOVERIES THAT HAVE EXCITED YOU.
Spanish reds from Catalonia. Wine from Montsant, Priorat and Costers del Segre reflect value, quality and style.

WHAT WOULD YOU LIKE YOUR CUSTOMERS TO KNOW ABOUT YOU?
I love a good bottle of wine, a game of chess and a day on the lake.

IF YOU WERE NOT IN THIS PROFESSION, WHAT WOULD YOU BE DOING?
Building handcrafted wooden sailboats.

DESCRIBE YOUR WINE SELECTIONS, BOTH BY THE GLASS AND ON YOUR LIST.
We offer big red wines from all over the world. At a steakhouse, the bigger, the better.

WHAT IS ONE OF THE MOST UNIQUE FEATURES IN YOUR WINE PROGRAM?
We have an extensive selection of eclectic Napa Cabernets.

WHAT CATEGORY OF WINE IS THE BEST VALUE IN YOUR RESTAURANT?
Red Burgundy. It isn't ordered much in this steakhouse, so we try to offer it as a value.

NAME A COUPLE OF YOUR RESTAURANT'S SIGNATURE DISHES. WHAT TYPES OF WINE DO YOU PREFER TO RECOMMEND WITH EACH?
Jumbo lump crab cakes paired with Mâcon blanc that is rich but not oaky; beef short ribs served with Zinfandel.

WHAT WINES ARE CUSTOMERS NOW MORE WILLING TO ORDER?
Australian Shiraz and Spanish reds.

Northern Lakes Seafood Co.
at the Kingsley Hotel

39495 North Woodward Avenue
Bloomfield Hills, Michigan 48304
phone 248-646-7900 fax 248-646-8148
website www.uniquerestaurants.com/urc/northernlakes.asp

Michelle DeHayes
GENERAL MANAGER AND SOMMELIER
TEAM: MAUREEN SANDAY, SOMMELIER

WHAT INSPIRED YOU TO PURSUE A CAREER THAT INVOLVES WINE?
Working with a restaurant owner who has an informal, eclectic approach to
wine and a great palate.

NAME ONE OF YOUR FAVORITE WINE REGIONS FROM AROUND THE
WORLD.
Burgundy is my favorite region for both white and red wines.

NAME RECENT WINE DISCOVERIES THAT HAVE EXCITED YOU.
The diversity of Italian wines and their compatibility with different foods has
kept me busy recently.

IF YOU WERE NOT IN THIS PROFESSION, WHAT WOULD YOU BE DOING?
Does Aretha Franklin need a backup singer?

DESCRIBE YOUR WINE SELECTIONS, BOTH BY THE GLASS AND ON YOUR LIST.
The wine list is always a work in progress. It is printed daily because changes
are made daily. This allows us to bring our guests new, interesting options in a
variety of price points.

WHAT CATEGORY OF WINE IS THE BEST VALUE IN YOUR RESTAURANT?
We strive to have great values in every category, but we love to share favorites.
It pays to ask for our recommendations.

NAME A COUPLE OF YOUR RESTAURANT'S SIGNATURE DISHES. WHAT
TYPES OF WINE DO YOU PREFER TO RECOMMEND WITH EACH?
Seared, rare ahi tuna with seaweed salad ponzu and wasabi caviar with Oregon
Pinot Noir; Maryland crab and lobster cakes with California Chardonnay.

IN THE PAST YEAR, WHAT WINES IN YOUR WINE PROGRAM HAVE CUS-
TOMERS BECOME MORE WILLING TO ORDER?
Pinot Noir, because of its compatibility with our seafood menu. Also, offbeat
whites from Italy, Spain and France.

The Rattlesnake Club

300 River Place
Detroit, Michigan 48207
phone 313-567-4400 fax 313-567-2063
website www.rattlesnake.com

Kirby Pope
SOMMELIER
TEAM: DAVID MAZELLA, SOMMELIER

NAME ONE OR TWO OF YOUR FAVORITE WINE DISTRICTS OR WINE REGIONS FROM AROUND THE WORLD.
Alsace, for its tremendous food-friendly wines, and Burgundy, because of that region's ultimate development of my beloved Pinot and Chardonnay.

NAME RECENT WINE DISCOVERIES THAT HAVE EXCITED YOU.
Kabinett-style Rieslings from top German producers, such as the 2000 Weingut Haus Klosterberg Zeltinger Sonnenuhr Kabinett. They are racy, intense and incredible with food. Australia has impressed me like no other region with its amazing and radical use of different varietals, like the 1999 Brokenwood "Graveyard Vineyard" from South Australia.

WHAT BITS OF INFORMATION WOULD YOU LIKE YOUR CUSTOMERS TO KNOW ABOUT YOU?
I worked as a stand-up comic for nine years and opened for the Kinks, Dolly Parton and Crosby, Stills & Nash, among others.

WHAT CATEGORY OF WINE IS THE BEST VALUE IN YOUR RESTAURANT?
Viognier, Merlot and Loire Valley wines.

NAME A COUPLE OF YOUR RESTAURANT'S SIGNATURE DISHES. WHAT TYPES OF WINE DO YOU PREFER TO RECOMMEND WITH EACH?
Herb-crusted and roasted Michigan spring lamb with artichokes, couscous, braised fennel, chive oil and Pinot essence paired with Nuits-Saint-Georges; Malpeque oysters with a citrus vodka mignionette with premier cru Chablis; Jimmy's famous white chocolate ravioli paired with late-harvest Viognier.

Shiraz

30100 Telegraph Road
Bingham Farms, Michigan 48025
phone 248-645-5289 fax 248-645-5484
website www.uniquerestaurants.com/urc/shiraz

Jeff P. Zimmerman
SOMMELIER

NAME RECENT WINE DISCOVERIES THAT HAVE EXCITED YOU.
The increasing of many Michigan wines has thrilled me. In 2002 Michigan produced its largest ice wine harvest to date.

WHAT WOULD YOU LIKE YOUR CUSTOMERS TO KNOW ABOUT YOU?
I took a break from restaurant work to be a truck owner and operator for three years. As a hobby, I enjoy comparing ancient and modern cosmologies in an effort to find the enduring qualities of our humanity.

IF YOU WERE NOT IN THIS PROFESSION, WHAT WOULD YOU BE?
A photographer for National Geographic or a performer with Cirque du Soleil.

WHAT ARE THE MOST UNIQUE FEATURES IN YOUR WINE PROGRAM?
Our "Flights of Shiraz/Syrah," and wine pairings that are listed with the Prime Courses for easy ordering. We offer twenty-four wines by the glass, 390 choices in full bottles and twenty-seven in half-bottles.

WHAT WINES ARE THE BEST VALUES IN YOUR RESTAURANT?
Great values abound, especially older Bordeaux and cru Burgundies that are priced at retail.

NAME A COUPLE OF YOUR RESTAURANT'S SIGNATURE DISHES. WHAT TYPES OF WINE DO YOU PREFER TO RECOMMEND WITH EACH?
Maine Lobster risotto with asparagus and tomato paired with Sonoma Chardonnay; prime beef short ribs with horseradish-whipped potatoes paired with Barossa Valley Shiraz.

WHAT WINES ARE CUSTOMERS NOW MORE WILLING TO ORDER?
Australian Shiraz, Austrian Grüner Veltliner and German Scheurebe.

WHAT ARE SOME OTHER ULTIMATE WINE AND FOOD PAIRINGS?
Demi-sec Champagne and crème brûlée; duck confit and Russian River Pinot Noir; fava bean and wild mushroom gratin with Vino Nobile di Montepulciano.

Tapawingo
9502 Lake Street
Ellsworth, Michigan 49729
phone 231-588-7971 fax 231-588-6175
website www.tapawingo.net

Ron Edwards
MANAGER AND SOMMELIER

NAME TWO OF YOUR FAVORITE WINES.
German whites, because they are such great food wines; Burgundy, because it is elegance in liquid form.

NAME RECENT WINE DISCOVERIES THAT HAVE EXCITED YOU.
The neon style of Grüner Veltliner has been an exciting discovery. Then there was the re-exploration of Tokaji. Wow!

WHAT BITS OF INFORMATION WOULD YOU LIKE YOUR CUSTOMERS TO KNOW ABOUT YOU?
I must admit that it is really more about them and not me.

IF YOU WERE NOT IN THIS PROFESSION, WHAT WOULD YOU BE DOING?
Either an engineer or a house dad.

DESCRIBE YOUR WINE SELECTIONS, BOTH BY THE GLASS AND ON YOUR LIST.
The by-the-glass list represents fairly standard choices, but the 650 additional choices by the bottle make it hard not to find whatever you want.

WHAT ARE THE MOST UNIQUE FEATURES IN YOUR WINE PROGRAM?
It is unique to find a wine list as broad as ours. It is also fun and interesting to have the tasting menus with matched wines.

NAME A COUPLE OF YOUR RESTAURANT'S SIGNATURE DISHES. WHAT TYPES OF WINE DO YOU PREFER TO RECOMMEND WITH EACH?
Nine-spice roasted loin of lamb with Côte-Rôtie; seared diver scallop with zucchini crab roll and orange sabayon with Hunter Valley Sémillon.

IN THE PAST YEAR, WHAT WINES IN YOUR WINE PROGRAM HAVE CUSTOMERS BECOME MORE WILLING TO ORDER?
Non-California Chardonnay, Spanish reds and wines from southern France.

WHAT ARE SOME OTHER ULTIMATE WINE AND FOOD PAIRINGS?
Brie soup and Alsace Pinot Gris; ballotine of rabbit and Pinot Noir.

Andante Restaurant

LORI STARK, WINE BUYER
321 Bay Street, Petosky
231-348-3321

Bostwick Lake Inn

JIM WEBB, WINE BUYER
8521 Belding Road, Rockford
616-874-7290

Capital Grille

BOB LOOMIS, WINE BUYER
2800 West Big Beaver Road, Troy
248-649-5300

Earle

STEVE GOLDBERG, WINE BUYER
121 West Washington, Ann Arbor
734-994-0211

Epic Bistro

BILL WEIR, WINE BUYER
359 South Burdick, Suite 103,
Kalamazoo
616-342-1300

Forte

MICHAEL KORN, WINE BUYER
210 South Woodward, Birmingham
248-594-7300

Giovanni's Ristorante

RANDY TRUANT, OWNER
AND WINE BUYER
330 South Oakwood Boulevard,
Detroit
313-841-0122

Golden Mushroom

BRIAN CISLO, SOMMELIER
18100 West Ten Mile Road,
Southfield
248-559-4230

Morel's

MADELINE TRIFFON,
MASTER SOMMELIER
30100 Telegraph Road,
Bingham Farms
248-642-1094

Opus One

JAMES KOKAS, CO-OWNER
AND WINE BUYER
565 East Larned Street, Detroit
313-961-7766

Rowe Inn

KURT VAN SUMEREN, WINE BUYER
AND SOMMELIER
6303 Country Road, Ellsworth
231-588-7351

Walloon Lake Inn

DAVID BEIER, PROPRIETOR, CHEF
AND WINE BUYER
Walloon Lake Village, Walloon Lake
231-535-2999

Lord Fletcher's

3746 Sunset Drive
Spring Park, Minnesota 55384-0446
phone 952-471-8513 fax 952-471-8937
website www.lordfletchers.com

Steve M. Michalski
SOMMELIER

WHAT ARE SOME OF YOUR ULTIMATE FOOD AND WINE PAIRINGS?
Jumbo diver sea scallops with pancetta bacon, Yukon gold potatoes and bell peppers with Dijon mustard paired with Rhône white wine or New World Chardonnay; cast iron–seared beef tenderloin medallions with lobster meat ravioli and ricotta cheese, grilled asparagus spears and hollandaise sauce paired with Bordeaux or California Cabernet; vine-ripened tomatoes and goat cheese salad with Sancerre; Dijon-encrusted lamb and Yukon gold potatoes with Rhône red; barbecued ribs with California Zinfandel or Australian Shiraz; Argentina steak with Argentina Malbec.

DESCRIBE YOUR WINE SELECTIONS.
We have two wine lists: a short list which is well-stocked with familiar wines, and a reserve list for our Chart Room which is literally a book.

WHAT CATEGORIES OF WINE ARE THE BEST VALUES ON YOUR WINE LIST?
"Periphery" French wine regions, such as the Loire Valley, Provence and Beaujolais.

NAME RECENT WINE DISCOVERIES THAT HAVE EXCITED YOU.
Cassis from Provence, Malbec from Argentina and Saumur-Champigny rouge from the Loire Valley.

WHAT IS YOUR FAVORITE WINE REGION IN THE WORLD TODAY?
France, because of the tremendous diversity of its wines and their exceptional compatibility with food.

WHAT ARE THE BEST ASPECTS OF YOUR JOB?
Encouraging conservative customers to try new and unfamiliar wines.

IF YOU WERE NOT IN THE WINE PROFESSION, WHAT WOULD YOU BE DOING?
Something in international business.

D'Amico Cucina

DALE PETERSON, WINE DIRECTOR

100 North Sixth Street, Minneapolis

612-338-2401

Oceanaire at the Hyatt Regency

RICK KIMMES, CHEF

AND WINE BUYER

1300 Nicollet Mall, Minneapolis

612-333-2277

St. Paul Grill at St. Paul Hotel

SCOTT IDA, WINE BUYER

350 Market Street, St. Paul

651-224-7455

Bravo! Restaurant and Bar

LESLEY TOLAR, SOMMELIER
244 Highland Village, Jackson
601-982-8111

The American Restaurant

2450 Grand Boulevard
Kansas City, Missouri 64108
phone 816-426-1133 fax 816-426-1190
website www.theamericanrestaurantkc.com

Dan W. Tutko

MANAGER AND SOMMELIER

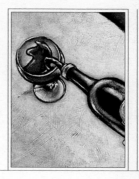

NAME ONE OR TWO OF YOUR FAVORITE WINE DISTRICTS OR WINE REGIONS FROM AROUND THE WORLD.

Bordeaux, for its history, longevity, influence and the magnificent wines it produces; Australia, for its wonderfully different wines and the winemakers' willingness to experiment with almost anything from packaging to winemaking.

IF YOU WERE NOT IN THIS PROFESSION, WHAT WOULD YOU BE?

An airline pilot.

DESCRIBE YOUR WINE SELECTIONS, BOTH BY THE GLASS AND ON YOUR LIST.

Our wines by the glass reflect our American cuisine, with a collage of choices from many different countries. The wine list has depth in California Cabernet Sauvignon, Bordeaux, Burgundy, the Rhône, Italy (super-Tuscans) and Champagne. We also feature wines from Germany, South Africa, South America, Australia, New Zealand, Spain, Portugal, Austria and Missouri.

WHAT WINES ARE THE BEST VALUES IN YOUR RESTAURANT?

Southern France, particularly reds.

NAME A COUPLE OF YOUR RESTAURANT'S SIGNATURE DISHES. WHAT TYPES OF WINE DO YOU PREFER TO RECOMMEND WITH EACH?

Butter-poached whole Maine lobster on pommes Maxime with carrot sauce and seared foie gras served with rich Chardonnay; four-hour braised veal shank, served in a shallow bowl with pot roast vegetables paired with Cabernet Sauvignon.

IN THE PAST YEAR, WHAT WINES IN YOUR WINE PROGRAM HAVE CUSTOMERS BECOME MORE WILLING TO ORDER?

The classic wines of Germany and Alsace, like Riesling, Pinot Gris and Pinot Blanc.

Annie Gunn's

16806 Chesterfield Airport Road
Chesterfield, Missouri 63005
phone 636-532-7684 fax 636-532-0561

Patricia Wamhoff
SOMMELIER

WHAT PART OF YOUR JOB DO YOU ENJOY THE MOST?
Interacting with people. One evening a couple that happened to be "wine vir-gins" asked for a wine recommendation. They never had wine before! Because they didn't know the differences between wines, I sampled different styles and let them choose what they liked. They fell in love with Pinot Noir and our grilled yellowfin.

NAME TWO OF YOUR FAVORITE WINE REGIONS FROM AROUND THE WORLD.
Austria for Grüner Veltliner; the fresh fruit and crisp acidity pairs well with many of our chef's fresh seafood daily selections. And Spain, for its range of impressive medium to full-bodied red wines from multiple regions.

NAME RECENT WINE DISCOVERIES THAT HAVE EXCITED YOU.
Italian wines, like Tuscan reds from Maremma and Veneto whites.

WHAT CATEGORY OF WINE IS THE BEST VALUE IN YOUR RESTAURANT?
Petits Châteaux Bordeaux and Italian red.

NAME A COUPLE OF YOUR RESTAURANT'S SIGNATURE DISHES. WHAT TYPES OF WINE DO YOU PREFER TO RECOMMEND WITH EACH?
Our chef features dry-aged steaks that need full-bodied red wines, such as Brunello di Montalcino and Australian Shiraz.

IN THE PAST YEAR, WHAT WINES IN YOUR WINE PROGRAM HAVE CUS-TOMERS BECOME MORE WILLING TO ORDER?
German wines. We added several wines, including Spätlese by the glass.

WHAT ARE SOME OTHER ULTIMATE WINE AND FOOD PAIRINGS?
Braised loin of rabbit on creamy polenta with pearl onions and a wild mush-room sauce with a medium-full California Pinot Noir.

The Blue Heron

Highway HH
Lake Ozark, Missouri 65049
phone 573-365-4646 fax 573-365-5743
website www.blueheronpottedsteer.com

Joseph H. Boer

OWNER AND OPERATOR

WHAT INSPIRED YOU TO PURSUE A CAREER THAT INVOLVES WINE?
I was inspired by my father, brother and brother-in-law.

NAME TWO OF YOUR FAVORITE WINE REGIONS FROM AROUND THE WORLD.
Howell Mountain and the Sierra Foothills, because of the character and depth of flavors of their wines.

NAME RECENT WINE DISCOVERIES THAT HAVE EXCITED YOU.
Zinfandels from Lava Cap and Amphora, and Sobon Estate Viognier.

WHAT BITS OF INFORMATION WOULD YOU LIKE YOUR CUSTOMERS TO KNOW ABOUT YOU?
I was born in Holland, went to chef's school, and served in the army in Holland. I served on the U.S. waitstaff at the Belgium Embassy.

IF YOU WERE NOT IN THIS PROFESSION, WHAT WOULD YOU BE DOING?
Professional art and architecture. I would also travel more.

DESCRIBE YOUR WINE SELECTIONS.
I began our wine list twenty-five years ago and wanted all varieties represented on it. I found the French wines the most important until I first went to the Monterey Wine Festival and discovered American wines.

WHAT IS THE MOST UNIQUE FEATURE IN YOUR WINE PROGRAM?
I started offering one-third bottles at one-third the price.

WHAT CATEGORY OF WINE IS THE BEST VALUE IN YOUR RESTAURANT?
California Zinfandel.

NAME A COUPLE OF YOUR RESTAURANT'S SIGNATURE DISHES. WHAT TYPES OF WINE DO YOU PREFER TO RECOMMEND WITH EACH?
It is all a matter of taste. My motto is "No Rules."

WHAT WINES ARE CUSTOMERS NOW MORE WILLING TO ORDER?
Cabernet Sauvignon, Zinfandel and Viognier.

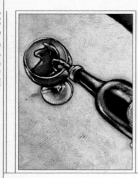

Tony's Restaurant

410 Market Street
St. Louis, Missouri 63102-2735
phone 314-231-7007 fax 314-231-4740
website www.tonysstlouis.com

Vincent P. Bommarito

EXECUTIVE CHEF AND PRESIDENT

WHAT INSPIRED YOU TO PURSUE A CAREER THAT INVOLVES WINE?
Tony's is a family business, so I have been around wine and food for as long as I can remember.

NAME ONE OF YOUR FAVORITE WINE REGIONS FROM AROUND THE WORLD.
Piedmont. Its Barolos are big wines with lots of character. I like the Nebbiolo grape because it refuses to flourish in any other part of the world.

NAME A RECENT WINE DISCOVERY THAT EXCITED YOU.
Quattrocentenario, Castello della Paneretta. I think it is a great wine for the price.

DESCRIBE YOUR WINE SELECTIONS, BOTH BY THE GLASS AND ON YOUR LIST.
Wines by the glass are mostly Italian, along with California and German wines and French Champagnes. The wine list is well-balanced. We have a good selection of Italian wines, both red and white, mostly from Tuscany and Piedmont. We also have a really nice French selection that features many first growths in varied vintages, along with some impressive red and white Burgundies. Our California selection is mostly comprised of producers who focus on low production, and includes a good selection of Cabernets and Chardonnays.

WHAT WINE ARE THE BEST VALUES IN YOUR RESTAURANT?
Red Burgundies and Tuscan blends.

NAME A COUPLE OF YOUR RESTAURANT'S SIGNATURE DISHES. WHAT TYPES OF WINE DO YOU PREFER TO RECOMMEND WITH EACH?
Osso buco Milanese with Barbaresco; linguine with lobster and shrimp with California Pinot Noir.

IN THE PAST YEAR, WHAT WINES IN YOUR WINE PROGRAM HAVE CUSTOMERS BECOME MORE WILLING TO ORDER?
Whatever we recommend. Customers are now very open to trying new wines.

Trattoria Marcella

3600 Watson Road
St. Louis, Missouri 63109-1232
phone 314-352-7706 fax 314-352-0848

Blake Shelton
SOMMELIER

WHAT ARE SOME OF YOUR ULTIMATE FOOD AND WINE PAIRINGS?
Braised veal cheeks with semolina gnocchi and Italian parsley salad paired with
Claudio Alario Dolcetto di Diano d'Alba "Costa Fiore"; pan-seared sweetbreads
with Champagne; ossobuco with Barolo or Barbaresco; foie gras with Pinot
Noir or Sauternes.

DESCRIBE YOUR WINE SELECTIONS.
We have a broad selection of Italian wines and a strong emphasis on California
wine from Monterey to Lake County.

WHAT CATEGORY OF WINE IS THE BEST VALUE IN YOUR RESTAURANT?
Piedmont wines, especially Dolcetto and Barbera. They offer great quality and
are not yet overpriced.

NAME A RECENT WINE DISCOVERY THAT EXCITED YOU.
Falesco Merlot from Umbria. The wine has the complexity of a Pomerol, with
good extraction, for less than forty dollars.

WHAT IS YOUR FAVORITE WINE REGION IN THE WORLD TODAY?
Vosne-Romanée in Burgundy. It is a magical place that produces the world's
most majestic wines.

WHAT LED YOU TO PURSUE A CAREER THAT INVOLVES WINE?
When I discovered Burgundy, it changed my whole perspective on wine and
the industry. A passion arose.

WHAT IS THE BEST ASPECT OF YOUR JOB?
Being able to introduce common restaurant diners to new wines that they perhaps have never seen or tasted.

IF YOU WERE NOT IN THE WINE PROFESSION, WHAT WOULD YOU BE
DOING?
Something in the music business or radio, unless I was on the PGA tour.

630 North and South Restaurant

Joseph King, Wine Buyer
630 North and South, University City
314-863-6013

Balaban's Restaurant

Steve McIntyre, Wine Buyer
405 North Euclid, Saint Louis
314-361-8085

Café Allegro

Steve Cole, Wine Buyer
1815 West 39th Street, Kansas City
816-561-3663

Café Eau

Mike Ward, Wine Buyer
212 North Kings Highway, St. Louis
314-454-9000

Duff's

Tim Kirby, Owner
and Wine Buyer
392 North Euclid Avenue, St. Louis
314-361-0522

Grand St. Café

Dennis Dickey, Wine Buyer
4740 Grand Street, Kansas City
816-561-8000

The Grill at the Ritz-Carlton Saint Louis

Neil Christensen, Wine Buyer
100 Carondelet Plaza, Clayton
314-863-6300

JJ's

Matt Nichols, General
Manager and Wine Buyer
910 West 48th Street, Kansas City
816-561-7136

The Potted Steer Restaurant

Joseph Boer, Owner
and Wine Buyer
5085 Highway 54, Lake Ozark
573-348-5053

Saint Louis Club

Robert Buehler, Sommelier
7701 Forsyth Boulevard, St. Louis
314-726-1964

Starker's Restaurant

Cliff Bath, Owner
and Wine Buyer
201 West 47th Street, Kansas City
816-753-3565

Buck's T-4 Lodge

46621 Gallatin Road
Big Sky, Montana 59716
phone 406-995-4111 fax 406-995-2191
website www.buckst4dining.com

David R. O'Connor
GENERAL MANAGER
AND WINE DIRECTOR

WHAT INSPIRED YOU TO PURSUE A CAREER THAT INVOLVES WINE?
Wine was always part of dinner in my family. Through trips to wine regions in America, I became very interested in all aspects of the industry.

NAME SOME OF YOUR FAVORITES WINES.
I enjoy Spanish reds for their complexity and intensity, Côtes du Rhône for the food-friendliness and rustic style and Washington Cabernets for sheer muscle and fruit quality.

NAME RECENT WINE DISCOVERIES THAT HAVE EXCITED YOU.
California red blends, which use new combinations of grapes; also, South American Malbecs.

WHAT WOULD YOU LIKE YOUR CUSTOMERS TO KNOW ABOUT YOU?
I enjoy skiing and fly-fishing and have become addicted to Montana.

IF YOU WERE NOT IN THIS PROFESSION, WHAT WOULD YOU BE?
Involved in the production end of the wine industry.

DESCRIBE YOUR WINE SELECTIONS, BOTH BY THE GLASS AND ON YOUR LIST.
Our list focuses on full-bodied reds that complement the menu's steak and wild game theme. I try to present a wide selection of varietals and regions.

WHAT ARE THE MOST UNIQUE FEATURES IN YOUR WINE PROGRAM?
We offer an extensive half-bottle selection, hold regular winemaker dinners and feature "flight nights" in summer.

NAME A FEW OF YOUR RESTAURANT'S SIGNATURE DISHES. WHAT TYPES OF WINE DO YOU PREFER TO RECOMMEND WITH EACH?
Pancetta-wrapped pheasant breast with Oregon Pinot Noir; bison tenderloin with Ribera del Duero; New Zealand red deer with Australian Shiraz.

WHAT WINES ARE CUSTOMERS NOW MORE WILLING TO ORDER?
Syrah and Shiraz and Washington wines.

Arthur's Grill
at the Pollard

DARCY KELLY, MANAGER
AND WINE BUYER

Two North Broadway, Red Lodge
406-446-0001

Aureole at the Mandalay Bay Resort

3950 Las Vegas Boulevard South
Las Vegas, Nevada 89119
phone 877-632-7800 fax 702-632-7443
website www.ewinetower.com

Andrew Bradbury
WINE DIRECTOR

NAME TWO OF YOUR FAVORITE WINE REGIONS FROM AROUND THE WORLD.
Austria and Germany, which make some of the world's greatest wines and at sensible prices.

NAME RECENT WINE DISCOVERIES THAT HAVE EXCITED YOU.
Spain and Portugal have been the source of some amazing wines, with new regions and young producers are contributing new treasures to the wine world.

IF YOU WERE NOT IN THIS PROFESSION, WHAT WOULD YOU BE DOING?
Scuba diving full-time in the tropics and being quite content.

DESCRIBE YOUR WINE SELECTIONS, BOTH BY THE GLASS AND ON YOUR LIST.
Aureole offers nearly four thousand selections from around the world that complement Chef Charlie Palmer's bold cuisine. We offer many great collections and verticals from some of the top wine producers in the world, and hundreds of half-bottle selections.

WHAT ARE THE MOST UNIQUE FEATURES IN YOUR WINE PROGRAM?
In addition to the world's coolest cellar, the "Wine Tower," we offer a one-of-a-kind wireless electronic wine list on Tablet PC that allows guests to surf and discover great wines from all over the planet! It is interactive and educational, and it's a great sales tool for our wine staff. I believe it is the future of wine sales and service and will allow customers to make more informed selections with more confidence.

WHAT CATEGORY OF WINE IS THE BEST VALUE IN YOUR RESTAURANT?
Austria and Germany for whites, and Italy and Spain for reds.

IN THE PAST YEAR, WHAT WINES IN YOUR WINE PROGRAM HAVE CUSTOMERS BECOME MORE WILLING TO ORDER?
New Zealand Sauvignon Blanc and Oregon Pinot Noir.

Aureole
at the Mandalay Bay Resort
3950 Las Vegas Boulevard South
Las Vegas, Nevada 89119
phone 877-632-7800 fax 702-632-7443
website www.ewinetower.com

Jaime Smith
HEAD SOMMELIER

NAME ONE OR TWO OF YOUR FAVORITE WINE DISTRICTS OR WINE
REGIONS FROM AROUND THE WORLD.
Champagne, for a region, and Riesling, for a variety. Riesling is the most noble
of all the varietals, and its results are stunning.

NAME RECENT WINE DISCOVERIES THAT HAVE EXCITED YOU.
Small-production Champagne houses and the resurgence of white wine from
Friuli.

WHAT BITS OF INFORMATION WOULD YOU LIKE YOUR CUSTOMERS TO
KNOW ABOUT YOU?
I was born to ride a bicycle.

IF YOU WERE NOT IN THIS PROFESSION, WHAT WOULD YOU BE?
An astronaut.

DESCRIBE YOUR WINE SELECTIONS, BOTH BY THE GLASS AND ON YOUR
LIST.
We have one of the greatest, if not the most circular and comprehensive "liquid
art" collections on earth. Our by-the-glass list is an extensive flavor profile.

WHAT ARE THE MOST UNIQUE FEATURES IN YOUR WINE PROGRAM?
We are the creators and developers of the first digital wine list ever.

WHAT CATEGORY OF WINE IS THE BEST VALUE IN YOUR RESTAURANT?
Some of the most quality-to-value wines are coming out of the Mediterranean
basin, particularly Italy, Greece and Portugal.

NAME A COUPLE OF YOUR RESTAURANT'S SIGNATURE DISHES. WHAT
TYPES OF WINE DO YOU PREFER TO RECOMMEND WITH EACH?
Caramelized sea scallops atop crimini mushrooms, fennel, baby spinach leaves
and a touch of Pernod with a top Barbera-Nebbiolo blend from Piedmont.

Aureole at the
Mandalay Bay Resort

3950 Las Vegas Boulevard South
Las Vegas, Nevada 89119
phone 877-632-7800 fax 702-632-7443
website www.ewinetower.com

Darius Allyn
SOMMELIER

NAME SOME OF YOUR FAVORITE WINE DISTRICTS.
Savennières, Saar and Wachau for whites, and Côte-Rôtie for red. They are
incredibly unique in their own way, and their pure, clean flavors make them a
hit with food pairing.

NAME RECENT WINE DISCOVERIES THAT HAVE EXCITED YOU.
Bierzo wines in Spain, especially the Corullon. They are high-quality, reasonably priced and completely distinctive wines.

IF YOU WERE NOT IN THIS PROFESSION, WHAT WOULD YOU BE DOING?
A musician. It's my other infatuation.

**DESCRIBE YOUR WINE SELECTIONS, BOTH BY THE GLASS AND ON YOUR
LIST.**
By-the-glass wines are uncommon, food-friendly selections that maintain bal-
ance and individualism. We supply the world's top wines and several rare wines.

WHAT ARE THE MOST UNIQUE FEATURES IN YOUR WINE PROGRAM?
Our forty-two-foot wine tower located inside the restaurant is unique. It epito-
mizes Las Vegas.

**NAME A FEW OF YOUR RESTAURANT'S SIGNATURE DISHES. WHAT TYPES
OF WINE DO YOU PREFER TO RECOMMEND WITH EACH?**
Our pan-seared scallop with shaved black truffles with a top Barbera-Nebbiolo
blend from Piedmont; Maine lobster with Thai curry sauce and coconut-
scented jasmine rice cake with German Riesling Spätlese or Alsace Pinot
Gris; roasted guinea hen breast with foie gras with great Rioja or Brunello.

**IN THE PAST YEAR, WHAT WINES IN YOUR WINE PROGRAM HAVE CUS-
TOMERS BECOME MORE WILLING TO ORDER?**
Spanish reds from Priorat, Australian Shiraz-Grenache blends, Argentine
Malbecs, German Rieslings and Austrian Grüner Veltliners.

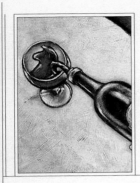

Craftsteak
at the MGM Grand Hotel

3799 Las Vegas Boulevard South
Las Vegas, Nevada 89109
phone 702-891-7318 fax 702-891-5899
website www.mgmgrand.com

Alison E. Fisher
MANAGER AND SOMMELIER

WHAT INSPIRED YOU TO PURSUE A CAREER THAT INVOLVES WINE?
A trip to Tuscany.

NAME TWO OF YOUR FAVORITE WINE REGIONS FROM AROUND THE WORLD.
Veneto, because it's where Amarone is made, and Mendoza, Argentina, which
makes some of the best wines I've ever tasted.

NAME RECENT WINE DISCOVERIES THAT HAVE EXCITED YOU.
Pinotage. It's very distinct and easy to identify in blind tasting.

WHAT WOULD YOU LIKE YOUR CUSTOMERS TO KNOW ABOUT YOU?
I'd really rather be drinking Bourbon.

IF YOU WERE NOT IN THIS PROFESSION, WHAT WOULD YOU BE DOING?
Public relations and diplomacy.

DESCRIBE YOUR WINE SELECTIONS, BOTH BY THE GLASS AND ON YOUR LIST.
We look for artisinal, esoteric producers whose wines complement the foods we
serve and the philosophy behind Tom Colicchio's cooking.

WHAT ARE THE MOST UNIQUE FEATURES IN YOUR WINE PROGRAM?
We have a large by-the-glass selection and extravagant wine dinners.

WHAT CATEGORY OF WINE IS THE BEST VALUE IN YOUR RESTAURANT?
The "Spicy, Full-Bodied Reds" section.

NAME A FEW OF YOUR RESTAURANT'S SIGNATURE DISHES. WHAT TYPES
OF WINE DO YOU PREFER TO RECOMMEND WITH EACH?
Braised short ribs with Barbera d'Alba; braised red king crab with grand cru
Chablis; Kobe flatiron steak with Amarone della Valpolicella.

WHAT WINES ARE CUSTOMERS NOW MORE WILLING TO ORDER?
Rioja and Priorat from Spain and Gewürztraminer from Alsace.

Craftsteak
at the MGM Grand Hotel

3799 Las Vegas Boulevard South
Las Vegas, Nevada 89109
phone 702-891-7318 fax 702-891-5899
website www.mgmgrand.com

Heather M. Branch
BEVERAGE DIRECTOR

NAME ONE OR TWO OF YOUR FAVORITE WINE DISTRICTS OR WINE REGIONS FROM AROUND THE WORLD.

I am an Austrian white fanatic, especially wines from Wachau. I also adore Savennières from the Loire Valley.

NAME RECENT WINE DISCOVERIES THAT HAVE EXCITED YOU.

Some of the new still red wines from Portugal are excellent. Jerry Luper, formerly of Diamond Creek, is making a voluptuous red, Quinta da Carolina, using only indigenous varieties.

IF YOU WERE NOT IN THIS PROFESSION, WHAT WOULD YOU BE DOING?

I would be in the Peace Corps.

DESCRIBE YOUR WINE SELECTIONS, BOTH BY THE GLASS AND ON YOUR LIST.

Craftsteak has twenty-one selections by the glass. These wines are somewhat esoteric, representing unusual varietals from as many different regions as possible. Our wine list focuses on boutique wineries that are family-run. And we always try to offer good values.

WHAT CATEGORY OF WINE IS THE BEST VALUE IN YOUR RESTAURANT?

Our Grenache section, which includes a spectacular range of styles and regions, from France and Spain to California and Australia.

NAME A COUPLE OF YOUR RESTAURANT'S SIGNATURE DISHES. WHAT TYPES OF WINE DO YOU PREFER TO RECOMMEND WITH EACH?

Our soft-shell crabs with Austrian Pinot Blanc; our braised short ribs with top Languedoc red.

Del Frisco's Double Eagle Steak House

3925 Paradise Road
Las Vegas, Nevada 89109
phone 702-796-0063 fax 702-796-0081
website www.delfriscos.com

Stephen Walker
SOMMELIER

WHAT INSPIRED YOU TO PURSUE A CAREER THAT INVOLVES WINE?
In 1982 I was between restaurant server positions when the manager of Bernard's at the Biltmore Hotel in Los Angeles offered me my first sommelier position.

NAME TWO OF YOUR FAVORITE WINE REGIONS FROM AROUND THE WORLD.
New Zealand, because I really enjoy its Sauvignon Blanc and Pinot Noir; I also like Australia for its rich Shiraz and Shiraz blends.

NAME RECENT WINE DISCOVERIES THAT HAVE EXCITED YOU.
Peregrine Pinot Noir from New Zealand is delicious; also, Morellino di Scansano, Costanza Malfatti, is a classy wine from an emerging region in Tuscany.

IF YOU WERE NOT IN THIS PROFESSION, WHAT WOULD YOU BE DOING?
Sales and marketing of high-value family education programs.

DESCRIBE YOUR WINE SELECTIONS, BOTH BY THE GLASS AND ON YOUR LIST.
We offer more than 800 selections from around the world, from more than thirty varietals.

WHAT ARE THE MOST UNIQUE FEATURES IN YOUR WINE PROGRAM?
Our extensive selection of Cabernet and Bordeaux; our large format bottles; and our world-class winemaker dinners. We also feature a page on the wine list with descriptions and special value offers.

NAME A COUPLE OF YOUR RESTAURANT'S SIGNATURE DISHES. WHAT TYPES OF WINE DO YOU PREFER TO RECOMMEND WITH EACH?
USDA prime Double Eagle strip steak or rib-eye with Napa Cabernet, Australian Shiraz, red Bordeaux or Tuscan red; Australian cold-water rock lobster tails with white Burgundy or New Zealand Sauvignon Blanc.

IN THE PAST YEAR, WHAT WINES IN YOUR WINE PROGRAM HAVE CUSTOMERS BECOME MORE WILLING TO ORDER?
Unclassified Bordeaux, Tuscan reds and Australian blends.

Delmonico's Steakhouse at the Venetian Resort

3355 Las Vegas Boulevard South
Las Vegas, Nevada 89109
phone 702-414-3737 fax 702-414-3838
website www.emerils.com

Kevin M. Vogt
MASTER SOMMELIER

WHAT INSPIRED YOU TO PURSUE A CAREER THAT INVOLVES WINE?
While working as a bartender at the Eldorado Hotel in Santa Fe, New Mexico, I started studying wine under my mentor, Peter C. Handler, who was one of the sharpest minds in the industry. Peter inspired me to take on the challenges of a career in the wine industry.

WHAT IS YOUR FAVORITE WINE REGION?
Piedmont, for its warm people, great wines and incredible scenery.

NAME RECENT WINE DISCOVERIES THAT HAVE EXCITED YOU.
Chile is making dramatic steps in increasing wine quality while still offering value. Some of its wines are amazing.

WHAT BITS OF INFORMATION WOULD YOU LIKE YOUR CUSTOMERS TO KNOW ABOUT YOU?
I was once held at gunpoint for four hours after accidentally wandering onto the Area 51 military base in the Nevada desert.

IF YOU WERE NOT IN THIS PROFESSION, WHAT WOULD YOU BE DOING?
My first degree was in computer science, so maybe something in the tech industry.

NAME A COUPLE OF YOUR RESTAURANT'S SIGNATURE DISHES. WHAT TYPES OF WINE DO YOU PREFER TO RECOMMEND WITH EACH?
Emeril's barbecue shrimp with a medium-sweet German Riesling; our bone-in rib steak, also known as the Cowboy Steak, is the single greatest steak I have ever had, and is incredible with Brunello di Montalcino or California Cabernet Sauvignon.

IN THE PAST YEAR, WHAT WINES IN YOUR WINE PROGRAM HAVE CUS-TOMERS BECOME MORE WILLING TO ORDER?
Italian wines. Italy has had a great run of vintages recently.

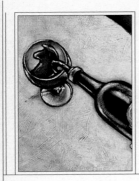

Elements and Tremezzo at Aladdin Resort and Casino

3667 Las Vegas Boulevard South
Las Vegas, Nevada 89109
phone 702-785-9003 fax 702-785-9058
website www.aladdincasino.com

Luis E. Reyneri
DIRECTOR OF FINE DINING
AND WINE AND SOMMELIER

NAME TWO OF YOUR FAVORITE WINE REGIONS FROM AROUND THE WORLD.
I love Burgundy for its style and tradition, and northern California for its innovation in winemaking styles, specifically with red varietals, and for its potential.

NAME RECENT WINE DISCOVERIES THAT HAVE EXCITED YOU.
Northstar Merlot from the Colombia Valley in Washington is fruit-driven and a great value. Col Solare, a joint venture between Piero Antinori and Chateau Ste. Michelle, uses Italian tradition in blending red varietals.

WHAT BITS OF INFORMATION WOULD YOU LIKE YOUR CUSTOMERS TO KNOW ABOUT YOU?
I was born in Cuba and raised in Miami, and attended Boston University. I enjoy wine and teaching about it, and am excited about my new consulting venture, Grape Advice at www.grapeadvice.com, where I also host private tasting parties.

DESCRIBE YOUR WINE SELECTIONS, BOTH BY THE GLASS AND ON YOUR LIST.
Our wines cover an array of varietals from wine regions around the world, with a focus on France, Italy and the United States, and an emphasis on California Cabernet Sauvignon, Merlot and Chardonnay. We recently constructed a wine bar, which offers rotating monthly features and a wide range of wines by-the-glass.

WHAT WINES ARE THE BEST VALUES IN YOUR RESTAURANTS?
Chilean Cabernet Sauvignon and Australian Shiraz.

NAME A FEW OF YOUR RESTAURANTS' SIGNATURE DISHES. WHAT TYPES OF WINE DO YOU PREFER TO RECOMMEND WITH EACH?
At Elements: Alaskan king crab legs with New Zealand Sauvignon Blanc; poached pear foie gras with Oregon Pinot Noir; and peppered rib-eye steak with California Zinfandel. At Tremezzo: lobster ravioli with an Italian Pinot Grigio; bone-in veal Parmesan with Brunello di Montalcino.

Galena Forest Restaurant

17025 Mount Rose Highway
Reno, Nevada 89511
phone 775-849-2100 fax 775-786-1314
website www.galenaforestrestaurant.com

Craig S. Cunningham
OWNER AND
WINE MANAGER

WHAT INSPIRED YOU TO PURSUE A CAREER THAT INVOLVES WINE?
Working in the food industry for more than twenty years, I fell in love with the
notion of wine and the nuances of the extensive varietals.

WHAT PART OF YOUR JOB DO YOU ENJOY THE MOST?
I enjoy making recommendations to customers and helping to introduce them
to a wide variety of styles.

NAME TWO OF YOUR FAVORITE WINES FROM AROUND THE WORLD.
Spanish reds and South African Cabernets.

NAME RECENT WINE DISCOVERIES THAT HAVE EXCITED YOU.
Spanish reds and South African Cabernets, because their value and quality are
exceptional.

IF YOU WERE NOT IN THIS PROFESSION, WHAT WOULD YOU BE DOING?
Architecture and design for both commercial and residential buildings.

DESCRIBE YOUR WINE SELECTIONS, BOTH BY THE GLASS AND ON YOUR LIST.
We have approximately 250 wines on our list. Most of our wines are from
California, but we also have representations from France, Italy, Spain, South
Africa, Australia and Oregon.

WHAT ARE THE MOST UNIQUE FEATURES IN YOUR WINE PROGRAM?
We have an extensive selection of half-bottles. We offer weekly wine tastings,
with each selection paired with food.

WHAT WINES ARE THE BEST VALUES IN YOUR RESTAURANT?
Spanish reds and Australian wines.

NAME A COUPLE OF YOUR RESTAURANT'S SIGNATURE DISHES. WHAT
TYPES OF WINE DO YOU PREFER TO RECOMMEND WITH EACH?
Wild boar with blackberries and golden chanterelles paired with red Hermitage;
black walnuts and Roquefort cheese with Sauternes.

Hugo's Cellar
at the Four Queens Hotel

202 Fremont Street
Las Vegas, Nevada 89101
phone 702-385-4011 fax 702-387-5120
website www.fourqueens.com

Vincent K. Wiggins
SOMMELIER

WHAT ARE SOME OF YOUR ULTIMATE FOOD AND WINE PAIRINGS?
"Queens Lobster" with sun-dried tomatoes and mushrooms, beurre blanc, and crushed red peppers with Pinot Blanc; salmon with herb butter and classic Chardonnay; grilled veal chop with Pinot Noir; a thick New York strip steak with crushed peppercorn and garlic paired with Sangiovese.

DESCRIBE YOUR WINE SELECTIONS.
Our 250-item wine list concentrates on an array of Californian, French and Italian wines, with selections from several other countries, as well.

WHAT CATEGORY OF WINE IS THE BEST VALUE IN YOUR RESTAURANT?
South American wines. They offer a huge variety of wines and styles at great prices.

WHAT IS YOUR FAVORITE WINE REGION IN THE WORLD TODAY?
Burgundy, for its Pinot Noir grape, which comes in a wide variety of styles. Pinot Noir is one of the most food-friendly varietals.

WHAT LED YOU TO PURSUE A CAREER THAT INVOLVES WINE?
I have a food and beverage management background, and while living in Northern California, I was surrounded by avid wine enthusiasts.

WHAT ARE THE BEST ASPECTS OF YOUR JOB?
Turning guests on to new varietals and then, on later visits, having them tell me those varietals have become their favorites.

IF YOU WERE NOT IN THE WINE PROFESSION, WHAT WOULD YOU BE DOING?
Music. I was a drummer and singer in a Bay Area rock and funk band and I still sit in with a few local bands. How does it go? "Wine, women and song!"

Lone Eagle Grille
at Lake Tahoe Hyatt Regency Hotel

111 Country Club Drive
Incline Village, Nevada 89451
phone 775-832-1234 fax 775-831-7508
website www.hyattahoe.com

Robert G. Vicale
SENIOR SOMMELIER

WHAT INSPIRED YOU TO PURSUE A CAREER THAT INVOLVES WINE?
My father's only hobby was wine, and he imparted his love for and interest in it to me.

WHAT PART OF YOUR JOB DO YOU ENJOY THE MOST?
Constantly changing the list to keep it fresh and intriguing for our guests.

NAME TWO OF YOUR FAVORITE WINE DISTRICTS.
Napa and Amador.

IF YOU WERE NOT IN THIS PROFESSION, WHAT WOULD YOU BE DOING?
Teaching Greek and Roman mythology.

DESCRIBE YOUR WINE SELECTIONS, BOTH BY THE GLASS AND ON YOUR LIST.
We are known for our California Cabernet Sauvignon and Oregon Pinot Noir selections. We offer fifteen selections by the glass, including two of each of the major varietals.

WHAT ARE THE MOST UNIQUE FEATURES IN YOUR WINE PROGRAM?
Because of our proximity to the California and Oregon wine country, we are able to constantly change our list to reflect current availability and complement our guests' ever-changing tastes.

WHAT CATEGORY OF WINE IS THE BEST VALUE IN YOUR RESTAURANT?
The greatest values on our list currently are Zinfandel, Syrah and Petit Syrah.

NAME A FEW OF YOUR RESTAURANT'S SIGNATURE DISHES. WHAT TYPES OF WINE DO YOU PREFER TO RECOMMEND WITH EACH?
Venison chop and Dry Creek Zinfandel; Angus filet or porterhouse with Howell Mountain Cabernet; Chilean sea bass with Oregon Pinot Noir.

WHAT WINES ARE CUSTOMERS NOW MORE WILLING TO ORDER?
Howell Mountain Cabernet, Amador Zinfandel and Oregon Pinot Noir and Pinot Gris.

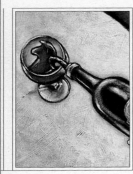

MGM Grand Hotel

3799 Las Vegas Boulevard South
Las Vegas, Nevada 89109
phone 702-891-7777 fax 702-891-7330
website www.mgmgrand.com

Kim Beto
DIRECTOR OF BEVERAGE

WHAT ARE SOME OF YOUR ULTIMATE FOOD AND WINE PAIRINGS?
Banyuls and chocolate; Sauternes and Stilton.

DESCRIBE YOUR WINE SELECTIONS.
We have various programs at MGM. Individual restaurants have different wine programs. There are some amazing wines on the hotel's reserve list.

NAME RECENT WINE DISCOVERIES THAT HAVE EXCITED YOU.
Priorat in Spain. Insane wines! Alvaro Palacios is awesome.

WHAT IS YOUR FAVORITE WINE REGION IN THE WORLD TODAY?
Champagne. Incredible history and great food and wine. Also, both Alsace and Burgundy, which produce phenomenal wines.

WHAT LED YOU TO YOUR CURRENT POSITION?
I've loved wine since I was very young. My father introduced me to wine and Fred Dame got me "hooked."

WHAT ARE THE BEST ASPECTS OF YOUR JOB?
Seeing someone selling or talking about something you showed them. Developing people.

IF YOU WERE NOT IN THIS PROFESSION, WHAT WOULD YOU BE?
A tennis player.

Morton's of Chicago
Las Vegas

400 East Flamingo Road
Las Vegas, Nevada 89109
phone 702-893-0703 fax 702-893-3020

Pierre A. Gendebien

ASSISTANT MANAGER AND SOMMELIER

WHAT ARE SOME OF YOUR ULTIMATE FOOD AND WINE PAIRINGS?
Filet Oskar with a well-defined Cabernet; scallops wrapped in bacon with a spicy apricot chutney paired with Zinfandel.

DESCRIBE YOUR WINE SELECTIONS.
We offer a very diverse selection of wines to our guests. Red wines dominate our offerings, since we are a steakhouse.

WHAT CATEGORY OF WINE IS THE BEST VALUE IN YOUR RESTAURANT?
Pinot Noirs.

NAME RECENT WINE DISCOVERIES THAT HAVE EXCITED YOU.
Australian wines. They offer quality for great value.

WHAT IS YOUR FAVORITE WINE REGION IN THE WORLD TODAY?
France. It offers so many different terroirs and wines that pair well with food.

WHAT LED YOU TO PURSUE A CAREER THAT INVOLVES WINE?
I grew up in a European family and wine was always part of our lives. It grew into a passion.

WHAT IS THE BEST ASPECT OF YOUR JOB?
People. From guests to vendors, people make my job challenging and very rewarding.

IF YOU WERE NOT IN THIS PROFESSION, WHAT WOULD YOU DO?
Become a pilot and travel the world.

Olives
at the Bellagio Resort
3600 Las Vegas Boulevard South
Las Vegas, Nevada 89109
phone 702-693-1111 fax 702-693-8511

Tammie W. Ruesenberg
SOMMELIER

WHAT IS ONE OF YOUR ULTIMATE FOOD AND WINE PAIRINGS?
Spicy tuna tartare with Domaines Schlumberger 1998 Pinot Gris from Alsace.

DESCRIBE YOUR WINE SELECTIONS.
We pour twenty premier wines by the glass and have a 300-item wine list,
which includes wines from around the world. We also have access to the
Bellagio master list of another 900 wines.

WHAT IS YOUR FAVORITE WINE REGION IN THE WORLD TODAY?
California. I love the New World style of the wines, as do most of our guests.

WHAT LED YOU TO PURSUE A CAREER THAT INVOLVES WINE?
I had worked both in the restaurant industry and as a sales rep for a wine dis-
tributor.

WHAT IS THE MOST CHALLENGING ASPECT OF YOUR JOB?
Being able to buy wines I want to keep on our list. Many are in short supply.

IF YOU WERE NOT IN THIS PROFESSION, WHAT WOULD YOU BE DOING?
I just can't imagine doing anything else.

Pamplemousse

400 East Sahara Avenue
Las Vegas, Nevada 89104
phone 702-733-2066 fax 702-733-9139
website www.pamplemousserestaurant.com

Reggie King
MANAGER, MAÎTRE D'
AND SOMMELIER

WHAT INSPIRED YOU TO PURSUE A CAREER THAT INVOLVES WINE?
We serve no hard liquor at Pamplemousse, so it became necessary right away to learn about wine.

NAME TWO OF YOUR FAVORITE WINES.
White Burgundy and California Pinot Noir. Pinot Noir improves there every year, and is a great value for such quality wines.

NAME RECENT WINE DISCOVERIES THAT HAVE EXCITED YOU.
Robert Sinskey Pinot Noir and Reserve Pinot Noir. The new releases are superb.

WHAT BITS OF INFORMATION WOULD YOU LIKE YOUR CUSTOMERS TO KNOW ABOUT YOU?
I have been employed at Pamplemousse since September 1984. Wine is my number one professional focus.

IF YOU WERE NOT IN THIS PROFESSION, WHAT WOULD YOU BE DOING?
Acting or writing.

DESCRIBE YOUR WINE SELECTIONS, BOTH BY THE GLASS AND ON YOUR LIST.
Our wines by the glass, as well as wine list selections, pair with our cuisine of fresh fish, veal medallions, prime beef and our house specialty, roast duckling.

WHAT IS A UNIQUE FEATURE IN YOUR WINE PROGRAM?
We have a list of wines in half-bottle.

WHAT CATEGORY OF WINE IS THE BEST VALUE IN YOUR RESTAURANT?
California Chardonnay.

NAME A COUPLE OF YOUR RESTAURANT'S SIGNATURE DISHES. WHAT TYPES OF WINE DO YOU PREFER TO RECOMMEND WITH EACH?
Salmon with orange and curry sauce and California Sauvignon Blanc; roast duck with a cranberry and Chambord French raspberry liquor sauce with California Pinot Noir.

Pearl at the MGM Grand

3799 Las Vegas Boulevard South
Las Vegas, Nevada 89109
phone 702-891-7380 fax 702-891-7610
website www.mgmgrand.com

Piotr S. Szczurko
SOMMELIER

NAME RECENT WINE DISCOVERIES THAT HAVE EXCITED YOU.
New Zealand's white wines have great acidity, turbo-charged fruit and a long finish; its reds also are excellent, especially Pinot Noir.

IF YOU WERE NOT IN THIS PROFESSION, WHAT WOULD YOU BE DOING?
In Poland, I attended agricultural school. I would probably be some sort of gardener, or maybe even have my own vineyard.

DESCRIBE YOUR WINE SELECTIONS, BOTH BY THE GLASS AND ON YOUR LIST.
We try to keep things simple. Our regular wine list has about 180 wines and our reserve list has about forty-five selections. Plus, we have twelve wines that we feature by the glass.

WHAT IS THE MOST UNIQUE FEATURE IN YOUR WINE PROGRAM?
The wines we offer have an international appeal and are food-friendly.

WHAT CATEGORIES OF WINE ARE THE BEST VALUES IN YOUR RESTAURANT?
Wines on our reserve wine list and in our mid-priced category wines ($100–$250), especially in the California Meritage category.

NAME A COUPLE OF YOUR RESTAURANT'S SIGNATURE DISHES. WHAT TYPES OF WINE DO YOU PREFER TO RECOMMEND WITH EACH?
Steamed Maine and Australia lobster paired with Napa Valley Chardonnay; crispy garlic chicken paired with Mosel Riesling Spätlese; wok-fried filet of venison and asparagus with Napa Valley Cabernet Sauvignon; spiced king crab legs with Riesling from Washington or Germany.

IN THE PAST YEAR, WHAT WINES IN YOUR WINE PROGRAM HAVE CUSTOMERS BECOME MORE WILLING TO ORDER?
German Riesling, Italian Pinot Grigio and California Pinot Noir.

Red Square at the Mandalay Bay Resort

3950 Las Vegas Boulevard South
Las Vegas, Nevada 89119
phone 702-632-7407 fax 702-632-6925
website www.mandalaybay.com

Steve Moberly
CO-MANAGER

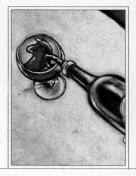

WHAT INSPIRED YOU TO PURSUE A CAREER THAT INVOLVES WINE?
My first job out of college was working for a hotel that was owned by Don Carano of the Ferrari-Carano Winery. Everyone at the hotel was into wine. I was almost forced to learn about it just to hold a conversation with my peers.

NAME ONE OF YOUR FAVORITE WINE REGIONS FROM AROUND THE WORLD.
South Africa, Stellenbosch in particular. It's what Australia was eight years ago with its high-quality wines at great values.

WHAT BITS OF INFORMATION WOULD YOU LIKE YOUR CUSTOMERS TO KNOW ABOUT YOU?
I am an avid mountain biker, rock climber and adventure traveler. Whenever I travel, I am known for bringing a couple of bottles of nice wine. Nothing beats sharing a nice bottle with friends and family.

IF YOU WERE NOT IN THIS PROFESSION, WHAT WOULD YOU BE?
A professional mountain biker or in some kind of guiding service.

DESCRIBE YOUR WINE SELECTIONS, BOTH BY THE GLASS AND ON YOUR LIST.
Our wine list includes big-name wines and hard-to-find wines from quality producers and new regions that have great potential.

WHAT CATEGORY OF WINE IS THE BEST VALUE IN YOUR RESTAURANT?
South African wine.

NAME ONE OF YOUR RESTAURANT'S SIGNATURE DISHES. WHAT WINE DO YOU PREFER TO RECOMMEND WITH IT?
Roquefort-crusted filet mignon with Stellenbosch Cabernet Sauvignon from South Africa.

IN THE PAST YEAR, WHAT WINES IN YOUR WINE PROGRAM HAVE CUSTOMERS BECOME MORE WILLING TO ORDER?
Cabernet Sauvignon and Merlot.

Renoir
at the Mirage Hotel
3400 Las Vegas Boulevard South
Las Vegas, Nevada 89109
phone 702-791-7353 fax 702-791-7437
website www.mirage.com

Stewart G. Patchefsky
WINE DIRECTOR
AND SOMMELIER

WHAT ARE SOME OF YOUR ULTIMATE FOOD AND WINE PAIRINGS?
Sautéed foie gras with Tokaji Aszú; salads that combine fresh apples or pears with Roquefort cheese and German Kabinett Riesling.

DESCRIBE YOUR WINE SELECTIONS.
We have a classical wine list, with approximately 650 selections, that focuses on quality French and Californian wines.

WHAT CATEGORY OF WINE IS THE BEST VALUE IN YOUR RESTAURANT?
German wines. Germany offers some perfectly balanced wines that are also modestly priced.

NAME A RECENT WINE DISCOVERY.
I have come to realize that the wine industry, or shall I say community, is much smaller than I had first anticipated.

WHAT IS YOUR FAVORITE WINE REGION IN THE WORLD TODAY?
Champagne. I love the history, the people and, most of all, the wine.

WHAT LED YOU TO PURSUE A CAREER THAT INVOLVES WINE?
When I was a waiter at The Phoenician Resort in Arizona, I became fascinated with the sommelier position. It was obviously the best job in the resort. After attending an organized wine trip to Napa Valley, I knew that I would become a sommelier.

WHAT IS THE BEST ASPECT OF YOUR JOB?
The exposure I have to such a wide range of interesting people. I learn so much about life from other people's experiences.

IF YOU WERE NOT IN THIS PROFESSION, WHAT WOULD YOU BE DOING?
Real estate.

Rosemary's Restaurant

8125 West Sahara Avenue
Las Vegas, Nevada 89117
phone 702-869-2251 fax 702-869-2283
website www.rosemarysrestaurant.com

Nick W. Hetzel
RESTAURANT MANAGER
AND WINE STEWARD

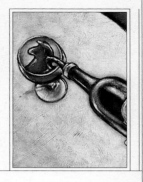

WHAT INSPIRED YOU TO PURSUE A CAREER THAT INVOLVES WINE?
A college buddy who is a sommelier opened a bottle of 1982 Bollinger R.D. to taste my first Champagne. It's been downhill since!

NAME YOUR FAVORITE WINE REGIONS.
Burgundy. I always go back to Burgundy. Its wines are the best food wines.

NAME RECENT WINE DISCOVERIES THAT HAVE EXCITED YOU.
Russian River and Sonoma Coast Pinot Noir and Santa Barbara Sauvignon Blanc.

WHAT BITS OF INFORMATION WOULD YOU LIKE YOUR CUSTOMERS TO KNOW ABOUT YOU?
My passion is golf; however, most outdoor activities excite me. Spending eighty hours a week inside these walls make me appreciate fresh air.

IF YOU WERE NOT IN THIS PROFESSION, WHAT WOULD YOU BE?
A PGA teaching professional or financial planner.

DESCRIBE YOUR WINE SELECTIONS, BOTH BY THE GLASS AND ON YOUR LIST.
Approximately 250 selections with an emphasis on American and French wines to mirror our style of cuisine. Most of the depth and excitement comes from Pinot Noir and Chardonnay.

WHAT ARE THE MOST UNIQUE FEATURES IN YOUR WINE PROGRAM?
We have fifty to seventy-five half-bottles and fifty percent off bottles of wine on Sunday night.

WHAT WINES ARE THE BEST VALUES IN YOUR RESTAURANT?
Sauvignon Blanc and red Bordeaux.

NAME A COUPLE OF YOUR RESTAURANT'S SIGNATURE DISHES. WHAT TYPES OF WINE DO YOU PREFER TO RECOMMEND WITH EACH?
Goat cheese–stuffed Piquillo peppers with an off-dry Gewürztraminer; crispy-skin striped bass with andouille and Creole Meunière with Gigondas.

Valentino Restaurant at the Venetian Resort

3355 Las Vegas Boulevard South
Las Vegas, Nevada 89109
phone 702-414-3000 fax 702-414-3099

Steve Hua
SOMMELIER

WHAT INSPIRED YOU TO PURSUE A CAREER THAT INVOLVES WINE?
The desire to taste the best wines in the world.

WHAT PART OF YOUR JOB DO YOU ENJOY THE MOST?
Making suggestions to guests and seeing their eyes light up when they sip the wines.

YOUR FAVORITE WINE REGION?
Piedmont. I especially like super-Piedmont wines (blends of Barbera, Dolcetto, and/or Nebbiolo with a splash of Cabernet or Merlot).

NAME RECENT WINE DISCOVERIES THAT HAVE EXCITED YOU.
Super-Piedmont blends.

IF YOU WERE NOT IN THIS PROFESSION, WHAT WOULD YOU BE DOING?
Something involving computers.

DESCRIBE YOUR WINE SELECTIONS, BOTH BY THE GLASS AND ON YOUR LIST.
We have sixty wines by the glass, 2,400 selections on the wine list and 150 wines in half-bottles.

WHAT IS THE MOST UNIQUE FEATURE IN YOUR WINE PROGRAM?
Our list of 150 half-bottles, which is still expanding.

WHAT CATEGORY OF WINE IS THE BEST VALUE IN YOUR RESTAURANT?
Old vintages of Italian wine. We don't increase the prices of these wines as we update the list.

NAME A COUPLE OF YOUR RESTAURANT'S SIGNATURE DISHES. WHAT TYPES OF WINE DO YOU PREFER TO RECOMMEND WITH EACH?
White truffles with Barolo; crab salad with Vermentino.

IN THE PAST YEAR, WHAT WINES IN YOUR WINE PROGRAM HAVE CUSTOMERS BECOME MORE WILLING TO ORDER?
Super-Tuscan wines.

White Orchid
at the Peppermill Hotel and Casino

2707 South Virginia Street
Reno, Nevada 89502
phone 775-689-7300 fax 775-689-7189
website www.peppermillreno.com

John R. Sanders
MAÎTRE D'HÔTEL AND SOMMELIER

NAME YOUR FAVORITE WINE DISTRICTS.
Stags Leap District and Oakville capture the essence of my favorite variety, Cabernet Sauvignon.

WHAT RECENT WINE DISCOVERIES HAVE EXCITED YOU?
New Zealand's Sauvignon Blanc and Chilean Cabernet Sauvignon and Merlot blends for value, quality, freshness and excitement.

IF YOU WERE NOT IN THIS PROFESSION, WHAT WOULD YOU BE DOING?
I would probably be sitting in the Ivory Tower, surrounded by impressionable young minds, or living in a Zapotec village.

DESCRIBE YOUR WINE SELECTIONS, BOTH BY THE GLASS AND ON YOUR LIST.
Of our 800 wine selections, the majority are from California. We are known for our vertical collections of California Cabernet Sauvignon and Bordeaux-style blends.

WHAT ARE THE MOST UNIQUE FEATURES IN YOUR WINE PROGRAM?
We offer thirty wines by the glass, and every month we feature a different winery, serving almost all offerings by the glass. Our monthly winemaker dinners always sell out.

NAME A COUPLE OF YOUR RESTAURANT'S SIGNATURE DISHES. WHAT TYPES OF WINE DO YOU PREFER TO RECOMMEND WITH EACH?
Filet mignon on portobello mushroom cap with Roquefort cheese and Cabernet syrup served with Sonoma County Cabernet Sauvignon; butter-poached live Maine lobster with chive butter sauce served with Carneros Chardonnay.

IN THE PAST YEAR, WHAT WINES IN YOUR WINE PROGRAM HAVE CUSTOMERS BECOME MORE WILLING TO ORDER?
Syrah, Zinfandel and Pinot Noir.

Alize at the Top of the Palms
CLAUDIO VIGANI, SOMMELIER
4321 West Flamingo Road, Las Vegas
702-951-7000

Andre's
CLAUDIO VIGANI, SOMMELIER
401 South Sixth Street, Las Vegas
702-385-5016

Andre's French Restaurant at the Monte Carlo
CLAUDIO VIGANI, SOMMELIER
3770 Las Vegas Boulevard South,
Las Vegas
702-798-7151

Aqua at the Bellagio Resort
CALEB DIAL, SOMMELIER
3600 Las Vegas Boulevard South,
Las Vegas
702-693-7111

Caesars Palace
LISA LEROUX, BEVERAGE DIRECTOR
3570 Las Vegas Boulevard South,
Las Vegas
702-731-7110

Caesars Tahoe
DIANE DOMINGUEZ,
PROPERTY SOMMELIER
55 Highway 50, Lake Tahoe
775-588-3515

Charlie Palmer Steak at Four Seasons Hotel
JASON WADE, WINE DIRECTOR
AND SOMMELIER
3960 Las Vegas Boulevard South,
Las Vegas
702-632-5000

China Grill at Mandalay Bay Resort
STEVE TORGASON, WINE BUYER
3950 Las Vegas Boulevard South,
Las Vegas
702-632-7777

Chinois Las Vegas at the Forum Shops at Caesars
LUIS DE SANTOS, MASTER
SOMMELIER AND DIRECTOR
OF WINE
3500 Las Vegas Boulevard South,
Las Vegas
702-737-9700

Circo at the Bellagio Resort
PAOLO BARBIERI, MASTER
SOMMELIER AND WINE DIRECTOR
ROBERT BIGELOW, SOMMELIER
PATRICK PRETZ, SOMMELIER
3600 Las Vegas Boulevard South,
Las Vegas
702-693-8150

Crown Point Restaurant at Gold Hill Hotel
NICK FAIN, BEVERAGE MANAGER
1540 South Main, Gold Hill
775-847-0111

Eiffel Tower Restaurant at the Paris Resort

DEANA ERICKSON, SOMMELIER
GULNARA JANZ, SOMMELIER
3655 Las Vegas Boulevard, Las Vegas
702-948-6937

Emeril's New Orleans Fish House at the MGM Grand

RICHARD FLETCHER, SOMMELIER
3799 Las Vegas Boulevard South,
Las Vegas
702-891-7777

Ferraro's

GINO FERRARO, WINE BUYER
5900 West Flamingo Road,
Las Vegas
702-364-5300

Fiore Rotisserie and Grille at the Rio

RYAN VOSS, SOMMELIER
3700 West Flamingo Road, Las Vegas
702-252-7702

The Grill at Quail Corners

SAM FRANCOVICH, WINE BUYER
6520 South McCarran Boulevard,
Reno
775-827-6262

Llewellyn's at Harvey's

GREG PSILOPOULOS, SOMMELIER
U.S. Highway 50 and
Stateline Avenue, Stateline
775-588-2411

Mayflower Cuisinier

THERESA WOO, MANAGER
AND WINE BUYER
4750 West Sahara, Suite 27,
Las Vegas
702-870-8432

Nob Hill at MGM Grand Hotel

RAJAT PARR, SOMMELIER
3799 Las Vegas Boulevard South,
Las Vegas
877-793-7111

Picasso at the Bellagio Resort

JAY JAMES, MASTER SOMMELIER
AND WINE DIRECTOR
ROBERT SMITH, SOMMELIER
3600 Las Vegas Boulevard South,
Las Vegas
702-693-7111

Pinot Brasserie at the Venetian Resort

JOSEPH HELPHINSTINE,
WINE BUYER
3355 Las Vegas Boulevard South,
Las Vegas
702-735-8888

Postrio at the Venetian Resort

LUIS DE SANTOS, MASTER
SOMMELIER AND WINE DIRECTOR
3355 Las Vegas Boulevard South,
Las Vegas
702-796-1110

Prime
at the Bellagio Resort

JOHN BURKE, SOMMELIER
JASON QUINN,
ASSISTANT SOMMELIER
3600 Las Vegas Boulevard South,
Las Vegas
702-693-7223

Roxy's
at the El Dorado
Hotel

ALAIN GREGOIRE, MAÎTRE D'
345 North Virginia Street, Reno
800-648-5966

Smith & Wollensky

SPENCER BRINTON,
CELLAR MASTER
NOEL CULLEN,
BEVERAGE MANAGER
3767 Las Vegas Boulevard South,
Las Vegas
702-862-4100

Spago Las Vegas
at the Forum Shops
at Caesars

LUIS DE SANTOS, DIRECTOR OF
WINE AND MASTER SOMMELIER
3500 Las Vegas Boulevard South,
Las Vegas
702-369-6300

Trattoria del Lupo
at the Mandalay
Bay Resort

LUIS DE SANTOS, MASTER
SOMMELIER AND WINE DIRECTOR
3950 Las Vegas Boulevard South,
Las Vegas
702-740-5522

Treasure Island

RICK GOLDSTEIN, FOOD AND
BEVERAGE DIRECTOR
3400 Las Vegas Boulevard South,
Las Vegas
702-894-7111

The 1785 Inn and Restaurant

3582 White Mountain Highway
North Conway, New Hampshire 03860
phone 603-356-9025 fax 603-356-6081
website www.the1785inn.com

Charles D. Mallar

OWNER AND SOMMELIER

NAME YOUR FAVORITE WINE DISTRICTS OR WINE REGIONS FROM AROUND THE WORLD.
Bordeaux, Tuscany and Napa Valley. I like big, bold reds.

NAME RECENT WINE DISCOVERIES THAT HAVE EXCITED YOU.
Australian reds. They are still good values, as are South American reds.

WHAT WOULD YOU LIKE YOUR CUSTOMERS TO KNOW ABOUT YOU?
I'm an organic gardener and grow organic herbs and vegetables for the restaurant.

IF YOU WERE NOT IN THIS PROFESSION, WHAT WOULD YOU BE DOING?
Teaching at a college.

DESCRIBE YOUR WINE SELECTIONS, BOTH BY THE GLASS AND ON YOUR LIST.
We have a wide range of wines available by the glass or bottle. We're known for our wines from California and France, as well as those from Italy and other wine regions.

WHAT IS THE MOST UNIQUE FEATURE IN YOUR WINE PROGRAM?
We offer rare wines by the ounce so that customers can afford to sample them.

WHAT CATEGORY OF WINE IS THE BEST VALUE IN YOUR RESTAURANT?
California Merlot.

NAME A COUPLE OF YOUR RESTAURANT'S SIGNATURE DISHES. WHAT TYPES OF WINE DO YOU PREFER TO RECOMMEND WITH EACH?
Rack of lamb with red Bordeaux or Napa Meritage; elk chop with Napa Meritage.

WHAT WINES ARE CUSTOMERS NOW MORE WILLING TO ORDER?
Oregon Pinot Noir.

WHAT ARE SOME OTHER ULTIMATE WINE AND FOOD PAIRINGS?
Asian cuisine with acidic Riesling; barbecue with big, fruity Zinfandel.

Kingston 1686 House Inc

MARLENE GILLESPIE, OWNER
AND WINE BUYER
127 Main Street, Kingston
603-642-3637

Ya Mama's

MICHELLE FERRAZANNI,
OWNER AND WINE BUYER
75 Daniel Webster Highway,
Merrimack
603-578-9201

The Bernards Inn

27 Mine Brook Road
Bernardsville, New Jersey 07924
phone 908-766-0002 fax 908-766-4604
website www.bernardsinn.com

Terri A. Baldwin
WINE DIRECTOR
AND SOMMELIER

NAME ONE OR TWO OF YOUR FAVORITE WINE DISTRICTS OR WINE
REGIONS FROM AROUND THE WORLD.
Burgundy's Côte de Nuits for its elegant Échezeaux and both Napa Valley and
Alexander Valley for their proprietary and red Meritage blends.

NAME RECENT WINE DISCOVERIES THAT HAVE EXCITED YOU.
New Zealand Sauvignon Blanc and Pinot Noir, and Washington State and
Portuguese reds.

WHAT BITS OF INFORMATION WOULD YOU LIKE YOUR CUSTOMERS TO
KNOW ABOUT YOU?
I participate in bowling tournaments when time allows, and I belong to WASA
(Women's All-Star Association), a semi-professional bowling organization.

NAME A FEW OF YOUR RESTAURANT'S SIGNATURE DISHES. WHAT TYPES
OF WINE DO YOU PREFER TO RECOMMEND WITH EACH?
Hudson Valley foie gras, sweet corn pancake, quince sauce paired with Vidal Ice
Wine from Canada; baked New York State goat cheese on brioche with grilled
vegetables paired with New Zealand Sauvignon Blanc; seared ahi tuna paired
with red Burgundy or Pinot Noir; dry-aged New York sirloin, potato and
Georgia onion gratin, demi-glaze paired with proprietary red or red Meritage.

IN THE PAST YEAR, WHAT WINES IN YOUR WINE PROGRAM HAVE CUS-
TOMERS BECOME MORE WILLING TO ORDER?
High-end wines by the glass. I also find that customers are always pleasantly
surprised when introduced to a proprietary red or red Meritage.

WHAT ARE SOME OTHER ULTIMATE WINE AND FOOD PAIRINGS?
Pizza and Edna Valley Pinot Noir.

Fromagerie
26 Ridge Road
Rumson, New Jersey 07760
phone 732-842-8088 fax 732-842-6625

Markus Peter
OWNER AND SOMMELIER

WHAT ARE SOME OF YOUR ULTIMATE FOOD AND WINE PAIRINGS?
Seared foie gras and vanilla compote with Alois Kracher 1997 Beerenauslese
from Austria.

DESCRIBE YOUR WINE SELECTIONS.
Our wine list has many selections from California and reflects my interest in
white and red Burgundies, but the rest of the world can be tasted here, too.

WHAT IS YOUR FAVORITE WINE REGION IN THE WORLD TODAY?
Alsace. I love the food and the wines, and the towns and villages are beautiful.

WHAT LED YOU TO PURSUE A CAREER THAT INVOLVES WINE?
Winery visits to Burgundy, Germany, Alsace, Bordeaux and California.

WHAT IS THE MOST CHALLENGING ASPECT OF YOUR JOB?
Not being able to help every customer with his wine selection. I want everyone
to get the most enjoyment from their experience here.

IF YOU WERE NOT IN THE WINE PROFESSION, WHAT WOULD YOU BE?
Travel writer.

Diamond's
TOMMY ZACHETTI, OWNER
AND WINE BUYER
132 Kent Street, Trenton
609-393-1000

The Dining Room at Hilton Short Hills
ISAAC ALEXANDER, SOMMELIER
41 J.F.K. Parkway, Short Hills
973-379-0100

Grand Café
DESMOND LLOYD, OWNER
AND WINE BUYER
42 Washington Street, Morristown
973-540-9444

La Griglia
CHRIS TOCCI, SOMMELIER
Boulevard and 26th, Kenilworth
908-241-0031

The Manor
MIKE CAMARANO, WINE BUYER
KURT KNOWLES, WINE BUYER
111 Prospect Avenue, West Orange
973-731-2360

Panico's
JOSE SOLANO, WINE BUYER
103 Church Street, New Brunswick
732-545-6100

Park and Orchard
BUDDY GEBHARDT, OWNER
AND WINE BUYER
240 Hackensack Street,
East Rutherford
201-939-9292

The Ryland Inn
CRAIG SHELTON, CHEF,
OWNER AND WINE BUYER
Route 22, Whitehouse
908-534-4011

Verve American Bar and Restaurant
RICK ST. PIERRE, OWNER
AND WINE BUYER
18 East Main Street, Somerville
908-707-8655

Billy Crews
Dining Room
1200 Country Club Road
Santa Teresa, New Mexico 88008
phone 505-589-2071 fax 505-589-9463
website www.billycrews.com

Billy Crews
OWNER AND WINE BUYER

WHAT IS ONE OF YOUR ULTIMATE FOOD AND WINE PAIRINGS?
Great steak with a great wine.

DESCRIBE YOUR WINE SELECTIONS.
We have 2,200 wines on our list, including many of the world's finest, with an emphasis on Cabernet Sauvignon and Bordeaux.

WHAT CATEGORIES OF WINE ARE THE BEST VALUES ON YOUR WINE LIST?
Wines from Australia and Chile.

NAME RECENT WINE DISCOVERIES THAT HAVE EXCITED YOU.
Many small French châteaus are now producing quality wines at good prices.

WHAT IS YOUR FAVORITE WINE REGION IN THE WORLD TODAY?
All regions are making great wines now. It is really hard to choose one.

WHAT LED YOU TO YOUR CURRENT POSITION?
I inherited the family restaurant. Because of my love for wine, I wanted to learn more about food and wine pairing and build a more extensive wine list.

WHAT IS THE BIGGEST CHALLENGE IN YOUR JOB?
Keeping the wine list current and the waitstaff informed.

IF YOU WERE NOT IN THIS PROFESSION, WHAT WOULD YOU BE DOING?
Hunting, fishing and drinking good wine.

Coyote Café

132 West Water Street
Santa Fe, New Mexico 87501
phone 505-983-1615 fax 505-989-9026
website www.coyotecafe.com

Quinn M. Stephenson
BEVERAGE MANAGER
AND WINE BUYER

NAME TWO OF YOUR FAVORITE WINES.
The reds from Hermitage and Côte-Rôtie; they age so gracefully.

NAME RECENT WINE DISCOVERIES THAT HAVE EXCITED YOU.
Spanish reds from lesser-known regions, like Priorat and Bierzo, which produce beautiful wines from varietals such as Grenache, Carignane and Mensilla, from vineyards that are more than a hundred years old.

DESCRIBE YOUR WINE SELECTIONS, BOTH BY THE GLASS AND ON YOUR LIST.
California is the anchor of our list, though we have a nice balance between Old World and New World regions.

WHAT ARE THE MOST UNIQUE FEATURES IN YOUR WINE PROGRAM?
We offer one-of-a-kind barrel samplings from the Hospice du Rhône in a wine flight. We also offer several rare boutique wines.

NAME A COUPLE OF YOUR RESTAURANT'S SIGNATURE DISHES. WHAT TYPES OF WINE DO YOU PREFER TO RECOMMEND WITH EACH?
Tuna tartare on top of a baked brioche and microgreens with vintage Champagne; our in-house dry-aged, 24-ounce rib-eye with a Napa Cabernet Sauvignon.

IN THE PAST YEAR, WHAT WINES IN YOUR WINE PROGRAM HAVE CUSTOMERS BECOME MORE WILLING TO ORDER?
Imported wines; customers have been experimenting with Old World varietals other than Cabernet Sauvignon and Chardonnay.

WHAT ARE SOME OTHER ULTIMATE WINE AND FOOD PAIRINGS?
Foie gras and Tokaji Aszù; roasted lamb grilled on vine cuttings with older Syrah from the Rhône; Champagne sabayon with fresh berries and Champagne; chocolate and vintage Porto.

La Casa Sena

BYRON RUDOLF, WINE MANAGER

125 East Palace, Santa Fe

505-988-9232

Rancher's Club
at the Hilton Inn
Albuquerque

RALPH GARCIA, GENERAL

MANAGER AND WINE BUYER

1901 University Boulevard East,
Albuquerque

505-884-2500

Alain Ducasse
at the Essex House

155 West 58th Street
New York, New York 10019
phone 212-265-7300 fax 212-265-5200
website www.alain-ducasse.com

André Compeyre
SOMMELIER

NAME ONE OR TWO OF YOUR FAVORITE WINE DISTRICTS OR WINE
REGIONS FROM AROUND THE WORLD.
Languedoc for true expression of terroir and tradition, and wines from Santa
Barbara.

NAME RECENT WINE DISCOVERIES THAT HAVE EXCITED YOU.
Argentina for the right quality of Malbec.

WHAT BITS OF INFORMATION WOULD YOU LIKE YOUR CUSTOMERS TO
KNOW ABOUT YOU?
I'm an ambassador of the winemaker. My only credit is to enjoy the wine I taste
and share it with my customers.

IF YOU WERE NOT IN THIS PROFESSION, WHAT WOULD YOU BE DOING?
Growing grapes in the middle of nowhere.

DESCRIBE YOUR WINE SELECTIONS, BOTH BY THE GLASS AND ON YOUR
LIST.
We have a "Prestige" (Reserve) list, a "La Montée de Cave" that changes daily,
weekly or as often as needed, and by-the-glass wine pairings that complement
the tasting menu.

WHAT ARE THE MOST UNIQUE FEATURES IN YOUR WINE PROGRAM?
Large verticals of the finest Burgundian producers and many verticals from
Bordeaux.

NAME ONE OF YOUR RESTAURANT'S SIGNATURE DISHES. WHAT WINE DO
YOU PREFER TO RECOMMEND WITH IT?
Scallops with golden osetra caviar and watercress with North Fork of Long
Island Pinot Blanc.

IN THE PAST YEAR, WHAT WINES IN YOUR WINE PROGRAM HAVE CUS-
TOMERS BECOME MORE WILLING TO ORDER?
Our customers are flexible to our suggestions.

Alfama Fine Portuguese Cuisine

551 Hudson Street
New York, New York 10014
phone 212-645-2500 fax 212-645-1476
website www.alfamarestaurant.com

Tarcisio Costa
WINE DIRECTOR

NAME ONE OF YOUR FAVORITE WINE REGIONS FROM AROUND THE WORLD.
The Alentejo in southern Portugal, which is Portugal's most exciting region right now.

NAME RECENT WINE DISCOVERIES THAT HAVE EXCITED YOU.
I am crazy about Rieslings from Alsace and Pinot Noirs from New Zealand. Quality is the number-one factor.

WHAT BITS OF INFORMATION WOULD YOU LIKE YOUR CUSTOMERS TO KNOW ABOUT YOU?
I love creating cocktails. I enjoy modern jewelry design, rings in particular, French lounge music and Patricia Kaas, but I also love Wagner and Strauss operas.

DESCRIBE YOUR WINE SELECTIONS, BOTH BY THE GLASS AND ON YOUR LIST.
We specialize in Portuguese wine and feature more than 100 of them, representing the best examples from each of Portugal's wine-producing regions.

WHAT ARE THE MOST UNIQUE FEATURES IN YOUR WINE PROGRAM?
A wine soirée is held on a daily basis with twenty-two selections by the glass. The second glass of wine is half-price.

WHAT CATEGORIES OF WINE ARE THE BEST VALUES IN YOUR RESTAURANT?
Vinhos Verdes and reds from the Douro.

NAME ONE OF YOUR RESTAURANT'S SIGNATURE DISHES. WHAT WINE DO YOU PREFER TO RECOMMEND WITH IT?
Mariscada Alfama, a seafood stew of shrimp, lobster, mussels, clams, squid and fish cooked in a tomato and wine sauce paired with Portuguese Alvarinho.

IN THE PAST YEAR, WHAT WINES IN YOUR WINE PROGRAM HAVE CUSTOMERS BECOME MORE WILLING TO ORDER?
Our entire list sells rather well in all categories and regions.

Aquagrill

210 Spring Street
New York, New York 10012
phone 212-274-0505 fax 212-274-0587
website www.aquagrill.com

Jeremy Cohen

MANAGER AND
WINE DIRECTOR

NAME SOME OF YOUR FAVORITES WINES.

Burgundy whites and reds. One thousand years of research and development really shows! And I'm a huge fan of Champagne as well. It's an excellent, all-around choice for general meals.

NAME A RECENT WINE DISCOVERY THAT EXCITED YOU.

Rosé Eiswein made with Pinot Noir or Spätburgunder. It's a new style to me.

WHAT BITS OF INFORMATION WOULD YOU LIKE YOUR CUSTOMERS TO KNOW ABOUT YOU?

I've traveled extensively throughout the United States.

DESCRIBE YOUR WINE SELECTIONS, BOTH BY THE GLASS AND ON YOUR LIST.

Our primary concern is making sure that the wines on the list are appropriate with our menu. We have a small list, but one that includes excellent wines across a range of values, varietals and countries of origin.

WHAT CATEGORY OF WINE IS THE BEST VALUE IN YOUR RESTAURANT?

Every category has excellent values.

NAME ONE OF YOUR RESTAURANT'S SIGNATURE DISHES. WHAT WINE DO YOU PREFER TO RECOMMEND WITH IT?

Falafel-crusted salmon over hummus with lemon coriander vinaigrette and a hearty Willamette Valley Pinot Noir.

Artisanal

Two Park Avenue
New York, New York 10016
phone 212-725-8585 fax 212-481-5455

Franck Bismuth
BEVERAGE DIRECTOR

WHAT INSPIRED YOU TO PURSUE A CAREER THAT INVOLVES WINE?
While working at a stock brokerage in Paris, my first boss handed me the wine list (this was our first lunch!) and I ordered Evian!

NAME TWO OF YOUR FAVORITE WINE REGIONS.
Burgundy, because of the complexity of the wines; Loire Valley for the excitement of a great, inexpensive white or red Sancerre.

NAME RECENT WINE DISCOVERIES THAT HAVE EXCITED YOU.
Spanish wines, especially those from Galicia.

WHAT WOULD YOU LIKE YOUR CUSTOMERS TO KNOW ABOUT YOU?
I love sports like soccer and basketball, and I'm very busy with my ten-year-old daughter.

NAME A COUPLE OF YOUR RESTAURANT'S SIGNATURE DISHES. WHAT TYPES OF WINE DO YOU PREFER TO RECOMMEND WITH EACH?
Rabbit au Riesling paired with Gigondas; crisp skate wings with blood orange grenobloise and cauliflower with Alsace Riesling grand cru.

WHAT WINES ARE CUSTOMERS NOW MORE WILLING TO ORDER?
Red Bordeaux, white and red Sancerre, Shiraz from Australia, Sauvignon Blanc from New Zealand and red Burgundy.

WHAT ARE THE MOST UNIQUE FEATURES IN YOUR WINE PROGRAM?
Cheese and wine pairings. We feature more than 250 cheeses and 150 wines by the glass. Every week, the cheese manager and I pair several wine and cheeses. We have a cheese class twice a month where we feature six cheeses paired with three wines.

WHAT ARE SOME OTHER ULTIMATE WINE AND FOOD PAIRINGS?
Our seafood tower with New Zealand Sauvignon Blanc; "stew" with an earthy wine like Cahors; grilled lamb with St. Joseph.

Aureole

34 East 61st Street
New York, New York 10021
phone 212-319-1660 fax 212-750-8613
website www.charliepalmer.com

Scott G. Brenner
WINE DIRECTOR

NAME TWO OF YOUR FAVORITE WINE DISTRICTS FROM AROUND THE WORLD.

The Wachau in Austria for the amazing depth and power its Grüner Veltliners achieve; Pinot Noir from Burgundy, because, for me, nothing can match the beauty and complexity of fine Burgundy.

WHAT BITS OF INFORMATION WOULD YOU LIKE YOUR CUSTOMERS TO KNOW ABOUT YOU?

I went from studying mechanical engineering and finance to running wine programs.

IF YOU WERE NOT IN THIS PROFESSION, WHAT WOULD YOU BE DOING?
Anything in Hawaii.

WHAT ARE THE MOST UNIQUE FEATURES IN YOUR WINE PROGRAM?
Our ever-changing pairings with the tasting menus and wine dinner series that feature a varietal or region. Also, our electronic wine tablet (as in Las Vegas), which allows unlimited information access, inventory control and flexibility.

WHAT CATEGORY OF WINE IS THE BEST VALUE IN YOUR RESTAURANT?
We provide several values in every category. Even so, Austrian whites, Côte Chalonnaise reds and whites, and Northern Italian reds are hard to beat for value.

NAME A COUPLE OF YOUR RESTAURANT'S SIGNATURE DISHES. WHAT TYPES OF WINE DO YOU PREFER TO RECOMMEND WITH EACH?
Roasted poussin with egg yolk ravioli, pea leaves and wood ear mushrooms with red Côte de Beaune; grilled lamb porterhouse with foie gras–stuffed morel mushroom with Piedmont Nebbiolo.

WHAT WINES ARE CUSTOMERS NOW MORE WILLING TO ORDER?
Spanish reds, especially Priorat, and reds and whites from the Rhône Valley.

WHAT ARE SOME OTHER ULTIMATE WINE AND FOOD PAIRINGS?
Champagne with just about anything—or nothing at all.

Balthazar

80 Spring Street
New York, New York 10012
phone 212-965-1785 fax 212-965-9590
website www.balthazarny.com

Chris Goodhart
WINE DIRECTOR
AND SOMMELIER

NAME TWO OF YOUR FAVORITE WINE DISTRICTS.

The Wachau and Priorat, whose wines are intensely flavored yet display a sense of elegance.

NAME RECENT WINE DISCOVERIES THAT HAVE EXCITED YOU.

The Sauvignon de St-Bris 2001 from J.M. Brocard, a mouthwatering wine at a ridiculously low price; and nineteenth and early twentieth-century Madeiras from d'Olivera, whose quality is off the charts.

WHAT BITS OF INFORMATION WOULD YOU LIKE YOUR CUSTOMERS TO KNOW ABOUT YOU?

In my past work life, I was creative services manager at Turner Broadcasting.

IF YOU WERE NOT IN THIS PROFESSION, WHAT WOULD YOU BE?

A stay-at-home dad and part-time wine writer anywhere in rural Italy, preferably with a view of the Mediterranean.

WHAT CATEGORIES OF WINE ARE THE BEST VALUES IN YOUR RESTAURANT?

Wines from the Languedoc and satellite appellations in Bordeaux and Burgundy.

NAME A COUPLE OF YOUR RESTAURANT'S SIGNATURE DISHES. WHAT TYPES OF WINE DO YOU PREFER TO RECOMMEND WITH EACH?

Chicken Riesling with sautéed spaetzle, mushrooms and pearl onions paired with grand cru Alsace Riesling or St-Joseph blanc; Jarret d'Agneau (braised lamb shanks with chickpeas, zucchini and tomatoes) paired with full-bodied Cabernet Sauvignon-based Vin de Pays de l'Hérault or Syrah-based Coteaux du Languedoc.

WHAT ARE SOME OTHER ULTIMATE WINE AND FOOD PAIRINGS?

Vin Jaune with pastas in cream sauce and a dash of white truffle oil; chocolate or rich chocolate desserts with Banyuls; Fino Sherry with plain, salted Ruffles potato chips.

Barolo Ristorante

398 West Broadway
New York, New York 10012
phone 212-226-1102 fax 212-226-1822
website www.nybarolr.com

Renzo Rapacioli
SOMMELIER

WHAT IS YOUR FAVORITE WINE DISTRICT?
Barolo is called the "King of Wines" for a reason.

WHAT ARE SOME RECENT WINE DISCOVERIES THAT HAVE EXCITED YOU?
Many wines from Sicily (Cabernet Sauvignon, Merlot, Syrah and Chardonnay) presented in new styles, of excellent quality and offering very good value.

DESCRIBE YOUR WINE SELECTIONS, BOTH BY THE GLASS AND ON YOUR LIST.
We carry more than twenty wines by glass. Our wine list is well-rounded internationally, with an emphasis on Piemonte and other regions of Italy, but California is also very well represented.

WHAT ARE THE MOST UNIQUE FEATURES IN YOUR WINE PROGRAM?
Our Barolo vintages date back to 1947, and our Barbarescos go back to the 1961 vintage.

WHAT CATEGORIES OF WINE ARE THE BEST VALUES IN YOUR RESTAURANT?
Popular Italian wines like Pinot Grigio, Dolcetto, Barbera; California Merlot and Syrah; Chilean Chardonnay.

NAME A FEW OF YOUR RESTAURANT'S SIGNATURE DISHES. WHAT TYPES OF WINE DO YOU PREFER TO RECOMMEND WITH EACH?
Filetto Barolo served with Barolo or Barbaresco; tuna tartare served with California Sauvignon Blanc; sautéed foie gras with caramelized wild asparagus drizzled with balsamic vinegar reduction with Brachetto d'Asti.

Bayard's

1 Hanover Square
New York, New York 10004
phone 212-514-9454 fax 212-514-9443
website www.bayards.com

Ivan T. Mitankin
MANAGER
AND WINE DIRECTOR

NAME TWO OF YOUR FAVORITE WINE DISTRICTS.
Alsace, for the distinctive floral bouquet of its white wines; Bordeaux, for the complexity and structure of its reds.

NAME A RECENT WINE DISCOVERY THAT EXCITED YOU.
California Rhône blends have caught my attention recently, like the Edmunds St. John 2000 Rocks and Gravel, an excellent blend of Grenache, Syrah and Mourvèdre.

WHAT WOULD YOU LIKE YOUR CUSTOMERS TO KNOW ABOUT YOU?
I enjoy cooking and pairing wines with the recipes I create.

IF YOU WERE NOT IN THIS PROFESSION, WHAT WOULD YOU BE?
A massage therapist.

DESCRIBE YOUR WINE SELECTIONS, BY THE GLASS AND ON YOUR LIST.
We offer fifteen wines by the glass, six whites, seven reds and two Champagnes—all at their best, thanks to our conscientious storage program.

WHAT ARE THE MOST UNIQUE FEATURES IN YOUR WINE PROGRAM?
We have an extensive list with 1,350 selections, of which 370 bottles are in large bottle formats. We also feature verticals of first growth Bordeaux back to 1961, verticals of California Cabernet Sauvignon back to 1980, forty Portos and twenty-eight Sauternes.

NAME A COUPLE OF YOUR RESTAURANT'S SIGNATURE DISHES. WHAT TYPES OF WINE DO YOU PREFER TO RECOMMEND WITH EACH?
Tuna tartare with sesame seeds, cilantro and mint paired with Alsatian Pinot Blanc; roasted pheasant with Champagne sauerkraut and foie gras sauce paired with California Pinot Noir.

WHAT ARE SOME OTHER ULTIMATE WINE AND FOOD PAIRINGS?
Sautéed foie gras with Calvados sauce paired with Sauternes; warm oysters with Champagne sauce and caviar paired with German Riesling Spätlese.

Le Bernardin

155 West 51st Street
New York, New York 10019
phone 212-489-1515 fax 212-265-1615

Michel R. Couvreux
WINE DIRECTOR
TEAM: OLIVER DUFEU, SOMMELIER

WHAT IS ONE OF YOUR ULTIMATE FOOD AND WINE PAIRINGS?
Sautéed scallops with foie gras and truffle sauce with Chambolle-Musigny Les Fuées, Ghislaine Barthod 1997.

DESCRIBE YOUR WINE SELECTIONS.
A large selection of international wines, which is very strong in Burgundy (white and red), followed by Bordeaux (red), and California wines (white and red). We also feature wines from the rest of France, and other countries like Spain, Italy and New Zealand.

WHAT IS YOUR FAVORITE WINE REGION IN THE WORLD TODAY?
The Rhône Valley in France, especially Côte Rôtie and Hermitage. I love the spices of the Syrah and the character of the terroir.

WHAT LED YOU TO PURSUE A CAREER THAT INVOLVES WINE?
The pleasure of opening a bottle of wine without knowing what will be inside.

WHAT IS THE BIGGEST CHALLENGE IN YOUR JOB?
Making sure every customer is satisfied with his wine selection and that it matches the food.

IF YOU WERE NOT WINE DIRECTOR, WHAT WOULD YOU BE DOING?
Cooking, because my pleasure in life is eating and drinking well.

Le Bernardin

155 West 51st Street
New York, New York 1009
phone 212-489-1515 fax 212-265-1615
website www.le-bernardin.com

Olivier Dufeu
SOMMELIER

WHAT PART OF YOUR JOB DO YOU ENJOY THE MOST?
I enjoy reading customers' tastes and helping them discover something new.

NAME TWO OF YOUR FAVORITE WINE REGIONS FROM AROUND THE WORLD.
Germany for the purity of its wines, and Burgundy.

NAME RECENT WINE DISCOVERIES THAT HAVE EXCITED YOU.
Slovenian Pinot Gris and Pinot Noir for their excellent value; Priorat for its complexity.

WHAT WOULD YOU LIKE YOUR CUSTOMERS TO KNOW ABOUT YOU?
I love to travel.

IF YOU WERE NOT IN THIS PROFESSION, WHAT WOULD YOU BE DOING?
Mathematics and sports.

DESCRIBE YOUR WINE SELECTIONS, BOTH BY THE GLASS AND ON YOUR LIST.
We have an international by-the-glass selection. Our bottle list is very classic, with forty-five percent from Burgundy, twenty-five percent from Bordeaux, twenty-five percent from California and five percent from other regions.

WHAT ARE THE MOST UNIQUE FEATURES IN YOUR WINE PROGRAM?
A selection of wines from Domaine de la Romanée-Conti, and a range of Portos available by-the-glass.

WHAT CATEGORY OF WINE IS THE BEST VALUE IN YOUR RESTAURANT?
Red Bordeaux (we are a seafood restaurant).

NAME A COUPLE OF YOUR RESTAURANT'S SIGNATURE DISHES. WHAT TYPES OF WINE DO YOU PREFER TO RECOMMEND WITH EACH?
Black bass with girolle and black trumpet in duck bouillon with excellent red Burgundy; skate wing with brown butter sauce with fine white Burgundy.

WHAT WINES ARE CUSTOMERS NOW MORE WILLING TO ORDER?
Oregon Pinot Noir and Rhône whites.

Café Boulud
at the Surrey Hotel

20 East 76th Street
New York, New York 10021
phone 212-772-2600 fax 212-772-7755
website www.danielnyc.com

Olivier Flosse

CHEF SOMMELIER

WHAT INSPIRED YOU TO PURSUE A CAREER THAT INVOLVES WINE?
The chance that one day somebody would show me what it was.

WHAT PART OF YOUR JOB DO YOU ENJOY THE MOST?
The purchase of wine and the recommendations to customers.

NAME ONE OF YOUR FAVORITE WINE REGIONS FROM AROUND THE WORLD.
I do love all the regions where people make an effort to make good wine, but my favorite is Burgundy.

NAME RECENT WINE DISCOVERIES THAT HAVE EXCITED YOU.
Meursault La Goutte d'Or Arnaud Ente 1998.

WHAT WOULD YOU LIKE YOUR CUSTOMERS TO KNOW ABOUT YOU?
The pleasure that I have getting them a wine that makes them happy.

IF YOU WERE NOT IN THIS PROFESSION, WHAT WOULD YOU BE?
A tennis player.

DESCRIBE YOUR WINE SELECTIONS, BOTH BY THE GLASS AND ON YOUR LIST.
We have been improving our wine list to 850 different wines from different regions. We offer twenty wines by glass.

WHAT ARE THE MOST UNIQUE FEATURES IN YOUR WINE PROGRAM?
This year we have magnums, double magnums and jeroboams.

WHAT CATEGORY OF WINE IS THE BEST VALUE IN YOUR RESTAURANT?
Languedoc, Burgundy and Bordeaux.

NAME ONE OF YOUR RESTAURANT'S SIGNATURE DISHES. WHAT WINE DO YOU PREFER TO RECOMMEND WITH IT?
Crab with apple gelée paired with Loire Valley Sauvignon Blanc.

WHAT WINES ARE CUSTOMERS NOW MORE WILLING TO ORDER?
American wines like Canepa and Peter Michael.

Capsouto Frères Bistro

451 Washington Street
New York, New York 10013
phone 212-966-4900 fax 212-925-5296
website www.capsoutofreres.com

Jacques Capsouto
CO-OWNER AND SOMMELIER

WHAT INSPIRED YOU TO PURSUE A CAREER THAT INVOLVES WINE?
I lived in Lyon, and being involved in the restaurant business at a young age, I
absorbed the knowledge of food and wine.

WHAT PART OF YOUR JOB DO YOU ENJOY THE MOST?
I enjoy seeing the customer leave thoroughly happy, and thanking the restaurant on top of that.

NAME SOME OF YOUR FAVORITE WINE DISTRICTS.
Burgundy, Beaujolais and Oregon.

NAME RECENT WINE DISCOVERIES THAT HAVE EXCITED YOU.
The discovery of vintage Burgundy and Beaujolais 2002.

WHAT BITS OF INFORMATION WOULD YOU LIKE YOUR CUSTOMERS TO
KNOW ABOUT YOU?
I work very hard to pick wines from all around the world and of good value.

IF YOU WERE NOT IN THIS PROFESSION, WHAT WOULD YOU BE DOING?
Growing grapes and making wine.

DESCRIBE YOUR WINE SELECTIONS, BOTH BY THE GLASS AND ON YOUR LIST.
We offer good-value wines, whether by the bottle or glass. Guests see the eccentricities on the wine list with the presence of wines like Beaujolais Blanc.

WHAT ARE THE MOST UNIQUE FEATURES IN YOUR WINE PROGRAM?
The work behind the list. We teach our staff and guests through the extensive
wine list.

NAME ONE OF YOUR RESTAURANT'S SIGNATURE DISHES. WHAT WINE DO
YOU PREFER TO RECOMMEND WITH IT?
Roasted ginger duck with Pinot Noir.

WHAT WINES ARE CUSTOMERS NOW MORE WILLING TO ORDER?
Loire Valley wines.

Chanterelle

2 Harrison Street
New York, New York 10013
phone 212-966-6960 fax 212-966-6143

Roger Dagorn
MASTER SOMMELIER
AND MAÎTRE D'

WHAT ARE SOME OF YOUR ULTIMATE FOOD AND WINE PAIRINGS?
Viognier with seafood sausages; southern Rhônes with lamb with Moroccan spices.

DESCRIBE YOUR WINE SELECTIONS.
Diversity of wines from different appellations, varietals and styles that go with David Waltuck's intense food, but mostly that satisfy the needs of the customer.

WHAT CATEGORY OF WINE IS THE BEST VALUE IN YOUR RESTAURANT?
The flight of wines that go with our tasting menu.

NAME RECENT WINE DISCOVERIES THAT HAVE EXCITED YOU.
The wines of the Wachau and Burgenland in Austria; the Veneto and Umbria in Italy; and Priorat, Rioja and Ribera del Duero in Spain.

WHAT IS YOUR FAVORITE WINE REGION IN THE WORLD TODAY?
Burgundy. Great wines, yet often elusive.

WHAT LED YOU TO PURSUE A CAREER THAT INVOLVES WINE?
Love of people.

WHAT ARE THE BEST ASPECTS OF YOUR JOB?
Working (playing) in a beautiful environment, surrounded by fun people, enjoying great food and great wines to match.

IF YOU WERE NOT IN YOUR CURRENT POSITION, WHAT WOULD YOU BE?
Assistant to a sommelier.

La Côte Basque
60 West 55th Street
New York, New York 10019
Phone 212-688-6525 Fax 212-258-2493

Emile Le Tennier
SOMMELIER

WHAT INSPIRED YOU TO PURSUE A CAREER THAT INVOLVES WINE?
The chemistry of how grapes become wine.

WHAT PART OF YOUR JOB DO YOU ENJOY THE MOST?
The whole scene.

NAME TWO OF YOUR FAVORITE WINE REGIONS FROM AROUND THE
WORLD.
Burgundy, because I love the scent of cherries, and California, because it offers
everything from the worst to the very best wines.

NAME RECENT WINE DISCOVERIES THAT HAVE EXCITED YOU.
Australian Shiraz. It's just awesome.

WHAT BITS OF INFORMATION WOULD YOU LIKE YOUR CUSTOMERS TO
KNOW ABOUT YOU?
I love the outdoors and botany.

IF YOU WERE NOT IN THIS PROFESSION, WHAT WOULD YOU BE DOING?
I'd have a financial career.

DESCRIBE YOUR WINE SELECTIONS, BOTH BY THE GLASS AND ON YOUR LIST.
Old and New World wine selections and wines by the glass. We have a great
wine for every purse.

WHAT ARE THE MOST UNIQUE FEATURES IN YOUR WINE PROGRAM?
Selections of Lafite-Rothschild, Mouton-Rothschild and verticals of Opus One.

WHAT CATEGORY OF WINE IS THE BEST VALUE IN YOUR RESTAURANT?
Red Bordeaux.

IN THE PAST YEAR, WHAT WINES IN YOUR WINE PROGRAM HAVE CUS-
TOMERS BECOME MORE WILLING TO ORDER?
Bordeaux and Napa Chardonnay.

Daniel

60 East 65th Street
New York, New York 10021
phone 212-288-0033 fax 212-396-9014
website www.danielnyc.com

Jean Luc S. Le Du
CHEF AND SOMMELIER

WHAT ARE SOME OF YOUR ULTIMATE FOOD AND WINE PAIRINGS?
Black sea bass in potato crust with red wine sauce paired with Saumur-Champigny "Les Poyeux" 1996 from Clos Rougeard; Fourme d'Ambert and pear tart with rich Coteaux du Layon.

DESCRIBE YOUR WINE SELECTIONS.
We have a comprehensive list with more than 1,500 selections. Sixty percent of these are French wines, but we are also strong in wines from the United States, Spain, Italy and Australia. We also pour twenty wines by the glass.

WHAT CATEGORY OF WINE IS THE BEST VALUE IN YOUR RESTAURANT?
Languedoc-Roussillon.

NAME RECENT WINE DISCOVERIES THAT HAVE EXCITED YOU.
Barrique-aged Barbera from Piedmont; 1998 St.-Émilions, for their richness and early drinkability.

WHAT IS YOUR FAVORITE WINE REGION IN THE WORLD TODAY?
Burgundy, for the charm and aromas of its wines.

WHAT LED YOU TO PURSUE A CAREER THAT INVOLVES WINE?
A chance encounter with a great bottle of wine (Cheval Blanc, 1964).

WHAT ARE THE BEST ASPECTS OF YOUR JOB?
Interacting with customers and winemakers.

Felidia Ristorante

243 East 58th Street
New York, New York 10022
phone 212-758-1479 fax 212-935-7687
website www.lidiasitaly.com

David Weitzenhoffer
WINE DIRECTOR

WHAT INSPIRED YOU TO PURSUE A CAREER THAT INVOLVES WINE?
A pairing of Copper River salmon and Oregon Pinot Noir.

NAME ONE OR TWO OF YOUR FAVORITE WINE REGIONS.
The Rhône Valley, because Syrah makes me happy; the Pacific Northwest,
because it's home.

NAME A RECENT WINE DISCOVERY THAT EXCITED YOU.
Spanish Albariño.

IF YOU WERE NOT IN THIS PROFESSION, WHAT WOULD YOU BE DOING?
Translating Russian for a law firm.

DESCRIBE YOUR WINE SELECTIONS, BOTH BY THE GLASS AND ON YOUR LIST.
Our wines by the glass are entirely Italian. Our 1,300-bottle list is approximately seventy-five percent Italian. We want to represent not only the best and most
exciting Italian wines and regions, but also the highest examples of all wines
from various regions in the world.

WHAT ARE THE MOST UNIQUE FEATURES IN YOUR WINE PROGRAM?
We age our wines until they are ready for consumption. For example, our
youngest Barolo currently available to customers is ten years old.

WHAT CATEGORY OF WINE IS THE BEST VALUE IN YOUR RESTAURANT?
Friulian wines from Italy. They are truly world-class.

NAME A COUPLE OF YOUR RESTAURANT'S SIGNATURE DISHES. WHAT
TYPES OF WINE DO YOU PREFER TO RECOMMEND WITH EACH?
Krafi-Istrian wedding pillows with dry Moscato from Sardinia; pasutice, a dia-
mond-shaped pasta, with a spicy lobster sauce with Piedmont Grignolino.

IN THE PAST YEAR, WHAT WINES IN YOUR WINE PROGRAM HAVE CUS-
TOMERS BECOME MORE WILLING TO ORDER?
Wines from Sicily and northeast Italy.

La Goulue

746 Madison Avenue
New York, New York 10021
phone 212-988-8169 fax 212-398-2552
website www.lagoulurestaurant.com

James E. Cawdron
MANAGER AND SOMMELIER

WHAT INSPIRED YOU TO PURSUE A CAREER THAT INVOLVES WINE?
I began working in a French restaurant, where I was exposed to great wines like Mouton and Lafite, and those from DRC.

NAME ONE OR TWO OF YOUR FAVORITE WINE REGIONS FROM AROUND THE WORLD.
Alsace, for its beautiful, floral notes; Australia, especially Petaluma from Piccadilly Valley.

NAME RECENT WINE DISCOVERIES THAT HAVE EXCITED YOU.
Bedell Viognier from Long Island; great value and quality.

WHAT WOULD YOU LIKE YOUR CUSTOMERS TO KNOW ABOUT YOU?
I was born in a pub in England, the Adam and Eve, built in 1250.

IF YOU WERE NOT IN THIS PROFESSION, WHAT WOULD YOU BE DOING?
Selling Rolls-Royce or Bentley cars.

DESCRIBE YOUR WINE SELECTIONS, BOTH BY THE GLASS AND ON YOUR LIST.
We have a rare and fun list of the best examples of each area in the world. We are known for our rare Burgundy and Bordeaux selection.

WHAT IS THE MOST UNIQUE FEATURE IN YOUR WINE PROGRAM?
Magnums of Chalk Hill.

WHAT CATEGORY OF WINE IS THE BEST VALUE IN YOUR RESTAURANT?
Bordeaux.

NAME ONE OF YOUR RESTAURANT'S SIGNATURE DISHES. WHAT WINE DO YOU PREFER TO RECOMMEND WITH IT?
French "grade A" foie gras terrine and grand cru Riesling from Alsace.

WHAT WINES ARE CUSTOMERS NOW MORE WILLING TO ORDER?
Long Island wines and Australian Shiraz.

Gramercy Tavern
42 East 20th Street
New York, New York 10013
phone 212-477-0777 fax 212-477-1160

Karen A. King
BEVERAGE DIRECTOR

WHAT INSPIRED YOU TO PURSUE A CAREER THAT INVOLVES WINE?
Working with Danny Meyer and Paul Bolles-Beaven, who introduced me to the wonderful world of wine.

WHAT PART OF YOUR JOB DO YOU ENJOY THE MOST?
Tasting, traveling and staff education.

YOUR FAVORITE WINE DISTRICT?
Piedmont. I love old Barolo!

WHAT WOULD YOU LIKE YOUR CUSTOMERS TO KNOW ABOUT YOU?
I'm a gal from Nashville, Tennessee, who loves to dance, roller-skate, read, and eat and drink good wine, of course.

IF YOU WERE NOT IN THIS PROFESSION, WHAT WOULD YOU BE DOING?
I'd be teaching.

DESCRIBE YOUR WINE SELECTIONS, BOTH BY THE GLASS AND ON YOUR LIST.
We try to represent most key wine regions with an emphasis on French, Italian and American wines. We lay wines down so we can offer older vintages.

WHAT ARE THE MOST UNIQUE FEATURES IN YOUR WINE PROGRAM?
We offer delicious wines, from a range of regions and price points that truly complement our menu.

WHAT CATEGORY OF WINE IS THE BEST VALUE IN YOUR RESTAURANT?
All of our wines are good values in their respective categories.

NAME A COUPLE OF YOUR RESTAURANT'S SIGNATURE DISHES. WHAT TYPES OF WINE DO YOU PREFER TO RECOMMEND WITH EACH?
Fresh bacon with Châteauneuf-du-Pape; fava bean salad with German Riesling.

WHAT WINES ARE CUSTOMERS NOW MORE WILLING TO ORDER?
Austrian whites.

Grand Central Oyster Bar

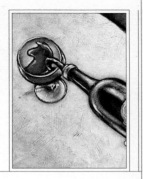

Grand Central Terminal
New York, New York 10017
phone 212-490-6650 fax 212-949-5210
website www.oysterbarny.com

Michael J. Garvey
GENERAL MANAGER

WHAT ARE SOME OF YOUR ULTIMATE FOOD AND WINE PAIRINGS?
Belon (or other briny) oysters on the half shell with Sauternes or Eiswein; bouillabaisse with red Meursault or Oregon Pinot Noir; Florida stone crab with Vouvray demi-sec; rare steak with Old World–style Pinot Noir; foie gras with Tokaji Aszú (4, 5 or 6 puttonyos); turkey sandwich with cold climate California Chardonnay.

DESCRIBE YOUR WINE SELECTIONS.
We have a diverse selection of wines, with something for everybody, from the novice to the pro.

WHAT CATEGORIES OF WINE ARE THE BEST VALUES ON YOUR WINE LIST?
Loire whites or reds, dessert wines and expensive wines, which are marked up less than at other establishments.

NAME RECENT WINE DISCOVERIES THAT HAVE EXCITED YOU.
A 1987 white Rioja, which held together magnificently; Long Island wines, whose quality-to-price ratio recently has improved markedly.

WHAT IS YOUR FAVORITE WINE REGION IN THE WORLD TODAY?
Loire Valley. The wines of the region are very diverse and reasonably priced.

WHAT LED YOU TO YOUR CURRENT POSITION?
Personal interest. I realized the more I learned about wine, the less I knew about it.

WHAT ARE THE BEST ASPECTS OF YOUR JOB?
Being a tour guide. I'm happy to take the standard tour through our list, but going off road is much more fun.

IF YOU WERE NOT IN THIS PROFESSION, WHAT WOULD YOU BE?
A Sherpa.

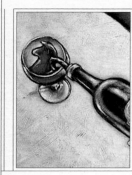

Henry's Evergreen

1288 First Avenue
New York, New York 10021
phone 212-744-3266 fax 212-744-2669
website www.henrysevergreen.com

Henry Leung
PROPRIETOR
AND GENERAL MANAGER

WHAT INSPIRED YOU TO PURSUE A CAREER THAT INVOLVES WINE?
I was challenged to prove that wine pairs with Chinese food in 1976, when I handed a wine list to a food critic and he remarked, "Young man, wine does not go with Chinese food," and gave me a curious look.

NAME ONE OR TWO OF YOUR FAVORITE WINE DISTRICTS OR WINE REGIONS FROM AROUND THE WORLD.
Napa and Bordeaux. I prefer Bordeaux varietals, especially Cabernet Sauvignon. Bordeaux has the perfect soil and Napa has the perfect climate.

NAME RECENT WINE DISCOVERIES THAT HAVE EXCITED YOU.
Switchback Ridge Cabernet Sauvignon and Petite Sirah. These wines are so thick you can cut them with a knife.

DESCRIBE YOUR WINE SELECTIONS, BOTH BY THE GLASS AND ON YOUR LIST.
We have twelve to sixteen wines by the glass and more than 400 selections on the list. The list's strength is in California Cabernet Sauvignon.

WHAT ARE THE MOST UNIQUE FEATURES IN YOUR WINE PROGRAM?
We have wine events once a week, which we list on our website.

WHAT CATEGORY OF WINE IS THE BEST VALUE IN YOUR RESTAURANT?
I have two wines in each category that are "best value" wines.

NAME A COUPLE OF YOUR RESTAURANT'S SIGNATURE DISHES. WHAT TYPES OF WINE DO YOU PREFER TO RECOMMEND WITH EACH?
Grand Marnier prawns with Gewürztraminer; Peking duck with Pinot Noir.

IN THE PAST YEAR, WHAT WINES IN YOUR WINE PROGRAM HAVE CUSTOMERS BECOME MORE WILLING TO ORDER?
California Cabernet Sauvignon.

I Trulli

122 East 27th Street
New York, New York 10016
phone 212-481-7372 fax 212-481-5785

Charles R. Scicolone
WINE DIRECTOR
AND SOMMELIER

WHAT INSPIRED YOU TO PURSUE A CAREER THAT INVOLVES WINE?
My love of Italian wines.

WHAT PART OF YOUR JOB DO YOU ENJOY THE MOST?
Talking one-on-one with my customers and matching wine and food.

WHAT ARE YOUR FAVORITE WINES?
Italian wines.

NAME RECENT WINE DISCOVERIES THAT HAVE EXCITED YOU.
Wines from southern Italy are not only great values but also of excellent quality.

WHAT WOULD YOU LIKE YOUR CUSTOMERS TO KNOW ABOUT YOU?
I have written books, like "Pizza Any Way You Slice It" and magazine articles
on food and wine with my wife, Michele Scicolone.

IF YOU WERE NOT IN THIS PROFESSION, WHAT WOULD YOU BE?
A pizza maker.

DESCRIBE YOUR WINE SELECTIONS, BOTH BY THE GLASS AND ON YOUR LIST.
We have an all-Italian wine list showing the great range and variety of Italian wines.

WHAT ARE THE MOST UNIQUE FEATURES IN YOUR WINE PROGRAM?
We have a large by-the-glass selection and a large number of wine flights.

WHAT CATEGORY OF WINE IS THE BEST VALUE IN YOUR RESTAURANT?
Southern Italian wines.

NAME WINES THAT ESPECIALLY COMPLEMENT YOUR RESTAURANT'S MENU.
Wines from Sicily's Apulia and Campagna go with our southern Italian dishes,
like orecchiete with broccoli rabe.

WHAT WINES ARE CUSTOMERS NOW MORE WILLING TO ORDER?
Wines from Sicily, Apulia and Campagna.

Industry (food)

509 East Sixth Street
New York, New York 10009
phone 212-777-5920 fax 212-777-5930
website www.industryfood.com

Benjamin E. Kirschner
WINE DIRECTOR

WHAT INSPIRED YOU TO PURSUE A CAREER THAT INVOLVES WINE?
My passion for food.

WHAT PART OF YOUR JOB DO YOU ENJOY THE MOST?
Going to auctions and buying mixed lots of older wines.

NAME ONE OR TWO OF YOUR FAVORITE WINE REGIONS.
Germany, because I love the secondary flavors that develop in older Rieslings;
Burgundy, because it's fun to compare producers' styles.

NAME RECENT WINE DISCOVERIES THAT HAVE EXCITED YOU.
A late-harvest 1971 German Riesling that was still fresh and had unusual flavors of sweet tobacco and smoked orange peel; old California Cabernets whose
fruit developed nice, earthy qualities.

WHAT WOULD YOU LIKE YOUR CUSTOMERS TO KNOW ABOUT YOU?
I take extra time just to pick out older wines.

DESCRIBE YOUR WINE SELECTIONS, BOTH BY THE GLASS AND ON YOUR LIST.
We offer unusual inexpensive wines, such as those from Savoie, Montpeyroux
and other lesser-known appellations.

WHAT ARE THE MOST UNIQUE FEATURES IN YOUR WINE PROGRAM?
Our older California wines.

WHAT CATEGORY OF WINE IS THE BEST VALUE IN YOUR RESTAURANT?
High-end Burgundy.

NAME ONE OF YOUR RESTAURANT'S SIGNATURE DISHES. WHAT WINE DO
YOU PREFER TO RECOMMEND WITH IT?
Monkfish in portobello mushroom broth with Burgundy.

WHAT WINES ARE CUSTOMERS NOW MORE WILLING TO ORDER?
California Cabernet between six and thirty years old.

Jean-Georges

One Central Park West
New York, New York 10023
phone 212- 299-3900 fax 212-358-0685
website www.jean-georges.com

Chuck A. Simeone

BEVERAGE DIRECTOR AND SOMMELIER
TEAM: JOSE MONTALVO, SOMMELIER

WHAT PART OF YOUR JOB DO YOU ENJOY THE MOST?
Turning guests onto new wines they've never experienced before. This elevates
their dining experience and helps them both remember the restaurant and the
sommelier.

NAME TWO OF YOUR FAVORITE WINE REGIONS FROM AROUND THE WORLD.
Sicily for its value and quality; Alsace for its great wines and their versatility.

NAME RECENT WINE DISCOVERIES THAT HAVE EXCITED YOU.
Wines from southern Italy and the Islands reflect a great price-to-quality ratio.

WHAT WOULD YOU LIKE YOUR CUSTOMERS TO KNOW ABOUT YOU?
I swim, golf and practice yoga.

IF YOU WERE NOT IN THIS PROFESSION, WHAT WOULD YOU BE DOING?
I'd be involved with Wall Street because I would need something with similar
energy.

DESCRIBE YOUR WINE SELECTIONS, BOTH BY THE GLASS AND ON YOUR LIST.
Our wines are priced from $25 to $17,000. There is something for everyone.

WHAT CATEGORY OF WINE IS THE BEST VALUE IN YOUR RESTAURANT?
The higher-end wines are a better value, giving guests the opportunity to experience some amazing wines.

NAME A COUPLE OF YOUR RESTAURANT'S SIGNATURE DISHES. WHAT
TYPES OF WINE DO YOU PREFER TO RECOMMEND WITH EACH?
Bay scallops with caper-raisin emulsion, caramelized cauliflower paired with
white Graves; broiled squab, onion compote paired with red Burgundy.

WHAT WINES ARE CUSTOMERS NOW MORE WILLING TO ORDER?
Alsatian whites, Austrian and southern Italian reds and German wines from the
2001 vintage.

Lutèce

249 East 50th Street
New York, New York 10022
phone 212-752-2225 fax 212-223-9050
website www.lutece.com

Raimundo C. Gaby, Jr.
DINING ROOM MANAGER
AND SOMMELIER

WHAT INSPIRED YOU TO PURSUE A CAREER THAT INVOLVES WINE?
The realization of how much the dining experience can be enhanced by an exciting pairing of food and wine and by the challenge of constantly having to learn more.

WHAT PART OF YOUR JOB DO YOU ENJOY THE MOST?
I enjoy tasting, increasing the wine knowledge and confidence of my staff, food and wine pairing, visiting wine regions and studying.

NAME RECENT WINE DISCOVERIES THAT HAVE EXCITED YOU.
Portuguese wines for their improved approachability; Long Island wines for their overall achievements in recent vintages.

WHAT BITS OF INFORMATION WOULD YOU LIKE YOUR CUSTOMERS TO KNOW ABOUT YOU?
I began cooking when I was thirteen years old in my family's restaurant in Brazil. I love to spend time with my daughter, play guitar, sing with friends, study foreign languages, watch movies and travel.

IF YOU WERE NOT IN THIS PROFESSION, WHAT WOULD YOU BE?
A singer, teacher or perhaps a bohemian.

WHAT ARE THE MOST UNIQUE FEATURES IN YOUR WINE PROGRAM?
We have ninety wines in the $30 to $60 range, as well as great verticals of red Bordeaux and Burgundies and many mature German Rieslings.

WHAT CATEGORIES OF WINE ARE THE BEST VALUES IN YOUR RESTAURANT?
Loire Valley white and red wines, wines from the south of France, Germany whites, and Spanish and Portuguese reds.

NAME A COUPLE OF YOUR RESTAURANT'S SIGNATURE DISHES. WHAT TYPES OF WINE DO YOU PREFER TO RECOMMEND WITH EACH?
Foie gras with chocolate paired with red Burgundy; sea bass with vanilla sauce paired with a lighter-style Rioja.

March Restaurant

405 East 58th Street
New York, New York 10022
phone 212-754-6272 fax 212-838-5108
website www.marchrestaurant.com

Joseph D. Scalice

CO-PROPRIETOR, WINE DIRECTOR
AND SOMMELIER

WHAT ARE SOME OF YOUR ULTIMATE FOOD AND WINE PAIRINGS?
Confit de foie gras (de canard) au tourchon with almonds, garam masala and
Sauternes glaze served with a Bodegas Dios Baco Oloroso Sherry; white asparagus on sweet pea purée with Château d'Auviernier Neuchâtel Blanc 2000; rack
of Colorado lamb with carrot and potato purée and Abadia Retuerta 1997.

DESCRIBE YOUR WINE SELECTIONS.
Our list consists primarily of boutique wines, both known and unknown, from
the United States, France and a selection of other international wines. Our
wine program is based on taste, not pretension.

WHAT CATEGORY OF WINE IS THE BEST VALUE IN YOUR RESTAURANT?
The lesser known communes of Burgundies, red and white.

NAME RECENT WINE DISCOVERIES THAT HAVE EXCITED YOU.
The wines of Chile and Argentina have gotten better and better while still
remaining great values.

WHAT IS YOUR FAVORITE WINE REGION IN THE WORLD TODAY?
Rioja, Spain. I love the elegance and food-friendliness of the wines.

WHAT LED YOU TO PURSUE A CAREER THAT INVOLVES WINE?
I have always loved wine.

WHAT ARE THE BEST ASPECTS OF YOUR JOB?
My "fun" begins when the guests arrive and I get to find, share and pour the
crowning jewels to their dining experiences.

IF YOU WERE NOT IN THIS PROFESSION, WHAT WOULD YOU BE?
A teacher.

March Restaurant

405 East 58th Street
New York, New York 10022
phone 212-754-6272 fax 212-838-5108
website www.marchrestaurant.com

Chuck Mason
ASSISTANT WINE DIRECTOR

WHAT INSPIRED YOU TO PURSUE A CAREER THAT INVOLVES WINE?
A passion for the pairing of food and wine.

NAME TWO OF YOUR FAVORITE WINE DISTRICTS FROM AROUND THE
WORLD.
The Toro district in Spain and the Curicu Valley in Chile. Both regions produce some great reds.

NAME A RECENT WINE DISCOVERY THAT EXCITED YOU.
A nice Sauvignon Blanc from Hungary that was a good value and had excellent crisp, fruity flavors.

IF YOU WERE NOT IN THIS PROFESSION, WHAT WOULD YOU BE?
A teacher.

DESCRIBE YOUR WINE SELECTIONS, BOTH BY THE GLASS AND ON YOUR LIST.
We specialize in limited-production wines from across the United States and France, complemented by an eclectic international selection to round out the list.

WHAT ARE THE MOST UNIQUE FEATURES IN YOUR WINE PROGRAM?
We offer tastings of about ten wines each night and have an excellent selection of sakes.

WHAT CATEGORY OF WINE IS THE BEST VALUE IN YOUR RESTAURANT?
We have great values in all categories, in wines ranging from $27 to $3,500 a bottle on our list.

NAME A COUPLE OF YOUR RESTAURANT'S SIGNATURE DISHES. WHAT
TYPES OF WINE DO YOU PREFER TO RECOMMEND WITH EACH?
Cold foie gras with Oloroso Sherry; lobster paired with Australian Marsanne.

IN THE PAST YEAR, WHAT WINES IN YOUR WINE PROGRAM HAVE CUSTOMERS BECOME MORE WILLING TO ORDER?
Oregon Pinot Noir, Chilean and Argentinean wines and Japanese sakes.

Mark's Restaurant at The Mark

25 East 77th Street
New York, New York 10021
phone 212-744-4300 fax 212-744-2749
website www.mandarinoriental.com

Richard E. Dean
MASTER SOMMELIER

WHAT INSPIRED YOU TO PURSUE A CAREER THAT INVOLVES WINE?
It's less boring than accounting.

WHAT PART OF YOUR JOB DO YOU ENJOY THE MOST?
I enjoy talking to customers and meeting new people.

NAME TWO OF YOUR FAVORITE WINE REGIONS FROM AROUND THE WORLD.
Alsace and Germany.

IF YOU WERE NOT IN THIS PROFESSION, WHAT WOULD YOU BE?
A stockbroker.

DESCRIBE YOUR WINE SELECTIONS, BOTH BY THE GLASS AND ON YOUR LIST.
Our summer Riesling Festival with 100 Rieslings by the glass, taste and bottle. Also, our Riesling dinners and classes.

WHAT ARE THE MOST UNIQUE FEATURES IN YOUR WINE PROGRAM?
We have many wine-tasting specials. Last summer, for example, we offered different Rieslings with lunch and dinner for $18 above prix fixe.

WHAT CATEGORY OF WINE IS THE BEST VALUE IN YOUR RESTAURANT?
California Cabernet Sauvignon.

NAME ONE OF YOUR RESTAURANT'S SIGNATURE DISHES. WHAT WINE DO YOU PREFER TO RECOMMEND WITH IT?
Beet salad with a bone-dry Riesling.

IN THE PAST YEAR, WHAT WINES IN YOUR WINE PROGRAM HAVE CUSTOMERS BECOME MORE WILLING TO ORDER?
German Rieslings. They are finally becoming popular.

Montrachet
239 West Broadway
New York, New York 10013
phone 212-219-2777 fax 212-274-9508

Daniel A. Johnnes
WINE DIRECTOR

WHAT ARE SOME OF YOUR ULTIMATE FOOD AND WINE PAIRINGS?
Volnay and grilled salmon; Sauternes and Roquefort.

DESCRIBE YOUR WINE SELECTIONS.
We are committed to providing wines from top growers and wines that are great values.

WHAT IS YOUR FAVORITE WINE REGION IN THE WORLD TODAY?
Burgundy, because of my passion for the wines.

WHAT LED YOU TO PURSUE A CAREER THAT INVOLVES WINE?
Love of wine and sharing knowledge with consumers.

WHAT IS THE MOST CHALLENGING ASPECT OF YOUR JOB?
Finding great value in wine.

Montrachet

239 West Broadway
New York, New York 10013
phone 212-219-2777 fax 212-274-9508
website www.myriadrestaurantgroup.com

Bernard Sun
HEAD SOMMELIER

NEW YORK, NEW YORK

WHAT INSPIRED YOU TO PURSUE A CAREER THAT INVOLVES WINE?
Tasting my first glass of Château d'Yquem after graduating from college. It was
something I will never forget.

**NAME ONE OR TWO OF YOUR FAVORITE WINE DISTRICTS OR WINE
REGIONS FROM AROUND THE WORLD.**
Burgundy. Taste an old Montrachet or something like a Comte de Vogüe
Musigny 1966 and you will understand elegance, beauty, delicacy and power.
No other wine has this combination.

NAME RECENT WINE DISCOVERIES THAT HAVE EXCITED YOU.
South African Sauvignon Blancs, for their high quality and wide range of styles.

IF YOU WERE NOT IN THIS PROFESSION, WHAT WOULD YOU BE?
A professional ice hockey player—or playing center field for the Yankees.

DESCRIBE YOUR WINE SELECTIONS, BOTH BY THE GLASS AND ON YOUR LIST.
We offer different varietals and styles available by the glass, including red and
white Burgundies.

WHAT ARE THE MOST UNIQUE FEATURES IN YOUR WINE PROGRAM?
Our Burgundy selection. We have also been a Grand Award winner since 1994.

WHAT CATEGORY OF WINE IS THE BEST VALUE IN YOUR RESTAURANT?
The "Off the Beaten Path" Burgundy section, which includes great values in
wines from communues like St-Aubin, St-Romain and Pernand-Vergelesses.

**NAME ONE OF YOUR RESTAURANT'S SIGNATURE DISHES. WHAT WINE DO
YOU PREFER TO RECOMMEND WITH IT?**
Truffle-crusted salmon with Burgundy.

**IN THE PAST YEAR, WHAT WINES IN YOUR WINE PROGRAM HAVE CUS-
TOMERS BECOME MORE WILLING TO ORDER?**
Pernand-Vergelesses.

Oceana Restaurant

55 East 54th Street
New York, New York 10022
phone 212-759-5941 fax 212-759-6076
website www.oceanarestaurant.com

Douglas Bernthal
WINE DIRECTOR

NAME ONE OF YOUR FAVORITE WINES OR WINE REGIONS.
Australian Shiraz from the Barossa Valley. The wines are reasonably priced, big
and powerful, but also approachable at a young age.

NAME RECENT WINE DISCOVERIES THAT HAVE EXCITED YOU.
The overall quality of Oregon wine has improved tremendously over the past
few years and can now rival Burgundy and California. And watch out for New
Zealand's Central Otago Pinot Noirs.

WHAT BITS OF INFORMATION WOULD YOU LIKE YOUR CUSTOMERS TO
KNOW ABOUT YOU?
I love the outdoors and really appreciate what Mother Nature has done for us.
Please do not destroy what has taken thousands of years to create.

IF YOU WERE NOT IN THIS PROFESSION, WHAT WOULD YOU BE DOING?
Running a bed-and-breakfast on Lake George in upstate New York, or involved
somehow with NASCAR.

DESCRIBE YOUR WINE SELECTIONS, BOTH BY THE GLASS AND ON YOUR
LIST.
We offer roughly eight white, eight red and twenty-five dessert wines by the
glass at any given time. Our wine list is very large, featuring the world's greatest
wines. We offer almost 100 selections in half-bottle, more than seventy-five
large-format bottles, roughly 225 white Burgundies and the largest selection of
Australian Shiraz available in New York City.

WHAT CATEGORY OF WINE IS THE BEST VALUE IN YOUR RESTAURANT?
Australian Shiraz.

IN THE PAST YEAR, WHAT WINES IN YOUR WINE PROGRAM HAVE CUS-
TOMERS BECOME MORE WILLING TO ORDER?
German Rieslings from the 2001 vintage and California Cabernets from 1997
and 1999.

Picholine

35 West 64th Street
New York, New York 10023
phone 212-724-8585 fax 212-875-8979

Jason Miller
WINE DIRECTOR
AND SOMMELIER

NAME ONE OR TWO OF YOUR FAVORITE WINE REGIONS FROM AROUND THE WORLD.
Southern Rhône, especially Châteauneuf-du-Pape and Gigondas, for their flexibility with food; Spain, in particular Ribera del Duero and Priorat, are great wines that are very underrated.

NAME RECENT WINE DISCOVERIES THAT HAVE EXCITED YOU.
Wines from Sicily, as well as areas in Spain other than Rioja and Ribera del Duero.

WHAT WOULD YOU LIKE YOUR CUSTOMERS TO KNOW ABOUT YOU?
I have ten years of cooking experience.

IF YOU WERE NOT IN THIS PROFESSION, WHAT WOULD YOU BE DOING?
I would be cooking in back-of-the-house. I've always been in love with the restaurant business.

DESCRIBE YOUR WINE SELECTIONS, BOTH BY THE GLASS AND ON YOUR LIST.
We have 650 selections, primarily French and American, as well as some very good Italian, Spanish and German wines.

WHAT ARE THE MOST UNIQUE FEATURES IN YOUR WINE PROGRAM?
We have more than fifty half-bottles and wine pairings that are available to match the tasting menu.

WHAT CATEGORY OF WINE IS THE BEST VALUE IN YOUR RESTAURANT?
We have a few different values in every major wine-producing area represented.

NAME A COUPLE OF YOUR RESTAURANT'S SIGNATURE DISHES. WHAT TYPES OF WINE DO YOU PREFER TO RECOMMEND WITH EACH?
Poached lobster in vanilla balsamic with Chassagne-Montrachet; cassoulet in the style of Toulouse with Côte-Rôtie.

WHAT WINES ARE CUSTOMERS NOW MORE WILLING TO ORDER?
Carmenère from Chile, Gigondas from Spain and whites from Italy.

La Pizza Fresca Ristorante

31 East 20th Street
New York, New York 10003
phone 212-598-0141 fax 413-280-8160

Massimo Vitiano
WINE DIRECTOR

NAME TWO OF YOUR FAVORITE WINE REGIONS FROM AROUND THE WORLD.

Sicily, for its indigenous varietals, quality of winemaking and overall wine value; Friuli, for its top-quality wines at very fair prices.

NAME RECENT WINE DISCOVERIES THAT HAVE EXCITED YOU.

Wines from the Aglianico grape, produced in southern Italy in Campania and further south.

DESCRIBE YOUR WINE SELECTIONS, BOTH BY THE GLASS AND ON YOUR LIST.

We try to offer the best wines we can find, exclusively from Italy, and offer them at a fair price. We are not trying to represent every region of Italy and have every price point. For this reason we like to call it a collection rather than a list. We always offer several choices by the glass at varying price points and have an apertivo such as Spumante or Prosecco and dessert wines like Moscato or Vin Santo.

WHAT CATEGORY OF WINE IS THE BEST VALUE IN YOUR RESTAURANT?

Red wines from the south of Italy, from regions such as Sicily, Molise and Apulia.

NAME A COUPLE OF YOUR RESTAURANT'S SIGNATURE DISHES. WHAT TYPES OF WINE DO YOU PREFER TO RECOMMEND WITH EACH?

Pesto lasagna with Tuscan Sauvignon Blanc; meat tortellini with fresh tomato sauce with Sangiovese or Chianti; polenta medallions with a mushroom cream sauce and thinly sliced, oven-baked veal topped with prosciutto and fontina cheese with Barolo, Barbaresco or Barbera.

San Pietro Ristorante

18 East 54th Street
New York, New York 10022
phone 212-753-9015 fax 212-371-2337
website www.sanpietro.net

Cosimo Bruno
SOMMELIER

WHAT INSPIRED YOU TO PURSUE A CAREER THAT INVOLVES WINE?
I love wine.

NAME ONE OR TWO OF YOUR FAVORITE WINE DISTRICTS.
Burgundy, France. Its exceptional soil produces remarkable wine.

NAME RECENT WINE DISCOVERIES THAT HAVE EXCITED YOU.
Wines from South Africa.

WHAT WOULD YOU LIKE YOUR CUSTOMERS TO KNOW ABOUT YOU?
I am an open-minded person, ready and eager to taste new wines.

IF YOU WERE NOT IN THIS PROFESSION, WHAT WOULD YOU BE?
A music engineer.

DESCRIBE YOUR WINE SELECTIONS, BOTH BY THE GLASS AND ON YOUR LIST.
We serve only top wines from California, Washington, France, Germany, Chile,
Spain, New Zealand and Italy. We specialize in the cuisine of Campania, in
southern Italy, and feature the most comprehensive selection of southern Italian
wines in America.

WHAT ARE THE MOST UNIQUE FEATURES IN YOUR WINE PROGRAM?
Presenting twenty different wine labels per week for our customers.

WHAT CATEGORY OF WINE IS THE BEST VALUE IN YOUR RESTAURANT?
The best category of wine is Italian, Spanish, American and Chilean.

NAME ONE OF YOUR RESTAURANT'S SIGNATURE DISHES. WHAT WINE DO
YOU PREFER TO RECOMMEND WITH IT?
A dish from antiquity in southern Italy, Bronzino al Sole, or sea bass with a soft
crust, served with great Chardonnay.

WHAT WINES ARE CUSTOMERS NOW MORE WILLING TO ORDER?
Wines from Italy and the United States.

Sushisamba Restaurant

87 Seventh Avenue South
New York, New York 10014
phone 212-691-7885 fax 212-691-2591
website www.sushisamba.com

Paul Tanguay
BEVERAGE MANAGER

WHAT PART OF YOUR JOB DO YOU ENJOY THE MOST?
Educating members of my staff at our two stores in New York, one in Miami and one in Chicago. There is nothing more rewarding than teaching and inspiring students to learn more about wine.

NAME ONE OF YOUR FAVORITE WINE REGIONS FROM AROUND THE WORLD.
Germany's Mosel-Saar-Ruwer. Its wines are steely, racy and feminine.

WHAT BITS OF INFORMATION WOULD YOU LIKE YOUR CUSTOMERS TO KNOW ABOUT YOU?
I'm the rock and roll sommelier. I just love music and am always playing it while in the cellar or office.

IF YOU WERE NOT IN THIS PROFESSION, WHAT WOULD YOU BE?
A chef, sweating and probably burning my hands in the kitchen.

DESCRIBE YOUR WINE SELECTIONS, BOTH BY THE GLASS AND ON YOUR LIST.
We offer many whites by the glass like Grüner Veltliner, Riesling and Viognier. The wine list is organized by body, with entertaining titles and informational boxes that describe wine and try to help educate patrons.

WHAT ARE THE MOST UNIQUE FEATURES IN YOUR WINE PROGRAM?
A large half-bottle selection and more than sixty sakes from Japan and the United States.

NAME A COUPLE OF YOUR RESTAURANT'S SIGNATURE DISHES. WHAT TYPES OF WINE DO YOU PREFER TO RECOMMEND WITH EACH?
Miso-marinated sea bass with Viognier; Yamato tuna sushi with foie gras and caviar, with German Riesling Spätlese.

IN THE PAST YEAR, WHAT WINES IN YOUR WINE PROGRAM HAVE CUSTOMERS BECOME MORE WILLING TO ORDER?
Crisp, medium-bodied wines like Sancerre and lesser-known varietals like Viognier, Grüner Veltliner and German Riesling.

Tribeca Grill

375 Greenwich Street
New York, New York 10013
phone 212-941-3900 fax 212-941-3915
website www.myriadrestaurantgroup.com

David Gordon
WINE DIRECTOR
TEAM: YOSHI TAKEMURA, SOMMELIER

WHAT INSPIRED YOU TO PURSUE A CAREER THAT INVOLVES WINE?
While working as a restaurant manager, I tasted the great 1971 Grange Hermitage and was hooked.

WHAT PART OF YOUR JOB DO YOU ENJOY THE MOST?
Tasting large quantities of wine without spitting.

YOUR FAVORITE WINE REGION?
The Rhône Valley, especially Châteauneuf-du-Pape and Côte-Rôtie.

NAME A RECENT WINE DISCOVERY THAT EXCITED YOU.
La Carraia Sangiovese from Umbria is better than many Chianti Classicos, for a fraction of the price.

WHAT WOULD YOU LIKE YOUR CUSTOMERS TO KNOW ABOUT YOU?
I was born in Brooklyn, so don't mess with me!

IF YOU WERE NOT IN THIS PROFESSION, WHAT WOULD YOU BE?
A point guard for the New York Knicks.

DESCRIBE YOUR WINE SELECTIONS, BOTH BY THE GLASS AND ON YOUR LIST.
We have 1,500 wines on the list with concentrations in California Cabernet Sauvignon and Zinfandel, as well as hundreds of Rhône wines including more than 150 wines from Châteauneuf-du-Pape.

NAME A COUPLE OF YOUR RESTAURANT'S SIGNATURE DISHES. WHAT TYPES OF WINE DO YOU PREFER TO RECOMMEND WITH EACH?
Braised short rib with foie gras paired with northern Rhône reds like Hermitage or Cornas; rare seared tuna with sesame noodles paired with German Riesling or Alsatian Gewürztraminer.

WHAT WINES ARE CUSTOMERS NOW MORE WILLING TO ORDER?
German Riesling and Spanish reds from Ribera del Duero and Toro.

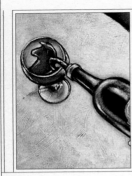

Tribeca Grill

375 Greenwich Street
New York, New York 10013
phone 212-941-3900 fax 212-941-3915
website www.myriadrestaurantgroup.com

Patrick T. Cappiello
SOMMELIER

WHAT INSPIRED YOU TO PURSUE A CAREER THAT INVOLVES WINE?
Fifteen years of restaurant experience and my love for food, wine and service.

WHAT PART OF YOUR JOB DO YOU ENJOY THE MOST?
I enjoy helping guests choose a wine that allows them to have a more memorable dining experience.

NAME ONE OR TWO OF YOUR FAVORITE WINE DISTRICTS OR WINE REGIONS FROM AROUND THE WORLD.
Rhône for its amazingly complex wines and good overall values; Burgundy for its expression of terroir.

NAME RECENT WINE DISCOVERIES THAT HAVE EXCITED YOU.
2000 Bordeaux, because it's hard to find a bad wine among them; 1999 Percarlo for its power and elegance; Aglianico is a world of new wine for me.

WHAT BITS OF INFORMATION WOULD YOU LIKE YOUR CUSTOMERS TO KNOW ABOUT YOU?
I have a B.A. in philosophy.

Union Pacific

111 East 22nd Street
New York, New York 10010
phone 212-995-8500 fax 212-460-5881
website www.unionpacificrestaurant.com

Fred Price
WINE DIRECTOR

WHAT INSPIRED YOU TO PURSUE A CAREER THAT INVOLVES WINE?
At the time, I thought it would be a really "cool" career, and that was confirmed after I met Fred Dame.

NAME TWO OF YOUR FAVORITE WINES FROM AROUND THE WORLD.
Mosel wines, because of their purity of flavor and variety of styles; Walla Walla for their New World sensibility and Old World restraint.

NAME RECENT WINE DISCOVERIES THAT HAVE EXCITED YOU.
Falanghina from Campania for its many nuances of flavor.

WHAT WOULD YOU LIKE YOUR CUSTOMERS TO KNOW ABOUT YOU?
I'm a jazz aficionado and an amateur drummer.

IF YOU WERE NOT IN THIS PROFESSION, WHAT WOULD YOU BE?
A jazz drummer.

DESCRIBE YOUR WINE SELECTIONS, BOTH BY THE GLASS AND ON YOUR LIST.
We specialize in cool-climate Northern German whites, as well as Pinot Noir and Syrah.

WHAT ARE THE MOST UNIQUE FEATURES IN YOUR WINE PROGRAM?
Our wine by-the-glass pairing program.

WHAT CATEGORY OF WINE IS THE BEST VALUE IN YOUR RESTAURANT?
Riesling.

NAME A COUPLE OF YOUR RESTAURANT'S SIGNATURE DISHES. WHAT TYPES OF WINE DO YOU PREFER TO RECOMMEND WITH EACH?
Taylor Bay scallops with mustard oil paired with Grüner Veltliner; rack of lamb with sour cherry mustard glaze with Dry Creek Valley Zinfandel.

WHAT WINES ARE CUSTOMERS NOW MORE WILLING TO ORDER?
Oregon Pinot Noir, Washington State red wines and Syrah from all around the world.

Veritas Restaurant
43 East 20th Street
New York, New York 10003
phone 212-353-3700 fax 212-353-1632

Tim Kopec
WINE DIRECTOR

WHAT IS ONE OF YOUR ULTIMATE FOOD AND WINE PAIRINGS?
Roasted artichokes with Manzanilla Sherry.

DESCRIBE YOUR WINE SELECTIONS.
We believe it is the greatest wine list in America, including more than 2,800 well-selected and fairly priced wines, including all the classics from California, France, Italy, Spain and Australia.

WHAT IS YOUR FAVORITE WINE REGION IN THE WORLD TODAY?
Burgundy. So few varietals expressing such diversity based on soil and wine-making.

WHAT LED YOU TO PURSUE A CAREER THAT INVOLVES WINE?
Passion for food and wine.

WHAT IS THE BEST ASPECT OF YOUR JOB?
Great wine directors and sommeliers work the floor.

Vine

25 Broad Street
New York, New York 10004
phone 212-344-8463 fax 212-344-1099
website www.vinefood.com

John J. Monagas

RESTAURANT DIRECTOR
AND SOMMELIER

NAME TWO OF YOUR FAVORITE WINE REGIONS FROM AROUND THE WORLD.

Napa Valley for its elegant Cabernet Sauvignons, and the Burgundy region for its always-surprising Pinot Noirs and delightful Chardonnays.

NAME RECENT WINE DISCOVERIES THAT HAVE EXCITED YOU.

The high quality and great wine values being produced by Chilean, Argentinean and South African vineyards.

WHAT BITS OF INFORMATION WOULD YOU LIKE YOUR CUSTOMERS TO KNOW ABOUT YOU?

I am an art collector and have a great deal of interest in the arts. I am also an avid gardener.

DESCRIBE YOUR WINE SELECTIONS, BOTH BY THE GLASS AND ON YOUR LIST.

Vine is a contemporary American restaurant. Our wine by-the-glass program has two Champagnes, one sparkling wine and one Riesling, one Sauvignon Blanc, one Sancerre, three Chardonnays, three Pinot Noirs, two Cabernets, one Côtes du Rhône, one Primitivo and one red Zinfandel. Our wine list includes 320 wines, mostly from the United States and France, representing both major and minor varietals. I'm expanding the list to include more international wines.

WHAT IS THE MOST UNIQUE FEATURE IN YOUR WINE PROGRAM?

Our popular wine dinners with guest speakers, which we offer each month.

NAME A COUPLE OF YOUR RESTAURANT'S SIGNATURE DISHES. WHAT TYPES OF WINE DO YOU PREFER TO RECOMMEND WITH EACH?

Dayboat scallops with truffles served with Carneros Pinot Noir; filet mignon wrapped in apple-smoked bacon with California Cabernet Sauvignon.

IN THE PAST YEAR, WHAT WINES IN YOUR WINE PROGRAM HAVE CUSTOMERS BECOME MORE WILLING TO ORDER?

Spanish Rioja, South African Pinotage and Californian Viognier.

Zoë Restaurant

90 Prince Street
New York, New York 10012
phone 212-966-6722 fax 212-966-6718
website www.zoerestaurant.com

Scott E. Lawrence
MANAGING PARTNER
AND WINE DIRECTOR

WHAT INSPIRED YOU TO PURSUE A CAREER THAT INVOLVES WINE?
Two consecutive tastings: Chateau Montelena Cabernet 1978–1993 and forty-five 1989 Bordeaux.

NAME RECENT WINE DISCOVERIES THAT HAVE EXCITED YOU.
Washington State Bordeaux varietals for their complexity, balance and acidity; German and Austrian whites for their minerality, acidity and the quality of the 2001 vintage.

IF YOU WERE NOT IN THIS PROFESSION, WHAT WOULD YOU BE?
A farmer or golfer.

DESCRIBE YOUR WINE SELECTIONS, BOTH BY THE GLASS AND ON YOUR LIST.
We have a 250-bottle all-American wine list. Our focus is to provide customers with site-specific wines and wines showing a range of flavor profiles for individual varietals.

WHAT ARE THE MOST UNIQUE FEATURES IN YOUR WINE PROGRAM?
We have thirty-five wines by the glass and all are available in 6-ounce or 3-ounce pours. We have wine flights featuring specific AVAs, and appellation-based winemaker dinners.

NAME ONE OF YOUR RESTAURANT'S SIGNATURE DISHES. WHAT WINE DO YOU PREFER TO RECOMMEND WITH IT?
Grilled lamb chop, lamb osso buco with butternut squash risotto and black trumpet mushrooms with Washington State Meritage or Syrah.

IN THE PAST YEAR, WHAT WINES IN YOUR WINE PROGRAM HAVE CUSTOMERS BECOME MORE WILLING TO ORDER?
American Syrah from Paso Robles, Sonoma and Washington; Oregon Pinot Noir; California Sauvignon Blanc; Riesling and Gewürztraminer from New York's Finger Lakes region.

"21" Club

PHILIP PRATT, SOMMELIER
CHRISTOPHER SHIPLEY,
BEVERAGE DIRECTOR
21 West 52nd Street, New York
212-582-7200

L'Acajou

DANIEL KOHN, OWNER
AND WINE BUYER
53 West 19th Street, New York
212-645-1706

Aigo

ROBERT GRGUREV, GENERAL
MANAGER AND WINE BUYER
1608 First Avenue, New York
212-327-4700

Alfredo of Rome

ROBERT MACDONALD, MANAGER
AND WINE BUYER
4 West 49th Street, New York
212-397-0100

Alouette

KENNETH GIN, OWNER
AND WINE DIRECTOR
2588 Broadway, New York
212-222-6808

Amuse

JEAN-LUC LAMETERIE,
CO-MANAGER AND WINE BUYER
108 West 18th Street, New York
212-929-9755

An American Place in the Benjamin Hotel

MARK MAGNOTTA, GENERAL
MANAGER AND WINE BUYER
565 Lexington Avenue, New York
212-888-5650

Aquavit Restaurant

KEVIN SHANNON, SOMMELIER
13 West 54th Street, New York
212-307-7311

Atelier at the Ritz-Carlton

WILLIAM SHERER, SOMMELIER
50 Central Park South, New York
212-521-6125

AZ

WARNER STREJAN, SOMMELIER
21 West 17th Street, New York
212-691-8888

Babbo

JOSEPH BASTIANICH, OWNER
AND WINE BUYER
DAVID LYNCH, DIRECTOR OF WINE
110 Waverly Place, New York
212-777-0303

Baraonda

ENRICO PROIETTI, WINE BUYER
1439 Second Avenue, New York
212-288-8555

Barbetta

LEO FROKIC, SOMMELIER
321 West 46th Street, New York
212-246-9171

Ben Benson's Steak House

BRIAN JANTOW, SOMMELIER
123 West 52nd Street, New York
212-581-8888

Beppe Trattoria

CESARE CASELLA, OWNER
AND WINE BUYER
45 East 22nd Street, New York
212-982-8422

Bid

OLIVIER SAINT-AMMAND,
WINE BUYER
1334 York Avenue, New York
212-988-7730

Bistro Ten 18

CRAIG SKIPTUNIS,
GENERAL MANAGER
1018 Amsterdam Avenue, New York
212-662-7600

Blue Fin

LAURA MANIEC, SOMMELIER
1567 Broadway, New York
212-918-1400

Blue Hill

PAM WATSON, WINE DIRECTOR
75 Washington Place, New York
212-539-1776

Blue Ribbon Restaurant

SEAN SAINT-AMOUR,
GENERAL MANAGER
97 Sullivan Street, New York
212-274-0404

Bobby Van's Steakhouse

STEVE BOATS, WINE BUYER
230 Park Avenue, New York
212-867-5490

Brasserie

DANA MADIGAN, WINE DIRECTOR
100 East 53nd Street, New York
212-751-4840

Brasserie 8 1/2

MICHEL BOYER, SOMMELIER
9 West 57th Street, New York
212-829-0812

Bubble Lounge

EMMANUELLE CHICHE,
OWNER AND WINE BUYER
228 West Broadway, New York
212-431-3433

Café Centro at the MetLife Building

RENAUD AMMON, WINE DIRECTOR
200 Park Avenue, New York
212-818-1222

Café Fiorello's

GULIE PIRRI, WINE BUYER
1900 Broadway, New York
212-595-5330

La Cantina Toscana

PIERLUIGI SACCHETTI, SOMMELIER
1109 First Avenue, New York
212-754-5454

Carmine's

ROBERT CASTLEBERRY,
BEVERAGE DIRECTOR
200 West 44th Street, New York
212-221-3800

Central Park Boathouse

BILL WEIGEL, WINE BUYER
East 72nd Street and Park Drive
North, New York
212-517-2233

Chiam Restaurant

DAVID NG, WINE BUYER
160 East 48th Street, New York
212-371-2323

China Grill

David Madison, Wine Buyer

CBS Building, New York

212-333-7788

Churrascaria Plataforma

Jean Frison, Manager
and Wine Buyer

Belvedere Hotel, New York

212-245-0505

Ciao Europa Ristorante

Raul Soria, Wine Buyer

63 West 54th Street, New York

212-247-1200

Le Cirque 2000

Ralph Hersom, Wine Director

Paul Altuna, Sommelier

Jeff Puccine, Assistant
Sommelier

455 Madison Avenue, New York

212-303-7788

Citarella The Restaurant

Peter Botti, Beverage Director

1240 Avenue of the Americas,
New York

212-332-1515

Cité

Bob Degroat, Sommelier

Michael McCann,
Beverage Manager

120 West 51st Street, New York

212-956-7100

City Crab

Mitchell Rosen, Wine Buyer

235 Park Avenue South, New York

212-529-3800

City Hall Restaurant

Eric Lilavois, Sommelier

131 Duane Street, New York

212-227-7777

City Lobster

David Chiong, Manager
and Wine Buyer

1251 Avenue of the Americas,
New York

212-354-1717

Club Guastavino

Andrew Barnett, Sommelier

409 East 59th Street, New York

212-421-6644

Craft

Matthew MacCartney,
Sommelier

43 East 19th Street, New York

212-780-0880

Cub Room

Stefanie Krzyzamiak,
Manager and Wine Buyer

131 Sullivan Street, New York

212-677-4100

Danube

Walter Kranjc, Maître d'

30 Hudson Street, New York

212-791-3771

DB Bistro Moderne

RYAN BUTTNER, WINE BUYER
55 West 44th Street, New York
212-391-1616

DeGrezia

JOSEPH DEGREZIA, OWNER
AND WINE BUYER
231 East 50th Street, New York
212-750-5353

Del Frisco's Double Eagle Steak House

DAVID O'DAY, WINE DIRECTOR
1221 Avenue of the Americas,
New York
212-575-5129

The Dining Room

JOHN EGAN, WINE DIRECTOR
154 East 79th Street, New York
212-327-2500

Dock's

DON BERLAND, WINE BUYER
2427 Broadway, New York
212-724-5588

Due Restaurant

ERNESTO CAVALLI, SOMMELIER
1396 Third Avenue, New York
212-772-3331

Dylan Prime

PETER KLEIN, WINE DIRECTOR
62 Laight Street, New York
212-334-2274

L'Express

ANN BRYNELL, WINE DIRECTOR
249 Park Avenue, New York
212-254-5858

Five Points

VICKI FREEMAN, OWNER
AND WINE BUYER
31 Great Jones Street, New York
212-253-5700

Four Seasons Hotel

JULIAN NICCOLINI, SOMMELIER
99 East 52nd Street, New York
212-754-9494

Frankie and Johnnie's Steakhouse NY

PETER CHIMOS, WINE BUYER
269 West 45th Street, New York
212-997-9494

Fresco

ANTHONY SCOTTO, OWNER
AND WINE BUYER
34 East 52nd Street, New York
212-935-3436

Gabriel's

RICHARD SHIPLEY,
WINE DIRECTOR
11 West 60th Street, New York
212-956-4600

Gallagher's Steak House

TERRY CONDON, WINE BUYER
228 West 52nd Street, New York
212-245-5336

Gotham Bar and Grill

MICHAEL GREENLEE, SOMMELIER
12 East 12th Street, New York
212-620-4020

Halcyon at the Rihga Royal Hotel

JAY JONES, RESTAURANT DIRECTOR
AND WINE BUYER
151 West 54th Street, New York
212-468-8858

The Harrison

PAUL MASTERS, WINE DIRECTOR
355 Greenwich Street, New York
212-274-9310

Heartbeat Restaurant

DAVID GORDON, WINE DIRECTOR
149 East 49th Street, New York
212-407-2900

Icon Restaurant at the W Court Hotel

MICHAEL TRENK, GENERAL
MANAGER AND WINE BUYER
130 East 39th Street, New York
212-592-8888

Judson Grill

BETH VON BENZ, WINE BUYER
152 West 52nd Street, New York
212-582-5252

JW's Steakhouse at the Marriott Marquis

RAYMOND DEPAUL, SOMMELIER
1535 Broadway, New York
212-704-8900

Keen's Steakhouse

JOHN MCCLEMENT, WINE BUYER
72 West 36th Street, New York
212-947-3636

Lenox Room

TONY FORTUNA, OWNER
AND WINE BUYER
1278 Third Avenue at 73rd,
New York
212-772-0404

Lentini Restaurant

ENZO LENTINI,
GENERAL MANAGER
1562 Second Avenue, New York
212-628-3131

Le Madeleine

NICK DIMINIO, SOMMELIER
403 West 43rd Street, New York
212-246-2993

Maloney and Porcelli

ANTHONY COTTINGHAM,
SOMMELIER
37 East 50th Street, New York
212-750-2233

The Manhattan Ocean Club

PETER KING, BEVERAGE MANAGER
57 West 58th Street, New York
212-371-7777

Marseille

LEONARD LARUSSO,
WINE DIRECTOR
630 Ninth Avenue, New York
212-333-2323

The Melrose Restaurant

STEPHANIE TEBORRI,
MANAGER AND SOMMELIER
995 Fifth Avenue, New York
212-650-4737

Mesa Grill

LAURENCE KRETCHMER,
WINE BUYER
102 Fifth Avenue, New York
212-807-7400

Michael's New York

RICHARD BILL, WINE BUYER
24 West 55th Street, New York
212-767-0555

Milos Restaurant

RENO CHRISTOU, SOMMELIER
125 West 55th Street, New York
212-245-7400

Le Monde

JOE JONES, GENERAL MANAGER
AND WINE BUYER
2885 Broadway, New York
212-531-3939

Monkey Bar

BOB HAYDEN, MANAGER
AND WINE BUYER
60 East 54th Street, New York
212-838-2600

Morton's of Chicago

SCOTT RUBEN, WINE BUYER
551 Fifth Avenue, New York
212-972-3315

New York Yacht Club

B. DALY, SOMMELIER
37 West 44th Street, New York
212-382-1000

Nobu

ORLANDO RAMOS, BEVERAGE
MANAGER AND SOMMELIER
105 Hudson Street, New York
212-219-0500

North Square at the Washington Square Hotel

CHAD SMYSER, WINE DIRECTOR
103 Waverly Place, New York
212-254-1200

The Oak Room at the Plaza Hotel NYC

ABDOU DIA, WINE DIRECTOR
Fifth Avenue at Central Park South,
New York
212-546-5200

Olica

CHRISTOPHE LAHAPHILIO,
OWNER AND WINE BUYER
145 East 50th Street, New York
212-888-1220

Olives New York

JOE BIBBO, SOMMELIER
West New York Union Square, 201
Park Avenue, New York
212-353-8345

One CPS

JOE MCGUIRE, MANAGER
AND WINE BUYER
1 Central Park South, New York
212-583-1111

One If By Land, Two If By Sea

MICHEL FLORANC, WINE BUYER
17 Barrow Street, New York
212-228-0822

Osteria Del Circo

KEVIN DEL CASALE,
WINE DIRECTOR
120 West 55th Street, New York
212-265-3636

Ouest

GODFREY POLISTINA, OWNER
AND WINE BUYER
2315 Broadway, New York
212-580-8700

The Palm

ALEX BALBUENA, WINE DIRECTOR
837 Second Avenue, New York
212-687-2953

Palm Too

KRISTINE WEHLER,
WINE DIRECTOR
840 Second Avenue, New York
212-697-5198

The Palm West

JEREMY LEBOW, SOMMELIER
250 West 50th Street, New York
212-333-7256

Park Avenue Café

PETER CREADON, WINE BUYER
100 East 63rd Street, New York
212-644-1900

Patria

JOSE PRADO, SOMMELIER
250 Park Avenue South, New York
212-777-6211

Patroon

THIERRY BRUNEAU, SOMMELIER
160 East 46th Street, New York
212-883-7373

Le Perigord

CHRISTOPHER BRIGUET,
MANAGER AND WINE BUYER
415 East 52nd Street, New York
212-755-6244

The Post House

JOSEPH FUNGHINI,
WINE DIRECTOR
28 East 63rd Street, New York
212-935-2888

Q56 Restaurant & Cocktails at the Swissotel

SABASTIAN LIEBOLD,
MANAGER AND WINE BUYER
65 East 56th Street, New York
212-756-3800

The Red Cat

CONNOR COFFEY,
GENERAL MANAGER
227 Tenth Avenue, New York
212-242-1122

Remi

NICK MAVRIC, SOMMELIER
1325 Avenue of the Americas,
New York
212-581-4242

The Restaurant of the French Culinary Institute

CHRISTIAN HAUSER, GENERAL
MANAGER AND WINE BUYER
462 Broadway, New York
212-219-3300

Rock Center Café

DAVID GORDON, SOMMELIER
600 Fifth Avenue, Building 17,
New York
212-332-7621

Les Routiers

SUSAN BENEDETTO,
WINE DIRECTOR
568 Amsterdam Avenue, New York
212-874-2742

Ruth's Chris Steak House

JESS HUBBELING, MANAGER AND
WINE BUYER
148 West 51st Street, New York
212-245-9600

San Domenico NY

PIERO TROUTTA, WINE STEWARD
240 Central Park South, New York
212-265-5959

The Sea Grill

EAMON MANLY, WINE DIRECTOR
19 West 49th Street, New York
212-332-7610

Shaffer City Oyster Bar & Grill

JAY SHAFFER, OWNER
AND WINE BUYER
5 West 21st Street, New York
212-255-9827

Shelly's New York

ROBERT ROSS, WINE DIRECTOR
104 West 57th Street, New York
212-245-2422

Shun Lee Palace

KENNY NG, GENERAL MANAGER
155 East 55th Street, New York
212-371-8844

Smith & Wollensky

PAT COLTON, WINE DIRECTOR
797 Third Avenue, New York
212-753-1530

Spark's Steakhouse

MIKE CETTA, WINE BUYER
210 East 46th Street, New York
212-687-4855

Strip House

BOGDAN CRUTA, SOMMELIER
13 East 12th Street, New York
212-328-0000

Tavern on the Green

DON MCHENRY, WINE AND
BEVERAGE DIRECTOR
One West 67th Street, Central Park
West, New York
212-873-3200

Tocqueville

JOANN MAKOVITZKY, SOMMELIER
15 East 15th Street, New York
212-647-1515

Trattoria Del Arte

BILL FUGERE, MANAGER
AND WINE BUYER
Seventh between 56th and 57th,
New York
212-245-9800

Tropica

JENNIFER HANCOX,
GENERAL MANAGER
200 Park Avenue, New York
212-887-6767

Tse Yang

LEE FLEMING, SOMMELIER
51st between Park and Madison,
New York
212-688-5447

Tuscan Steak

MARK SOMEN, GENERAL MANAGER
622 Third Avenue, New York
212-404-1700

Union Square Café

CHRISTOPHER RUSSELL,
SOMMELIER
21 East 16th Street, New York
212-243-4020

Verbena

AARON VON ROCK,
WINE DIRECTOR
54 Irving Place, New York
212-260-5454

Vong

ANNIE TURSO, WINE BUYER
200 East 54th Street, New York
212-486-9592

The Water Club

SAM CORRENTI,
BEVERAGE DIRECTOR
500 East 30th Street, New York
212-683-3333

West Bank Café

STEVE OLSEN, OWNER
AND SOMMELIER
407 West 42nd Street, New York
212-695-6909

Friends Lake Inn

963 Friends Lake Road
Chestertown, New York 12817
phone 518-494-4751 fax 518-494-4616
website www.friendslake.com

Thomas P. Burke

SOMMELIER

NAME YOUR FAVORITE WINE REGION FROM AROUND THE WORLD.
One smell of a northern Rhône wine always manages to bring me back to
Tournon-sur-Rhône, looking up at the Hermitage hills.

WHAT BITS OF INFORMATION WOULD YOU LIKE YOUR CUSTOMERS TO
KNOW ABOUT YOU?
I used to be a competitive ultra-runner when I lived in Park City, Utah.

IF YOU WERE NOT IN THIS PROFESSION, WHAT WOULD YOU BE?
An organic farmer.

WHAT ARE THE MOST UNIQUE FEATURES IN YOUR WINE PROGRAM?
We have three pages of the list devoted solely to half-bottles. I love the "Bring
Your Own Best Bottle" dinners we put on. We pick a region of the world with
vintage and quality restrictions; say first- through fifth-growth Bordeaux, 1989
and older, and guests bring one bottle per person. We pair courses with wines
and start popping bottles. Guests are eager to bring out their gems.

WHAT WINES ARE THE BEST VALUES IN YOUR RESTAURANT?
Languedoc wines and Italian wines from lesser-known regions.

NAME A COUPLE OF YOUR RESTAURANT'S SIGNATURE DISHES. WHAT
TYPES OF WINE DO YOU PREFER TO RECOMMEND WITH EACH?
Lobster and scallop-stuffed corn crepe with vanilla bean beurre blanc paired
with New World cool-climate Chardonnay; frutti di mare with squid ink risot-
to paired with Italian whites, white Châteauneuf-du-Pape or New World
Viognier.

IN THE PAST YEAR, WHAT WINES IN YOUR WINE PROGRAM HAVE CUS-
TOMERS BECOME MORE WILLING TO ORDER?
Syrah. It has been fun to take them to France to show them an expression of
Syrah they may not know.

Gage and Tollner

372 Fulton Street
Brooklyn, New York 11201
phone 718-875-5181 fax 718-243-0222
website www.gageandtollner.com

Nicola A. Vendola
BEVERAGE DIRECTOR

WHAT INSPIRED YOU TO PURSUE A CAREER THAT INVOLVES WINE?
While working at I Trulli Restaurant, the Beverage Director, Charles Scicolone, helped me discover this passion in me.

NAME YOUR FAVORITE WINE REGIONS FROM AROUND THE WORLD.
Wines from the Finger Lakes in New York. The wines are great.

NAME RECENT WINE DISCOVERIES THAT HAVE EXCITED YOU.
Wines from Spain, because their quality is excellent and they are great values.

IF YOU WERE NOT IN THIS PROFESSION, WHAT WOULD YOU BE DOING?
Teaching.

DESCRIBE YOUR WINE SELECTIONS, BOTH BY THE GLASS AND ON YOUR LIST.
Our selections are international, organized by varietal so guests see how a wine from a particular varietal changes in taste according to geographical origin.

WHAT ARE THE MOST UNIQUE FEATURES IN YOUR WINE PROGRAM?
Our half-bottle selection and the collections of Amarone Bertani from Italy, Far Niente from Napa, and Don Melchor from Chile.

WHAT CATEGORY OF WINE IS THE BEST VALUE IN YOUR RESTAURANT?
Primitivo from Italy's Apulia region.

NAME A COUPLE OF YOUR RESTAURANT'S SIGNATURE DISHES. WHAT TYPES OF WINE DO YOU PREFER TO RECOMMEND WITH EACH?
Virginia crab cake with Willamette Valley Pinot Noir; T-bone steak with older Amarone.

IN THE PAST YEAR, WHAT WINES IN YOUR WINE PROGRAM HAVE CUSTOMERS BECOME MORE WILLING TO ORDER?
Finger Lakes Riesling, Tasmania Pinot Noir, Alsace Pinot Blanc, and half-bottles of red Burgundy and Indian Cabernet-Shiraz.

The Grill at Strathallan

550 East Avenue
Rochester, New York 14607
phone 585-454-1880 fax 585-461-2845
website www.grill175.com

Milisav Tadich
OWNER AND
WINE DIRECTOR

WHAT ARE SOME OF YOUR ULTIMATE FOOD AND WINE PAIRINGS?
Carpaccio of Kobe beef over soft polenta, drizzled with white truffle oil, paired
with 1998 Gaja Sauvignon Blanc, "Alteni di Brassica."

DESCRIBE YOUR WINE SELECTIONS.
Our wine list has more than 1,200 selections, with a focus on California, Italy
(Toscana, Piemonte and Friuli) and France (Bourgogne and Champagne), but
most wine regions in the world are also represented, from Croatia to Lebanon.

WHAT IS YOUR FAVORITE WINE REGION IN THE WORLD TODAY?
Austria. Rieslings and Grüner Veltliners produced in Austria's Wachau Valley
and Burgenland's Neusiedlersee dessert wines are simply world-class.

WHAT LED YOU TO YOUR CURRENT POSITION?
I grew up in Europe tasting wines and being involved in the process, from vineyard to the table. It was captivating. Later, the "mystery" became a passion.

IF YOU WERE NOT IN THIS PROFESSION, WHAT WOULD YOU BE?
Worldwide food and wine tour guide.

Hemingway's American Bar and Grill

1885 Wantagh Avenue
Wantagh, New York 11793
phone 516-781-2700 fax 516-781-2781
website www.hemingwaysgrill.com

Gregory R. Bartolotta
PARTNER AND
WINE DIRECTOR

NAME TWO OF YOUR FAVORITE WINE REGIONS FROM AROUND THE
WORLD.
Carneros for its outstanding Pinot Noirs and Chardonnays; Tuscany for pro-
ducing some of Italy's greatest wines.

WHAT BITS OF INFORMATION WOULD YOU LIKE YOUR CUSTOMERS TO
KNOW ABOUT YOU?
I am blessed with a loving wife and three loving daughters and a personal
1,000-bottle home wine cellar!

DESCRIBE YOUR WINE SELECTIONS, BOTH BY THE GLASS AND ON YOUR
LIST.
Our list's emphasis is on California wines. We offer fifteen to eighteen wines by
the glass. We have a large selection of quality wines offered at reasonable prices.

WHAT ARE THE MOST UNIQUE FEATURES IN YOUR WINE PROGRAM?
Our prix fixe wine dinners every Monday evening. We pour exceptional wines
at no extra charge with a three-course dinner from our entire menu selection.

NAME A COUPLE OF YOUR RESTAURANT'S SIGNATURE DISHES. WHAT
TYPES OF WINE DO YOU PREFER TO RECOMMEND WITH EACH?
Baby back ribs with ginger barbecue sauce with Sonoma Zinfandel; double-cut
pork chop with Bourbon demi-glaze with Carneros Pinot Noir.

IN THE PAST YEAR, WHAT WINES IN YOUR WINE PROGRAM HAVE CUS-
TOMERS BECOME MORE WILLING TO ORDER?
California Chenin Blanc and California Rhône-style blends.

WHAT ARE SOME OTHER ULTIMATE WINE AND FOOD PAIRINGS?
Grilled salmon or sautéed pork loin with a light- to medium-bodied Pinot
Noir; tomato-based pastas with medium-bodied Sangiovese; braised lamb
shanks with full-bodied Syrah.

Jacques Cartier Dining Room at the Riveredge Resort Hotel

17 Holland Street
Alexandria Bay, New York 13607
phone 315-482-9917 fax 315-482-5010
website www.riveredge.com

Nicola A. Bonavita
MAÎTRE D' AND SOMMELIER

WHAT INSPIRED YOU TO PURSUE A CAREER THAT INVOLVES WINE?
I began as a bartender.

NAME SOME OF YOUR FAVORITE WINE REGIONS FROM AROUND THE WORLD.
Tuscany, Campania and Burgundy. My family is from the two Italian regions, and I have a personal love for Burgundy.

NAME RECENT WINE DISCOVERIES THAT HAVE EXCITED YOU.
Super-Tuscans and newer-style white wines from California.

WHAT WOULD YOU LIKE YOUR CUSTOMERS TO KNOW ABOUT YOU?
I've written two books, a training manual and Once Upon a Wine, a collection of experiences and stories concerning wine. I've been in the wine trade for thirty-three years involved with wholesale, wineries and suppliers.

DESCRIBE YOUR WINE SELECTIONS, BOTH BY THE GLASS AND ON YOUR LIST.
We offer American wines from New York, Washington State, Oregon and California and European wines from Austria, Germany, Italy, France and many others.

WHAT ARE THE MOST UNIQUE FEATURES IN YOUR WINE PROGRAM?
We have large by-the-glass and half-bottle selections, wine flights, wines available by the half-glass or taste, extravagant wine dinners and special wine pricing.

WHAT CATEGORY OF WINE IS THE BEST VALUE IN YOUR RESTAURANT?
California.

NAME A COUPLE OF YOUR RESTAURANT'S SIGNATURE DISHES. WHAT TYPES OF WINE DO YOU PREFER TO RECOMMEND WITH EACH?
Roasted sea bass and Touraine Rosé or Greco di Tufo.

WHAT WINES ARE CUSTOMERS NOW MORE WILLING TO ORDER?
Wine from Chile, California, Washington State, Alsace and unfamiliar Italian wines.

Old Drovers Inn

196 East Duncan Hill Road, Old Route 22
Dover Plains, New York 12522
phone 845-832-9311 fax 845-832-3403
website www.olddroversinn.com

Arthur L. Levin
EXECUTIVE WINEMASTER

WHAT INSPIRED YOU TO PURSUE A CAREER THAT INVOLVES WINE?
A taste of a mature Chambertin while dining at l'Auberge de Chambertin in
Burgundy.

NAME ONE OR TWO OF YOUR FAVORITE WINE DISTRICTS OR WINE
REGIONS FROM AROUND THE WORLD.
Burgundy for the ultra-finesse of both its whites and reds when the vintage is
au point; Bordeaux for consistency in producing extremely high-quality reds.

NAME RECENT WINE DISCOVERIES THAT HAVE EXCITED YOU.
California wines, across a spectrum of producers and grapes.

IF YOU WERE NOT IN THIS PROFESSION, WHAT WOULD YOU BE DOING?
I have had previous and parallel careers as a journalist, computer scientist and
information technologies consultant.

DESCRIBE YOUR WINE SELECTIONS, BOTH BY THE GLASS AND ON YOUR LIST.
By the glass we offer two sparkling wines, one Rosé, four whites (from France,
California, Italy), five reds (from France, California, Australia), and sixteen
dessert wines. Our red wines are from Bordeaux, Burgundy, California and
Italy, in that order.

WHAT CATEGORY OF WINE IS THE BEST VALUE IN YOUR RESTAURANT?
We have forty wines at $25 or less, all sommelier-tested to ensure they comple-
ment our cuisine.

NAME A COUPLE OF YOUR RESTAURANT'S SIGNATURE DISHES. WHAT
TYPES OF WINE DO YOU PREFER TO RECOMMEND WITH EACH?
Turkey hash with Barbera d'Alba or Barolo; double lamb chops with Brunello
di Montalcino or Ribera del Duero.

IN THE PAST YEAR, WHAT WINES IN YOUR WINE PROGRAM HAVE CUS-
TOMERS BECOME MORE WILLING TO ORDER?
New Zealand Pinot Noir.

Yono's Restaurant

64 Colvin Avenue
Albany, New York 12205
phone 518-436-7747 fax 518-437-3410
website www.yonos.com

Dominick H.V. Purnomo
MAÎTRE D'HÔTEL
AND SOMMELIER

WHAT ARE YOUR FAVORITE WINES?
German Rieslings, from the slatey, minerally style of the Mosel to the voluptuous style of the Rhein.

NAME RECENT WINE DISCOVERIES THAT HAVE EXCITED YOU.
Austrian Grüner Veltliners and Rieslings.

IF YOU WERE NOT IN THIS PROFESSION, WHAT WOULD YOU BE?
A Formula One race car driver with a large personal wine collection, maybe even my own vineyard.

DESCRIBE YOUR WINE SELECTIONS, BOTH BY THE GLASS AND ON YOUR LIST.
We offer wines from every major growing region. We specialize in hand-crafted, boutique wines that show the essence of the land that they come from and the people who make them. Our wines by the glass change daily, usually consisting of twenty to twenty-five wines, including Champagnes and white and red table wines.

WHAT ARE THE MOST UNIQUE FEATURES IN YOUR WINE PROGRAM?
We use Riedel crystal exclusively.

NAME A FEW OF YOUR RESTAURANT'S SIGNATURE DISHES. WHAT TYPES OF WINE DO YOU PREFER TO RECOMMEND WITH EACH?
Pan-seared Hudson Valley foie gras with Asian pear and a fifty-year-old balsamic reduction paired with Austrian Scheurebe Trockenbeerenauslese; hamachi and yellowfin tuna tartare with Champagne; pork tenderloin with coconut milk, orange, sweet soy and ginger with Sonoma County Zinfandel.

WHAT ARE SOME OTHER ULTIMATE WINE AND FOOD PAIRINGS?
Pizza and burgers with California Zinfandels and Spanish Riojas, and shellfish with Châteauneuf-du-Pape blancs.

The 1906 Restaurant
ROSEMARIE DE CRISTOFARO,
WINE BUYER
41 Lower Main Street, Callicoon
845-887-1906

75 On Main Street
JUNE SPIRER, OWNER
AND WINE BUYER
75 Main Street, Southampton
631-283-7575

Al Di La Trattoria
EMILIANO COPPA, OWNER AND
WINE BUYER
248 Fifth Avenue, Brooklyn
718-783-4565

Alberto Restaurant
JOE ARTHEY, SOMMELIER
SILVANA CHIAPPELLONI,
SOMMELIER
98-31 Metropolitan Avenue,
Forest Hills
718-268-7860

Alison by the Beach
ALISON HURT, OWNER
AND WINE DIRECTOR
3593 Montauk Highway, Sagaponack
631-537-7100

Allyn's Restaurant
ALLAN KATZ, OWNER,
CHEF AND WINE BUYER
4258 Route 44, Millbrook
845-677-5888

American Hotel
TED CONKLIN, OWNER
AND WINE BUYER
Main Street, Sag Harbor
631-725-3535

Anthony's Restaurant
ANDREW SABELLA, OWNER
AND WINE BUYER
Route 3 and Interstate 87, Plattsburgh
518-561-6420

Arad Evans Inn
JASON THOMAS, WINE DIRECTOR
7206 Genesee Street, Fayetteville
315-637-2020

Argyle Grill and Tavern
MEGAN YATES, MANAGER
AND WINE BUYER
90 Deer Park Avenue, Babylon Village
631-321-4900

Barney's
JOHN ARON, GENERAL MANAGER
315 Buckram Road, Locust Valley
516-671-6300

The Bear Café
PETER CANTINE, OWNER
AND WINE BUYER
295A Tinker Street, Route 212,
Bearsville
845-679-5555

The Belhurst Castle
KELLY LYNCH, BAR MANAGER
Belhurst Castle and White Springs
Manor, Geneva
315-781-0201

Bella Vita City Grill
ANTHONY CAMBRIA, JR.,
GENERAL MANAGER
430-16 North Country Road,
Saint James
631-862-8060

Brewster Inn
RICHARD HUBBARD, OWNER
AND WINE BUYER
6 Ledyard Avenue, Route 20,
Box 507, Cazenova
315-655-9232

Burton and Doyle Steakhouse
GIL TRAVALIN, WINE DIRECTOR
661 Northern Boulevard, Great Neck
516-487-9200

Café on the Green
JOE FRANCO, OWNER
AND WINE BUYER
201-10 Cross Island Parkway,
Bayside
718-423-7272

La Caravelle Restaurant
ANDRE AND RITA JAMMET,
PROPRIETORS AND WINE BUYERS
46 Bedford-Banksville Road, Bedford
212-586-4252

The Carltun at Eisenhower Park
NATALIE ZALEVSKA, SOMMELIER
Eisenhower Park, East Meadow
516-542-0700

Casa Di Copani
JOHN COPANI, OWNER
AND WINE BUYER
3414 Burnet Avenue, Syracuse
315-463-1031

City Grill
MIKE DEPUE, SOMMELIER
268 Main Street, Buffalo
716-856-2651

Cosimo's Brick Oven
TONY POLANCO, WINE BUYER
620 Route 211 East, Middletown
845-692-3242

Crabtree's Kittle House Inn
DON CASTALDO, SOMMELIER
11 Kittle Road, Chappaqua
914-666-8044

Cripple Creek Restaurant
PATRICK HAYES, CO-OWNER
AND WINE BUYER
22 Garden Street, Rhinebeck
845-876-4355

Culinary Institute of America
STEVE KOLPAN, WINE BUYER
433 Albany Post Road, Hyde Park
845-471-6608

Depuy Canal House
LEE HARRINGTON, SOMMELIER
Route 213, High Fallas
845-687-7700

Eastchester Fish Gourmet
RICK ROSS, WINE BUYER
837 White Plains Road, Scarsdale
914-725-3450

Emerson Inn and Spa
LAURENT ERTLE, WINE BUYER
146 Mount Pleasant Road,
Mount Tremper
845-688-7900

Equus at the Castle at Tarrytown

GILBERT BAERISWIL, WINE BUYER
400 Benedict Avenue, Tarrytown
914-631-1980

Fiamma Osteria

GREG HARRINGTON,
WINE DIRECTOR
206 Spring Street, Astoria
212-653-0100

Fiddleheads American Fish House & Grill

EILEEN O'LEARY, OWNER
AND WINE BUYER
62 South Street, Oyster Bay
516-922-2999

The Fine Foods Café

SHANNON MCKINNEY, OWNER
AND WINE BUYER
10 Charles Colemann Boulevard,
Pawling
845-855-3875

The Ginger Man

SHANNON KELLEY,
RESTAURANT MANAGER
234 Western Avenue, Albany
518-427-5963

The Heights Café and Grill

JAMES LAROUNIS, OWNER
AND WINE BUYER
903 Hanshaw Road, Ithaca
607-257-4144

Henry's End Restaurant

MARK LAHM, OWNER
AND WINE BUYER
44 Henry Street, Brooklyn Heights
718-834-1776

Hudson House River Inn

BERTRAM STEWART, MANAGER
AND WINE BUYER
2 Main Street, Cold Spring
845-265-9355

Hudson's Ribs and Fish

ED BOGDAN, SOMMELIER
1099 Route 9, Fishkill
845-297-5002

Inn at Stone Creek

WAYNE PANZA, OWNER
AND WINE BUYER
31 Route 376, Hopwell Junction
845-227-6631

Irises Café and Wine Bar

CAROL MCLEAN, OWNER
AND WINE BUYER
20-22 City Hall Place, Plattsburgh
518-566-7000

James Lane Café at Hedges Inn

LARRY BRYANT, MANAGER
AND WINE BUYER
74 James Lane, East Hampton
631-324-7100

Kettle Lakes Restaurant
TORREY GRANT, WINE BUYER
5785 Route 80, Tully
315-696-3663

King Umberto
ROSARIO FUSCHETTO, OWNER
AND WINE BUYER
1343 Hempstead Turnpike, Elmont
516-352-3232

Lake Placid Lodge
MARK STEBBINGS, SOMMELIER
Whiteface Inn Road, Lake Placid
518-523-2700

Lincklaen House
IAN KUPER, WINE DIRECTOR
79 Albany Street, Cazenovia
315-655-3461

Longfellows Restaurant
YVONNE SINNAMON, CO-OWNER
AND WINE BUYER
500 Union Avenue, Saratoga Springs
518-587-0108

Luigi's Restaurant & Bar
ROGER BAJANA, WINE DIRECTOR
265-21 Union Turnpike, New Hyde Park
718-347-7136

Lusardi's Restaurant
MAURO LUSARDI, OWNER
AND WINE BUYER
1885 Palmer Avenue, Larchmont
914-834-5555

The Maidstone Arms Inn
CYNTHIA GATTIE, MANAGER
AND WINE BUYER
207 Main Street, East Hampton
631-324-5006

Mamma Lombardi's
GUY LOMBARDI, OWNER
AND WINE BUYER
400 Furrows Road, Holbrook
631-737-0774

Mario's Via Abruzzi
ANTHONY DANIELE, OWNER
AND WINE BUYER
2740 Monroe Avenue, Rochester
585-271-1111

Maxie's Supper Club & Oyster Bar
DEWI EVANS, CO-OWNER
AND WINE BUYER
635 West State Street, Ithaca
607-272-4136

Mazzi
KATHY CATANZARO, OWNER
AND WINE BUYER
493 East Jericho Turnpike,
Huntington
631-421-3390

Mirabelle
JULIE PASQUIER, SOMMELIER
404 North Country Road, St. James
631-584-5999

Mirror Lake Inn
KATIE WELCH,
DINING ROOM MANAGER
5 Mirror Lake Drive, Lake Placid
518-523-2544

Number Five
JAMES MCCOY, OWNER
AND WINE BUYER
33 South Washington Street,
Binghamton
607-723-0555

Oliver's Restaurant

HENRY GORINO, OWNER
AND WINE BUYER
2095 Delaware Avenue, Buffalo
716-877-9662

The Omaha Steakhouse

FRANK PEPPINO, MANAGER
AND WINE BUYER
566 East 187th Street, Bronx
718-584-6167

Oznots Dish

ERIC BAUM, OWNER AND
WINE BUYER
Berry and North Ninth, Brooklyn
718-599-6596

P.S. Restaurant

RICHARD DODD, OWNER
AND WINE BUYER
Giant Plaza, 100 Rano Boulevard,
Vestal
607-770-0056

The Palm at Huntting Inn

ARGELYS CRUZ, ASSISTANT
MANAGER AND WINE BUYER
94 Main Street, East Hampton
631-324-0410

Pascale Wine Bar

CHUCK PASCALE, WINE BUYER
204 West Fayette Street, Syracuse
315-471-3040

Pat Russo's Dugout

DIANNE RUSSO, OWNER
AND WINE BUYER
43 Main Street, South Glens Falls
518-793-9560

Pierce's 1894 Restaurant

JOE PIERCE, WINE BUYER
228 Oakwood Avenue, Elmira Heights
607-734-2022

The Plaza Café

DOUGLAS GULIJIA, OWNER
AND CHEF
61 Hill Street, Southampton
631-283-9323

The Prospect Restaurant at Scribner Hollow Lodge

GUY CHIRICO,
RESTAURANT MANAGER
Route 23A, Hunter
518-263-4211

Provence Restaurant

TAMAR SHAHINIAN, GENERAL
MANAGER AND WINE DIRECTOR
Stuyvesant Plaza, Albany
518-689-7777

Richard's Freestyle Cuisine

JAMIE NICHOLSON, WINE STEWARD
51 Main Street, Lake Placid
518-523-3680

The Rio Bamba

JAMES BROWN, MANAGER
AND WINE DIRECTOR
282 Alexander Street, Rochester
716-244-8680

River Café

JOSEPH DELISSO, SOMMELIER
1 Water Street, Brooklyn
718-522-5200

Ruth's Chris Steak House at the Marriott

Chris Limburg, Manager
and Wine Buyer
670 White Plains Road, Tarrytown
914-631-3311

Ruth's Chris Steak House

Mariola Kensington,
Manager and Wine Buyer
600 Old Country Road, Garden City
516-222-0220

San Marco Ristorante

Orlando Andreani, Owner
and Wine Buyer
658 Motor Parkway, Hauppauge
631-273-0088

Scrimshaw at the Desmond

Rob Wentworth,
Restaurant Manager
660 Albany-Shaker Road, Colonie
518-452-5801

Tequila Sunrise

Rich Perez, Owner
and Wine Buyer
145 Larchmont Avenue, Larchmont
914-834-6378

Three Village Inn

Dan Laffitte, General Manager
150 Main Street, Stony Brook
631-751-0555

Troutbeck Inn and Confrence Center

Garret Corcoran,
General Manager
Leedsville Road, Amenia
845-373-9681

Union House

Regina Bei, Owner
and Wine Buyer
1108 Main Street, Fishkill
845-896-6129

Village Tavern Restaurant & Inn

Suzanne Geisz, Wine Director
30 Mechanic Street, Hammondsport
607-569-2528

Water's Edge Restaurant

Philipe Crespi, Sommelier
44th Drive and East River,
Long Island City
718-482-0033

The Willett House

Dennis Gallagher,
General Manager
20 Willett Avenue, Port Chester
914-939-7500

The Wine Bar

Melissa Evans, Sommelier
417 Broadway, Saratoga Springs
518-584-8777

The Would Restaurant at the Inn at Applewood

Debra Dooley, Sommelier
120 North Road, Highland
845-691-9883

Xaviar's

William Rattner, Sommelier
506 Piermont Avenue, Piermont
845-359-7007

The Angus Barn

9401 Glenwood Avenue
Raleigh, North Carolina 27617
phone 919-781-2444 fax 919-783-5568
website www.angusbarn.com

Hendrik P. Schuitemaker
WINE AND BEVERAGE DIRECTOR

NAME YOUR FAVORITE WINE DISTRICTS OR REGIONS FROM AROUND THE WORLD.
The Rhône Valley. Its wines are truly wonderful with food.

NAME RECENT WINE DISCOVERIES THAT HAVE EXCITED YOU.
Wines from South African and North Carolina are really starting to come online.

WHAT BITS OF INFORMATION WOULD YOU LIKE YOUR CUSTOMERS TO KNOW ABOUT YOU?
I enjoy the outdoors very much and I love to garden. I have also adopted six dogs from very bad situations.

IF YOU WERE NOT IN THIS PROFESSION, WHAT WOULD YOU BE DOING?
Working with the mentally handicapped in some capacity.

DESCRIBE YOUR WINE SELECTIONS, BOTH BY THE GLASS AND ON YOUR LIST.
We have more than 1,300 selections on our wine list representing wine-growing regions from all over the world. We also have more than thirty wines by the glass.

WHAT ARE THE MOST UNIQUE FEATURES IN YOUR WINE PROGRAM?
Our wine flights and the Adventure Page in the wine list featuring unusual wines with descriptions are very popular with our guests. We also have a thirty-seat wine cellar dining room for multi-course wine dinners.

NAME A FEW OF YOUR RESTAURANT'S SIGNATURE DISHES. WHAT TYPES OF WINE DO YOU PREFER TO RECOMMEND WITH EACH?
Barbecued baby-back ribs with Sonoma or Alsatian Gewürztraminer; rack of lamb with Châteauneuf-du-Pape; 22-ounce cut of prime rib with South African Pinotage.

IN THE PAST YEAR, WHAT WINES IN YOUR WINE PROGRAM HAVE CUS-TOMERS BECOME MORE WILLING TO ORDER?
Wines from Spain and California red Zinfandels, as well as unusual varietals that represent good value on our list.

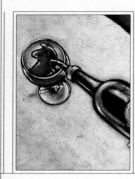

The Angus Barn

9401 Glenwood Avenue
Raleigh, North Carolina 27617
phone 919-781-2444 fax 919-783-5568
website www.angusbarn.com

Jefferson S. Napier
WINE EDUCATOR

NAME ONE OR TWO OF YOUR FAVORITE WINE DISTRICTS OR WINE
REGIONS FROM AROUND THE WORLD.
Spanish wines. Local North Carolina wineries have had promising results with
Viognier, my favorite white varietal.

NAME RECENT WINE DISCOVERIES THAT HAVE EXCITED YOU.
The wines of New Zealand, particularly Pinot Noir.

WHAT BITS OF INFORMATION WOULD YOU LIKE YOUR CUSTOMERS TO
KNOW ABOUT YOU?
I do stand-up comedy on open-mike nights at the local clubs. I am point man
on my restaurant's bid to win the Malcolm Baldrige National Quality Award.

DESCRIBE YOUR WINE SELECTIONS, BOTH BY THE GLASS AND ON YOUR
LIST.
We have nearly 1,300 selections. About forty percent of the collection is
Californian and thirty percent is French. Our cellar program is not limited to
"collectibles," but also lesser-known wines that we deem ageworthy.

WHAT ARE THE MOST UNIQUE FEATURES IN YOUR WINE PROGRAM?
The "Adventure Page" on our list, where we feature varietals and regions that
many guests might have only read about; our monthly themed wine dinners,
held in our wine cellar dining room. For example, we did a re-creation of the
last dinner served aboard the Titanic.

NAME A COUPLE OF YOUR RESTAURANT'S SIGNATURE DISHES. WHAT
TYPES OF WINE DO YOU PREFER TO RECOMMEND WITH EACH?
Sirloin strip topped with a little Gorgonzola cheese and a drizzle of balsamic
glaze with Brunello di Montalcino or a super-Tuscan; herb-crusted rack of lamb
with Côte-Rôtie or Châteauneuf-du-Pape.

Beef Barn

400 Saint Andrews Drive
Greenville, North Carolina 27834
phone 252-756-1161 fax 252-756-7655

Robert M. Simon
OWNER

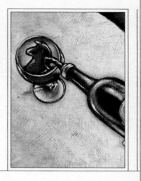

WHAT ARE SOME OF YOUR ULTIMATE FOOD AND WINE PAIRINGS?
Smoked pork chops with big California Pinot Noir; our New York strip topped
with shallot sauce with California Meritage.

DESCRIBE YOUR WINE SELECTIONS.
The list has been developed over the last 18 years. We have more than 650
selections, with a focus on vertical selections of California Cabernet
Sauvignons.

WHAT IS YOUR FAVORITE WINE REGION IN THE WORLD TODAY?
California. I developed my taste for wine in the late 1970s and early 1980s and
grew up with the California explosion.

WHAT LED YOU TO YOUR CURRENT POSITION?
General interest, and desire to match food and wine at my restaurant.

WHAT ARE THE BEST ASPECTS OF YOUR JOB?
Educating the public about the fun of drinking wine.

IF YOU WERE NOT IN THIS PROFESSION, WHAT WOULD YOU BE DOING?
Running a golf resort.

Camel City Café and Wine Bar

878 West Fourth Street
Winston-Salem, North Carolina 27101
phone 336-734-1797 fax 336-734-1796

John Hughes
OWNER AND PRESIDENT

NAME ONE OF YOUR FAVORITE WINE REGIONS FROM AROUND THE WORLD.
Sonoma County for its Pinot Noir and obscure white wines.

NAME RECENT WINE DISCOVERIES THAT HAVE EXCITED YOU.
Santa Rita Casa Real; its quality is very high and it is an affordable wine. Nga Waka Sauvignon Blanc from New Zealand; awesome, as well.

IF YOU WERE NOT IN THIS PROFESSION, WHAT WOULD YOU BE DOING?
Teaching athletics, being a motivational speaker or working with kids on self-esteem.

DESCRIBE YOUR WINE SELECTIONS, BOTH BY THE GLASS AND ON YOUR LIST.
Our list explores the world of wine. We represent all regions.

WHAT ARE THE MOST UNIQUE FEATURES IN YOUR WINE PROGRAM?
We offer wines by the glass and half-bottle, wine flights and wine dinners.

WHAT CATEGORIES OF WINE ARE THE BEST VALUES IN YOUR RESTAURANT?
Côtes du Rhône, Australian whites and Barbera d'Asti.

NAME A FEW OF YOUR RESTAURANT'S SIGNATURE DISHES. WHAT TYPES OF WINE DO YOU PREFER TO RECOMMEND WITH EACH?
Barbecued shrimp with Australian Sémillon-Sauvignon Blanc; snapper Orleans with Santa Lucia Highlands Chardonnay or Spanish Cabernet-Grenache-Carignane blend; grilled breast of duck with Napa Valley Chardonnay.

IN THE PAST YEAR, WHAT WINES IN YOUR WINE PROGRAM HAVE CUSTOMERS BECOME MORE WILLING TO ORDER?
Alsatian wines, Portuguese Vinho Verde, Canadian ice wines, Piedmont and Tuscan wines, New Zealand whites and Pinot Noirs.

Horizons at Grove Park Inn Resort and Spa

290 Macon Avenue
Asheville, North Carolina 28804
phone 828-252-2711 fax 828-252-6442
website www.groveparkinn.com

Kevin D. Schwartz

GENERAL MANAGER

NAME ONE OR TWO OF YOUR FAVORITE WINE DISTRICTS OR WINE
REGIONS FROM AROUND THE WORLD.

For whites, the wines of Alsace. You can't beat the quality-to-price ratio. For
reds, the wines of Burgundy, because you can get quality and a ton of versatility.

WHAT BITS OF INFORMATION WOULD YOU LIKE YOUR CUSTOMERS TO
KNOW ABOUT YOU?

My parents left the Amish at about the same time they were married. (It's a
good thing because I can't grow a beard.)

IF YOU WERE NOT IN THIS PROFESSION, WHAT WOULD YOU BE DOING?

I like doing nothing, but the pay isn't good. I suppose I could have ended up in
construction, but I don't know how long any houses I built would remain
standing.

DESCRIBE YOUR WINE SELECTIONS, BOTH BY THE GLASS AND ON YOUR
LIST.

We offer twenty wines by the glass and 630 selections on the list, including 100
wines in half-bottle. We have particularly good representations of California
Cabernet Sauvignon and Merlot-based wines and Burgundy on the list.

WHAT ARE THE MOST UNIQUE FEATURES IN YOUR WINE PROGRAM?

We offer a few wine dinners throughout the year culminating in our Asheville
Wine and Food Festival in November.

NAME ONE OF YOUR RESTAURANT'S SIGNATURE DISHES. WHAT WINE DO
YOU PREFER TO RECOMMEND WITH IT?

Horizons' signature lobster bisque paired with buttery California Chardonnay.

IN THE PAST YEAR, WHAT WINES IN YOUR WINE PROGRAM HAVE CUS-
TOMERS BECOME MORE WILLING TO ORDER?

Red and white Burgundies.

Liberty Oak Wine and Cheese

JOHN FANCORT, SOMMELIER

100 East Washington, Greensboro

336-273-7057

Lucky 32

JULIE BAIRD, BAR MANAGER

1421 Westover Terrace, Greensboro

336-370-0707

Second Empire at the Dodd-Hinsdale House

DANIEL SCHURR, EXECUTIVE CHEF AND WINE BUYER

330 Hillsborough Street, Raleigh

919-829-3663

Classics Restaurant at the Intercontinental Hotel

Carnegie Avenue
Cleveland, Ohio 44106
phone 216-707-4157
website www.intercontinental.com

Manuel G. Nieves

SOMMELIER TEAM: CHRIS OPPEWALL,
ASSISTANT SOMMELIER

WHAT INSPIRED YOU TO PURSUE A CAREER THAT INVOLVES WINE?

I was given a Château Latour 1990 as a gift in 1993 and enjoyed it more than anything I had ever had.

NAME ONE OR TWO OF YOUR FAVORITE WINE REGIONS FROM AROUND THE WORLD.

Italy and Spain. There is such a diversity in wines from these countries that there is a wine for just about any palate in every price range.

IF YOU WERE NOT IN THIS PROFESSION, WHAT WOULD YOU BE DOING?

I was on the road to becoming an international attorney when the restaurant and wine bug bit me.

DESCRIBE YOUR WINE SELECTIONS, BOTH BY THE GLASS AND ON YOUR LIST.

We offer thirty wines by the glass from six countries. Our list consists of 400 selections from twelve countries and is growing every day.

WHAT ARE THE MOST UNIQUE FEATURES IN YOUR WINE PROGRAM?

We offer all our wines by the glass in three- and five-ounce portions. Last September we began hosting winemaker dinners with a winery representative present to guide us through the wines.

NAME A COUPLE OF YOUR RESTAURANT'S SIGNATURE DISHES. WHAT TYPES OF WINE DO YOU PREFER TO RECOMMEND WITH EACH?

Turbot Vaudovan, baked with marinated Indian spices, julienned snow peas and sautéed langoustine with crab cappuccino, paired with Sonoma County Chardonnay; various foie gras preparations paired with California late-harvest wines, Sauternes and Stags Leap District Sauvignon Blancs.

Giovanni's
25550 Chagrin Boulevard
Beachwood, Ohio 44122
phone 216-831-8625 fax 216-831-4338

Pierre Gregori
GENERAL MANAGER

WHAT ARE SOME OF YOUR ULTIMATE FOOD AND WINE PAIRINGS?
Veal chop with Barbera; lamb with Châteauneuf-du-Pape; pasta cavatelli and
gnocchi with Chianti; halibut with Verdicchio; duck breast–stuffed foie gras
with Burgundy; lamb shank with Nebbiolo.

DESCRIBE YOUR WINE SELECTIONS.
We have more than 600 selections from every great wine region in the world.
We also offer thirty wines by the glass.

WHAT CATEGORY OF WINE IS THE BEST VALUE IN YOUR RESTAURANT?
Italian wines, from varieties like Primitivo and Negroamaro, and producers like
Falesco and Zardetto.

NAME RECENT WINE DISCOVERIES THAT HAVE EXCITED YOU.
Italian wines from Umbria, the south and the islands.

WHAT IS YOUR FAVORITE WINE REGION IN THE WORLD TODAY?
Italy. They have never been so good.

WHAT LED YOU TO YOUR CURRENT POSITION?
A passion for great food and wine.

WHAT IS THE BEST ASPECT OF YOUR JOB?
Pulling the cork of a great bottle of wine with the people who are going to
enjoy it.

IF YOU WERE NOT IN THIS PROFESSION, WHAT WOULD YOU BE DOING?
I don't know. I love this industry and I love food and people.

Swingos on the Lake

12900 Lake Avenue
Lakewood, Ohio 44107
phone 216-221-6188 fax 216-221-9878
website www.swingos.com

Matthew J. Swingos

PRESIDENT, EXECUTIVE CHEF
AND SOMMELIER

NAME TWO OF YOUR FAVORITE WINE DISTRICTS OR WINE REGIONS
FROM AROUND THE WORLD.
Burgundy, because it's the pinnacle of Pinot Noir and Chardonnay, and wines
from the Wachau, for their ability to pair with a wide variety of food.

NAME RECENT WINE DISCOVERIES THAT HAVE EXCITED YOU.
Ohio Riesling, and Austrian Muskateller and Zweigelt.

IF YOU WERE NOT IN THIS PROFESSION, WHAT WOULD YOU BE DOING?
Coaching high school football.

DESCRIBE YOUR WINE SELECTIONS, BOTH BY THE GLASS AND ON YOUR LIST.
Our wine selections number 1,800 from more than thirty countries and 100
appellations, including 100 half-bottle selections, and large-format offerings
from three-liter to eighteen-liter sizes.

WHAT ARE THE MOST UNIQUE FEATURES IN YOUR WINE PROGRAM?
We have wine dinners with unique feature pours such as 1982 Château Lafite-
Rothschild by the glass.

WHAT WINES ARE THE BEST VALUE IN YOUR RESTAURANT?
Wines from the Loire Valley, Alsace and Spain.

NAME A COUPLE OF YOUR RESTAURANT'S SIGNATURE DISHES. WHAT
TYPES OF WINE DO YOU PREFER TO RECOMMEND WITH EACH?
Tenderloin of veal presented over caramelized walnut polenta, dried cranberry
and tawny Port wine risotto paired with top Ribera del Duero; curry and
cumin–encrusted salmon over curry risotto with red pepper and pineapple relish paired with great red Burgundy.

IN THE PAST YEAR, WHAT WINES IN YOUR WINE PROGRAM HAVE CUS-
TOMERS BECOME MORE WILLING TO ORDER?
German Riesling, Austrian Riesling and Grüner Veltliner, and Greek
Xynomavro and Syrah.

Alana's Food and Wine

KEVIN BERTSCHI, PROPRIETOR
AND WINE BUYER
2333 North High Street, Columbus
614-294-6783

Alberini's Restaurant

ANTHONY CHANCE, SOMMELIER
1201 Youngstown Warren Road, Niles
330-652-5895

L'Antibes

DALE GUSSETT, CO-OWNER AND
WINE BUYER
772 North High Street, Columbus
614-291-1666

Inn at Turner's Mill

BRAD BUCHANAN, WINE BUYER
36 East Streetsboro Street, Hudson
330-656-2949

Johnny's Bar

ANTHONY "BO" SANTOSUOSSO,
WINE BUYER
3164 Fulton Road, Cleveland
216-281-0055

Maisonette Restaurant

LARA MORGAN, WINE DIRECTOR
114 East Sixth Street, Cincinnati
513-721-2260

Palace Restaurant at the Cincinnati Hotel

SCOTT JONES, MAÎTRE D'
601 Vine Street, Cincinnati
513-381-3000

The Refectory

DAVID McMAHON, SOMMELIER
1092 Bethel Road, Columbus
614-451-9774

La Baguette Bistro

MICHEL BUTHION, OWNER
AND WINE BUYER
7408 North May Avenue,
Oklahoma City
405-840-3047

Boulevard Steakhouse

SAGE SHURWADY, WINE BUYER
505 South Boulevard, Edmond
405-715-2333

The French Hen

RICHARD CLARK, OWNER,
CHEF AND WINE BUYER
7143 South Yale, Tulsa
918-492-2596

The Heathman Restaurant and Bar

1001 Southwest Broadway
Portland, Oregon 97205
phone 503-790-7752 fax 503-790-7105
website www.heathmanhotel.com

Tysan Pierce
RESTAURANT MANAGER
AND SOMMELIER

NAME ONE OR TWO OF YOUR FAVORITE WINE DISTRICTS OR WINE
REGIONS FROM AROUND THE WORLD.

Burgundy, particularly Chambolle-Musigny, followed by Mosel-Saar-Ruwer.

NAME RECENT WINE DISCOVERIES THAT HAVE EXCITED YOU.

Jerez (Sherry). We have an afternoon high tea on the weekends at the
Heathman where it's really fun to see people trying and really appreciating
Sherry again.

WHAT ARE THE MOST UNIQUE FEATURES IN YOUR WINE PROGRAM?

Our extensive Oregon Pinot Noir list is impressive. We also have a program
called "Sommelier Round Tables," an informal tasting each month with some
of our guests who want to learn more about different regions and wines.

NAME A FEW OF YOUR RESTAURANT'S SIGNATURE DISHES. WHAT TYPES
OF WINE DO YOU PREFER TO RECOMMEND WITH EACH?

Foie Gras Cappuccino (yellow-foot chanterelle mushrooms and port soup) with
Coteaux du Layon, British Columbia ice wine; roasted halibut with organic
blood orange salad with shaved fennel fricassee of spring vegetables, purple fingerling potatoes and agrumato olive oil, with Austrian Riesling or drier Alsace
whites; Canard à l'Orange (grilled Peking duck breast and leg confit, sable
potatoes, green beans and orange sauce) with Pinot Noir.

IN THE PAST YEAR, WHAT WINES IN YOUR WINE PROGRAM HAVE CUS-
TOMERS BECOME MORE WILLING TO ORDER?

It's nice to see customers venturing out of the New World and back into France.

WHAT ARE SOME OTHER ULTIMATE WINE AND FOOD PAIRINGS?

Oysters and Champagne; goat cheese and Sancerre; braised leg of lamb with
Rioja; foie gras and British Columbia ice wine.

Southpark Seafood Grill and Wine Bar

901 Southwest Salmon Street
Portland, Oregon 97205
phone 503-326-1300 fax 503-326-1301
website www.southpark.citysearch.com

David B. Holstrom
WINE CONSULTANT

WHAT ARE SOME OF YOUR ULTIMATE FOOD AND WINE PAIRINGS?
Braised beef or lamb with southern Rhône red; Catalan fish stew with Greek white wine.

DESCRIBE YOUR WINE SELECTIONS.
Our program specializes in varieties and wine regions that are not well-known to most Americans. We search out regions that offer wines with a great price-to-value ratio that taste good.

WHAT CATEGORIES OF WINE ARE THE BEST VALUES ON YOUR WINE LIST?
Mosel Riesling, and wines from southwestern France, the Languedoc and Austria.

NAME RECENT WINE DISCOVERIES THAT HAVE EXCITED YOU.
Greek white wines and German Sekt.

WHAT ARE YOUR FAVORITE WINE REGIONS IN THE WORLD TODAY?
The Mosel and Austria.

WHAT LED YOU TO YOUR CURRENT POSITION?
It was a way to meet women in college. It became evident (more times than not) that the wines were, over time, more interesting.

WHAT IS THE BEST ASPECT OF YOUR JOB?
Introducing a new wine, variety or region to guests that they have never experienced, and having them love it.

IF YOU WERE NOT IN THIS PROFESSION, WHAT WOULD YOU BE DOING?
Teaching or cooking.

The Dining Room at The Westin Salishan Resort

LISA POPHAME, MAÎTRE D'
7760 North Highway 101,
Glenedon Beach
541-764-2371

Higgins

ANDREW ZALMAN, WINE STEWARD
1239 Southwest Broadway, Portland
503-222-9070

Morton's of Chicago

JOHN MITCHELL,
BEVERAGE DIRECTOR
213 Southwest Clay Street, Portland
503-248-2100

Three Doors Down

KATHY BERGIN, CO-OWNER
AND WINE BUYER
1429 Southeast 37th, Portland
503-236-6886

Wildwood Restaurant

RANDY GOODMAN, DIRECTOR
OF SERVICES AND WINE
1221 Northwest 21st Avenue,
Portland
503-248-9663

Le Bec-Fin

1523 Walnut Street
Philadelphia, Pennsylvania 19102
phone 215-567-1000 fax 215-568-1151
website www.lebecfin.com

Gregory Castells

SOMMELIER AND WINE DIRECTOR
TEAM: LOIC BEAUMAVIN,
ASSISTANT SOMMELIER

WHAT INSPIRED YOU TO PURSUE A CAREER THAT INVOLVES WINE?
My family has always been involved in wine and winemaking. It became a passion very quickly.

NAME TWO OF YOUR FAVORITE WINE REGIONS FROM AROUND THE WORLD.
Languedoc in France and Washington State.

NAME A RECENT WINE DISCOVERY THAT EXCITED YOU.
Movia Veliko Bianco, from Slovenia for the depth and unique style.

IF YOU WERE NOT IN THIS PROFESSION, WHAT WOULD YOU BE?
An art dealer.

DESCRIBE YOUR WINE SELECTIONS, BOTH BY THE GLASS AND ON YOUR LIST.
We have 600 selections and our focus is French and California wine. We are expanding into other countries and expect a total offering of more than 1,000 wines. We have a monthly tasting menu that always changes and offer a regular wine flight of eight different wines.

WHAT ARE THE MOST UNIQUE FEATURES IN YOUR WINE PROGRAM?
Our wine flights and our outstanding wine dinners have become very well known and appreciated in this city.

WHAT CATEGORIES OF WINE ARE THE BEST VALUES IN YOUR RESTAURANT?
Rhône and Languedoc.

NAME A COUPLE OF YOUR RESTAURANT'S SIGNATURE DISHES. WHAT TYPES OF WINE DO YOU PREFER TO RECOMMEND WITH EACH?
Truffle risotto, crisp shrimp with Slovenia white; saddle and shoulder of venison with quince and cabbage paired with top Côte-Rôtie.

IN THE PAST YEAR, WHAT WINES IN YOUR WINE PROGRAM HAVE CUSTOMERS BECOME MORE WILLING TO ORDER?
White Burgundy, red Rhône and Bordeaux.

The Fountain at Four Seasons

1 Logan Square
Philadelphia, Pennsylvania 19103
phone 215-963-1500 fax 215-963-2748
website www.fourseasons.com/philadelphia

Melissa B. Monosoff

SOMMELIER
TEAM: STEPHANE CASTERA, SOMMELIER;
CHERIE VALLANCE, SOMMELIER

WHAT ARE SOME OF YOUR ULTIMATE FOOD AND WINE PAIRINGS?
Roasted halibut with sweetbreads, morels, baby white asparagus and veal jus paired with Meursault or Puligny-Montrachet; smoked salmon and caviar crème fraîche with Savennières; and chèvre with Sancerre or Pouilly-Fumé.

DESCRIBE YOUR WINE SELECTIONS.
We are known for depth in the heavy-hitting French and California wines, but I balance the rest of the list with wines from under-recognized regions and from smaller, lesser-known producers.

WHAT CATEGORIES OF WINE ARE THE BEST VALUES ON YOUR WINE LIST?
Southern Italy, southern France and Australia.

NAME RECENT WINE DISCOVERIES THAT HAVE EXCITED YOU.
Pinot Noirs and Sauvignon Blancs from South Africa.

WHAT IS YOUR FAVORITE WINE REGION IN THE WORLD TODAY?
I have several: Alsace and the Loire for elegance, the Rhône for intensity and value, and southern Italy for great new wines that show a huge improvement in quality.

WHAT LED YOU TO PURSUE A CAREER THAT INVOLVES WINE?
When I was at the Striped Bass, Marnie Old, the sommelier, took me under her wing while I was a cook. I have followed this path ever since.

WHAT ARE THE BEST ASPECTS OF YOUR JOB?
Teaching the staff and interacting with the guests. It's fun opening people's eyes to new things, teaching and sharing information.

IF YOU WERE NOT IN YOUR CURRENT POSITION, WHAT WOULD YOU BE DOING?
In the kitchen, cooking.

Kansas City Prime
4417 Main Street
Philadelphia, Pennsylvania 19127
phone 215-482-3700 fax 215-483-1515
website www.kansascityprime.com

Charles A. Grayson
ASSISTANT MANAGER
AND SOMMELIER

NAME TWO OF YOUR FAVORITE WINE DISTRICTS OR REGIONS FROM
AROUND THE WORLD.
Spring Mountain and Marlborough, New Zealand.

NAME RECENT WINE DISCOVERIES THAT HAVE EXCITED YOU.
Sauvignon Blancs from New Zealand. For such a small wine-growing area, it
has great potential.

IF YOU WERE NOT IN THIS PROFESSION, WHAT WOULD YOU BE DOING?
An outdoor adventure therapy program for at-risk youth.

DESCRIBE YOUR WINE SELECTIONS, BOTH BY THE GLASS AND ON YOUR
LIST.
We offer 450 wines by the bottle specializing in red wines, Cabernet Sauvignon
in particular. We also have twenty-five wines by the glass including sparkling,
red, white and dessert wines.

WHAT ARE THE MOST UNIQUE FEATURES IN YOUR WINE PROGRAM?
Each Sunday, every bottle on our list is available at half-price. Each Friday we
offer a three-course dinner where any item from our menu and a glass of wine
is available for only $60 per person.

WHAT CATEGORY OF WINE IS THE BEST VALUE IN YOUR RESTAURANT?
The Italian selection, where many of the wines are under $60 a bottle.

NAME A COUPLE OF YOUR RESTAURANT'S SIGNATURE DISHES. WHAT
TYPES OF WINE DO YOU PREFER TO RECOMMEND WITH EACH?
Kobe beef with Rutherford Cabernet Sauvignon; steamed whole Maine lobster
with Rhône Valley Viognier.

IN THE PAST YEAR, WHAT WINES IN YOUR WINE PROGRAM HAVE CUS-
TOMERS BECOME MORE WILLING TO ORDER?
Washington State Merlots, Argentinean Malbecs, Chilean Cabernet
Sauvignons, New Zealand Sauvignon Blancs and Australian Chardonnays.

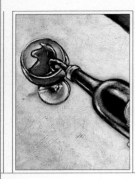

Savona Cucina Della Costa

100 Old Gulph Road
Gulph Mills, Pennsylvania 19428
phone 610-520-1200 fax 610-520-2045
website www.savonarestaurant.com

Evan Lambert
MANAGING PARTNER AND WINE DIRECTOR
TEAM: THOMAS COMDESCOT-LEPERE,
SOMMELIER

WHAT PART OF YOUR JOB DO YOU ENJOY THE MOST?
Seeing the satisfied faces of guests in my restaurant and feeling the achievement of a seamlessly orchestrated evening on the dining room floor.

YOUR FAVORITE WINE REGION?
Piedmont. I am in love with the Nebbiolo grape and the wonderful people of Alba who care for it.

NAME RECENT WINE DISCOVERIES THAT HAVE EXCITED YOU.
Wines from Chile and from Spain, especially Priorat.

IF YOU WERE NOT IN THIS PROFESSION, WHAT WOULD YOU BE DOING?
A career in psychology.

DESCRIBE YOUR WINE SELECTIONS, BOTH BY THE GLASS AND ON YOUR LIST.
We offer approximately fifteen wines by the glass in different styles from many regions. We try to make sure all wines match our cuisine, offering many different types of wines. We have an extensive wine list of more than 1,200 selections from all over the world. Our list offers many vertical presentations from benchmark producers.

WHAT CATEGORY OF WINE IS THE BEST VALUE IN YOUR RESTAURANT?
Chile. Chilean wines offer enormous quality at affordable prices.

NAME ONE OF YOUR RESTAURANT'S SIGNATURE DISHES. WHAT WINE DO YOU PREFER TO RECOMMEND WITH IT?
Plancha seared Dover sole with Sonoma County Chardonnay, a match made in heaven.

IN THE PAST YEAR, WHAT WINES IN YOUR WINE PROGRAM HAVE CUSTOMERS BECOME MORE WILLING TO ORDER?
Wines from Alsace, Spain, Australia and New Zealand.

Vallozzi's

Route 30 East and George's Station Road
Greensburg, Pennsylvania 15601
phone 724-836-7663 fax 724-836-7917
website www.vallozzis.com

Jim Manolakos

GENERAL MANAGER AND
WINE DIRECTOR

NAME ONE OR TWO OF YOUR FAVORITE WINE DISTRICTS OR WINE
REGIONS FROM AROUND THE WORLD.
Piedmont reds and Napa Cabernet Sauvignon for their quality, and Tuscany for
the unique and diverse flavors in its Sangiovese and Cabernet Sauvignon.

NAME RECENT WINE DISCOVERIES THAT HAVE EXCITED YOU.
The quality of some California Barberas and Sangioveses, and Spanish
Tempranillo-based wines that reflect quality and value.

WHAT BITS OF INFORMATION WOULD YOU LIKE YOUR CUSTOMERS TO
KNOW ABOUT YOU?
I'm a baseball junkie. I love to garden and I appreciate beer almost as much as wine!

DESCRIBE YOUR WINE SELECTIONS, BOTH BY THE GLASS AND ON YOUR LIST.
We have more than 520 different selections, focused on California, Italy and
France, but with a grouping of international wines. We have a comprehensive
by-the-glass selection and wine flight program.

WHAT ARE THE MOST UNIQUE FEATURES IN YOUR WINE PROGRAM?
Our wine by-the-glass program, along with flights, are often time-created or
suggested by our guests. We also have our own wine club, Gioco di Amici (circle of friends). Our list and by-the-glass offerings are changed and completely
updated every thirty days, always presenting diverse choices for both new and
regular customers.

NAME ONE OF YOUR RESTAURANT'S SIGNATURE DISHES. WHAT WINE DO
YOU PREFER TO RECOMMEND WITH IT?
Roast veal shank served au jus with braised potatoes and peppers with Vino
Nobile di Montepulciano.

IN THE PAST YEAR, WHAT WINES IN YOUR WINE PROGRAM HAVE CUS-
TOMERS BECOME MORE WILLING TO ORDER?
Oregon Pinot Noir and Australian Shiraz.

Wooden Angel Restaurant and Café

308 Leopard Lane
Beaver, Pennsylvania 15009
phone 724-774-7880 fax 724-774-7994
website www.wooden-angel.com

Alex E. Sebastian
RESTAURATEUR

NAME ONE OR TWO OF YOUR FAVORITE WINES FROM AROUND THE
WORLD.
Rhône blends, New Zealand Sauvignon Blancs and the whites of Alsace.

WHAT BITS OF INFORMATION WOULD YOU LIKE YOUR CUSTOMERS TO
KNOW ABOUT YOU?
I have tried to give back to the community as a volunteer fireman for more
than thirty years, a member of the local planning commission, hospital board
and fundraiser, Penn State HRIM advisory board, past president of the local
restaurant association—the dues we pay for space in our industry.

DESCRIBE YOUR WINE SELECTIONS, BOTH BY THE GLASS AND ON YOUR LIST.
Our list is all-American and has been for the past thirty-three years. It is an
ever-changing list of varietals with an emphasis on ABC (anything but
Cabernet, Chardonnay and Merlot). Our wines by the glass selections of eight
to twelve labels feature a different winery each month.

WHAT ARE THE MOST UNIQUE FEATURES IN YOUR WINE PROGRAM?
We have no half-bottles due to our extensive wine by-the-glass program. We
have Friday Fine Wine dinners featuring four courses with four glasses of the
wines we are promoting.

NAME A COUPLE OF YOUR RESTAURANT'S SIGNATURE DISHES. WHAT
TYPES OF WINE DO YOU PREFER TO RECOMMEND WITH EACH?
Rack of American lamb with Zinfandel or Syrah; Maryland crab cakes with an
herbaceous Sauvignon Blanc.

IN THE PAST YEAR, WHAT WINES IN YOUR WINE PROGRAM HAVE CUS-
TOMERS BECOME MORE WILLING TO ORDER?
Viognier, Seyval and Vidal and blends, which was considered un-American
for years.

Yangming

1051 Conestoga Road
Bryn Mawr, Pennsylvania 19010
phone 610-527-3200 fax 610-527-0229

James T. Mullen, III
SOMMELIER AND
BEVERAGE MANAGER

DESCRIBE YOUR WINE SELECTIONS.
We have an extensive wine list featuring California Chardonnays and Cabernet Sauvignons, and wines from France, Italy, Australia, Germany, New Zealand, Spain, Chile and Japan.

WHAT IS YOUR FAVORITE WINE REGION IN THE WORLD TODAY?
California. I believe California produces the best wines in the world. Some of my favorites come from the Carneros region.

WHAT LED YOU TO PURSUE A CAREER THAT INVOLVES WINE?
I started with the company as a bartender and worked my way up the "corporate ladder."

WHAT IS THE BIGGEST CHALLENGE IN YOUR JOB?
Trying to get guests from always thinking "mainstream." Everybody knows Chardonnay and Merlot. I want them to try Chenin Blanc and Syrah.

IF YOU WERE NOT IN YOUR CURRENT POSITION, WHAT WOULD YOU BE DOING?
Bartending.

Alma de Cuba
LAUREND ABRAHIM,
BEVERAGE DIRECTOR
1623 Walnut Street, Philadelphia
215-988-1799

La Bonne Auberge
GERARD CARONELLO, WINE BUYER
LINO FUENTES, SOMMELIER
Village 2, Mechanic Street, New Hope
215-862-2462

Brasserie Perrier
JEAN-FRANCOIS HENRI,
SOMMELIER
1619 Walnut Street, Philadelphia
215-568-3000

The Carlton
KEVIN JOYCE, WINE BUYER
500 Grant Street, Pittsburgh
412-391-4099

Circa
DAVID MANTELMACHER,
WINE BUYER
18 Walnut Street, Philadelphia
215-545-6800

La Collina
ENZO VALENT, WINE BUYER
37-41 Ashland Avenue, Belmont Hills
610-668-1780

Creed's Seafood and Steaks
BEDROS KAYSER, WINE BUYER
499 North Gulph Road,
King of Prussia
610-265-2550

Deux Cheminees
JIM PETRIE, WINE BUYER
1221 Locust Street, Philadelphia
215-790-0200

Dilworthtown Inn
HENRY DAWSON, SOMMELIER
1390 Old Wilmington Pike,
West Chester
610-399-1390

Evermay on the Delaware
BILL MOFFLY, WINE BUYER
889 River Road, Erwinna
610-294-9100

La Famiglia Restaurant
MARIO FATTORINI, SOMMELIER
GUSIPPE SENA, WINE BUYER
8 South Front Street, Philadelphia
215-922-2803

Founders Restaurant at the Park Hyatt Bellevue
EVAN EVANS, FOOD AND
BEVERAGE DIRECTOR
Broad and Walnut Streets,
Philadelphia
215-790-2814

The Grill at the Ritz-Carlton Hotel
VINCE PRESCITI, WINE DIRECTOR
10 Avenue of the Arts, Philadelphia
215-523-8000

Hayden Zug's Restaurant
TERRY LEE, WINE BUYER
1987 State Street, East Petersburg
717-569-5747

Hyeholde Restaurant
JAMES BRINKMAN,
DINING ROOM MANAGER
190 Hyeholde Drive, Moon Township
412-264-3116

Jake's

CYRIL ADDISON, GENERAL
MANAGER AND WINE BUYER
4365 Main Street, Manayunk
215-483-0444

Morton's of Chicago

JOSEPH HART, WINE BUYER
1411 Walnut Street, Philadelphia
215-557-0724

New Orleans Café

DANIEL FUNK, OWNER,
CHEF AND WINE BUYER
4 West State Street, Media
610-627-4393

The Palm

KEVIN FRANKLIN, GENERAL
MANAGER AND WINE BUYER
200 South Broad Street,
Philadelphia
215-546-7256

Panorama Ristorante at the Penn's View Hotel

WILLIAM ECCLESTON,
WINE BUYER
Front and Market Streets,
Philadelphia
215-922-7800

Passerelle

ROBERT FENIMORE, MANAGER
AND WINE BUYER
175 King of Prussia Road, Radnor
610-293-9411

The Prime Rib at the Warwick

BRENDON KOTULAK, BEVERAGE
MANAGER AND SOMMELIER
1701 Locust Street, Philadelphia
215-735-6000

Smith & Wollensky

PAUL DUMONT,
BEVERAGE MANAGER
210 West Rittenhouse Square,
Philadelphia
215-545-1700

Strawberry Hill

DENNIS KEREK, PROPRIETOR
AND WINE BUYER
128 West Strawberry Street,
Lancaster
717-393-5544

Striped Bass

JASON TAYLOR,
BEVERAGE MANAGER
1500 Walnut Street, Philadelphia
215-732-4444

Susanna Foo

KENNETH JOHNSON,
WINE BUYER
1512 Walnut Street, Philadelphia
215-546-9106

Charleston Grill at the Charleston Place Hotel

224 King Street
Charleston, South Carolina 29401
phone 843-577-4522 fax 843-724-8405
website www.charlestongrill.com

Roberto Fuschi
SOMMELIER

WHAT ARE SOME OF YOUR ULTIMATE FOOD AND WINE PAIRINGS?
Maine lobster tempura over lemon grits and fried mini green tomatoes in a yellow tomato tarragon butter paired with white Burgundy; poached fresh turbot fillet over caramelized fennel and Vidalia onions with Maine lobster in Dijon mustard and thyme sauce with Santa Barbara Pinot Noir; chilled duck breast with a citrus truffle oil dressing with spinach and duck crackling paired with Tocai Friulano from Collio.

DESCRIBE YOUR WINE SELECTIONS.
Our selection is extensive (1,200) and includes a strong representation of California Chardonnay and Cabernet Sauvignon, Burgundy and Bordeaux. We also have fifty wines by the glass.

WHAT CATEGORY OF WINE IS THE BEST VALUE IN YOUR RESTAURANT?
Italian reds.

NAME RECENT WINE DISCOVERIES THAT HAVE EXCITED YOU.
White wines from the Collio region and Sangiovese from Napa Valley.

WHAT IS YOUR FAVORITE WINE REGION IN THE WORLD TODAY?
The Rhône Valley, for the character of the wines.

WHAT LED YOU TO PURSUE A CAREER THAT INVOLVES WINE?
The search for the ultimate wine and food pairings; the love of dining room service; the desire to work with a great chef.

WHAT ARE THE BEST ASPECTS OF YOUR JOB?
Satisfying guests and creating a perfect tasting menu with wine pairings.

IF YOU WERE NOT A SOMMELIER, WHAT WOULD YOU BE DOING?
Cooking again.

CQ's Restaurant

140 Lighthouse Road
Hilton Head Island, South Carolina 29928
phone 843-671-2779 fax 843-671-6787
website www.celebrationusa.com

Scott E. Entrup
WINE DIRECTOR

WHAT ARE SOME OF YOUR ULTIMATE FOOD AND WINE PAIRINGS?
Our version of a grilled cheese sandwich: house brioche slices, Boursin cheese, chunks of filet mignon all made into a sandwich then sautéed in duck fat and served with a tomato jam paired with a Napa Valley Cabernet; any blue-veined, hearty cheese and a flight of Ports from around the world.

DESCRIBE YOUR WINE SELECTIONS.
We select wines that complement our cuisine. We feature American cuisine with a French influence. Two-thirds of our list is American, the other third is international.

WHAT CATEGORY OF WINE IS THE BEST VALUE IN YOUR RESTAURANT?
California Chardonnay.

NAME RECENT WINE DISCOVERIES THAT HAVE EXCITED YOU.
South African wines. The quality has improved over the last five years and there are a number of great values.

WHAT IS YOUR FAVORITE WINE REGION IN THE WORLD TODAY?
Oregon. The wines reveal terroir more so than California wines.

WHAT LED YOU TO YOUR CURRENT POSITION?
An interest in learning more about wine.

WHAT IS THE BEST ASPECT OF YOUR JOB?
Seeing the guests enjoy a wine I've suggested.

IF YOU WERE NOT IN YOUR CURRENT POSITION, WHAT WOULD YOU BE DOING?
Anything in food and beverage.

Cypress Low Country Grill

167 East Bay Street
Charleston, South Carolina 29401
phone 843- 727-0111 fax 843-722-0035
website www.magnolias-blossom-cypress.com

William H. Netherland
WINE DIRECTOR

WHAT INSPIRED YOU TO PURSUE A CAREER THAT INVOLVES WINE?
Six years in Italy and Germany. They have the good wine life; they've figured it all out.

NAME ONE OF YOUR FAVORITE WINE REGIONS FROM AROUND THE WORLD.
Tuscany.

NAME RECENT WINE DISCOVERIES THAT HAVE EXCITED YOU.
Languedoc, Roussillon, Cabardès, Minervois, Corbières: all offer complexity and value.

IF YOU WERE NOT IN THIS PROFESSION, WHAT WOULD YOU BE?
A vineyard manager.

DESCRIBE YOUR WINE SELECTIONS, BOTH BY THE GLASS AND ON YOUR LIST.
We try to strike a balance between high-profile varietals, winemakers and lesser-known grapes and regions.

WHAT ARE THE MOST UNIQUE FEATURES IN YOUR WINE PROGRAM?
Our extremely wide selection. We have a lot of depth in first-growth Bordeaux, 1960s to 1980s California cult wines, and a wonderful large-format selection.

WHAT CATEGORY OF WINE IS THE BEST VALUE IN YOUR RESTAURANT?
Although some of our Bordeaux is very expensive, I believe that this is still where the value is.

NAME A COUPLE OF YOUR RESTAURANT'S SIGNATURE DISHES. WHAT TYPES OF WINE DO YOU PREFER TO RECOMMEND WITH EACH?
Crispy wasabi tuna with fine Mosel Riesling; lamb with Oregon Pinot Noir.

IN THE PAST YEAR, WHAT WINES IN YOUR WINE PROGRAM HAVE CUS-TOMERS BECOME MORE WILLING TO ORDER?
Austrian whites and South African reds.

Old Fort Pub
at Hilton Head Plantation

65 Skull Creek Drive
Hilton Head Island, South Carolina 29926
phone 843-681-2386 fax 843-681-9287
website www.celebrationusa.com

Christopher L. Tassone

VICE PRESIDENT OF OPERATIONS
AND SOMMELIER

NAME TWO OF YOUR FAVORITE WINES.
New World–style Chardonnay that is lightly oaked from California and
Australia and, for red wine, big Cabernet Sauvignons from Napa Valley that
ooze jammy black currants and end with a sweet tannin finish.

NAME RECENT WINE DISCOVERIES THAT HAVE EXCITED YOU.
California Syrah and Zinfandel. They are rich yet affordable, and ready to drink
on release.

IF YOU WERE NOT IN THIS PROFESSION, WHAT WOULD YOU BE?
A karate instructor with my own studio and gym.

DESCRIBE YOUR WINE SELECTIONS, BOTH BY THE GLASS AND ON YOUR LIST.
We have more than thirty wines available by the glass and almost 400 selections
by the bottle. Our wine list complements our menu while offering value and
quality.

WHAT ARE THE MOST UNIQUE FEATURES IN YOUR WINE PROGRAM?
We have a very extensive wine program including a wine club with weekly wine
tastings that we call "Wine and Dine Wednesday." The club also offers discount
wine purchasing, free consulting and gourmet wine dinners.

WHAT CATEGORIES OF WINE ARE THE BEST VALUES IN YOUR RESTAURANT?
California Zinfandel and Australian Cabernet Sauvignon.

NAME A COUPLE OF YOUR RESTAURANT'S SIGNATURE DISHES. WHAT
TYPES OF WINE DO YOU PREFER TO RECOMMEND WITH EACH?
Maple Leaf Duck Elegante with feijoa chutney and a wild blackberry sauce
paired with a robust, velvety Oregon Pinot Noir; grilled American red snapper
with a porcini beurre blanc paired with big Sonoma Chardonnay.

IN THE PAST YEAR, WHAT WINES IN YOUR WINE PROGRAM HAVE CUS-
TOMERS BECOME MORE WILLING TO ORDER?
Oregon Pinot Noir.

Woodlands Resort and Inn

125 Parsons Road
Summerville, South Carolina 29438
phone 843-875-2600 fax 843-875-2603
website www.woodlandwinn.com

Stephane Peltier
SOMMELIER

NAME TWO OF YOUR FAVORITE WINE REGIONS.
Spain, for Rias Baixas (Albariño) and Priorat (Garnacha), two up-and-coming wine regions offering great value; South Africa for Cabernet Sauvignon from Stellenbosch and Gewürztraminer from Robertson.

DESCRIBE YOUR WINE SELECTIONS.
We have 1,100 wines on our list, with verticals of Silver Oak, Spottswoode, Shafer Hillside and many others. We have a great selection of white and red Burgundies and real depth in Bordeaux. We also offer 120 wines in half-bottle.

WHAT WINES ARE THE BEST VALUES IN YOUR RESTAURANT?
Rhône Valley white and Sicilian Nero d'Avola.

NAME A FEW OF YOUR RESTAURANT'S SIGNATURE DISHES. WHAT TYPES OF WINE DO YOU PREFER TO RECOMMEND WITH EACH?
Twice-baked fingerling potato, applewood-smoked salmon, Iranian osetra caviar, Meyer lemon cream with Champagne; slow-cooked whole Maine lobster, stir-fry of honshimeji mushrooms, asparagus, spiced coconut broth with Central Otago Pinot Noir; seared foie gras, apricot vinegar sauce with vanilla-poached Texas sweet onions and spiced pecans with Alsace Gewürztraminer; pomegranate barbecue, rack of lamb, crispy Anson Mills white grits with Napa Valley Zinfandel.

IN THE PAST YEAR, WHAT WINES IN YOUR WINE PROGRAM HAVE CUS-TOMERS BECOME MORE WILLING TO ORDER?
White Burgundy and Pinot Noir from Russian River Valley.

WHAT IS ANOTHER UNIQUE ASPECT OF YOUR WINE PROGRAM?
We offer a special menu known as "A Meal Around Your Wine." At Woodlands we encourage our guests to choose a wine that ultimately sets the tone for the dining experience. The wine then becomes our chef's muse that inspires him to create personalized dishes.

Boat House on East Bay

MONIQUE BAILEY, WINE BUYER

549 East Bay Street, Charleston

843-577-7171

Boathouse II Restaurant

DAVID SMITH, WINE DIRECTOR
AND SOMMELIER

397 Squire Pope Road,
Hilton Head Island

843-681-3663

Magnolia's Restaurant

WILLIAM NETHERLAND,
WINE DIRECTOR

185 East Bay Street, Charleston

843-577-7771

Penninsula Grill

DENNIS PERRY, SOMMELIER

112 North Market Street,
Charleston

843-723-0700

Mario's

2005 Broadway Street
Nashville, Tennessee 37203
phone 615-327-3232 fax 615-321-2675
website www.mariosfinedining.com

Daniel Mora
PART OWNER AND
SOMMELIER

WHAT ARE SOME OF YOUR ULTIMATE FOOD AND WINE PAIRINGS?
Rack of lamb with heavy Cabernet or Zinfandel; veal piccata with Pinot Noir;
sea bass with Chardonnay or Italian white.

DESCRIBE YOUR WINE SELECTIONS.
We have 392 selections on our wine list, plus additional rare wines that I sell
verbally. Sixty percent of our wines are Italian and the remainder are from
California and the rest of the world.

WHAT ARE YOUR FAVORITE WINE REGIONS IN THE WORLD TODAY?
Piedmont and Tuscany. They make outstanding wines.

WHAT LED YOU TO PURSUE A CAREER THAT INVOLVES WINE?
I was born in San Remo, Italy, and was stomping grapes by the time I was ten
years old. My love of wine started there.

WHAT IS THE BEST ASPECT OF YOUR JOB?
Every day is exciting with so many new wines in the market. As soon as I learn
about one, it seems that another one comes along.

IF YOU WERE NOT IN YOUR CURRENT POSITION, WHAT WOULD YOU BE?
A chef.

Midtown Café

102 19th Avenue South
Nashville, Tennessee 37203
phone 615-320-7176 fax 615-320-0920
website www.midtowncafe.com

Mark C. Johnson
SOMMELIER

NAME ONE OF YOUR FAVORITE WINE COUNTRIES.
Spain, for the small regions like Yecla, Jumilla and Rias Baixas that are beginning to make world-class wines.

WHAT BITS OF INFORMATION WOULD YOU LIKE YOUR CUSTOMERS TO KNOW ABOUT YOU?
I went to college to study opera and I'm a volunteer fire fighter and EMT. I write a weekly wine and spirits article for the Nashville City Paper and host a local weekly program on Comcast called All Things Wine.

DESCRIBE YOUR WINE SELECTIONS, BOTH BY THE GLASS AND ON YOUR LIST.
Our wine list has 125 wines and we pour more than fifty by the glass, mostly New World selections. We are now adding more Spanish, Italian and German wines to match new menu items.

WHAT IS A UNIQUE FEATURE IN YOUR WINE PROGRAM?
Pairing special wines with the nightly prix fixe menu.

NAME A COUPLE OF YOUR RESTAURANT'S SIGNATURE DISHES. WHAT TYPES OF WINE DO YOU PREFER TO RECOMMEND WITH EACH?
Maine lobster Napa slaw and tropical salsa with aromatic, full bodied white wine; Kobe beef filet with butter-poached lobster tail, roasted garlic Yukon gold, mashed potatoes and wild mushroom demi-glaze with Napa Valley Cabernet Sauvignon.

IN THE PAST YEAR, WHAT WINES IN YOUR WINE PROGRAM HAVE CUSTOMERS BECOME MORE WILLING TO ORDER?
Santa Barbara Pinot and Chardonnay, Spanish reds and Chenin Blanc.

WHAT ARE SOME OTHER ULTIMATE WINE AND FOOD PAIRINGS?
Asian cooking with Oregon Pinot Noir and Pinot Gris; venison or antelope with well-aged northern Rhône reds; Champagne and popcorn.

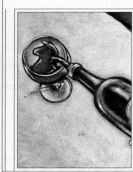

Opryland Hotel

2800 Opryland Drive
Nashville, Tennessee 37214
phone 615-871-6000 fax 615-871-7872
website www.gaylordhotels.com

Gina R. Hendrix
BEVERAGE MANAGER
AND WINE BUYER

WHAT INSPIRED YOU TO PURSUE A CAREER THAT INVOLVES WINE?
I fell in love with wine after my first glass of wine (yes, from a box!) and found myself intrigued by it.

NAME ONE OF YOUR FAVORITE WINE REGIONS FROM AROUND THE WORLD.
Paso Robles, home of some great Zinfandels.

WHAT BITS OF INFORMATION WOULD YOU LIKE YOUR CUSTOMERS TO KNOW ABOUT YOU?
I am a knowledge buff. I love to learn about food and beverages. I also love to play basketball and tennis—a true competitor!

DESCRIBE YOUR WINE SELECTIONS, BOTH BY THE GLASS AND ON YOUR LIST.
Right now, in all of our restaurants (Old Hickory, Volares, Cascades and Rachel's), we are very heavy in California wines, but we are beginning to take a more worldly approach to wine.

WHAT ARE THE MOST UNIQUE FEATURES IN YOUR WINE PROGRAM?
All of our lists are progressive by body and weight. The whites are listed sweetest to driest. I like to do what's easiest for the guests to understand, and it helps servers suggest wines with confidence.

NAME A FEW OF YOUR RESTAURANT'S SIGNATURE DISHES. WHAT TYPES OF WINE DO YOU PREFER TO RECOMMEND WITH EACH?
Filet mignon or rack of lamb with truffles paired with Malbec from Argentina; cedar-plank salmon with Oregon Pinot Noir; grilled ahi tuna with ponzu sauce and German Gewürztraminer.

IN THE PAST YEAR, WHAT WINES IN YOUR WINE PROGRAM HAVE CUSTOMERS BECOME MORE WILLING TO ORDER?
Oregon Pinot Noir, and wines from Argentina and New Zealand.

Sunset Grill

2001 Belcourt Avenue
Nashville, Tennessee 37212
phone 615-386-3663 fax 615-386-0495
website www.sunsetgrill.com

Craig Clifft
GENERAL MANAGER AND
DIRECTOR OF WINE

NAME ONE OF YOUR FAVORITE WINE DISTRICTS.
McLaren Vale. The Shiraz coming from that part of Australia is fabulous and a great value.

NAME RECENT WINE DISCOVERIES THAT HAVE EXCITED YOU.
Spanish wines offer not only quality, but also value.

WHAT BITS OF INFORMATION WOULD YOU LIKE YOUR CUSTOMERS TO KNOW ABOUT YOU?
I like traveling, flying, skiing, sailing and deep-sea fishing.

IF YOU WERE NOT IN THIS PROFESSION, WHAT WOULD YOU BE?
An airline pilot. I began working in restaurants to pay for flight time to become a commercial pilot. I have my commercial license and a degree in aerospace.

DESCRIBE YOUR WINE SELECTIONS, BOTH BY THE GLASS AND ON YOUR LIST.
We have seventy-five wines by the glass and 300 by the bottle. We focus mainly on New World wines.

WHAT ARE THE MOST UNIQUE FEATURES IN YOUR WINE PROGRAM?
Two times a year we run a discount on our entire wine list, usually at thirty percent off. This brings in customers in at slower times of year and allows me to move through stagnant inventory.

WHAT CATEGORY OF WINE IS THE BEST VALUE IN YOUR RESTAURANT?
ABC, Anything but Chardonnay.

NAME A COUPLE OF YOUR RESTAURANT'S SIGNATURE DISHES. WHAT TYPES OF WINE DO YOU PREFER TO RECOMMEND WITH EACH?
Grilled Tennessee freshwater prawns served with yucca salad and a five-fruit relish with Washington State Riesling; wasabi-crusted ahi tuna served rare with carrot-infused jasmine rice, stir-fry snow pea salad and a chilled mango-chili sauce with Alsatian Gewürztraminer.

By the Tracks Bistro
MARK HAWKINS, HEAD WAITER
520 Kingston Pike, Knoxville
865-558-9500

Chez Philippe
JAY TURNEY, MAÎTRE D'
149 Union Avenue, Memphis
901-529-4188

The Orangery
STEWART KENDRICK, WINE BUYER
5412 Kingston Pike, Knoxville
865-588-2964

Stock Yard Restaurant
ANDREW PENLAND, WINE BUYER
901 Second Avenue North, Nashville
615-255-6464

La Tourelle
GLEN HAYES, WINE BUYER
2146 Monroe Avenue, Memphis
901-726-5771

The Wild Boar Restaurant
BRETT ALLEN, SOMMELIER
2014 Broadway, Nashville
615-329-1313

Bamboo Bamboo

5150 Keller Spring Road
Dallas, Texas 75248
phone 972-239-8988 fax 972-239-0090

Philip C. Natale
WINE DIRECTOR

NAME ONE OF YOUR FAVORITE WINES.
Amarone from the Veneto region of Italy, one wine that thrills me every time I have the opportunity to consume it.

NAME RECENT WINE DISCOVERIES THAT HAVE EXCITED YOU.
The wines of Sicily. There is great promise in these wines.

WHAT BITS OF INFORMATION WOULD YOU LIKE YOUR CUSTOMERS TO KNOW ABOUT YOU?
I studied chemical engineering at the University of Michigan before graduating with a degree in economics.

DESCRIBE YOUR WINE SELECTIONS, BOTH BY THE GLASS AND ON YOUR LIST.
We feature mainly New World wines from boutique producers.

WHAT ARE THE MOST UNIQUE FEATURES IN YOUR COMPANY'S WINE PROGRAMS?
Our 1,300-selection wine list has depth in past vintages of California Cabernet, Bordeaux, Burgundy, Italian and vintage Port.

NAME ONE OF YOUR RESTAURANT'S SIGNATURE DISHES. WHAT WINE DO YOU PREFER TO RECOMMEND WITH IT?
Kobe beef short rib with a full-structured Shiraz-Cabernet Sauvignon blend from South Eastern Australia.

IN THE PAST YEAR, WHAT WINES IN YOUR WINE PROGRAM HAVE CUS-TOMERS BECOME MORE WILLING TO ORDER?
Pinot Grigio from the United States.

WHAT ARE SOME OTHER ULTIMATE WINE AND FOOD PAIRINGS?
Rich Napa Valley Chardonnay and sweet corn grits.

Café on the Green
at Four Seasons
4150 North MacArthur Boulevard
Irving, Texas 75038
phone 972-717-0700 fax 972-717-2550
website www.fourseasons.com

James E. Tidwell
SOMMELIER

NAME TWO OF YOUR FAVORITE WINE REGIONS FROM AROUND THE
WORLD.
Burgundy and Willamette Valley, or any other region that grows quality Pinot
Noir.

NAME RECENT WINE DISCOVERIES THAT HAVE EXCITED YOU.
Northern Italian reds for their absolute quality; lesser-known areas of France,
Spain and Italy are producing excellent wines and real values.

WHAT BITS OF INFORMATION WOULD YOU LIKE YOUR CUSTOMERS TO
KNOW ABOUT YOU?
I grew up in northern Louisiana, which is not the fun Cajun part. My father
was a preacher, and my family didn't drink. I have a culinary degree from the
Culinary Institute of America and several wine certifications.

DESCRIBE YOUR WINE SELECTIONS, BOTH BY THE GLASS AND ON YOUR LIST.
The by-the-glass selection and the wine list are weighted toward California.
Currently, we are diversifying our selections.

WHAT ARE THE MOST UNIQUE FEATURES IN YOUR WINE PROGRAM?
We have a nice and ever-expanding selection of half-bottles. Also, we offer
wine-tasting receptions one Friday evening per month. Each reception has a
focus, such as "A Wine Tasting Tour of Spain."

NAME A COUPLE OF YOUR RESTAURANT'S SIGNATURE DISHES. WHAT
TYPES OF WINE DO YOU PREFER TO RECOMMEND WITH EACH?
Tuna sashimi in a light tomato and wasabi sauce with a semi-dry California or
German Kabinett Riesling; seared salmon with wasabi mashed potatoes in a
miso broth with Carneros Pinot Noir or a rustic Burgundy appellation.

IN THE PAST YEAR, WHAT WINES IN YOUR WINE PROGRAM HAVE CUS-
TOMERS BECOME MORE WILLING TO ORDER?
Wines from regions other than California, especially European wines.

The Green Room

2715 Elm Street
Dallas, Texas 75226
phone 214-748-7666 fax 214-748-7704

R. Whitney Meyers, Jr.

PROPRIETOR
AND WINE BUYER

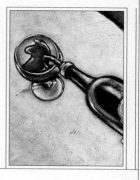

WHAT ARE SOME OF YOUR ULTIMATE FOOD AND WINE PAIRINGS?
Swiss Chasselas and lobster rolls; red Zinfandel and Texas barbecue; Savennières
and pâté de foie gras.

DESCRIBE YOUR WINE SELECTIONS.
An eclectic, award-winning list, featuring wines from fifteen countries.

WHAT IS YOUR FAVORITE WINE COUNTRY?
Lebanon. Chateau Musar is my favorite wine.

WHAT LED YOU TO YOUR CURRENT POSITION?
Chef laziness.

WHAT IS THE MOST CHALLENGING ASPECT OF YOUR JOB?
Time management. Trying to juggle responsibilities for each business while
making time for staff training, product selection and wine list updates at each
restaurant.

IF YOU WERE NOT IN THIS PROFESSION, WHAT WOULD YOU BE DOING?
Litigating ACLU cases or running political campaigns.

Lonesome Dove Western Bistro

2406 North Main Street
Fort Worth, Texas 76110
phone 817-740-8810 fax 817-740-8632
website www.lonesomedovebistro.com

Brad Ludington

GENERAL MANAGER
AND WINE DIRECTOR

WHAT INSPIRED YOU TO PURSUE A CAREER THAT INVOLVES WINE?
I stumbled upon the world of fine wine while working in steakhouses across the country. I've been fascinated by it ever since.

NAME TWO OF YOUR FAVORITE WINES.
Australian Shiraz, because each region creates such diverse wines; California Cabernet Sauvignons, because they are so rich and full-bodied.

NAME RECENT WINE DISCOVERIES THAT HAVE EXCITED YOU.
Oregon Pinot Noirs, so intriguing with their rich fruit.

IF YOU WERE NOT IN THIS PROFESSION, WHAT WOULD YOU BE DOING?
I don't think I'm suited for anything else.

DESCRIBE YOUR WINE SELECTIONS, BOTH BY THE GLASS AND ON YOUR LIST.
Our wine list offers a wide selection of fine American wines and introduces the best that Australia has to offer. Our twenty-four wines by the glass represent thirteen different wine types. We also hold wine dinners where Chef Tim Love creates unique menus to pair with specific wines.

WHAT CATEGORY OF WINE IS THE BEST VALUE IN YOUR RESTAURANT?
Shiraz. The prices are very reasonable.

NAME A COUPLE OF YOUR RESTAURANT'S SIGNATURE DISHES. WHAT TYPES OF WINE DO YOU PREFER TO RECOMMEND WITH EACH?
Roasted garlic-stuffed beef tenderloin with McClaren Vale Shiraz; seared sweet lobster cakes with New Zealand Sauvignon Blanc.

Mansion on Turtle Creek

2821 Turtle Creek Boulevard
Dallas, Texas 75219
phone 214-559-2100 fax 214-526-5345

Kent Rice

SOMMELIER

WHAT IS ONE OF YOUR ULTIMATE FOOD AND WINE PAIRINGS?
A simple roasted chicken with great California Cabernet Sauvignon or Château Haut-Brion.

DESCRIBE YOUR WINE SELECTIONS.
Our list is one of the best in the nation. It is fairly evenly divided between French and California wines, with representations from many other regions and countries as well. The selections include many unusual and rare vintages and a large number from small, boutique producers.

WHAT IS YOUR FAVORITE WINE REGION IN THE WORLD TODAY?
Napa Valley, because of the quality of wines and the natural beauty of the region.

WHAT LED YOU TO PURSUE A CAREER THAT INVOLVES WINE?
As a youngster, I lived in a Texas vineyard. I was always curious about wines and vineyards. Eventually, I began to study wine and dreamed of going to Paris by way of Dallas—but in Dallas he stays!

WHAT ARE THE MOST CHALLENGING ASPECTS OF YOUR JOB?
First, overcoming the "fear factor" that some guests have about consulting a sommelier. Second, matching the food to the appropriate wine, within the guest's budget.

IF YOU WERE NOT IN THIS PROFESSION, WHAT WOULD YOU BE?
A playwright.

Al Biernat's Restaurant

TODD LINCICOME, SOMMELIER

4217 Oak Lawn Avenue, Dallas

214-219-2201

Beau Nash at the Hotel Crescent Court

LUIGI ROMANELLI, WINE BUYER

400 Crescent Court, Dallas

214-871-3200

Bistro Louise

LOUISE LAMENSDORF, OWNER

AND WINE BUYER

2900 South Hulen, Southgate

Commons, Fort Worth

817-922-9244

Café Pacific

JEAN-PIERRE ALBERTINETTI,

SOMMELIER

24 Highland Park Village, Dallas

214-526-1170

Chamberlain's

JEFF BARKER, SOMMELIER

5330 Belt Line Road, Dallas

972-934-2467

Chaparral Club in the Adams Mark Hotel

WES HARRELL,

BEVERAGE DIRECTOR

400 North Olive Street, Dallas

214-777-6539

Cool River

JEFF IVY, SOMMELIER

1045 Hidden Ridge Road, Irving

972-871-8881

Del Frisco's Double Eagle Steak House

BRIAN SOLOWAY, WINE DIRECTOR

5251 Spring Valley Road, Dallas

972-490-9000

The French Room at Hotel Adolphus

AUGUSTINE YBARRA, SOMMELIER

1321 Commerce Street, Dallas

214-742-8200

Morton's of Chicago

JOHN BENTON, WINE CAPTAIN

501 Elm Street, Dallas

214-741-2277

Nana at the Wyndham Anatole Hotel

FABIAN HERNANDEZ,

WINE STEWARD

2201 Stemmons Freeway, Dallas

214-761-7470

Newport's Restaurant

ROBERT WRIGHT, MANAGER

AND SOMMELIER

703 McKinney Avenue, Dallas

214-954-0220

Nick and Sam's

NATE BIDDICK, SOMMELIER

3008 Maple Avenue, Dallas

214-871-7444

The Palm

PETER MACVAK, SOMMELIER

701 Ross Avenue, Dallas

214-698-0470

Pappa's Brothers Steakhouse

ROBERT SMITH, WINE BUYER

10477 Lombardy Lane, Dallas

214-366-2000

The Riviera

JOSEPH ICHO, SOMMELIER

7709 Inwood Road, Dallas

214-351-0094

Ruth's Chris Steak House

RON WYLICK, MANAGER

AND SOMMELIER

5922 Cedar Springs Road, Dallas

214-902-8080

Steel Restaurant & Lounge

MAREK VON SPRINGER,

CELLAR MASTER

3102 Oak Lawn Avenue, Dallas

214-219-9908

Sullivan's Steakhouse

RANDY BRANDON, WINE STEWARD

17795 North Dallas Parkway, Dallas

972-267-9393

III Forks Steakhouse

KYLE KEPNER, MANAGER

AND SOMMELIER

17776 Dallas Parkway, Dallas

972-267-1776

Arcodoro and Pomodoro

5000 Westheimer at Post Oak
Houston, Texas 77056
phone 713-621-6888 fax 713-621-6859
website www.arcodoro.com

Efisio Farris
OWNER AND CHEF

NAME TWO OF YOUR FAVORITE WINE REGIONS FROM AROUND THE WORLD.
Sardinia. It is my home. Second, Piedmont, which produces Italian wine masterpieces.

WHAT BITS OF INFORMATION WOULD YOU LIKE YOUR CUSTOMERS TO KNOW ABOUT YOU?
My devotion to my home in Sardinia, and my passion to bring the flavors of my home to America with new products.

IF YOU WERE NOT IN THIS PROFESSION, WHAT WOULD YOU BE DOING?
My first career path was architecture, which lent a hand when designing my two restaurants.

DESCRIBE YOUR WINE SELECTIONS, BOTH BY THE GLASS AND ON YOUR LIST.
We specialize in Italian wine. Our wines by the glass expose customers to various wines and styles in a range of prices.

WHAT ARE THE MOST UNIQUE FEATURES IN YOUR WINE PROGRAM?
My loyalty to Italian wine, our extensive list and reserve selections that include many boutique and independent wineries. Also unique is our Chef's Wine Room with humidity and temperature control where we have our Chef's Table dinners with wine pairings.

NAME A FEW OF YOUR RESTAURANT'S SIGNATURE DISHES. WHAT TYPES OF WINE DO YOU PREFER TO RECOMMEND WITH EACH?
Costolette al Vino Cotto with old-vine Cannonau; Sa Fregnla with Vermentino di Gallura; Seadas with Lughente Passito.

IN THE PAST YEAR, WHAT WINES IN YOUR WINE PROGRAM HAVE CUSTOMERS BECOME MORE WILLING TO ORDER?
Sardinian wines and small, little-known producers from other regions, such as Soave in Veneto and Foresco in Umbria.

Brennan's of Houston

3300 Smith Street
Houston, Texas 77006
phone 713-522-9711 fax 713-522-9142
website www.brennanshouston.com

Martin W. Korson
"THE WINE GUY"

NAME ONE OF YOUR FAVORITE WINES.
Grower-producer Champagnes with their sense of soul and heart, such as René Geoffroy and Gimonnet.

NAME RECENT WINE DISCOVERIES THAT HAVE EXCITED YOU.
German Rieslings continue to amaze me in both quality and value. They seem to go with so many different kinds of dishes.

WHAT WOULD YOU LIKE YOUR CUSTOMERS TO KNOW ABOUT YOU?
I am a Culinary Institute graduate, but I have more fun working in the front of the house.

IF YOU WERE NOT IN THIS PROFESSION, WHAT WOULD YOU BE?
Chef-instructor at the Culinary Institute of America or a history professor.

DESCRIBE YOUR WINE SELECTIONS, BOTH BY THE GLASS AND ON YOUR LIST.
We have fifty-seven wines by the glass and 390 wines on the list from fourteen different countries and five different states.

WHAT ARE THE MOST UNIQUE FEATURES IN YOUR WINE PROGRAM?
We now have more than fifty half-bottles, and we do a "wine table" experience custom-designed for diners.

WHAT CATEGORY OF WINE IS THE BEST VALUE IN YOUR RESTAURANT?
My special listing of "Martin's Affordable Alternatives" offers great wines from around the world.

NAME ONE OF YOUR RESTAURANT'S SIGNATURE DISHES. WHAT WINE DO YOU PREFER TO RECOMMEND WITH IT?
American artisanal cheese selection with Austrian Grüner Veltliner.

IN THE PAST YEAR, WHAT WINES IN YOUR WINE PROGRAM HAVE CUSTOMERS BECOME MORE WILLING TO ORDER?
Spanish reds and grower-producer Champagnes.

Lynn's Steakhouse
955 Dairy Ashford Road
Houston, Texas 77079
phone 281-870-0807 fax 281-870-0888

Loic Carbonnier
PROPRIETOR AND WINE BUYER
TEAM: LYNN FOREMAN, PROPRIETOR
AND WINE BUYER

WHAT ARE SOME OF YOUR ULTIMATE FOOD AND WINE PAIRINGS?
Prime beef Châteaubriand with Napa Cabernet (especially from the Stag's Leap
District); Cajun snapper étouffée with Alsatian Riesling.

DESCRIBE YOUR WINE SELECTIONS.
Our wine list is focused on reds, since we're a steakhouse. We have a great selection of red Burgundies, and at reasonable prices.

WHAT CATEGORY OF WINE IS THE BEST VALUE IN YOUR RESTAURANT?
Burgundy.

NAME RECENT WINE DISCOVERIES THAT HAVE EXCITED YOU.
New Zealand Sauvignon Blancs, for their bouquets and crispness.

WHAT IS YOUR FAVORITE WINE REGION IN THE WORLD TODAY?
Burgundy, for the challenge it represents. (Who could stay married to a Pinot
Noir wife!)

WHAT LED YOU TO YOUR CURRENT POSITION?
When I started cooking, I soon discovered my love for wine. I was fortunate to
meet the right people and was given the opportunity to pursue it.

WHAT IS THE MOST CHALLENGING ASPECT OF YOUR JOB?
Finding the right wines and making customers happy, whether it is with a
twenty-dollar or two thousand–dollar bottle of wine.

IF YOU WERE NOT IN YOUR CURRENT POSITION, WHAT WOULD YOU BE
DOING?
Cooking or fly fishing.

Mark's American Cuisine

1658 Westheimer Road
Houston, Texas 77006
phone 713-523-3800 fax 713-523-9292
website www.marks1658.com

Matthew T. Pridgen
MANAGER AND
WINE DIRECTOR

WHAT INSPIRED YOU TO PURSUE A CAREER THAT INVOLVES WINE?
Tasting a 1938 Château Palmer, a great, mature wine. It inspired and intrigued me.

DESCRIBE YOUR WINE SELECTIONS, BOTH BY THE GLASS AND ON YOUR LIST.
Mark's features more than thirty selections by the glass and more than 260 wines in bottles and half-bottles. We are a family-owned restaurant and our focus is small, family-owned and -operated wineries from around the world.

WHAT ARE THE MOST UNIQUE FEATURES IN YOUR WINE PROGRAM?
We offer a number of wines by the glass and around twenty half-bottles. Wines are offered with our six-course tasting menu on a nightly basis.

WHAT WINES ARE THE BEST VALUES IN YOUR RESTAURANT?
German Rieslings and Côtes du Rhône.

NAME A COUPLE OF YOUR RESTAURANT'S SIGNATURE DISHES. WHAT TYPES OF WINE DO YOU PREFER TO RECOMMEND WITH EACH?
Roasted garlic and cauliflower flan with Avruga caviar with Blanc de Blancs sparkling wine; hearth roasted Maple Leaf duck with blueberry with Barbera d'Asti.

IN THE PAST YEAR, WHAT WINES IN YOUR WINE PROGRAM HAVE CUS-TOMERS BECOME MORE WILLING TO ORDER?
Northern Italian wines, German Riesling and New Zealand reds.

O'Rourke's Steak House

4611 Montrose
Houston, Texas 77006
phone: 713-523-4611 fax 713-523-0033

John O'Rourke
OWNER

NAME TWO OF YOUR FAVORITE WINE DISTRICTS OR REGIONS FROM AROUND THE WORLD.
Côte de Nuits and Côte-Rôtie, whose wines are particularly subtle and intricately layered.

NAME RECENT WINE DISCOVERIES THAT HAVE EXCITED YOU.
Jean-Marc Boillot Rully premier cru Mont-Palais 1999 is a beautifully structured Chardonnay at a good price; Domaine Leflaive Blagny premier cru Sous Le Dos d'Ane 1997 has a rich, velvety texture and is another good value.

WHAT BITS OF INFORMATION WOULD YOU LIKE YOUR CUSTOMERS TO KNOW ABOUT YOU?
I am a marathoner and triathlete.

DESCRIBE YOUR WINE SELECTIONS, BOTH BY THE GLASS AND ON YOUR LIST.
Our clientele and our cuisine generally direct our wine list toward Cabernet Sauvignon and Chardonnay. However, we have begun to see a broader support for other varietals, and we are strengthening our Burgundy and Rhône selections, as well as those from Italy and Spain.

WHAT ARE THE MOST UNIQUE FEATURES IN YOUR WINE PROGRAM?
We have a strong by-the-glass program that features three price tiers for each varietal. We regularly host wine dinners in our private wine room.

NAME A COUPLE OF YOUR RESTAURANT'S SIGNATURE DISHES. WHAT TYPES OF WINE DO YOU PREFER TO RECOMMEND WITH EACH?
Gulf red snapper with grilled leeks and tomato-fennel broth with Carneros Chardonnay; Grilled veal chop with roasted corn polenta, wild mushroom sauté and tarragon butter with Côte-Rôtie.

IN THE PAST YEAR, WHAT WINES IN YOUR WINE PROGRAM HAVE CUSTOMERS BECOME MORE WILLING TO ORDER?
Wines from Burgundy and the Rhône Valley.

Pappas Brothers
Steakhouse

5839 Westheimer Road
Houston, Texas 77057
phone 713-780-7352 fax 713-780-8119

Scotti A. Stark

SOMMELIER AND
WINE DIRECTOR

WHAT ARE SOME OF YOUR ULTIMATE FOOD AND WINE PAIRINGS?
Gooey pecan pie with Fonseca twenty-year-old tawny Port; pizza and big
Zinfandel.

DESCRIBE YOUR WINE SELECTIONS.
Very extensive. We have more than 1,700 wines from around the world on our
list.

WHAT ARE YOUR FAVORITE WINE REGIONS IN THE WORLD TODAY?
Napa Valley and Sonoma County, where the weather is spectacular year-round
and the wines are consistently great.

WHAT LED YOU TO PURSUE A CAREER THAT INVOLVES WINE?
I started here as a server and had never worked in a restaurant with sommeliers.
I was fascinated!

WHAT ARE THE MOST CHALLENGING ASPECTS OF YOUR JOB?
Keeping the wine list updated and making enough time for training, tasting
and traveling.

IF YOU WERE NOT IN THIS PROFESSION, WHAT WOULD YOU BE DOING?
Probably something similar, selling and/or educating.

Rotisserie for Beef and Bird

2200 Wilcrest Street
Houston, Texas 77042
phone 713-977-9524 fax 713-977-9568
website www.rotisserie-beef-bird.com

Vincent S. Baker
CELLAR MASTER AND SOMMELIER

NAME ONE OR TWO OF YOUR FAVORITE WINE DISTRICTS OR WINE REGIONS FROM AROUND THE WORLD.
Sonoma County, and Portugal in general for the sheer diversity of styles of its wines.

NAME RECENT WINE DISCOVERIES THAT HAVE EXCITED YOU.
2001 Forefathers Shiraz, the Paul Hobbs 2000 Cuvée Agustina Pinot Noir and Shafer 1999 Relentless Syrah; all wines of quality and style.

WHAT BITS OF INFORMATION WOULD YOU LIKE YOUR CUSTOMERS TO KNOW ABOUT YOU?
I enjoy running, cooking and home-schooling our children.

DESCRIBE YOUR WINE SELECTIONS, BOTH BY THE GLASS AND ON YOUR LIST.
By the glass, we serve quality wines that are good values. On the list, we provide flavors for all palates. We emphasize New World wines, especially those that are new and up-and-coming.

WHAT ARE THE MOST UNIQUE FEATURES IN YOUR WINE PROGRAM?
Our Vintner's Dinners and Theme Dinners. They encompass the entire facility (approximately 180 covers) with a six-course dinner with six wines. It is always a Sunday sell-out.

WHAT WINES ARE THE BEST VALUES IN YOUR RESTAURANT?
Chilean Merlot and Australian Shiraz.

NAME ONE OF YOUR RESTAURANT'S SIGNATURE DISHES. WHAT WINE DO YOU PREFER TO RECOMMEND WITH IT?
Grilled seafood, especially heavy fish like tuna or swordfish, with Howell Mountain Cabernet Franc.

IN THE PAST YEAR, WHAT WINES IN YOUR WINE PROGRAM HAVE CUSTOMERS BECOME MORE WILLING TO ORDER?
New Zealand Sauvignon Blanc, Australian Shiraz and Argentine Malbec.

Tony's

1801 Post Oak Boulevard
Houston, Texas 77056
phone 713-622-6778 fax 713-626-1232

Armando Dawdy
CORPORATE SOMMELIER

WHAT INSPIRED YOU TO PURSUE A CAREER THAT INVOLVES WINE?
I grew up in Texas and did not develop a taste for beer. Wine was my favorite alternative.

WHAT PART OF YOUR JOB DO YOU ENJOY THE MOST?
I enjoy most everything, but tasting is always a lot of fun.

NAME ONE OF YOUR FAVORITE WINES FROM AROUND THE WORLD.
Burgundy for its excellent wines with finesse and elegance.

NAME RECENT WINE DISCOVERIES THAT HAVE EXCITED YOU.
The 2001 German wines are of great quality and very food-friendly.

WHAT BITS OF INFORMATION WOULD YOU LIKE YOUR CUSTOMERS TO KNOW ABOUT YOU?
I play a lot of golf and tennis.

IF YOU WERE NOT IN THIS PROFESSION, WHAT WOULD YOU BE DOING?
Pharmaceutical sales.

DESCRIBE YOUR WINE SELECTIONS, BOTH BY THE GLASS AND ON YOUR LIST.
We have a large selection of French, Italian and Californian wines with an emphasis on old Burgundy.

WHAT CATEGORY OF WINE IS THE BEST VALUE IN YOUR RESTAURANT?
Red Bordeaux with vintages from 1844 to 1999.

NAME A COUPLE OF YOUR RESTAURANT'S SIGNATURE DISHES. WHAT TYPES OF WINE DO YOU PREFER TO RECOMMEND WITH EACH?
Osso buco with Brunello di Montalcino; foie gras with Sauternes.

IN THE PAST YEAR, WHAT WINES IN YOUR WINE PROGRAM HAVE CUSTOMERS BECOME MORE WILLING TO ORDER?
German wines, in all styles.

America's

RIGO ROMERO, WINE BUYER
1800 South Post Oak, Houston
713-961-1492

Café Annie

MARIANNA BERRYHILL,
WINE DIRECTOR AND SOMMELIER
1728 Post Oak Boulevard, Houston
713-840-1111

The Palm

JEREMY CALVERT, SOMMELIER
6100 Westheimer Road, Houston
713-977-2544

Quattro at the Four Seasons

MICHAEL SAVINO, WINE BUYER
1300 Lamar Street, Houston
713-652-6250

Rainbow Lodge

TIM NEELY, GENERAL MANAGER
AND WINE BUYER
One Birdsall Street, Houston
713-861-8666

La Reserve

IVO NIKIC, SOMMELIER
4 Riverway Drive, Houston
713-871-8177

River Oaks Grill

2630 Westheimer Road
Houston, Texas 77098
713-520-1738

Sierra Grill

LEE BENNETT, GENERAL MANAGER
4704 Montrose, Houston
713-942-7757

La Tour d'Argent

GIANCARLO CAVATORE,
OWNER AND WINE BUYER
2011 Ella Boulevard, Houston
713-864-9864

Bohanan's Prime Steak and Seafood

219 East Houston Street
San Antonio, Texas 78205
phone 210-472-2600 fax 210-472-2276
website www.bohanans.com

André H. Mack

SOMMELIER

WHAT PART OF YOUR JOB DO YOU ENJOY THE MOST?
Introducing guests to new and interesting wines.

NAME ONE OR TWO OF YOUR FAVORITE WINE DISTRICTS OR WINE REGIONS FROM AROUND THE WORLD.
Burgundy for its complexity and elegance.

NAME RECENT WINE DISCOVERIES THAT HAVE EXCITED YOU.
Still white wines from the Dâo region of Portugal. Its wines are clean and fresh in style, great values and excellent with food.

WHAT WOULD YOU LIKE YOUR CUSTOMERS TO KNOW ABOUT YOU?
I have a collection of 5,000 corks.

IF YOU WERE NOT IN THIS PROFESSION, WHAT WOULD YOU BE DOING?
Slowly dying.

DESCRIBE YOUR WINE SELECTIONS, BOTH BY THE GLASS AND ON YOUR LIST.
Our list has a strong emphasis on boutique wines from California, with regions represented from around the world. Our by-the-glass collection of fifteen wines is small but changes weekly.

WHAT ARE THE MOST UNIQUE FEATURES IN YOUR WINE PROGRAM?
We have a half-bottle selection of more than twenty-five wines.

WHAT CATEGORY OF WINE IS THE BEST VALUE IN YOUR RESTAURANT?
Texas wines and wines over $100, which have a lower markup.

NAME A COUPLE OF YOUR RESTAURANT'S SIGNATURE DISHES. WHAT TYPES OF WINE DO YOU PREFER TO RECOMMEND WITH EACH?
Mesquite-grilled red snapper with sauce royale paired with Santa Maria Valley Pinot Noir.

WHAT WINES ARE CUSTOMERS NOW MORE WILLING TO ORDER?
Cabernet Franc, Petit Verdot and Malbec from around the world!

The Grille at the Westin La Cantera Resort

16641 La Cantera Parkway
San Antonio, Texas 78256
phone 210-558-6500 fax 210-558-1529
website www.westinlacantera.com

Steven A. Krueger
LEAD SUPERVISOR AND RESORT SOMMELIER

NAME ONE OF YOUR FAVORITE WINE REGIONS FROM AROUND THE WORLD.
South Africa. Its wines are high in quality and excellent value. They have all the juicy, fruity expression of California wines with the intriguing complexity of European wines.

NAME RECENT WINE DISCOVERIES THAT HAVE EXCITED YOU.
Texas wines! They are improving every year, by leaps and bounds. Watch for "Super-Texans" as vineyards begin bottling hot-climate blends from varietals like Sangiovese, Tempranillo and Syrah.

WHAT BITS OF INFORMATION WOULD YOU LIKE YOUR CUSTOMERS TO KNOW ABOUT YOU?
I originally worked in graphic arts and comic books, but the wonder and excitement of the restaurant business got into my blood.

IF YOU WERE NOT IN THIS PROFESSION, WHAT WOULD YOU BE DOING?
It does not get any better than this.

DESCRIBE YOUR WINE SELECTIONS, BOTH BY THE GLASS AND ON YOUR LIST.
Our wine list is predominately Californian with many other wines from all over the world. We're constantly training all service staff to be knowledgeable and well-informed about our wines.

NAME ONE OF YOUR RESTAURANT'S SIGNATURE DISHES. WHAT WINE DO YOU PREFER TO RECOMMEND WITH IT?
Cowboy cut rib-eye with limited-production California Cabernet Sauvignon from the 1997 vintage.

IN THE PAST YEAR, WHAT WINES IN YOUR WINE PROGRAM HAVE CUSTOMERS BECOME MORE WILLING TO ORDER?
Syrah/Shiraz.

Ruth's Chris Steak House

7720 Jones-Maltsberger Street
San Antonio, Texas 78216
phone 210-821-5051 fax 210-821-5095
website www.ruthschris-sanantonio.com

Janet M. Easterling
SOMMELIER

NAME ONE OF YOUR FAVORITE WINES FROM AROUND THE WORLD.
Napa Valley Cabernet Sauvignon. I love the power and ripe flavors.

NAME RECENT WINE DISCOVERIES THAT HAVE EXCITED YOU.
Priorat in Spain is an exciting wine with great depth, and Malbec, especially
from Argentina, is a great value.

WHAT BITS OF INFORMATION WOULD YOU LIKE YOUR CUSTOMERS TO
KNOW ABOUT YOU?
I love gardening, my dogs, other animals and birds. I love to travel. Porto and
chocolate are my favorite snack!

IF YOU WERE NOT IN THIS PROFESSION, WHAT WOULD YOU BE?
A volunteer at the Humane Society. I'd also have beautiful flower gardens.

DESCRIBE YOUR WINE SELECTIONS, BOTH BY THE GLASS AND ON YOUR LIST.
Our list covers the globe with 425 selections. We specialize in hearty red wines predominately from California and Bordeaux that complement our steakhouse menu.

WHAT ARE THE MOST UNIQUE FEATURES IN YOUR WINE PROGRAM?
We have an extensive half-bottle list, an impressive number of older verticals
and many small-production, hard-to-find wines.

WHAT WINES ARE THE BEST VALUES IN YOUR RESTAURANT?
California Zinfandel and red Rhône.

NAME A COUPLE OF YOUR RESTAURANT'S SIGNATURE DISHES. WHAT
TYPES OF WINE DO YOU PREFER TO RECOMMEND WITH EACH?
Cowboy rib-eye with California Cabernet Sauvignon; filet mignon with red
Bordeaux; crème brûlée with German Auslese.

WHAT WINES ARE CUSTOMERS NOW MORE WILLING TO ORDER?
Australian Shiraz, Rhône reds, premium California Zinfandels and premium
wines in half-bottles.

Cuvée

LEN WHITE, WINE BUYER

342 West Main Street, Fredericksburg

830-990-1600

Little Rhein Steakhouse

MOE LAZRI, WINE BUYER

231 South Alamo Street, San Antonio

210-225-1212

Le Rêve

ANDREW WEISSMAN, OWNER,

CHEF AND WINE BUYER

152 East Pecan Street, San Antonio

210-212-2221

Ruth's Chris Steak House

ALEX BOLAND, MANAGER

AND WINE BUYER

1170 East Commerce Street,

San Antonio

210-227-8847

Stein Eriksen Lodge

7700 Stein Way
Park City, Utah 84060
phone 435-649-3700 fax 435-645-6465
website www.steinlodge.com

Cara Schwindt
BEVERAGE MANAGER
AND SOMMELIER

WHAT LED YOU TO PURSUE A CAREER THAT INVOLVES WINE?
Wine chose me.

WHAT IS YOUR FAVORITE REGION IN THE WORLD TODAY?
Italy. I love the vast array of flavors, textures and styles.

NAME RECENT WINE DISCOVERIES THAT HAVE EXCITED YOU.
Recently, finding a simple Merlot with a vibrant blueberry nose, a rich, lush texture and an easy-to-drink nature that my customers will love.

IF YOU WERE NOT IN THE WINE PROFESSION, WHAT WOULD YOU BE DOING?
Teaching Pilates.

DESCRIBE YOUR WINE PROGRAM AND WINE SELECTIONS.
We offer a broad range of wines from a worldwide viewpoint. I want everyone who joins us to be able to find a wine he or she will enjoy.

WHAT CATEGORY OF WINE IS THE BEST VALUE IN YOUR RESTAURANT OR IN YOUR RESTAURANT?
There are good values in every category.

WHAT ARE SOME OF YOUR FAVORITE WINE AND FOOD PAIRINGS?
Caribou tenderloin and northern Rhône red; salmon chowder and dry Alsatian Riesling.

IN THE PAST YEAR, WHAT WINES IN YOUR WINE PROGRAM HAVE CUSTOMERS BECOME MORE WILLING TO ORDER?
Wines from the southern Rhône.

Chez Betty

TOM BELL, OWNER
AND WINE BUYER
1637 Shortline Road, Park City
435-649-8181

Deer Valley Resort

SYNDEY KEEL, WINE BUYER
2250 Deer Valley Drive South,
Park City
435-649-1000

Goldener Hirsch Inn

JEFF DUKES, RESTAURANT
MANAGER AND WINE BUYER
7570 Royal Street East, Park City
435-649-7770

Market Street Broiler

ADAM MARTY, WINE BUYER
260 South 1300 East, Salt Lake City
801-583-8808

Sai-Sommet at the Deer Valley Club

PETE BARQUIN, WINE BUYER
7720 Royal Street East, Park City
435-645-9909

The Colonnade at the Equinox

JOHN ALEXOPOULOS, DIRECTOR
OF PURCHASING AND WINE BUYER
3567 Main Street,
Manchester Village
802-362-4747

Hemingway's Restaurant

TIM DRISCOLL, SOMMELIER
Route 4, Killington
802-422-3886

The Hermitage Inn

JIM MCGOVERN, WINE BUYER
Coldbrook Road, Wilmington
802-464-3511

The Inn at Sawmill Farm

BRILL WILLIAMS, WINE BUYER
Mount Snow Valley No. 100,
West Dover
802-464-8131

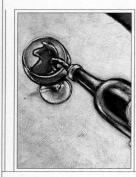

Colvin Run Tavern
8045 Leesburg Pike
Vienna, Virginia 22182
phone 703-356-9500 fax 703-356-1008

Richard D. Mahan, Jr.
BEVERAGE MANAGER
AND SOMMELIER

NAME SOME OF YOUR FAVORITE WINES FROM AROUND THE WORLD.
Oregon Pinot Noir, because they show remarkable improvement; Priorat for its unique depth and concentration of flavor; Burgundy, because nothing is better when it is made right.

NAME RECENT WINE DISCOVERIES THAT HAVE EXCITED YOU.
Domaine Serene Pinot Noir, Evenstad Reserve 1999 for its texture and bouquet; Peachy Canyon Zinfandel, Benito Dusi Ranch 1999 has understated elegance.

WHAT BITS OF INFORMATION WOULD YOU LIKE YOUR CUSTOMERS TO KNOW ABOUT YOU?
I was a chef in fine dining restaurants for twenty years.

IF YOU WERE NOT IN THIS PROFESSION, WHAT WOULD YOU BE?
Cooking, in sports management or coaching.

DESCRIBE YOUR WINE SELECTIONS, BOTH BY THE GLASS AND ON YOUR LIST.
Our by-the-glass selection is diverse and offers very good value. Our 300-bottle list has wines encompassing popular and esoteric selections from around the world.

WHAT ARE THE MOST UNIQUE FEATURES IN YOUR WINE PROGRAM?
Our half-bottle list, our monthly wine flights and reasonable wine markups.

NAME A COUPLE OF YOUR RESTAURANT'S SIGNATURE DISHES. WHAT TYPES OF WINE DO YOU PREFER TO RECOMMEND WITH EACH?
Seared sea scallops with smoked bacon arugula salad and parsley caper purée with Central Coast Pinot Noir; pan-roasted squab with truffled potato gnocchi, wild mushrooms, squab confit and foie gras emulsion with Oregon Pinot Noir; crispy Thai squab with spicy green papaya salad and California Syrah.

IN THE PAST YEAR, WHAT WINES IN YOUR WINE PROGRAM HAVE CUSTOMERS BECOME MORE WILLING TO ORDER?
Oregon Pinot Noir, Austrian Grüner Veltliner, and New Zealand and Virginia reds.

The Dining Room at Ford's Colony

240 Ford's Colony Drive
Williamsburg, Virginia 23188
phone 757-258-4107 fax 757-258-4168
website www.fordscolony.com

Adam Steely
RESTAURANT MANAGER

NAME RECENT WINE DISCOVERIES THAT HAVE EXCITED YOU.
Old-vine Syrahs from Languedoc for their quality, intensity and value; Austrian whites and reds for their value and richness.

IF YOU WERE NOT IN THIS PROFESSION, WHAT WOULD YOU BE?
Professional Gater? Movie star?

DESCRIBE YOUR WINE SELECTIONS, BOTH BY THE GLASS AND ON YOUR LIST.
Our wine list has 1,400 selections including Spanish, Italian, Australian, New Zealand and German wines, although our focus is upon American and French wines. We offer fifteen whites and fifteen reds by the glass.

WHAT ARE THE MOST UNIQUE FEATURES IN YOUR WINE PROGRAM?
Depth and breadth of selection. We offer so many great wines from around the world that I am confident we have surprises for everyone.

WHAT WINES ARE THE BEST VALUES IN YOUR RESTAURANT?
Red Bordeaux, Alsatian wines and American Syrah, Cabernet and Pinot Noir.

NAME A FEW OF YOUR RESTAURANT'S SIGNATURE DISHES. WHAT TYPES OF WINE DO YOU PREFER TO RECOMMEND WITH EACH?
Grilled breast of pigeon with red onion confit served with Oregon Pinot Noir; Yukon gold potato and black truffle soup with shaved truffles served with Alsatian Pinot Gris; seared foie gras paired with Alsatian grand cru Gewürztraminer

IN THE PAST YEAR, WHAT WINES IN YOUR WINE PROGRAM HAVE CUSTOMERS BECOME MORE WILLING TO ORDER?
German Riesling, Alsatian Pinot Gris and Australian Shiraz.

Lansdowne Grille
at Lansdowne Resort

44050 Woodridge Parkway
Leesburg, Virginia 20176
phone 703-729-4073 fax 703-729-4096
website www.lansdowneresort.com

Mary L. Watson-DeLauder
RESORT SOMMELIER

WHAT ARE SOME OF YOUR ULTIMATE FOOD AND WINE PAIRINGS?
Pinot Noir with filet mignon; big Cabernet Sauvignon with ribeye; Zinfandel with New York strip; Champagne with caviar or smoked salmon; big, ripe Zinfandel with lamb.

DESCRIBE YOUR WINE SELECTIONS.
The wine list is predominantly American. I am very proud of the wines we are making in the United States.

WHAT CATEGORIES OF WINE ARE THE BEST VALUES ON YOUR WINE LIST?
Zinfandel, Syrah/Shiraz and Meritage.

NAME RECENT WINE DISCOVERIES THAT HAVE EXCITED YOU.
Austrian Grüner Veltliner, Ribera del Duero reds from Spain.

WHAT IS YOUR FAVORITE WINE REGION IN THE WORLD TODAY?
California, especially Napa Valley, Sonoma County and Mendocino County. Every year, we see more quality wines and new producers and innovators from here.

WHAT LED YOU TO PURSUE A CAREER THAT INVOLVES WINE?
I love wine. I love everything about it, from grape growing all the way to making it, aging it, serving it and enjoying it with food.

WHAT ARE THE BEST ASPECTS OF YOUR JOB?
I especially enjoy staff wine training and guest interaction. Hearing one of the servers relate something we have talked about to a guest is incredibly satisfying.

IF YOU WERE NOT IN THIS PROFESSION, WHAT WOULD YOU BE?
A chef, a gardener or landscaper. Maybe even a farmer or grape grower.

Maestro
at the Ritz-Carlton
Tysons Corner

1700 Tysons Boulevard
McLean, Virginia 22102
phone 703-506-4300 fax 703-917-5499
website www.ritzcarlton.com

Vincent Feraud
SOMMELIER

WHAT ARE SOME OF YOUR ULTIMATE FOOD AND WINE PAIRINGS?
Trio of tartan fish with Venica Sauvignon Blanc from Collio; roasted potatoes wrapped around John Dory with Chalk Hill Chardonnay.

DESCRIBE YOUR WINE SELECTIONS.
Our wine list is French, Italian and American and includes a number of producers from Virginia.

WHAT CATEGORY OF WINE IS THE BEST VALUE IN YOUR RESTAURANT?
Italian white wines.

NAME RECENT WINE DISCOVERIES THAT HAVE EXCITED YOU.
Valpolicella Ripasso from Zenato and 2000 Tocai Friulano from Venica.

WHAT IS YOUR FAVORITE WINE REGION IN THE WORLD TODAY?
Burgundy. I enjoy its flavors and terroir. I also enjoy Amarone.

WHAT LED YOU TO PURSUE A CAREER THAT INVOLVES WINE?
When I was an apprentice waiter at sixteen years old, one of the sommeliers in the restaurant in which I worked broke too many glasses. They fired him and I started my sommelier training.

WHAT ARE THE BEST ASPECTS OF YOUR JOB?
Having a good time at night in the restaurant and selling the right wine to the right person.

IF YOU WERE NOT IN THIS PROFESSION, WHAT WOULD YOU BE DOING?
I'd live on a windy island and try to make a living off the water.

Palm Court Restaurant at the Westfield Conference Center

14750 Conference Center Drive
Chantilly, Virginia 20151
phone 703-818-3522 fax 703-818-0363

David J. Pennell
MAÎTRE D' AND SOMMELIER

WHAT PART OF YOUR JOB DO YOU ENJOY THE MOST?
Sharing new discoveries or unusual varietals with our guests.

NAME SOME OF YOUR FAVORITE WINES FROM AROUND THE WORLD.
Santa Barbara Chardonnay and Pinot Noir have fullness and rich flavors.
Virginia's Viognier and Cabernet Franc are local treasures.

NAME RECENT WINE DISCOVERIES THAT HAVE EXCITED YOU.
Chrysalis Virginia Viognier, an excellent local wine, and Portuguese reds, which
are great values.

WHAT BITS OF INFORMATION WOULD YOU LIKE YOUR CUSTOMERS TO
KNOW ABOUT YOU?
I worked as a carpenter for fifteen years while moonlighting in this business.

IF YOU WERE NOT IN THIS PROFESSION, WHAT WOULD YOU BE DOING?
Teaching, since my job involves training and education already.

DESCRIBE YOUR WINE SELECTIONS, BOTH BY THE GLASS AND ON YOUR LIST.
Our list consists of international wines offering well-known favorites, as well as
obscure and allocated wines.

WHAT ARE THE MOST UNIQUE FEATURES IN YOUR WINE PROGRAM?
We offer highly discounted wines nightly, such as 1996 Calon-Segur for $75.

WHAT CATEGORY OF WINE IS THE BEST VALUE IN YOUR RESTAURANT?
California reds, particularly the higher-end Cabernet Sauvignons and Pinot Noirs.

NAME A COUPLE OF YOUR RESTAURANT'S SIGNATURE DISHES. WHAT
TYPES OF WINE DO YOU PREFER TO RECOMMEND WITH EACH?
Buffalo with California Syrah; lobster bisque with Pinot Blanc.

WHAT WINES ARE CUSTOMERS NOW MORE WILLING TO ORDER?
New Zealand Pinot Noir and Virginia wines.

Williamsburg Inn
Regency Dining Room

136 Francis Street
Williamsburg, Virginia 23187-1776
phone 757-229-2141 fax 757-220-7096
website www.colonialwilliamsburg.com

Paul B. Austin
SOMMELIER

WHAT ARE SOME OF YOUR ULTIMATE FOOD AND WINE PAIRINGS?
Foie gras with Sauternes; lobster with Loire Valley white; crab Randolph with white Burgundy; roast rack of lamb with Syrah or Shiraz; cheese samplers after dinner with vintage Port; Iranian Beluga caviar with huge white Burgundy (Montrachet, Corton-Charlemagne).

DESCRIBE YOUR WINE SELECTIONS.
We have an international selection of 400 wines. To help guide customers through the list, we have a sommelier and wine stewards on the floor at dinner and brunch.

WHAT CATEGORIES OF WINE ARE THE BEST VALUES ON YOUR WINE LIST?
Wines in the international section from Chile, Argentina, Australia, New Zealand, South Africa and other regions, and from California's Central Coast.

NAME RECENT WINE DISCOVERIES THAT HAVE EXCITED YOU.
Jurançon (Petit Manseng varietal) and Mendocino Charbono.

WHAT IS YOUR FAVORITE WINE REGION IN THE WORLD TODAY?
Burgundy. The whites and reds range from light as a feather to full and earthy.

WHAT LED YOU TO PURSUE A CAREER THAT INVOLVES WINE?
A chance meeting with a publisher and wine journalist who was a customer at a restaurant I ran. He let me taste wonderful wines and complimented my palate. I was hooked.

WHAT ARE THE BEST ASPECTS OF YOUR JOB?
Making people feel at home with wine; seeing the child of a guest I first met when he was eight years old, now old enough to order wine.

IF YOU WERE NOT A SOMMELIER, WHAT WOULD YOU BE DOING?
Designing and building restaurants.

Clifton Inn

ARNAUD DEWEVER, FOOD
AND BEVERAGE DIRECTOR
1296 Clifton Inn Drive,
Charlottesville
434-971-1800

Elysium
at the Morrison
House Hotel

ALBERT LEROUX, FOOD
AND BEVERAGE DIRECTOR
116 South Alfred Street, Alexandria
703-838-8000

Inn at Little
Washington

SCOTT CALVERT, WINE DIRECTOR
AND SOMMELIER
Middle and Main Street, Washington
540-675-3800

Sam & Harry's

KIM FERGUSON, GENERAL
MANAGER AND WINE BUYER
8240 Leesburg Pike, Vienna
703-448-0088

Café Juanita

9702 Northeast 120th Place
Kirkland, Washington 98034
phone 425-823-1505 fax 425-823-8500
website www.cafejuanita.com

Judith E. Ham-Conces
GENERAL MANAGER
AND WINE DIRECTOR

NAME TWO OF YOUR FAVORITE WINES FROM AROUND THE WORLD.
Piedmont wines have such an unusual complexity with layers of character. I also love wines from Tuscany for the same reason.

NAME A RECENT WINE DISCOVERY THAT EXCITED YOU.
Sagrantino di Montefalco from Umbria. It's a very dry wine with delicate fruit subtleties that explode mid-palate.

DESCRIBE YOUR WINE SELECTIONS, BOTH BY THE GLASS AND ON YOUR LIST.
Our focus is on Italian wine (eighty-five percent Italian). Our wines by the glass are Italian, and include Lagrein, Dolcetto, Barco Reale di Carmignano, Grechetto and Roero Arneis.

WHAT ARE THE MOST UNIQUE FEATURES IN YOUR WINE PROGRAM?
Our focus on Italian wine. We also make available plenty of Northwest and California wines in half-bottles.

WHAT CATEGORY OF WINE IS THE BEST VALUE IN YOUR RESTAURANT?
Dolcetto.

NAME A COUPLE OF YOUR RESTAURANT'S SIGNATURE DISHES. WHAT TYPES OF WINE DO YOU PREFER TO RECOMMEND WITH EACH?
Braised rabbit with Roero Arneis or Teroldego Rotaliano; roasted quail with Brunello di Montalcino.

IN THE PAST YEAR, WHAT WINES IN YOUR WINE PROGRAM HAVE CUSTOMERS BECOME MORE WILLING TO ORDER?
Barolo and Barbaresco. Recent vintages have inspired a lot of curiosity.

WHAT ARE SOME OTHER ULTIMATE WINE AND FOOD PAIRINGS?
Grilled octopus with Vermentino; seared foie gras with sweet white passito; crisp veal sweetbreads with Nebbiolo Langhe; roast squab with Apulia Primitivo; saddle of lamb with Barolo or Barbaresco.

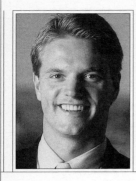

Canlis Restaurant

2576 Aurora Avenue North
Seattle, Washington 98119
phone 206-283-3313 fax 206-283-1766
website www.canlis.com

Shayn E. Bjornholm
WINE MANAGER
AND SOMMELIER

WHAT INSPIRED YOU TO PURSUE A CAREER THAT INVOLVES WINE?
One great incident with Sauternes, and one great experience with fellow professionals learning about the sommelier profession.

WHAT PART OF YOUR JOB DO YOU ENJOY THE MOST?
Helping guests realize the perfect evening at Canlis with the joys of food and wine.

NAME ONE OR TWO OF YOUR FAVORITE WINE DISTRICTS OR WINE REGIONS FROM AROUND THE WORLD.
Washington State Syrah for its world-class potential and varietal typicity combined with clarity and ebullient flavors; aged German Riesling from the Mosel for its complexity and brightness.

NAME RECENT WINE DISCOVERIES THAT HAVE EXCITED YOU.
Quality Malbecs from Argentina that have depth, purity and age well, as opposed to just plush fruit!

IF YOU WERE NOT IN THIS PROFESSION, WHAT WOULD YOU BE?
A landscape architect or actor.

DESCRIBE YOUR WINE SELECTIONS, BOTH BY THE GLASS AND ON YOUR LIST.
We have a Wine Spectator Grand Award list, featuring world-class wines from major growing regions, priced from $19 to $3,000 a bottle.

WHAT CATEGORY OF WINE IS THE BEST VALUE IN YOUR RESTAURANT?
German Riesling!

NAME A COUPLE OF YOUR RESTAURANT'S SIGNATURE DISHES. WHAT TYPES OF WINE DO YOU PREFER TO RECOMMEND WITH EACH?
Canlis salad with top Sancerre; Wasyugyu tenderloin with Walla Walla Syrah.

IN THE PAST YEAR, WHAT WINES IN YOUR WINE PROGRAM HAVE CUSTOMERS BECOME MORE WILLING TO ORDER?
Red Burgundies.

Cascadia Restaurant

2328 First Avenue
Seattle, Washington 98109
phone 206-448-8884 fax 206-448-2242
website www.cascadiarestaurant.com

Jake Kosseff

SOMMELIER

WHAT ARE SOME OF YOUR ULTIMATE FOOD AND WINE PAIRINGS?
Oregon white truffle bisque with Willamette Valley Dijon clone Chardonnay;
mature tête-de-cuvée Champagne and movie theater popcorn; ice wine or
Eiswein with salty, creamy cheeses.

DESCRIBE YOUR WINE SELECTIONS.
We specialize in handcrafted wines from very small producers. In keeping with
our food, we also try to keep at least 60 percent of the list from the Cascadia
region (Pacific Northwest).

WHAT CATEGORY OF WINE IS THE BEST VALUE IN YOUR RESTAURANT?
Cascadia whites (Pacific Northwest).

NAME RECENT WINE DISCOVERIES THAT HAVE EXCITED YOU.
1998 Strangeland "Silver Leaf" Pinot Noir: complex, earthy, perfect balance.
2000 Buty Semillon/Sauvignon Blanc from the Columbia Valley: rich, crisp
and intense.

WHAT IS YOUR FAVORITE WINE REGION IN THE WORLD TODAY?
Willamette Valley. It has great farming practices and small producers who make
fabulous, handcrafted wines.

WHAT LED YOU TO PURSUE A CAREER THAT INVOLVES WINE?
A fascination with and love for wine, food and restaurants.

WHAT ARE THE BEST ASPECTS OF YOUR JOB?
Making people truly happy and showing them new things. Also, putting
together the wine list. I believe that there is such a thing as a perfect wine list.

IF YOU WERE NOT IN THIS PROFESSION, WHAT WOULD YOU BE?
Smoke jumper or something intellectual like professor of classical philosophy.

Earth and Ocean

1/2 Fourth Avenue
Seattle, Washington 98101
phone 206-264-6060 fax 206-264-6070

Marc S. Papineau
SOMMELIER

NAME TWO OF YOUR FAVORITE WINE REGIONS FROM AROUND THE WORLD.
Pinot Noir from Burgundy and the variation in styles and profiles that can be
found there; and wines from Washington.

NAME RECENT WINE DISCOVERIES THAT HAVE EXCITED YOU.
Recently I spent time in Sonoma's Russian River Valley, where I tasted some
wonderful Pinot Noirs and Chardonnays.

WHAT BITS OF INFORMATION WOULD YOU LIKE YOUR CUSTOMERS TO
KNOW ABOUT YOU?
I received a degree in French language and English literature. I'm a road cyclist,
formerly a racer, and an artist.

IF YOU WERE NOT IN THIS PROFESSION, WHAT WOULD YOU BE DOING?
Painting and, perhaps, starving.

DESCRIBE YOUR WINE SELECTIONS, BOTH BY THE GLASS AND ON YOUR LIST.
We focus on Northwest wines both by the glass and by the bottle. We specialize
in Northwest Syrah and carry benchmark wines from all the major wine-growing regions of the world.

WHAT CATEGORY OF WINE IS THE BEST VALUE IN YOUR RESTAURANT?
Our "Going Native" list offers premium wines from outside Washington at a
great price.

NAME A COUPLE OF YOUR RESTAURANT'S SIGNATURE DISHES. WHAT
TYPES OF WINE DO YOU PREFER TO RECOMMEND WITH EACH?
Scallops and savoy cabbage and ham hocks with Washington Chardonnay or
Oregon Pinot Noir; shepherd's pie of oxtail with braising liquid reduction
paired with Washington Syrah.

IN THE PAST YEAR, WHAT WINES IN YOUR WINE PROGRAM HAVE CUS-
TOMERS BECOME MORE WILLING TO ORDER?
Washington Bordeaux blends, Oregon Pinot and Rhône Valley.

Flying Fish Restaurant

2234 First Avenue
Seattle, Washington 98121
phone 206-728-8595 fax 206-728-1551

Brian K. Huse
GENERAL MANAGER
AND WINE BUYER

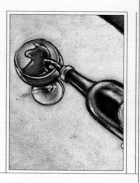

WHAT ARE SOME OF YOUR ULTIMATE FOOD AND WINE PAIRINGS?
Salt-and-pepper crab with Alsace Gewürztraminer; oysters and Champagne;
lamb and Rhône red.

DESCRIBE YOUR WINE SELECTIONS.
We offer wines in a variety of styles, from a range of regions, and at multiple
price levels. We seek out wines that match our food and that are a sheer pleasure to drink.

WHAT CATEGORY OF WINE IS THE BEST VALUE IN YOUR RESTAURANT?
Sauvignon Blanc from New Zealand and the Loire Valley.

WHAT ARE YOUR FAVORITE WINE REGIONS IN THE WORLD TODAY?
France, all of it, and New Zealand.

WHAT LED YOU TO YOUR CURRENT POSITION?
I love the stuff.

WHAT IS THE BEST ASPECT OF YOUR JOB?
Seeing that our customers enjoy their entire restaurant experience.

IF YOU WERE NOT IN THIS PROFESSION, WHAT WOULD YOU BE?
A stay-at-home dad.

El Gaucho

2505 First Avenue
Seattle, Washington 98121
phone 206-728-1337 fax 206-728-4477
website www.elgaucho.com

Michael R. Kaminski
WINE CAPTAIN

WHAT ARE SOME OF YOUR ULTIMATE FOOD AND WINE PAIRINGS?
Châteaubriand with red Burgundy, especially Pommard; porterhouse steak with big Napa Cabernet Sauvignon; crisp Provence Rosé with salad (in Marseilles); a ripe white peach with Viognier.

DESCRIBE YOUR WINE SELECTIONS.
Our list is constantly evolving. As a steakhouse, we specialize in big red wines from regions all over the world, from those with solid reputations to those with cult followings, and from the obscure to the offbeat.

WHAT CATEGORY OF WINE IS THE BEST VALUE IN YOUR RESTAURANT?
Spanish red.

NAME A RECENT WINE DISCOVERY THAT EXCITED YOU.
Betz Family Cabernet Sauvignon, from the Columbia Valley, Washington. It is rich and elegant with a supple, long finish, at a great price.

WHAT IS YOUR FAVORITE WINE REGION IN THE WORLD TODAY?
Spain. Wines from Rioja, Ribera del Duero and Priorat offer real quality and value.

WHAT LED YOU TO PURSUE A CAREER THAT INVOLVES WINE?
A B.A. in Film Studies guaranteed me a career in the restaurant industry. Wine became a tool, hobby and passion.

WHAT IS THE BEST ASPECT OF YOUR JOB?
Seeing the wine program evolve and have a favorable impact on my customers and the local marketplace.

IF YOU WERE NOT IN THIS PROFESSION, WHAT WOULD YOU BE?
Rock star.

The Herbfarm
14590 Northeast 145th Street
Woodinville, Washington 98072
phone 425-485-5300 fax 206-789-2279
website www.theherbfarm.com

Christine Mayo
SOMMELIER

WHAT ARE SOME OF YOUR ULTIMATE FOOD AND WINE PAIRINGS?
Seared sea scallops and spiced carrot sauce with Riesling; duck with Oregon black truffles and mature Pinot Noir; foie gras and Sauternes.

DESCRIBE YOUR WINE SELECTIONS.
We have 1,400 selections, specializing in the wines of the Pacific Northwest, including very deep selections of Oregon Pinot Noir. Our nightly, nine-course prix fixe dinner includes six paired wines.

WHAT CATEGORY OF WINE IS THE BEST VALUE IN YOUR RESTAURANT?
The wines of the Pacific Northwest.

NAME RECENT WINE DISCOVERIES THAT HAVE EXCITED YOU.
Austrian white wines. They are precise and expressive wines with great character and flavor.

WHAT IS YOUR FAVORITE WINE REGION IN THE WORLD TODAY?
The Pacific Northwest. Its pioneering spirit, camaraderie and potential greatness make it a very exciting place to be.

WHAT LED YOU TO PURSUE A CAREER THAT INVOLVES WINE?
Dumb luck. I was just out of grad school and was very lucky to be working at a restaurant that had an outstanding wine program.

WHAT ARE THE BEST ASPECTS OF YOUR JOB?
With our nine-course, fixed menu we do precise pairings of five or six wines each night. It is wonderful to see our guests' faces when they hit the "ah-ha" moment, when they realize that the wine is not incidental to their meal.

IF YOU WERE NOT IN THIS PROFESSION, WHAT WOULD YOU BE DOING?
More painting.

Metropolitan Grill

820 Second Avenue
Seattle, Washington 98104
phone 206-624-3287 fax 206-389-0042
website www.themetropolitangrill.com

David Coyle
HEAD SOMMELIER

WHAT PART OF YOUR JOB DO YOU ENJOY THE MOST?
When a customer hands back our wine list and says, "I'm in your hands. You have never steered me wrong." That's job satisfaction.

NAME ONE OR TWO OF YOUR FAVORITE WINE REGIONS.
Columbia Valley for its rich, opulent reds and consistent vintages. Also, the Stags Leap District in Napa Valley.

NAME RECENT WINE DISCOVERIES THAT HAVE EXCITED YOU.
As wine prices come down on some wines, I am happy to pass the savings on to our guests.

WHAT WOULD YOU LIKE YOUR CUSTOMERS TO KNOW ABOUT YOU?
I have accumulated thirty years of experience in the restaurant business and still enjoy coming to work every day.

IF YOU WERE NOT IN THIS PROFESSION, WHAT WOULD YOU BE DOING?
I can't imagine any other profession.

DESCRIBE YOUR WINE SELECTIONS, BOTH BY THE GLASS AND ON YOUR LIST.
We offer 1,000 wines, thirty-five by the glass, with an emphasis on West Coast reds from America, yet still covering the great wine regions of the world.

WHAT IS THE MOST UNIQUE FEATURE IN YOUR WINE PROGRAM?
Our staff of five certified sommeliers with fifteen to thirty years of experience. They keep wine fun!

WHAT CATEGORY OF WINE IS THE BEST VALUE IN YOUR RESTAURANT?
Australian Shiraz.

NAME ONE OF YOUR RESTAURANT'S SIGNATURE DISHES. WHAT WINE DO YOU PREFER TO RECOMMEND WITH IT?
Prime beef served with great Cabernet Sauvignon, Merlot or a blend from Washington State.

Metropolitan Grill

820 Second Avenue
Seattle, Washington 98104
phone 206-624-3287 fax 206-389-0042

William Dave Prigmore
SOMMELIER AND CAPTAIN

WHAT ARE SOME OF YOUR ULTIMATE FOOD AND WINE PAIRINGS?
Porterhouse steak with 1996 Alexander Valley Silver Oak Cabernet Sauvignon;
Delmonico steak with 1999 Januik Winery Cabernet Sauvignon; peppercorn
New York steak with Petite Sirah; mesquite-grilled salmon with Yakima Valley
Syrah.

DESCRIBE YOUR WINE SELECTIONS.
We offer principally Bordelais varietals from the classic regions, including
Bordeaux, California and Washington. However, we feature wines from all classic wine regions worldwide, from Hungary to Argentina and from South Africa
to British Columbia.

WHAT CATEGORY OF WINE IS THE BEST VALUE IN YOUR RESTAURANT?
California Cabernet Sauvignon.

NAME A RECENT WINE DISCOVERY THAT EXCITED YOU.
Vega Sicilia. One of the best red wines I've tasted.

WHAT IS YOUR FAVORITE WINE REGION IN THE WORLD TODAY?
Washington. Cabernet Sauvignon and Merlot from the Columbia Valley and
Syrah from the Yakima Valley are outstanding.

WHAT LED YOU TO PURSUE A CAREER THAT INVOLVES WINE?
I worked as a sous-chef with a CIA graduate on over forty winemaker dinners.

WHAT ARE THE BEST ASPECTS OF YOUR JOB?
Every day I meet fifty to one hundred diners and wine enthusiasts who are
interesting, engaging and full of curiosity about the kaleidoscopic world of
wines.

IF YOU WERE NOT IN THIS PROFESSION, WHAT WOULD YOU BE DOING?
More winemaking; greater involvement in a wholesale nursery, featuring peren-
nials, alpine plants and conifers.

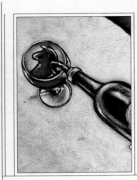

Rover's

2808 East Madison Street
Seattle, Washington 98112
phone 206-325-7442 fax 206-325-1092

Cyril R. Frechier
MANAGER AND SOMMELIER

WHAT IS ONE OF YOUR ULTIMATE FOOD AND WINE PAIRINGS?
Seared Hudson Valley foie gras and a foie gras nage with Zind-Humbrecht 1997 Pinot Gris, Clos Windsbuhl.

DESCRIBE YOUR WINE SELECTIONS.
An extensive coverage of French, Californian and Pacific Northwestern vineyards.

WHAT IS YOUR FAVORITE WINE REGION IN THE WORLD TODAY?
Burgundy. No other region gives me that toe-curling sensation that I get when I taste a truly great Burgundy.

WHAT LED YOU TO PURSUE A CAREER THAT INVOLVES WINE?
My love of food and wine and the restaurant world. It's a great industry.

WHAT IS THE MOST CHALLENGING ASPECT OF YOUR JOB?
Staying current with the ever-expanding wine world. All these great new wine regions and winemakers; too many wines, too little time!

IF YOU WERE NOT IN THIS PROFESSION, WHAT WOULD YOU BE DOING?
Working the vineyard, making wine.

Salish Lodge and Spa

6501 Railroad Avenue Southeast
Snoqualmie, Washington 98065
phone 425-888-2556 fax 425-888-2533
website www.salishlodge.com

Mark A. Kieras
SOMMELIER

WHAT PART OF YOUR JOB DO YOU ENJOY THE MOST?
Pairing wine with food, an artisan synergy that I enjoy. Flavors, textures and weight are just a few of the variables I consider while pairing.

NAME TWO OF YOUR FAVORITE WINE DISTRICTS.
Red Mountain, Washington, for its beautiful and opulent reds; McLaren Vale, Australia, for its appealing, intense reds.

NAME RECENT WINE DISCOVERIES THAT HAVE EXCITED YOU.
Washington Viognier and New Zealand Pinot Noir. Both are beginning to command attention.

WHAT WOULD YOU LIKE YOUR CUSTOMERS TO KNOW ABOUT YOU?
I enjoy making wine and beer in my free time, and I read extensively about them to improve my knowledge.

IF YOU WERE NOT IN THIS PROFESSION, WHAT WOULD YOU BE DOING?
Computer programming or wine distributing.

DESCRIBE YOUR WINE SELECTIONS, BOTH BY THE GLASS AND ON YOUR LIST.
We have a Northwest focus and feature regional varietals that best represent each specific area. Our Northwest collection is one of the most comprehensive in the area.

WHAT CATEGORY OF WINE IS THE BEST VALUE IN YOUR RESTAURANT?
Northwest Merlot.

NAME ONE OF YOUR RESTAURANT'S SIGNATURE DISHES. WHAT WINE DO YOU PREFER TO RECOMMEND WITH IT?
Truffle-crusted monkfish with parsley risotto paired with Oregon Pinot Noir.

IN THE PAST YEAR, WHAT WINES IN YOUR WINE PROGRAM HAVE CUS-TOMERS BECOME MORE WILLING TO ORDER?
Spanish whites, particularly Albariño, and Washington Syrah.

Seastar Restaurant

205 108th Avenue Northeast
Bellevue, Washington 98004
phone 425-456-0010 fax 425-456-0020
website www.seastarrestaurant.com

Erik A. Liedholm

WINE DIRECTOR
AND SOMMELIER

WHAT PART OF YOUR JOB DO YOU ENJOY THE MOST?
I enjoy inspiring staff and guests and helping them understand that wine enhances life at the table.

NAME ONE OF YOUR FAVORITE WINE REGIONS FROM AROUND THE WORLD.
Loire Valley. I love the diversity of its wines.

NAME RECENT WINE DISCOVERIES THAT HAVE EXCITED YOU.
Austrian wine—a wine revolution and revelation! Look out, Germany!

WHAT WOULD YOU LIKE YOUR CUSTOMERS TO KNOW ABOUT YOU?
I love to run, play soccer and make really mediocre wine.

IF YOU WERE NOT IN THIS PROFESSION, WHAT WOULD YOU BE?
A chef.

DESCRIBE YOUR WINE SELECTIONS, BOTH BY THE GLASS AND ON YOUR LIST.
Our glass list reflects the rest of our wine list, which is known for its diversity and value, and includes a very broad range of wines from around the world, with an emphasis on Burgundy, Germany and Austria.

WHAT ARE THE MOST UNIQUE FEATURES IN YOUR WINE PROGRAM?
We hold intimate winemaker dinners and large wine-tasting events.

WHAT CATEGORIES OF WINE ARE THE BEST VALUES IN YOUR RESTAURANT?
Wines from Spain and the Languedoc.

NAME A COUPLE OF YOUR RESTAURANT'S SIGNATURE DISHES. WHAT TYPES OF WINE DO YOU PREFER TO RECOMMEND WITH EACH?
Scallop ceviche and Austrian Grüner Veltliner; Idaho Kobe-style beef tenderloin with red Burgundy.

WHAT WINES ARE CUSTOMERS NOW MORE WILLING TO ORDER?
Austrian Riesling and Grüner Veltliner and the wines of Spain.

Serafina

2043 Eastlake Avenue East
Seattle, Washington 98102
phone 206-323-0807 fax 206-325-2766
website www.serafinaseattle.com

John S. Neumark
EXECUTIVE CHEF
AND WINE DIRECTOR

NAME TWO OF YOUR FAVORITE WINE DISTRICTS OR REGIONS.
Piedmont, Italy, offers a diversity of wine styles at different price points that are food-friendly, and Soave in the Veneto is a terrific alternative to Chardonnay.

NAME RECENT WINE DISCOVERIES THAT HAVE EXCITED YOU.
Wines from Piedmont, such as Deltetto's 2001 Sarvai, made from the Vermentino grape.

WHAT WOULD YOU LIKE YOUR CUSTOMERS TO KNOW ABOUT YOU?
I am an unabashed hedonist and revel in engaging my sensorial universe.

IF YOU WERE NOT IN THIS PROFESSION, WHAT WOULD YOU BE DOING?
Creating perfumes and fragrances; a sea-kayaking guide on Vancouver Island, B.C.

DESCRIBE YOUR WINE SELECTIONS, BY THE GLASS AND ON YOUR LIST.
We emphasize Italian regional wines and pour everything from Dolcetto to Terlodego by the glass. We have a Vini di Meditazione section that features Italian dessert wines. We have lots of half-bottles, wine dinners eight times a year and a "Wine of the Week" program that offers more expensive wines by the glass.

WHAT CATEGORY OF WINE IS THE BEST VALUE IN YOUR RESTAURANT?
White Italian wine.

NAME A COUPLE OF YOUR RESTAURANT'S SIGNATURE DISHES. WHAT TYPES OF WINE DO YOU PREFER TO RECOMMEND WITH EACH?
Duck ragout with potato gnocchi with Piedmont Barbera; semolina gnocchi with wild mushrooms with Morellino di Scansano.

IN THE PAST YEAR, WHAT WINES IN YOUR WINE PROGRAM HAVE CUS-TOMERS BECOME MORE WILLING TO ORDER?
Red and white wines from Alto Adige, Friuli and Sicily.

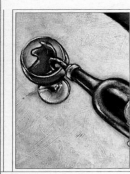

Sun Mountain Lodge
Patterson Lake Road
Winthrop, Washington 98862
phone 509-996-2211 fax 509-996-4711

Hector A. Garibay
FOOD AND BEVERAGE MANAGER

DESCRIBE YOUR WINE SELECTIONS.
Our wine list is very strong on Washington wines.

WHAT IS YOUR FAVORITE WINE REGION IN THE WORLD TODAY?
Spain. The Basque region has great wines that now compare with the quality of French wines.

WHAT IS THE MOST CHALLENGING ASPECT OF YOUR JOB?
Following all the new wines from all over the world.

IF YOU WERE NOT IN THE WINE PROFESSION, WHAT WOULD YOU BE DOING?
Enjoying a full bottle of wine.

Tulio Ristorante

1100 Fifth Avenue
Seattle, Washington 98101
phone 206-624-5500 fax 206-623-0568

Michael Degano
GENERAL MANAGER
AND SOMMELIER

WHAT ARE SOME OF YOUR ULTIMATE FOOD AND WINE PAIRINGS?
Roasted salmon with spinach, mascarpone and grilled lemons paired with
Piedmont Barbera; foie gras with late-harvest Semillon; venison with Australian
Shiraz; asparagus with Sauvignon Blanc.

DESCRIBE YOUR WINE SELECTIONS.
We have wines from every wine region in Italy and the Northwest. Our wine
by-the-glass program shows off the best of Washington.

WHAT CATEGORY OF WINE IS THE BEST VALUE IN YOUR RESTAURANT?
Southern Italian reds (Primitivo, Nero d'Avola, Salento).

NAME RECENT WINE DISCOVERIES THAT HAVE EXCITED YOU.
Washington Syrahs from 1998. They are unbelievable, with balance and fruit.
Excellent juice.

WHAT IS YOUR FAVORITE WINE REGION IN THE WORLD TODAY?
Piedmont. I love the wines. Winemakers combine a passion for tradition and
the desire to make drinkable wine.

WHAT LED YOU TO PURSUE A CAREER THAT INVOLVES WINE?
My passion for wine and knowledge. It was the natural progression in my
career.

WHAT IS THE MOST CHALLENGING ASPECT OF YOUR JOB?
Wine list maintenance. Keeping it balanced and inspired.

IF YOU WERE NOT IN THIS PROFESSION, WHAT WOULD YOU BE?
A physical therapist.

Brasa
BRYAN HILL, OWNER
AND WINE GUY
2107 Third Avenue, Seattle
206-728-4220

Campagne
SHAWN MEAD, WINE BUYER
86 Pine Street, Seattle
206-728-2800

Le Gourmand
BRUCE NAFTALY, OWNER,
CHEF AND WINE BUYER
425 Northwest Market Street, Seattle
206-784-3463

Lombardi's Cucina of Ballard
JENNIFER BUSHMAN,
WINE DIRECTOR
2200 Northwest Market Street,
Seattle
206-783-0055

Place Pigalle
BILL FRANK, PROPRIETOR
AND WINE BUYER
81 Pike Street, Seattle
206-624-1756

Ray's Boathouse
DAVID CARREON, WINE DIRECTOR
AND SOMMELIER
6049 Seaview Avenue Northwest,
Seattle
206-789-3770

Ten Mercer
BRIAN CURRY, GENERAL MANAGER
AND WINE BUYER
10 Mercer Street, Seattle
206-691-3723

W Hotel
CARL BRUNO, BEVERAGE MANAGER
1112 Fourth Avenue, Seattle
206-264-6000

Wild Ginger
BRUCE STURGEON, GENERAL
MANAGER AND WINE BUYER
1401 Third Avenue, Seattle
206-623-4450

The Bavarian Inn

Route 480
Shepherdstown, West Virginia 25443
phone 304-876-2551 fax 304-876-0435
website www.bavarianinnwv.com

Christian Asam

GENERAL MANAGER
AND SOMMELIER

NAME TWO OF YOUR FAVORITE WINE REGIONS FROM AROUND THE WORLD.
Spain for its great quality and good prices; Santa Barbara for its great Pinot
Noir and Syrah.

NAME RECENT WINE DISCOVERIES THAT HAVE EXCITED YOU.
German Riesling. It is so compatible with food and had a great 2001 vintage;
Grüner Veltliner is a great wine many have not experienced.

WHAT WOULD YOU LIKE YOUR CUSTOMERS TO KNOW ABOUT YOU?
I play tennis and golf and love to travel and dine out, experiencing others'
hospitality.

IF YOU WERE NOT IN THIS PROFESSION, WHAT WOULD YOU BE?
A meteorologist. I am addicted to the Weather Channel.

DESCRIBE YOUR WINE SELECTIONS, BY THE GLASS AND ON YOUR LIST.
We have 400 labels on our list, with a large selection of wines from all around
the world, especially Germany, Bordeaux and Napa.

WHAT ARE THE MOST UNIQUE FEATURES IN YOUR WINE PROGRAM?
We have verticals of Lafite-Rothschild, Montelena, and Léoville-Las-Cases. We also
hold wine dinners once a month, and I think we have extremely fair prices on wines.

WHAT CATEGORY OF WINE IS THE BEST VALUE IN YOUR RESTAURANT?
German Riesling.

NAME A COUPLE OF YOUR RESTAURANT'S SIGNATURE DISHES. WHAT
TYPES OF WINE DO YOU PREFER TO RECOMMEND WITH EACH?
Venison medallions with goat cheese and black currants with Australian Grenache;
Gulf shrimp and caviar with tarragon and Parmesan crisps with Champagne.

WHAT WINES ARE CUSTOMERS NOW MORE WILLING TO ORDER?
German Riesling, Australian Shiraz and Grenache, New Zealand Sauvignon
Blanc and Italian Pinot Grigio.

The Greenbrier Dining Room at the Greenbrier Hotel

KEVIN DOTT, BEVERAGE DIRECTOR
AND SOMMELIER

300 West Main Street,
White Sulphur Springs
304-536-1110

Red Fox Restaurant

JOHN BETZ, DIRECTOR
OF WINE SERVICE

One Whistlepunk Village, Showshoe
Mountain Resort, Showshoe
304-572-1111

Bartolotta's Lake Park Bistro

PETER DONAHUE,
CORPORATE WINE DIRECTOR
SUSAN WELLER, GENERAL
MANAGER AND WINE BUYER
3133 East Newberry Boulevard,
Milwaukee
414-962-6300

The Immigrant Room at the American Club

DEAN SCHAAP, BEVERAGE
COORDINATOR
Highland Drive, Kohler
800-344-2838

Karl Ratzsch's

TOMAS ANDERO, WINE BUYER
320 East Mason Street, Milwaukee
414-276-2720

Blue Lion Restaurant
KYLE THOMPSON, WINE BUYER
160 North Millward Street, Jackson
307-733-3912

Cadillac Grille
SUZANNE GRAVES, WINE BUYER
Post Office Box 925, Jackson
307-733-3279

Snake River
BOB MERRIMAN, GENERAL
MANAGER AND WINE BUYER
84 East Broadway Street, Jackson
307-733-0557

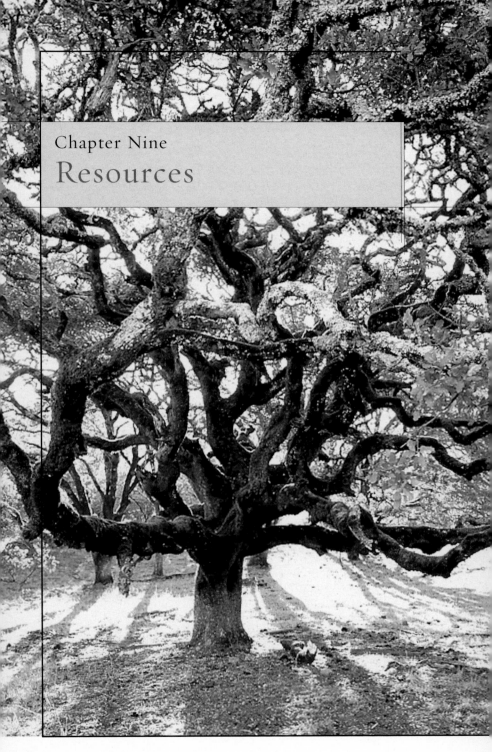

Chapter Nine
Resources

Confrérie de la Chaîne des Rôtisseurs

Chaîne House in Residence
Fairleigh Dickinson University
Madison, New Jersey
Email: chaine@chaineus.org
Website: www.chaineus.org

The Chaîne des Rôtisseurs is an international gastronomic society founded in Paris in 1950. It is devoted to promoting fine dining and "les arts de la table" (the arts of the table) in the broadest sense. The Chaîne is based on the traditions and practices of the old French Royal Guild of Geese Roasters, "les Ayeurs" (geese were particularly appreciated in those days). Its authority gradually expanded to the roasting of all poultry, meat and game. The written history of "les Ayeurs" has been traced back to the year 1248.

Today, the Society has professional and non-professional members in more than 70 countries around the world. Each chapter, called a "Bailliage" (in English, bailiwick), is headed by a "bailli" (bailiff) and other officers who plan the individual chapter's activities. All bailliages offer fine dining events, often black tie, in the best local restaurants and hotels. The menus and dishes are created exclusively for these dinners by the chefs, many of whom are also members of the confrérie.

An important arm of the Chaîne des Rôtisseurs is L'Ordre Mondial des Gourmets Dégustateurs, an organization within the Society which focuses on enjoying, studying and appreciating fine wines and crafted beverages and provides recognition to those professionals who are beverage-oriented. L'Ordre events are often less formal than those of the Chaîne, with wine the primary focus.

L'Ordre Mondial is also proud to sponsor a national Young Sommelier Competition. This competition is open to participants between the ages of 23 and 32 who have won their regional competitions, and are sponsored by Chaîne members. The national competition provides them with the opportunity to display their knowledge through blind tastings, a written test and a verbal exam that often includes questions dealing with food and wine pairing.

The 2004 Young Sommelier Competition finals will be held May 22, 2004, at Chalk Hill Estate in Sonoma County, California. For further information, please contact National Director Dan Gulbronsen at dan4wines@msn.com.

For decades, sommeliers have competed against one another in various competitions throughout the world. Today, the preeminent sommelier competition is the Meilleur Sommelier du Monde Competition, or Concours Mondiale. The Best Sommelier in America Competition is held to select one individual to represent the USA in this competition. Virginia Philip won the 2002 event.

The 2002 Best Sommelier in America Competition
Comments by Virginia Philip, Master Sommelier

Competitions such as the Best Sommelier in America Competition bring the sommelier profession into the public eye, and allow recognition for a profession that is highly regarded in Europe and finally becoming more so here, in the United States.

It is very difficult and takes a bit of self-appraisal to enter such a competition and say, "I think I am good enough, and if I am not, I shall take this experience and learn from it." I was impressed with the sportsmanship attitude of all the participants. Within moments of meeting one another, we began discussing favorite wines and their regions and sharing stories as if we were old friends. I had a great time and thoroughly enjoyed myself.

Preparing for the competition is, and probably always will be for most sommeliers, a labor of love. You are studying and tasting so much, your passion for wine becomes a bit blurred and you find yourself asking, "Why am I doing this?"

October 2002 was a critical month as my preparation overlapped with my studies for my Master Sommelier exam that was also scheduled in November (I only found out in early October that I was sitting for the Master's in November). With less than a month to go, I had to kick into high gear and really give myself a strong push to taste and study as much as possible.

I had been told the two exams would be vastly different, but they were similar in a lot of ways. I believe my success in the sommelier competition was the result of the intense and thorough standards of the Court of Master Sommeliers, especially in the tasting requirements needed to pass that exam.

Initially, I had never really thought that I would win the sommelier competition, because I knew it would be very difficult to do so. There were too many strong competitors. Getting to the finals became my new goal. I held to it and found myself the winner.

Winning has been more rewarding than I could ever have imagined. I am an avid watcher of the Olympics. I have always admired the determination and courage of those competitors and always wondered what it must be like to be there, competing for something you love to do so much. Now I know. This competition for me was the Olympics for Wine. I am thrilled and honored to have won such a prestigious award.

I encourage all sommeliers to participate in the next sommelier competition and to support the next Best Sommelier in the World Competition.

Virginia Philip is Chef Sommelier at The Breakers resort in Palm Beach, Florida. In addition to winning the 2002 Best Sommelier in America Competition, she also passed, in the same month, the Master Sommelier Diploma Examination in London, making her the 52nd American, and the ninth American woman, to do so.

The Breakers
One South County Road
Palm Beach, Florida 33480
phone 561-659-8466, x1522
email virginia.philip@thebreakers.com

Ten years ago a sommelier in North America had very few resources with which to further his or her education and career. Today there are numerous wine training and certification programs available across the nation. The following includes the significant professional wine training programs, consumer-oriented programs and a list of wine education–related resources.

I. ASSOCIATION DE LA SOMMELLERIE INTERNATIONALE MEMBERS

Every three years, A.S.I. hosts the Meilleur Sommelier du Monde Competition, or "Concours Mondiale." Giuseppe Vaccarini is President of the Milan-based organization. Only one sommelier association in each nation is recognized by A.S.I.

AUSTRIA
AUSTRIAN SOMMELIERS
ASSOCIATION
Siegfried Brudermann, President
Skilftstrasse 315, A-5753
Saalbach
phone +43-6541-6284
fax +43-6541-6284-20
email sommelier@saalbach.at

BELGIUM
BELGIUM SOMMELIERS GUILD
Alain de Mol, President
c/o Teverne du Passage
30 Galerie de la Reine
phone 32-2-512-37-32
fax 32-2-511-08-82

BRAZIL
BRAZILIAN SOMMELIERS
ASSOCIATION
Danio Braga, President
Paia do Flamengo, 66,
Bloco B, sala 307
Rio de Janeiro RJ CEP: 22228-900
phone 55-21-285-0497
fax 55-21-265-2157
email abs@abs.rio.com.br
website www.abs-rio.com.br

CANADA
CANADIAN ASSOCIATION OF
PROFESSIONAL SOMMELIERS
Guénaël Revel, President
150, rue Lesage, Sainte-Adèle,
Quebec J8B 2R4
phone 450-229-7604
fax 450-229-5771

CHILE
CHILEAN SOMMELIERS
ASSOCIATION
Héctor Vergara F., President
c/o El Mundo del Vino
Jorge Alessandri, 514, La Reina
Santiago de Chile
phone 56-2-758-58-00
fax 56-2-758-58-08

CHINA
HONG KONG SOMMELIERS
ASSOCIATION
19-21 Nathan Road, Hong Kong
phone 852-2369-8698
fax 852-2739-9811
email khh@peninsula.com
website www.peninsula.com

CROATIA
CROATIAN SOMMELIERS
ASSOCIATION
Ninoslav Dusper, President
c/o Vinoteka Vinum, Hotel Opera
Krsnjavoga, 1
10000 Zagreb
phone 385-1-4811-532
fax 385-1-4836-572
email hrvatski-sommelier-
klub@zg.hinet.hr

THE CZECH REPUBLIC
THE CZECH REPUBLIC
SOMMELIER ASSOCIATION
Martin Pastyrík, President
Rest. Palac Kinski,
Staromëstské nám. 12,
110 00 Praha 1
phone 420-2-2481-0750
fax 420-2-232-61-37

DENMARK
DANISH SOMMELIERS
ASSOCIATION
Jesper Boelskifte, President
Kirkebroen, 44
2650 Hvidovre
phone 45-36-75-40-10
email mail@lesommelier.dk

FINLAND
FINNISH SOMMELIERS
ASSOCIATION
Kristiina Laitinen, President
Pengerkatu 19 A 15,
00500 Helsinki
phone +358-9-726-0386

FRANCE
FRANCE SOMMELIERS
ASSOCIATION
Georges Pertuiset, President
Les Hameaux du Suzon, 12 rue
Paul-Delouvrier, 21000 Dijon
phone 33-80-70-92-10
fax 33-80-71-62-11
email catherine.dore@wanadoo.fr
website www.udsf.net

GERMANY
GERMAN SOMMELIERS
ASSOCIATION
Bernd Glauben, President
Romantik Hotel, Goldene
Traube, Am Viktoriabrunnen, 2
96450 Coburg
phone 49-9561-8760
fax 49-9561-8762-22
email goldene-traube@roman
tikhoteles.com

GREAT BRITAIN
THE ACADEMY OF FOOD AND
WINE SERVICE
Richard Edwards, President
Burgoine House, 8 Lower
Teddington Road Hampton
Wick,
Kingston on Thames KT1 4ER
phone 44-208-943-10-11
fax 44-208-977-55-19
email richardedwards@acfws.org

GREECE
GREEK SOMMELIERS
ASSOCIATION
Kostas Touloumtzis, President
L. Pentelis, 113, 152 34,
Halandri-Athènes
phone 30-1-68-90-238
fax 30-1-61-38 651

ICELAND
ICELANDIC SOMMELIERS
ASSOCIATION
Sigurdur Bjarkason, President
Sommelier/Vinthonninn ehf,
Hverfisgata, 46
101 Reykjavik
phone 354-511-44-55
fax 354-511-44-56
email sommelier@sommelier.is

IRELAND
THE IRISH GUILD OF
SOMMELIERS
Mary O'Callaghan, President
Catering Services, 11, Elmwood
Road, Swords Co. Dublin
phone 353-1-84-01-839
fax 353-1-84-03-107
email mary.ocallaghan@ireland.com

ITALY
ITALIAN SOMMELIERS
ASSOCIATION
Terenzio Medri, President
Viale Monza, n. 9, 20125 Milano
phone 39-02-2846-2378
fax 39-02-2611-2328
email ais@sommeliersonline.it
website www.sommeliersonline.it

JAPAN
JAPAN SOMMELIERS
ASSOCIATION
Takashi Atsuta, President
6-1, Jingumae 2–Chome
Shibuya-ku Tokyo 150-0001
phone 81-3-57-850-442
fax 81-3-57-850-443
email vin@sommelier.or.jp
website www.sommelier.or.jp

KOREA
IN VINO VERITAS SOCIETY
Sun-Tschu Theodor Lie,
President
724-35, Yeoksam-2-dong,
Kangnam-gu, Seoul 135-082
phone 822-555-8158
fax 822-569-8158
email theolie@united.co.kr

LUXEMBURG
LUXEMBURG SOMMELIER
ASSOCIATION
Claude Hilbert, President
Boîte Postale 3046,
1030 Luxemburg
phone 352-46-03-11
fax 352-46-52-07

MEXICO
MEXICAN SOMMELIERS
ASSOCIATION
Manuel Orgaz Tapia, President
c/o Vinoteca, Victor Absalon
Lopez
Lago Bolsena nº159, Col.
Anahuac, Miguel Hidalgo
C.P. 11320 Mexico D.F.
phone 52-5254-6051
fax 52-5254-5587
email fernando7ru@
infosel.net.mx

MONACO
MONACO SOMMELIERS
ASSOCIATION
Jean Pallanca, President
3, passage St-Michel, 98000
Monaco
phone/fax 377-93-30-75-00
email amsommelier@monaco
377.com

NETHERLANDS

NETHERLANDS SOMMELIER
ASSOCIATION
Cees Vos, President
De Acedemie voor Gastronomie,
Amersfoorts weg 86
7346 AA Hoog Soeren
phone 31-55-519-14-29
fax 31-55-519-14-09
email info@echoput.nl and
wijnmess@worldonline.nl

NORWAY

DEN NORSKE VINKELNER
FORENING
Remi Madsen, President
c/o Hotel Continental, P.B. 1510
Vika
0117 Oslo
phone 47-6684-99-29
fax 47-6684-68-18

POLAND

POLISH SOMMELIERS
ASSOCIATION
Wojciech Gogolinski, President
UI. Litewska 24/64, 30-014
Krakow
phone 48-12-423-40-69
fax 48-12-429-18-56

PORTUGAL

PORTUGUESE SOMMELIER
ASSOCIATION
Joaquim Santos, President
Avenida Almirante Reis,
58 r/c-Dt.
1150-019 Lisboa
phone/fax +351-21-813-25-42

ROMANIA

NATIONAL SOMMELIER CLUB
OF ROMANIA
Prof. Radu Nicolescu, President
Bucuresti, Sect 1, P-ta W.
Mārācineanu, nr. 1-3, intr. 5
Rt 6, camera 397, 394
Bucuresti, CP 1-234
phone/fax +401-313-52-88

SLOVAKIA

SLOVAK SOMMELIERS
ASSOCIATION
Stefan Valovic, President
c/o Hotel Devin, Riecna, 4,
81102 Bratislava
phone 421-7-54-41-23-07
fax 421-7-54-41-82-39

SLOVENIA

SLOVENIAN SOMMELIER
ASSOCIATION
Franko Rutar, President
Delpinova 7A, 5000 Nova Gorica
phone 386-5-3364000
email davorin.skarabot@hit.si
and sommelier.slovenije@amis.net
website www.sommelier-assoc.si

SPAIN

SPANISH SOMMELIERS
ASSOCIATION
Juan Muñoz Ramos, President
Riera Bonet, 5, At. 3.a, 08750
Molins de Rei, Barcelona
phone/fax 34-9-3-6686586
email munoz@eurovid.es

SWEDEN

SWEDISH SOMMELIERS
ASSOCIATION
Åsa Wahlström, President
Postfack 256, 116 74 Stockholm
phone/fax 46-86-63-19-37
email asa.wa@swipnet.se
website www.sommelier
foreningen.org

SWITZERLAND

SWISS ASSOCIATION OF
PROFESSIONAL SOMMELIERS
Piero Tenca, President
ASSP, P.O. Box 39, 6943
Vezia-Suisse
phone 0041-91-966-66-27
fax 0041-91-966-66-28
email info@sommelier-suisse.ch
website www.sommelier-suisse.ch

TURKEY

TURKISH SOMMELIER
ASSOCIATION
Randolph Ward Mays, President
Göktürk Köyü, Istanbul Cad.
Kumlugeçit Mevkii No. 14
Kemerburgaz, 34993 Istanbul
phone 90-212-239-95-44
fax 90-212-239-74-40

USA

AMERICAN SOMMELIER
ASSOCIATION
Andrew Bell, President
580 Broadway, Suite 716
New York, NY 10012
phone 212-226-6805
fax 212-226-6407
email andrewbell@bellwines.com
website www.american
sommelier.com

VENEZUELA

VENEZUELAN SOMMELIERS
ASSOCIATION
Leonardo D'Addazio, President
Edificio Sada—Planta Baja
Avenida Las Americas,
Puerto Ordaz
phone 58-86-22-25-57
fax 58-86-23-23-14
email leoenot@telcel.net.ve

II. THE BRITISH MASTER PROGRAMS

The Master Sommelier and the Master of Wine are professional titles earned after several years of examinations and tastings. Both the Court of Master Sommeliers and the Institute of Masters of Wine are based in the U.K. and are modeled on the trade guilds of the 19th century. As the titles imply, the Master Sommelier program emphasizes wine service skills while the Master of Wine program requires a broad understanding of all aspects of the industry, from viticulture and vinification to finance, marketing and contemporary issues. Both programs examine the wine world at large, from an international standpoint. North America is important but takes a backseat to Old World areas such as France, and to New World areas such as Australia. Only 105 have earned the M.S. (ten women) and 250 the M.W. (forty-six women). Three men—North America's Ronn Wiegand and Doug Frost, and France's Gerard Basset—have earned both titles.

Master Sommelier

Established in 1969 "to encourage improved standards of beverage knowledge and service in hotels and restaurants," and internationally recognized in 1977, the Court of Master Sommeliers is an educational body. The Court explains: "In the service of wine, spirits and other alcoholic beverages, the Master Sommelier Diploma is the ultimate professional credential that anyone can attain worldwide." The M.S. syllabus includes production methods of wines and spirits, international wine laws, harmony of food and wine, wine tasting skills, and practical service and salesmanship, including service of liqueurs, brandies, ports and cigars. In a blind tasting of six wines in twenty-five minutes, candidates must correctly identify grape varieties, country and region of origin, age and quality.

All exams after the Basic Introductory Course are verbal and in the presence of a panel of judges. Prerequisites to sitting for the M.S. Diploma are successful completion of the Introductory Sommelier Course and the Advanced Sommelier Course, which require several years of practical experience in the restaurant industry. After passing the Advanced level you are invited to sit for the M.S. Diploma. You will have three years or three tries to pass all three sections at the Master's level—Theory, Tasting and Practical Service. If your clock runs out without passing all of the three parts you may start again. Once you pass all three, you are invited to join the Court as a Master Sommelier.

Court of Master Sommeliers

North American Chapter, Kathleen Lewis
1200 Jefferson Street
Napa, California 94559
phone 707-255-7667
fax 707-255-1119
email courtofms@aol.com
website www.mastersommeliers.org

American Master Sommeliers

Nunzio Alioto, Alioto's Restaurant, San Francisco, CA
Paolo Barbieri, Le Cirque/Circo-Bellagio Hotel & Casino, Las Vegas, NV
Robert Bath, The RLB Wine Group, St. Helena, CA
Wayne Belding, Boulder Wine Merchant, Boulder, CO
Richard Betts, Montagna at The Little Nell, Aspen, CO
Robert J. Bigelow, Le Cirque/Circo-Bellagio Hotel & Casino, Las Vegas, NV
Michael Bonaccorsi, Bonaccorsi Wine Company, Santa Monica, CA
Scott Carney, Brooklyn, NY
Matthew Citriglia, Vintage Wine, Columbus, OH
Roger Dagorn, Chanterelle, New York, NY
Fredrick Dame, Paterno Wines International, San Francisco, CA
Gilles de Chambure, Robert Mondavi Winery, Oakville, CA
Richard Dean, The Mark Hotel, New York, NY
Luis DeSantos, Spago, Las Vegas, NV
Catherine Fallis, Planet Grape LLC, San Francisco, CA
Jay Fletcher, Southern Wine & Spirits of Colorado and Aspen Wine
Sense Consulting, Aspen, CO
Sarah Floyd, Partners in Wine/Fine Estates from Spain, San Francisco, CA
Kenneth Fredrickson, Nevada Wine Agents, Las Vegas, NV
Doug Frost, Strong Water, Kansas City, MO
Chuck Furuya, Wine Consultant, Honolulu, HI
Tim Gaiser, San Francisco, CA
Steven Geddes, Vintage Consultants, Las Vegas, NV
Evan Goldstein, Allied Domecq Wines USA, Healdsburg, CA
Keith Goldston, Alexandria, VA
Peter Granoff, Napa, CA
Ira Harmon, Southern Wine & Sprits, Las Vegas, NV
Greg Harrington, BR Guest, New York, NY
Eric Hemer, Southern Wine & Spirits of Florida, Miami, FL
Andrea Immer, French Culinary Institute of New York City, Stamford, CT
Jay James, Bellagio Resort & Casino, Las Vegas, NV

Robert Jones, Kysela Pere et Fils Ltd., Richmond, VA
Emmanuel Kemiji, Miura Vineyards, San Francisco, CA
Fran Kysela, Kysela Pere et Fils Ltd., Winchester, VA
Michael McNeill, Ritz Carlton-Buckhead, Atlanta, GA
Sally Mohr, Boulder Wine Merchant, Boulder, CO
Steve Morey, Southern Wine & Spirits of Nevada, Las Vegas, NV
Ron Mumford, Southern Wine & Spirits of Nevada, Las Vegas, NV
Lawrence O'Brien, Orlando, FL
David O'Connor, McCall Associates-Events Management, Inc.,
San Francisco, CA
Damon Ornowski, Paterno Wines International, Chicago, IL
Ed Osterland, Osterland Enterprises, La Jolla, CA
Virginia Philip, The Breakers, Palm Beach, FL
Paul Roberts, French Laundry, Yountville, CA
Elizabeth Schweitzer, Beverly Hills, CA
William Sherer, Ritz Carlton, New York, NY
Alpana Singh, Everest, Chicago, IL
Cameron Sisk, Milo's Best Wine Cellar, Las Vegas, NV
Joseph Spellman, Paterno Wines International, Chicago, IL
Larry Stone, Rubicon, San Francisco, CA
Angelo Tavernaro, Wine and Service Consultant, Las Vegas, NV
Greg Tresner, Mary Elaine's at the Phoenician Resort, Scottsdale, AZ
Madeline Triffon, Unique Restaurant Corp., Bingham Farms, MI
Claudia Tyagi, Milo's Best Wine Cellar, Las Vegas, NV
Kevin Vogt, Delmonico Steak House at the Venetian Resort, Las Vegas, NV
Barbara Werley, The Homestead, Hot Springs, VA
Ronn Wiegand, Restaurant Wine, Napa, CA

III. OTHER PROFESSIONAL RESOURCES

Master of Wine

Like the Court of Master Sommeliers, the Institute of Masters of Wine is an educational body. The first examination was held in 1953. The M.W. syllabus includes three units of theory—Production of Wine, Business of Wine and Contemporary Issues, plus one wine analysis unit, the Practical, or blind, tasting.

A separate U.K. organization, the Wine and Spirit Education Trust, offers three courses to educate and train the trade and public: the Certificate, the Higher Certificate and the Diploma. Successful completion of these courses is highly recommended for anyone wishing to begin the M.W. program. WSET courses are currently available in

Boston, New York City and Philadelphia, or by correspondence course. Mary Ewing-Mulligan, M.W. at NYC's International Wine Center, has arranged a Home Study Program in conjunction with the WSET.

The Institute of Masters of Wine North America Ltd.
Roger Bomrich, M.W., President
phone 212-355-0700
website www.masters-of-wine.org

Wine and Spirit Education Trust North America Offered at:

New York:
Mary Ewing-Mulligan, M.W., President
Linda G. Lawry, Director
May Matta-Aliah, Wine Program Coordinator
International Wine Center
1133 Broadway, #520
New York, New York 10010
phone 212-627-7170
fax 212-627-7116
email iwcny@aol.com
website www.learnwine.com

Boston:
Sandy Block, M.W.
Bill Nesto, M.W.
Boston University, Special Programs
Elizabeth Bishop Wine Resource Center
808 Commonwealth Avenue, Boston, Massachusetts 02215
phone 617-353-9852
fax 617-353-4130
email boswine@aol.com

Philadelphia:
Neal Ewing
Independent Wine Club of Delaware Valley
P.O. Box 1478, Havertown, Pennsylvania 19083
phone 610-649-9936
fax 610-649-9936
email IWCwine@aol.com

Wine and Spirit Education Trust UK:
Caroline Finch, M.W., Education Officer
email institute_of_masters_of_wine@compuserve.com
website www.masters-of-wine.org

Sommelierjobs.Com

Listing of sommelier schools and courses, competitions and events, articles, guest articles, and links to sommelier resources and supplies.
website www.sommelierjobs.com

Society of Wine Educators

The Society of Wine Educators is dedicated to the advancement of wine education through professional development and certification. As a not-for-profit organization formed in 1977, S.W.E. has supported the efforts of those who teach about wine in structured educational programs or who otherwise seek to spread knowledge of wine. Membership in the Society is open to individuals and organizations all over the world that share in the Society's dedication to wine knowledge and learning.

Bonnie Fedchock, Executive Director
1200 G Street N.W., Suite 360
Washington, District of Columbia 20005
phone 202-347-5677
fax 202-347-5667
email vintage@erols.com
website www.wine.gurus.com

Wine Institute

The mission of the Wine Institute is to initiate and advocate state, federal and international public policy to enhance the environment for the responsible consumption and enjoyment of wine. The institute has a library open to the trade with vast resources including wine books and current publications.

425 Market Street, Suite 1000
San Francisco, California 94105
website www.wineinstitute.org

IV. CONSUMER RESOURCES

Andrea Immer, M.S., Dean of Wine Studies
French Culinary Institute of New York City
160 Rockrimmon Road
Stamford, Connecticut 06903
phone 646-254-7516
email andrea@greatwinesmadesimple.com

Chicago Wine School

Chicago wine writer and educator Patrick Fegan is the main instructor.
website www.wineschool.com